THE FUNCTION OF DOCUMENTS IN ISLAMIC LAW

THE FUNCTION OF DOCUMENTS IN ISLAMIC LAW

The Chapters on Sales

from

ṬAḤĀWĪ'S *KITĀB AL-SHURŪṬ AL-KABĪR*

Edited with an Introduction and Notes by

Jeanette A. Wakin

STATE UNIVERSITY OF NEW YORK PRESS
ALBANY

The Function of Documents in Islamic Law

First Edition

Published by State University of New York Press
99 Washington Avenue, Albany, New York 12210

Printed in Lebanon by the IMPRIMERIE CATHOLIQUE
Designed by Zahi N. Khuri

Library of Congress Cataloging in Publication Data
al-Ṭaḥāwī, Aḥmad ibn Muḥammad, 852?-933
The function of documents in Islamic law)

Bibliography: p.

1. Legal instruments (Islamic law) 2. Sales (Islamic law)
I. Wakin, Jeanette A., ed.
II. Title. III. Title: Kitāb al-shurūṭ al-kabīr.
LAW 346.07'2'0917671 75-171178
ISBN 0-87395-100-X
ISBN 0-87395-104-2 (microfiche)

CONTENTS

PREFACE

> We know from experience that someone may study traditions for fifty years, occupy himself with Qur'ānic exegesis, and spend his time among religious scholars. Yet he is not considered one of the *fuqahā'* and could never obtain a position as a judge. He would reach this position only after he has studied the works of Abū Ḥanīfa and other doctors of this kind, and learned by heart the practical legal formulas. For that, one or two years are required. Then only a short amount of time would elapse before such a man would be named judge of a city or even of a province.

WITH THIS QUOTATION from Jāḥiẓ, Ignáz Goldziher called to the attention of European scholarship the important branch of legal literature known as *shurūṭ*, or formularies for drawing up private legal documents. Underscoring Jāḥiẓ's remarks, he noted (in *Muhammedanische Studien*, II, 233) that the knowledge of *shurūṭ* was one of the essential qualifications of a qadi, and that the earliest authors made themselves specialists on the subject. Further, he pointed to the existence of a manuscript in the former Khedivial library in Cairo, which was the oldest surviving work on *shurūṭ*. It was written at the end of the third/ninth century by the great Egyptian Ḥanafī scholar, Abū Ja'far Aḥmad b. Muḥammad al-Ṭaḥāwī.

In the late 1920's, Joseph Schacht made a substantial addition to the study of Islamic law in practice when he published this Cairo manuscript, which was actually two fragments of a large work. These were the section on claims for debts and pledges, and the section on pre-emption. At about the same time, Schacht's research in the libraries dispersed in and about Istanbul brought to light two more fragments of the same manuscript, as well as four copies of Ṭaḥāwī's abridgement of his long work. The abridgement had been preserved in its entirety. One of the two Istanbul fragments of the long work contained formulas for the qadi and his court. The other was the first chapter of the work, the "Kitāb al-Buyū'," or section on contracts of sale.

Scholars concerned with the history of Islamic institutions have often acknowledged the importance of Schacht's contribution, yet there have been no studies of this important branch of legal literature, nor have additional texts been published. Thus I hope that this work, an edition of the "Kitāb al-Buyūʿ," will add to that earlier research and help bring us closer to understanding the institutions on which it has bearing.

The chief aim of the Introduction is to identify the purposes served by written contracts and the function of the handbooks that instruct the notary in drawing up private legal documents. Second, an attempt is made to sketch the early history of the genre in Islamic law, particularly in the Ḥanafī school. I have also drawn attention to the continuity of practice by placing the writing of contracts within the context of older Near Eastern practice; by no means does this aim at a comprehensive comparative study, but is intended to suggest further lines of research. Finally, to add support to the conclusions made in the Introduction, I have attempted a more detailed analysis of the Arabic formulary, with an emphasis on the contract of sale.

The Notes to the text accompany parts one and two of Ṭaḥāwī's work, which contain the more important models for contracts of sale, while parts three, four and five are offered for purposes of documentation. In place of a translation, the text is analyzed in the Notes; however, the formulas discussed in the Introduction are translated there. In the Notes, I have given parallel references from the actual contracts of the published papyri found mainly in Egypt. However, I have been selective in my use of the papyri so as not to overburden the Notes unnecessarily. I regret not having had the opportunity to make direct use of the relevant unpublished Geniza records, but I do not think the main lines of the thesis have suffered on this account.

The system of transliteration adopted here for Arabic words corresponds to that used by the *Encyclopaedia of Islam*, except that the consonants *d̲j̲* and *ḳ* are rendered *j* and *q*. The spelling of certain names, especially place names, has been retained in the form under which they are generally known in English, without transliteration or diacritical marks. Thus I have preferred Mecca, Damascus, qadi, dirham and dinar. Dates are usually given in both Muslim and Christian eras, the Hijra date coming first. In the Notes, Hijra dates are used alone, since these are of more interest to the specialist reader in referring to the sources. I have used the conventional letters A.H. and A.D. only where there is a likelihood of confusion.

The system of textual citation requires a few words of explanation. The "Kitāb al-Buyūʿ" was divided by the author himself into five parts (*juz'*) with the subject matter loosely grouped in each. Each of these is designated by a Roman numeral. To aid the reader, I have subdivided each part into sections and paragraphs, indicated by an Arabic numeral to the left and to the right of a decimal point, respectively. Each section deals with a separate contract. If the paragraph is the *formula* for a contract, this is shown by a zero to the right of the decimal point; if it is Ṭaḥāwī's commentary, it is shown by a numeral. Thus III 17.0 is the formula for the seventeenth contract in Part III, while III 17.9 is the ninth paragraph of Ṭaḥāwī's commentary on that contract. I have preferred to subdivide the text rather than furnish punctuation of a modern variety, both because it helps preserve the identity and integrity of the text as much as possible and because Ṭaḥāwī's style is clear enough without punctuation.

I am happy to express my thanks to the many who have helped me in the preparation of this work. A grant from the American Association of University Women permitted me to begin the project and the Columbia University Council for Research in the Humanities provided funds so that I was able to examine original unedited documents, as well as a small collection of *shurūṭ* manuscripts, deposited in the Egyptian National Library. I am particularly grateful to Professor S. D. Goitein who read through the work and made many valuable comments. Professor Maan Madina and Mr. Mansour Ajami, both of Columbia, gave much of their time in helping me proofread the Arabic text. I am also grateful to Professors Charles Issawi and Douglas M. Dunlop, of Columbia, Abraham Udovitch of Princeton, and George Makdisi of Harvard, who read through all or parts of this work, and I am particularly indebted to my friend Yochanan Muffs of the Jewish Theological Seminary, for his encouragement and thoughtful advice. Finally, I would like to express my deep gratitude and affection for my late teacher, Professor Joseph Schacht, whose guidance and inspiration extend far beyond these pages. He was responsible for the better part of my training and I hope that this study is faithful to the spirit of his scholarship.

INTRODUCTION

1. WRITTEN DOCUMENTS IN ISLAMIC LAW.

The study of the literature of *shurūṭ* and of individual forms for documents [1] is rewarding from many points of view. The economic historian, who is particularly hindered by the scarcity of source materials, should find much in them, for there is little doubt that most of the commercial contracts were used in practice. [2] Not only do surviving documents from different times and places show a close correspondence with *shurūṭ* models, but in addition, these fixed forms established by the jurists allowed businessmen few alternative procedures. It is a generally admitted principle that contracts, legally correct and following used forms, had a certain value: no one could suspect the parties of illegal ends.

Because of its early date, Ṭaḥāwī's work is important for the history of Islamic law and especially for the early history of the Ḥanafī school. The extensive commentary records many examples of *ikhtilāf*, or diversity of doctrine, among individual scholars and the several schools of law. Thus, as an early comparative account of doctrine, at least on the points at issue, it is a valuable source of information.

Quite apart from their legal content, the documents may be considered from the point of view of their formal aspects. Although there is a substantial

[1] The term *shurūṭ* is used by the authors themselves to apply equally to the literature as a whole, the model document, or to one or more formulas within a document. In addition, Ṭaḥāwī refers to a single document as *sharṭ* or *sharā'iṭ* (in this plural form, he is perhaps thinking of a collection of formulas), while *sharā'iṭ* can also be a plural of either *sharṭ* or *shurūṭ* (e.g., I 2.156; V 5.0, 20.0, 21.0). *Shurūṭ* is the usual Ḥanafī term, although occasionally a written document is called *wathīqa*, *ṣakk al-shirā* or *kitāb al-shirā* (for sale), *bayāḍ* (Sarakhsī, *Mabsūṭ*, XXX, 168, 179, 187); *kitāb al-'uhda* (II 3.4, 17.1); *'uqūd* (in the book titles below, pp. 18 and 22); *dhukr* or *dhukr ḥaqq*, pl. *adhkār al-ḥuqūq*; *masṭūr* (Ṣayrafī, 17); *ḥujja* (APEL II, 186; Grohmann, *Einführung*, 108). In the eastern part of the Islamic world and in the Ottoman period, documents and forms for documents are more often called *ṣakk*, pl. *ṣukūk* (to Ṭaḥāwī this can only mean a document recording a debt), and in the west, *wathīqa*, pl. *wathā'iq*.

[2] That legal treatises can be a source for the study of economic and social conditions in the medieval Muslim world has been convincingly shown most recently by A. Udovitch in his *Partnership and Profit in Medieval Islam* (Princeton, 1970); discussion, 3-7.

literature on documentary practice in other legal systems, little is known about that practice in Islam. For private legal acts, our main source of information has always been the Arabic papyri,[1] the actual documents that have survived since the earliest times, and to which we must now add the Geniza records. However, the nature of these materials has not permitted a systematic study of documentary practice. The finds are haphazard, and for the earlier period, almost entirely limited to Egypt. Because the papyri are often inaccessible, scattered as they are all over the world, and extremely difficult to read, only a relatively small proportion has been published.

The edited papyri, as the notes to this text will show, are often a help in understanding individual formulas and clauses. Yet a great deal has gone unnoticed even in Grohman's monumental work and, conversely, the *shurūṭ* are an important aid to reading and understanding the papyri and surviving contracts.

Arabic documentary practice gains another dimension when it is compared with other systems in the pre-Islamic Near East[2] and later in Europe.[3] There is considerable evidence of cultural continuity, not only in individual formulas, but also in the structure of the documents. Grohmann has shown, for example, that Arabic notaries borrowed certain stylistic details from Greco-Egyptian

[1] For papyrology and its connection with the study of documentary practice, see Grohmann, *Einführung*, 107-126.

[2] The extent of influence or dependence is difficult to assess and beyond the scope of this Introduction. However, in order to gain perspective on the Arabic formulary, it is useful to refer to studies on pre-Islamic Near Eastern law and documents. Not only Coptic legal practice (and its immediate predecessor, the Greco-Egyptian law of Byzantine times) but also Semitic Near Eastern legal systems contributed to the Arabic formulary. The literature is extensive; the study of documentary practice was stimulated by the need to discover the law itself, for documents often provided the only source. For some general remarks on determining the influence of older usage, see the last two chapters in R. Yaron, *Introduction to the Law of the Aramaic Papyri* (London, 1961). The fundamental treatment of ancient Near Eastern law of sale is M. San Nicolò, *Die Schlussklauseln der altbabylonischen Kauf- und Tauschverträge* (Munich, 1922), where the principles of Old Babylonian law are explained through a study of final settlement clauses. Yaron's articles, many of them summarized in the book just mentioned, discuss the practice at Elephantine. The valuable recent work by Y. Muffs, *Studies in the Aramaic Legal Papyri from Elephantine* (Leiden, 1969), a model of method in comparative studies, is a broad investigation of "satisfaction" clauses, i.e., quittance clauses. Demotic documents have been studied by E. Seidl; see his contribution to *Orientalisches Recht* (Leiden, 1964) and references there. For Coptic documents and references to Byzantine forms in Egypt, A. Steinwenter's *Das Recht der koptischen Urkunden* (Munich, 1955) is valuable, as are the many articles of A. Schiller cited in this Introduction. While these works, as well as others used here, are not all necessarily definitive, I have depended on them because they conveniently sum up previous research or present useful arguments.

[3] Among a number of works on documentary practice in early medieval Europe, perhaps the best known is H. Steinacker's *Die antiken Grundlagen der frühmittelalterlichen Privaturkunde* (Leipzig, 1927).

models,[1] while Hoenerbach, in a systematic study of Islamic and Christian documents in Spain after the reconquest, has demonstrated a complex process of exchange.[2]

In Egypt, at least, and perhaps in the other formerly Byzantine provinces, the Arab conquerors most likely took over the prevailing notarial practice.[3] This practice was already the heir to a very ancient system, composed of many different streams. Terms had accumulated through the ages, new expressions added as the meaning of old ones changed or were forgotten, while others were lost through the process of transfer to a new legal context. Many other expressions lay embedded in the formulary, fossilized.

Similarly, the Arabic formulary, having acquired many of these stylistic elements, had to be interpreted according to Islamic law and adapted to its needs. The contracts offer us a superb example of how a foreign institution was taken over intact, assimilated, and reinterpreted in an Islamic context. Many examples of this reinterpretation occur in Ṭaḥāwī's text, and there we can see one more instance of the creativity of the early legal scholars.

[1] In notes to his several editions for the most part, but a short statement in *FWAP*, 189. The relationship is not difficult to understand. The Coptic notaries were strongly influenced by the authors of the fifth and sixth century Byzantine documents, and during this period, at least, even co-existed with them. Similarly, the Arabic notary practiced side by side with his colleague writing in Coptic and using Coptic notarial forms, in the early Islamic period. A. Steinwenter has emphasized the dependence of the Coptic on the late Byzantine notarial forms. See *Die Bedeutung der Papyrologie für die koptische Urkundenlehre* (Munich, 1934), 302-313. E. Seidl sees more than mere borrowing; even though the legal documents were drawn up in the Egyptian (i.e., now the Coptic) language, he says, "on closer examination it becomes evident that the phrases used there were nothing but translations of those used in Greek documents." See his article "Law" in *The Legacy of Egypt*, ed. S.R.K. Glanville (Oxford, 1942), 216. For some remarks on the parallelisms in these documentary forms and the literature summing up the discussion, see A. Schiller, "Prolegomena to the Study of Coptic Law," *Archives d'Histoire du Droit Oriental*, II (1938), 360-361.

[2] *Spanisch-islamische Urkunden aus der Zeit der Naṣriden und Moriscos* (Berkeley and Los Angeles, 1965).

[3] The development in the formerly Persian provinces is much more obscure, partly because few private legal documents have survived, but more because *shurūṭ* handbooks written in the east are a later development and are based directly on forms established by Ḥanafī scholars in Egypt, Syria and Iraq.

Iraq was, of course, a Persian province, but there is no reason why local documentary practice had to derive from Sassanian practice. If we are to look for influences, it would be more useful to seek them in other sources. The schema that San Nicolò has given for neo-Babylonian documents shows many characteristics identical with the *shurūṭ* formulas. (See Schacht "Vom babylonischen zum islamischen Recht," *OLZ*, 1927, cols. 663-669.) Moreover, it was Hellenistic learning that prevailed when Islamic law, and the first discussions on *shurūṭ*, began to be formulated in Iraq.

However, the question that must finally concern us is how a fully developed branch of technical legal literature arose out of this documentary practice and served its needs. Some general lines of approach can be suggested. First, the question of origins must go back to the related institutions of notarial practice and *shahāda*, or witnessing. Second, the reasons why the legal scholars found it necessary to produce a body of works as an instrument of the practice must be sought in the broader consideration of the conflicting claims of theory versus practice in Islamic law. Both of these explanations must be seen in the light of the ambiguous status of written documents in Islam.

It is now well established that Islamic law came into being as an idealistic system, independent of current legal practice and sometimes even opposed to it.[1] Even though much of the raw material of early Islamic law may have come from the existing practice of Syria, Iraq and the Hijaz, local custom was never recognized as one of the Sharī'a's sources. On the contrary, classical Islamic law was based on a pure religious standard, the main concern being how a Muslim ought to live in this world in order to attain the everlasting joys of Paradise.

One of the consequences of this approach was that Islamic legal theory demanded that the believers abandon those practices and standards of conduct that had evolved out of millennia-old experience and that had adjusted to current social needs. The ideal religious law, as it crystallized in the doctrine of the texts, was formally to replace this tradition. But in many legal spheres, the realities of everyday life were too compelling to permit conformity to these standards. This was particularly true in commercial law, where the demands of an urban and increasingly complex society placed a further strain on doctrine. Eventually the scholars, eager to maintain the inviolability of the Sharī'a, found ways to assimilate the practice when they could, and to accommodate it by realistic means when they could not.

Thus, many institutions, never quite recognized by theory, learned to live with it. One of these was the practice of using written documents for private transactions. On the one hand, doctrine discouraged their use by refusing to allow documents as legal proof, and accepting only the oral testimony of witnesses. This rule denying the validity of the written act

[1] A comprehensive statement on the relationship between theory and practice will be found in Schacht, *Introduction*, 76-85, a summary of his many previous discussions. A bibliography of various aspects of this conflict, compiled by him, on 239-244. For the historical and dialectical processes by which Islamic law absorbed local custom, see his *Origins*.

originated during the first century, for it is mentioned by John of Damascus.[1]

Yet, private contracts of all kinds depended on written instruments, and from the earliest Islamic times they were used extensively.[2] This was only natural, for the use of legal documents is an institution in the Near East that has an unbroken tradition since cuneiform times. As Tyan suggests, it is difficult to believe that the populations of the former Byzantine provinces would relinquish such a convenient, legally necessary and thoroughly established custom simply because they had changed their religion and language.[3] In pre-Islamic Arabia, the written document was also known, serving the bustling commercial activity and financial operations of the Meccans.

The rule against the validity of written documents not only ignored custom, it contradicted an explicit ruling of the Qur'ān (Sur. 2:282) that obviously demanded written documents in some circumstances, at least:

> "When you contract a debt for a fixed term, record it in writing. Let a scribe record it in writing between you.... Be not averse to writing down [the contract], whether [the amount] be small or great, with its term."

The verse adds that if the merchandise is transferred in a direct cash sale, "it is no sin if you do not write it down," implying that the parties ought to do so.

The other textual source for Islamic law, the *ḥadīth*, also supports the use of documents. A number of traditions establish the precedents: the Prophet ordered 'Alī to draw up a document in his name at Ḥudaybiya, he bought

[1] Schacht, *Origins*, 188, citing Migne, *Patrologiae Cursus Completus, Series Graeca*, XCIV, 768. We know nothing about the means by which this rule came into being. But perhaps it is not too far-fetched to suggest that the ideological milieu that gave rise to it is one that is attested in many traditions, namely, the attempt on the part of many early Muslims to put forth the image of the rude, illiterate bedouin as the ideal of piety. Apart from the genesis of the rule, the reasons for its persistence are discussed below, 6-8.

[2] For example, Mālik mentions that in the time of Marwān (i.e., when he was governor of Madīna), *ṣukūk*, or documents for subventions being doled out by the state (foodstuffs in this case), were being traded by the Madinese among themselves. It was not the *ṣukūk* that Mālik objected to, but the *ribā* involved in speculation. *Muwaṭṭa'*, with the commentary of Zurqānī (Cairo, 1310), III, 118.

The title deeds that appear inscribed on wood or stone on private houses, buildings of pious foundations and other structures, are nothing less than legal documents, too, drawn up in the same legally valid form as a contract. A list of the most important is given in J. David-Weill, "Un nouveau titre de propriété daté," *Mél. Gaudefroy-Demombynes* (Cairo, 1935-1945), 141-146. See also his *Catalogue général du Musée arabe du Caire: Les bois épigraphes jusqu'à l'époque mamlouke* (Cairo, 1931), *passim*, for further examples. A recently published *waqf* inscription on stone from Palestine is written in the conventional form for *waqf* documents: M. Sharon, "A Waqf Inscription from Ramlah," *Arabica*, XIII (February, 1966).

[3] *Notariat*, 7.

a slave from a Companion and drafted a written contract,[1] he ordered his *'āmils*, his representatives abroad, to draft documents,[2] and so on.

Despite all this, the jurists never modified their attitude toward written documents and managed to avoid the Qur'ānic injunction by interpreting it as a simple recommendation. Documents, says Ṭaḥāwī, are not enjoined as a duty, nor are they forbidden; they are a useful support for oral testimony in that they help keep the debtor and creditor from forgetting the terms of their agreement. Moreover, the traditions are cited by Ṭaḥāwī not in support of documents at all, but as precedents to justify the wording of one clause or another.

Thus, oral testimony provided the only form of proof in the Sharī'a. In the earlier period of Islamic law, the religious scholars tried to ensure that its exclusive use would be maintained by rejecting written evidence. This attitude was in keeping with their idealistic approach to the law and their tendency to treat such questions in the light of religious and ethical standards. For not only was written evidence unacceptable, so too was circumstantial evidence. The personal word of an upright Muslim was deemed worthier than an abstract piece of paper or a piece of information subject to doubt and falsification. This reliance on religious standards is also apparent in the judicial oath (*yamīn*), for the assumption was that no Muslim would lie under oath.

Related to this characteristic Islamic tendency is another, in the field of proof, that has been observed by Brunschvig. It is less important, he notes, to pursue the strict truth, the knowledge of which belongs only to God, than it is to establish by regulated means and in a humane fashion, what is most probable.[3]

Second, if the Qur'ān enjoins written evidence, it also strongly supports the evidence of witnesses, who ought to confirm recognition of the debt as soon as the debtor has dictated its terms to the scribe. The Qur'ān also recommends that certain other legal acts be established by witnesses,[4] and its emphasis on witnesses to prove crimes punishable by *ḥadd*[5] may have influenced the attitude toward oral testimony in civil transactions.

Furthermore, although Islamic law developed the witness system to a high degree, the jurists did not invent it. Witnesses were common in the pre-Islamic Near East. There need not be a direct correlation between the use

[1] I 2.4, 2.8 and ff.

[2] Sarakhsī, 168.

[3] *EI*², "Bayyina."

[4] *SEI*, "Shāhid"; *EI*², "Bayyina."

[5] Fixed penalties, stated in the Qur'ān, for certain crimes.

of writing and the presence of a legal system, and often writing is known for long periods of time before it becomes common in legal transactions.[1] In the primitive law of Arabia, the use of witnesses for giving evidence was surely the more common form of proof, and legal transactions may even have been accompanied by a ceremony performed for the benefit of witnesses.[2] Witnesses were also required in the legally advanced societies of the ancient Near East even though their testimony only augmented the validity of the document itself. Their names and attestations were usually furnished in the documents so that they might be called upon to give evidence in a future lawsuit.[3]

At first this exclusive reliance on witnesses in Islamic law led to certain inconveniences that impaired the efficiency of the system. Most important was the possibility that the moral and religious character of the witnesses would be challenged and the transaction upset. This flaw in the system gave rise, at an early date,[4] to the institution of fixed witnesses, the *shahāda*, in the abstract sense of the term. The moral uprightness (*'adāla*) of an individual was determined by a qadi once and for all through a regulated procedure of screening and formal certification. If established, he was qualified to be a witness whose testimony, in principle, could not be doubted. In this way there arose a permanent body of accredited witnesses[5] who not only testified for and against private claims, but who also became personnel of the court.

Among their duties, one of the most important was to witness and furnish proof of the proceedings of the court and of the qadi's judgments. At the same time, clerks of the court also recorded these proceedings and judgments according to fixed forms.[6] The obvious duplication of function came about because even the documents and archives of the tribunal were not considered valid unless they were duly witnessed. Just as in the case of private documents, which had no value without the attestation of two or more witnesses to their contents, the text of public documents also required oral testimony.

[1] W. Seagle, *The Quest for Law* (New York, 1941), 34, 116.

[2] For example, the *ṣafqa*, striking of hands.

[3] Greco-Roman practice in the Near East, Tyan, *Notariat*, 10 and references there; Coptic documents, Schiller, "Coptic Law," *The Juridical Review*, XLIII (1931), 217 and n. 12; Aramaic and demotic practice, Yaron, *Aramaic Papyri*, 16-24; Mesopotamian practice, San Nicolò, *Schlussklauseln*, 22.

[4] According to Kindī, in Egypt in the year 174/790. Quoted by Tyan, *Organisation*, 239-241. This important work contains the best treatment of the institution of *shahāda*, 236-252.

[5] *shāhid 'adl* (pl. *shuhūd 'udūl*), usually shortened to *shuhūd* in Cairo and Baghdad and to *'udūl* in the Maghrib and the east. On the lists of witnesses drawn up to recruit court personnel, see the remarks of C. Cahen, "A propos des Shuhūd," *SI*, XXXI, 75-77.

[6] *maḥāḍir* and *sijillāt*; see below, pp. 11-12.

Thus, the refusal to recognize written documents, originally intended to safeguard oral testimony, acted in turn to reinforce the witness system. Before long, the number of witnesses in any given city greatly increased.[1] At the same time, the witness played a significant social role in the Muslim community. The qadi, who determined his good moral character, was able to insure that Islamic standards would be maintained and carried forward. The function of witness was a religious one (*waẓīfa dīniyya*, as opposed to administrative) because he was attached to the Sharīʿa court.[2] And though in later times many people complained of their corruption,[3] as members of the literate and professional élite of the urban bourgeoisie, they were persons to be emulated with respect to ethical and social standards. Witnesses were counted among the notables of the town, the *aʿyān al-nās* or the *aʿyān al-bilād*,[4] and were in touch with many of the economic and social concerns of the community. Ibn Khaldūn hints at this when he says that witnesses were useful to the qadi in finding out about the probity of other men in a large and complex city.[5] In short, the witness, a person certified to be of good moral character, penetrated the whole of society and was influential in preserving and spreading Islamic norms. The latent contributions he made to Islamic society, together with a certain degree of social inertia and the operation of vested interests, may help explain why he continued to flourish for so long.

The importance of oral testimony and the position of witnesses help us appreciate the reasons for the continued rejection of the written instrument as a form of proof. That it eventually did become more widely accepted by doctrine has been shown by Tyan in his valuable monograph. However, this

[1] About the year 300/912 there were 1800 witnesses in Baghdad; A. Mez, *The Renaissance of Islam* (Patna, 1937), 228-229. In 383/993 the number was cut down to 303. The figure of 36,000 nominated by a single qadi (although only 16,000 availed themselves of the honor) must be considered fanciful (Mez, 228, citing Amedroz's reading of Tanūkhī). Several other figures are given by Mez. In Mamlūk Cairo, the qadis were ordered to clear their rolls regularly to curb excessive expansion; I. Lapidus, *Muslim Cities in the Later Middle Ages* (Cambridge, Mass., 1967), 137. Also, see Tyan, *Organisation*, 243-244.

[2] Tyan, *Notariat*, 27; Grohmann, *Einführung*, 112.

[3] In particular, see the treatise of Lisān al-Dīn b. al-Khaṭīb, *Mutlā al-ṭarīqa fī ḏamm al-wathīqa*, recently edited and studied by A. Turki in *Arabica*, XVI (1969). Apart from its linguistic and literary interest, the treatise tells us a good deal about the role of the notary in fourteenth century North Africa.

[4] Lapidus, 80-81, 264-265, n. 1.

[5] *The Muqaddima*, trans. F. Rosenthal (New York, 1958), I, 462. Witnesses could have other professions besides. Some witnesses were Kārimis or spice merchants (Lapidus, 211, 213), and in a sampling of merchants who had part-time careers as members of the broadly-based *ʿulamā*' class, a large number were found to be witnesses (109).

was a development that took place mostly in the Mālikī school; documents were proof only under restricted circumstances, and only after qualified witnesses had attested their contents.[1]

The Ḥanafīs were more hesitant in accepting written evidence but eventually the principle of *istiḥsān* ("juristic preference") prevailed. Some jurists conceded that in certain cases, if there were absolutely no possibility of a document being falsified—if it had been preserved in the court archives, for example, as were the *maḥāḍir*, the minutes of the court—it may be valid evidence, provided it had already been duly witnessed. Thus it became common to draw up witnessed documents before the qadi and then deposit them in his archives for safekeeping.[2] Even though the exception was narrowly defined, then, its effect was significant for the practice. The acceptance was finally confirmed, albeit in a negative way, in the *Mejelle*, the Ottoman Civil Code of 1877, which declared that the witnessed document had no value in itself—unless it met those requirements mentioned above. However, legal tradition dies hard, and the *Mejelle* still regarded as the basic type of evidence that given by witnesses whose *'adāla* had to be established.

While doctrine may have neglected the written instrument, in practice it was indispensable. Not only did written contracts serve an imperative economic function, but they touched more private areas of life as well. Such acts as marriage contracts, legacies, the emancipation of slaves, were recorded in writing.

It was important, of course, that these contracts be witnessed so that evidence could be produced in case of litigation, but in addition they had to be drawn up in the correct form. Thus it was natural that the professional witness often exercised the function of notary. The dual role of the *shuhūd* is described by Ibn Khaldūn:

> "In every city, [the witnesses] have their own shops and benches where they always sit, so that people who have transactions to make can engage them to function as witnesses and register the (testimony) in writing."[3]

[1] Tyan, *Notariat*, 76, 82-84.

[2] Tyan, *Notariat*, 79; Ḥanafī position summed up on 78-79.

[3] *The Muqaddima*, I, 462. On the development of the *shuhūd* into notaries, a development that occurred especially among the Mālikīs, see the references in *SEI*, art. "Shāhid," at the end. *Shurūṭ* handbooks sometimes provide preliminary sections on the qualifications of the notary; Tyan draws on these for his discussion of the profession (*Notariat*, 14-41). These prefaces are most interesting for what they reveal about the approach of their authors. For instance, Nuwayrī's introduction to Ṣayrafī's *shurūṭ* work (in the *Nihāyat al-Arab*, IX, 1-9; below, p. 13, n. 3), with its emphasis on outward forms (good calligraphy, the public impression the notary ought to make while he is in court, and so on), shows how different this

There were many practical advantages in consulting a witness/notary to have a document drawn up, but the most important was that he would be likely to have the technical knowledge to produce a sound document, stylistically correct and recording a legally valid operation. Thus, one of his obligations, as we will see, was to act as legal advisor to his clients. Once the profession became established, it was only one more step to provide him with a manual standardizing his professional activity and reducing the effort of creating a new, acceptable instrument on each occasion. From this point of view, the *shurūṭ* literature was a direct outgrowth of the practice.

2. ṬAḤĀWĪ AND THE SHURŪṬ TRADITION IN THE ḤANAFĪ SCHOOL.

In a broader sense, the *shurūṭ* literature grew out of the attempt by jurists to bring ideal theory and practice closer together. They were aware of the growing separation from the very beginning, for even while they were elaborating their doctrine, they were creating ways to make room for the practice, although without specifically admitting that this could be done. The aim was to keep practice under the control of doctrine, for otherwise their own system would have been undermined.

One of the ways by which the jurists, particularly the scholars of the Ḥanafī school, tried to accommodate practice was to create certain forms of literature that had as their immediate purpose the smooth operation of law and legal procedures in everyday life. This literature consisted of a variety of practical works, intended not to discover or even explain the law, but to help the qadi and other concerned persons in the law's application.

The works on *shurūṭ* are an outstanding example of this literature. These handbooks, or formularies, were designed especially for the professional notary, and contained model contracts, legally correct in every detail, for all possible needs. The notary had only to select the model that suited the particular need of his client, fill in the "blank spaces" (that is, their equivalents, *kadhā* and *fulān*, "such-and-such" and "so-and-so"), and add the signatures of the witnesses. If the paradox in the official rejection and widespread use of written

author's aims are from those of Ṭaḥāwī. Ṭaḥāwī ignores such matters altogether, and is interested only in the notary's ability to bring about certain legal effects, using the document as a means to this, and the consequences should he fail to do so. Further, compare the excerpt from a Mālikī work in Hoenerbach (*Urkunden*, 49-50), a straightforward list of the qualifications set by religious law, and the first chapter of the *Fatāwā ʿĀlamgīriyya* (below, p. 27), on technical terminology.

contracts epitomizes the conflict between theory and practice, the very existence of these *shurūṭ* works shows us how the scholars tried to make that conflict less sharply felt.

Another outstanding example of this practical literature are the treatises on *ḥiyal*,[1] legal devices or evasions. Often compiled by the great jurists themselves, *ḥiyal* works were handbooks showing interested persons, particularly the merchants, how they could follow the letter of the law and yet arrive at a different result than that intended by the law.

The *shurūṭ* formularies, of course, were not meant in themselves to evade the formal prescriptions of the law. They also differed from the *ḥiyal* works in that they had a much broader application in the practice, simply because the legal subject matter covered by documents is more extensive. It was natural, then, that the *shurūṭ* treatises would be more widely distributed.

But the two were alike in that their effectiveness depended on a fool-proof legal validity that would pass the scrutiny of the qadi who had to apply the Sharī'a. The purpose was to carry out the intentions of the client—regardless of whether these were legal or illegal—and to avoid the transaction being upset in any way. The *shurūṭ* served the *ḥiyal* in a direct way, for each step of a complicated transaction was, as a matter of course, recorded in a separate witnessed document. Most important, like the *ḥiyal* works, the *shurūṭ* treatises expressed the unequivocal acknowledgement by the Ḥanafī jurists that the needs of the practice had to be met in the most direct way possible.

Books on *shurūṭ* and *ḥiyal* were two important subdivisions within this category of practical literature. Another group of works were the *maḥāḍir* and *sijillāt*, formularies containing model documents for use of the qadi and his clerks acting in the capacity of notaries.[2] More exactly, the *maḥāḍir* were the written records of the proceedings before the qadi, the minutes of the court, and the *sijillāt* were the written judgments containing the qadi's decisions.[3]

[1] The subject was studied several years ago by Schacht, first in "Die arabische *ḥijal*-Literatur," *Der Islam*, XV (1926), and then in his "Zur soziologischen Betrachtungen des islamischen Rechts," *Der Islam*, XXII (1935). For his several editions of Arabic *ḥiyal* works, see *EI*², s.v. "Ḥiyal."

[2] Above, p. 7. See Tyan, *Notariat*, 38, 44, and for his discussion of the notarial functions of the qadi, 86-89; Schacht, *Introduction*, 83, 189, for definitions.

[3] For the meaning of the term *sijill* (certificate of safe conduct) in pre-Islamic Egypt, see A. Schiller, "The Coptic Word of God Documents," in *Studi in Memoria di Aldo Albertoni*, I (Padova, 1933). Once the term passed into Arabic it acquired a variety of meanings related to one another. In the Qur'ān it is (mistakenly) the "registrar" or "recorder" (Sur. 21:104) from Lat. *sigillum*. Then it was used to mean the text of a judgement and by extension the register of judicial decisions and even any official register (Kindī, *Wulāt*, 397; Tyan, *Organisation*, 181, n. 7). It also meant the diploma of investiture of a qadi (*Organisa-*

These formularies were, by their very nature, closely connected with *shurūṭ* works. In fact, they often appear as separate chapters at the end of *shurūṭ* treatises.[1] An author of one frequently will have composed a separate work on the other. On the other hand, the treatment of each in the commentaries of the handbooks differs to some extent, because the *maḥāḍir* and *sijillāt* were not private deeds, but were documents preserved in the official court archives.

Several other subjects of practical importance completed this branch of legal literature. Among them were works on the duties of the qadi (*adab al-qāḍī*, *wilāyat al-qāḍī*), on pious endowments (*waqf*), legacies (*waṣāyā*) and the law of succession (*farā'iḍ*), and maintenance of a wife (*nafaqāt*).[2] They were all loosely tied together by the fact that they tended to appear in connection with the same authors and because a certain literary continuity was maintained over the centuries.

The scholars of the Ḥanafī school in the older period played a special role in the creation of this literature.[3] Perhaps it was the common sense characteristic of the Ḥanafī jurists, combined with their tendency toward speculative reasoning, that prompted them to cultivate these themes. Whatever the reason, a continuing tradition was established, and with one important exception, none of the other schools was able to produce a comparable body of literature.

It has been shown, for example, that although Shāfi'ī authors eventually produced *ḥiyal* works themselves, these were a later synthetic creation made

tion, 181-182) and a document drawn up by a qadi nominating a witness (244). The verb *sajjala* usually means "to draft a document." Finally, *sijill* commonly appears in the Egyptian papyri for a contract of lease, because these were entered in the land registers of the local tax offices (*APEL* II, 51, note to l. 18).

[1] One of the last chapters of Ṭaḥāwī's long version of his book is, in fact, his "Kitāb al-Maḥāḍir." Transcribed by the same two copyists as the "K. al-Buyū'," it is a long chapter of about 260 folios, in three parts (*juz'*). Immediately preceding the "K. al-Maḥāḍir" and catalogued with it is Ṭaḥāwī's "K. Wilāyat al-Qaḍā'," on the jurisdiction of the qadi, another subdivision within his *shurūṭ* work.

The abridged version of Ṭaḥāwī's text contains corresponding chapters and, in addition, his "K. al-Sijillāt," followed by other chapters pertaining to documents used by the courts. We can assume that these, too, formed part of the larger work but have been lost.

The other important extant work on *maḥāḍir* and *sijillāt* is contained in a separate chapter of the *Fatāwā 'Ālamgīriyya*, VI, 247-371; see below, p. 26.

A brief but interesting handbook with some relation to these works has been published by R.B. Serjeant. It is a Shāfi'ī formulary for pleas, written by a qadi of the Ḥaḍramaut who died in 930/1524. "Forms of Plea, a Šāfi'ī Manual from al-Šiḥr," *Revista degli Studi Orientali*, XXX (1955).

[2] For the titles and authors of some of these, see Schacht, *Introduction*, 264.

[3] See Schacht, "Ḥiyal," 216-217, 221, and the article "Ḥanafiyya" in *EI*².

possible largely by the success of the Ḥanafī works.[1] In the case of treatises on *shurūṭ*, the Shāfiʿīs were also far behind. Although the Imām al-Shāfiʿī was himself the author of a *shurūṭ* work,[2] the number produced and the quality of those that have survived allow us to make the same judgment as was made in the case of the *ḥiyal* works.[3]

The Ḥanbalīs, in keeping with their highly idealistic and uncompromising approach to religious law, produced no *shurūṭ* works that we know of, while they took a distinctively negative attitude toward *ḥiyal*. This is not to say that the actual use of written documents was not equally widespread in all schools. The Ḥanbalīs undoubtedly drew up written contracts to the same extent as everyone else,[4] even though the practice of so doing was not complemented for them by a field of intellectual speculation.[5]

The one exception to these remarks, however, applies to the independent development in the Mālikī school of *wathāʾiq* literature, as *shurūṭ* was called in the west. For although the Mālikī jurists were in fact hostile to the subject of *ḥiyal*, their interest in the formularies began at a very early date. However, the Mālikī tradition went through a somewhat different process of development. Gradually, the science of *shurūṭ* was pursued not only for its own sake, as a subject of intellectual interest, but even more as a practical outcome of

[1] "Ḥiyal," 224-225 for the Shāfiʿī contribution.

[2] *Fihrist*, II, 210. Two original documents, a *waqf* endowed by him and his *waṣiyya*, both dated in the year 203, have been incorporated in his *Kitāb al-Umm*; for texts and translations, see F. Kern, "Zwei Urkunden vom Imām aš-Šāfiʿī," *Mitt. d. Sem. f. Orient. Sprachen*, VII (1904).

[3] There are many manuscripts extant, but the one Shāfiʿī *shurūṭ* work that is readily accessible is that of al-Ṣayrafī (d. 330/941). It is a somewhat superficial, formalistic work, with little interest in the law as such; the formulas, often based more on literary considerations than on solid practical grounds, could not have had great importance for the practice. See above, p. 9, n. 3.

[4] For mention of a Ḥanbalī qadi who was considered the expert of his time in drawing up *shurūṭ*, see G. Makdisi, *Ibn ʿAqīl et la résurgence de l'Islam traditionaliste au XIe siècle*, Damascus (1963), 491, citing Ibn Rajab's *Dhayl ʿalā Ṭabaqāt al-Ḥanābila*.

[5] We ought to keep in mind Laoust's observation that the Ḥanbalī formula for strictness in prescribed religious practice is combined with wide tolerance in matters of usage (*EI*², s.v. "Ḥanābila" and "Aḥmad b. Ḥanbal").

A short manuscript in the Ẓāhiriyya library (Fiqh Ḥanbalī 70) begins with a strong statement in favor of *shurūṭ* works. The author, ʿAlāʾ al-Dīn b. Mufliḥ (d. 884; see *EI*², s.v. "Ibn Mufliḥ" for information on various members of the family) reviews the position of the other schools on accepting witnessed documents as evidence. He complains that since other schools will admit them under certain circumstances, strictly defined, then the Ḥanbalīs should do so too. He cites a number of traditions in support of documents and points out that the community would not even have these traditions had they not been transmitted in written form.

customary law in North Africa.[1] The *wathā'iq* works eventually became closely connected with the *'amal*, the practice of the courts, because the terms of documents were always drafted in accordance with this judicial practice, regardless of whether or not it agreed with classical doctrine.[2] The opinions of the jurists in defining this practice were thus expressed in these *wathā'iq* formularies and particularly in the commentaries to these works (as well as in other handbooks), and they became an authoritative source for establishing and expounding the *'amal*.

Mālikī *wathā'iq* and Ḥanafī *shurūṭ*, then, may be studied and discussed separately without loss of understanding. But there is a positive reason for doing so, related to the nature of Islamic legal literature in general. For just as continuity within the *madhhab* was maintained, so too did certain kinds of literature develop in isolation, within any given school, with little reference by one school to that of another.

Ṭaḥāwī's text is itself a revealing example. The sources upon which he drew for his book form a clear line of tradition for the drafting of written documents, going back several generations. This tradition is both oral and written, and the strands that make it up are many. Furthermore, it never crosses the borders of the *madhhab*: one cannot find an instance in the entire "K. al-Buyū'" where Ṭaḥāwī has gone outside his school to cite an authority on *shurūṭ*.[3] This is particularly striking especially when we recall that Ṭaḥāwī had been a member of the Shāfi'ī school and must have been acquainted with Shāfi'ī's book on the subject. Indeed, Muzanī, Ṭaḥāwī's uncle, former teacher, and renowned disciple of Shāfi'ī, is known to have composed a *shurūṭ* handbook himself.[4] Certainly Shāfi'ī and Mālikī handbooks circulated in Egypt and Syria at the time, yet there is no reference to them at all, nor to their authors, or the formulas their authors preferred. So although it might be useful, in studying individual contracts, to compare formulas as they were used in the

[1] The oldest known work is that of Ibn 'Abdūs, who died in 258, 260, or 261; it is mentioned in the *Wathā'iq al-Majmū'a* of M. b. Aḥmad b. al-'Aṭṭār al-Andalūsī (d. 399). For a description of the existing fragments of this work and the contents of the parts that survive, see J. Schacht, "Sur quelques manuscrits de la bibliothèque de la mosquée d'al-Qarawiyyīn à Fès," *Etudes d'Orientalisme dédiées à la mémoire de Lévi-Provençal*, I (Paris, 1962), 276, No. 7. The list of Mālikī *wathā'iq* authors given in Hoenerbach, *Urkunden*, xxvii ff., should be corrected from the information in this article.

[2] Coulson, 146.

[3] Of course, Ṭaḥāwī sometimes mentions the authorities of other schools (and frequently, Ḥanafī jurists) on points of legal doctrine, but this is related to his concern with the *ikhtilāf*, or difference of opinion among scholars on points of positive law.

[4] *Fihrist*, II, 212; Ḥajjī Khalīfa, IV, 47.

actual practice, there is little to be gained in treating *shurūṭ* literature as a single entity.

The Ḥanafī *shurūṭ* tradition was already firmly established by the time Ṭaḥāwī composed his handbook in the second half of the third century. Several specialists had composed written works before this date, but the representatives of the *shurūṭ* tradition also included a number of persons whose opinions on the writing of formulas were handed down orally.

As far as is known, these persons were all practicing qadis, and drafting documents of various kinds was part of their professional routine. Ṭaḥāwī occasionally supports a statement on how a formula should be worded with "This is how our contemporaries write [the formula] in their *maḥāḍir* and *sijillāt*,"[1] or, "[*x* and *y*] wrote, in their documents of *iqrār* and *barā'āt*..."[2] In the Arabic sources on the early qadis, we often come across information of this kind.[3] To be sure, the formulas were remembered; they became part of the general stock in circulation, and could be referred to by a conscientious judge relying on accepted usage.

Furthermore, Ṭaḥāwī's text clearly shows that there were others who—although they wrote no works on *shurūṭ*—were very popular oral sources for the science of drawing up documents. These persons appear to be more than just casually interested in the subject because it served their own professional needs; they occupied themselves with it to the degree that they can be called true specialists. Such a person was Yūsuf b. Khālid (d. 189), one of the frequently cited names in the "K. al-Buyū'."

Ṭaḥāwī's sources reach back to the formal beginnings of the Ḥanafī school, to the teachings of Abū Ḥanīfa himself.[4] Although Abū Ḥanīfa wrote no works on law, his doctrine is preserved in the writings and teachings of some of the many disciples who gathered around him in Kufa. Some of these disciples transmitted his teachings on *shurūṭ*,[5] with the result that Abū Ḥanīfa's

[1] For example, I 4.3, 2.185.

[2] I 2.185.

[3] 'Īsā b. Abān (d. 220; see below, p. 18) for instance, wrote *sijillāt* for the family of Ja'far b. Sulaymān; he drafted legacies, worked out the calculations for the shares of inheritance, and drew up documents for cases when an heir dies before a legacy is divided (*munāsakhāt*). Wakī', *Quḍāt*, II, 172.

[4] Abū Ḥanīfa died in 150/767, at the age of 70. See the article on him in *EI*^{2}, "Abū Ḥanīfa al-Nu'mān."

[5] Ṭaḥāwī often repeats his formulas without documentation. Otherwise, the usual *isnād* for his opinions on *shurūṭ* is: Sulaymān b. Shu'ayb — his father, Shu'ayb b. Sulaymān al-Kaysānī — Shaybānī — Abū Yūsuf — Abū Ḥanīfa. Less frequently, the first two names are M. b. al-'Abbās b. al-Rabī' al-Lu'lu'ī and 'Alī b. Ma'bad. Other persons connected

"formulary," containing his opinions on the precise manner of phrasing clauses in written documents, has been preserved for us embedded in Ṭaḥāwī's text.[1]

The two most famous disciples of Abū Ḥanīfa, Abū Yūsuf[2] and Shaybānī,[3] also stand out prominently in the Ḥanafī *shurūṭ* tradition. Abū Yūsuf's interest in the practical side of Islamic law is reflected in the titles of some of his works, among which were his *K. al-Ḥiyal*[4] and *K. Adab al-Qāḍī.*[5] No book on written documents is attributed to him, but it would be possible to reconstruct a detailed formulary (just as in the case of Abū Ḥanīfa), based on Ṭaḥāwī's frequent citations.

Having studied as a youth with Abū Ḥanīfa, and trained in *fiqh* by Abū Yūsuf, Muḥammad b. Ḥasan al-Shaybānī naturally absorbed their teachings on *shurūṭ*. In Ṭaḥāwī's treatise, Shaybānī not only acts as a transmitter of their opinions, but his own formulas are discussed and evaluated by Ṭaḥāwī. Further, Shaybānī's work on *shurūṭ* has been preserved for us, and in one sense can be called the oldest formulary known. It exists in extracts incorporated into the commentary of Sarakhsī's *Mabsūṭ*,[6] perhaps the best known systematic presentation of Shaybānī's doctrine. Another source for his formulas are the contracts scattered here and there in Shaybānī's important

with the transmission of *shurūṭ* from Abū Ḥanīfa are M. b. Samā'a, Bakkār b. Qutayba, and Ḥasan b. Ziyād al-Lu'lu'ī. Nearly all these persons wrote *shurūṭ* and are themselves quoted for their opinions.

[1] It is important to note that even at this time there was a fully developed, and even highly stereotyped, Arabic formulary. The sureness and precision of Abū Ḥanīfa's formulas, and the technical sophistication he can apply to the subject, show that such discussions must have been familiar in Iraqi legal circles. Also, Abū Ḥanīfa always refused to accept an appointment as a qadi; his objective interest shows the strong tradition of learning in matters concerning the application of the law in practice.

[2] Abū Yūsuf Ya'qūb lived in Kufa until he was appointed chief qadi in Baghdad, possibly by Hārūn al-Rashīd. He died in the capital in 182/798. See the article on him in *EI*², s.v., and further references there.

[3] Muḥammad b. Ḥasan al-Shaybānī was also a qadi for Hārūn, particularly at Raqqa, and at Rayy in Khurāsān where he died in 189/805 at the age of 58. For his life and work, see *SEI*, s.v. "Shaibānī," and M. Khadduri's introduction to his translation of Shaybānī's *K. al-Siyar*; *The Islamic Law of Nations* (Baltimore, 1966), 22-38. Like Abū Yūsuf, Shaybānī's literary output was extensive; many of his works have survived, and accompanied by lengthy commentaries, have become the standard texts of the *madhhab*.

[4] Extracts are preserved in Shaybānī's *K. al-Makhārij fi'l-Ḥiyal*, ed. Schacht (Leipzig, 1930).

[5] *Classen*, 282-283; the work was dictated. There is a MS in the Tunis National Library; Sezgin, I, 421.

[6] Shams al-A'imma al-Sarakhsī (d. 483/1090). The authoritative treatises of the Ḥanafī school are listed in N.P. Aghnides, *Mohammedan Theories of Finance* (New York, 1916; reprinted Lahore, 1961). Also, *EI*², s.v. "Ḥanafiyya".

work, the *K. al-Aṣl.*[1] It is worth noting in passing how early these contracts found their way into theoretical works.

Another scholar whose name was closely associated with that of Abū Ḥanīfa, and who was at the same time a prominent authority on *shurūṭ*, was Abū Khālid Yūsuf b. Khālid al-Sumtī al-Baṣrī (d. 189/905).[2] For a time Yūsuf was governor of Basra, but withdrew from public life after he made the acquaintance of Abū Yūsuf and turned to the study of religious law. Nothing is known about his writings, except that a *K. al-Rahn* is attributed to him.[3] However, he must have been a great expert on *shurūṭ*; Ṭaḥāwī cites his opinions frequently. His name is nearly always mentioned together with that of Hilāl b. Yaḥyā, not because they necessarily held the same opinions, but because Hilāl was his pupil and the two became identified with one another.

At about the same time that Shaybānī wrote (or dictated) his *shurūṭ*, two leading representatives of the Iraqi school also composed treatises on forms for written documents. These books are, in fact, the first mentioned in the Arabic bio-bibliographical sources.[4]

One of these authors was Muḥammad b. Samā'a, qadi of the west side of Baghdad[5] for many years under Ma'mūn. The *Fihrist* reports that in addition to having related the books of Shaybānī, Muḥammad b. Samā'a himself composed a *K. Adab al-Qāḍī* and a *K. al-Maḥāḍir wa'l-Sijillāt.*[6] Muḥammad, born at about the same time as Shaybānī, died in 233 at an advanced age.

[1] Several incomplete MSS of the *Aṣl* exist, but there is no guide or index to the chapters they contain. I have seen these contracts in a photocopy of a MS in the Dār al-Kutub al-Miṣrīyya (Fiqh Ḥanafī, 34). Chafik Chehata has begun an edition of the *Aṣl* with the parts on *buyū'* and *salam* (Cairo, 1954).

[2] 'Abd al-Qādir, II, No. 711; *Classen*, 286, where Flügel erroneously gives his death date as 179. It was to Yūsuf that the falsely attributed *Waṣiyyat Abī Ḥanīfa* was addressed. This is the "Yūsuf al-Shamanī" of the *Fatāwā 'Ālamgīriyya*, e.g., 423. For his name (al-Samtī?), see Sezgin, I, 417.

[3] 'Abd al-Qādir, II, No. 711.

[4] In the section he devotes to the science of *shurūṭ*, Ḥajjī Khalīfa mistakenly asserts that the first person to compose a book on the subject was Hilāl b. Yaḥyā (*Kashf*, IV, 45; his source on 46).

[5] That is, the *madīnat al-Manṣūr*, the original administrative complex, and therefore the more important post.

[6] Abū 'Abd Allāh M. b. Samā'a al-Tamīmī; *Fihrist*, II, 205. For his biography, see the longer notices in 'Abd al-Qādir, II, No. 189; Ibn Quṭlūbughā, No. 160; Laknawī, No. 354; *Classen*, 287. All these mention his two books, the earliest ('Abd al-Qādir) naming the *Fihrist* as its source.

The *Fihrist* is also our source of information for Qutayba b. Ziyād.[1] Ibn al-Nadīm remarks that he was particularly proficient in composing books on *shurūṭ* and notes a *K. al-Shurūṭ*, the whole of which Ibn al-Nadīm had seen personally, as well as a large work with the comprehensive title of the *K. al-Maḥāḍir wa'l-Sijillāt wa'l-Wathā'iq wa'l-'Uqūd.* It appears somewhat unusual that Ṭaḥāwī does not quote Qutayba b. Ziyād's formulas. Similarly, although he draws on M. b. Samā'a's knowledge of Shaybānī's legal opinions, his formulas are not mentioned.

Neither Ismā'īl b. Ḥammād b. Abī Ḥanīfa (d. 212/827)[2] nor 'Īsā b. Abān b. Ṣadaqa (d. 220/835) composed works on *shurūṭ*, but they are indirectly connected with the tradition through their teachers and pupils. They must be included because Ṭaḥāwī sometimes quotes the formulas they preferred, or devised in their capacity as qadis. Furthermore, 'Īsā b. Abān, who had studied with Shaybānī and who held an important post as qadi of Basra for at least ten years,[3] counted among his foremost pupils two who distinguished themselves as authors of *shurūṭ*. One of these was Ṭaḥāwī's teacher in Damascus, Abū Khāzim;[4] the other was Bakkār b. Qutayba, the noted qadi of Miṣr, friend and mentor of Ṭaḥāwī.[5]

Similarly, Ṭaḥāwī draws on the formulas of the qadis Bishr b. al-Walīd (238/852)[6] and Yaḥyā b. Aktham (243/857).[7] Although no handbooks are

[1] Qutayba b. Ziyād al-Khurāsānī, *Fihrist*, II, 207. The date of his death is not known, but 'Abd al-Qādir (I, No. 1146) comments that he became qadi of the east side of Baghdad at the same time that M. b. Samā'a became qadi of the west side. That was in the year 192. Also, he took part in the questioning of Bishr al-Marīsī to force the latter to retract his views. Bishr died in 218. *EI*², s.v. "Bishr al-Ghiyāth," and Wakī', *Quḍāt*, III, 269-270, 326.

[2] Ismā'īl did not know his grandfather, but handed on his doctrine in at least three works ('Abd al-Qādir, I, No. 329). He was qadi in Basra, Raqqa and the east side of Baghdad. Other notices in Ibn Quṭlūbughā, No. 46, *Classen*, 286. Some interesting decisions of his concerning evidence and procedure are reported by Wakī', *Quḍāt*, II, 167-170, 308.

[3] *Classen*, 288; 'Abd al-Qādir, I, No. 1113; Wakī' makes him qadi of Basra for twenty years and is rather disparaging about 'Īsā's reported contacts with Shaybānī and Abū Yūsuf (II, 170-172). His works, mostly on *uṣūl*, are listed in the *Fihrist*, II, 205. Ṭaḥāwī wrote a refutation of one of them.

[4] In Laknawī's notice of 'Īsā, No. 298.

[5] Kindī, *Wulāt*, 505, in his biography of Bakkār. Bakkār's other teacher was Hilāl b. Yaḥyā.

[6] Bishr is well known as one of the traditionists who experienced the *mihna* of Mutawakkil. He was qadi of both districts of Baghdad. 'Abd al-Qādir, I, No. 374; Laknawī, No. 93; Wakī', *Quḍāt*, III, 272-273, 325-326.

[7] In his notice on the three *shurūṭ* works composed by Dāwūd b. 'Alī al-Isfahānī (Dāwūd al-Ẓāhirī), Ḥajjī Khalīfa mentions that Dāwūd discusses his criticisms of Yaḥyā's *shurūṭ* (*Kashf*, IV, 47). Yaḥyā b. Aktham began his career as a Shāfi'ī and is usually identified as such (C. Brockelmann, *History of the Islamic Peoples* [New York, 1947], 132), but we should

attributed to them, they were apparently skilled in the science and looked to as authorities in the correct manner of drawing up documents. Bishr was the author of a *K. Adab al-Qāḍī*,[1] which may have been Ṭaḥāwī's source.

At about the middle of the third century, the groundwork that had been established by the first two generations of Ḥanafī scholars began to be built up into a more specialized and highly finished structure. Not only did the number of works on *shurūṭ* increase at this time, but there was also a tendency for authors to restrict their fields of interest to related subjects. Accumulation of learning in the science and—undoubtedly—increasing demand for these works inevitably led to specialization.

One of the more influential contributions was made by Hilāl b. Yaḥyā,[2] or Hilāl al-Ra'y, as he was later called because of his identification with the Iraqi school of Abū Ḥanīfa. Hilāl, who died in Basra in 245/858, is an important link in the *shurūṭ* tradition. Having studied with Yūsuf b. Khālid,[3] Abū Yūsuf and Zufar, he later taught the science of *shurūṭ* to Bakkār b. Qutayba in Basra,[4] before Bakkār went to Egypt to become its qadi and chief representative of the Ḥanafī school there. Bakkār transmitted his knowledge of *shurūṭ* directly to Ṭaḥāwī.

The authority Hilāl's opinions commanded is reflected in the frequency with which Ṭaḥāwī refers to them. He probably was able to draw on Hilāl's book, as well as Bakkār's knowledge, for Hilāl was the author of a work mentioned in most of the bio-bibliographic sources,[5] the *K. Tafsīr al-Shurūṭ*. Another of the practical works that he wrote, on the principles of *waqf*, has survived.[6]

A scholar of the third century, whose epithet testifies to his reputation as an expert in his subject, was Abū Zayd Aḥmad b. Zayd al-Shurūṭī. The Arabic biographical sources are silent on his background and training, but

include him among the Ḥanafīs. The Ḥanafī *ṭabaqāt* authors all claim him as their own; further evidence is given by Wakī' (*Quḍāt*, III, 281); and Kindī (*Wulāt*, 518) mentions that the first Shāfi'ī to become qadi of Miṣr was appointed in the year 284, whereas Yaḥyā was appointed by Ma'mūn in 217 (*Wulāt*, 442).

[1] *Classen*, 287.

[2] Abū Bakr Hilāl b. Yaḥyā al-Baṣrī. 'Abd al-Qādir, II, No. 647; Ibn Quṭlūbughā, No. 246 and p. 101, n. 186.

[3] 'Abd al-Qādir, II, No. 711.

[4] Ibn Quṭlūbughā, 14.

[5] Besides the above, *Fihrist*, II, 205; Ḥajjī Khalīfa, IV, 45, who gives his death date erroneously as 249 (p. 46).

[6] *GAL*, G I, 173, S I, 292.

we may gather from Ṭaḥāwī's text that he was a prominent Ḥanafī in his own time. The *Fihrist* identifies him as an Iraqi[1] and names three works on *shurūṭ*, the *K. al-Shurūṭ al-Kabīr*, the *K. al-Shurūṭ al-Ṣaghīr*, and the *K. al-Wathā'iq.*[2] Abū Zayd's *shurūṭ* have been extensively incorporated into Ṭaḥāwī's text. His opinions on the drafting of formulas enter almost every discussion, and if Ṭaḥāwī does not always agree, he takes them carefully into account.

Abū Bakr Aḥmad b. 'Amr al-Khaṣṣāf[3] occupies a special place in the history of Ḥanafī literature, particularly for the number of works he produced devoted to practical subjects.[4] Some of these achieved a considerable reputation, and at least one, his *K. Adab al-Qāḍī*, a comprehensive work of 120 chapters,[5] attracted several commentaries. At least two of these were by *shurūṭ* authors of the sixth century.[6] This handbook, as well as his important *K. Aḥkām al-Waqf* and another work, on maintenance, still survives.[7]

Khaṣṣāf also wrote a *K. al-Maḥāḍir wa'l-Sijillāt*, and two works on *shurūṭ*, a *K. al-Shurūṭ al-Kabīr* and a *K. al-Shurūṭ al-Ṣaghīr*. These are lost, unfortunately, and because Ṭaḥāwī does not quote Khaṣṣāf extensively in the "K. al-Buyū'," except perhaps, indirectly, as "one of the Baghdadis," we are unable to gain an idea of what his formulas were like. It is possible, of course, that Ṭaḥāwī never had access to these works. Khaṣṣāf had been court lawyer to Muhtadī, and when the caliph was murdered in 256/869, Khaṣṣāf's house was sacked by the Turkish guard. Although he managed to escape to Baghdad, his library was destroyed, and some of his own manuscripts may have disappeared in this way. It is more likely, however, that Ṭaḥāwī does not rely on Khaṣṣāf as much as we would expect because, even though they are close

1 Indications in Ṭaḥāwī and Sarakhsī (170) make it certain that he was a Baghdadi. His name is not associated with that of anyone else, and it is therefore difficult to assign him an approximate date of death. However, Laknawī, citing the *K. al-Irshād* of Abū Ya'lā al-Khalīlī (d. 446), says that a Muḥammad b. Aḥmad al-Shurūṭī (Abū Zayd's son?) had asked Ṭaḥāwī why he left Muzanī's school (*Fawā'id*, 41). The story is also found in Ibn Khallikān (ed. de Slane), I, 26-27.

2 *Fihrist*, II, 208. Ḥajjī Khalīfa, IV, 45, mentions a *K. al-Shurūṭ al-Mutawassiṭ* instead of the *K. al-Wathā'iq*; they are, perhaps, identical. 'Abd al-Qādir (I, No. 109) cites the *Fihrist* but adds no new information. Also, see Ibn Quṭlūbughā, 91, n. 89.

3 'Abd al-Qādir, I, 161; Ibn Quṭlūbughā, No. 12.

4 The *Fihrist*, II, 206, gives the most complete list. See also Ḥajjī Khalīfa, IV, 46 (where he is called Abū Bakr Aḥmad b. 'Alī).

5 *Classen*, 291-292.

6 See below, pp. 28-29.

7 *GAL*, G I, 173, S I, 292. A work on *ḥiyal* attributed to Khaṣṣāf, but presumably composed in Iraq in the fourth century, has been edited by Schacht (Hanover, 1923); the *Fihrist* lists a work on *ḥiyal*. Also see Sezgin, I, 436-438.

together in time (Khaṣṣāf died in 261/874), Khaṣṣāf stands somewhat outside that branch of the *shurūṭ* tradition, the line of teachers and pupils that leads directly to Ṭaḥāwī in Egypt.

Other Ḥanafī *shurūṭ* authors were active at this time. The Arabic bio-bibliographical sources mention at least four, but we have less information on them; and because Ṭaḥāwī does not include them among his sources, their places in the tradition are not clear.

The first, Abu'l 'Abbās M. b. 'Abd Allāh b. 'Abdūn, was a prominent Ḥanafī who was appointed qadi of Ifrīqiyā (at Qayrawān) in 275.[1] He withdrew from that office two years later and died in Ifrīqiyā in 299. Ibn 'Abdūn wrote a number of works, but according to 'Abd al-Qādir,[2] he was a specialist in the science of *shurūṭ* and wrote some excellent books on the subject. Further, Ṭaḥāwī heard traditions from Ibn 'Abdūn and received his *ijāza*, but when and where this took place is not known. Possibly it was after Ṭaḥāwī wrote his own books, but before Ibn 'Abdūn wrote his, which might account for the fact that he is not mentioned in Ṭaḥāwī's works.

'Alī b. Muqātil al-Rāzī was the author of a *K. al-Sijillāt*.[3] An older contemporary of Ṭaḥāwī, he lived in Egypt.[4] The *Fihrist* is our source for two other Ḥanafī authors, Yaḥyā b. Bakr, who wrote a *K. al-Shurūṭ*,[5] and Ibn Mawṣil, to whom is attributed a *K. al-Shurūṭ al-Kabīr* and a *K. al-Wathā'iq wa'l-Sijillāt*.[6] Both were from Iraq; their dates are suggested by the position of their names in Ibn al-Nadīm's list.

Among Ṭaḥāwī's companions and teachers in Egypt, none enjoyed greater esteem than the qadi Abū Bakr (or Abū Bakra) Bakkār b. Qutayba.[7] Born

[1] During the first centuries of Islam, the Ḥanafīs had adherents in North Africa alongside the Mālikīs. This was especially true under the Aghlabids. See *EI*², s.v. "Aghlabids," ii.

[2] II, No. 208. Ibn Quṭlūbughā (No. 188) repeats the same information on his *shurūṭ* works, but not on his relationship with Ṭaḥāwī.

[3] 'Abd al-Qādir, I, No. 1044.

[4] 'Alī's father, Muqātil b. Manṣūr al-Rāzī, was a well-known Ḥanafī scholar who died in 211/826 (*Classen*, 287). Muḥammad b. Muqātil, problably 'Alī's brother, was a pupil of Shaybānī and qadi of Ramla; his dates are not known but Flügel notes that he is usually connected with the *ṭabaqa* of Sulaymān b. Shu'ayb (*Classen*, 289; see note to text, I 2.22). And it was undoubtedly 'Alī's son, M. b. 'Alī b. Muqātil al-Rāzī, who served as vizier to the Ikhshīd in 333 and was arrested in 335 when the Ikhshīd died (Kindī, *Wulāt*, 294, 491, 567).

[5] *Fihrist*, II, 208; Ḥajjī Khalīfa, IV, 45; and repeating the first, Ibn Quṭlūbughā, No. 257.

[6] *Fihrist*, II, 208.

[7] For his name Abū Bakra, which is sometimes given by the biographers, and his family background, see *EI*², s.v. "Abū Bakra." The longest notice on him is in Kindī's *Wulāt* (505-514). See also 'Abd al-Qādir, I, No. 378; Ibn Quṭlūbughā, No. 50; Laknawī, No. 95; *Classen*, 293.

in Basra in 182, he studied there with 'Īsā b. Abān and Hilāl al-Ra'y. But Bakkār was to be identified with Egypt after 246, the year he came to Fusṭāṭ to become qadi of Egypt and the acknowledged head of the Egyptian Ḥanafīs.[1] As his influence grew, he played an increasingly important role in spreading the doctrine of the *madhhab* in general, and the views of the scholars of Basra in particular. His book refuting Shāfi'ī's criticism of Abū Ḥanīfa, the *Kitāb al-Naqd 'alā al-Shāfi'ī*, won him high praise. At the same time, Bakkār sat at the center of a wide circle of Egyptian lawyers, and a smaller but active circle of *ghurabā'*, Basrians who had emigrated to Egypt. Among these last were many names prominent in Ṭaḥāwī's text: Sulaymān b. Shu'ayb and his father, Aḥmad b. Abī 'Imrān, Ibrāhīm b. Marzūq, Yazīd b. Sinān, and several others.

Bakkār was the author of at least two works on forms for documents, the *K. al-Maḥāḍir wa'l-Sijillāt* and the *K. al-Wathā'iq wa'l-'Uqūd*; some also attribute to him a *K. al-Shurūṭ*.[2] His relationship with Ṭaḥāwī must have been enduring and close. Ṭaḥāwī had been Bakkār's *kātib*, or legal secretary. It was from him, according to the biographers, that Ṭaḥāwī learned the science of *shurūṭ*, and after his death in 270, he assumed Bakkār's position as the leading Ḥanafī in Egypt.

Ṭaḥāwī's journey to Syria in 268 put him in touch with Abū Khāzim 'Abd al-Ḥamīd b. 'Abd al-'Azīz (d. 292/904).[3] Born in Basra, Abū Khāzim received his education from some of that city's leading *shaykhs*, among whom was 'Īsā b. Abān.[4] He later went on to a successful career as qadi of Karkh, the chief suburb of Baghdad, then of Kufa, and Damascus, the post he held when Ṭaḥāwī began his studies with him. Abū Khāzim's best known works are his *K. al-Maḥāḍir wa'l-Sijillāt*, *K. Adab al-Qāḍī*, and a work on the dividing of legacies, the *K. al-Farā'iḍ*,[5] reflecting his interest in the practical applications of mathematics. Although Abū Khāzim is frequently named as Ṭaḥāwī's *shaykh*, their association may not have continued for long, because Ṭaḥāwī

[1] His position did not prevent his being the victim in a political affair for which Aḥmad b. Ṭulūn, who had always honored Bakkār, had him imprisoned. Ṭaḥāwī says that he was so popular that the scholars crowded around the arched windows of his prison quarters to hear *ḥadīth* from him. (Ṭaḥāwī, quoted in Kindī, *Wulāt*, 513-514.) Various versions of the affair are repeated in the biographies.

[2] Ibn Quṭlūbughā, Laknawī.

[3] Sometimes spelled Abū Ḥāzim, as in the *Fihrist*, 208. Longer notices in 'Abd al-Qādir, I, No. 786; Ibn Quṭlūbughā, No. 95.

[4] Laknawī, No. 186.

[5] *Classen*, 293-294: *Lubāb al-Farā'iḍ*. Only Flügel lists other works as well as these three.

was back in Egypt in 270, the year that Bakkār died.[1] We cannot tell whether *shurūṭ* was a subject of interest between them: Ṭaḥāwī cites Abū Khāzim's opinion only once in the "K. al-Buyū'."[2]

Ṭaḥāwī's works on *shurūṭ* can now be placed in the context of this mature Ḥanafī tradition that he was to bring to its peak. In later times, his books commanded the greatest authority, combining as they did the most esteemed opinions of the school with the broad knowledge, the originality, and above all, the reputation of the author.

Ṭaḥāwī, or to give him his full name, Abū Ja'far Aḥmad b. Muḥammad b. Salāma b. Salama al-Azdī al-Ṭaḥāwī, is considered to be one of the great religious and legal scholars of Islam, yet only the bare outlines of his life can be sketched.[3] He was born in Ṭaḥā, in Upper Egypt,[4] sometime between the years 229 and 239 (843-853).[5] Ṭaḥāwī began his career as a Shāfi'ī and had the good fortune to be trained by the great disciple of Shāfi'ī himself, al-Muzanī, who was Ṭaḥāwī's maternal uncle. His celebrated shift to the Ḥanafī school must have taken place before Muzanī's death in 264/878 and therefore while Ṭaḥāwī was still young.[6] Be that as it may, four years later in 268,

[1] Kindī, *Wulāt*, 514.

[2] *Wa-qad kataba aṣḥābunā* (I 2.185); and once in "Adhkār al-Ḥuqūq," (*wa-sami'tu Abā Ḥāzim yaqūlu...*).

[3] Biographical notices are given in the standard works, especially the Ḥanafī *ṭabaqāt*: 'Abd al-Qādir, I, No. 205; Ibn Quṭlūbughā, No. 15; Laknawī, No. 48; *Classen*, 296-297. These and many more sources have been collected by the modern scholar, Muḥammad Zāhid al-Kawtharī, for his biography, *al-Ḥāwī fī Sīrat al-Imām Abī Ja'far al-Ṭaḥāwī* (Cairo, 1368/1948).

Some of the most valuable information can be found in the histories of the early qadis, and particularly in Kindī's *K. al-Quḍāt wa'l-Wulāt* (and the appended *Raf' al-Iṣr* by Ibn Ḥajar) in Rhuvon Guest's critical edition (Leiden and London, 1912) because Ṭaḥāwī himself was a primary source for that book.

[4] Even this is disputed by the biographers; further, as Grohmann points out, there are at least eleven places of this name in Egypt, the best known of which is described in his "Probleme der arabischen Papyrusforschung," 387-390 (*Archiv Orientální*, Prague, 1931).

[5] Ṭaḥāwī relates in Kindī (*Wulāt*, 457) that he was present at an interview with the qadi of Egypt, M. b. Abī Layth, who held that post from 226 to 237. This would suggest that the earliest date is correct and that Ṭaḥāwī heard him as a boy. This would also make him in his early nineties when he died, which would not be impossible.

[6] The evidence of various anecdotes suggests this. This break with Muzanī, incidentally, was probably what gave rise to the accusation repeated by Ḥajjī Khalīfa (IV, 45) that Ṭaḥāwī plagiarized M. b. Jarīr al-Ṭabarī's work on *shurūṭ*. Ṭabarī may very well have written a *shurūṭ* work, but Ṭabarī's doctrine was based on the Shāfi'ī, and only a glance at Ṭaḥāwī's book will show how deeply rooted in the Ḥanafī school it is.

The biographers try to explain the "conversion" in somewhat simplified, and not impartial, terms: When asked why he left Muzanī, Ṭaḥāwī replied, "Because my uncle was forever poring over the works of Abū Ḥanīfa"; or sometimes, Ṭaḥāwī was provoked when Muzanī said of him, "Nothing good will ever come of you!"

Ṭaḥāwī went to Syria as a Ḥanafī, and after travelling through Jerusalem, Ghazza and 'Asqalān to hear traditions,[1] began studying *fiqh* with Abū Khāzim in Damascus. Back in Egypt, he resumed his association with the qadi Bakkār and with Aḥmad b. Abī 'Imrān (d. 280/893),[2] the Ḥanafī scholar to whom he first turned when he broke with his uncle. There is no evidence that he ever lived outside Egypt after that. Much respected during his time, Ṭaḥāwī died in Fusṭāṭ (where his tomb still stands) in 321/933 (or 322) when he was in his eighties or early nineties.

Ṭaḥāwī wrote a considerable number of works during his long and successful life, many of which are still extant.[3] They span an unusually broad range of subjects in religious law, and may have even included a large work of history.[4] The popularity of some—his short *'aqīda*, or creed, for instance—is attested to by the number of commentaries they attracted over the centuries.

The Arabic bio-bibliographical sources give us little more than the names of Ṭaḥāwī's handbooks on forms for documents. In addition to his *Kitāb al-Maḥāḍir wa'l-Sijillāt*,[5] they mention three versions of a work on *shurūṭ*: the *Kitāb al-Shurūṭ al-Kabīr*[6]—or to give it the title usually mentioned in the sources—the *Jāmi' al-Kabīr fi'l-Shurūṭ*, the *Kitāb al-Shurūṭ al-Awsaṭ*,[7] and an abridgement of the longest work, the *Kitāb al-Shurūṭ al-Ṣaghīr*.[8] The last is

[1] Kawtharī, 19; no source.

[2] See note to I 2.9; for the names of others, see Kawtharī, 8-11.

[3] *GAL*, G I, 173-174, S I, 293-294; Kawtharī, 31-37; *Classen*, 296-297; Sezgin, I, 439-442.

[4] Mentioned in Ibn Kathīr's (d. 774) *al-Bidāya wa'l-Nihāya*, XI, 174 (Cairo, 1351-1358/1932-1939), and cited by H. Laoust, "Ibn Kaṯīr Historien," *Arabica*, II (1955), 79. Ibn Kathīr knew Ṭaḥāwī's *Ta'rīkh al-Kabīr*. See R. Guest's introduction to Kindī's *Wulāt*, 17, where the history is also mentioned.

[5] Usually mentioned separately, but which actually formed part of his *shurūṭ* work. See above, p. 12, n. 1. *Fihrist*, II, 207; Ibn Quṭlūbughā, No. 15; *Classen* erroneously mentions a work on *shurūṭ* and *sijillāt*, 297.

[6] *Fihrist*, II, 207; Ibn Quṭlūbughā, No. 15. For the two extant Cairo fragments, see *GAL*, G I, 174, and *Fihrist al-Kutub al-'Arabiyya al-Maḥfūẓa bi'l-Kutubkhāna al-Khidīwiyya al-Miṣriyya* (Cairo, 1306-1309), III, 102. These were edited by Schacht in "Das kitāb aḏkār al-ḥuqūq war-ruhūn aus dem al-ǧāmi' al-kabīr fiš-šurūṭ des abū Ǧa'far Aḥmad ibn Muḥammad aṭ-Ṭaḥāwī," and "Das kitāb aš-šuf'a aus dem... aṭ-Ṭaḥāwī," *Sitzungsber. Heidelberger Akad. Wiss.*, Phil.-hist. Klasse, 1926-1927, No. 4, and 1929-1930, No. 5.
The two fragments in Istanbul were first reported in Schacht's *Bibliotheken* I and III. For these, see also Sezgin, I, 441.

[7] This work of medium size is mentioned only by Ibn Quṭlūbughā.

[8] As Ṭaḥāwī says in the opening lines, *qad waḍa'tu hādhā mukhtaṣaran...*, Mehmet Murat 997, fol. 1 b. *Fihrist*, II, 207; Ibn Quṭlūbughā, No. 15. Ḥajjī Khalīfa (IV, 45) mentions only one *shurūṭ* work, in 40 parts (*juz'*); the shortest version actually has 32 chapters (*bābs*), and we assume the longest rescension had the same arrangement. For the MSS of the short version, see *Bibliotheken*, I and III; Sezgin, I, 441.

called, on the title page of the extant manuscripts, the *Kitāb al-Shurūṭ wa'l-Warāqa*. The chronology of his writings in general is not at all clear, but we can, at least, date the shortest version from the opening lines in the Mehmet Murat manuscript, which indicate that it was completed by the year 305. This date, then, is likely the *terminus ad quem* for his *shurūṭ* works.

Fortunately, the entire manuscript of the *Shurūṭ al-Ṣaghīr*, as well as four complete chapters of the *Jāmiʿ al-Kabīr*, have been preserved, so that we are in a position to compare and make certain judgements about both.

First of all, how do the two differ? In size, the short work is less than one-eighth the length of the longer, if we take the extant chapters in the longer work as a sample and assume that each chapter in the long text is proportionately longer than the corresponding chapter in the *Shurūṭ al-Ṣaghīr*.[1] In content, as we might expect, the *Jāmiʿ al-Kabīr* not only included many more model documents, but presents the basic contracts in fuller form. To be sure, the abridgement covers the same general categories, but the contracts are usually trimmed to their essential formulas. In the short text we also miss the wide variety of contracts: alternative models for special situations; additional documents or inserts as the circumstances of the contracts vary; models for transactions not common in everyday commercial life, perhaps, but of great interest to a person concerned with the theory of writing documents. But most of all, the commentary suffers. A practicing notary, following the *Shurūṭ al-Ṣaghīr*, would receive sufficient instruction to help him avoid the pitfalls of wording a formula incorrectly; but a jurist, wishing to relate the details of the formulas to the prescriptions of the law, would be less satisfied.

The essential difference between the two versions, then, is that each had a separate purpose. One was a handbook, to be kept at the notary's elbow, and used as a professional aid.[2] The other was a speculative work, devoted to the theory of drafting documents, which the scholar and jurist studied; the notary may have referred to it on occasion, but it was surely too unwieldy for everyday use.

Second, the existence of a complete abridgement of the work enables us to know the parts of the *Jāmiʿ al-Kabīr* that have perished. Thirty-two chapters present model documents for what would appear to be every possible need. The classification of subject matter is, on the whole, comparable to

[1] The longer chapter on sale, for example, is 214 folios, with an average of 17 lines to a page, while the abridged chapter on sale is 42 folios, with about 23 lines to a page. The entire shorter work in the Mehmet Murat MS is 170 folios.

[2] The actual contracts of the papyri are usually drafted as they occur in the shorter form.

that in the Ḥanafī *fiqh* works, although the same order of chapters is not maintained.[1]

Besides the chapter on sale, the first in the book, there are also chapters on how to draft documents for transactions of pre-emption (*shuf'a*) and hire and lease (*ijāra*); claims for debts and pledges (*adhkār al-ḥuqūq wa'l-ruhūn*), formal binding acknowledgements (*iqrār*) and declarations of quittance (*barā'āt*) are documents seen frequently enough in the published papyri. Agency and dismissal of an agent from his commission (*wakāla, 'azl 'an wakāla*) form two separate chapters, while division of property and division of the use of property (*qisma, muhāya'a*) are together. Legacies (*waṣāyā*), gifts (*hibāt*), and two chapters on charitable gifts and trusts (*ṣadaqāt al-mamlūkāt, al-mawqūfāt*) form separate *kitābs*. There are two chapters dealing with slaves that include documents for various forms of manumission (*'itāq, tadbīr, mukātaba*) and for slaves given a peculium and permission to trade (*ma'dhūn lahū*). The chapter on contracts of clientship (*muwālāt*) deals not with manumitted slaves, but with converted non-Muslims. Marriage contracts and documents for repudiation (*nikāḥ, ṭalāq*) form relatively long sections. Various kinds of partnership are dealt with under two main subdivisions (*muḍāraba, sharika*). Criminal offenses (*jināyāt*), found objects (*luqaṭa*), loan of non-fungible property without interest (*'āriyya*) are treated separately, as are fiduciary relationships (*amānāt*), conciliation (*ṣulḥ*) and appointment of arbitrators (*taḥkīmāt*). Finally, several *kitābs* are devoted to the documents that the qadi or his assistants will have to draw up themselves: *maḥāḍir, sijillāt*, rules for the jurisdiction of Mecca, and forms for pleas and various judicial procedures.

The *Jāmi' al-Kabīr* surely exceeds in scope, not to mention length, any surviving Ḥanafī text that we know of written since Ṭaḥāwī's time. It should not surprise us to find that the detailed works of a later period were to draw heavily on it. For some, at least, Ṭaḥāwī would seem to be the final authority, closing the list that began with Abū Ḥanīfa. The seventeenth century *Fatāwā 'Ālamgīriyya*, for example, in its chapter on *shurūṭ*, always designates as the *ahl al-shurūṭ*, the main authorities only, up to and including *Ṭaḥāwī*.[2] The text never refers to formulas of individuals beyond that time, although it

[1] Also, *shurūṭ* works differ from one another in this respect, the ordering of subject matter varying considerably.

[2] This is also true of Marghīnānī's work on *shurūṭ*, which was used as a basic source for the *Fatāwā 'Ālamgīriyya*. For both of these, see below. These authorities are Abū Ḥanīfa, Abū Yūsuf, Shaybānī (most frequently), Abū Zayd al-Shurūṭī, Yūsuf b. Khālid, Hilāl b. Yaḥyā, and Ṭaḥāwī. Both works usually mention Shaybānī by name, but on a few occasions use Sarakhsī's name instead, suggesting the derivation.

occasionally opposes to the *ahl al-shurūṭ* writers who go by the highly impersonal designation of the *muta'akhkhirūn*, "the moderns." Sarakhsī, too, in his commentary to Shaybānī's work on *shurūṭ*, written before 483, mentions only one other name (once) in connection with a formula, that of a contemporary of Ṭaḥāwī who did not write a *shurūṭ* work.[1]

However, despite the existence of Ṭaḥāwī's formulary, the demand for new handbooks on *shurūṭ* did not cease, for Ḥanafī scholars continued to produce them for a long time to come. Many of these are lost, and only their titles and the names of their authors are known. But many others, a good proportion of them from the Ottoman period, survive in manuscript libraries.[2] Some of these extant works were composed by outstanding Ḥanafīs, some by authors whose dates cannot be precisely determined, and a large number are anonymous.

Extracts of some of these works (excluding the Ottoman ones) have been preserved in the collection mentioned above, the *Fatāwā 'Ālamgīriyya.*[3] Compiled by the order of the Mughal emperor Awrangzīb ('Ālamgīr) during the years 1075-1083/1664-1672, the *Fatāwā 'Ālamgīriyya* is not a collection of *fatwās* at all, but an enormous compendium of Ḥanafī law. The intention was to gather together the authoritative opinions of the school scattered in the various works of *fiqh*, and this included, in the mind of the Shaykh Niẓām, its chief editor, works on documentary practice. The collection thus contains two extensive chapters on *maḥāḍir* and *sijillāt* and on *shurūṭ*.[4]

The primary source from which the chapter on *shurūṭ* is derived is easily identified as a work composed in the sixth/twelfth century, by Ẓahīr al-Dīn Abu'l-Maḥāsin al-Ḥasan b. 'Alī al-Marghīnānī.[5]

[1] Sarakhsī, 173. He is Abu'l Qāsim al-Ṣaffār al-Balkhī, Aḥmad b. 'Iṣma. ('Abd al-Qādir, I, No. 142, and *Classen*, 298.)

[2] The most important, from the libraries of Cairo and Istanbul, were found and described by Schacht in the three parts of his *Bibliotheken*.

[3] *EI*², s.v. "al-Fatāwā al-'Ālamgīriyya," and Schacht, *Introduction*, 91, 243.

[4] Calcutta edition (1251/1835), VI, 247-371 ("K. al-Maḥāḍir wa'l-Sijillāt"), 371-559 ("K. al-Shurūṭ"); Bulāq edition (1310/1892), VI, 160-248 and 248-389.

[5] References to his *shurūṭ* works, the second part of a collection of *fatāwā*, in *GAL*, G I, 379, S I, 651; Ḥajjī Khalīfa, IV, 46; Laknawī, No. 117. The MS used here is the Br. Mus. Suppl. 4305.

Marghīnānī's relationship to the author of the *Hidāya*, the *fiqh* work most esteemed in India, is not clear. The more famous Marghīnānī was 'Alī b. Abī Bakr b. 'Abd al-Jalīl (d. 593/1196). Flügel erroneously calls him 'Alī b. 'Abd al-'Azīz (*Classen*, 316) who was actually Ḥasan's (our author's) father. 'Abd al-Qādir mentions that Ḥasan is known for his transmission of Tirmidhī's work to the author of the *Hidāya* ('Abd al-Qādir, I, No. 487).

As for Marghīnānī's dates, we can note further that his father, a well-known scholar, died in 506. See Ibn Quṭlūbughā, No. 56 (in the biography of Qāḍīkhān), and 'Abd al-Qādir, I, No. 1010. References to the son's pupils in Ibn Quṭlūbughā, Nos. 59 and 155.

The two works are similar in a number of ways. Most important is that the formulas agreed upon as correct are more or less the same. Second, the arrangement of the subject matter follows the same general outlines. Third, although Marghīnānī's work is not mentioned, his commentary obviously forms the framework for that of the *Fatāwā 'Ālamgīriyya*. And finally, both texts open with an interesting section on terminology, reflecting the eastern provenance of a work that depended on others born in the central Islamic lands. However, the chapter in the *Fatāwā 'Ālamgīriyya* is by no means a mere reproduction of Marghīnānī's text, for there are many more subdivisions in the Indian work (28 *faṣls*, as opposed to 11), while the formulas and commentary are both more detailed.

At approximately the same time that Marghīnānī composed his book on *shurūṭ*, other scholars produced works that easily may have been related to his. The first was Fakhr al-Dīn al-Ḥasan b. Manṣūr al-Uzjandī Qāḍīkhān (d. 592/1196),[1] the author of a *K. al-Maḥāḍir.*[2] Qāḍīkhān was the teacher of Marghīnānī, and had been a pupil of Marghīnānī's father before that. He is best known for his collection of *fatwās*, but in the field of practical legal literature, he wrote a commentary on Khaṣṣāf's *Adab al-Qāḍī* as well.

Another jurist of the time whose name can be linked with that of Marghīnānī was Burhān al-A'imma 'Umar b. 'Abd al-'Azīz b. Māza (d. 536/1141),[3] a member of the well-known family of the Banū Māza in Bukhārā.[4] His writings for the most part concerned practical affairs, so that later jurists frequently used excerpts in their own works.[5] Among these was a work on *shurūṭ*[6] and like Qāḍīkhān, he wrote a commentary on Khaṣṣāf's *Adab al-Qāḍī*. His son, also a well-known scholar, was Marghīnānī's teacher.

Another *shurūṭ* scholar, whose work seems to have been popular at about this time, was Jalāl al-Dīn (or Jamāl al-Dīn) Ḥāmid b. Rukn al-Dīn Muḥammad al-Rīghdamūnī.[7] His detailed formulary, the *Ghurar al-Shurūṭ wa-Durar*

[1] Ibn Quṭlūbughā, No. 56; 'Abd al-Qādir, I, No. 507; Laknawī, No. 121.

[2] *Classen*, 314; Laknawī, No. 121. See also *GAL*, G I, 376, S I, 643-644.

[3] 'Abd al-Qādir, I, No. 1081; Laknawī, No. 289; *Classen*, 311-312.

[4] For their political role there, see *EI*², s.v. "Ḥanafiyya."

[5] *Classen*, 312.

[6] Ḥajjī Khalīfa, IV, 46, where the date is wrong and his name misspelled (Māzin).

[7] 'Abd al-Qādir, I, No. 183; Laknawī, No. 155. The date of his death is not known, but his father, who was *imām* of the mosque of Bukhārā, died in 518. See 'Abd al-Qādir, II, No. 40; Laknawī, No. 27.

al-Sumūṭ, is preserved in a number of manuscripts.[1] One of the main sources for Rīghdamūnī's work was the *Fā'iq fī Shurūṭ al-Wathā'iq* by Najm al-Dīn Abū Ḥafṣ 'Umar b. M. b. Aḥmad al-Nasafī (d. 537/1147),[2] a famous and prolific author from Samarqand, known chiefly for his *'aqīda*, or creed.

The titles given here by no means exhaust the list of works on documentary forms written after Ṭaḥāwī's *Jāmi' al-Kabīr*. Nor do they take account of the numerous printed texts of Ottoman Ḥanafī *ṣukūk*, collections based on older works and used in the modern period.[3] But they will give some idea of the close relationship among these works, and their growth out of the earlier tradition.

3. THE PURPOSE OF THE "KITĀB AL-BUYŪ'"

The origin of *shurūṭ* handbooks as a direct outgrowth of the practice can best be discovered in the forms for documents themselves. For the justifications offered by the *shurūṭ* authors barely suggest the important practical ends their models served.

Ṭaḥāwī opens his *Jāmi' al-Kabīr* with a comparison of the relative merits of oral testimony and written documents. Confining himself to the two transactions mentioned in Sur. 2:282, contracts of sale with delayed payment and those payable immediately (*tijāra ḥāḍira*, lit. present trade),[4] he remarks that in the second, Allah did not call for documents, because this would have been oppressive; no one would buy anything, not even food or water, without feeling obliged to draw up a written instrument. However, Allah did recommend calling for witnesses (*amara bi'l-ishhād*), whether the price was payable

[1] For these, see *Bibliotheken* I, No. 51, and III, No. 36. Laknawī calls his work a *K. al-Maḥāḍir wa'l-Shurūṭ*, and Ḥajjī Khalīfa, IV, 46, mentions that it was arranged in 26 *faṣls*; *GAL* S I, 638.

[2] See *Bibliotheken*, III, No. 39 and note to I, No. 51. For his life and writings, Ibn Quṭlū-bughā, No. 140; 'Abd al-Qādir, I, No. 1090; Laknawī, No. 292; *GAL*, G I, 427, S I, 758-760.

[3] A number of European works that drew upon collections of Ḥanafī *ṣukūk* and Mālikī *wathā'iq* were published as early as the beginning of the nineteenth century. The purpose of these printed texts and translations was to serve as guides to language and procedure of the courts for the British Indian official and for the French civil servant in North Africa. For some of these works, see Schacht, *Introduction*, 243-244.

[4] *Tijāra ḥāḍira* includes cash transactions, barter, and any other form of direct exchange, as opposed to sale on credit or a transaction in which performance is incomplete on one or both sides. In the same context, Ṭaḥāwī also uses the expressions *naqd*, *'ājila*, vs. *ājila*, *naqdan* vs. *nasī'an* (I 1.4, 1.7, 1.8), and the discussion makes explicit that this is how he understands the Qur'ānic term. He does not mean local trade as opposed to long distance trade (cf. Udovitch's reading of Sarakhsī, 79-80), although these may imply direct and delayed payment.

immediately (*athmān ʿājila*) or payable in a specified period (*athmān ājila*), because they could testify later if the merchandise had to be returned to the seller on account of a hidden defect or a prior claim. Since the purpose of a document in the case of a debt is to eliminate distrust and forgetfulness, then a document of *shahāda* ought to be drawn up for *all* contracts of sale for the same reason.[1] Ṭaḥāwī's model contracts bear this out, for they provide for recording the smallest details of the transaction in order to keep conflicts between the parties at a minimum.

Neither Ṭaḥāwī nor the other *shurūṭ* authors discuss documents in the light of their lega effects, but we may ask whether these model documents, with their "blank spaces" filled in, ever served the parties as contracts in practice. In the strict sense of the word, they are not contracts at all, except retrospectively. They are not constitutive instruments, for the legal obligations exist whether or nor they are spelled out in the documents. In other words, the document itself does not give rise to legal obligations; the transaction has already been completed and nothing remains to be done on either side.

However, they may be called contracts in the sense that they are the written record of the terms of a concluded contract.[2] Furthermore, even when the essential provisions of the contract have been carried out, the document contains clauses which may bind the parties in the future. Some of these are not necessary to a valid sale, but they guarantee complete performance, such as clauses insuring the buyer against future claims by a third party. While it is true that the testimony of witnesses would suffice to establish proof of these guarantees, the document emphasized them and preserved their terms in writing.

Recording all the details in writing not only lessened the possibility of conflict between the parties, but also established the validity of the transaction. Thus, no third person would be likely to appear in the future, to challenge it on the grounds that it was irregular or invalid. For the document itself acted as confirmation that all the conditions required for a valid contract existed

[1] Sarakhsī (168) is more specific. The document prevents dispute because it can be referred to should one of the parties try to repudiate the rights of the other. The document can be produced, the witnesses testify, and the deception is exposed.

[2] That is, they are declarative instruments. All of Ṭaḥāwī's formulas in the "K. al-Buyūʿ" are conveyances in that they transfer or confirm property rights. But all conveyances are not included in this section of the book, for gift, *waqf*, and other subjects are treated in separate chapters. However, they all share the same general structure, even though some are unilateral declarations. For the contract in Islamic law, which must be verbally expressed, see *EI*², s.v. "ʿAḳd." The author of this article, Chafik Chehata, provides a more detailed treatment of the subject in his *Essai d'une théorie générale de l'obligation en droit musulman hanéfite* (Paris, 1969).

and that all the necessary steps had been taken by the co-contractors in orderly progression. The emphasis on the validity of the transaction, the care for being legally correct, brings out another feature of the *shurūṭ*. It shows how closely the Sharī'a was followed in these *shurūṭ* works, at least in its details. If occasionally Ṭaḥāwī suggests ways to avoid uncomfortable situations, there is no attempt to draft contracts in such a manner as to evade the law while appearing to follow it. This care for the letter of the law, of course, made them potentially effective instruments for carrying out legal evasions.

Another purpose must have been to reduce the possibility of conflicting testimony on the part of witnesses in case they were called upon to testify in a lawsuit. This was essential, because if the witnesses disagreed in their testimony, the depositions of both were usually invalid. The legal system would seek to keep procedure running smoothly.

Finally, although the document may have been subordinate to oral testimony, or even unnecessary, what would happen if the witnesses were no longer available, if they should die or be distant from the town where the litigation takes place?[1] The practice of calling upon secondary witnesses, to affirm the testimony of the primary witnesses (the *shahāda 'alā shahāda*), solved this difficulty for a while. But eventually, the document itself, with merely the signatures of the witnesses affixed to it, would have to be consulted.[2] In this connection we should note that the notary did not merely record the name of the witness; the witness himself had to sign the document, at the end of clauses declaring that he had given his oral deposition.[3]

If there were important advantages in drawing up a written document, there were even more compelling reasons for the parties to consult a professional notary for that purpose. Naturally, there was nothing to prevent them from drafting a contract themselves, but as Sarakhsī warns, most people would not know how to avoid a defective contract, whereas the notary can take that responsibility off their shoulders.[4]

As a person trained in the law—or at least with a handbook such as Ṭaḥāwī's at his elbow—the notary is the person best qualified to help people carry out

[1] Sarakhsī (168) rightly remarks that the *heirs* of the parties will want to know the contents.

[2] A solution to this problem was sought in the Mālikī school by calling upon secondary witnesses to testify to the *handwriting* of the primary witnesses. There are various arguments on when this procedure could be applied, and whether the witnesses verifying the signature had to know the signing witnesses personally. It should be noted that these persons were not experts, but merely other certified *shuhūd*. See Tyan, *Notariat*, 68-69, 71-72, and references there.

[3] See below, p. 66 and n. 3.

[4] Sarakhsī, 168.

their intentions. But the contract must not only be effective, it must also be perfectly valid in the Sharīʿa. Ṭaḥāwī constantly reminds the user of his book that he must therefore act as counsel to his clients, acquainting them with the legal rules and informing them of any potential risks.[1] If the notary himself does not know these rules, or the proper expressions to convey exactly what he means, not only will these shortcomings injure his clients but he will be sinning against Allah for obstructing such meritorious legal acts as making charitable gifts and freeing slaves.[2]

However, a written contract could appear to be free of fault both in outward form and inner content, and yet the transaction might still be jeopardized. This risk was a consequence of the *ikhtilāf*, the diversity of views among the legal scholars on details of positive law. For if the contract were disputed before a qadi who followed the opinion of one scholar or school, while a single clause or element in the document was an expression of another opinion, the qadi might declare the entire contract invalid. A model contract had to be valid in all schools simply because business itself cut across the borders of all schools. Thus it was up to the notary to satisfy every view, or at least avoid offending any one of them. In other words, he had to draw up a contract that would be absolutely safe in court.

The guiding principle, and one on which Ṭaḥāwī insists throughout his book, is *iḥtiyāṭ* (or *taḥarruz*), precaution. By this he does not mean the religious scruples of a pious Muslim that would, for example, lead him to pay his alms rate based on the higher of two assessments, but precaution that had considerable practical importance. For the notary it meant not only knowing the differences of opinion, but knowing the techniques for making them innocuous, and even for preventing misinterpretation on the part of ignorant or careless qadis.[3] Instructing the notary in this respect was, as we shall see, Ṭaḥāwī's chief reason for writing his book.

No element of the written document escapes Ṭaḥāwī's attention as a possible means of dealing with the *ikhtilāf*. The structure of the contract, order of clauses, wording of formulas, and even the manipulation of the transaction itself are all brought to bear on the resolution of the problem. Ṭaḥāwī's book is well furnished with examples of *iḥtiyāṭ*, applied in a number of ways:

(1) First of all, Ṭaḥāwī advises the notary to be deliberately ambiguous whenever necessary so the qadi can construe the clause any way he likes.

[1] For example, I 6.34, II 21.3, III 44.3.

[2] I 1.11, 1.12.

[3] For example, I 2.188-2.190.

A concern that appears in many contexts is the opinion of Ibn Abī Laylā, Zufar, and the scholars of Madīna, that once the buyer makes his formal acknowledgement—his binding and irreversible *iqrār*—that the seller owns the property, the buyer will have, in effect, denied his own ownership even in the future. Having done this, he may not be able to demand return of the price from the seller should a third party establish a rightful claim to the property.[1] Thus the formula avoids mention of the seller's possession or ownership altogether; but when the contract demands it, the notary, instead of writing "A bought the entire house property belonging to B," should formulate the clause obliquely: "A bought from B everything that B had stated was owned by him and was his property."[2]

Further, if there is disagreement concerning which person, the buyer or his agent, receives a guarantee for a fault in ownership (the *darak*), the notary does not specify either one, but says "the party who is entitled to take possession [of the guarantee]."[3] To avoid differences of opinion on what rights and appurtenances are inseparable from the property, and to insure that all of them will be transferred to the new owner, Ṭaḥāwī suggests strengthening the transfer clause with "[he delivers] everything this sale entails," rather than "the entire house."[4]

(2) Another way of resolving the *ikhtilāf* is to add to the formula details, or even whole clauses, that will meet the requirements of one opinion but appear unobjectionable to another. For instance, when agricultural land is sold, the fruit on the trees is normally retained by the seller, unless the buyer stipulates otherwise. This rule is based on a well-known tradition of the Prophet and is unquestioned by the community of scholars—with one exception. Ibn Abī Laylā includes the fruit in the sale, whether the buyer stipulates it or not. Out of fear that the sale might some day be disputed before a qadi who follows Ibn Abī Laylā's view, Ṭaḥāwī inserts a clause in the contract excluding the fruit from the sale and reserving it for the seller. Standing crops are also covered by the clause because of a possible analogy with the fruit.[5]

Another instance of the same kind of resolution is seen in a formula for *shahāda* in which witnesses testify to the number of heirs to a man's estate. It is inadequate to say that there are no heirs except those mentioned in the

[1] See notes to text, I 2.18, 4.0.

[2] *Passim*; *jamī'u mā dhakara annahū lahū wa-milkuhū.*

[3] Examples in III 45.13-45.14, IV 5.2; *ilā alladhī yajibu lahū al-qabḍ.*

[4] Notes to text, I 2.42-2.55; *jamī'u mā waqa'a 'alayhi hādha'l-bay'.*

[5] III 2.0-2.1.

document: the witnesses are obliged to testify that "they do not *know of* any heirs other than those named," because a qadi might take the first to be mere conjecture and the testimony, in his eyes, would be imperfect.[1]

Sometimes, rather than deliberately formulate a clause ambiguously, it is preferable to state all the possibilities. In a case where the jurists disagree over whether the acting buyer or the principal pays the price to the seller, Ṭaḥāwī names them both: "the agent paid the price out of the capital of the one who commissioned him."[2] Thus a qadi could not object to the formula, no matter what view he holds. Similarly, does the buyer, the seller, or both, have the option to cancel the sale after the property has been inspected? Since agreement has never been universal on this point, Ṭaḥāwī mentions both parties.[3]

Continual repetition of the phrase *'alā anna* ("on condition that [*x* and *y* has taken place, or is true]") is an outstanding example of Ṭaḥāwī's use of precaution. It may be repeated several times throughout any given contract, and now and then Ṭaḥāwī points out its importance in certain contexts. For instance, if agricultural land is sold it will be described as either *'ushr* or *kharāj* land, depending on whether it is subject to the tithe or the land tax; but the notary must write "on condition that it is *'ushr*," because if it turns out to be *kharāj*, the seller will not have fulfilled the conditions stipulated by the buyer and the sale can be cancelled. On the other hand, if *'alā anna* is left out, the buyer has no redress and has paid for land that he can only use but never own.[4]

(3) *Iḥtiyāṭ* sometimes demands that the notary avoid phrases he might normally consider acceptable. For instance, the sale must not be described as being sound and valid, for if the buyer gives his *iqrār* or formal acknowledgement to this, and it turns out not to be so, the buyer will have released the seller from the obligation to return the price.[5] Again, ownership of the seller must never be directly acknowledged by the buyer, but care for this view can be extended in application: when describing the boundaries of the property sold, do not even mention a neighbor's ownership of adjacent property, because some day one of the contracting parties may wish to purchase

[1] V 11.5-11.10.

[2] III 45.5-45.11; *dafa 'a al-wakīlu al-thamana min māl al-āmir.*

[3] The *khiyār al-ru'ya*; I 2.77-2.82.

[4] III 1.1; cf. an interesting distinction in V 5.1-5.2. Another case of precaution enters in here: the *kharāj* land is always treated as unowned land only because of an opinion of the Madinese, III 7.2.

[5] I 2.102.

it, and they will already have given their *iqrār* to the fact that it belongs to someone else. This would, of course, interfere with the potential buyer's claim to redress in case of a future fault in ownership.[1] Following the same principle in the sale of a slave, the notary should not call the slave by the usual term *mamlūk*, or even *'abd*, but must use *ghulām* or *nasama* or some other evasive expression, because the slave must not be acknowledged as "owned."[2]

(4) A somewhat unexpected way of dealing with the *ikhtilāf* is to have the notary draw up *two* documents; the parties keep the second in reserve and produce it only as needed, when the qadi's views are discovered. The second might be a document of *shahāda* establishing the seller's possession of the property (and by implication, his ownership) and his right to dispose of it before the sale. This supplementary instrument can be produced should the lawsuit be heard before a judge who holds the opinion of the Basrians, that the sale is not valid if the seller does not have the object of sale in his possession when it is sold.[3] The basic contract, however, reflects precaution against the opposite and stricter view. A similar solution occurs in the *Fatāwā 'Ālamgīriyya* in a different context: a second instrument guarantees the value of improvements to the property in case of a claim, and is shown to a qadi who holds that these expenditures can be recovered by the buyer.[4]

(5) The notary's role as legal advisor to his clients becomes even more apparent when he is called upon to interfere with the transaction itself in order to reconcile two or more diverging opinions. Sometimes this entails separating the transaction into two contracts, as when a person wishes to sell his own house property to his minor son. In general this is permitted, but one view holds that it would be equivalent to selling it to himself (since he has the right of disposal of his son's property), and selling to or buying from one's self is not possible. Ṭaḥāwī's solution is to conclude a sale whereby the property is sold to a third person; another contract then makes it possible to buy it back on his son's behalf and the *ikhtilāf* is avoided.[5] Marghīnānī's solution to this same problem is less elaborate, but shows the real reasons behind objections to the transaction. Several phrases are added to the description of the price, guaranteeing that it is equal to or even less than the value of the

[1] I 2.38; see notes to text.

[2] III 38.1; cf. V 13.0, 14.0, 16.0.

[3] Contract in I 3.0; see notes to text.

[4] *Fat. 'Ālam.*, 422.

[5] IV 5.5; presumably there is some assurance that the purchaser will relinquish it, although Ṭaḥāwī does not say how to provide for that.

property. In the opposite case, buying property from one's son on one's own behalf, Marghīnānī suggests weighing the price in the presence of witnesses.[1]

Another instance where the notary's solution lies not in an element of the document itself, but in avoiding the *ikhtilāf* before the contract is even made, occurs in an agreement to reverse a sale, a contract of *iqāla*. In a special case of *iqāla*, the original buyer has not taken possession of the property; but in the view of jurists who construe the *iqāla* as a new sale, the transaction would then be invalid. The notary should suggest to the co-contractors that they complete the transfer of the property, and then make a new agreement. The buyer's interests will not be affected, for he merely reverses his role to become a seller, while his burden of guarantees is limited to his own actions regarding the property.[2]

Similarly, in the sale of a fruit crop, most jurists would permit the buyer to leave the fruit on the trees until it ripened as long as this was stipulated as a condition of the sale. Others, however, refuse to allow any conditions to be attached to the sale, and would declare such a contract voidable. The correct solution, then, in Ṭaḥāwī's opinion, is to change the nature of the sale by introducing a contract of *ʿāriyya* into the transaction. This is a gratuitous loan, the transfer of the use of the trees for a limited period; the permission of the seller thus replaces a stipulation made by the buyer. Further clauses are added guaranteeing that no conditions are attached to the sale, and the contract remains intact, safe from the risks imposed by the *ikhtilāf*.[3]

(6) Finally, there will inevitably be situations where it is impossible to neutralize the effect of divergent opinions. For example, in the sale of house property in exchange for garments or cloth, the strictest opinion says that it is unlawful to sell objects at term if they cannot be measured or weighed. Ṭaḥāwī's attitude is an important clue to his purposes in the book: reconciling the *ikhtilāf* is not feasible in the document, he says (*lā yatahayyaʾu fī hādhaʾl-kitāb*); and since documents are only drawn up because of precaution against the *ikhtilāf*, then there is no reason at all for drafting them when this is impossible.[4]

Ṭaḥāwī's continual preoccupation with the differences of opinion among jurists was no formal intellectual pursuit, but was obviously an attempt to

[1] Both contracts, fols. 20b-21a.

[2] Since it presumably will not have left his hands; IV 7.20-7.21.

[3] III 25.1; insert to contract, 25.0.

[4] III 44.1: *wa-innamā tuktab al-kutubu iḥtiyāṭan min al-ikhtilāf fa-idhā lam yaqdir ʿalā dhālika fa-lā maʿnā li-iktitābihā.* Further examples in IV 17.3, 17.8 and V 1.0 bis.

meet a severe problem in court practice. It has often been claimed that the differences in positive law are relatively unimportant compared to the essential unity they share. This thesis was partly the outcome of later formulations in Islamic legal theory which attempted to rationalize and understate the differences and which *could* do so because it did not recognize a historical process of development. In fact, the earlier rivalry among the schools was reflected in the courts, legal practice emphasized this rivalry, and despite the later emphasis on the equal legitimacy of alternative interpretations of the Qur'ān and traditions, considerable diversity in substantive law continued to exist.[1]

Ṭaḥāwī's text gives ample evidence of how widely disparate some of these judgements could be on matters of decisive practical importance.[2] From the point of view of a person engaged in legal proceedings, the *ikhtilāf* must have caused serious inconvenience and frustration, for he could never be certain which line of thought a qadi would pursue or whether his decisions would be reversed by his successors in the future.[3] Moreover, when the courts in different geographical areas began to apply the doctrine of one particular school, litigants themselves often could not choose the school they wished, but had to plead before the established one. And even when they could choose, they might find that wide variations in opinion separated qadis within the same school.

It is in this light that we must view Ṭaḥāwī's concern with reconciling or neutralizing the effect of these variations in opinion. But even more, it was by means of the written document that the removal of these obstacles was definitively established before the qadi. The fact that documents were not accepted as proof in the technical sense begins to recede in importance as we discover again how vital they were to the functioning of law in practice.

4. THE ARABIC FORMULARY AND THE CONTRACT OF SALE.

Forms for documents in the chapter on sale may be considered representative of Ṭaḥāwī's other *shurūṭ* and, indeed, of the Arabic formulary as a

[1] Although they are not systematic accounts of legal practice, biographical works such as Wakī''s *Akhbār al-Quḍāt* give us many valuable glimpses into this aspect of Islamic law.

[2] Several examples of conflict that cannot be called minor are given by Coulson, 94-99, to illustrate just this point.
I thank S.D. Goitein for the observation that many Geniza documents referring to differing decisions given by various Muslim judges in the same case confirm the fact that the *ikhtilāf* was real and not merely theoretical.

[3] See Coulson (88) for a lawsuit concerning the "House of the Elephant" which involved the decisions of successive Egyptian qadis for over a century.

whole.[1] For apart from particulars concerning the subject matter, there is not a great deal of difference among marriage contracts, agreements creating partnerships, claims for debts, or deeds of sale. Even instruments recording bilateral obligations seem very much like those containing unilateral declarations. It is not difficult to account for the outward similarity: the feature that strikes us at once is their formalism—the rigid structure and repetition of stereotyped phrases.[2]

Formalism is common to most archaic legal systems,[3] but the Arabic formulary does seem to have become excessively overburdened in this respect. It is longer and more complex than formularies from pre-existing legal systems in the Near East. Like these, it was an adaptation of elements assimilated from many sources, and so in addition to taking over fixed stylistic practices, the Arabic formulary acquired a number of legally synonymous terms that had piled up over time.[4] This quality is consistent with the formalism of the documents.

Eventually, however, cultural borrowings become the property of the society that has borrowed them. From Ṭaḥāwī's point of view, rigidity in structure is but one dimension of precaution: i.e., formulas are not stereotyped but are highly differentiated and are the *only* way of expressing the intention; because terms are carefully chosen to cover every possibility, in his mind there are no superfluous phrases. An analysis of the document itself will suggest

[1] It should be pointed out, in fact, that sale is usually considered the typical contract in Islamic law, after which other contracts are patterned. Islamic law never developed a general theory of contracts.

[2] The uniformity this imposed was not limited to private legal documents; documents of state were subject to the same formalism. Grohmann has shown (in the letters of Qurra b. Sharīk, for example) how the standardized style of the chancellery was already well developed in the Egyptian provinces by the end of the first century (*FWAP*, 113-137). In a later period, the large number of detailed *inshā'* manuals for drafting official acts (the complement of our *shurūṭ* handbooks) testifies to the stage of development the science had reached. See the art. "Diplomatic" in *EI*² and C. Cahen, "Notes de diplomatique arabo-musulmane," *JA* (1963), which also mentions *shurūṭ* works.

On formalism in documents, see Schiller, "Coptic Law," 215-216, and the references cited there to formalism in "primitive" legal systems.

[3] That is, the ancient and classical legal systems, as well as early European law that preceded the law of modern capitalism. For the distinctions between primitive, archaic and mature systems, see W. Seagle, *The Quest for Law* (New York, 1941), xv-xvi.

[4] Multiplicity of terms to mean the same thing is discussed by Schiller, "Coptic Documents," *Zum gegenwärtigen Stand der juristischen Papyrusforschung*, *ZVRW*, LX (1957), 203, and in his "Coptic Law," 222. He points out that the words "deceit, fraud, artifice, ruse" in the same formula had probably accumulated because it was uncertain whether the existing terms would say all that was intended by the formula.

how the Muslim jurists created and, in part, refashioned, the written contract for their own particular needs.[1]

Ṭaḥāwī treats the ordinary contract of sale primarily in Parts I and II of his work, and his discussion of the more important formulas and clauses can be found in them. A good many of the notes to the text of these two parts analyse individual formulas. However, the very nature of a commentary precludes a systematic treatment of the subject; Ṭaḥāwī could not anticipate (or "cross-reference" we might say), for the convenience of his readers, many features of the formulary that are brought up only later in the book. In addition, it is natural that we will often place the emphasis on different aspects of the formulary than did Ṭaḥāwī, observing it in its historical setting and especially for its place in the history of Islamic legal institutions. Therefore, for the sake of a more systematic study, we can divide the contract of sale into broad divisions, parts of which are discussed in the notes where relevant, or below where not. These are:

1. The Scheme.
   a. Order of Clauses.
   b. Stylization and Point of View.
   c. Number of Copies.
   d. Dating Formula.

2. Descriptive Formulas.
   a. Opening Formula.
   b. Formulas Identifying the Parties.
   c. Formulas Defining the Property.

3. Transfer Clauses.
   a. Formulas Describing the Transfer of Property.
   b. Formulas Guaranteeing the Validity of the Transaction.
   c. Quittance Clauses.

[1] The divisions within the document and the terminology observed vary considerably among scholars. I have drawn my terminology from many sources, guided by what seemed most appropriate to the Arabic formulary. For the classification of Arabic documents in general, Grohmann's scheme (*Einführung*, 108-110) which follows the precedents established for European documents (e.g., Steinacker, *Privaturkunde*, 6-14) seems suitable. In general, they are: documents with and without legal content, public and private, witnessed and non-witnessed, mandates, diplomas, and so on. Further, private legal documents are usually divided into evidential (*Beweisurkunde*, corresponding to those in Ṭaḥāwī's work) and "dispositive" or "constitutive" documents (*Geschäftsurkunde*) which not only serve as proof, but create and erase legal relationships (Steinacker, 10-11).

4. Final Settlement Clauses.
   a. Guarantees Against a Fault in Ownership.
   b. Clauses Denying Rights and Claims.
   c. Other Guarantees.

5. Witnessing Clauses.
   a. Testimony of Primary Witnesses.
   b. Testimony of Secondary Witnesses.
   c. Separate Document of *shahāda*.

1. The Scheme.

a. *Order of Clauses*. The main part of the contract of sale[1] is a narrative written in the past tense, relating in order the various steps taken by the parties to conclude the transaction.[2] Following the general outlines of an ancient scheme, already established in cuneiform deeds,[3] the Arabic documents maintain and even stress the rigid sequence. If special clauses have to be inserted, Ṭaḥāwī leaves nothing to the notary's imagination.

This rigidity may have been observed originally to prevent tampering with or making insertions in the document, but in explaining the sequence of clauses, Ṭaḥāwī often imposes Islamic norms and offers rationalizations to conform to Islamic legal practice. His reasons are usually attributed to *iḥtiyāṭ*. For instance, the order of clauses transferring the property is standard in the pre-Islamic documents[4] and is preserved in the Arabic formulary: payment of price, receiving of price, quittance for price; delivery of property, taking possession of property. Ṭaḥāwī instructs the notary to state that the seller takes the price *before* he mentions the buyer taking possession of the property

[1] The "operative section" as opposed to the sections containing final guarantees. This useful term seems to have been first used by Yaron, "The Schema of the Aramaic Legal Documents," *JSS*, II (1957), to apply to those parts of the conveyance that record the creation of a new legal status as a result of the parties' actions. It corresponds roughly to the sections containing the descriptive clauses and the transfer clauses, as they are set out in this outline.

[2] Facts about the complex negotiations that may have preceded the transaction are never mentioned, although certain kinds of contracts that depend on prior agreements (transfer of a debt, divorce) may allude to the original agreements or even incorporate all their information.

[3] San Nicolò, 14 ff., for Old Babylonian scheme; Muffs, 18-19, for other non-Old Babylonian sale deeds; Schiller, "Coptic Law," 217-218; Yaron, n. 1 above.

[4] At least in those formulas that describe counter-performance as well as performance. The Old Babylonian deeds, for example, record only the buyer's actions as a static, one-sided event.

because of the opinion of some scholars that the second can occur only with the permission of the seller;[1] taking the price implies that he has given his permission.[2] Further, the notary must say that the seller delivers the property (and not simply that the buyer takes possession of it) in order to protect the buyer against charges that he acquired it by usurpation (*ghaṣb*).[3]

However, the order of clauses can be linked to the principle of *iḥtiyāṭ* in a more significant way than the above examples show. An excellent illustration of this, and one that also demonstrates how the document acted as a firm record and even proof of the transaction, is the question of the order in which various parties give their *iqrār* at the end of the witnessing clauses.

All the scholars agree, says Ṭaḥāwī, that the *iqrār* of the seller precedes that of the buyer, because it is the seller who initiates the sale and the buyer who accepts it.[4] But the question becomes urgent in cases where the scholars disagree on the respective roles allotted to the parties in a court action. Briefly, one of these is the party whose assertion runs counter to the presumption (of freedom from debt, in our examples) and the other is the party whose assertion is supported by the presumption. When there is no proof,[5] the presumption operates in favor of the second, although the rules are most elaborate and this party cannot always be clearly defined. That is, it is the statement of the second, supported by the oath, that holds good (*al-qawl qawluhū*). Consequently, in a *salam* contract (prepayment, with delivery of merchandise at the end of a specified period), Ṭaḥāwī makes the *iqrār* of the *musallim* (the one advancing the cash) precede the *iqrār* of the *musallam ilayhi*, in order that the first can specify the date on which the merchandise is to be delivered to him.[6] The reason for this is that according to the dominant Ḥanafī view, the presumption operates in favor of the *musallim*; having the

[1] I 2.76. Referring to the same steps but shifting the emphasis, the seller must receive the price before delivery of the property, since the view of the Madinese is that the seller's *iqrār* that the buyer took the property by his having delivered it is the same as his *iqrār* that he has received the price (III 42.1).

[2] It is likely, in fact, that payment of the price always comes first because the document is drawn up primarily for the buyer's protection and at his request.

[3] I 2.75. Other discussions on the order of clauses in I 6.1-6.3, 7.1 ff., II, 7.1 ff., 23.4-23.5.

[4] Ṭaḥāwī's explanation is made too simple. As the following examples will show, the real reason for putting the *iqrār* of the buyer second is to protect him against false claims on the part of the seller in a lawsuit.

[5] As frequently happens in Islamic law because of the stringent rules regarding evidence. See Schacht, *Introduction*, 191. For some of the complex rules regarding presumptions, 190-192.

[6] V 19.34; clauses in 19.0, end.

advantage in a lawsuit, he may use his potential position to either deny that he has been paid when the term expired, or more likely, to prematurely claim the term over and demand delivery of the merchandise. If, however, the notary establishes in the document that the *musallim* gave his *iqrār* first, and in so doing specified the term before the exchange of promises proceeded any farther, he will have no such advantage over the *musallam ilayhi*.

Similarly, the *iqrār* of the creditor should precede that of the debtor, so that the creditor can be the first to commit himself by specifying the date when the debt is payable. The *iqrār* of a woman who has been divorced or a slave who has been manumitted, both with the promise that a sum of money will be handed over to them, is mentioned before that of the former husband or the *mawlā*; the first two will have to state the amount, and although the presumption operates in their favor, they will not be able to take advantage of this to deny that they received the sums owed them.[1] All these solutions, of course, are designed to protect the buyer-debtor, and it is up to the notary to insure these safeguards by maintaining the proper order of clauses in his contract.

b. *Stylization and Point of View.* These two formal aspects of written documents are rather complex, and have been the subject of considerable discussion particularly in connection with tracing cultural influences and lines of development. In general, documents can be cast in an impersonal, objective style, or as subjective, first-person declarations.[2] Sometimes, as is the case in certain Arabic documents, both styles can be combined in the same deed.[3]

Apart from this distinction, another is made based on the point of view of the document: one or the other party can be the subject of the deed, the other remaining in the background and appearing, perhaps, when it is his

[1] V 19.35-19.38. The opposite view on presumptions (i.e., the *qawl* belongs to the debtor, etc.) in all these cases is held by the Madinese, Ibn Abī Laylā, and Shāfi'ī. This is one of the few instances where Ṭaḥāwī does not attempt to resolve the *ikhtilāf*, since that is impossible, but instead conforms to the dominant opinion and hopes for the best. Certainly in this case, the notary contributes more to safeguarding the rights of the parties than he risks in permitting them to confront the *ikhtilāf*.

[2] Steinacker, *Privaturkunde*, 18, discusses the broad differences. We may draw an example from an objective cuneiform deed, "A bought a cow from B. He weighed out *x minas* of silver," as opposed to a subjective Coptic formulation, "I, Aristophanes, sell to you, Komes, the room which is off the foyer..." There are also shades of difference in between; compare the transition to a more subjective style in the Aramaic deed: "The house is owned by you," and "You are the owner of the house" (Muffs, 23, note).

[3] The demotic documents, for example, begin as one-sided declarations in objective style, stating the person who draws up the document; his declaration then follows in subjective style. See Seidl, *Ptolemäische Rechtsgeschichte* (Second edition, Gluckstadt-Hamburg, 1962), 50.

turn to give a guarantee.[1] Or the document can be written in the form of a dialogue (*Zweigesprächsurkunde*), describing the actions and reactions of the parties as a two-sided event.[2] Quite apart from the point of view, where one person is the subject of the deed, the document may be *drawn up* by one party or the other.[3]

However, these are matters of outward form, of notarial practice, and while they may be interesting for helping to determine the sources of the Arabic deed, they do not contribute much to the study of written documents in practice. Ṭaḥāwī himself is not much interested in such matters. He is certainly aware of broad distinctions in form, but tends to take them for granted and only mentions that they do occur in different circumstances.

In keeping with their testimonial character, most Arabic documents are cast in an objective style. They are drawn up by the seller, or the party undertaking the obligation, but the statements are formulated *ex latere emptoris*, with the buyer as the subject and the transaction recorded from his point of view (A has bought, rather than B has sold). Many contracts, however, are drawn up in an objective-subjective style, beginning as usual, but switching to a

[1] The transaction is from the point of view of the buyer, for instance, in the Old Babylonian deeds; the seller does not even appear for the quittance or transfer of property, but only if he must give a guarantee. San Nicolò, 27-28.

[2] As in the subjectively-formulated neo-Babylonian deeds. Schacht (*OLZ*, 1927) has noted that the Arabic documents alone share this characteristic of writing in both offer and acceptance, based on mutual consent, and this has led him to link the later cuneiform and the Islamic deeds. This fundamental point, "the moment of mutual consent as the basis of obligation," in his view overrides the external differences, such as the fact that the Arabic documents do not record the offer in direct speech.

San Nicolò (30-31) on the other hand, denies all Mesopotamian origins for the Arabic deed (as against Carusi and others looking for Semitic origins), and concludes that it is derived from Egyptian formularies (including Aramaic practice at Elephantine) with their overlay of imported Greco-Roman styles. He bases his conclusion mainly on the fact that the entire development in Egypt is based on declarations of the seller, for in the Arabic documents, it is the seller who undertakes the obligations and draws up a deed in favor of the buyer, even though the contract is formulated from the point of view of the buyer.

[3] It is impossible to state any general rules connecting all these variables. A document may be unilateral in form, one party drawing up the contract, but stating bilateral obligations. Also, it may be executory on one side only, the other party having fulfilled his obligations, with one party speaking in the deed. For a convenient summary of some of these elements in the scheme, see Yaron, 124-125.

Bilateral obligations may even be recorded in parallel documents, as sometimes occurs in Assyrian and Babylonian practice: for example, in a sale on credit, the transaction is embodied in two separate tablets, one recording the transfer (the sale tablet) and the other the terms of the loan making the sale possible (the obligation tablet). For an interesting interpretation of this practice and its implications for the theory of contract in archaic law, see W. Seagle, *The Quest for Law* (New York, 1941), 259-260.

The distinction in point of view may even be based on whether the property transferred is movable (seller) or immovable (buyer) as in documents of the neo-Babylonian period. San Nicolò, 28-30.

first person formulation and then closing objectively, as they began, with the testimony of witnesses.[1] What is the difference?

There are basically only two styles, says Ṭaḥāwī in connection with his discussion of a contract of *iqāla*, an agreement to reverse a sale, and all *shurūṭ* fall into one category or the other.[2] The first is the style that Yūsuf b. Khālid employs, beginning:

> "This is a document in favor of A, the seller, which B, the buyer, has had drawn up in his favor: 'I bought from you, O Fulān, the entire house property...' "

The sale is described and the attesting witnesses named, all in the first person and spoken by the original buyer (now become the "seller"). The deed then continues with the new agreement:

> "Then, after that, you asked me, O Fulān, to grant you a contract of *iqāla* for the property you sold me... on condition that I return the price to you...; I agreed to your request, and I granted you an *iqāla*..."

The second contract, including all the guarantees, is also recorded in the first person, except for the witnessing clauses at the end; here, the testimony to the *iqrār* of the two parties to the *iqāla* is given in objective style.

The other type of formulation is Abū Zayd's model for the same transaction, the contract beginning with *hādhā mā* and carried through to the end in objective style, or the usual style of the deeds.[3] This is quite appropriate for transactions in which the parties conclude an original agreement, says Ṭaḥāwī, for the document is a confirmation (*ījāb*) of the rights of each party toward the other. However, certain contracts are based upon prior legal arrangements (*asbāb mutaqaddima*); divorce, for example, must refer to a previous marriage, and manumission of a slave depends on prior ownership of that slave. The same is true of the contract for *iqāla*, for without the original sale, the *iqāla* would not exist. All these contracts, then, must be drawn up so that they express the *iqrār* of one party[4] toward the other, and not of the two together.

[1] There are no fully subjective documents, as in the later Byzantine and Coptic *tabellio* deeds, drawn up as declarations of the seller.

[2] IV 7.4. The contract for *iqāla* is the first *shurūṭ* in Ṭaḥāwī's book given in subjective style.

[3] IV 7.2. Abū Zayd begins with *hādhā mā shahida 'alayhi al-shuhūd*, while other authors might begin with *hādhā mā istaqāla*, but Ṭaḥāwī is right in pointing out that it comes down to the same thing: both formulations introduce objective contracts and contain the acknowledgements of both parties together.

[4] The acknowledgement of the party creating the obligation, and responsible for additional guarantees, is in this case the *muqīl*, the original buyer, who grants the *iqāla*. Both parties still give their acknowledgements for their respective roles in the transaction, and because the usual objective style expresses the double *iqrār*, the conclusion of the *iqāla* contract (and others like it) is framed in the third person.

However, the question that may be asked at the outset is why these two criteria, prior legal arrangements and the *iqrār* of one in favor of another (rather than a double *iqrār*) should require stylization in direct speech. There is no reason why the obligation could not be recorded in the usual objective fashion, following the formula *hādhā kitāb li-fulān katabahū lahū fulān.*[1] Ṭaḥāwī's explanation for the use of the subjective style is tautological: certain contracts, based on prior arrangements, are formulated in this way by all *shurūṭ* authors; therefore, on analogy with these, all contracts that meet the criteria should be formulated in the same way.

Furthermore, the rule is not strictly applied. Some contracts that do not depend on others that were concluded previously are formulated subjectively,[2] while other contracts, meeting both requirements, may be formulated either way, according to Ṭaḥāwī's own instructions.[3] The evidence of the papyri confirms these variations. Indeed, there probably are no hard and fast rules governing this manner of stylization. The first-person formulation is certainly more emphatic.[4] The person undertaking the obligation in the second transaction is usually reversed, and so the shift in diction has the effect of stressing the shift in obligation.

c. *Number of Copies.* Arabic documents were often drawn up in two or more copies. There is no evidence from the papyri that the witness received a copy of the contract, although he probably kept his own notes. If he had to repeat his testimony later on, he would want to have the facts on hand.

The copies were made for the contracting parties, but not merely for the sake of their convenience. Ṭaḥāwī translates this feature of notarial usage into a formula that is planted in the document itself, as one of its formal elements.[5] Furthermore, the position of the clause within the document is

[1] This form, in fact, is used in a model from "Adhkār al-Ḥuqūq," II, 5. Ṭaḥāwī's term for objective styling is *'alā khiṭāb al-ithnayni*, as opposed to *'alā khiṭāb al-wāḥid*, which shows that he expects the notary to be consistent in recording the *iqrār* of both parties in the objectively styled contract.

[2] As in a *salam* transaction, where the party who promises to deliver merchandise at a later date drafts a contract in favor of the one advancing the cash (V 19.0). Presumably, as in analogical cases, the roles will be reversed and another document will be drawn up in favor of the first when he performs his part of the transaction. A second example occurs when a document is lost and the buyer asks the seller to draw up another for him; the transfer clauses are framed subjectively by the seller (IV 18.0).

[3] For example, *shurūṭ* in V 1.0, 4.0, 18.0.

[4] We may compare the striking preference for the energetic mood in the documents of the papyri. Grohmann, *FWAP*, 94.

[5] The clause is introduced in III 11.0 and appears quite regularly thereafter; examples in III 17.0, 40.0, IV 19.0, V 13.0.

meaningful. It is not simply tacked on at the end, but purposefully placed immediately after the final guarantee clauses and before the witnessing formulas; thus the clause is comprehended by the *shahāda.*

The first part of the formula specifies the number of copies made, but in effect it is also a stamp of validity,[1] affirming the external correctness of the document:

> "This document has been drawn up in two copies, according to the same order and arrangement. Neither copy exceeds the other by a single letter that might alter a rule or add to its meaning..."

It is the second half that reveals the intrinsic value of the document as proof of the transaction:

> "And one of the two copies is in the possession of Fulān, serving him as a written confirmation and a document of proof (*thiqatan lahū wa-ḥujjatan*), and the other copy is in the possession of Fulān, serving him as a written confirmation and a document of proof."[2]

If more than two parties are involved, Ṭaḥāwī's instructions regarding the distribution of copies are usually explicit.

One example will show why it was important merely to have a written document in one's hands. An agreement is made to rescind a sale when the right of option is exercised. Abū Ḥanīfa and others call for a separate document (*ḥujja*) that specifically cancels the sale, to be given to the buyer; possession of the document will prevent the seller from demanding the price at a later date, claiming that the contract was binding and the transaction must be completed.[3]

Commenting on Abū Ḥanīfa's solution, Ṭaḥāwī touches on another matter of form, namely, how two related agreements are to be drafted so that each supports the other as proof. Always more cautious than his teachers, Ṭaḥāwī advises that a safer procedure is to write up the sale together with the

[1] Notaries often placed legalization formulas at the head of the document. For examples of these, see Grohmann, *Einführung*, 122, and *APEL* I, 210 and 215, note to 1.1.

[2] It would be possible to translate *thiqa* and *ḥujja* simply as "confirmation and proof" but for the usage noted in the next paragraph, and but for the fact that in some formulas from the papyri, the term *wathīqa* occurs in place of *thiqa*. See Grohmann, *Einführung*, 109. In any case, the meaning remains much the same.

Other *shurūṭ* authors (cited by Tyan, *Notariat*, 73; Nuwayrī, 9) give detailed instructions to the notary concerning the number of copies, number of pages, lines to a page, and so on, but these are strictly matters of form and are not discussed with reference to the nature of the written document itself.

[3] III 17.1-17.2; contract in 15.0. Another example in V 13.0-13.1, concerning a slave manumitted by the executor of an estate.

cancellation in a single document (*ḥujja*), make two copies, and give one to each party. This achieves Abū Ḥanīfa's purpose, and also insures that a detail in one of Abū Ḥanīfa's two separate documents (the sale and the cancellation) will not be altered nor disagree with a detail in the other. This is the solution that Ṭaḥāwī consistently adopts, not only to insure that the documents will correspond, but for a number of technical reasons, related to *iḥtiyāṭ*, as well. Deeds containing the testimony of secondary witnesses are, by preference, incorporated in the original contract.

An interesting practice that Ṭaḥāwī recommends on occasion, and one that we find often enough in the papyri, is to draft a supplementary document on the *verso* of the contract. If, for instance, an acting buyer wishes to add his acknowledgement that he bought property on behalf of someone else and that he has no rights in it whatever, his witnessed *iqrār* is added on the back of the contract of sale. The important facts recorded on the *recto* are mentioned, and the legal relationship between the agent and the person commissioning him, their mutual rights and duties, is defined. This calls for a double *iqrār* as well, written in and attested at the end of the document.[1]

d. *Dating Formula.* The relevant date was that on which the document was drawn up, and only secondarily the date on which it was witnessed. This is clear from the dating formula, typically "[This document] has been written in the month of Ramaḍān of the year 441," placed sometimes at the head of the document above the *basmala*, and sometimes at the end before the names of the witnesses.[2]

[1] IV 1.0. These documents on the *verso* all seem to be cases where the attestation is made by primary witnesses. Of the many examples in the papyri, we may mention a long and well preserved contract of sale for land with date palms on it (edited by Dietrich, *Papyri*, 12-27); the *verso* is a separate contract between buyers and agent (who happens to be one of the buyers), appointing the agent.

Documents written on the *verso* are not to be confused with the endorsements that commonly appear on the outside of a rolled or folded papyrus. These were short memorandums giving the names of the parties and some general idea of the contents, so the owner would be able to distinguish them in his files. They were also quite different from the *scriptura exterior* of the "double documents" (*Doppelurkunden*) of the ancient Near East, in which the entire transaction was rewritten on the outside of the sheet, which was then folded in half, sealed, and rolled. The purpose of these was exactly the same as Ṭaḥāwī's in combining two documents in one and giving a copy to each party—to prevent the *scriptura interior* from being falsified. Some scholars (e.g., Grohmann, *Einführung*, 121-122; Steinacker, *Privaturkunde*, 165, n. 6) consider endorsements as abbreviated *scripturae exteriores*. However, each of the three "outside writings" differs so in function, that it seems impossible to state any certain connection or unifying principle other than that they all took advantage of the empty back of the sheet.

[2] For the term *kutiba* in the passive, see Dietrich, *Briefe*, 74. Date at the top, e.g., *APEL*, I, 210; at the end, all of Ṭaḥāwī's *shurūṭ* where the dating formula is given (these begin in III 11.0) and *APEL* I, 222, 232, 246, 258, for examples.

Ṭaḥāwī's *shurūṭ* cannot show this, but in the papyri, a second dating formula was written in following the signature of each witness; occasionally, it is "[Fulān] gave his testimony to everything contained in the document... on its date (*fī ta'rīkhihī*)." Usually, however, this date is recorded by month and year, as in the body of the document. Presumably the witnessing date coincides with the drafting of the deed, and in the few instances where the *day* of the month is mentioned in both places, and they do agree, there is no difficulty.

But why was it necessary to repeat the date after the name of each witness? Did the drafting of the deed and part of the witnessing, at least, take place at different times? First of all, since most documents of the papyri are dated by naming the month only, or at best, the decade of the month, these two events could have taken place within ten days or more of one another without the discrepancy being apparent. In fact, the expression *fī ta'rīkhihī* may have been another way of saying that the deed was drawn up and witnessed on the very same day, and not another. Second, a few papyri do give us real evidence that depositions were given over a short period of time; in one example, the list of witnesses is long, and signatures are recorded over a period that occurs in two consecutive months.[1]

Third, the logic of the circumstances suggests that the date the document was drawn up did not necessarily coincide with the date all the depositions were given. Two parties who wished to draw up a contract preserving their transaction presented themselves to a notary and told him the facts. The notary then drew up the instrument or assigned it to an assistant. Considering the length of some of the contracts, he may have instructed the parties to go about their business and call for their document sometime later. Once the deed was prepared, the parties were ready to submit it to the witnessing procedure, part of which consisted of having the entire document read out to them in the presence of the witnesses. Two were required, one of them likely to be the notary himself.[2] But as we know from the surviving documents, the

[1] Dietrich, *Papyri*, 20, and note on 26. Dietrich does not distinguish this procedure from that of witnessing over a period of years, the purpose of which was quite different. The alert co-contractors, seeking to assure the continuing value of the document as proof of their transaction, simply replaced or added to the earlier witnesses, some of whom may have died or disappeared. An example is found in *APEL* I, 105, and note on 117, in which twenty-two witnesses testify over a period of twelve years.

[2] We can only presume this, since naming the writer of the document was rare in Arabic documentary practice. See *APEL* I, notes on 82, 116, and II, 152, 231; Dietrich, *Papyri*, 11, n. to l. 14; Serjeant, "Ḥabbān," 125. When he is named, more often than not his name appears at the head of the list of witnesses. Yaron makes an interesting distinction in this

parties were rarely satisfied with the minimum number, and it was up to them to go out and find supplementary witnesses.[1] These activities would surely take some time, especially since the deed would have to be read out to them again before each witness or group of witnesses. It would have been surprising if, at the end of the day, all this could have been accomplished. It is likely, then, that the essential two witnesses signed on the day the deed was written only because circumstances permitted it, but we cannot take for granted a single witnessing date for the document.

The dating formula in Ṭaḥāwī's contracts appears at the end of the document and names only the month and the year.[2] His discussion of dating is brief, and limited to those passages within a document where a date occurs as one of the terms of the transaction. Since incorrect wording may affect the way the contract is interpreted, precaution requires that the notary choose his terminology with care; for example, when he has to define the period during which the parties can exercise their option to rescind a sale, or the length of time land is leased when only the standing crop is purchased. The *method* of dating also prevents misinterpretation. Thus, the notary is instructed to use certain conventional styles and not others: dating according to the days of the month passed (*khalā*) rather than those remaining (*baqiya*), and mentioning the first lunation (*istihlāl*, *mustahall al-shahr*) or night of the month. Both of these are commonly found in the preserved documents.[3]

2. Descriptive Formulas.

At first glance, the significance of the descriptive clauses may seem slight relative to the number of lines devoted to them in the contract, as well as in the commentary. Their purpose, to define the nature of the transaction, identify the parties, and describe the property, is certainly not unique to

connection. The practice of putting the witnesses' names first accords with demotic and Aramaic (but not Coptic) usage; in these the witnesses signed with their own hand. On the other hand, if the names are only listed by the scribe, as is invariably the case in the cuneiform documents, the scribe completes his work by putting his own name at the end. The placing of the scribe's name at the end has the advantage that it will immediately be obvious if the document is not complete (Yaron, 12).

[1] We find notarized deeds with the testimony of as many as forty-two witnesses. Tyan (*Notariat*, 51) refers to anecdotes in historical works that tell of individuals, their written contracts already in hand, presenting themselves before professional witnesses to request their depositions.

[2] But never the decade, even though this is often found in the papyri; see *APEL* I, 85. Nuwayrī (7) recommends that the notary specify even the hour, because another contract drawn up on the same day may conflict with the first.

[3] Terminology, III 41.3-41.5; styles, III 13.0, 13.2-13.4, 15.0, 28.0.

Arabic documents. But apart from these apparent purposes, the clauses have hidden functions that are revealed in the light of Ṭaḥāwī's broader aims.

a. *Opening Formula.* The most common introductory formula in the objective style deeds is *hādhā mā* (lit. this is what...) followed by a verb in the perfect tense, indicating the nature of the contract (*hādhā mā ishtarā*, *shahida 'alayhi*, *awṣā bihi*, etc.). We can venture to explain the verb as the written counterpart of the oral declaration which, together with the *niyya* (intention), is necessary to bring about the legal obligation. While the use of the verb is not even mentioned, the formula *hādhā mā* is discussed by the Ḥanafī *shurūṭ* writers to an extent that seems out of proportion to its significance. After all, it was a common formal phrase, used even to introduce chancery documents;[1] there were few meaningful alternatives that one could prefer or defend.[2] But more important, it contributed nothing in terms of its legal effect.

Ṭaḥāwī's commentary mostly consists of traditions citing precedents for the phrase in the documents drawn up by the Prophet and others.[3] We may wonder why he did not use these same traditions in his introduction where they would have been dramatic support for the practice of writing down contracts. In this context they have little impact: the Prophet used the phrase *hādhā mā*, and so should we. But if they are not as effective here, at least they are more subtly introduced, and this could have been Ṭaḥāwī's intention. However, we should not press this point too far. Ṭaḥāwī took the existence of written documents for granted, and nowhere is he willing to engage in more than perfunctory arguments either for or against them.

b. *Formulas Identifying the Parties.* The individuals who have concluded the contract must be identified as accurately as possible, but not merely for the sake of describing them. The identification is important both for the inner structure of the document and for safeguarding the rights of the parties. First of all, the formula is an objective statement of fact, comparable to any other in the document. Identity is established: it is A and B, and no others, who have concluded the present agreement. This sets the stage for the depositions at the end, where the witnesses, referring back to this original

[1] See above, p. 38, n. 2.

[2] For these alternatives, see notes to I 2.3-2.13, the paragraphs devoted to the introductory formula.

[3] Including an interesting and rare testament establishing a *waqf*, purportedly drawn up by 'Alī b. Abī Ṭālib. It is curious that Ṭaḥāwī should quote this document in its entirety just for the sake of the two words that introduce it, but in any case, we are glad to have it. It appears to be the most detailed version extant. See the notes to I 2.11.

identification in effect, will testify that it is indeed the same A and B whose identity and legal competence they verify.

Second, the parties ought to be described as fully as is necessary to prevent their being confused with someone else of the same name. The *shurūṭ* authors do not always agree on the best way of doing this, and in addition to specifying a man's *nisba*, or genealogy, it is suggested that the notary name his profession, residence, tribal affiliation, distinguishing physical characteristics and even his *laqab*, or nickname, if this does not anger or dishonor him.[1]

Furthermore, Ṭaḥāwī points out that an exact identification will show whether the individual is present, dead, or has departed the town. Although the intention is not made explicit, Ṭaḥāwī probably had in mind a situation in which a third person might assume the identity of someone who is not able to appear to claim his rights. It is conceivable, for example, that an unscrupulous person, claiming to be someone else, would wrongfully collect a debt from one of the parties or his heirs. The witnesses, if they are still available to testify, cannot be expected to remember the face of every single client for whom they have given their depositions. This does not, of course, lessen the value of their testimony, but identity based on a number of objective facts can more readily be the subject of inquiry.

c. *Formulas Defining the Property*. The written document also served as a record of the property conveyed. It was essential, then, that it be defined as fully as possible, first by a restricting formula (*Begrenzungsformel*) and second, by an accessory clause (*Pertinenzformel*). The restricting formula established the location (if it were immovable property), beginning with the town and gradually proceeding to a more narrow designation; all four boundaries were then defined with reference to bordering property and to the four cardinal points. These definitions and the proper way of expressing them to avoid controversy are discussed in detail in the *shurūṭ* commentaries.

Even more elaborate are the rules for notaries governing the accessory clauses, for these defined the *ḥuqūq* and *marāfiq*, the abstract rights and the material appurtenances, that are sold with the property. If house property (a *dār*) is sold, the notary must know what fixed constituent parts are automatically included in the sale, and what is included if the terms *ḥuqūq* and *marāfiq*

[1] See note to I 2.14. Sarakhsī's discussion, 169-170. In practice, notaries often went beyond the minimum requirements of the *shurūṭ* authors. The handwriting of the parties is of no consequence, of course, as a distinguishing feature, and the subject is not even brought up. The parties never signed the document because their signatures would have had no effect.

are added.[1] Baths, mills, ships, and so on, and the equipment that is essential to their definition, give rise to detailed distinctions; slaves and movables must be discussed whenever model contracts for their sale are introduced.[2] Included in these accessory clauses are provisions for easements, such as an access road to a neighbor's house, or the *ḥarīm* of a well or canal, the perimeter of land around the property that is necessary for its use. Although the *ḥuqūq* and *marāfiq* and the other rights are fairly well defined by custom, and even by law, the notary's task was complicated by differences of opinion among the scholars on individual details. Conscious use of ambiguity was one solution adopted, but at the same time, the skillful notary should be able to express exactly what was intended by the parties.

Ṭaḥāwī does not discuss the essential purposes of the descriptive clauses, but these can be readily observed. First of all, the clauses lessened the likelihood of future conflicts between the parties. In addition to defining exactly what the buyer could expect the seller to deliver, the actual condition of the property at the time of the sale was recorded. This is most apparent in contracts for movable property. A future quarrel over a detail might serve as an excuse to overturn the entire transaction.

Second, the descriptive clauses helped establish the validity of the sale. No one could accuse the parties of having violated any of the numerous rules that defined what things could be the objects of ownership and transfer.[3] The clauses might establish, for example, that property such as fruit on the trees or crops in the field was in existence on the day the sale was concluded,[4] or that the property was exactly known, or that it was in actual possession of the seller.

Finally, these clauses, and especially the restricting formulas, were most important as a way of establishing ownership. It is significant that when the notary has to express the prior ownership and possession of the seller, but cannot do so explicitly because of the *ikhtilāf* mentioned earlier, he draws up

[1] A *dār* without *ḥuqūq*, as the formula states, includes among other things, all the dwellings and rooms (*manāzil*, *buyūt*) within it; but these two can also be sold separately, and will then be subject to other sets of rules determining how they are to be defined if sold with and without *ḥuqūq*. For Ṭaḥāwī's discussion of the descriptive clauses for the basic contract, see I 2.22-2.41 (restricting clauses) and I 2.42-2.55 (accessory clauses), and notes to these paragraphs.

[2] Because the descriptive clauses will vary according to the type of property treated, discussion is scattered throughout the work, but see especially Parts II and III. These include distinctions the notary must make when parts of the property are sold, for divided and undivided joint shares, and when exceptions are made in a sale.

[3] See Schacht, *Introduction*, 134-135.

[4] III 2.1-2.2.

a document containing the testimony of secondary witnesses confirming the *boundaries* of the property sold.[1]

3. Transfer Clauses.

a. *Formulas Describing the Transfer of Property.* This section is the heart of the contract and its longest part. Here are all the facts: the transfer of the property and the creation of a new legal status are recorded in a step-by-step description. The action stands out as a dramatic episode against the static quality of the rest of the document: the stage has been set, the cast of characters named, and now the parties are to perform their interacting roles.

The purpose of these clauses is not merely to describe the reciprocal actions of the parties, but to prove that the contract they concluded was complete, valid, and not open to challenge. Therefore, none of the steps the parties had taken can be left out of the written document, or the contract itself might be suspect. According to stricter opinions, the omission of any element would make the contract void or, at least, would weaken it. Thus the seller not only delivers the property, the buyer takes possession of it. This is one reason why all the clauses in the section play a part, no matter how repetitive or superfluous they may seem.

The most important formulas, if we are to judge by the elaborateness of some of the *shurūṭ* formulas and the actual practice of the papyri, are those expressing the price. In Ṭaḥāwī's text, the price is described, and the quality of the coin is also established with the formula "of standard weight [i.e., seven *mithqāls*] in gold, in minted coin of full weight and good alloy."[2] Often the formula has to be modified to take account of special situations,[3] or certain safeguards will be added if the nature of the contract does not permit the price to be specified.[4] In practice, frequently half the stipulated sum was

[1] I 4.0 and notes to this document.

[2] *bi-kadhā kadhā dīnāran mathāqīla dhahaban ʿaynan wāzinatan jiyādan.* This formula was for dinars, of course; the special difficulties connected with it are discussed in the notes to I 2.69-2.70. For dirhams, see IV 6.0, where the formula is introduced. Ṣayrafī (25) claims that his own formula, given in rhyme, will "improve [the notary's] mode of expression, ornament the document and make it longer" without having a harmful effect on the document or the validity of the sale.

[3] For example, when payment is made by handing over a *ṣakk* for a debt, rather than cash (V 3.0, 4.0), or in a contract for resale of merchandise at a fixed profit (*murābaḥa*, IV 11.0), where the profit is paid in another coin.

[4] A common formula in the text is *wafāʾ bi-qīmatihā*, referring to paying the full value of the property when, for instance, the principal does not specify a price to his agent and acting seller, but directs him to get as much as he can for it (V 15.0 bis). Another formula, often added as a safeguard in such cases (or when a minor is involved, or an executor sells

mentioned immediately after the price formula to help prevent falsification of the amount in the document, but Ṭaḥāwī does not mention this usage.[1]

Next, the buyer hands over the price[2] and the seller receives it in full: (*istawfāhu minhū tāmman kāmilan*); the seller delivers the property[3] and the buyer takes possession.[4] The order of clauses must be strictly maintained.[5]

The formula for the actual transfer of the property is straightforward compared with that for inspection of the property (the *ru'ya*). The second is a veritable net for divergent opinions, from which Ṭaḥāwī must extract a satisfactory formulation by the most careful attention to details. The clause states that prior to the transfer, the parties had:

> "... inspected together (*ra'ayā jamī'an*) the entire *dār*, defined [by its boundaries] in this document, all its *ḥuqūq*, all the structures and dwellings that are in it and form part of it, no matter how few or many they may be; they have examined everything themselves (*'āyanāhā*) inside and out. All of that was apparent to them [while they were] together, and they were cognizant of it at the time the contract for this sale, mentioned in this document, was concluded between them, as well as before that time. Then, they concluded their contract of sale on the basis of that [inspection]."

It is evident at once how many elements must be comprehended by the clause. First, stress is placed on the fact that both parties together inspect the property, despite the general rule in Islamic law that it is the buyer only, and not the seller, who has the right to rescind the sale at the time he sees the

on behalf of the heirs, etc.) is *lā waks wa-lā shaṭaṭ*, "without undue loss or gain [on either side]"; e.g., V 7.0, 15.0 bis, Marghīnānī, fol. 22a. Sarakhsī (179) defines "fair value" as *huwa mā fawq al-waks wa-dūn al-shaṭaṭ*.

[1] Ṣayrafī (25), *tanṣīf al-thaman*. See *APEL* I, 152-153, where Grohmann points out that this practice was already in full vogue in the demotic and Greek documents; examples on 146, 238. S.D. Goitein observes that the fact that Ṭaḥāwī does not mention this is paralleled in the Geniza documents where the practice becomes common only in later documents.

[2] The *thaman* and not a specified number of dinars, because paying dinars does not discharge the buyer's obligation; the kind of coin may not be to the liking of the seller, who has the right to refuse what the buyer offers him (I 2.67-2.71).

[3] Again, the notary must take care how he expresses this: if he uses the term *dār*, for example, he would be obliged to repeat all the details concerning the rights, appurtenances, and boundaries, and this would be most tiresome (I 2.74). This is why a circumlocution is used whenever possible in the contract; most often it is *jamī'u mā waqa'a 'alayhi hādha'l-bay'*, "everything that this sale entails."

[4] The buyer not only takes possession (*qabaḍahū minhū*), but the property itself "moves," as it were, into his hands by virtue of the purchase (*ṣāra fī yadihī wa-qabḍihī bi-hādha'l-shirā*). There are variants (e.g., as in V 1.0, *bi-ḥaqqi ibtiyā'ihī iyyāhā minhū*) but no difference in meaning.

[5] I 2.75-2.76. See above, p. 40 ff.

property he has bought. However, there are good reasons for strictness that goes beyond the requirements of the majority view. The first is simple precaution against one opinion that holds that both parties have the option for what they have not seen until the time of the contract.[1] The second is that the clause insures that the sale has not taken place for something that is not in actual possession;[2] if both parties have to look at the property, and this is confirmed by testimony, any accusation to the contrary can be automatically dismissed.

The third point is not mentioned by Ṭaḥāwī, but is in keeping with the character of the documents. As long as the option of inspection has not been extinguished, the sale is not complete; the clause dealing with inspection formally establishes this quality of completeness and thus prevents conflict between the parties in the future. If they give their formal acknowledgement to the fact that they were both present when the property was inspected, and this acknowledgement is confirmed by the testimony of witnesses, it becomes impossible for the buyer to state at a later date that he had not seen the property at the time and now wishes to cancel the sale. Also, the seller will be unable to claim that the buyer had indeed exercised his option to cancel but had not returned the property. This is undoubtedly also the reason for the phrase at the end of the clause, declaring that the two were cognizant of the property even before the sale took place, for this in itself would extinguish the option.

Another of Ṭaḥāwī's requirements, not shared by other *shurūṭ* authors, is that the *ru'ya* be stated in the form of an *iqrār* rather than a simple affirmation that it has taken place. Seeing is subjective, he says, and neither witnesses nor any amount of outside evidence can establish the fact that a person has truly "seen" something.[3] The *iqrār* takes it beyond the bounds of subjectivity and, as it were, makes the *ru'ya* watertight.

The variety of opinions on the nature of inspection also helps determine the wording of the formula. When does it take place, and exactly how much of the property must be seen? In order to satisfy the strictest views, and not the more realistic ones usually held, Ṭaḥāwī's clause states that the *ru'ya* takes place at the very time the contract is concluded, and defines

[1] I 2.77-2.83. The seller may, for example, inherit a piece of property and then sell it without having looked at it.

[2] I 2.83.

[3] I 2.84-2.89.

the parts of the *dār* that must be inspected in the broadest way possible.[1]

Similarly, separation of the parties (*tafarruq*) to bring to an end the meeting in which the contract was concluded must be formally expressed in the document. Like inspection of the property, this act also extinguishes the option to ratify or cancel the sale (the *khiyār al-majlis*). Thus, the clause not only establishes that this step had been taken, again stressing the validity of the contract, but also that neither party had rejected the sale before separation took place.[2]

One difficulty, however, is the interpretation a qadi might give to the term *tafarruq*. While one might construe it as actual physical separation (*bi'l-abdān*), another qadi might take a less literal view and define *tafarruq* as the completion of offer and acceptance (*tafarruq bi'l-aqwāl*, "separation with the words of the parties"). The notary is therefore obliged to comprehend both definitions in his formula, and Ṭaḥāwī accomplishes this nicely with

> "The two parties separated physically after this sale, mentioned in this document, [was concluded], in mutual agreement (*'an tarāḍin minhumā*) and with the intention to carry it out on the part of both of them together (*wa-infādh minhumā lahū*) with respect to all of [its provisions]."

Thus, the Qur'ānic phrase *'an tarāḍin minhumā*,[3] and the words *wa-infādh minhumā lahū*, express not merely the state of mind of the parties and satisfy the requirement for *tafarruq bi'l-aqwāl*, but in a practical way facilitate one of the aims of the document, reconciling divergent views.

b. *Formulas Guaranteeing the Validity of the Transaction.* Phrases advertising that the contract is sound, and valid in Islamic law, are avoided by Ṭaḥāwī for reasons connected with *iḥtiyāṭ*,[4] even though they were commonly employed in practice and by other *shurūṭ* authors.[5] Precaution, however, outweighs other considerations, and even the negative formulation, "[a sale] in which there is no condition or promise [stipulated]" (*lā sharṭ fīhi wa-lā 'ida*) wins only his begrudging approval. The words *lā sharṭ* do, it is true, prevent a future claim by one of the parties that a condition had been attached to the

[1] I 2.90-2.99. In some circumstances it would be impossible to look at the property together at the time of the sale (i.e., during the *majlis*, or "session"), as when two pieces of house property are exchanged in a barter transaction. Ṭaḥāwī's solution is the *iqrār* of the parties that before the contract was concluded they had inspected the two *dārs*. The word "together" is avoided. III 40.0 ter.

[2] It is for this reason that Yaḥyā b. Aktham writes in both separation and a statement that the option is no longer operative. Ṭaḥāwī considers the second superfluous, since the first effectively expresses the same thing. I 2.104, 2.110-2.111.

[3] Sur. 4:29, 2:233.

[4] See above, p. 34. The formulas are dismissed by Ṭaḥāwī in I 2.100-2.110.

[5] These are discussed in the notes to I 2.56-2.60.

sale, making it invalid, but "no promise" is merely a concession to a few scholars who do not realize that a person making an agreement may legitimately refuse to live up to a promise if he retains an option. The phrase, therefore, does not prejudice the document, but is superfluous in Ṭaḥāwī's opinion.

c. *Quittance Clauses.* An essential part of the written contract is the *barā'a* (*Entlastungsformel*), the quittance given by the seller to the buyer for the price. It is included here among the transfer clauses, and not with the final guarantees, because its function is to insure perfect performance, rather than provide against *future* attempts to interfere with the transaction. The seller declares that he has cleared the buyer of obligation, having received payment in full; that is, nothing more is wanted of him and nothing more can be demanded. Furthermore, to avert a future claim on the part of the seller that the price he received was not that agreed upon, or that the coin was unsatisfactory, the full formula for the price is repeated in the quittance clause.[1]

The seller's release of the buyer is, to be sure, withheld if the nature of the contract permits delayed payment. Frequently in such cases the quittance formula is not merely omitted, but a clause formally expressing this fact is inserted in the contract.[2] When delivery of the price finally takes place, quittance is given in a separate document of *shahāda.*[3]

The *shurūṭ* authors sometimes refer to quittance for the price as the *barā'at al-qabḍ wa'l-istīfā'*, to distinguish it from the *barā'at al-'ayb.*[4] The second is given by the buyer, freeing the seller from obligation, in the event a defect (that would normally allow the sale to be cancelled) is later discovered in the sold property. The quittance for defects was not necessary for a valid contract, but could be incorporated in the contract of sale if the parties so wished.[5]

[1] I 2.61-2.65 and notes to these pars.

[2] See, for example, a *salam* contract (V 19.0) in which the party who promises to deliver merchandise at a future date affirms that he has not received a *barā'a*, and will not receive one, except when he settles his debt (*illā bi'l-khurūj ilayka minhū*).

[3] e.g., III 11.0.

[4] Marghīnānī makes the distinction (fols. 16b-17a), while the terminology is used by Ṭaḥāwī and others.

[5] At least, Ṭaḥāwī suggests that it be written in after the formulas stating the separation of the parties; see his formula and discussion in I 5.0-5.10, and notes to these pars. A feature of Ṭaḥāwī's formula is that acceptance of the quittance for defects is also required, and is stated formally by the seller; see notes to I 6.20.

In practice, a separate witnessed document was usually drawn up. For example, see Hoenerbach, *Urkunden*, 307-308; Dietrich, *Papyri*, 39-40 (in subjective style); *APEL* II, 152-154. In fact, the term *barā'a* or *barā'āt* (or *barāwāt*) came to denote written documents themselves, of various kinds. See *EI*², s.v. "Barā'a."

Quittance clauses clearing the buyer of the price had greater importance in documents of the pre-Islamic Near East. This is apparent not only from the consistency with which they appear in nearly all conveyances, but also because the usual clauses are frequently supplemented with formulas having a similar function. In the Islamic deeds, the quittance is clearly part of the transfer section; it looks back to the exchange and emphasizes its completion. In the ancient Near Eastern deeds, however, it plays a dual role. Satisfaction clauses[1] not only look back to the transfer, but also look forward to other guarantees, and even anticipate the final relinquishment of rights expressed in the final settlement clauses. In other words, the quittance acts as a bridge between performance and the obligatory effects of the final clauses.

But such satisfaction formulas were apparently considered inadequate by the scribes to express the seller's intention to withdraw, and so among the supplementary formulas we find, for example, the oath or declaration of no-contest. The former owner or rightholder promises that having taken the full price, neither he nor his heirs (sometimes all the possibilities are expressed) will ever dispute the transaction or interfere with the buyer's enjoyment of his property.[2] A penalty clause is nearly always added to this, stating that in the event of so doing, the seller will have to pay a fine or, sometimes, undergo some other kind of punishment.[3] Another form of quittance supplementing the satisfaction formulas are clauses stating that the seller "removes" himself,

[1] The standard quittance formula is "You have given me *x* and my heart is satisfied," "You have satisfied my heart with *x*." Normally the seller makes the statement, but if the buyer's heart is satisfied, this can be understood to mean that he will not make a claim if he finds faults or imperfections. This second, however, does not seem to be common. For the seller's quittance, and the Akkadian, Aramaic and demotic forms of this satisfaction formula, see Muffs, *passim.*

[2] Discussions of the no-contest clauses are found in Muffs, 48-52, 65-66; Yaron, 84-86; San Nicolò, 20 ff.; Schiller, "Coptic Law," 236-237, 239.

[3] Penalty clauses were so common in Aramaic deeds that their absence is considered rare. Not only were they usual in deeds of conveyance, but they also appeared in manumission, adoption, marriage, and contracts of loan. They were, in fact, the main safeguard, in the absence of a promissory oath, insuring the discharge of obligations. See Yaron, 86. Coptic conveyances and other kinds of documents usually included penalty clauses. Both money penalties and spiritual sanctions were imposed: the penalty of exclusion from the oath of the Father, Son and Holy Ghost meant a prohibition against taking the oath employed in settling a dispute. See A. Schiller in "Coptic Documents," *Zum gegenwärtigen Stand der juristischen Papyrusforschung*, *ZVRW*, LX (1957), 200. For the formulas themselves, see Schiller's "Coptic Dialysis," *Revue d'Histoire du Droit*, VII (1927), 437, 450-452, and "Coptic Law," 236, 239. The monetary fines were heavy, sometimes more than twice the purchase price, as in the document cited in the last reference.

from the buyer or from the property, thereby relinquishing all rights and claims.[1]

What is particularly interesting is that these forms of quittance, so prominent in pre-Islamic documentary practice, are by and large missing in the Arabic contract. And when those that have survived do appear, they are only incidental to the contract.[2] Why they should have lost their importance is not easy to explain,[3] but perhaps a partial answer can be put forward, based on what has been suggested for the cuneiform and Aramaic documents.

The cuneiform conveyance, according to San Nicolò, was not an instrument that in itself obliged two parties to complete their promised performance. This was accomplished by an instrument outside the transaction, namely the oath, by the god or the king or both.[4] Sanctions were imposed by the threat of death, physical punishment, or in the mildest cases, heavy fines. Thus, in the cuneiform deeds, quittance was a comparatively weak instrument. The Aramaic conveyance, on the other hand, not having the oath to enforce the obligation, had to rely on the force of the document itself, and the accumulation of quittance formulas, penal stipulations, and other safeguards, enhanced the obligatory powers of the document.[5] But the Arabic instrument had neither the oath with its dreadful consequences to back up performance, nor was there any inherent binding force in the document that would make such stipulations effective. There was, however, another means of creating an

[1] For example, "I hereby remove myself from you; it [the property] is yours." The distinction is made between transfer-removal and litigation-removal formulas. The second is operative usually after litigation and means that the losing party is forbidden to challenge the judgement; these were often embodied in separate "deeds of submission, or removal," executed by the party renouncing a claim (Yaron, 33-35). The clause pertinent here, the transfer-removal formula, is regarded by Yaron as substantive, expressing the fact that in a conveyance of land, the seller abandons his land, or "removes" himself from it (81-82). Muffs, on the other hand, considers it the Aramaic quittance term *par excellence* (48).

[2] These are discussed below, with the final settlement clauses, in accordance with the role they play in the Arabic documents.

[3] Penalty clauses would be automatically excluded because of the Islamic prohibition against *ribā*, or any unjustified enrichment. In the Coptic documents, the money seems to have been paid over to the state, and this would not be quite the equivalent of *ribā*. However, Schiller ("Coptic Documents," 200) points out that in some cases the evidence is for stipulated damages. The penalty for breach of contract (*Konventionalstrafe*) is found in the Ptolemaic and Roman papyri from Egypt (E. Seidl, *Ptolemäische Rechtsgeschichte*, 163), in Mesopotamia (V. Korošec, "Keilschriftrecht," in *Orientalisches Recht*, 51), and in the Aramaic deeds (Yaron, 88), where the penalty is paid to the person acquiring the rights.

[4] San Nicolò, 76 ff. Consistent with this is the fact that penalty clauses were unknown in the older cuneiform deed, but the no-contest clause, relinquishing the right to dispute the contract in the future, played an important role (San Nicolò, 20).

[5] Muffs, 44-45; Yaron, 84-88.

obligation that was final and irreversible: this was, of course, the *iqrār*, a powerful device because it was absolutely binding on the person who made it, without any reference to its origin or to the circumstances in which it was made.[1] The quittance was contained in the witnessed *iqrār*, and needed nothing further to give it maximum effect.

4. Final Settlement Clauses.

A group of clauses prominent in both the pre-Islamic and the Arabic documents are the *Schlussklauseln*,[2] incidental to the conveyance, but essential in guaranteeing the inviolability of the transaction. More precisely, these are the guarantees aimed at protecting the new legal status, evidenced by the written document, from future attempts to upset it. The range of obligations conveyed by the clauses is wide, but the formulas can be separated into two groups: (1) formulas protecting the buyer against interference by a third party challenging his ownership, and (2) those denying any future rights or claims. In the main, these guarantees are undertaken by the seller (or alienor), although there are some exceptions to this in the Arabic deeds with respect to the second group.

a. *Guarantees against a Fault in Ownership.* By far the most important final settlement clause in the Arabic contracts, and the only essential one, is the guarantee against the *darak* or fault in ownership.[3] The important place given to this guarantee in the written deed reflects a prominent feature in Islamic law, the protection of ownership through a series of rules, among which is the protection of bona fide acquisition.[4]

Essentially, the *darak* guarantee is a guarantee given by the seller to make good should the buyer's title be contested by a third party.[5] Such instances can easily be imagined. It is possible, for example, that prior to the transaction, and without the knowledge of the buyer (or seller), a third party had inherited all or part of the property sold, it had been given as a *waqf*, a slave had been manumitted, a neighbor exercises his right of pre-emption, or a

[1] See Schacht, *Introduction*, 151.

[2] This term is not translated in the literature on documentary practice when these clauses are dealt with as a whole, but "final settlement clauses" seems a reasonable compromise between an accurate description and a close translation.

[3] See notes to I 2.116-2.158, where the *darak* is discussed more fully.

[4] See Schacht, *Introduction*, 139.

[5] Thus Yaron has called this provision in the contract the "defension" clause, because the seller undertakes to come to the defense of the buyer. See his "On Defension Clauses of Some Oriental Deeds of Sale and Lease, from Mesopotamia," *Bibliotheca Orientalis*, XV (1958).

creditor appears with a debt against the seller and declares his right to the property. If such a claim (*istiḥqāq*) is proven valid, the ownership of the property newly acquired by the *bonae fidei emptor* is thus defective. In the Arabic contracts, the seller is accordingly bound to return to the buyer either the property itself, its price, its equivalent (if it is fungible), or its value with the value of such improvements as were made by the buyer himself.[1] A rightful claim resides in the property before the contract is concluded, and only the buyer is entitled to the guarantee for the *darak*; it does not extend to anyone who may subsequently acquire it from him. Thus, the *ḍamān al-darak* (or simply *darak*, as the Arab authors abbreviate the term) is a special kind of guarantee and is treated separately from the others.

The formulas for the *darak* exhibit more variety in practice, perhaps, than any other clause. To assure the effectiveness of the guarantee, the Arab notaries often felt obliged to enumerate all the possibilities with regard to the persons who might make a claim, the circumstances under which it might occur, and the obligations of the seller.[2] The last, for example, can include "delivery, recuperation, redemption, and indemnification" in a single formula. Ṭaḥāwī's *darak* clause is comparatively simple:

> "Should any claim be made against Fulān [the buyer][3] with respect to whatever is entailed in this sale, mentioned in this document, or any part of it or any rights attached to it, proceding from any person whatsoever, then it is the responsibility of Fulān [the seller] to deliver what is incumbent upon him as a duty, and what is required of him because of this sale, mentioned in this document. [He is responsible] until he delivers that to Fulān, according to whatever this sale, mentioned in this document, makes binding on him in [the buyer's] favor."

[1] This represents a considerable advance over the Aramaic documents, in which the seller promises to "clean" (*bereinigen*) the property sold (i.e., clean it from the contamination of a claim by taking legal action), and then give back the *property* to the buyer. Provisions in case the seller is not successful are missing in these and other ancient Near Eastern documents (see the discussion in Yaron, 90-91); in contrast, the Arabic clause is construed by the Muslim scholars to include these alternatives. In Ṭaḥāwī's commentary all the possibilities are discussed at some length, and it appears that in practice, return of the price (as we would expect) was the norm (I 2.128 and note to 2.140). There is one instance where the parties agree beforehand on the return of the property only, and this is contained in a contract that engages a third party as a guarantor; if the property itself cannot be delivered, the sale is cancelled (II 5.0-5.1).

[2] For translations of some of these, see notes to I 2.116 and 2.140.

[3] *fa-mā adraka fulān... min darakin*; Grohmann translates more literally, perhaps following Lane's definition (s.v. *d-r-k*), "and whatever [evil] consequence may befall Fulān..." (Ṭaḥāwī writes *fulān* and not *fulānan* throughout, indicating that this formal word was pronounced without case endings.)

The ambiguity of some of the phrases (whatever is entailed in this sale, what is incumbent upon him, whatever this sale makes binding on him, etc.) is deliberate and reflects Ṭaḥāwī's efforts to avoid the *ikhtilāf* concerning the precise definitions of the various provisions.

Although the *darak* guarantee is normally given in favor of the buyer and is written into the document only when real property is transferred, these applications are extended in Ṭaḥāwī's contracts. First, the function of the clause to protect against incomplete ownership is brought out in several contracts where the buyer becomes responsible for the *darak* if he has had the property in his possession and it is, or might be, returned. Since the claim of a third party does not enter in unless the buyer himself turns the property over to another, formulas singling out the buyer as the only source of a fault in ownership are added.[1] Sometimes longer formulas are furnished after these, stating that he has done nothing that would disturb legal ownership in the future.[2] Often the steps the buyer might have taken (an *iqrār* in favor of a third person, a *ḥīla* or legal device, admitting someone else into partnership, and so on) are made explicit.

Second, Ṭaḥāwī points out that *shurūṭ* scholars do not ordinarily write a *darak* formula into the contract except in the sale of immovable property (*'aqārāt*); but guided by his sense of precaution, he adds "there is no harm if you do write it in."[3] Certainly the seller of movables was obliged to undertake the same guarantees, but movables are generally of less value than real property, and this is probably the reason *darak* clauses could be omitted in such contracts. This is borne out by the fact that in the case of some movables of considerable value—slaves, a wall, date palms[4]—the *darak* formula is carefully included in the contract.

[1] This problem is discussed in several places in the commentary. For the formulas, see the notes to I 2.116 at the end, and 2.119. Some examples where the *darak* is written in favor of the seller are: the property has been delivered but the buyer still has the option to cancel the sale (III 19.0); the transaction was declared a sale with *talji'a* (V 17.0, see note to I 2.165); the property is sold back to the original seller before he takes the price (V 1.3, 1.0 ter, 2.0); in a contract of *iqāla*, the *muqīl* gives a guarantee to the *mustaqīl*, the party asking for a reversal of the sale (IV 7.0, 7.16-7.19). Even in a contract of *sharika* the buyer gives a guarantee for half the property to the person he admits into partnership (IV 8.0).

[2] Examples of this longer formula are found in III 19.0, IV 1.0 and 7.0.

[3] Thus the *darak* is not identical with the term "eviction" unless this is used in its loosest sense to mean the ousting of a person from the possession of chattels.

[4] Slave: III 38.0. The contract in V 14.0 is a special case where both the seller of a slave and the executor of an estate (who manumits the slave on behalf of the deceased) are involved. Writing the *darak* clause protects the deceased. The wall is movable property because it can be dismantled for its materials; contract in II 30.0. The trees (III 22.0-22.1) are to be uprooted from the land, which is not sold.

Finally, the *darak* clause does not appear in contracts in which the property is to be delivered at a later date;[1] in such cases a separate document of *shahāda* is drawn up after delivery takes place, and the guarantee is included in this. Nor is the *darak* given in conveyances in which the alienor receives no consideration, as in a deed of gift.

b. *Clauses Denying Rights and Claims.* Various developments have taken place with respect to the final settlement clauses in the transition from pre-Islamic Near Eastern to Arabic documentary practice. First, as was pointed out in the preceding section, some of these clauses have fallen into disuse. Second, there has been a considerable shift in emphasis, not only with respect to the relative importance given to the different guarantees, but also in the way they are used. While the guarantee against a *darak* was not a prominent feature of the pre-Islamic Near Eastern conveyance, it is essential in the Arabic deeds. On the other hand, there are other final settlement clauses that are found regularly in the older documents, and which are always given by the seller. In the Arabic documents, these are incidental; they are included in the contract for special reasons, and the party who undertakes the obligations they express is not usually the seller, but is defined by the circumstances.

Within this last group, the formulas that appear most frequently in Ṭaḥāwī's text are those acknowledging the relinquishment of future rights and claims. They contain a number of separate elements which can be described by the names usually given to these formulas in studies of documents from other legal systems: no-suit-or-process clause, non-interference, no-challenge, *Klageverzicht*, *Streitbeendigung*, and so on. A typical formula is contained in a document in which a buyer of house property exercises his option and cancels the sale within the stipulated three-day period. The acknowledgement declaring his relinquishment of future rights is inserted into the written contract:

> "Fulān, the buyer, has no rights in this property [whose boundaries are] defined in this document, nor in any part of it, neither its land nor any building constructed on it. He has no right of claim (*da'wā*) nor can he make any demands (*ṭaliba*) by reason of [alleged] ownership, sale, or anything else, for any cause or reason whatsoever. Any legal claim he might put forward concerning this property..., any part of it, its land, buildings, and anything else besides, or any claim that someone else might put forward on his behalf, witnesses who might testify to that [action] in his favor, any document he might produce, any proof he might bring to

[1] For example, III 10.1, the parties do not take possession of either the property or the price; III 13.0, sale with option to rescind.

bear, any judicial oath he might offer Fulān [the seller] to swear in court, any claim, dispute, litigation, or vindication (*muṭālaba, munāza'a, 'ulqa, tabi'a*), all that [shall be considered] false and invalid, a fiction, and an arbitrary proceeding (*fa-dhālika kulluhū zūr wa-bāṭil wa-ifk wa-ẓulm*). And Fulān [the seller] is declared exempt from all [such actions] and is free to dispose of that over which he has power (*fī ḥilli wus'ihī*) both in this world and the next, because Fulān [the buyer] knows and is cognizant of the fact that he has no right of claim over that property, nor any part of it, nor has anyone else the right of claim due to his initiative, without its being an offense against the law and a wrongful action."[1]

Such guarantees were not stated in the most succinct manner possible. Yet it is not easy for us to judge to what extent the notaries distinguished between seemingly synonymous terms, if they did so at all. While *muṭālaba, munāza'a, 'ulqa* and *tabi'a* may not have implied different forms of challenge in the technical sense, they may very well have occupied different places within a given semantic range.[2] Other phrases, such as "both in this world and the next," are not mere literary flourishes, but guarantee (in this case) that ownership shall remain intact and undisturbed even after the death of the legal rightholder.

There are no other *Schlussklauseln* of importance in Ṭaḥāwī's *shurūṭ*. Clauses stating that the buyer has free disposition over his property are naturally avoided because this would constitute a formal acknowledgement of ownership, which Ṭaḥāwī is at pains to avoid.[3] Such a formula is contained in one docu-

[1] III 17.0. Other situations where this clause is included in the written document are: in a contract of *muḍāraba*, the acting buyer gives the silent partner a guarantee that he has no future rights in the property he has bought except those to which he is entitled (IV 6.0); a *muqīl* who grants an *iqāla* contract acknowledges that he has no rights in the house property he has returned to the seller (IV 7.0); a buyer acting as agent for another has no rights in the property and no claims against the principal (IV 1.0); the principal is absent and the acting buyer acnowledges that the price he paid belonged to the person who authorized him to carry out the purchase, and that he has, therefore, no future claim on the property (III 47.0); a seller has no future rights in *kharāj* land whose fruit he has sold (III 9.0), nor in land belonging to a third party on which stands a building he has sold (II 18.0); two heirs acknowledge that a third heir had bought property from the deceased before he died, and that they have no future rights or claims in it (V 9.0).

[2] Had Ṭaḥāwī discussed these terms in his usual thorough manner, we would know how they were distinguished in his mind, at least. The absence of any such discussion may imply either that he accepted the formula as set and formal and had no quarrel with the way it was phrased, or (more likely) that it was not a pre-established subject for commentary within the tradition of the authors of *shurūṭ* handbooks.

[3] Clauses referring to the alienee's power of subsequent alienation are not even brought up in discussions that would warn against them. For avoidance of stating ownership or possession, see above, pp. 33-35 and note to I 2.18. There are no negative statements concerning the seller's loss of control ("he may not hereafter sell it, give it as a gift, etc.") as in some ancient Near Eastern deeds; but see note to II 18.0.

ment only, drawn up explicitly for that purpose. The passage is quite similar to other such formulas in earlier Near Eastern documents and in the Arabic papyri. The owner of the house property may:

> "... dwell in it or in any part of it, or allow anyone else he wishes to dwell in it or any part of it, for a remuneration or otherwise. He may tear it down, or any part of it, or build on it. There is no impediment between him and [free disposal of his property] that they [the witnesses] know of, nor anything to prevent him from it."[1]

The papyri sometimes contain other means by which the new owner can dispose of his property: "he may sell it, give it as a gift, leave it empty, make it over as a pious endowment." But these do not appear frequently and, to be sure, not regularly as in the earlier Near Eastern deeds. It would seem that the expression of ownership as control over property represents a more archaic stage of legal development. In Islamic law, the concept of ownership was well-defined; consequently, it was hardly necessary to spell out, in the written document, the various types of control the new owner was entitled to exercise. This may be a partial explanation of why such formulas are not at all prominent in the Arabic deed.

5. Witnessing Clauses.

a. *Testimony of Primary Witnesses.* The term *shahāda*, in the sense of testimonial proof, can mean either testimony or witnessing. In the system of procedure and evidence, it refers to the deposition made before a qadi, of a witness supporting the claim of one person against another in a lawsuit. But since this testimony must be based upon prior knowledge, *shahāda* is also used to refer to a witness's previous statements about a fact or facts. It is these previous statements that are the *shahāda* of notarial practice.

Strictly speaking, this prior testimony evidencing a transaction was not necessary for the validity of that transaction, but was a convenience of which the parties could avail themselves. In the event the contract were challenged, the same persons who gave their evidence at the time the written document

[1] The formula occurs in I 3.0; the document concerns the seller's, and not the buyer's, ownership, but this would not make any difference in the phrasing of the clause. Another formula in the papyri affirms the new ownership in a more general way: "The *dār* became part of his own wealth and property," "He has free disposition of it according to the free disposition of proprietors over their property," etc. (Grohmann's translation). For examples, see *APEL* I, 146, 162, 169, 181, 189, 269; Hoenerbach, *Urkunden*, 273, note; Serjeant, "Ḥabbān," 125.

was drawn up would be summoned to repeat their testimony orally in court.[1] It was this oral testimony which alone was acceptable to legal theory. However, in practice, calling upon witnesses to evidence the contract was essential. No transaction of any importance would have been concluded without them, because oral testimony was the surest means of proof.[2] And just as the written document recorded directly the terms of the transaction, and indirectly its validity and universal acceptability, it also recorded the fact of this testimony and the identity of the *shuhūd* who gave it. Indeed, as if to give substance to his identity, the witness himself signed the document, a fact that was stated in the formula itself by the words *bi-khaṭṭihī* ("in his own handwriting"). And to forestall any doubts, he was described not only by his patronymics but also by his *kunya*, or familiar name.[3]

It was not necessary for the witnesses to verify the facts of the transaction by such acts as visiting the property or by being present when the transfer took place. When two persons wished to conclude a contract of sale, they applied to a notary, described what they wanted, and he drafted the document in the form of a double *iqrār*. The witnesses then gave their testimony to this double *iqrār*, the acknowledgement by both parties of the part each played in the transaction. The witnesses also testified to the identity of the parties and their legal competence to conclude a transaction:

[1] It has been pointed out that in North Africa, at least, this procedure was the starting point for the development of the notary-witness. In order to prevent inconvenience should the need for litigation arise, the *'udūl* witnessed the contracts and at the same time kept notes of their terms; eventually, they drew up the written contract themselves. Coulson, 146; Schacht, *Introduction*, 194.

[2] The *iqrār*, if it were to gain its full effect in creating obligations, had to be proved by the testimony of witnesses. For this see Schacht, *Introduction*, 192 ff.

[3] Both of these are left out of the basic contract of sale in I 2.0, either by the copyist, or by Ṭaḥāwī himself because the *shahāda* is given there in somewhat abbreviated form. They are found regularly in other complete contracts (e.g. *kunya* in I 9.0, at the beginning, and *katabū shahādātihim bi-khuṭūṭihim* in I 4.0, at the end) and in the Arabic papyri. The signatures of witnesses had no legal effect, of course, except under certain conditions in the Mālikī school when secondary testimony could be applied to verify them (see Tyan, *Notariat*, 70-72). But the practice was an ancient one and there was no reason why the Arabs should have discarded it. In the Aramaic and demotic papyri, while the signatures of the parties had no legal effect and are almost never found, the signatures of witnesses, in their own hand, is usual. Yaron (p. 17) conjectures that a rule requiring they sign themselves did not seem to exist because illiteracy would exclude part of the population from acting as witnesses. This is also true in the Arabic documents, where we sometimes find another person signing for an illiterate witness and noting that fact alongside the name. (See IV 16.1, where Ṭaḥāwī takes the practice for granted, but cites authorities for it as well.) As a rule, patronymics of witnesses were given at Elephantine. In the Coptic documents an additional feature is a clause appointing both scribe and witness at the beginning of the document; witnesses usually signed themselves and patronymics are frequently added.

"[The witnesses whose names are written below][1] testify to the *iqrār* of Fulān... the seller, and Fulān... the buyer, acknowledging the entire contents of this document, after everything contained in it had been read out to them together from beginning to end. [The parties] then gave their *iqrār* to the fact that they had understood and were cognizant of [the contents], letter for letter, while they were in a state of sound mind and body and legally capable of conducting their affairs, voluntarily and not under compulsion. [They also testify that] they are acquainted with the parties in a valid manner, [i.e.] personally, by name, and by *nisba*."[2]

Ṭaḥāwī insists on a formula that mentions the *iqrār* of the parties, rather than the phrasing of other *shurūṭ* writers, whose formulas simply state that the witnesses "testify to all the terms contained in the document."[3] Testimony to the true facts of the case (*shahāda ʿalā ḥaqāʾiqihā*) or based on a simple assertion (*ithbāt*) by the parties is inadequate, he says, because the witness has no way of knowing whether or not the buyer and seller had actually carried out all the necessary steps.[4] Nor can he know the inner intentions of the parties who might wish to misrepresent the sale or engage in fraud. Perhaps because he is not concerned with the witness as such, Ṭaḥāwī does not add that this procedure protects the witness against giving false evidence or against charges casting suspicion on his probity.

The clauses verifying the identity of the parties follow, rather than precede testimony to the *iqrār*, because the witness testifies to the persons who made that *iqrār*, not the persons who concluded the transaction. Again, this protects the witness who, despite the formulas to the contrary, could not have personally known[5] every client who came to him for his services.

[1] The subject of the verb *shahida* is sometimes expressed in this way, but more often the names of the witnesses at the end of the document are the subject.

[2] The formulas, as well as variants common in practice, are discussed in the notes to I 2.159-2.186, and I 9.1, 9.9-9.12. Volition formulas (*Spontanitätsformeln*) are, of course, part of the requirements for legal capacity. They have a very old history in Near Eastern documentary practice, the ancient terminology being preserved almost intact in the Arabic deeds. See Muffs, 128-139; for Latin expressions, Hoenerbach, *Urkunden*, 58, n. 1.

[3] I 2.162.

[4] There are some exceptions to this. In a document establishing the prior ownership of the seller without explicitly stating it, witnesses testify to their having personally inspected the boundaries (*ʿalā muʿāyanatihā*) and not to the *iqrār* of the parties for the boundaries. See Ṭaḥāwī's explanation in I 4.3. Special cases arise in transactions made by parties in their last illness. It is important, for example, to establish that witnesses actually saw a man on his deathbed take the price of a house he had previously bought for 200 dinars but which he now sells (as a concession) for 100 dinars. The transaction takes place in the presence of witnesses: *bi-maḥḍarihim wa-bi-ruʾyati aʿyunihim* (V 7.0, 8.5). On the other hand, if a man dies before the witnesses can reach his bedside, the formula states nonetheless that they knew him personally, by name and by *nisba*, *after his death* (V 11.0).

[5] The minimum requirements are described; see note to I 9.9-9.12.

b. *Testimony of Secondary Witnesses.* A most interesting feature of Islamic legal practice is the *shahāda ʿalā shahāda*, the indirect evidence of secondary witnesses who are called upon to give evidence concerning the testimony of primary witnesses.[1] Normally, this practice was intended as a safeguard in case the primary witnesses were unable to give their depositions in court because they were ill, absent (more than a three-day journey away), or dead. It was also used to establish that the primary witnesses were men of good moral character if it happened that the qadi was not satisfied with their integrity. So much weight was placed on the evidence of witnesses that it was important to guard against individuals who would tend to give false evidence.[2]

However, in Ṭaḥāwī's documents, the *shahāda ʿalā shahāda* in its practical application protected the parties in a much more direct way. It was not merely second-degree proof or indirect evidence. The secondary witnesses do testify to the *shahāda* of the original witnesses, but they also have another function: they act as supplementary primary witnesses whenever there is some element within a contract, or added to it, that might weaken the contract or expose it to a claim. The secondary witnesses serve to strengthen the potential vulnerable spots. In so doing, they may act on behalf of one of the parties or both of them.

Ṭaḥāwī's *shurūṭ* show us how this worked in practice. For example, in a contract of *sharika* in which one person admits another into partnership after having bought a piece of property, primary witnesses testify to the *iqrār* for the original sale and secondary witnesses give evidence that the first have indeed so testified. Then all the witnesses together give their depositions to the *iqrār* of the two parties who concluded the contract of partnership. The weak element in this case is a potential claim on the part of the original seller directed against the new partner. He may confront the partner one day with a demand for the return of his half of the property, saying that he

[1] Called the *shuhūd al-aṣl* and the *shuhūd al-farʿ* by other writers (e.g., Ṣayrafī especially p. 149, n. 1, where the editor's definition is not accurate). Further, *EI*[1], s.v. "Shāhid." Ṭaḥāwī does not employ any technical terms to distinguish primary and secondary witnesses, and consequently the discussion is frequently ambiguous with "some witnesses, the rest of the witnesses, other witnesses," etc.

[2] Two secondary witnesses are needed for one primary witness, but the same individuals can also testify to the other primary witnesses. (It may have been common practice to have several, for Ṭaḥāwī always refers to the secondary witnesses in the plural, rather than the dual, just as the primary witnesses are mentioned in the plural in the commentary.) Another requirement is that the secondary witnesses are always called upon to testify (*ashhadū ʿalā shahādātihim sāʾira al-shuhūd*); they cannot take the initiative, and normally the parties do not invite them.

had not actually sold it, that he did not receive the price from the buyer, or that the buyer took possession without his having delivered it.[1]

Similarly, secondary witnesses enter in on behalf of a father who buys a house for his minor son with the son's money. Because the father fears that the son will later claim that he was not a minor at the time (and that the father bought it without his authorization), or will claim that the father did not discharge his obligations toward him, the *shahāda 'alā shahāda* is employed. The sequence of witnessing is the same as in the example above. Primary witnesses testify to the minority of the boy, to his father's guardianship, and to the fact that the father bought the house and paid for it in a legal manner. These witnesses then invite a second group of witnesses to give evidence to their testimony; then both groups of witnesses together give their testimony to the *iqrār* of the acting buyer (the father) and seller for the sale.[2] Similar documents preserve secondary testimony to the fact that a woman is of age and has legal capacity, or that an individual appointed an agent to carry out a sale on his behalf.[3]

It should be noted that the secondary witnesses not only give their testimony to the evidence of the primary witnesses, but to the identity of the parties, their legal capacity, and to their *iqrār*. Thus, if the primary witnesses do not or cannot appear in court, the parties are protected not only against the weakening element, but for the entire transaction. The written document serves as a record and a proof of this and helps prevent their intentions being thwarted in any way.

c. *Separate Document of shahāda.* Another kind of written contract related to these and common in notarial practice is the supplementary document of *shahāda*. The particular contracts just mentioned incorporate the secondary testimony in the written document that records the original transaction. This procedure is possible only when some fact or circumstance that might render the contract liable to challenge *can be anticipated* by the notary; the secondary witnesses needed to lend additional support are summoned in advance. In many other cases, however, the *shahāda* must be recorded in a separate deed. It would be impossible to insert additional clauses or extra guarantees into a deed already witnessed, yet these require the testimony of witnesses themselves. These contracts all begin *hādhā mā shahida 'alayhi al-shuhūd*; the details of the original contract must be included so that there will be no doubt about the

[1] IV 8.0, 8.5.

[2] IV 4.0.

[3] Woman, I 9.0; agent, V 15.0.

transaction referred to in the supplementary witnessing deed.[1] And, of course, the *shahāda 'alā shahāda* may operate in this kind of deed as well as an ordinary document of sale.[2]

For example, two persons may make a contract of sale for a piece of property with delivery of both price and property at a future date. The sale is binding, but since the buyer has not turned over the price he cannot receive quittance for it; and since the seller has not delivered the property he is not obliged to give a guarantee for a *darak*. Both of these acts are dealt with in a separate document containing the testimony of witnesses when the time comes for it.[3] Again, two persons may conclude a sale with the option to rescind within three days; when the sale is ratified, the *ijāza* or ratification of the sale is formulated as a separate document of *shahāda.*[4]

Ṭaḥāwī often recommends an alternate procedure: drawing up a document of *shahāda,* incorporating in it the original witnessed contract of sale, and then calling upon secondary witnesses to go through the usual procedures. In this way there will not be any dispute about the terms of the original contract of sale, nor doubt that it was the very same transaction.[5] Needless to say, some of these documents can be extremely long and complex but the cautious businessman, according to Ṭaḥāwī, would consider it well worth the trouble.

5. THE MANUSCRIPT.

The manuscript on which this edition is based is the only known copy of the "Kitāb al-Buyū'" and one of the four extant chapters of the *Kitāb al-Shurūṭ al-Kabīr.*[6] It is preserved in the Süleymaniye library in Istanbul. It is

[1] The extra wordage can be partly avoided by writing up the separate document on the *verso* of the original contract. See, for example, IV 1.0 and III 14.0. Sarakhsī objects to beginning a document with *hādhā mā shahida*, commenting tersely that the witnessing formula ought to be put where it belongs—with the names of the witnesses at the end. However, his commentary covers a much narrower range of contracts than does Ṭaḥāwī's book, and he does not appear to have occasion to use a separate document of *shahāda* (p. 173).

[2] Examples in III 40.0 (a barter transaction, to avoid giving the name of one party precedence over the other); V 10.0 and 11.0 (a *ṣakk* for a debt as payment of the price; the seller is ill and creditors for debts made while he was in good health are more entitled to payment.

[3] III 11.0.

[4] III 14.0.

[5] III 12.1-12.2, for his explanation. Examples of such contracts are found throughout the book.

[6] See above, p. 12, n. 1, and pp. 24-25. The authenticity of the manuscript has been established by Schacht, "Adhkār al-Ḥuqūq," vi.

quite a long manuscript of 214 folios[1] with an average of seventeen lines to a page, and is divided into five parts of unequal length. That its provenance was Egypt is indicated on the title page of each of the five sections, where the name of one of the owners, Muḥammad b. M. b. M. al-Sābiq al-Ḥanafī, is followed by *al-Qāhirat al-Maḥrūsa*, and by the date he acquired it, Monday, the sixteenth of Dhu'l-Ḥijja, 849 (or the seventeenth of March, 1446 A.D.).

The manuscript was copied for a certain 'Ubayd Allāh M. b. 'Abd al-Wahhāb b. Tammām al-Ṣāni' and was the work of two copyists transcribing alternate sections.[2] The penmanship of both leaves something to be desired. In the case of the first (Parts I, III and V), it is small and intricate, but legible (Plate I); the handwriting of the second scribe is crude, unattractive, and difficult to read (Plates II and III). Vowels are lacking and diacritical points distinguishing consonants are capricious, the second copyist having dispensed with them almost entirely.

The condition of the manuscript is not particularly good. The entire copy is disfigured by humidity stains and wormholes, but except in places where the ink is washed away completely, this does not seriously interfere with the reading. Occasionally there are places where parts of folios have stuck together because of the humidity and the ink was transferred from one page to another; this occurs mostly in the marginal notes and these can be read with the aid of a mirror. In some places, the binder's scissors have done more damage than the humidity.

There are no lacunae in the text, for the copyists took pains to provide, at the bottom of the *verso* of each folio, the first word of the *recto* of the next. They also collated the text themselves, recovering omissions and inserting corrections. Despite this evidence of care, the manuscript has many errors and there are signs that the copyists did not always know what they were reading.

The orthography of the manuscript bears features common to manuscripts of the period. For example, *hamza* is completely lacking, long *alif* is often omitted, and the imperfect singular of *verba tertiae wāw* frequently appears with an *alif wiqāya* at the end. The copyists have also written a *yā'* at the end of indefinite participles of weak *lām* verbs and at the end of the jussive form of these verbs. Frequently words are run together that should be separated, and in other cases, words that are usually joined in writing are written as two

[1] The chapters on *shuf'a* and *ḥuqūq* of the edited Cairo manuscript are considerably shorter (80 and 62 folios) partly because features common to contracts as a whole are treated in the first chapter on sale. The Cairo fragments have the same title pages.

[2] Their names and the date on which they completed their work are not mentioned.

words. On the whole, the orthographical peculiarities are consistent, and I have modified them to conform to modern usage without making note of the changes.

To avoid burdening the text with an extensive critical apparatus, I have made certain other changes without indicating them. Specifically, I noted obliterated words or letters only when words I supplied were not readily apparent from the context or when I could not read them at all. The marginal notes are nearly always in the hand of the copyists and serve to supply omitted words or to correct mistakes. If I judged these corrections to be sound, I incorporated them into the text. Missing diacritical points were of such frequent occurence that I noted these only when there was a possibility of two readings.

In general, my approach to the text has been conservative, and I have made as few changes as possible. Thus I have been careful to preserve certain usages in language[1] that were common Ḥanafī technical terms and modes of expression, current before the relative standardization of terminology that took place in a later period.

[1] Some of these interesting linguistic features are mentioned in "Adhkār al-Ḥuqūq," vii-viii; others are pointed out in the Notes to the present text.

NOTES TO THE ARABIC TEXT

PART I

I 1.2 - 1.10 Qur'ān passages and references are from Sūra 2:282, except the verse at the beginning of 1.5, which is from Sūra 2:283.

In the introduction to the abridged version of his text (Mehmet Murat 997, fol. 1b), Ṭaḥāwī limits his discussion to brief comments on a few quotations from Sūra 2:282. Missing are the *ḥadīth* interpreting the Qur'ānic passages, the discussion of whether drawing up written documents is a duty or merely recommended, and significantly, the many practical arguments for doing so.

I 1.5. Ibrāhīm b. Marzūq b. Dīnār al-Baṣrī was one of the scholars from whom Ṭaḥāwī heard traditions and legal opinions within the Ḥanafī school (Kawtharī, 8). He was a member of the community of legal scholars and qadis from Iraq living in Fusṭāṭ, and died in Egypt in 270 (*Tahdhīb* I, No. 290).

'Affān b. Muslim, Abū 'Uthmān al-Baṣrī, lived in Baghdad and died there in 220 (*Tahdhīb* VII, No. 423). Wuhayb b. Khālid al-Bāhilī, d. 165 or 167 (*Tahdhīb* XI, No. 290). Dā'ūd b. Abī Hind al-Qushayrī, d. 140 (*Tahdhīb* III, No. 388). 'Āmir is 'Āmir b. Shurāḥīl al-Sha'bī, a well-known traditionist of Kufa who died in 109 (*Tahdhīb* V, No. 110).

I 1.6. Abū Shurayḥ M. b. Zakariyyā' b. Yaḥyā was one of Ṭaḥāwī's *shuyūkh* (Kawtharī, 6, citing Ibn 'Asākir's biography of Ṭaḥāwī in the *K. Ta'rīkh Dimashq*). His father was the Kātib al-'Umarī, an Egyptian qadi who died in 241 (*Tahdhīb* III, No. 625).

M. b. Yūsuf al-Firyābī was one of Sufyān al-Thawrī's companions, having learned traditions from him in Kufa. He resided in Qaysariyya and died in the year 212 (*Tahdhīb* IX, No. 878). Sufyān al-Thawrī, the prominent Kufan scholar and founder of a school of law, died in 161. See Schacht, *Introduction*, 58, and his biography in the *Tahdhīb* (IV, No. 199). Ismā'īl b. Abī Khālid al-Aḥmasī, d. 146 (*Tahdhīb* I, No. 543). Sha'bī is 'Āmir b. Shurāḥīl; see above, note to 1.5.

I 1.7. Al-Rabī' is al-Rabī' b. Ṣabīḥ, d. 160, a Basra traditionist and companion of Ḥasan of Basra, who is meant here. For Rabī', see *Tahdhīb* III, No. 474, and for Ḥasan, II, No. 488 and *EI*², s.v.

I 1.8. Layth is Layth b. Abī Salīm al-Qurashī, al-Kūfī, who died in 143 or 148 (*Tahdhīb* VIII, No. 833). He frequently appears as a transmitter to Thawrī from Mujāhid b. Jabr. Mujāhid, an authority of the Meccans, died in 104. See Schacht, *Origins*, 114, n. 8, and *Tahdhīb* X, No. 68.

I 1.11. Sūra 24:63.

I 1.13. Sūra 2:282. Abū Hudhayfa Mūsā b. Mas'ūd al-Baṣrī, d. 220 or 221 (*Tahdhīb* X, No. 657). Yazīd b. Abī Ziyād al-Qurashī, d. 136 (*Tahdhīb* XI, No. 630). Miqsam b. Bujra, a traditionist of Medina who died in 101, was the *mawlā* of Ibn 'Abbās (*Tahdhīb* X, No. 507). For 'Abd Allāh b. 'Abbās (d. 68), companion and authority of the Meccans, see Schacht, *Origins*, 249 ff., and *EI*², s.v.

I 2.3 - 2.13 is Ṭaḥāwī's commentary on the phrase used to introduce the objective style contracts, *hādhā mā ishtarā*. See Grohmann, *Einführung*, 115-116; Introduction, p. 50. The phrase is usually translated literally by editors of the published papyri ("this is what Fulān bought"), but as Sarakhsī points out (169), "everyone knows that it means 'this is a written form (*kitāb*) containing a document (*dhukr* [incorrectly *dhikr* in Lane]) for what Fulān bought.' " For the use of *dhukr* (pl. *adhkār*) in this sense, see Fagnan, *Additions*, s.v. In the context of the contracts and Ṭaḥāwī's commentary, the verb *dhakara* is best translated "declare formally."

Sarakhsī notes that the reason some *shurūṭ* scholars object to the phrase and prefer *hādhā kitāb mā ishtarā* is that the shorter formula might be taken to mean that it is the copy of the document itself (*bayāḍ*) that is for sale (168)! Marghīnānī objects to the *longer* formula for the same reason: the document will be considered the thing bought (*mushtarā*, fol. 16a). Ṭaḥāwī ignores such arguments here, but engages in the same kind of reasoning when he discusses the term *fī hādha'l-kitāb*, which occurs so frequently in the written contract (I 2.48 - 2.49). The opening formula is discussed here in terms of precedent and the practice of his colleagues. Cf. Mehmet Murat 997, fol. 2b.

I 2.3. The authorities on whom Ṭaḥāwī relies for the wording and drafting of contracts are not mentioned in these notes, since they have been discussed in the Introduction. For their biographies and the role they played in transmitting the *shurūṭ* tradition, see the Introduction, pp. 15-23.

I 2.4. 'Umar b. Yūnus al-Yamāmī, d. 206 (*Tahdhīb* VII, No. 845). 'Ikrima b. 'Ammār of Basra, d. 159 (*Tahdhīb* VII, No. 474). Abū Zumayl, a member of the (tribe of) 'Abd Allāh b. al-Dūl, is unidentified; for the Banū al-Dūl, see Dhahabī, *Mushtabih* I, 292.

I 2.5. Yazīd b. Sinān, one of Ṭaḥāwī's Egyptian contemporaries, was a merchant of Basra who came to Egypt and decided to settle there. In Fusṭāṭ he wrote down *ḥadīth* that he had heard in his native town, especially those from his brother Muḥammad (below, I 2.9). He became prominent in the Egyptian community of jurists and scholars (see the narrative in Kindī, *Wulāt*, 199-200, 463-464) and when he died in 264 at the age of eighty, the chief qadi of Egypt, Bakkār b. Qutayba, performed the *ṣalāt* (*Tahdhīb* XI, No. 639).

Ḥibbān b. Hilāl Abū Ḥabīb al-Muqri' (or al-Kinānī as in the *Tahdhīb* II, No. 307) was one of the *shaykhs* of Basra who indirectly provided traditions for Bakkār, Ṭaḥāwī, and other Egyptian Ḥanafīs (Kindī, *Wulāt*, 505). He died in Basra in 216. Mubārak b. Faḍāla attended the circle of Ḥasan of Basra, who is the Ḥasan meant here, for some 13 or 14 years. He died in 165 (*Tahdhīb* X, No. 50). Al-Aḥnaf b. Qays is well known for his influential political role during the 'Alī-Mu'āwiya dispute and later under the first Umayyads. See *EI*², s.v.

I 2.6. Aḥmad b. Dā'ūd b. Mūsā al-Sadūsī is identified by Kawtharī as one of Ṭaḥāwī's *shuyūkh* (p. 8), but remains otherwise unknown to me. 'Abd al-A'lā b. Ḥammād al-Narsī, d. 237 (*Tahdhīb* VI, No. 196). Hishām b. Khālid's identity is not certain; see *Tahdhīb* XI, No. 77. Rabī' b. Khuthaym, d. 61 or 63 (*Tahdhīb* III, No. 467). For 'Ubayd Allāh b. 'Iyāḍ, see *Tahdhīb* XII, No. 75. 'Abd Allāh b. Shaddād, a traditionist born during the lifetime of the Prophet, is given a notice in Ibn ʿAbd al-Barr, *Istīʿāb* III, No. 1573, as is Suhayl b. ʿAmr al-Anṣārī (II, No. 1105).

I 2.7. Abu'l-Fatḥ Naṣr b. Marzūq al-ʿUtaqī (Dhahabī, *Mushtabih* II, 446) was an Egyptian traditionist and contemporary of Ṭaḥāwī. See Kawtharī, 10, and Kindī, *Wulāt*, index, s.v. *Naṣr*, where his name occurs frequently as a transmitter. Asad b. Mūsā was the grandson of the Umayyad caliph Ibrāhīm b. al-Walīd. He died in Egypt in 212 (*Tahdhīb* I, No. 494).

Yaḥyā b. Zakariyyā' b. Abī Zā'ida was appointed qadi of Madina by Hārūn al-Rashīd, but lived in Baghdad for some time before he died in 183 or 184 (ʿAbd al-Qādir II, 541-542). His father, Zakariyyā' (d. 147, 148 or 149) transmitted *ḥadīth* to Sufyān al-Thawrī (ʿAbd al-Qādir I, 244). Abū Isḥāq is ʿAmr b. ʿAbd Allāh al-Sabīʿī, a well-known traditionist of Kufa, who died about 128 (*Tahdhīb* VIII, No. 100). Al-Barā' b. ʿĀzib al-Awsī died in Kufa in 72; he is a well-known Companion. See Ibn ʿAbd al-Barr, *Istīʿāb* I, No. 173; Ibn al-Athīr, *Usd* I, No. 389; *EI*², s.v. "al-Barā'."

I 2.8. The tradition from al-ʿAddā', which comes to Ṭaḥāwī from three sources, is widely quoted. See Sarakhsī, 168-169; Marghīnānī, fol. 16a; *Fat. ʿĀlam.*, 406; and the biographical notice given to al-ʿAddā' b. Hawdha in Ibn ʿAbd al-Barr, *Istīʿāb* III, No. 2024. Also, see III 38.2.

Abū Khālid ʿAbd al-ʿAzīz b. Muʿāwiya al-Qurashī, al-ʿAttābī. As qadi of Damascus, he lived in Syria, but traveled or lived elsewhere as well. Iraqi scholars related traditions on his authority (the name ʿAttābī derives from a quarter in Baghdad, *Classen*, 315-316), while Ṭaḥāwī must have sat in his circle before 284, the year of his death. See his biographical notice in *Tahdhīb* VI, No. 683. In Kawtharī (9) he is called al-Ghassānī. ʿAbbād b. Layth al-Baṣrī, *Tahdhīb* V, No. 171. ʿAbd al-Majīd Abū Wahb al-ʿUqaylī, *Tahdhīb* VI, No. 720.

I 2.9. Abū Jaʿfar Aḥmad b. Abī ʿImrān Mūsā b. ʿĪsā al-Baghdādī, d. 280, was a qadi of Egypt and one of Ṭaḥāwī's teachers in religious law. He himself was the pupil of two well-known Egyptian Ḥanafīs, cited frequently for their opinions in Ṭaḥāwī's text, M. b. Samāʿa and Bishr b. al-Walīd. (Laknawī, No. 11; *Classen*, 292; Ibn Quṭlūbughā, in his entry for Ṭaḥāwī, No. 15; Kawtharī, 8.) Isḥāq b. Abī Isrā'īl lived in Baghdād and died in 240 (*Tahdhīb* I, No. 415).

Abū Umayya M. b. Ibrāhīm b. Muslim was originally from Baghdad, lived in Egypt, and died in Ṭarsūs in 273. *Tahdhīb* IX, No. 20. Ibrāhīm b. M. b. ʿArʿara, d. 231 (*Tahdhīb* I, No. 279). M. b. Sinān, unlike his brother Yazīd who was one of Ṭaḥāwī's companions (see above I 2.5), made his home in Baghdad where he died in 271. Kawtharī, 9, calls him al-Shayzarī, but this *nisba* is not mentioned elsewhere (*Tahdhīb* IX, No. 323).

I 2.10. Abū ʿĪsā Mūsā b. ʿĪsā b. Bashīr al-Kūfī is so far unidentified. Ḥusayn b. ʿAlī al-Juʿfī, d. 203 or 204 (*Tahdhīb* II, No. 616). Hishām b. Ḥassān of Basra, d. 148, is credited with transmitting many traditions from Ibn Sīrīn (*Tahdhīb* XI, No. 75). M. b. Sīrīn, d. 110, and Anas b. Mālik, d. 91-93, both well known and prolific traditionists. On the second, see *EI*², s.v.

Sūra 2:131.

I 2.11. The *waṣiyya*, or testament, establishing a *waqf*, and attributed to ʿAlī b. Abī Ṭālib, does not seem to be as well-known a document as its contents would lead one to expect. Apart from brief traditions appearing in two early works on *waqf* (Khaṣṣāf's *Aḥkām al-Waqf*, Cairo 1904, and Hilāl b. Yaḥyā's *Aḥkām al-Waqf*, Hydarābād 1936) the *waṣiyya* does not seem to be preserved in the standard Sunni sources, nor in the several collections containing 'Alī's sayings and writings. Caetani does not include it in his *Annali*, IX and X. It is, however, preserved in two recensions in one later Shi'ite source, at least, the *Biḥār al-Anwār*, a compendium of Shi'ite theology by M. Bāqir al-Majlisī al-Iṣfahānī, who died in 1700 A.D. (Lith. Tabrīz, 1270-5, 14 vols.; the *waṣiyya* in IX, pp. 517-518 and 615-616). For the author, *GAL* II, 411, S II, 572-573).

The first third of the *waṣiyya* is also found in the Qāḍī Nu'mān's work on law written for one of the Ismā'īlī Fāṭimid caliphs, the *Da'ā'im al-Islām* (ed. A.A.A. Fyzee, Cairo, 1951-60, 2 vols.) II, 339-341.

On the whole, there is little correspondence among the three full versions—the two published texts in the *Biḥār al-Anwār* and Ṭaḥāwī's document. Apart from the standard expressions found in many documents creating a *waqf*, only the main outlines for disposition of the property are common to all three. The text in the *Da'ā'im al-Islām* is useful only for the first several lines, after which it turns to another subject. Of all the versions, Ṭaḥāwī's is the most detailed.

Two other testaments attributed to 'Alī and addressed to Ḥasan and Ḥusayn are much better known, but they are of moral and religious content. One was supposed to have been written down just after it was uttered on 'Alī's deathbed, and the other was delivered on the eve of Ṣiffīn. For references to these, see W. Ivanow, *Guide to Ismā'īlī Literature* (London, 1933), 29.

The *isnād* for Ṭaḥāwī's text is: M. b. al-'Abbās b. al-Rabī' al-Lu'lu'ī, one of Ṭaḥāwī's authorities for *shurūṭ*, who is unidentified thus far. Abū Yaḥyā Zakariyyā' b. Mubārak al-Wāsiṭī, also unidentified. 'Ubayd Allāh b. M. b. 'Umar is given a brief notice in the *Tahdhīb* (VII, No. 86); his father, Muḥammad, was 'Alī's grandson. 'Umar was one of 'Alī's sons by a Taghlibī woman captured in the *ridda* engagements (Muḥibb al-Dīn Ṭabarī, *Al-Riyāḍ al-Nādira fī Manāqib al-'Ashara*, II, 153-334, [Cairo, 1327]).

The *isnād* in Majlisī's version is Abū 'Alī al-Ash'arī — M. b. 'Abd al-Jabbār and M. b. Ismā'īl — al-Faḍl b. Shādhān — Ṣafwān b. Yaḥyā — 'Abd al-Raḥmān b. al-Ḥajjāj — Abu'l-Ḥasan Mūsā.

Line 4. The village of Yanbu' was one of 'Alī's estates near Madina, which he either bought (Saleh El-Ali, "Muslim Estates in Hidjaz," *JESHO* II (1959), 254, 257 and references there) or which was given to him by the Prophet (Yāqūt, *Mu'jam al-Buldān* VI, index, 236, s.v.; Ibn Hishām, *Sīra* I and II, index, s.v.). The editor of the *Da'ā'im* reads *yanbu'* as a verb.

Line 7. Rabāḥ, Abū Nayzar and Jubayr, and on l. 11, Ruzayq, are 'Alī's freed slaves. The only one who can be positively identified is Abū Nayzar, a person well known in tradition as the son of the Abyssinian Negus (Najāshī). See Yāqūt, *Mu'jam al-Buldān* III, 757, where he is mentioned in connection with 'Alī making over two of his estates as *waqf* property. Also, see Ibn Hishām, *Sīra* II, 341. The editor of the *Da'ā'im* reads Riyāḥ, Abū Bīzad, Habtar and Zurayq.

Line 9. Wādī al-Qurā was a Jewish settlement close by Madina, which the Prophet conquered in the year 7. (Yāqūt, *Mu'jam al-Buldān* VI, index, 225, s.v.; Nuwayrī, *Nihāya* XVII, 268 ff. The Qāḍī Nu'mān adds *thulthuhū māl Banī Fāṭima*, and Majlisī, *min māl Banī Fāṭima*.

Line 10. Udhayna, also known as Taytad. See Yāqūt, *Mu'jam al-Buldān* I, 180, 904, and Saleh El-Ali, *JESHO* II, 250 and references there. Burqa belonged to the Prophet personally and was one of his "seven *ṣadaqāt*"; he acquired it from the Banū Naḍīr. Yāqūt, *Mu'jam al-Buldān* I, 575. There seems to be no reason to read Ri'a as in the manuscript. Majlisī has Dīha and Dīma.

Line 12. Here the contents of both published versions of the document differ from Ṭaḥāwī's to the extent that they can no longer be compared. Majlisī's text begins to correspond with ours again, in content if not in wording, with the appended document beginning *ammā ba'd* on l. 25.

lā yuba'na wa-lā yūhabna wa-lā yu'addayna (or more commonly for the last, *lā yūrathna*), "they may not be sold, given away, nor used to discharge an obligation (nor bequeathed)." The phrase makes explicit one of the essential conditions for a *waqf* : once founded, the endowment cannot be alienated. The expression is often extended to include other economic transactions; see, for example, an interesting *waqf* inscription on stone from the year 301 (913 A.D.) in M. Sharon, "A Waqf Inscription from Ramlah," *Arabica* XIII (1966), 81. The term *batlatan* two lines below, "irrevocable" or, literally, "cut off from its giver or from the rest of the property" (Lane, s.v. *b-t-l*) serves the same purpose.

Another condition, that the *waqf* must be in perpetuity, is not stated here by using the usual verb *abbada* (or the adverb *abadan*), but by the reference to the last day, *yawma taswaddu wujūh wa-tabyaḍḍu wujūh*, "on the day some faces will become black and others white," i.e., grieved and joyous.

Further, 'Alī's endowment makes his immediate descendants the beneficiaries, and in accordance with the rules for *waqf* property, permanent secondary beneficiaries are named should the descendants die out. In this case, proceeds are used to support the expenses of the holy war and the fighter in the *jihād*, the *dhawū al-raḥim* (see below, note to l. 21), and the poor and the unfortunate. See Schacht, *Introduction*, 125-126, and *EI*[1], s.v. "Waqf," for details.

Line 14. Maskin is either a place in Kufa (Majlisī, 616) or in Iraq near the Dujayl canal, between Baghdad and Sāmarrā (Yāqūt, *Mu'jam al-Buldān* IV, 529).

Lines 17-18. *wa-lā tubā'u... ghirāsan*: the passage may be translated "Not a single palm tree of these four estates, [even though it be still] a young shoot, is to be sold to [their] descendants until their land is ready for cultivation."

Line 21. The *dhawū al-raḥim*, one of the categories of persons to benefit from the *waqf* are, roughly speaking, relatives on the maternal side. Specifically, these are the Banū Hāshim and the Banū 'Abd al-Muṭṭalib, named in both published versions.

Line 25. This second, appended document, beginning with *ammā ba'd*, makes provisions for 'Alī's nineteen concubines, "whom I am visiting in turns" (*ataṭawwaf*). Those who have borne him a child (the *ummahāt al-awlād*) would automatically be free on his death but those who have not had children are set free here. Majlisī mentions seventeen concubines. Mme. L. Veccia Vaglieri counts fourteen sons and nineteen *daughters* by nine wives and several concubines (*EI*[2], s.v. " 'Alī b. Abī Ṭālib").

The two witnesses are 'Ubayd Allāh b. Abī Rāfi' (*Tahdhīb* VII, No. 21) and Hayyāj (or Hayāj) b. Abī Hayyāj, unidentified. Four persons witness the *waṣiyya* in Majlisī's text. An error in the longer of his two recensions puts the date in the year 37; 'Alī was killed in Ramaḍān of the year 40, or January, 661.

I 2.12. M. b. Khuzayma b. Rāshid al-Asadī, unidentified, but mentioned in Kawtharī, 9. Abū Rabī'a, unidentified. Abū 'Awāna, identity uncertain; see the notice for Ḥibbān b.

Hilāl in the *Tahdhīb*, referred to in I 2.5. Sa'īd b. Masrūq (*Tahdhīb* IV, No. 142) died in 126 or 128.

I 2.14. Identification of the parties by giving their genealogies and *nisbas* will show whether they are present, absent (more than a three-day journey away) or dead. The name itself will not lead to that information, but describing the parties fully will help distinguish them from other persons in the town with the same familiar names and the same patronymics; this more exact identification, then, will tell us about their physical whereabouts.

In practice, from the evidence of the published papyri, patronymics and descriptive names were multiplied often far beyond Abū Ḥanīfa's and Ṭaḥāwī's requirements, even when the transaction was made in towns of relatively small size. There was good reason for this, namely the practice of the continuity of *kunyas*. Since Muslim genealogies often followed certain fixed patterns for two generations or more, it would not be unusual for two men to have the same names and for their fathers to have the same names as well. Sarakhsī (170) suggests naming some physical feature for identification. This is also seen in the papyri, as "[Fulān] the flat-nosed" (al-Afṭas, *APEL* I, 181) or "the snub-nosed" (al-Dhalīf, *APEL* I, 141). However, naming the profession or trade was the most common practice. The witnesses, but not the parties to the contract, should be identified further, in Ṭaḥāwī's opinion, by their more familiar *kunya* (e.g., I 10.0).

I 2.15. Abū Ḥanīfa does not lower his own strict standards in this passage. It is only when an individual's social or professional standing is high enough that he can do without his father's name.

I 2.18. Ṭaḥāwī here introduces the subject of whether or not the notary should mention the seller's possession of the thing sold (*yad al-bā'i' 'ala'l-mabī'*), a concern that will appear frequently in other contexts (Introduction, pp. 33, 35). In his opinion, the better course is to steer clear of the doctrine of Ibn Abī Laylā and the scholars of Madina that once the buyer formally acknowledges that the seller owns the property, the seller can withdraw his guarantee (or simply ignore his obligation concerning it) should a third party step in and establish a rightful claim to the property. Thus the buyer, bound by his *iqrār* in favor of the seller and unable to reverse its effect, will not be able to demand return of the price from the seller (I 2.20). But Abū Zayd is also aware of the risk to which the notary might expose his clients and prefers to do the opposite: mention possession as a precaution against the opinion of certain Basrians who might declare the sale invalid because the seller sells property not in his possession (I 2.18).

In fact, formulas affirming the seller's possession do not occur often in the published documents. When they do, the wording usually avoids an explicit acknowledgement by the buyer that the seller owns or possesses the property. For example, a common formula is *mā dhakara annahū lahū wa-milkuhū*, "[he bought all the land] that he [the seller] declared was owned by him and was his property." Similar formulas are "all that he [the seller] informed him that it was [sic] belonging to him and in his possession and in his hand(s) as a legal possession, and a declared right" (*milkan ṣaḥīḥan wa-ḥaqqan wājiban*; *APEL* I, 210, 219, 229; Grohmann's translation. Also, see Ṣayrafī in Nuwayrī, *Nihāya* IX, 20, for a similar, Shāfi'ite formula, *mā dhakara annahū lahū wa-fī milkihī wa-yadihī wa-taṣarrufihī*). These formulas, of course, all solve the problem of the *ikhtilāf*, satisfying both opinions.

Ṭaḥāwī's solution is more elaborate. He rescues the parties from this conflict of opinion by providing a model for a separate document of *shahāda* (I 3.0). Reference is made to the sale, but the object of the document is to establish that the seller owned the property until it was transferred to its new owner, and that until then, he had complete freedom of disposition. Furthermore, the buyer need not give his own *iqrār* to the seller's possession, but this is established independently by the testimony of witnesses. Note that no distinction is made here between ownership and possession, the term *yad* being used to signify both.

I 4.0 does not necessarily provide an alternative to a separate document of *shahāda*, as Ṭaḥāwī's opening words would imply. What is "more reliable and preferable" is a contract of sale improving on the one given in I 2.0, the basic instrument. Ṭaḥāwī suggests copying out the original document in full, then adding the deposition of secondary witnesses to strengthen the testimony of the primary witnesses, especially with respect to the boundaries of the property. The primary witnesses have already testified to the *iqrār* of the parties for the contents of the deed and the role played by each in the transaction. But the primary witnesses were not bound to look at the property itself and ascertain the truth of the parties' acknowledgements. They had only to hear their *iqrār*. Lest their testimony seem insufficient during a litigation, secondary witnesses are called to strengthen this part of the contract. These inspect the property itself (*waqafa 'alā* here means "to see," not merely "to stand on" or "be acquainted with"; see I 4.2); they look at the outermost limits of the boundaries (*nihāyat al-ḥudūd*). The purpose of strengthening this element—the definition of the boundaries—with additional testimony, is to affirm the prior ownership and possession of the seller without explicitly stating these. And of course, the secondary witnesses also verify the identity of the parties and confirm the depositions of the primary witnesses in order to make their testimony inseparable from the original contract.

Again, Ṭaḥāwī's words "until you finish [writing down] the names of those who witness possession of the seller" are not to be taken as referring to the separate document for possession in I 3.0 (which has not been incorporated into this document). He means all secondary witnesses in addition to the three unspecified "*fulāns*."

I 2.22. Sulaymān b. Shu'ayb b. Sulaymān al-Kaysānī was one of Ṭaḥāwī's most important personal sources for the doctrine of Abū Ḥanīfa, appearing throughout the text at the head of the same impressive list of authorities. (The omission of Abū Yūsuf's name may be a copyist's error.) Sulaymān and his father were *ghurabā'*, immigrants in Egypt, and both are counted particularly among the disciples of Shaybānī. Shu'ayb was a companion of both Shaybānī and his teacher Abū Yūsuf, and although the son could not have known Shaybānī himself, he collected his *nawādir*, or legal decisions on unusual cases. For Sulaymān, who died in 278, see 'Abd al-Qādir I, No. 652, and *Classen*, 289 (where he is called al-Kisā'ī). His father, (d. 204) is noted in the *Jawāhir* I, No. 673, and *Classen*, 292.

I 2.22 - 2.55. Real property must be strictly defined so there will be no dispute that might invalidate the sale. In the case of house property, the location (2.22 - 2.23), the boundaries (2.24 - 2.41) and the material and abstract rights belonging to it (2.42 - 2.55) must be specified. The sequence, Sarakhsī says (170), should always be from the general to the particular.

I 2.22 - 2.23. *Kindat al-Kūfa*, *Miṣr*, and *al-qabīlat al-suflā*, *'ulyā*, all refer here to the tribal quarters within the town; *suflā* and *'ulyā*, meaning "lower" and "upper" with respect to territory, distinguish two different quarters in the lower or upper parts of the town occupied by the same tribal group. (See the discussion of the *ḥamūla*, a family unit, and its relationship to specific residential quarters, in G. Baer, *Population and Society in the Arab East* [New York,

1964], 169-70.) Sarakhsī (170) also describes the location of the property by naming the tribal quarters (*fī banī fulān*). Ṭaḥāwī considers this kind of designation inadequate; he supplies only "in *x* place, known as *y*," although later, orchards and cultivated lands will be defined by their district (*kūra*) and village (*qarya*), as in III 1.0. Marghīnānī's formula comes closest to the practice in the papyri (and reminds us of usage in the Near East today) in naming the district, thoroughfare (*darb*), street (*sikka*), lane (*zuqāq*) and relationship to the nearest mosque (fol. 16a).

I 2.24 - 2.28. The boundaries are defined by referring to all four cardinal points, a practice which appears to have been standard in both the Arabic documents from Egypt and those of the pre-Islamic Near East. Thus Ṭaḥāwī takes this for granted and the question of how the boundaries are to be established does not even arise. (However, see Sarakshsī, 171, for other opinions.) The subject under discussion here is which of the four cardinal points is to be given preference. Grohmann has shown (*APEL* I, 143 f.) that the sequence South-North-East-West, the order most often seen in the Egyptian Arabic papyri, corresponds with older Egyptian legal practice as it is frequently found in the demotic, Greek and Coptic papyri. See A. Schiller, "Coptic Law," 234, n. 1; Hoenerbach, "Notes," 35; Dietrich, *Papyri*, 23-24; Grohmann, *FWAP*, 189. For references to Spanish Arabic usage, see *APEL* I, 144, and Hoenerbach, *Urkunden*, 273-274. (It should also be pointed out that maps were also oriented toward the south.) Of course, variations within the sequence of cardinal points are common. For example, Sarakhsī prefers to put east before north, and this is also the order in three contracts from Damascus (Sourdel-Thomine and Sourdel, "Damascus," 167, 173, 178). Ṭaḥāwī's orientation, too, is toward the south, called *qibla* from the direction toward Mecca taken by Muslims living north of that city. For Sarakhsī, therefore, who would justify this old and established usage from an Islamic point of view, the south is first in the sequence because it is the most noble direction (*ashraf al-jihāt*), although he adds that the sequence is not as important as specific references to what constitutes these boundaries (178). Another Islamic context for older documentary forms is found by Ṭaḥāwī in the Qur'ān, allowing him to express his preference for the east over the west. North is usually expressed in the Egyptian documents by *al-baḥrī*, with the orientation toward the Mediterranean, while in the Spanish documents it is commonly *al-jawf* (Dozy, *Suppl.*, s.v.). In deeds from Damascus, the northern boundary is *al-shām* (Sourdel-Thomine and Sourdel, "Damascus," 167, 173, 178 and n. 6 on 178).

I 2.26. There are two *riwāyas* of Abū Yūsuf's opinion here; the first is explained in 2.24.

I 2.28. Sūras 2:115 and 2:142; 55:17; 70:40.

I 2.29 - 2.41. One of the problems in formulating the restricting clauses is how to express the boundaries of the property so as not to include anything beyond them, which the seller does not own, in the sale. The difficulty here is that Ṭaḥāwī is bound by an older Latin formula (see Hoenerbach, "Notes," 35) in its corresponding Arabic form, expressed a few lines farther on in the contract: "Fulān bought... the entire property... with all its boundaries (*bi-ḥudūdihā*)." The Latin "boundaries" expressed the bordering on adjacent property; and Sarakhsī, seeing the contradiction but not the reason for it, rightly says "I don't think [the notary] should write 'with its boundaries' for the boundary is not that which is bounded, while the object of the sale *is* that which is bounded, excluding its boundary" (171).

However, established usage must be reconciled with meaning, and this is the reason for

Ṭaḥāwī's insistence on using the verb *intahā* (2.29 - 2.31), which has the meaning of coming up to the very edge of something but not including it. The *ḥudūd* or boundaries, then, are identical with the *nihāyāt*, the outermost limits of the property conveyed. Sarakhsī emphasizes that the notion of connection (*ittiṣāl*) must be present. (In a modern contract from South Arabia, the word *taṣillā* [for *taṣilu ilā*] is, indeed, used in this formula; see Serjeant, "Ḥabbān," 125.) Sarakhsī also mentions the preferences of other *shurūṭ* scholars: *aḥadū ḥudūdihā lazīq kadhā*, or *yulāṣiqu kadhā*. (Cf. Sourdel-Thomine and Sourdel, "Damascus," 167).

Ṭaḥāwī's disagreement with Shaybānī (2.34 - 2.36) concerns only the meaning of the verb *waliya* and is not an argument on what the terms should convey.

In the published papyri, we often find the verb omitted altogether ("the northern boundary [is] the property of Fulān..."), a practice to which Ṭaḥāwī objects at the outset of his discussion (2.29) because of the possible interpretation that the neighbor's property will be included in the sale. When a verb is used, it is most often *yantahī* and less frequently, *yalī* (e.g., a document of the II/III century in *APEL* I, 141).

I 2.32. Zufar is Zufar b. al-Hudhayl, one of the more prominent pupils of Abū Ḥanīfa. His views on legal matters are greatly esteemed by Ṭaḥāwī, and are cited perhaps as often as those of the two great disciples, Shaybānī and Abū Yūsuf. Zufar died in Basra in 158, at the age of 48. 'Abd al-Qādir I, No. 622 and *manāqib* in II, 534-6; *Classen*, 282; Ibn Quṭlūbughā, No. 78.

I 2.32 - 2.33. *Ṣafqa wāḥida*, "in a single transaction." Ṭaḥāwī, in fact, recommends using the formula in all contracts (II 3.4). Concluding one contract as part of another (*ṣafqa fī ṣafqa*) is prohibited for fear of disguising unjustified enrichment.

I 2.38. In phrasing the clauses that describe the boundaries, Ṭaḥāwī carries his rules of precaution even farther than he did in 2.29. Here he warns the notary against saying that "the boundaries extend to the property of Fulān" because this could be interpreted as a formal acknowledgement, given in advance, of the neighbor's ownership of his own property. As potential buyers of that property, the parties to our contract might not be able to hold the neighbor, the potential seller, to his guarantee for a fault in ownership (*darak*), having already acknowledged that *he* (the neighbor) is the owner of the property.

Ṭaḥāwī's precaution is more formal than realistic. It would be difficult to define a boundary in any other way, since adjacent property did indeed usually belong to another person and there were few other ways of identifying it. In documentary practice, this was the normal way to describe a boundary. The only exceptions I know of are contracts where an estate was so large that the desert and "the Nile flowing past" could be boundaries (e.g., in Dietrich, *Papyri*, 18-19).

'uhda here is synonymous with *ḍamān al-darak*. Elsewhere (I 2.121, 2.123, and IV 7.8) Ṭaḥāwī points out that the *'uhda* refers to the document itself, which contains the guarantee. Sarakhsī emphasizes that *'uhda* means either *ṣakk* (written contract) or *'aqd*, and should not be used in place of *darak* (173).

I 2.39 - 2.40. *bi-asrihī*, or *bi-asrihī wa-kamālihī*, "entirely," "altogether," are not uncommon in the Egyptian papyri but both usually appear in connection with the property sold rather than the boundaries (e.g., *APEL* I, 229, 243). This is a good example of how, in practice, these stereotyped phrases shift about from one clause to another.

I 2.42 - 2.55. In defining house property (the *dār*), it is important for the notary to know which elements belong to the house and are to be included in the sale. Specifically, these are the *ḥuqūq*, the abstract rights residing in the property or particular to it, and the *marāfiq*, the conveniences and appurtenances that are not, like doors and beams, fixed parts of the house itself. Together, the *ḥuqūq* and *marāfiq* include such things as access roads, courtyards, water drains, kitchens or privies. They exclude anything that cannot legally be the object of sale or that would prevent a neighbor from enjoyment of his own rights.

In these paragraphs, Ṭaḥāwī only sketches the outlines of these matters. In parts II and III he describes in more detail the *ḥuqūq* and *marāfiq* for various types of property, because they are especially important when contracts are drawn up for selling parts of a *dār*, for divided and undivided joint shares, and when exceptions are made in a sale.

To insure that all the rights and accessories will be transferred to the new owner, Ṭaḥāwī advises the notary to affirm these in the transfer clause by saying that the seller delivers "everything that this sale entails" (*jamīʿa mā waqaʿa ʿalayhī hādha'l-bayʿ*), rather than "the entire house" (I 2.73).

For parallels to *ḥuqūq* and *marāfiq* in the Greek documents from Egypt and late Latin documents from Spain, see Hoenerbach, "Notes," 35-37, and *Urkunden*, 38-40, n. 1.

I 2.42 - 2.44. *sufl wa-ʿulūw* has been translated in various ways by the editors of the Arabic papyri, most of them following Grohmann's "what is below and above the surface." Grohmann has discussed the phrase and has concluded that it is a survival from the demotic and Greek formulary. Because it often occurs with *arḍuhā wa-samā'uhā*, "its land and its sky," found in many Arabic documents, the expression means, he says, that the air above the property is one of its appurtenances. (*APEL* I, 152 and references there; Dietrich, *Papyri*, 61; Sourdel-Thomine and Sourdel, "Damascus," 167 and 170. For the vocalization of *ʿulūw*, see Dozy, *Suppl.*, s.v., and Wright I, 121 D). Further, Serjeant reports that he has heard of the formula *al-bayt hawwuh wa-djawwuh wa'l-samā lī tawwuh*, "the house, its air (*hawāhu*) and atmosphere and the sky adjoining it" ("Ḥabbān," 127).

However, *arḍuhā wa-samā'uhā* also suggests a usage familiar in Arabic and other Semitic languages, the employment of two words at extreme ends on the scale of meaning to exhaust the whole range of meaning. An example would be the Qur'ānic phrase *mā taqaddama min dhanbika wa-mā ta'akhkhara*, "[that Allāh may forgive thee, Muḥammad] of thy sins, those which are past and those which are to come" (i.e., all his sins; Sūra 48:2). See Wright II, 284 D to 285 C for further examples. In this light, the expression *sufl wa-ʿulūw* would mean "the entire house," much as we would say "the whole house from top to bottom" or *de haut en bas*. The true purpose of these phrases, then, is to stress the fact that there are no exceptions to the sale; all the *ḥuqūq* and *marāfiq*, even though they may not be explicitly named in the contract, are sold with the house. A similar expression in the accessory formula is *kullu qalīl wa-kathīr* with the meaning of "everything, no matter how few or many, scant or abundant" (Grohmann: "all of little and much"); that is, everything that belongs with the property. For other, parallel formulas, see below, notes to I 2.50 - 2.51.

The discussions among the earlier scholars of *shurūṭ* indicate that there was some uncertainty even then about the phrase *sufl wa-ʿulūw*. They seem to agree, and this is certainly Ṭaḥāwī's opinion, that it was to be read "the lower and upper stories [of a building]." But these discussions reflect the fact that the *shurūṭ* writers were themselves influenced by such parallel formulas as "the land and the sky" and thus sought to read *sufl wa-ʿulūw* in a literal way. For example, Yūsuf and Hilāl object that the *ʿulūw* might be taken to mean the air space (*hawā'*) above a structure, the sale of which would be *fāsid*. or voidable (I 2.42; Sarakhsī, 171; Hilāl's opinion concerning the *'anān al-samā'*, "clouds of the sky," in *Fat. 'Ālam.*, 410).

In addition, references to the air above a house may reflect an earlier desire, since forgotten, to define or emphasize the right of the new owner and no one else to build a second story above his house. But in Islamic law, the right to be above a house cannot be sold because it is not *māl*, or property, and so the *shurūṭ* authors are forced to seek a concrete and plausible meaning for the word. Abū Zayd, in fact, is aware of the possibility that the *'ulūw* represents an abstract right, but rejects it as incorrect (I 2.43).

For Ṭaḥāwī, the *'ulūw* can only be the upper story of a structure that by definition can have more than one story (such as a *dār* or a *manzil*, but not a *bayt*; see below, note to II 7.0 and 15.0, and Sarakhsī, 171, 178-81; nor can it apply to a *binā'* which is an abstract term for any structure within the house complex). In a contract of sale for a one-story house, the empty space, representing a hypothetical upper story, is called a *barāḥ* (II 7.0 bis; see Muṭarrizī, *Mughrib* I, 33). The sale of an upper story if it has not yet been constructed is, of course, unlawful.

In the same way, the word *sufl* means the ground floor of a building which may or may not have an upper story. To scholars writing in Iraq and Persia, this definition is extended to include the cool underground chamber known as the *sardāb* (Pers. *sard* & *āb*; Ar. *sirdāb*, Lane, s.v.; known in Persia today as the *būm-kand*; for details, see H. E. Wulff, *The Traditional Crafts of Persia*, Cambridge, Mass., 1966). Usually it was used for food storage, but after the eleventh century it was often a summer living room (Mez, *Renaissance*, 379-380; *EI*², s.v. "Dār"). The *sardāb*, it is pointed out, is one of the appurtenances of the *dār* (Sarakhsī, 171; Marghīnānī, fol. 17a), or of the *'arṣa*, an open area without buildings (*Fat. 'Ālam.*, 410), and not an appurtenance of any single structure.

I 2.45 - 2.47 and **2.52 - 2.55.** Three categories of roads (*ṭuruq*), water channels (*masāyil*) and conveniences (*marāfiq*) must be distinguished in order to appreciate Ṭaḥāwī's discussion: (1) those which are strictly private (*khāṣṣ*) and, according to most opinions are normal *ḥuqūq* of the property and need not be stipulated as such, (2) public roads (*al-ṭuruq al-'āmma, al-mārra*) and large streams that carry water to neighboring houses and cannot be sold, and (3) those which share the characteristics of both public and private property. These last include the access road (*ṭarīq nāfidh*; see Dietrich, *Papyri*, 61) leading out of the property to a neighbor's house or to become a public highway; water channels which serve a neighboring house; and such conveniences as the *finā'* (here pl. *afniya*, 2.45), a perimeter of land around the house (Fagnan, *Additions*, s.v. *f-n-y*) or an open court in front of it (*'arṣa*, pl. *'irāṣ*) that may merge into other private or public land (the owner of the house could not build on such outside ground although most scholars held that it was his property; however, Abū Ḥanīfa defines it as public property [*Fat. 'Ālam.*, 412]); and the *ẓulla* or portico extending from the wall of the house being sold to the neighbor's house (I 2.55).

Clearly, ownership of some of these last can be disputed (I 2.55). Furthermore, if they are considered parts of the house sold, some scholars hold that they are automatically included in the term *ḥuqūq* while others say they must be stipulated as *ḥuqūq* in the contract. Hence, Ṭaḥāwī takes the precaution of writing in *fī ḥuqūqihā* (I 2.45) and other safeguards (I 2.55) whenever necessary, whereas Sarakhsī (172, 175) avoids the differences of opinion by not mentioning specific appurtenances at all. (See also Marghīnānī, fols. 17a, 17b; *Fat. 'Ālam.*, 410-411, following Sarakhsī for the most part.)

I 2.50 - 2.51. *kullu qalīl wa-kathīr* is the phrase most commonly used to state the comprehensive nature of the sale (see above, note to 2.42 ff.). Other expressions, not referring to specific appurtenances but intended to include them all, are: *ẓāhirihī wa-bāṭinihī*, "[anything, be it] conspicuous or hidden," (or perhaps, as Grohmann translates, "[anything] outside or inside [the house]"; *'āmirihī wa-ghāmirihī*, "inhabited or empty" (or when referring to land, "cultivated or uncultivated," III 1.0); *ṭūbuhū wa-khashabuhū, abwābuhū wa-ḥijāratuhū*, "its bricks and timbers, wooden doors and stones." A rhymed formula occurs in a contract of sale from South Arabia: *wa-ṭīn wa-'ūd wa-ḥadd wa-ḥudūd wa-abwāb wa-akhshāb wa-ḥadīd wa-jarīd wa-ḥajār wa-madār* (for *aḥjār wa-amdār*), and the editor translates it "mud and wattle, borne and bounds, doors and timbers, iron and palm-branches, stone and clay" (Serjeant, "Ḥabbān," 125-126).

Objections to *kullu qalīl wa-kathīr* are based on the fear that even things not intended to be sold, such as household furniture, will be included. Sarakhsī is amused by an opinion of Zufar that along with the house, the buyer will acquire the wife and children of the seller, as well as the insects within, because these are "few and many" (172).

I 2.56 - 2.60. Clauses declaring that the sale is valid appear far more frequently in the preserved contracts than we would gather from Ṭaḥāwī's remarks and from his brief and cautious *shiran lā sharṭ fīhi wa-lā 'ida*, "a sale in which neither condition nor promise [is stipulated]." See the Introduction, pp. 56-57.

Ṭaḥāwī cautions the notary to avoid any positive statement by the buyer that the sale is sound, because if the claim of another person (an heir, perhaps, or a creditor) should be recognized, then obviously the sale was not sound and the buyer will have taken the property wrongfully. What Ṭaḥāwī means, of course, is that only the true owner can make a valid sale. The buyer, according to one opinion (see above, note to I 2.20), will then be unable to recover the price he paid to the seller (I 2.57 and 2.102). In drafting the contract, the notary was not responsible for verifying the seller's ownership, except in the theory of the Mālikī school (Tyan, *Notariat*, 63-64). None of the contracts in Grohmann's collection of the Egyptian papyri mention that the notary has done so. Yet he does have a professional obligation, at least, to avoid using phrases in his contracts that might prejudice the rights of one of the parties.

Declaring the sale to be sound is only one obstacle preventing the buyer from securing a refund from the seller. The other, according to the same opinion, is giving his *iqrār* that the seller is the owner of the property, an act that might deprive the buyer himself of his claim to ownership in the future.

But this was a minority opinion and probably not commonly followed, because clauses that explicitly confirm validity are quite common. Apart from Abū Zayd's formula quoted by Ṭaḥāwī (I 2.56, "a sound, valid and completed sale"), we find: (1) synonyms for *ṣaḥīḥ* and *thābit*, "valid or legally effective," *wājib*, *lāzim*, "binding on the parties," *sharī'ī*, "in conformity with Sharī'a law" (usually a Shāfi'ite formula), *nāfidh*, "legally operative," *jā'iz*, "valid or permitted"; (2) synonyms of *tāmm*, "complete or fully completed," such as *māḍī* and other terms to indicate that a period of time, within which the right to cancel the sale is given, is over; and (3) terms which express the opposite of something that would make the sale defective, such as *bayān*, "clear, open," meaning that there is no *talji'a*, that is, misrepresentation or attempt to conceal the terms of the sale from others (see I 2.163 and note to I 2.165, V 17.0 and 18.0 for Ṭaḥāwī's definition; Grohmann renders *talji'a* as "exclusive bequest," and Sourdel-Thomine and Sourdel, "*protection*"; as a widespread economic practice, see *EI*², s.v. "Ḥimāya").

Even more profuse are terms advertising that flaws are absent, and the notaries are quite specific as to what these could be. In addition to Ṭaḥāwī's formula declaring that the contract contains no stipulated conditions or promises inadmissible in a transaction, the parties announce that there is no *talji'a*, no *fasād*, imperfection (in the form of the contract), nor *khiyār*, or option (i.e., to cancel the sale; Ṭaḥāwī, 2.60, refers to something else, the *khiyār al-majlis*). Nor are there any reservations or exceptions in the sale: *istithnā'*, exceptions [to what is sold], or *mathnawiyya*, *lā li-raddihī wa-lā li-faskhihī*, *lā li-ajalin wa-lā li-abadin*, "no reservations of the right to return the property or cancel the sale, after a specified period, or for good."

The contract is not intended as a pledge (*'alā sabīli rahnin*, *bi-sababi rahnin*), nor as a gift (*hiba*). There has been no agreement of *iqāla* to rescind the sale at a future date, nor *i'āda* or *raj'a*, return to the former legal status (Grohmann: "recurrence or right of reversal"). The parties deny that there is any *ghirra*, inadvertence, or *itwā*, anything that can bring about destruction of the property, or *khilāba*, giving out that one has sold at a loss by exaggerating the purchase price (see Fagnan, *Additions*, s.v.). There is no *wadī'a*, deposit (i.e., no deposit outstanding, given by the owner of the property to another to hold it in safe keeping).

An interesting and somewhat puzzling group of clauses appears in the contracts of the papyri, although they are not mentioned in Ṭaḥāwī's text. They state that the transaction has been concluded "according to the Muslim law of sale" (*'alā sharṭ bay' al-islām*), or "according to the regulations and contractual obligations necessary under Islamic law" (*'alā mā yūjibuhū ḥukmu bay' al-islām wa-'uhdatuhū*). These and a variety of other expressions are found, for example, in *APEL* I, 146, 162, 169, 175, 182, 199, 257.

It is possible that these clauses were inserted in the contracts when one of the parties was a non-Muslim, to stress that Islamic law would prevail in such a case. This is Tyan's suggestion (*Notariat*, 62-63). Yet the usage shows little consistency in this respect, and the same formula appears when both parties are Muslims and, indeed, when both parties are Christians. The only explanation seems to be that model contracts in circulation among the notaries were used by Christians, Jews, and Muslims alike. Just as non-Muslims commonly applied to Muslim witnesses to have their deeds attested, as the papyri show, they also went to Muslim notaries to have them drawn up. The formula was formal, a set phrase, serving only to indicate that the sale was correct, and probably had no immediate significance. (For Jews as clients of Muslim notaries, especially in the sale or gift of houses, see S.D. Goitein, *A Mediterranean Society* [Berkeley and Los Angeles, 1967], I, 196).

A comparable phrase, *bay' al-muslim min al-muslim*, "the sale by a Muslim to a Muslim," occurs in Marghīnānī's lengthy formula for validity; it affirms, he says, that nothing ritually impure, such as wine or pork or other things lawful to non-Muslims, had been exchanged (fol. 17b; the *Fat. 'Ālam.* mistakenly ascribes this formula to Ṭaḥāwī, 414). This is another case where the formula may have been an old, formal expression, and Marghīnānī, writing in the middle of the sixth/twelfth century, gives it a characteristic explanation.

Ṭaḥāwī's *bay' al-muslim al-muslim* (III 38.0) refers to the sale of a slave, and it is to be read as "a sale in which a Muslim is sold to a Muslim." It is used as a formula for validity because it affirms the important rule that a non-Muslim cannot be the owner of a Muslim slave.

I 2.61 - 2.112. Ṭaḥāwī's commentary on the transfer section of the simple contract may be analyzed as follows: (1) exchange of the price and the property, 2.61 - 2.76; (2) quittance (*barā'a*) for the price, 2.61 - 2.65 and 2.72 - 2.73; (3) inspection of the property and the *khiyār al-ru'ya*, 2.77 - 2.99; and (4) separation of the parties and the *khiyār al-majlis*, 2.100 - 2.112. Aspects of these various steps in the transaction will be discussed in more detail as they come up in the text.

I 2.61. Formulas for the *barā'a*, releasing the buyer from further responsibility for the price, do not vary much in practice. (See the Introduction, pp. 57-60.) All the documents use form I or IV of the verb *b-r-'*, and the clause may be expanded to state that the seller has taken the price (Ṭaḥāwī's *barā'at al-qabḍ wa'l-istīfā'*), or to enumerate some of the responsibilities from which the buyer has been acquitted (e.g., *min jamī'i dhālika wa-min waznihī wa-min naqdihī wa-min al-yamīn 'alayhi aw 'alā shay'an* [*sic*] *minhū*; Grohmann, "[he has released him] from all of [the price] and from its weight and ready money and from the oath with regard to it or any portion thereof," *APEL* I, 146).

Formulas declaring the seller cleared for delivery of the sold object are rare. A Mālikī text says *wa-ḥālla al-mubtā'u... fi'l-mabī' al-madhkūr 'ala'l-bā'i'...*, "the buyer declares the seller quit of the above-mentioned object of sale." (Formula in Hoenerbach, *Urkunden*, 273, n. 1.)

I 2.64. *abra'tuka*, in an active sense, meaning "I have given you quittance [for the price]," does not constitute an *iqrār* that the seller has received the price because there are many circumstances where transfer of the price does not take place. The seller may, for example, give the price to the buyer as a gift before taking possession of it. (A model contract for this transaction is supplied in IV 13.0, with a further discussion of the *barā'a*.) Or the property may be sold in exchange for a debt which the seller owes to a third party; the buyer transfers the price to the creditor and the seller receives a *barā'a* for the debt (contract in V 3.0 ff.; Sarakhsī, 186-187).

'Alī b. Ma'bad b. Shaddād, a Ḥanafī scholar who emigrated to Egypt with his father, is known chiefly for his close association with Shaybānī. He met Shaybānī when the latter was qadi of Raqqa and later transmitted two of his more important works. 'Alī b. Ma'bad died in 218 or 228. His name always appears in this text in connection with that of M. b. al-'Abbās as transmitter of Abū Ḥanīfa's doctrine. ('Abd al-Qādir I, No. 1042; Laknawī, No. 271.)

I 2.67. The tradition is cited again in III 45.10 to prove much the same point; for a variant, see the biographical notice of Hind in Ibn 'Abd al-Barr, *Istī'āb* IV, No. 4114. M. b. 'Amr b. Yūnis al-Sūsī (Dhahabī, *Mushtabih* I, 376 for his name) is not identified. Abū Mu'ā-wiya al-Ḍarīr is M. b. Khāzim, a Kufan traditionist who died in 113 or later (*Tahdhīb* IX, No. 191). Hishām b. 'Urwa, d. about 145 (*Tahdhīb* XI, No. 89), is the son of 'Urwa b. Zubayr, one of the "seven scholars of Madina" (d. 94; *Tahdhīb* VII, No. 351; see Schacht, *Origins*, 243 ff.).

I 2.69. Note the unusual use of *kadhā* in this formula and throughout the text: as a definite noun in the feminine, and then followed by a definite noun. See I 2.72 where it is used as we would expect, with a following indefinite noun, in the accusative singular (Wright II, 127 D, 128 A).

I 2.69 - 2.70. In cash transactions, coins were usually weighed out, although Muslim lawyers seem never to have really decided whether coins passed by weight or by tale. This ambiguity is reflected in the formulas describing the price. For instance, Ṭaḥāwī's formula says that the price is "*x* number of dinars, of standard weight (*mathāqīl*, i.e., each weighing one *mithqāl*) in gold, in minted coin of full weight and good alloy." Many other examples from the papyri include words describing both standards. For example, *'adad* or *ma'sūl*, correctly counted out (Grohmann, *APEL* I, 173, 181; II, 49-50, 51-53; David-Weill, "Louvre," 281-282); *wazn sab'a* for dirhams, of the weight of seven *mithqāls* for every ten dirhams (IV 6.0; Sarakhsī, 172; Lane, s.v. *s-b-'*); *qā'im*, of prescribed weight (*APEL* II, 77; David-Weill, "Louvre," 290); *bi'l-ṣaḥīḥ*, correctly minted (*APEL* I, 257, 263).

Yet, many of these terms would seem to be purely formal. For while the weight standard and the alloy of the dinar was maintained in most parts of the Islamic world for some time (*EI*², s.v. "Dīnār"), by the period of most of these documents the preserved specimens of coins show great irregularity in both weight and fineness. "Of full weight," for instance, ceased to be meaningful, for there was no single standard by which a coin could be judged. The *shurūṭ* texts, of course, acknowledged this; the *Fat. 'Ālam.* (412-413) mentions several weight standards, such as the *mithqāl* of Mecca, Samarqand, and Khwārizm, and points out that it differed from place to place. Also, clipping was a widespread practice and the papyri themselves even mention pieces of coins used in payment (*qiṭ'a*: *APEL* IV, 226; David-Weill, "Louvre," 279), not legal, according to the doctrine of the jurists, but admitted in practice (David-Weill, "Louvre," 281; Dozy, *Suppl.*, s.v. *q-ṭ-'*).

And so we can see why Ṭaḥāwī must insist that the notary mention the word "price" rather than specify the number of dinars to be paid. Dinars alone do not fully discharge the obligation to pay the price (*al-wafā' bihī li'l-thaman*); the dinars must be of a quality or mint issue (*jins*) that satisfies the seller, and the word *thaman* expresses this obligation. Sarakhsī points out that "if coins are of different kinds, and all of them are in circulation at the same time [and place], one must distinguish the kind of dirham, because the contract is not valid without it" (172). Marghīnānī demands mention of the exact mint issue (*ḍarb*) itself (fol. 16b). See the valuable section on the use of money in business in S.D. Goitein, *A Mediterranean Society* (Berkeley and Los Angeles, 1967), I, 229-240. Goitein points out that the practice of handling money in sealed purses, the exact value of which was stamped on the outside, helped solve the problem of the variety of coins in circulation, especially where large sums were concerned. For other aspects of the problem, see R. Brunschvig, "Conceptions monétaires chez les juristes musulmans," *Arabica*, XIV, 134.

The preserved contracts, indeed, do usually distinguish the coins in one way or another. If they are not called by their popular names (Mustanṣirī, Mu'izzī, Ḥākimī, etc., referring to their *jins*), or designated by their place of minting (e.g., Hoenerbach, *Urkunden*, 117), a number of terms serve as a substitute, if a rather loose one, for defining a standard. For example, we find *al-muta'āmal bihā yawma'idhin*, [dinars] with which one does business at the time (Ṣayrafī, p. 10); *min ḥaqq al-sūq*, according to the market value (*APEL* I, 220), *bi-wazni tujjār*, according to the weight standard of businessmen (*APEL* I, 227); *bi'l-jadīd*, of new weight standard (Grohmann: "newly minted," *APEL* I, *passim*, and note on p. 116; David-Weill, "Louvre," 281-282); *ṭarī*, "fresh" or unworn (*APEL* I, 71, and *EI*², s.v. "Dīnār"); *al-jāriyat al-āna*, now in circulation (Hoenerbach, *Urkunden*, 307 and *passim*); *'ala'l-rasm al-jārī fi'l-balad, fi'l-ṣarf al-ajwad wa'l-hīna wa'l-āna*, according to the current rate in the town, at the best exchange [both] anytime and now (*APEL* II, 52); *jā'iz* or *jawāz*, valid, in circulation (see Dietrich, *Briefe*, 108-109, n. 14, and Goitein ["legal tender"], p. 234); and *naqd bayt al-māl* *wa-waznihī*, money [estimated according to] the standard weight value of the treasury (i.e., referring to the glass weights deposited there; *APEL* II, 47, note).

Specifying the type of coin that may be used as payment is advised here primarily from the point of view of satisfying the seller. The issue gains another dimension when there is a risk of unlawful gain. Certain transactions, such as a *murābaḥa* sale, resale with a fixed profit, require that the resale price be paid in the same coin which the original buyer gave as payment. But the *ribḥ*, or profit, may be paid in the coin current in the country in which the resale contract is made. The notary, then, must name two prices in his contract, one for the property and one for the *ribḥ*. These matters of price are discussed further in IV 11.1-11.4.

I 2.71. In connection with the above, note that *istīfā'*, receiving payment [of the price] in full, includes not just the amount, but also the good quality (*jūda*) of the coin.

I 2.79. Sawwār b. 'Abd Allāh al-'Anbarī became qadi of Baghdad in 237, having previously served as qadi of Ruṣāfa. According to Wakī', he was also something of a literary figure (*Quḍāt* III, 278-280). He died in 245 (*Tahdhīb* IV, No. 463; this is the "Sawād [or Sawwād] b. 'Abd Allāh al-'Arī" mentioned in the *Fat. 'Ālam.*, 419).

I 2.81. Muḥammad b. Shādhān, known as the Qāḍī Abū Bakr al-Naṣrī, was a prominent Egyptian Ḥanafī, assistant to Bakkār b. Qutayba and then qadi of Miṣr himself when Bakkār went to Damascus. He died in 274 ('Abd al-Qādir II, No. 191). 'Abd al-Raḥmān b. Mahdī, traditionist and *faqīh*, d. in 198 (*Tahdhīb* VI, No. 549). Rabāḥ b. Abī Ma'rūf al-Makkī (*Tahdhīb* III, No. 454). Ibn Abī Malīka is 'Abd Allāh b. 'Ubayd Allāh, d. 117 in Bukhara (*Tahdhīb* V, No. 523). 'Alqama b. Waqqāṣ al-Laythī, a Companion who died in Madina during the caliphate of 'Abd al-Mālik (Ibn 'Abd al-Barr, *Istī'āb* III, No. 1852). Ṭalḥa b. 'Ubayd Allāh, d. 36, and Jubayr b. Muṭ'im al-Qurashī, d. 57 or 59, were both Companions from Madina (Ibn 'Abd al-Barr, *Istī'āb* II, No. 1280 and I, No. 311).

I 2.96. Ḥasan b. Ziyād al-Lu'lu'ī was one of the famous pupils of Abū Ḥanīfa and a jurist of Kufa. He was the author of several practical works on law, among them a handbook for qadis, and works on maintenance, land tax, inheritance and testaments (*Fihrist* II, 204). Ḥasan died in 204 in Kufa. (See 'Abd al-Qādir I, No. 449; Ibn Quṭlūbughā, No. 55; and *Classen*, 284-285.)

I 2.104. For *ghāba 'an ṣāḥibihī* as a way of expressing separation of the parties, see 2.111.

I 2.106. *mā 'aqada lahū 'alā nafsihī*: "the [conditional] obligation which he had imposed on himself in the other's favor."

The three opinions Ṭaḥāwī cites on separation of the parties and the effect it has on making the option no longer operative (*ḥadhf al-takhyīr*) are presented as follows: the first is given in pars. 106-108, the second and third at the beginning of par. 109. It is the second (*idhā ta'āqada al-mutabāyi'āni fa-qad tafarraqā*) that is separation *bi'l-aqwāl*, simple offer and acceptance rather than physical separation.

I 2.116. The *ḍamān al-darak*, or simply *darak* as it is often abbreviated by the *shurūṭ* authors, is a guarantee given to the buyer alone and does not extend to anyone who may subsequently acquire the property from the buyer. This is because the *darak*, properly speaking, rises from a claim (i.e., a rightful claim of ownership) which existed before the contract came into being. A claim established after that (because a defect is discovered or because the sold object perishes before delivery, for instance) is not covered by the *darak*. One consequence of this is that the buyer's right to the guarantee exists even after his death (Sarakhsī, 173; Marghīnānī, fol. 19a; Ṭaḥāwī alludes to this in 2.117; cf. Mehmet Murat 997). Thus, in order to exclude a claim for the *darak* on the part of the buyer's heirs, or someone to whom the buyer may sell or give the property, the notary must state that the *darak* is given to the buyer, naming him specifically, and not for the property sold (2.118 - 2.119).

The opposite view, that the guarantee is a fixed right residing in the property and may therefore be extended to others, is mentioned by Sarakhsī. (He ascribes it to Abū Yūsuf, perhaps mistakenly, since Abū Yūsuf's formula as Ṭaḥāwī quotes it does not reflect this view; 2.115.) The appropriate designation for the buyer then becomes *man yaḥiqqu lahū al-rujū' min darak*, "he who has a right to demand return [of the price] on account of a *darak*." But such formulas are not at all usual in the papyri, although a contract from the fifth century adds to the name of the buyer *aw aḥad min nasabihī*, "or one of his family" (*APEL* I, 193).

On the other hand, the potential sources of a claim are often enumerated in the deeds of the Egyptian papyri. For example, part or all of the following formula may be written to cover the possibilities: *fa-mā kāna min 'ulqa aw khuṣūma aw tabi'a* [or *tibā'a*] *aw ṭārī bi-dayn aw mustaḥiqq bi-mīrāth aw rāghib qarīb am ba'īd shāhid am ghā'ib* (*fa-inqādh dhālika 'alā* [*fulān*]). Grohmann translates, "But if there should be any contention or litigation or vindication or one who suddenly appears with a debt or who makes a claim on the basis of an inheritance, or someone desiring it, be he near or far, present or absent (then the recuperation therefor are incumbent upon [Fulān]."

There are some cases in which only the property itself can be returned. For example, the buyer may be the one to give a guarantee of *darak* to the seller, in the expectation that he will return the property to the seller for one reason or another. Technically, these are guarantees for a *darak* because they insure against a fault in ownership; the property must remain intact, secure against any claim, until it is delivered back to the seller. The formulas do not differ from the formulas given in these paragraphs, except for the fact that *min qibalihī wa-bi-sababihī* may be substituted for *min aḥad min al-nās kullihim*, reflecting the fact that since the property has not left his hands (in these contracts), only the buyer can be the source of a fault in ownership, and not "any person whatsoever." For examples of the above, see III 19.0, IV 7.0, V 1.0 ter, and V 17.0.

I 2.119. *kullu wāḥid bi-sababihī* (or *min qibalihī*), "every person on account of him," is an ellipsis for "every person who acquires the property on account of him." The plural *asbāb* is used a few lines further on in a similar way, but here *fa-wajabat lahū asbābuhū* means that whatever may happen to the property (i.e., to improve it) on account of the buyer is incumbent upon the seller in the buyer's favor. Ṭaḥāwī's point is that the person who pays the price is the one who is entitled to a guarantee against a *darak*. Since the buyer did not pay the price for improvements made by his heir, the seller is not responsible to the buyer's executor for their value. The *darak* for the improvements is given by the heir to the person to whom *he* sells the property.

I 2.121. The use of the term *'uhda* was somewhat ambiguous, as this paragraph shows. As a technical term to denote various kinds of guarantees given by the seller, it is, first of all, "an isolated, archaic survival" (Schacht, *Introduction*, 8) that persisted in the Mālikī school for a special kind of guarantee applied to the sale of slaves (e.g., in Mālik's *Muwaṭṭa'*, "Kitāb al-Buyū'," *Bāb* 3). Secondly, it came to mean a guarantee both for hidden defects and in case of a claim (i.e., for a *darak*) according to Mālikī examples attested by Fagnan (*Additions*, s.v. '*-h-d*; a similar definition in Muṭarrizī, *Mughrib* II, 64).

Ṭaḥāwī, who is not always consistent in his terminology, sometimes uses *'uhda* in place of *darak* and sometimes to mean the contract itself, even though he advises the notary against both (examples of the first in I 2.38, II 11.4, 13.1, and the second in II 3.4). But to Abū Ḥanīfa, the term is equivalent to *ḍamān al-ṣaḥīfa*, the actual document on which the guarantee for the sale is written (see IV 7.8 for definition). Sarakhsī calls attention to the ambiguity in meaning: to some the *'uhda* is the document (*ṣakk*, 179, 187) and to others, the [written or unwritten] contract (*'aqd*, 173).

I 2.121 - 2.141. In the event a claim for the property is recognized, how does the seller extinguish his obligation toward the buyer? The question is discussed in two of its aspects, the nature of what he returns to the buyer (2.123 - 2.130), and the nature of the property claimed (2.131 - 2.139; improvements, 2.142 - 2.158).

The prevailing opinion is that if the property itself cannot be delivered, then the seller is liable to the amount of the price paid. This is Ṭaḥāwī's view (his arguments in 2.127 - 2.130), but other opinions demand return of exactly the same thing (a model contract for this, with the guarantee given by the third party, is offered in II 5.0), return of another piece of property as nearly like it as possible, or return of the value of the property on the day the claim was made (contract in I 6.0). Moreover, should the buyer be compensated for improvements, such as additional structures or standing crops (2.142 - 2.158)? What are the seller's obligations if part of a piece of property held in joint ownership is claimed (undivided shares, 2.137 - 2.139; divided shares, 2.140 - 2.141)?

Because there are a variety of opinions applied to each of these questions, it is vital that the notary word his formula so that the qadi will not be restricted by the notary's stipulations, but will be free to decide according to his own views and thus uphold the validity of the contract. Ṭaḥāwī's preferences are stated in 2.140 - 2.141 and 2.158.

I 2.125. Little is known about 'Uthmān al-Battī, despite the fact that it was he to whom Abū Ḥanīfa addressed a letter defending his views as a Murji'ite (*EI*[2], s.v. "Abū Ḥanīfa"). He appears in *isnāds* as a transmitter from Ḥasan of Baṣra. (Ibn al-Athīr, *Lubāb* I, 96; he is the " 'Uthmān al-Laythī" mentioned in the *Fat. 'Ālam.*, 419, 425.)

I 2.140. Ṭaḥāwī is referring here to part of the formula drafted by Abū Ḥanīfa and Abū Yūsuf and quoted in 2.115: *fa-'alā fulān khalāṣu dhālika aw radd al-thaman.* Abū Zayd's formula, also some pages back, was *wa-'alā fulān taslīmu mā yajibu li-fulān... ḥattā yusallima dhālika lahū* (2.114).

Strictly speaking, *khalāṣ* or *takhlīṣ* is delivery of the property (at least insofar as that is possible), according to Abū Ḥanīfa. But Ṭaḥāwī points out that this really comes down to the next best thing, return of the price ("that is the very *takhlīṣ* that Abū Ḥanīfa and Abū Yūsuf meant," 2.128) because the seller is not free to choose, but must depend on the *ijāza*, ratification of the sale, by the person making the claim. (The same argument is found in the *Fat. 'Ālam.*, 417.) Sarakhsī interprets *khalāṣ*, as Shaybānī uses it, to mean return of the price when the sold object is claimed, and mentions other opinions as well (173, 174).

The term *khalāṣ*, to express the seller's obligation, appears very often in the published papyri, sometimes in combination with other words of approximately the same meaning. For example, *fa-inqādhuhū wa-fakākuhū wa-khalāṣuhū 'alā* [*fulān*] (Grohmann: "then its recuperation, redemption and indemnification are incumbent upon [Fulān]," *APEL* I, 146, 187, 200). Variations are *fa-ḍamānu mā yajrī fī dhālika 'alā* [*fulān*] (Sourdel-Thomine and Sourdel, "Damascus," 174); *wa-taḍammanū bi-hā jamī' al-darak fī dhālika kullihī* (*APEL* I, 257, 264). For western Arabic forms, see Hoenerbach, *Urkunden*, 41-42, n. 1, and examples given there; in these, the entire *darak* clause is usually much briefer (e.g., [he delivered the property] *'alā marja' bi'l-darak*, 42).

I 2.144 - 2.145. The objection of Abū Zayd and others to the formulas given in 2.142, defining the *darak* guarantee for improvements, is based only on the omission of *fī mā yustaḥaqqu min dhālika* (in two places), "with respect to those [improvements] that may be claimed." It is not because the formula leaves out reference to the value of improvements in dirhams (see below). As Ṭaḥāwī explains, if only part of the property is claimed, but the seller is obliged to compensate the buyer for improvements that apply to the entire piece of property, the sale will be *fāsid*. The formula, in effect, specifies that the *darak* will be given only for those improvements connected with the claim.

Another argument that comes to mind, but which Ṭaḥāwī does not mention, arises from the fact that there are some improvements for which the buyer is not compensated because it is not possible to return them to the seller (or to the person making the claim) for their value. So the formula limits improvements to crops or buildings and does not include such alterations as digging wells, clearing land, or cleaning out drains. It would seem that, just as in the case of defining the *ḥuqūq* of property, there would be arguable borderline cases here as well. The authors of the *Fat. 'Ālam.* are perhaps referring to this when they say that the phrase *wa-ghayru dhālika*, "and other things," ought to be excluded from the formula (p. 420; Marghīnānī, fol. 19b).

Ṭaḥāwī makes no comment here, in his general discussion of the *darak*, on the practice of stating the amount of money that is guaranteed. Other *shurūṭ* scholars call attention to Ibn Abī Laylā's view that the *darak* is not valid unless the amount is specified, and so notaries are advised to protect their clients by writing in *min dirhamin fa-mā fawqahā* (Sarakhsī, 173) or *mā bayna dirhamin ilā kadhā wa-aqalla wa-akthara* (Marghīnānī, fol. 19a). Both formulas allow the greatest flexibility in fixing the actual amount to be paid when the time comes, and the second even puts a tentative ceiling (*ilā kadhā*) on the value of the property.

Abū Zayd's formula (2.143) and the preferred view expressed in the *Fat. 'Ālam.* (422) is to name the amount for the improvements. Here, too, they are guided by precaution against the same opinion. And since no one can tell what the value of these might amount to over a period of time, necessity requires the same flexibility in the way the clause is phrased. The *Fat. 'Ālam.* suggests a *ḥīla*: write a separate document (*'alā ḥidatin*) in which the value of improvements in dirhams is mentioned, and present it to a qadi if he should happen to follow the opinion of Ibn Abī Laylā. An alternative is to incorporate this clause in the deed of sale, but add as a safeguard that the seller's guarantee for improvements is not stipulated as a condition of the sale (see Ṭaḥāwī's first argument below, note to 2.146) and that the guarantee is made after the sale has taken place (*Fat. 'Ālam.*, 422). For Ṭaḥāwī's remarks on specifying the value of improvements, see I 6.4 - 6.12.

In practice, contracts seldom mention the amount, but substitute such expressions as *kā'inun mā kāna wa-bālighun mā balagha*, "whatever it may be or amount to." These formulas may comprehend additions to the value because of improvements, but they do not fulfill Ibn Abī Laylā's requirements.

I 2.146. Ṭaḥāwī "prefers" the formula drafted by Abū Ḥanīfa and Abū Yūsuf, but only because it is briefer and therefore contains fewer pitfalls than Abū Zayd's. His real preference, in fact, is to avoid mention of improvements altogether, and this is why he supplies *mā yajibu ʻalayhi fī dhālika*, "what [the seller] is obliged to do respecting that [delivery]" (2.156). A qadi can interpret this to mean anything he pleases.

Ṭaḥāwī's arguments may be summed up as follows: (1) the Madinese (2.151 - 2.154) and Shāfiʻī as well (2.155) relieve the seller of all responsibility for guaranteeing the value of improvements, so following the principle of *iḥtiyāṭ*, he should not be charged with it in the contract. (This point is also made in the *Fat. ʻĀlam.*, 420, although the commentary incorrectly ascribes mention of improvements to Ṭaḥāwī.) (2) Abū Zayd's formula refers to the value of the "standing" crop or an "existing" building (*qā'im*), but in some cases the *darak* is paid for the value in an uprooted or demolished state (*maqlūʻan, manqūḍan*, 2.147, 2.148, 2.153). (3) The seller must not be bound by conditions imposed by the buyer as he would be were Shaybānī's solution applied (2.149 - 2.152).

I 2.159 - 2.186. The commentary on the basic contract of sale is concluded in these paragraphs with a discussion of the witnessing formulas. In Ṭaḥāwī's instrument, these are testimony to (1) the *iqrār* of the parties to the contents of the document (2.159 - 2.167) and to their understanding of its terms (2.168); (2) the legal competence of the parties (2.169 - 2.184), especially including the affirmation that they have entered into the contract voluntarily (2.174 - 2.184); and (3) the identity of the parties (2.185 - 2.186). Because this model contract contains only the most essential elements, other details such as formulas for the date, the number of copies and the signature of the witnesses are taken up later.

I 2.160. Three contracting parties are mentioned here because Ṭaḥāwī means his remarks to apply to any document of *shahāda* and not necessarily to the formulas closing a bilateral sale contract. The arguments in the following paragraphs, to support his point that witnesses must testify to the formal acknowledgement (*iqrār*) made by the parties and not just their positive affirmation (*ithbāt*), essentially repeat what was said in I 2.84 - 2.89. See also *Fat. ʻĀlam.*, 423, for a summary.

Note that here and throughout the section on the *shahāda*, Ṭaḥāwī draws on illustrations from three sources only: Yūsuf, Hilāl and Abū Zayd. Some of the earliest authorities, among whom were Abū Ḥanīfa, Abū Yūsuf and Shaybānī, wrote no formula at all beyond the single word *shahida* (or *shahida ʻalā dhālika*) followed by the names of the witnesses (*Fat. ʻĀlam.*, 422), and this is reflected in the absence of longer formulas in many of the preserved documents. But a large number of these papyri, originating especially in Egypt and Syria, follow Ṭaḥāwī's formula quite closely. Most of these mention testimony for the *iqrār* of the parties rather than for the contents of the documents. Indeed, often the term *iqrār* is repeated after the name of each witness signing the deed (*shahida fulān ʻalā iqrār fulān...*), as if to underscore the intention.

The witnessing formula in Arabic deeds from the west differs in wording somewhat, although it too is stereotyped. Of the many formulas quoted in Hoenerbach's notes, none mention the *iqrār*. However, another feature appears in the Spanish formulary, which is absent in the Egyptian deeds (and which is undoubtedly why Ṭaḥāwī does not mention it). The witnesses "hear" the contents of the contract from the parties (*samiʻahū* [*al-madhkūr*] *minhumā*). (Hoenerbach, *Urkunden*, 2, 35, n. 1, 273, and *passim.*) The opening phrases vary as well. A Spanish handbook says that the only way to begin the *shahāda* is with *yashhadūna man yatasammā*, "the above-named witnesses testify," and only uninformed notaries (*juhhāl al-'aqqādīn*) would begin with such expressions as *ya'rifu shuhūduhū*, "the witnesses [to this document] know..." (Hoenerbach, *Urkunden*, 28.)

I 2.165. Despite this variant opinion from Abū Ḥanīfa, and despite other cases discussed in the *fiqh* works in which a sale with *talji'a* can be valid, one must take precautions and assume that *talji'a* makes a sale *bāṭil* (see above, note to 2.61 - 2.112). If it is declared invalid, or if the parties agree to cancel the sale, they are advised to have a contract drawn up in which the *talji'a* is acknowledged and the price and property returned. For this, Ṭaḥāwī gives the notary a choice of two models, a document of *shahāda* in V 17.0, and one cast in the form of an *iqrār* by the buyer in V 18.0.

I 2.172. Abū Nujayd 'Imrān b. Ḥusayn lived in Baṣra and died there in the year 52 (Ibn 'Abd al-Barr, *Istī'āb* III, No. 1969).

I 2.178 - 2.184. Ṭaḥāwī reviews the consequences of revoking or limiting the legal capacity to dispose, because he wishes to make the point that Abū Zayd's negative formulation, *ghayr maḥjūr 'alayhim* (end of 2.160) covers only a limited number of cases. Even a man imprisoned for debt, for example, is not subject to *ḥajr* and may sell his property or otherwise dispose of it by *iqrār*, according to one opinion (2.179 - 2.180). Since these rules vary, the best course for the notary is to write a single phrase that includes legal capacity and at the same time rules out a condition of slavery or minority, or imprisonment for a debt, without explicitly saying so (2.178 and 2.184). This is to say that the parties are *jawāz al-amr*, or legally competent. For the various procedures discussed here, see E. Tyan, "*Iflās* et procédure d'exécution sur les biens en droit musulman (maḏhab ḥanafite)," *SI* XXI (1964); Schacht, *Introduction*, 197-198; *EI*², s.v. "Hadjr."

In practice, formulas verifying capacity do not show much variety. Nearly all contain *jā'iz al-amr*, or some form of the phrase; see M. Sharon in *Arabica* XIII, 79-80, n. 6 and references there. *Ṣiḥḥat al-badan* and *ṣiḥḥat al-'aql* (or *thabāt al-'aql*, Marghīnānī, fol. 21a) are the usual terms to denote soundness of body and mind, although the Spanish Arabic formula commonly includes the sense of both in *fī ḥāl al-ṣiḥḥa* (cf. Yūsuf and Hilāl's formulas in 2.169).

Because of the rules governing the effect of an *iqrār* made by a person in his last illness (here, *marīḍ*), some scholars recommend adding, as a safeguard, *lā 'illa bi-himā min maraḍin wa-lā ghayrihī*, "[the parties] have no malady, neither illness nor anything else [to prevent their making a valid *iqrār*]" (2.171; Marghīnānī, fol. 21a). Ṭaḥāwī finds such phrases redundant (see his discussion in V 6.1 - 6.3). Circumlocutions, such as *jā'iz al-bay'*, *jā'iz al-waṣiyya*, "capable of entering into a sale, bequeathing a legacy," are also unnecessary, because one may arrive at the same meaning, just as safely, with *jā'iz al-amr* (V 6.1 - 6.3).

Another group of formulas that form part of the *shahāda* are those that deny coercion (*nafy al-ijbār*) and affirm that the contract was freely concluded. Besides Ṭaḥāwī's *ṭā'i'ayni ghayr mukrahayni*, "voluntarily, not under compulsion," notaries used several phrases: *ṭaw'an*, "voluntarily," (Sourdel-Thomine and Sourdel, "Damascus," 174); *ṭālibāni lā mujbarāni wa-lā muḍṭahadāni*, "demanding [it], not against their will and not under constraint" (*APEL* I, 146, 182, and *passim*; Grohmann's translation); *rāghibatan*, "[her] desiring [it]" (*APEL* I, 169, 176); *ṭībatan bi-dhālika anfusahum*, "willingly, liberally" (*APEL* I, 187; Dietrich, *Papyri*, 6; Lane, s.v. *ṭāba*, first par.).

I 2.182. Al-Qāsim b. Ma'n, chief qadi of Kufa after Sharīk b. 'Abd Allāh (below), was learned in poetry and grammar as well as *fiqh*. Shaybānī was one of his pupils for a time, as was Ismā'īl b. Ḥammād (Ibn Quṭlūbughā, in Ismā'īl's biography; see Introduction, p. 18). Qāsim died in 175. 'Abd al-Qādir I, No. 1144; Laknawī, No. 354.

Sharīk b. 'Abd Allāh al-Nakha'ī, one of Abū Ḥanīfa's companions, was qadi of Wāsiṭ and then of Kufa, where he died in 177 or 178. *Tahdhīb* IV, No. 577; 'Abd al-Qādir I, No. 669.

I 2.185. *ma'rifa bi-a'yānihimā*, "knowing them personally," means looking at the faces of the parties so that they may be recognized at a later date. According to the *Fat. 'Ālam.* (423), this is important because the *iqrār* of the parties to their own names and patronymics is not adequate; people can assume identities or exploit the fact that they have the same name as another in order to acquire property illegally. Women are not excluded from this requirement by some scholars; the witnesses must look at their faces for an effective *shahāda* (*Fat. 'Ālam.*, 423). Occasional examples are found: e.g., *wa-ra'āhā sāfirat al-wajh wa-'arafahumā bi'l-'ayn wa'l-ism*, "[the witness] saw her face unveiled, and he knows the two [parties] personally and by name" (Hoenerbach, *Urkunden*, 118).

Here Ṭaḥāwī has passed over a phrase that appears in most of his model documents, namely, that the witnesses are acquainted with the parties *ma'rifatan ṣaḥīḥatan*, "with a knowledge that is legally correct (*ṣaḥīḥ*)." The phrase strikes us as formal and imprecise, perhaps a survival from an older time. Aware of this himself, perhaps, Ṭaḥāwī later raises the question of how well and how long (cf. a variant, *ma'rifatan qadīmatan*) the witness must know a person before he can give effective testimony. The formula is discussed in I 9.9. - 9.12 (see note to these paragraphs) and IV 1.2 - 1.3. Occasionally, a synonym for *shuhūd* is *ahl al-ma'rifa bi-himā* (e.g., in an Egyptian contract of the third century; Dietrich, *Papyri*, 19).

I 5.0 - 5.10. In addition to the *barā'at al-qabḍ*, the quittance given to the buyer for the price (I 2.61 - 2.65, 2.72 - 2.73), which is an essential part of the contract, the parties may choose to insert a clause releasing the seller from responsibility for defects in the object sold. The *barā'at al-'ayb* is a general waiver of the right to return what the buyer has purchased should he discover a defect in the object or a quality below the standard he expected to receive. (See Schacht, *Introduction*, 152-153.) In phrasing his formula, Ṭaḥāwī must take account of two problems created by the *ikhtilāf*: first, is the *barā'a* valid if given before the buyer has inspected the property, or is he obliged to acquaint himself with the defects before the parties separate (5.1 - 5.7)?; second, must the seller explicitly accept the *barā'a* (5.8 - 5.10)? The contract is not discussed separately in other *shurūṭ* handbooks, although the *barā'at al-'ayb* sometimes appears in connection with the sale of slaves (III 38.4), fruit (III 29.0), and so forth. Ṭaḥāwī's short text devotes only four lines to the contract (Mehmet Murat 997, fol. 4a).

I 5.2. "Hilāl was accustomed to write [the formula] in this manner, and this is preferable to the first" means, we may gather from the discussion that follows, that Hilāl and Ṭaḥāwī wrote similar versions, and that Hilāl's is preferable to the version given in 5.1. This is actually the second and not the first, as the text says, and the confusion may simply represent an oversight or a copyist's error.

I 5.4. Yūnis b. 'Abd al-A'lā, traditionist, ascetic, and specialist in variant readings of the Qur'ānic text, died in Egypt in 264 (*Tahdhīb* XI, No. 853). Anas b. 'Iyāḍ al-Laythī, a Madinese traditionist, died in 185 or 200 (*Tahdhīb* I, No. 689). Sālim b. 'Abd Allāh b. 'Umar, the grandson of the second caliph, died about 106, and is included among the "seven scholars of Madina" (Schacht, *Origins*, s.v., index; *Tahdhīb* III, No. 807). Yaḥyā b. Sa'īd b. al-'Āṣ was a second-generation Madinese and one of Mālik's authorities (Schacht, *Origins*, 248; *Tahdhīb* XI, No. 357).

I 5.6. Fahd b. Sulaymān's name is mentioned in Kawtharī, 9, ("al-Makkī"), and in Yāqūt, *Mu'jam al-Buldān* II, 220, but nothing is known about him. M. b. Sa'īd al-Iṣbahānī is unidentified, but there is reason to believe he is the Kufan Ibn al-Iṣbahānī (d. 220) who is given a notice in the *Tahdhīb* (IX, No. 282; see also Yāqūt I, 677, and II, 386). 'Āṣim b. 'Ubayd Allāh, a traditionist of Madina, was the great-grandson of the second caliph (*Tahdhīb* V, No. 79). Two companions bear the name 'Abd Allāh b. 'Āmir b. Rabī'a, and it is difficult to know which of the two are meant here. See Ibn 'Abd al-Barr, *Istī'āb* III, Nos. 1585, 1586.

I 5.8 - 5.9. For the formula *bi-mukhāṭaba minhū iyyāhu*, see the note to I 6.20 - 6.22.

I 6.0 - 6.34. It is possible, of course, for a third person to give a guarantee against a *darak* on behalf of the seller. But because the buyer's rights will be affected (though not the terms of the sale itself), such provisions must be written into the contract of sale. The long insert of thirty-five lines (in the manuscript) which the notary introduces after the *darak* clauses is intended to set forth the guarantor's role in the transaction.

However, the passage has another purpose, and that is to define in writing the relationship between the seller and the *ḍamīn* (or *ḍāmin*, guarantor) and to describe their mutual obligations. Taken apart, the insert is, in fact, a general document of *ḍamāna*. We see this reflected in Ṭaḥāwī's commentary as he gradually abandons the terminology of sale and purchase and slips into that of suretyship and agency. For here are the more important characteristics of such a relationship, to be elaborated in contracts presented later on in the book. The seller and guarantor act as surety (*kafīl*) for one another; each makes the other his deputy (*wakīl*) in case of litigation, and his executor (*waṣī*) for the property concerned should one of them die. For detailed contracts, see especially III 46.0 - 47.2, IV 1.0, and V 13.0 - 15.0.

Discussion of the insert continues in the sections following: I 7.1 - 7.8 shows the notary how to write the *shahāda* for the *iqrār* of the guarantor; special cases are provided for in 8.0 (more than one guarantor) and in 9.0 (a woman acts as a guarantor).

Ṭaḥāwī introduces his commentary with remarks on the order of the clauses (6.1 - 6.3). The liability of the *ḍamīn* is discussed only in connection with the amount he must guarantee for improvements to the property, because here is where differences of opinion, important for phrasing the formula, are felt (6.4 - 6.12). The guarantor's role vis-à-vis the buyer and the appropriate language to be used is the subject of paragraphs 6.13 - 6.17 and 6.20 - 6.22. And finally, his position vis-à-vis the seller, and the way this must be formulated, is discussed in the longest section (6.18 - 6.19: authorization of the seller; 6.23 - 6.30: the *kafāla*, *wakāla*, *wiṣāya*; 6.31 - 6.34: cancellation of these). For parallel discussions, see the *Fat. 'Ālam.*, 424-426; Sarakhsī, 174. A much shorter document, without commentary, is in Mehmet Murat 997, fol. 5b.

I 6.0. The *ḍamīn* is liable for everything owed to the buyer by virtue of the sale contract, "*min taslīmin, darakin, raddi thamanin,* etc." Strictly speaking, the word *darak* (standing for *ḍamān al-darak*) is out of place here, because it is equivalent to *taslīm* or *radd al-thaman* (see note to I 2.140). That is, the guarantee against a fault in ownership *is* delivery of the property or return of the price. Either Ṭaḥāwī is being particularly cautious or a copyist has made a slip, more likely the second.

Radd al-thaman is to be read here only in connection with the *darak* and is not return of the price for a defect, for instance. *Raddi qīmati binā'in wa-qalīlin wa-kathīrin* refers to the improvements made by the buyer. Note that none of these obligations is stated in the ordinary formula for the *darak* given by the seller himself (see I 2.113 ff.).

Ṭaḥāwī takes for granted that the guarantee will include improvements. The *Fat. 'Ālam.*, however, makes a careful distinction between a guarantee for return of the price of the property only (424-425) and a guarantee that includes the value of improvements. The distinction is emphasized even more strongly by Sarakhsī (187-188). If only the *darak* is mentioned, Sarakhsī says, then the buyer has no right to ask to be compensated for improvements. The buyer's claim is based upon elements of uncertainty; that is, it is not known whether or not the improvements will exist, and what their value will be, at the time the guarantee is given. A guarantee for uncertain elements is like a guarantee for hidden defects, and the *kafīl* for the *darak* is not responsible for them.

I 6.1 - 6.3. The reason that Ṭaḥāwī writes this section separately from that stating the obligations of the seller is to avoid the risk that the guarantee will be taken as one of the conditions of the sale. Sarakhsī finds it adequate for the notary to write in the words *min ghayri an yakūna dhālika sharṭan fi'l-'aqd*, "without that [*kafāla*] being a condition of the sale" (174; quoted by the *Fat. 'Ālam.*, 424).

I 6.7. By *faḍl* Ṭaḥāwī means an excess number, a margin of safety; that is, the number of dinars that are specified should be somewhat more than the value of the improvements.

I 6.10. "We wrote 'and less than a dinar' " is a slip on Ṭaḥāwī's part. He does not mention dinars at all in his formula (6.4) and, in fact, strongly disapproves of specifically stating the *darak* for improvements, let alone by naming an amount (see note to I 2.146). What he undoubtedly had in mind was that *if* a notary were to mention an amount, he would be safest in adding *wa-aqalla min dīnārin*, to take account of Zufar's opinion that to say "from one to ten" is to exclude the first and the tenth.

I 6.20 - 6.22. The phrase *bi-mukhāṭaba minhū iyyāhu* is always included in Ṭaḥāwī's formula for acceptance. Here it is out of care for Abū Ḥanīfa's opinion that the person in whose favor the *ḍamān* is given (the *maḍmūn lahū*, i.e., the buyer, here) must signify his acceptance "by addressing himself directly to [the seller and guarantor]." A personal, face-to-face encounter is what Ṭaḥāwī means, as is clear from the example making an exception in the case of a dying man who acknowledges a debt (6.20).

The formula is also required for acceptance of the agreement made between the guarantor and the seller, and so is written into the contract a second time. For a witnessed contract of *wakāla*, with the formula for acceptance placed right at the beginning, see Dietrich, *Papyri*, 12-18; the contract of sale which the agent has been appointed to carry out is written on the *verso* of the document. For the formula *bi-mukhāṭaba minhū iyyāhu* in connection with acceptance of a quittance for defects, see the discussion in I 5.8 - 5.9.

I 6.23 - 6.24. Suretyship here is both for the person, guaranteeing his appearance in court in case of a lawsuit (*kafāla bi'l-nafs*), as well as for the claim (*kafāla bi'l-māl*). For the non-appearance of a litigant, see *EI*[2], s.v. "Ghā'ib."

I 6.26 - 6.30. For *jarī* and *jarāya*, instead of *wakīl* and *wakāla*, see the discussion in III 46.6 - 46.7. Muṭarrizī, *Mughrib* I, 81, explains the term, as does Lane, s.v.

I 6.28. M. b. Isḥāq, d. in Baghdad about 150. His famous biography of the Prophet is preserved in the work of Ibn Hishām (for both men, see *EI*², s.v.). Jahm b. Abī Jahm appears in the *Sīra* of Ibn Hishām (I, 162) as the *mawlā* of Ḥārith b. Ḥāṭib (Ibn al-Athīr, *Usd*, No. 865) but is not mentioned in the biographies. ʿAqīl b. Abī Ṭālib, ʿAlī's brother and some twenty years his senior (Ibn ʿAbd al-Barr, *Istīʿāb* III, No. 1834). ʿAbd Allāh b. Jaʿfar b. Abī Ṭālib, son of ʿAlī's brother, died in the year 80 (Ibn ʿAbd al-Barr, *Istīʿāb* III, No. 1488).

I 6.29. Fāṭima bint Qays al-Fihriyya was a Companion of Madina. The tradition given here concerning her divorce is mentioned in her biographical notices (Ibn ʿAbd al-Barr IV, No. 4062) as well as in those of her husband, ʿAbd al-Ḥamīd Abū ʿAmr b. Ḥafṣ (Ibn ʿAbd al-Barr IV, No. 3104). ʿAyyāsh b. Abī Rabīʿa emigrated to Abyssinia and afterwards lived in Madina (Ibn ʿAbd al-Barr III, No. 2009).

I 7.8. Sūra 16:91.

I 9.1. Ṭaḥāwī's introduction to the following paragraphs makes it appear that he is adding detail to the document for suretyship. But this is his way of making a transition to a new subject and, in fact, the section is a commentary on a general document of *shahāda* if one of the transacting parties happens to be a woman. The formula itself appears after eight paragraphs of preliminaries.

The notary is advised to add one more fact to the formula verifying capacity of the parties, which is that "you substantiate their status as adult women" (*tu'akkidu umūr al-nisā'*, 9.1) For if nothing in the contract itself (such as her name, "the mother of so-and-so") or in another existing document (that might mention her menstruation, for example) indicates that she is of age to manage her own affairs (9.2), then the document requires her *iqrār* stating her majority (9.8). A woman's legal status with respect to her age is more easily concealed than a man's and that is why she must make the acknowledgement, while he need not do so (Mehmet Murat 997, fol. 4a). Ṭaḥāwī writes the formula for several women, but it is intended, of course, to serve for one woman as well.

This part of the testimony is given by secondary witnesses; the full witnessing formula, the *shahāda ʿalā shahāda*, is presented in 10.0, the final section of Part I.

I 9.5. *Kitāb al-Amālī al-Kaysāniyyāt*, by his pupil Sulaymān b. Shuʿayb. Partly edited Ḥydarābād, 1360/1930. See *GAL* S I, 291.

I 9.9 - 9.12. For the witnessing formula *maʿrifatan ṣaḥīḥatan*, see note to I 2.185. Ṭaḥāwī makes it clear that the term *maʿrifatan qadīmatan* ("of long acquaintance") is unacceptable because it cannot be precisely defined. But it would be interesting to know exactly what he expects *ṣaḥīḥ* to mean (technically, fully valid in law): how well acquainted, how deep must that knowledge go? The minimum requirements at least, are explained in IV 1.4: it is possible for the witness to testify he knows someone if he has been introduced to him personally, by a group of reliable persons who themselves know that person, personally, by name, and by *nisba*.

I 9.13. *al-bulūgh minhinna lā yuʿlam illā bi-qawlayni.* That is, her majority cannot be known unless the notarity writes, in addition to her *iqrār*, a positive statement (*ithbāt*) confirming her acknowledgement that she is an adult. The witness, then, testifies further that her majority is apparent, something that can be visualized (*mawhūm*, 9.14 - 9.15); (e.g., *inbāt*, in par. 9.6, refers to the stage of physical development characterized in women by the protuberance of breasts). For the opposite case, where the *ithbāt* alone is not sufficient but needs an *iqrār* in addition, see I 2.84 - 2.89, 2.160.

I 9.10. Sūra 36:39.

I 10.1 - 10.2. It is important to note that the primary witnesses testify to the fact that the secondary witnesses have given their testimony, and not to that testimony itself. See also I 4.4 - 4.5.

PART II

II 1.0 - 4.1. The subject of these four sections is the contract of sale in which two or more persons act as one contracting party. Frequently such contracts give rise to a joint relationship, but in these pages there is no clear distinction between the true joint contract and that called (in modern legal terminology) "several." In the first, the parties are jointly bound to fulfill their obligations, and in the same way, can require performance in common. The second is more usual in Islamic law; each party acts independently to enforce his individual interest, and is liable separately from his partner.

Ṭaḥāwī's models combine elements of both types of contracts. For example, in a discussion of which of two sellers (the acting seller or the principal) is liable for the *darak*, he raises the question of whether each seller owns half the house independently, in which case he can act on his own, or whether each seller owns both halves in common with his partner (1.1 - 1.3). Again, in connection with the use of the term *ṣafqa wāḥida* (see note to I 2.32 - 2.33), may two partners act independently in their claim because of a hidden defect, or must they act together (II 3.1 - 3.4)? The discussion of consent (*idhn*; see especially 1.9 - 1.10), and providing an alternative to mentioning consent (2.0), also reflect the absence of clearly drawn lines.

The contracts in 1.0 and 2.0 are for two or more sellers; the two following (3.0 and 4.0) are models for two or more buyers. 2.0 and 4.0 show how the contract is written for unequal shares. A corresponding section, much abbreviated, is given in Mehmet Murat 997, fols. 5b - 6b.

II 1.3. Sarakhsī's solution for this difference of opinion is slightly different. He recommends stating explicitly in the document that each seller is the *wakīl* and the *ḍamīn* for the other (174-175). Thus they both become liable for the *darak* (or in his text, the *'uhda*, by which he means any other guarantee in favor of the buyer, as well), and one seller will then have recourse to the other.

II 1.9 - 1.10. The sale of jointly-owned property requires that one seller give a mandate to the others to sell to an outside person. This is because each partner owns a portion of the property of his co-partners; since the shares which constitute the whole cannot actually be separated from one another, each thus sells a fraction of his partners' shares. The secondary question raised here is, if the shares are unequal, how does this rule apply?

According to Abū Ḥanīfa and others, the one who owns the larger of two shares gives his permission. Each sells one-half of the property in the sense that each participates equally in the sale. But seller A, owning two-thirds of the property, will sell his half separately (*khāṣṣatan*), entirely out of his larger share. Seller B, in order to sell one-half, sells his third plus one-sixth of the property belonging to his partner. This can be represented in the following way:

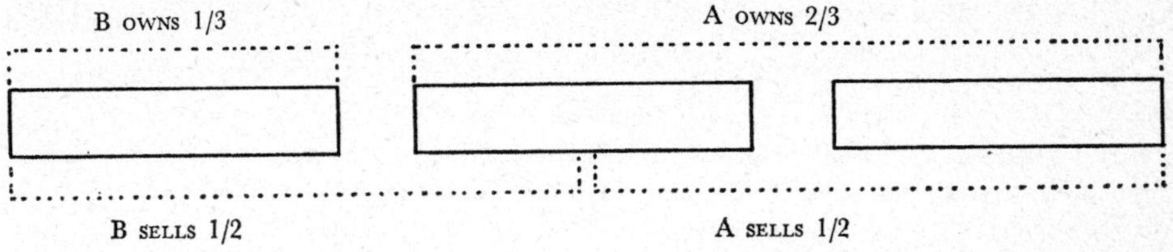

Therefore B, the owner of the smaller share, must have the consent of A to sell A's property.

Zufar (1.10) has a different view. The shares of each are intermingled, and no matter how large or small the relative proportions, each sells part of the others's property:

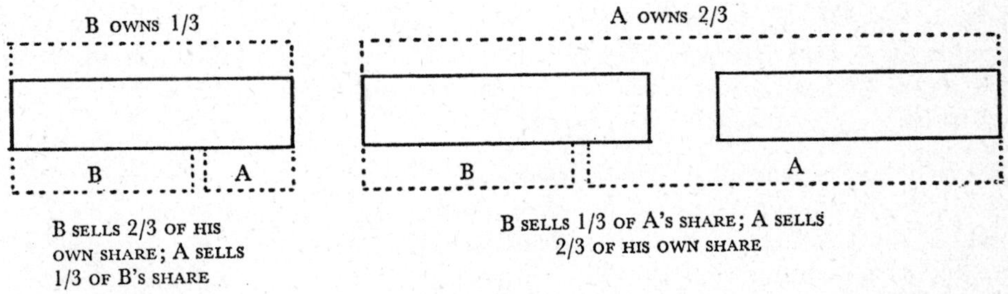

Therefore, it is not a matter of one giving permission to the other, although the implication is that both do so.

Ṭaḥāwī embraces both opinions in his formula by mentioning the consent of each seller in the most general terms possible. But if the notary would avoid the difference of opinion altogether, he is advised to follow the model inserted after the clause naming the total price (2.0). Instead of mentioning the proportion of the whole that each sells, for a corresponding proportion of the price, the notary specifies the number of shares and the exact price each receives (2.3, 4.1). Then, even though the shares are joint and indivisible (*shā'i'atan ghayr maqsūmatin*), each sells his own separately (*khāṣṣatan*) and consent need not be mentioned.

An interesting document following just this scheme is preserved in the collection of the Egyptian Library (*APEL* II, 15-21). Four owners, two men and two women, apparently not related to one another , sell a house to another person. They hold unequal, indivisible shares, whose total number (as is common) is twenty-four. The contract specifies their respective shares and the prices they receive according to Ṭaḥāwī's order of clauses.

II 5.0. This contract appears, at first glance, very much like the one provided in I 6.0. But there are two important differences. Here, Ṭaḥāwī provides a model for a sale in which the buyer has not yet taken possession of the thing sold, but in which a third party guarantees its delivery in the future. Second, if the property itself cannot be delivered, the guarantor need not undertake to furnish an equivalent on behalf of the seller. Instead, the sale, as well as the agreement between *ḍamīn* and seller, is cancelled.

II 6.0. The formula for the purchase of more than one piece of property in a single transaction requires only a simple adjustment in the description of the boundaries. Ṭaḥāwī has already discussed problems of wording raised by the *ikhtilāf* (I 2.24 - 2.40), and his main concern here is how the notary is to distinguish between houses that have common boundaries and those that are located in various places. The *Fat. ʿĀlam.* considers the same contract, but emphasizes instead identifying the location of the property (426-427).

II 7.0 - 8.0. The brief formula for making an exception of part of the property sold is introduced in these two sections. The formula will appear as an important clause in many contracts scattered throughout the book. For example, the land is excepted in the sale of a shop (II 20.0), date palms (III 22.0), a standing crop (III 27.0), a wall (II 31.0); in the sale of land, the fruit on the trees or the crop in the field can be the objects of exception (III 2.0) as can a small plot of land (*buqʿa*) within a larger area (II 28.0). The beams in a wall (II 32.0) and a building constructed after purchase of the property and before resale (IV 10.0) may also be excluded.

Here Ṭaḥāwī is concerned with a contract in which the seller wishes to reserve for himself part of a *dār* (7.0), or exclude from the sale a road running through two adjacent pieces of property (8.0). In the first case, Ṭaḥāwī's aim is to delineate the *ḥukm* of various component parts of the *dār*: how the *bayt*, *manzil* and *ghurfa* are to be treated. In the second case, Ṭaḥāwī establishes a way of dealing with an easement.

II 7.0. It will be noted that a *bayt*, although it is normally only one room, can have all the rights and appurtenances that belong to the entire house complex, or *dār*. Of course, this will be the case only if the *bayt* is defined as a room on the ground floor of a building, or as a single-storied structure with an open space (*barāḥ*) above. If a *bayt* is a room on the upper floor, it will not have all these *ḥuqūq*. If both lower and upper *bayts* are excluded from the sale (7.0 bis), the *ḥuqūq* go with the lower. Further, the *daraja*, or staircase that leads to the upper *bayt* is here defined as one of the appurtenances of the *dār*; but it would be possible, of course, for it to be within the boundaries of the lower *bayt* (Mehmet Murat 997, fol. 6b), in which case it need not be mentioned in the deed.

The *Fat. ʿĀlam.* (427) adds to the description of the *bayt* by stating its function: e.g., the entire *bayt* which is for summer use (*bayt ṣayfī*), used only in the winter (*shatawī*), a *bayt* that is used as a kitchen (*bayt al-maṭbakh*), to keep firewood (*bayt al-ḥaṭab*), as a privy (*bayt al-khalāʾ*) a subterranean room (*bayt al-ṭabāq*).

In the fourth and last contract, the *ghurfa* to which Ṭaḥāwī refers is simply a term for an upstairs room, synonymous with *bayt ʿulūw* (see the long discussion in the *Fat. ʿĀlam.*, 428-430). It and the *bayt sufl* together comprise the *manzil*, which is usually a two-storied structure (see II 15.1, 16.3). For *ḥujra*, *maskin*, and so forth, see notes to II 9.0.

The *barāḥ* is here an open space above a one-story house, representing a hypothetical upper story. From its more general meaning as an open area of any kind (Muṭarrizī, *Mughrib* I, 33), it can denote land without trees (as in Sarakhsī, 189) or an open tract of land (II 28.1). For the use of *zuqāq* (by-street, alley) in Egyptian documents and parallels in the Greek papyri from Egypt, see Dietrich, *Papyri*, 60-61, n. 5.

Some terms for dwellings have been noted here because just as usage varied considerably in different times and places, so their definitions in the standard lexicons will vary. In any case, it is important to know what they mean in the context of Ṭaḥāwī's formulas. Ṭaḥāwī himself continues to discuss these terms so that the notary may make the appropriate distinctions in his document. See especially II 15.0 - 17.2.

II 8.0. Ṭaḥāwī envisions a private road traversing two adjacent pieces of property and connecting with a highway on the opposite side of the plot being sold. The smaller road is one of the *ḥuqūq* or rights belonging to the neighbor's house and is jointly owned by both. Its sale would block the neighbor's access to the main highway. Therefore, it legally cannot be sold and this is why the notary must write it into the document as an exception to the sale. (Of course, the adjacent property may belong to the seller, who will want to maintain his right of access, but this is not the essential problem here.) Other examples of easements will be found in II 28.1 - 28.4, 30.1, and in Sarakhsī, 189-190. A parallel contract is in Mehmet Murat 997, fol. 8a.

II 8.1. Ṭaḥāwī here points out that the seller cannot make an exception by saying "I sell you this house on condition that (*'alā anna*) there be a road belonging to the neighboring house"; he must say " ... except for (*illā, ghayr, siwā, ḥashā al-ṭarīq*) the road on the property I sell you." His argument concerns the price: the notary must not word the formula in such a way that the total price includes both what is excepted and what is sold. The road would then be sold for an unknown price and that would make the sale void. (It is taken for granted that the sale would be void for another reason, namely that the seller has made a condition [in his saying *'alā anna*] to his own or another's advantage.) See the *Fat. 'Ālam.*, 468, for the same contract and discussion.

II 9.0 - 14.0. Connected with earlier sections on contracts for jointly-owned property are these paragraphs dealing with the purchase of part of a piece of joint property which has been divided into shares. Here, however, the emphasis is on the property itself and not on the ownership (see note to II 1.9 - 1.10), for the shares may be in the hands of one person as well as several. The first contract deals with divided shares; each share is equal to a known and physically defined part of the property. The other contracts concern the purchase of undivided joint shares, where no single structure or unit of land is sold separately, but a fraction of the whole is purchased.

II 9.0. The term *manzil* (here, pl. *manāzil*) in the title of the chapter is meant to refer to any dwelling which may be sold as a divided share of a *dār*. In the following contract, Ṭaḥāwī uses a *hujra* as his example, meant as a synonym of *manzil* (see the remark at the end of II 15.0 and Sarakhsī, 175). Although a *ḥujra* is usually defined as a single room (i.e., a *bayt*), here it is a fairly complex dwelling or a small house (one of the meanings given by Dozy, *Suppl.*, s.v.). That is, it has more than one story and its own road, as well as various appurtenances, as the descriptive formula shows.

The *manzil* itself is also defined as two *manzils*, one on top of the other, or two *bayts* (II 15.0, Sarakhsī, 176-177), although the upper story may be called one of the *ḥuqūq* of the lower *manzil* (II 15.1; see the contract in Sourdel-Thomine and Sourdel, "Damascus," 173 and 175, n. 2, where *manzilā* [*ishtarā manzilā*] should be read as an accusative rather than as an incorrectly written dual; the two *bayts* mentioned in this contract are another way of saying one *manzil*). The standard definition, repeated by Sarakhsī, "a place where a man lives with his family and belongings," implies that such household appurtenances as kitchens, water pipes and courtyards are included, and this is borne out by references in the papyri (*APEL* I, 267-272; II, 10-15, 15-21).

In its chief model for the sale of divided shares, the *Fat. 'Ālam.* avoids using the term *manzil* to represent a divisible entity. Instead, the expression *qiṭ'a muqaddara*, "a piece [of the property] that is measured [in terms of proportion to the whole]" is used (427). Specific terms are used, naturally, in instructing the notary in differences between various parts of the *dār.*

II 9.0 bis. If the shares that constitute the private road can be specified, then the notary ought to do so. The road is sold with the *ḥujra* because the purchaser must be guaranteed access to his property; and since the road will traverse the open courtyard of the main house property (*sāḥa, 'arṣa, qā'a*) and its entrance way (*dihlīz*), which are not being sold, it must be clearly separated from these two. Second, the notary must state that the property being sold and the access road are both parts of the same *dār* (9.5 - 9.6). Finally, he must word his accessory formula so that the farthest limits of the road include the entry gate, but not be interpreted to include the main road (9.4, 9.6 - 9.12). For the same easement, in connection with the purchase of a *bayt,* see II 17.0, and of a *buq'a,* II 28.0.

The word *ṭarīq* is used in these paragraphs to mean both the main thoroughfare and the private road, although *ṭarīq* and *zuqāq* (see note to II 7.0) are often qualified in the papyri: for example, *al-ṭarīq al-mārra minhā* (*APEL* I, 145), *ṭarīq ghayr nāfidhin* or *zuqāq ghayr bādin,* "blind alley, dead end" (Dietrich, *Papyri,* 60-61), *zuqāq nāfidh,* "thoroughfare" (*APEL* I, 268).

II 9.6. Sūra 2:187 and Sūra 5:6.

II 10.0. The standard contract for the purchase of joint, undivided shares should specify the number of shares bought (rather than the fraction or proportion of the *dār,* 10.12 - 10.15; the *Fat. 'Ālam.* consistently mentions a fraction, 427 and 428), and should contain certain formulas imposed by the nature of the transaction. Accordingly, to avoid difficulties about the effectual delivery of the property, Ṭaḥāwī introduces a new formula for transfer of possession: *kamā yuqbaḍ al-mushā'*, "in the way one takes possession of joint property." (Sarakhsī distinguishes between *qabḍ ḥukmī* and *qabḍ ḥissī,* 186; the *Fat. 'Ālam.* resolves the difficulty by having the notary write first that the buyer took possession of the thing sold, and second, that he took possession of the entire *dār,* 428-429). The second problem concerns the formulas for inspection and for definition of the boundaries. For either, the entire *dār,* and not just the shares sold, must be mentioned. An undivided share cannot, of course, be "seen." And although it has no boundaries, still, Ṭaḥāwī reasons, part of the boundaries of the *dār* are sold and so they must all be described.

The contracts following (11.0 - 14.0) provide for several variations in the ownership of either the shares sold or of the rest of the property. The main concern here is to define this ownership, but at the same time, to avoid the buyer's acknowledgement of it. Once again, this refers to the opinion of Ibn Abī Laylā, Zufar, and the Madinese scholars that the acknowledgement may prejudice the buyer's claim to the *darak* in the future (11.4 - 11.7, 13.1 - 13.4).

A version of 10.0, containing only the essential formulas, appears in Mehmet Murat 997 fols. 8b-9a. There are no corresponding documents in either Sarakhsī or Marghīnānī, but examples in the papyri are numerous. See, for example, *APEL* I, 255-267; II, 3-21. The *Fat. 'Ālam.* does not make a systematic distinction between contracts for divided and for undivided shares, but considers them together. Undivided shares on pp. 428, 429, 433, 434.

II 11.8 - 11.10. The term *sahm* is used for the unit share of the property itself, while *ḥiṣṣa* refers to the interest of the owner of that share in the property and is synonymous with *ḥaqq.*

Ṭaḥāwī's formula, using *ḥiṣṣa* and *ḥaqq*, avoids direct mention of ownership, and also satisfies two opposing opinions on the identity of the *sahm* and the *ḥiṣṣa*.

II 15.1 - 17.2. If the notary is to draw up an accurate document for the sale of parts of a *dār*, he must be aware of the rules governing the definition of various types of structures. 15.0 shows him how to draft a document for both stories of a *manzil*; 16.0 for an upper or lower *bayt*. In the second case, each *bayt* must be purchased separately, or at least distinguished in the contract as separate, if both are bought. Yet, even though the lower *bayt* alone may be specified in the contract, and carefully defined as such, Ṭaḥāwī makes doubly sure that the upper story is excluded by adding the formula for exception (16.0 and 17.0; a similar case appears in 20.0 ter, in which a shop is purchased without its upper story).

The subject of boundaries appears once again in a discussion of whether or not they can be defined when the upper *bayt* alone is sold (17.1 - 17.2). Ṭaḥāwī argues that these boundaries are "the upper stories of [other] people's houses" (*manāzil al-aqwām*); Sarakhsī, quoting Ṭaḥāwī, adds that "surrounding this upper story is a *ḥujra*," 178.

II 18.0 - 22.0. The title of the *bāb* introducing these contracts for the sale of a building without its land does not reveal a fact of some importance: the land is owned not by the seller, but by a third party. Consequently, certain steps must be taken to insure the buyer against future claims preventing his use of the land. Thus, besides the excepting clause (20.1), the contract will include the seller's *iqrār* renouncing all prior rights to the land. Second, transfer of possession of the land (i.e., the exclusive right to use it) must be made explicit (20.2).

II 18.0. The formula provided for the seller's *iqrār* belongs, like the *ḍamān al-darak*, to the final settlement clauses. It is intended to affirm the final relinquishment of rights by virtue of ownership, possession, or lease; hereafter the seller is barred from making any claim that might upset the transfer of these rights to use the land.

The same formula is found in more detail in III 9.0, in a contract in which the seller of a fruit crop gives up his rights to *kharāj* land, acknowledging that it is now in the possession of the buyer. In connection with other kinds of transactions, see III 15.0, 18.0, and IV 1.0, 6.0, and 7.0.

Neither this clause, nor the reverse formulation, declaring that the buyer now has free disposition over his property, appear in ordinary documents of sale in Ṭaḥāwī's text. But in practice it was not uncommon. For example, in a contract from Spain we see *wa-lam yabqa li'l-bā'i' fi'l-jamī'i ḥaqqun bi-wajhin wa-lā bi-ḥālin*, "and there remain no rights to the seller in the entire [thing sold] for any reason and in any way whatsoever" (Hoenerbach, *Urkunden*, 272). A Shāfi'ī formulation has *fa-lā 'āda baqā* [*sic*] *li'l-bayyā' ḥaqqun min al-ḥuqūq*, "the seller no longer retains any rights [therein]" (Serjeant, "Ḥabbān," 125).

The second formula introduced in this contract transfers the right to use the land to the new owner. However, Ṭaḥāwī suggests that this be reinforced by inserting an additional transfer clause which he gives at the beginning of 21.0. And as if this were not enough, the seller formally appoints the buyer his *wakīl* during his lifetime and executor after his death insofar as the land is concerned.

The term *ism fulān* which occurs in the transfer clause in 18.0 is somewhat ambiguous and does not appear again in the text to help us discover its meaning. It probably refers to the name of a previous owner, the name by which the plot is known. The usufruct, then, is a gratuitous loan and a voluntary act of assistance (*'āriyya wa-ma'ūna*) on his part, that becomes passed on from one to another. The seller had not rented the land before he sold his property, but he too had acquired the use of it through this means. In the papyri I have examined, the term occurs only twice, and both texts support this interpretation. In a document of *shahāda* for the sublease of state land, Grohmann reads "belonging to that [land] which passed under the name of [Fulān]," *APEL* II, 59. And in a request for information concerning the survey of a garden (*misāḥat al-janān*) the land is worked by one person, but it is in the name of, or goes by the name of, another (David-Weill, "Louvre," 283).

The remaining contracts in this section elaborate on 18.0 and 21.0. One concerns the sale of a *ḥānūt*, or shop, making exceptions of part of the *ḥānūt*; another names the *ḥuqūq* of the building in more detail, although not nearly to the extent that the parallel formula in the *Fat. 'Ālam.* (423) does. The inserted clauses in 22.0 protect the buyer from arbitrary cancellation of the *wakāla* or the *wiṣāya* on the part of the seller. The seller cannot remove the buyer from this position, Ṭaḥāwī argues, because he was obliged to appoint him on behalf of the owner of the land, not on his own behalf (22.2).

Ṭaḥāwī's abridged version combines the principal documents in this section, uninterrupted by a commentary (Mehmet Murat 997, fols. 9a-10a). Marghīnānī's text is quite brief, placing all the emphasis on describing the *ḥuqūq*. Although the formula excepting the land is included in the contract, he remarks that this is not necessary as long as the land is not listed among the *ḥuqūq* (fols. 25a-25b). The *Fat. 'Ālam.* leaves out the excepting clause altogether (432). In Ṭaḥāwī's opinion, this will make the sale *fāsid* (20.1). There is no parallel contract in Sarakhsī.

II 19.1 - 19.3. The term *nuqḍ* (rubble, debris; "materials that remain after something has been demolished," Dozy, *Suppl.*, s.v.) is frequently found in the papyri, usually as part of the appurtenance formula. Grohmann, however, reads *naqḍ* (pl. of *naqḍa*) and translates it "beams" and "timbers" because *khashab*, "timbers," occurs in similar passages. But *nuqḍ* (or *naqḍ*) always seems to appear in combination with *binā'* and *finā'* in a series of opposites (such as *'āmir* and *ghāmir*, *bāṭin* and *ẓāhir*, and so on). *Nuqḍ*, therefore, seems to be more appropriate to the context. In any case, Ṭaḥāwī's discussion leaves no doubt how we are to understand the word in these contracts. His objection to the notary using the word is repeated again in II 31.1, in connection with the purchase of a wall in order to demolish it for its materials. See also I 2.149 ff. (*manqūḍ, maqlū'; qā'im, mabnī*).

II 20.3 - 20.4. Although the MS clearly reads *arḍ al-jawn* (in five places), perhaps a better reading would be *arḍ al-juruf*, a term which has the meaning of land in a valley or on the bank of a river, that has been eroded or otherwise undermined by a torrent (see Lane, s.v., for a complete definition; also Fagnan, *Additions*; and O. Rescher, *Vocabulaire de recueil de Bokhārī*, Stuttgart, 1922). This would be justified not only by reference to the *nahr*, but also because of the mention of the *muqāsama* tax (the "share tax," A. Ben Shemesh, *Taxation in Islam* [Leiden, 1965], II, 37-41; or "proportional *kharāj*," Aghnides, 377). The *kharāj* tax levied on the produce would be proportionately lower where the land is difficult to cultivate or the yield is low or risky. (The same principle is applied when the land must be irrigated.) On the other hand, *arḍ al-jawn*, a hollow or depression in the land, makes little sense here.

II 23.0 - 29.0. Until now, Ṭaḥāwī's text has dealt with the sale of property as a single entity. In these paragraphs, a variation is introduced in which property is sold by the unit of measurement. The number of *dhirā'* (cubits, see below, note to 23.0) and the price for all of them are specified in the offer, the land is measured by professional surveyors (*dharrā'*; *qassām*, partitioners), transfer of price and property takes place, and the sale is concluded. These additional steps and the order in which they occur raise two points of importance for the notary.

First, the practical procedures for measuring the land must be reflected in the document. The surveying itself and the fees of the *dharrā'* are stipulated as a condition of the sale, and the seller must fulfill this performance just as he must meet his other obligations (23.1 - 23.3). Further, the presence of the seller, and especially of the buyer, at the surveying is necessary since both must give their *iqrār* to the fact of measuring as well as to the results, and the buyer must be able to give quittance (23.6 - 23.14; 24.1).

Second, the notary must be aware of the rules if it should turn out that the number of *dhirā'* stipulated by the seller does not correspond to the number determined by the surveyors after the property has been measured. If the buyer chooses to take the property at the specified price (in general, he has the option), two insertions to the document are provided as models for the notary, which he copies depending on whether the stipulated *dhirā'* are more or less than the actual number (24.0 and 25.0). The essential clause records the *iqrār* of the parties that "without any doubt whatsoever" they are aware of the number of cubits that constitute the property sold. Various reasons are given for not stating directly the actual discrepancy.

However, the notary might wish to advise his clients to avoid this problem, entailing risks and complications, by concluding the contract on a different basis altogether. A document is provided in which each cubit is sold separately, each for a specified price (26.0; "on condition that the *dār* consists of one thousand *dhirā'*, each *dhirā'* for *x* dirhams"). And because each unit is sold separately, the contract must mention that each has its own share, proportionately, of the *ḥuqūq* (26.1 - 26.4). The model contract for the sale of land that has a subterranean irrigation channel (*sarab*) is intended as an example of this. A contract of this kind has certain advantages: the price fluctuates according to the actual number of cubits found (26.2), and neither party has the right to cancel the sale if there is a discrepancy (25.6 - 25.7).

It is even possible that one piece of property will be sold in two ways, so Ṭaḥāwī furnishes a document in which a large piece of land is sold by the cubit, as in 26.0, but a small plot (*buq'a*) within it is sold at the same time as a single unit (28.0).

Finally, a variable is introduced which requires an additional document of *shahāda* (29.0). In this case, the variable is whether or not the parties have taken possession before the property was measured. If the land was measured after the contract of sale was concluded and the document recording it drawn up, but before the parties took possession, secondary witnesses are called. These testify to the *iqrār* of the parties that the land was measured and that both parties accept the surveyors' results; then a new deed is drafted incorporating the testimony of the secondary witnesses. For similar contracts, see Sarakhsī, 188-189. Mehmet Murat 997 contains the essential clauses only, with a very brief commentary (fols. 10a-10b).

II 23.0. The term *dār* is used in these contracts in the broadest sense, to include land alone, although the models given are meant to apply to house property as well. Here we may note Sarakhsī's definition of a *dār* as a noun that may mean empty land (*ṣaḥrā'*) as well as buildings (179). Presumably the land need not be surrounded by a wall, as is usually the case with a house complex.

Because a considerable variety of cubits were in common use, the notary had to specify which one was meant in the transaction. Normally, this would be the cubit employed by the *qassām* of the town, the dividers of joint or inheritance property. Ṭaḥāwī adds the qualification *mukassara*, which means a cubit of middling size (*wasaṭ*), compared to the *dhirā‘ al-malik*, the "king's cubit" (Sarakhsī, 188; Muṭarrizī defines the *mukassara* specifically as six handsbreadths, one short of the "king's cubit," and notes that it is the *dhirā‘ al-‘āmma*, the one in common use [*Mughrib*, I, 191]).

The task of measuring or surveying the land (*misāḥa*) was undertaken by professionals or semi-professionals appointed by the court (*dharrā‘ ‘udūl*). Their technical competence was the concern of the qadi who appointed them, and not of the parties who had to be present at the surveying (see 24.1).

For the different kinds of *dhirā‘*, see *EI²*, s.v.; Grohmann, *Einführung*, 171-176; Hinz, *Islamische Masse und Gewichte* (Leiden, 1955), 55-62; to the lists given in these, we may add the *dhirā‘ mukassara*. For official surveyors, partitioners (the *māsiḥ*, *qassāb*, but not the *dharrā’*, who were probably employed only for private transactions) see C. Cahen, "Contribution à l'étude des impôts dans l'Égypte médiévale," *JESHO* V (1962), 267 ff. For examples of *misāḥa* in the papyri, see Dietrich, *Papyri*, 51 and n. 4 on p. 54 with references there; David-Weill, "Louvre," 283 and n. on 284.

II 30.0 - 32.0. In these contracts for the purchase of a wall, Ṭaḥāwī is interested primarily in the clauses describing the property, because more often than not a wall will border on someone else's property. Inadequate definition could result in quarrels and litigation.

The concern is emphasized in cases where the beams in the wall are made an object of exception (32.0), for the wooden timbers, besides being valuable material in most parts of the Middle East, may also act as supports for a contiguous wall and for adjoining upper rooms. Furthermore, excepting the beams gives rise to a rather novel situation, and the contract must take account of this. Since the owner of the beams (i.e., the seller) has rights in the wall at the places where the beams join it, these places must be excepted as well. The seller thus becomes a co-owner in the wall he has just sold (32.3). The same concern would exist in the sale of a *sābāṭ*, a roof between two walls, or between two houses under which is a thoroughfare. The contract appears in the *Fat. ‘Ālam.* although these issues are not raised there (431).

For parallel contracts, see the *Fat. ‘Ālam.* (431-432), which adds nothing new to Ṭaḥāwī's text. Sarakhsī devotes only a few lines to the contract (181), but furnishes a long discussion of the rules pertaining to the division of a wall between two co-owners (191-192). A document of *shahāda* for such a division is found in *APEL* I, 133-137.

II 31.2. Ṭaḥāwī's authorities do not usually write the *darak* guarantee clauses in these contracts, presumably because a wall is not considered *‘aqār*, immovable property (see III 22.0, 38.0). But Ṭaḥāwī, always more conservative than they are, retains it as a precaution.

ABBREVIATIONS AND WORKS CITED

'Abd al-Qādir: 'Abd al-Qādir al-Qurashī, M. b. Abi'l-Wafā'. *Jawāhir al-Muḍiyya fī Ṭabaqāt al-Ḥanafiyya*. 2 vols. Ḥydarābād, 1332/1914.

"Adhkār al-Ḥuqūq": Schacht (ed.), "Das kitāb aḏkār al-ḥuqūq... des aṭ-Ṭaḥāwī."

Aghnides, N.P. *Mohammedan Theories of Finance*. New York, 1916 (reprinted Lahore, 1961).

APEL: Grohmann, *Arabic Papyri in the Egyptian Library*.

Baer, G. *Population and Society in the Arab East*. New York, 1964.

Ben Shemesh, A. *Taxation in Islam*. 3 vols. Leiden, 1965-1969.

Bibliotheken: Schacht, "Aus orientalischen Bibliotheken."

Brockelmann, C. *Geschichte der arabischen Litteratur*. 2nd ed., 2 vols. Leiden, 1943-1949; and *Supplement*, 3 vols. Leiden, 1937-1942.

——. *History of the Islamic Peoples*. Trans. M. Perlmann and J. Carmichael. New York, 1947.

Brunschvig, R. "Conceptions monétaires chez les juristes musulmans," *Arabica*, XIV (1967), 113-143.

Caetani, L. *Annali dell'Islam*. 10 vols. Milan, 1905-1926.

Cahen, C. "A propos des Shuhūd," *SI*, XXXI (1970), 71-79.

——. "Contribution à l'étude des impôts dans l'Égypte médiévale," *JESHO*, V (1962), 244-278.

——. "Notes de diplomatique arabo-musulmane," *JA*, 251 (1963), 311-325.

Chehata, C. *Essai d'une théorie générale de l'obligation en droit musulman hanéfite*. Paris, 1969.

Classen: Flügel, *Die Classen der ḥanefitischen Rechtsgelehrten*.

Coulson, N.J. *A History of Islamic Law*. Edinburgh, 1964 (*Islamic Surveys* 2).

Dār al-Kutub al-Miṣriyya. *Fihrist al-Kutub al-'Arabiyya al-Maḥfūẓa bi'l-Kutubkhāna al-Khidīwiyya al-Miṣrīyya*. 7 vols. Cairo, 1305-1308 / 1887-1890.

David-Weill, J. *Catalogue général du Musée arab du Caire*: *Les bois épigraphes jusqu'à l'époque mamlouke*. Cairo, 1931.

——. "Un nouveau titre de propriété daté," *Mélanges Gaudefroy-Demombynes*. Cairo, 1935-1945, 141-146.

——. "Papyrus arabes du Louvre," *JESHO*, VIII (1965), 277-311.

Dhahabī, *Mushtabih*: Dhahabī, M. b. Aḥmad. *Kitāb al-Mushtabih fi'l-Rijāl*: *Asmā'ihim wa-Ansābihim*. 2 vols. Beirut, 1962.

Dietrich, *Briefe*: Dietrich, A. *Arabische Briefe aus der Papyrussammlung der Hamburger Staats- und Universitäts-Bibliothek*. Hamburg, 1955 (*Veröffentlichungen aus der Hamburger Staats- und Universitäts-Bibliothek*, V).

Dietrich, *Papyri*: Dietrich, A. *Arabische Papyri aus der Hamburger Staats- und Universitäts-Bibliothek*. Leipzig, 1937 (*Abhandlungen für die Kunde des Morgenlandes*, XXII/3).

Dozy, *Suppl.*: Dozy, R. *Supplément aux dictionnaires arabes*. 2nd ed. Leiden and Paris, 1927.

EI[1]: *The Encyclopaedia of Islam*. 4 vols. and Supplement. Leiden, 1913-1938.

EI[2]: *The Encyclopaedia of Islam*. New edition. Leiden, 1954-.

El-Ali, Saleh. "Muslim Estates in Hidjaz in the first Century A.H.," *JESHO*, II (1959), 247-261.

Fagnan, *Additions*: Fagnan, E. *Additions aux dictionnaires arabes*. Algiers, 1923.

Fat. 'Ālam.: *Al-Fatāwā al-'Ālamgīriyya*. 6 vols. Calcutta, 1251/1835.

Fihrist: Ibn al-Nadīm, *Kitāb al-Fihrist*.

Flügel, G. *Die Classen der ḥanefitischen Rechtsgelehrten*. Leipzig, 1861 (*Abhandlungen der philologisch-historischen Classe der königlich sächsischen Gesellschaft der Wissenschaften*, III, 267-358).

FWAP: Grohmann, *From the World of Arabic Papyri*.

GAL: Brockelmann, *Geschichte der arabischen Litteratur*.

Goitein, S.D. *A Mediterranean Society, The Jewish Communities of the Arab World as Portrayed in the Documents of the Cairo Geniza*. Vol. 1, *Economic Foundations*. Berkeley and Los Angeles, 1967.

Goldziher, I. *Muhammedanische Studien*. 2 vols. Halle, 1888-1890.

Grohmann, A. (ed.). *Arabic Papyri in the Egyptian Library*. 5 vols. Cairo, 1934 ff.

Grohmann, *Einführung*: Grohmann, A. *Einführung und Chrestomathie zur arabischen Papyruskunde*. Vol. 1, *Einführung*. Prague, 1954 (*Monographie Archivu Orientálniho*, XIII).

Grohmann, A. *From the World of Arabic Papyri*. Cairo, 1952.

——. "Probleme der arabischen Papyrusforschung," *Archiv Orientální*. Prague, 1931.

Ḥajjī Khalīfa: Ḥajjī Khalīfa, Kātib Çelebī. *Kashf al-Ẓunūn*. Ed. with Latin trans. G. Flügel. 7 vols. Leipzig, 1835-1858.

Hinz, W. *Islamische Masse und Gewichte*. Leiden, 1955 (*Handbuch der Orientalistik*, I).

"Ḥiyal": Schacht, "Die arabische *ḥijal*-Literatur."

Hoenerbach, "Notes": Hoenerbach, W. "Some Notes on the Legal Language of Christian and Islamic Deeds," *JAOS*, 81 (1961), 34-38.

Hoenerbach, *Urkunden*: Hoenerbach, W. *Spanisch-islamische Urkunden aus der Zeit der Naṣriden und Moriscos*. Berkeley and Los Angeles, 1965 (*University of California Publications*, *Near Eastern Studies*, III).

Ibn 'Abd al-Barr, *Istī'āb*: Ibn 'Abd al-Barr, Yūsuf b. 'Abd Allāh. *Al-Istī'āb fī Ma'rifat al-Aṣḥāb*. 4 vols. Beirut, n.d.

Ibn al-Athīr, *Lubāb*: Ibn al-Athīr, 'Izz al-Dīn. *Al-Lubāb fī Tahdhīb al-Ansāb*. 3 vols. Cairo, 1357-1369 / 1938-1949.

Ibn al-Athīr, *Usd*: Ibn al-Athīr, 'Izz al-Dīn. *Usd al-Ghāba fī Ma'rifat al-Ṣaḥāba*. Cairo, 1964.

Ibn Ḥajar al-'Asqalānī. *Tahdhīb al-Tahdhīb*. 12 vols. Ḥydarābād, 1325-1327 / 1907-1909.

Ibn Hishām. *Al-Sīrat al-Nabawiyya*. 2 vols. Cairo, 1955.

Ibn Khaldūn. *The Muqaddima, An Introduction to History*. 3 vols. Trans. F. Rosenthal. New York, 1958.

Ibn Khallikān, Shams al-Dīn Aḥmad b. M. *Wafayāt al-A'yān wa Anbā' Abnā' al-Zamān* (*Vies des hommes illustres de l'Islamisme en Arabe par Ibn Khallikan*). Ed. W. MacG. de Slane. Paris, 1838-1842.

Ibn al-Nadīm, Abu'l-Faraj M. b. Isḥāq. *Kitāb al-Fihrist*. Ed. G. Flügel. 2 vols. Leipzig, 1871-1872.

Ibn Quṭlūbughā: Ibn Quṭlūbughā, Zayn al-Dīn Qāsim b. 'Abd Allāh. *Tāj al-Tarājim fī Ṭabaqāt al-Ḥanafiyya* (*Die Krone der Lebenschreibungen enthaltend die Klassen der Ḥanefiten*). Ed. G. Flügel. Leipzig, 1862 (*Abhandlungen für die Kunde des Morganlandes*, II/3).

Ivanow, W. *Guide to Ismā'īlī Literature*. London, 1933.

JA: *Journal Asiatique*.

JAOS: *Journal of the American Oriental Society*.

JESHO: *Journal of the Economic and Social History of the Orient.*

JSS: *Journal of Semitic Studies.*

Kawtharī: Kawtharī, M. Zāhid. *Al-Ḥāwī fī Sīrat al-Imām Abī Ja'far al-Ṭaḥāwī.* Cairo, 1368/1948.

Kern, F. "Zwei Urkunden vom Imām aš Šāfi'ī," *Mitteilungen des Seminars für Orientalische Sprachen*, VII (1904), 53-68.

Khadduri, M. *The Islamic Law of Nations, Shaybānī's Siyar.* Baltimore, 1966.

Kindī, *Wulāt*: Al-Kindī, Abū 'Umar M. b. Yūsuf. *Kitāb al-Wulāt wa-Kitāb al-Quḍāt* (*The Governors and Judges of Egypt or Kitāb El 'Umarā'* [*El Wulāh*] *wa Kitāb El Quḍāh of El Kindī*). Ed. Rhuvon Guest. Leiden and London, 1912 (*Gibb Memorial Series*, XIX).

Korošec, V. "Keilschriftrecht," *Orientalisches Recht.* Leiden, 1964, 49-219 (*Handbuch der Orientalistik*, I Abteilung, III).

Laknawī: Laknawī, M. 'Abd al-Ḥayy. *Al-Fawā'id al-Bahiyya fī Tarājim al-Ḥanafiyya.* Qazān (Kazan), 1321/1903.

Lane: Lane, E.W. *An Arabic-English Lexicon.* Book I, Parts 1-8. Ed. Stanley Lane-Poole. London, 1863-1893.

Laoust, H. "Ibn Kaṯīr Historien," *Arabica*, II (1955), 42-88.

Lapidus, I. *Muslim Cities in the Later Middle Ages.* Cambridge, Mass., 1967.

Al-Majlisī Al-Iṣfahānī, M. Bāqir b. M. *Biḥār al-Anwār.* 14 vols. Lith. Tabrīz, 1270-1275 / 1853-1858.

Makdisi, G. *Ibn 'Aqīl et la résurgence de l'Islam traditionaliste au XIe siècle.* Damascus, 1963.

Mālik b. Anas. *Al-Muwaṭṭa'* (with the commentary of Zurqānī). 4 vols. Cairo, 1310/1892.

Marghīnānī: Marghīnānī, Ẓahīr al-Dīn Abu'l-Maḥāsin. *Al-Fatāwā al-Ẓahīriyya* (Part II on *shurūṭ*). MS British Museum (Rieu Suppl. 4305).

Mez, A. *The Renaissance of Islam.* Trans. S. Khuda Bakhsh and D.S. Margoliouth. Patna, 1937.

Muffs: Muffs, Y. *Studies in the Aramaic Legal Papyri from Elephantine.* Leiden, 1969 (*Studia et Documenta ad Iura Orientis Antiqui Pertinentia*, VIII).

Muṭarrizī, *Mughrib*: Muṭarrizī, Nāṣir b. 'Abd al-Sayyid. *Kitāb al-Mughrib fī Tartīb al-Mu'rib.* 2 vols. Ḥydarābād, 1328/1910.

Al-Nu'mān b. M., Al-Qāḍī. *Da'ā'im al-Islām.* 2 vols. Ed. A.A.A. Fyzee. Cairo, 1951-1960.

Nuwayrī: Nuwayrī, Aḥmad b. 'Abd al-Wahhāb, *Nihāyat al-Arab fī Funūn al-Adab.* 18 vols. Cairo, 1923 ff.

OLZ: *Orientalische Literaturzeitung.*

Rescher, O. *Vocabulaire du recueil de Bokhārī.* Stuttgart, 1922.

San Nicolò, *Schlussklauseln*: San Nicolò, M. *Die Schlussklauseln der altbabylonischen Kauf- und Tauschverträge*: *Ein Beitrag zur Geschichte des Barkaufes.* Munich, 1922 (*Münchener Beiträge zur Papyrusforschung und antiken Rechtsgeschichte*, IV).

Sarakhsī: Sarakhsī, M. b. Abī Sahl. *Kitāb al-Mabsūṭ fi'l-Furū'.* 30 vols. Cairo, 1324-1331 / 1906-1913. (Chapter on *shurūṭ*, XXX, 167-209.)

Ṣayrafī: Ṣayrafī, Abū Bakr M. b. 'Abd Allāh. *Al-Mukātabāt al-Badī'a fīmā Yuktab min Umūr al-Sharī'a.* In Nuwayrī, *Nihāyat al-Arab*, IX, 9-160.

Schacht, J. "Die arabische *ḥiyal*-Literatur, Ein Beitrag zur Erforschung der islamischen Rechtspraxis," *Der Islam*, XV (1926), 211-232.

——. "Aus orientalischen Bibliotheken," *Abhandlungen der Preussischen Akademie der Wissenschaften, Phil.-hist. Klasse*; Part I (1928, 1-75), Part II (1929, 1-36), Part III (1931, 1-57).

Schacht, *Introduction*: Schacht, J. *An Introduction to Islamic Law*. Oxford, 1964.

Schacht, J. (ed.). "Das kitāb aḏkār al-ḥuqūq war-ruhūn aus dem ǧāmiʿ al-kabīr fiš-šurūṭ des abū Ǧaʿfar Aḥmad ibn Muḥammad aṭ-Ṭaḥāwī," *Sitzungsberichte der Heidelberger Akademie der Wissenschaften, Phil.-hist. Klasse*, 1926-1927, 4. Abhandlung.

——. (ed.). "Das kitāb aš-šufʿa aus dem ǧāmiʿ al-kabīr fiš-šurūṭ des abū Ǧaʿfar Aḥmad ibn Muḥammad aṭ-Ṭaḥāwī," *Sitzungsberichte der Heidelberger Akademie des Wissenschaften, Phil.-hist. Klasse*, 1929-1930, 5. Abhandlung.

Schacht, *Origins*: Schacht, J. *Origins of Muhammadan Jurisprudence*. Oxford, 1950.

Schacht, J. "Sur quelques manuscrits de la bibliothèque de la mosquée d'al-Qarawiyyīn à Fès," *Études d'Orientalisme dédiées à la mémoire de Lévi-Provençal*. 2 vols. Paris, 1962.

——. "Vom babylonischen zum islamischen Recht," *OLZ*, 1927, cols. 663-669.

——. "Zur soziologischen Betrachtungen des islamischen Rechts," *Der Islam*, XXII (1935), 217-221.

Schiller, A. "Coptic Documents," *Zum gegenwärtigen Stand der juristischen Papyrusforschung. ZVRW*, LX (1957), 190-221.

——. "Coptic Law," *The Juridical Review*, XLIII (1931), 211-240.

——. "The Coptic Word of God Documents," *Studi in Memoria di Aldo Albertoni*, I. Padova, 1933, 304-345.

——. "Prolegomena to the Study of Coptic Law," *Archives d'Histoire du Droit Oriental*, II (1938), 341-365.

Seagle, W. *The Quest for Law*. New York, 1941 (republished as *The History of Law*, 1946).

SEI: *Shorter Encyclopaedia of Islam*. Ed. H.A.R. Gibb and J.H. Kramers. Ithaca, 1961.

Seidl, E. "Altägyptisches Recht," *Orientalisches Recht*. Leiden, 1964, 1-48 (*Handbuch der Orientalistik*, I Abteilung, III).

——. "Law," *The Legacy of Egypt*. Ed. S.R.K. Glanville. Oxford, 1942, 198-217.

——. *Ptolemäische Rechtsgeschichte*. 2nd ed. Gluckstadt-Hamburg, 1962.

Serjeant, R.B. "Forms of Plea, a Šāfiʿī Manual from al-Šiḥr," *Revista degli Studi Orientali*, XXX (1955), 1-15.

Serjeant, "Ḥabbān": Serjeant, R.B. "A Judeo-Arabic House Deed from Ḥabbān," *Journal of the Royal Asiatic Society*, 1953, 117-131.

Sezgin: Sezgin, F. *Geschichte des arabischen Schrifttums*. Band I, Leiden, 1967.

Sharon, M. "A Waqf Inscription from Ramlah," *Arabica*, XIII (1966), 77-84.

Al-Shaybānī, M. b. al-Ḥasan. *Kitāb al-Makhārij fi'l-Ḥiyal*. Ed. J. Schacht. Leipzig, 1930.

"Shufʿa": Schacht (ed.), "Das kitāb aš-šufʿa... des aṭ-Ṭaḥāwī."

SI: *Studia Islamica*.

Sourdel-Thomine and Sourdel, "Damascus": Sourdel-Thomine, J. and D. Sourdel, "Trois actes de vente damascains du début du IVe/Xe siècle," *JESHO*, VIII (1965), 164-185.

Steinacker, *Privaturkunde*: Steinacker, H. *Die antiken Grundlagen der frühmittelalterlichen Privaturkunde*. Leipzig, 1927 (*Grundriss der Geschichtswissenschaft*, I).

Steinwenter, A. *Die Bedeutung der Papyrologie für die koptische Urkundenlehre*. Munich, 1934 (*Münchener Beiträge zur Papyrusforschung und antiken Rechtsgeschichte*, XIX).

——. *Das Recht der koptischen Urkunden*. Munich, 1955 (*Handbuch der Altertumswissenschaft*, X).

Ṭabarī, Muḥibb al-Dīn. *Al-Riyāḍ al-Nādira fī Manāqib al-ʿAshara*. 2 vols. Cairo, 1327/1909.

Ṭaḥāwī, Abū Jaʿfar Aḥmad b. M. *Kitāb al-Shurūṭ al-Kabīr* (*Al-Jāmiʿ al-Kabīr fi'l-Shurūṭ*). MS Süleymaniye (Şehid Ali Paşa 881: "Kitāb al-Buyūʿ").

——. MS Süleymaniye (Şehid Ali Paşa 882: "Kitāb al-Maḥāḍir" and "Kitāb Wilāyat al-Qaḍā' ").

——. *Kitāb al-Shurūṭ al-Saghīr* (*Kitāb al-Shurūṭ wa'l-Warāqa*). MS Murat Molla Kütüphanesi (Mehmet Murat 997).

Tahdhīb: Ibn Ḥajar al-'Asqalānī, *Tahdhīb al-Tahdhīb*.

Turkī, A. "Lisān al-Dīn Ibn al-Khaṭīb (713-76 / 1313-74) juriste d'après son œuvre inédite: *Muṯlā al-ṭarīqa fī ḏamm al-waṯīqa*," *Arabica*, XVI (1969); "Introduction," 155-211, "Texte arabe et glossaire," 279-312.

Tyan, É. "*Iflās* et procédure d'éxécution sur les biens en droit musulman (*maḏhab ḥanafite*)," *SI*, XXI (1964), 145-166.

Tyan, *Notariat*: Tyan, É. "Le Notariat et le régime de la preuve par écrit dans la pratique du droit musulman," *Annales de l'École Française de Droit de Beyrouth*, II(1945), 3-99. (Separately printed, Beirut, 1959).

Tyan, *Organisation*: Tyan, É. *Histoire de l'organisation judiciaire en pays de l'Islam*. 2nd ed. Leiden, 1960.

Udovitch, A. *Partnership and Profit in Medieval Islam*. Princeton, 1970.

Wakī', *Quḍāt*: Wakī', M. b. Khalaf. *Akhbār al-Quḍāt*. 3 vols. Cairo, 1366/1944.

Wright: Wright, W. *A Grammar of the Arabic Language*. 3rd ed., 2 vols. Cambridge, 1896-1898.

Wulff, H.E. *The Traditional Crafts of Persia*. Cambridge, Mass., 1966.

Yāqūt, Abū 'Abd Allāh, Al-Rūmī. *Kitāb Mu'jam al-Buldān* (*Geographisches Wörterbuch*). Ed. F. Wüstenfeld. 6 vols. Leipzig, 1866-1870.

Yaron: Yaron, R. *Introduction to the Law of the Aramaic Papyri*. London, 1961.

Yaron, R. "On Defension Clauses of Some Oriental Deeds of Sale and Lease, From Mesopotamia," *Bibliotheca Orientalis*, XV (1958), 15-22.

——. "The Schema of the Aramaic Legal Documents," *JSS*, II (1957), 33-61.

ZVRW: *Zeitschrift für Vergleichende Rechtswissenschaft*.

INDEX OF PROPER NAMES

SUBJECT INDEX

Acceptance formulas, 95, 96

Accessory clauses, 49-53; formulas, 33; house property, 79, 81-83, 100-102, 103, 105; road, 102; wall, 106

Acknowledgement (*iqrār*): by acting buyer, 47, 69; in barter transaction, 56n; of contents of document, 92; by guarantor, 95; of inspection of property, 55; of land survey, 105; and order of clauses, 41-42; of ownership, 33, 34-35, 78, 81, 102; in partnership, 68; of relinquishment of rights, 103; and stylization, 44n, 45; and testimony of witnesses, 55, 66-67, 92-93; of validity, 34; by women, 95, 97-98

Agency (*wakāla*): contracts for, 95-96; in jointly-owned property, 98; in transfer of use of land, 104. *See also* Agent.

Agent (*wakīl*): acknowledgement by, 47; dismissal of, 104; and payment of price, 34; relinquishes rights, 64n; and witnessing, 69

Archaic law, 38, 43n

Appurtenance formulas. *See* Accessory clauses

'āriyya (loan for use), 36, 104

Authorization, 36, 69, 95, 98, 99

barā'a. *See* Quittance clauses

Barter, 36, 56n, 70n

Boundaries: definition in contract, 34, 51, 80-81, 103; in establishing ownership, 53, 67n, 79; in jointly-owned property, 100, 102. *See also* Accessory clauses

Capacity: formulas, 92-93; testimony to, 51, 66-67, 69, 92; and volition formulas, 67n; of women, 69, 97-98

Chancellery documents (*inshā'*), 38n, 50

Consent. *See* Authorization

Contracts, and relationship to documents, 30-31. *See also* Documents; Validity of contract

Copies of document: copy on *verso*, 47, 70n; formula, 46; number of, 45-47

ḍamān al-darak (guarantee against defect in ownership), 60-62, 81, 88-91, 95; in document of *shahāda*, 70; formulas, 33, 61, 90-91; for improvements, 91-92, 96; for jointly-owned property, 98-99; for movable property, 62, 106; and *'uhda*, 81, 90. *See also* Final settlement clauses

Dating formulas, 47-49

Delivery of property, 53-54, 90

Description of property. *See* Accessory clauses

dīnār, 86-88. *See also* Price

Documents: "blank spaces" in, 10, 30, 86; classification of, 39n; as contracts, 30-31; copies of, 45-47, 70n; formalism in, 38, 64, 85; lost, 45n; in Near East, 2-3, 38; structure of, 38, 39-40; stylizaton of, 42-43; validity of, 4-10, 11, 29-30

Easements, 52, 100, 101, 102

Exceptions in a sale: of property, 82, 100-101 103, 104, 106; in validity formulas, 85

Final settlement clauses, 60-65, 88-89, 90-91 *See also ḍamān al-darak*

Formalism in documents, 38, 64, 85

Geniza documents, 2, 37n

Gift, 63, 85, 86

Ḥanafī school: attitude toward documents, 9-10; literary continuity in, 12, 14-15; and practical literature, 10-12; and *shurūṭ* tradition, 10-11, 15-23, 27-29

Hanbalī school, 13

ḥiyal (legal evasions), 11-13, 31

ḥuqūq and *marāfiq*. *See* Accessory clauses

Identification: formulas, 50-51; of parties, 70, 78, 79, 92-93, 97-98; of property, 79-81; by witnesses, 66-67

iḥtiyāṭ (precaution), 32-34; in dating formulas, 49; describing appurtenances, 83; describing price, 91; in expressing formulas, 38; order of clauses, 40-42; selling land by cubit, 105; stating possession, 78; and use of *'alā anna*, 34, 101

ikhtilāf (*-āt*) (diversity of doctrine): on boundaries, 100; and court practice, 37; on final guarantees, 62, 90; on inspection, 54, 55; in Islamic law, 32-36; on ownership, 78; on presumptions, 41-42; on appurtenances, 52-53, 83; on shares, 103; in Ṭaḥāwī's work, 1, 14n

Illness: *iqrār* made in, 93; transactions in, 67n, 70n

Improvements in property: guarantee for, 89, 90, 95; separate document for, 35; value of, 91, 96

PLATE I. Şehid Ali Paşa 881 (Fol. 121b-122a)

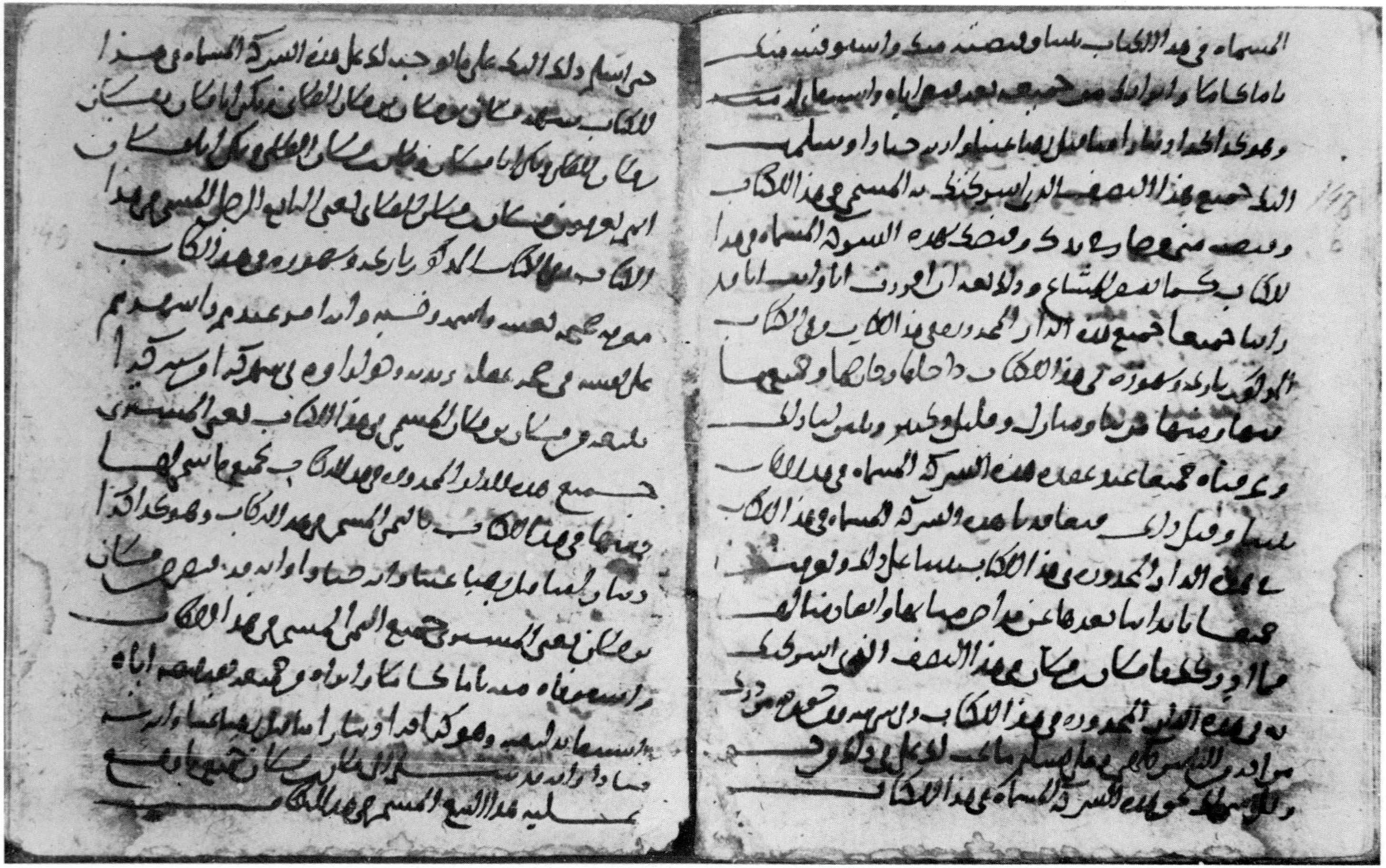

PLATE II. Şehid Ali Paşa 881 (Fol. 148b-149a)

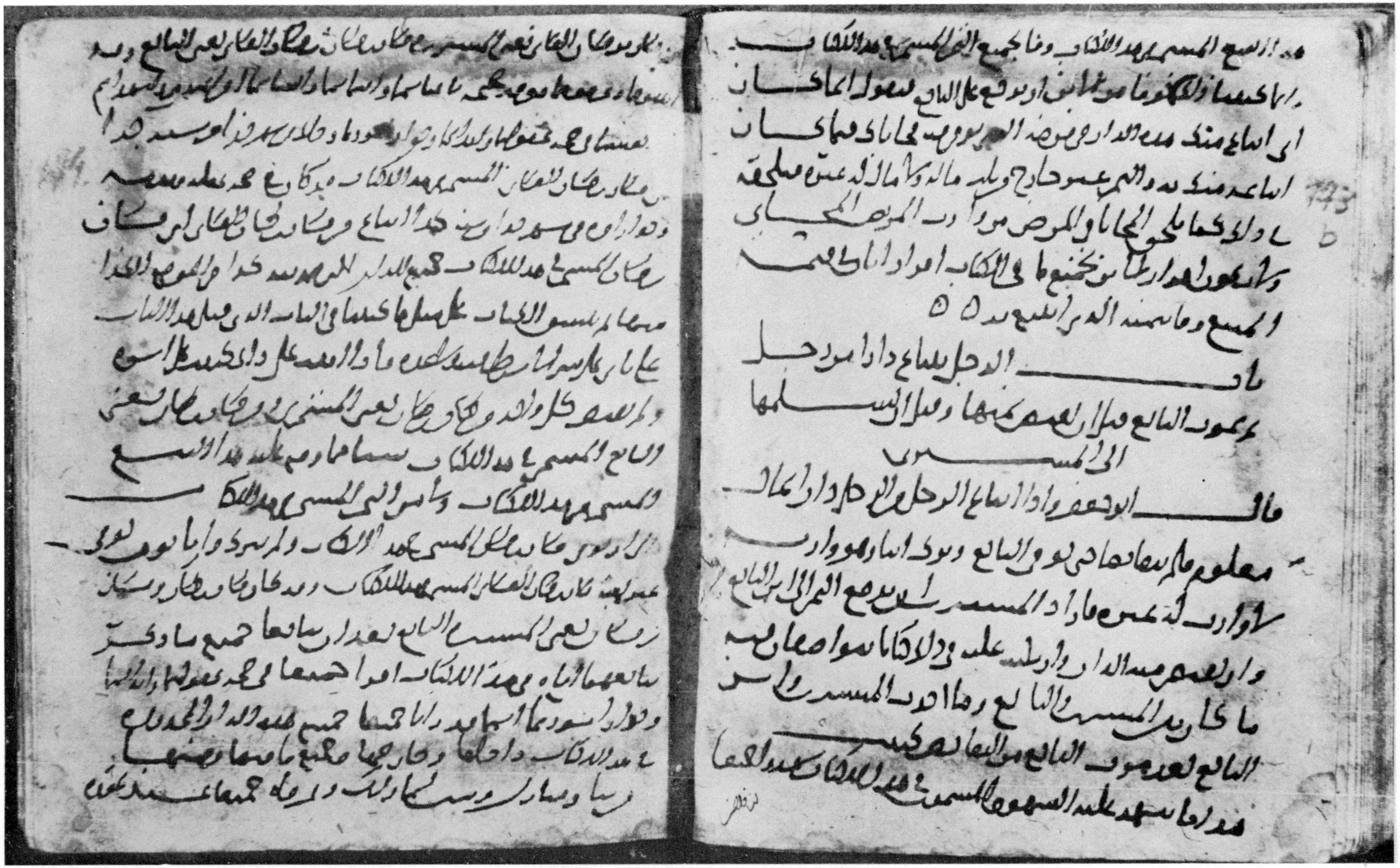

PLATE III. Şehid Ali Paşa 881 (Fol. 173b-174a)

الجُزْءُ الأولُ مِنَ البُيُوع

مِنْ

كِتَابِ الشُّرُوطِ الكَبِير

تأليف أبي جعفر أحمد بن محمد بن سلامة بن سلمة
الطحاوي الأزدي رحمه الله

بسم الله الرحمن الرحيم (1 b)

1.1 قال أبو جعفر أحمد بن محمّد بن سلامة بن سلمة الأزدى بحمد الله أبتدئ وإيّاه أستهدى
1.2 والله المستعان * أمّا بعد فإنّ الله جلّ ثناؤه قال فى كتابه (يا أيُّها الذينَ آمَنوا إذا تَدايَنْتُم بِدَيْنٍ إلى أجَلٍ مُسَمًّى فاكْتُبُوهُ) فأمر عزّ وجلّ بكتاب الدين ثمّ أخبرهم أنّ حكم ما قلّ منه كحكم ما كثر فقال (ولا تَسْأموا أنْ تَكْتُبُوهُ صَغيرًا أوْ كَبيرًا إلى أجَلِهِ) ثمّ بيّن بعد ذلك المعنى الذى له أراد ما أمرهم به من ذلك فقال (ذٰلِكُم أقْسَطُ عِنْدَ اللهِ وَأقْوَمُ لِلشَّهادَةِ وَأدْنَى ألاّ تَرْتابُوا) فأعلمهم أنّ فى كتابهم قوام الشهادة التى يثبت بها مال الطالب ويحصّن فيها دين المطلوب وينتفى عنهم الريب والشكّ فيما لهم وفيما عليهم وفيما يشهد به بعضهم لبعض *

1.3 ثمّ قال (إلاّ أنْ تَكُونَ تِجارَةً حاضِرَةً تُديرُونَها بَيْنَكُمْ فَلَيْسَ عَلَيْكُم جُناحٌ ألاّ تَكْتُبُوها) فوسّع عليهم فى ذلك لئلاّ يضيق عليهم أمر بياعاتهم فلا يشترى أحد شيئاً إلاّ احتاج الى كتابه فيدخل فى ذلك شرى الماء الذى يشربونه والطعام الذى يأكلونه وما أشبه ذلك *

1.4 ثمّ قال عزّ وجلّ (وأشْهِدُوا إذَا تَبَايَعْتُم) فأمر بالإشهاد فى كلّ بياعات بالأثمان العاجلة والأثمان الآجلة لما فى ذلك من الحقوق لبعضهم على بعض بسبب ردّ ما يتبايعون بعيب إن كان به أو رجوع لما يجب لمبتاعه باستحقاق مستحقّ له أو لشىء منه وفيما علّمهم عزّ وجلّ //
(2 a) فيما ذكرنا من كتاب الدين خوفاً من النسيان والريب دليل أنّ حكم الشهادة كذلك أيضاً وأنّه ينبغى أن يكتب خوف الريب والنسيان وفى كتاب الشهود لذلك صفة حكم البيع الذي تعاقد المتبايعان بينهما *

1.5 ثمّ قال عزّ وجلّ (فَإنْ أمِنَ بَعْضُكم بَعْضاً فَلْيُؤدِّ الّذِى اؤتُمِنَ أمانَتَهُ وَلْيَتَّقِ اللهَ رَبَّهُ) و (لاَ يَبْخَسْ مِنْهُ شَيْئاً) فدلّ ذلك إنّما كان ما أمر به من الكتاب والإشهاد فى أهل هذه الآية لم يكن على الحتم وأنّه كان على الإرشاد والندب منه لهم لما فيه من حفظ[1] حقوقهم وقد قال قوم إنّ ذلك نسخ لإيجاب الشهادة والكتاب المذكورين فى

[1] MS لما فيه حفظ

هذه الآية[1] ورَوَوْا فى ذلك عن المتقدّمين ما حدّثنا إبراهيم بن مرزوق بن دينار البصرى قال حدّثنا عفّان بن مسلم عن وُهَيب بن خالد عن داود بن أبى هند عن عامر (فَإِنْ أَمِنَ بَعْضُكُم بَعْضاً) قال إنْ شهد فحزم وإن ائتمنه ففى حلّ وسعه *

1.6 قال حدّثنا أبو شُرَيح محمّد بن زكريّاء بن يحيى قال حدّثنا محمّد بن يوسف الفريابى قال حدّثنا الثورى عن اسماعيل بن أبى خالد عن الشعبى قال اذا ائتمنه فلا يضرّه ألاّ يكتب

1.7 ويؤوّل هذه الآية (فَإِنْ أَمِنَ بَعْضُكُم بعضاً) * حدّثنا أبو شُرَيح قال حدّثنا الفريابى قال حدّثنا سفيان الثورى عن الربيع قال سألت الحسن قلت أبيعٌ بالنقد أشهد ؟ قال إن أشهدت

1.8 فهو ثقة وإن لم تُشهِد فلا بأس * حدّثنا أبو شُرَيح قال حدّثنا الفريابى قال حدّثنا سفيان الثورى عن ليث عن مجاهد (وأَشْهِدُوا إذَا تَبَايَعْتُم) قال اذا كان نسيئة كتب وإن كان نقدًا أشهد *

1.9 قال أبو جعفر فلم يكن فى هذه التأويلات // التى ذكرنا ما يمنع من كتاب الدين وكتاب (2 b) الشهادة لأنّ من ذهب الى أنّ الكتاب المأمور به فى أوّل الآية على الحتم ذهب الى أنّ هذا المذكور بعده نسخ للحتم لا منع للكتاب ومن ذهب الى أنّ هذا المذكور فى هذه الآية أخيرا على البيان لما أريد فى أوّلها ذهب الى أنّ كلّ ما فيها ليس على الحتم بالكتاب والإشهاد

1.10 وأنّهما على الإرشاد * ثمّ بيّن الله عزّ وجلّ ما على من تولّى كتاب ذلك فقال (وَلْيَكْتُبْ بَيْنَكُم كَاتِبٌ بِالعَدْلِ) فأمر عزّ وجلّ من تولّى الكتاب بين الناس أن يكتب بينهم بالعدل ومن العدل ألاّ يكتب بينهم إلاّ بعد علمه بالأسباب[2] التى يراد الكتاب من أجله وما أجمعت عليه العلماء واختلفت فيه الفقهاء والوجوه التى تحتاط بها من ذلك وتقويم الألفاظ التى تنبغى احتمال المعانى ليتوثّق المكتوب له والمكتوب عليه فإذا كان كذلك كتب كتابا لا يحيف فيه لأحد على أحد ولا يميل عنه فيه هوى ولا يخشى فيه أحدا حتّى يحوط فيه الطالب والمطلوب بغاية ما يقدر عليه من التوثّق لكلّ واحد منهما على صاحبه *

1.11 ومن اختلاف العلماء خوفا أن يُرفَع ما كُتب من ذلك الى قاض من قضاة المسلمين يرى غير ما كُتب فيُبطِل كتابه فيردّ الأمر فيما كان جرى بين الطالب والمطلوب الى ما رأى ولعلّهما فى بدء أمرهما لم يكونا أرادا المعنى الذى من أجله فسخ الحاكم البيع بينهما وانّما أراد صحّة البيع

(3 a) وتمامه وجوازه // فيكون الذى منع من ذلك تقصير هذا الكتاب ويدخل فى ذلك الصدقات والهبات والعتاقات والكتابات وسائر ما يدور بين الناس فمانع ذلك والممنوع من أجله إثم مخالف لأمر الله وقد حذّر الله عزّ وجلّ فى كتابه من خالف أمره فقال (فَلْيَحْذَرِ الّذِينَ يُخَالِفُونَ عَنْ أَمْرِهِ أَنْ تُصِيبَهُم فِتْنَةٌ أَوْ يُصِيبَهُم عَذَابٌ أَلِيمٌ) *

[1] فى هذه الآية unclear in MS

[2] بالاسباب unclear in MS

1.12 وأمر الله عزّ وجلّ الكاتب أن يكتب بينهم فقال (وَلاَ يَأْبَ كَاتِبٌ أنْ يَكْتُبَ كَمَا عَلَّمَهُ اللهُ) لما له فى ذلك من الثواب الجزيل اذا كان يريد فى كتابه التّماس ما ذكرنا ممّا على

1.13 الكاتب * ثمّ قال عزّ وجلّ (وَلاَ يُضَارَّ كَاتِبٌ وَلاَ شَهِيدٌ) قال فحدّثنا إبراهيم بن مرزوق قال حدّثنا أبو حُذَيفة موسى بن مسعود عن سفيان الثورى عن يزيد بن أبي زياد عن مِقْسَم عن ابن عبّاس فى قول الله عزّ وجلّ (وَلاَ يُضَارَّ كَاتِبٌ وَلاَ شَهِيدٌ) قال إنْ يَجِيئ فيدعو الكاتب والشهيد فيقولان إنّا على حاجة فيضارّهما فيقول قد أُمِرْتُما أن تجيئا *

1.14 قال أبو جعفر فأمر الله عزّ وجلّ ألاّ يفعلوا ذلك بكاتب ولا شهيد تخفيفا منه عمّن يكتب وعمّن يشهد لأنّه لو أطلق ذلك وأوجبه على الكاتب والشهيد لقطع ذلك منهما عن أمر معايشهما

1.15 وعن كثير ممّا يتقرّبان به الى ثوابها[1] * قال وقد وضعت هذا الكتاب على الاجتهاد منّى لإصابة ما أمر الله عزّ وجلّ به من الكتاب بين الناس بالعدل على ما ذكرت فى صدر هـذا

(3 b) الكتاب ممّا على الكاتب بين الناس وجعلت ذلك أصنافاً // ذكرت فى كلّ صنف منها اختلاف الناس فى الحكم فى ذلك وفى رسم الكتاب فيه وبيّنت حجّة كلّ فريق منهم وذكرت ما صحّ عندى من مذاهبهم وممّا رسموا به كتبهم فى ذلك والله أسأله الفوز والتوفيق بأنّه لا حول ولا قوة إلاّ به *

2.1 فأوّل ما نذكر من ذلك الكتب فى الأشرية والبياعات على النحو الذي وصفنا إن شاء الله *

2.0 كتاب رجل اشترى من رجل دارا * هذا ما اشترى فلان بن فلان بن فلان الفلانى من فلان ابن فلان بن فلان الفلانى اشترى منه جميع الدار التى بمدينة كذا فى الموضع الذي منها المعروف بكذا ويحيط بهذه الدار ويجمعها ويشتمل عليها حدود أربعة أحد حدود جماعتها الحدّ الأوّل وهو كذا ينتهى الى كذا والحدّ الثانى وهو كذا ينتهى الى كذا والحدّ الثالث وهو كذا ينتهى الى كذا والحدّ الرابع وهو كذا ينتهى الى كذا وفيه يشرع باب هذه الدار المحدودة فى هذا الكتاب اشترى فلان ابن فلان بن فلان من فلان بن فلان بن فلان جميع هذه الدار المحدودة الموصوف جماعتها فى هذا الكتاب بحدودها كلّها وأرضها وبنائها وسفلها وعلوّها ومرافقها فى حقوقها وطرقها التى هى لها

(4 a) فى حقوقها ومسايلها فى حقوقها وكلّ قليل وكثير هو لها فيها ومنها من حقوقها // وكلّ حقّ هو لها داخل فيها وكلّ حقّ هو لها خارج منها بكذا كذا ديناراً مثاقيل ذهبا عينا وازنة جيادا شرى لا شرط فيه ولا عدة ودفع فلان بن فلان الى فلان بن فلان جميع الثمن المسمّى فى هذا الكتاب وقبضه منه فلان بن فلان واستوفاه منه تامّا كاملا وأبرأه من جميعـه بعد قبضه إيّاه واستيفائه له منه وهو كذا كذا دينارا مثاقيل ذهباً عيناً وازنة جيادا وسلّم فلان بن فلان بن فلان الى فلان بن فلان بن فلان[2] جميع ما وقع عليه هذا البيع المسمّى فى هذا الكتاب وقبضه منه فلان

[1] MS ثوبها

[2] MS الى فلان بن فلان

ابن فلان وصار فى يده وقبضه بهذا الشرى المسمّى فى هذا الكتاب وذلك بعد أن أقرّ فلان بن فلان وفلان بن فلان أنّهما قد رأيا جميعا جميع هذه الدار المحدودة فى هذا الكتاب وجميع حقوقها وجميع ما فيها ومنها من بناء ومنازل وكلّ[1] قليل وكثير وعاينا ذلك كلّه داخله وخارجه وتبيّن لهما ذلك كلّه جميعا وعرفاه عند عقدة هذا البيع المسمّى فى هذا الكتاب بينهما وقبل ذلك فتبايعا على ذلك وتفرّقا جميعا بأبدانهما بعد هذا البيع المسمّى فى هذا الكتاب عن تراض منهما جميعا بجميعه وإنفاذ منهما له فما أدرك فلان بن فلان فيما وقع عليه هذا البيع المسمّى فى هذا الكتاب وفى شىء منه ومن حقوقه من درك من أحد من الناس كلّهم فعلى فلان بن فلان تسليم ما يجب

(4 b) عليه فى ذلك من حقّ ويلزمه بسبب هذا البيع المسمّى // فى هذا الكتاب حتّى يسلّم ذلك الى فلان بن فلان على ما يوجبه له عليه هذا البيع المسمّى فى هذا الكتاب شهد على إقرار فلان ابن فلان بن فلان الفلانى يعنى البائع وفلان بن فلان بن فلان الفلانى يعنى المشترى بجميع ما فى هذا الكتاب بعد أن قُرِئَ عليهما جميعا جميع ما فيه من أوّله الى آخره فأقرّا أن قد فهماه وعرفا جميع ما فيه حرفا حرفا فى صحّة عقولهما وأبدانهما وجواز أمورهما طائعين غير مكرهين[2] وعلى معرفتهما بأعيانهما وأسمائهما وأنسابهما وذلك فى شهر كذا من سنة كذا ٭

2.2 قال أبو جعفر هذا أوثق ما قدرنا عليه وأحوط وأحسن ألفاظا وأجمع معان من سائر كتب أهل العلم فى ذلك مع أنّهم قد اختلفوا فى أشياء من هذا الكتاب فكتبها بعضهم على خلاف ما كتبها الآخرون واحتجّ كلّ فريق منهم لمذهبه بحجّة وسأُبيّن ذلك كلّه وجميع ما يلزمه كلّ فريق منهم فى ذلك وما صلح عندى ممّا اختلفوا فيه من ذلك فى هذا الكتاب إن شاء الله ٭

2.3 قال فكان أبو خالد يوسف بن خالد السُمتى وهلال بن يحيى يبتدئان كتابهما هذا كتاب ما اشترى وكان أبو حنيفة وأبو يوسف ومحمّد بن الحسن وأبو زيد المعروف بالشّروطى وعامّة أصحاب أبى حنيفة ومن كتب الشروط من غيرهم يكتبون هذا ما اشترى فكان هذا أحبّ الينا ممّا كتب يوسف وهلال لأنّ كُتُب رسول الله عليه السلام وأصحابه جرت على ذلك ٭ //

2.4 (5 a) قال حدّثنا أبو بكرة بكّار بن قتيبة وإبراهيم بن مرزوق قالا حدّثنا عمر بن يونس اليمامى قال حدّثنا عِكرِمة بن عمّار قال حدّثنى أبو زُمَيل أحد بنى عبد الله بن الدُول قال حدّثني عبد الله ابن عبّاس أنّ نبىّ الله عليه السلام قال لعلىّ بن أبى طالب يوم الحُدَيبية أُكتُب يا علىّ هذا ما اصطلح عليه محمّد رسول الله فقال المشركون لا والله لا نعلم أنّك رسول الله لو نعلم أنّك رسول الله ما قاتلناك فقال رسول الله عليه السلام اللهمّ إنّك تعلم أنّى رسولك أُكتُب يا علىّ هذا ما اصطلح عليه محمّد بن عبد الله ٭

2.5 قال حدّثنا يزيد بن سِنان قال حدّثنا حِبّان بن هلال أبو حبيب المُقرئ قال حدّثنا مبارك ابن فَضالة عن الحسن قال حدّثنى الأحنف بن قيس أنّ معاوية كتب الى علىّ أن امْحُ عنك

[1] MS omits كلّ

[2] MS omits غير مكرهين

هذا الاسم إن أردتَ أن يكون صلحا فاستشار القومَ وكانت له قبّة يأذن لبنى هاشم فيها ويأذن لى معهم فقال ما ترون فيما كتب به معاوية الى أن أمْحُ هذا الاسم ؟ قال مبارك أمير المؤمنين فقال فلان قد سمّاه مبارك أترحِهْ أتْرِحهُ أتْرَحهُ الله فإنّ رسول الله عليه السلام كتب الى أهل مكّة محمّد رسول الله فأبَوا ذلك حتّى كتب هذا ما قاضى عليه محمّد بن عبد الله قال الأحنف فقلت له يا أمير المؤمنين إنّا والله ما حابَيْناك بَيْعَتَنا ولو نعلم أحدًا هو أحقّ بهذا الأمر منك لَبايعناه ولَقاتلناك معه وإنّى أُقسمُ بالله أنّى مَحوْتُ عنك هذا الاسم الذي
(5 b) قاتلت الناس عليه // ودعوتهم اليه ثمّ طلبت أن تعود اليه ولا يعود اليه فقال الحسن صدق يرحمه الله قَلَّ ما وُزِن رأيهُ برأيِ رجلٍ إلا ربح رأيُه برأيه *

2.6 قال حدّثنا أحمد بن داود بن موسى قال حدّثنا عبد الأعلى بن حمّاد النَّرْسِي[1] قال حدّثنا هشام بن خالد قال حدّثنى ابن خُثَيْم عن عبيد الله بن عِياض[2] أنّ عبد الله بن شدّاد دخل على عائشة مَرجِعَهُ من العراق ليالى قتل علىّ رحمة الله عليه فذكر حديثاً طويلاً فيه أنّ عليًا قال نقموا علَىَّ أنّى كاتبت معاوية فكتبت علىّ بن أبى طالب وقد جاءنا سُهَيل بن عمرو بالحديبية حين صالح قومه قريشاً فكتب رسول الله عليه السلام بسم الله الرحمن الرحيم قال لا أكتب بسم الله الرحمن الرحيم فقال رسول الله عليه السلام اكتبْ محمّد رسول الله قال لو أعلم أنّك رسول الله لم أخالفك فكتب هذا ما صالح عليه محمّد بن عبد الله قريشا *

2.7 قال أبو الفتح نصر بن مرزوق قال حدّثنا أسد بن موسى قال حدّثنى يحيى بن زكرياء ابن أبى زائدة قال حدّثنى أبى عن أبى اسحاق عن البراء بن عازب أنّ النبىّ عليه السلام قال لعلىّ اكتبْ الشرط بيننا فكتب بسم الله الرحمن الرحيم هذا ما قاضى عليه محمّد رسول الله فقال المشركون لو نعلم أنّك رسول الله بايعناك ما مانعناك شيئا ولكن اكتبْ محمّد بن عبد الله فقال أنا رسول الله وأنا محمّد بن عبد الله ثمّ قال لعلىّ امْحُ رسول الله قال والله لا أمْحوك أبدا فقال رسول
(6 a) الله أرنى مكاتبة[3] فأراه فمحاه وكتب // محمّد بن عبد الله *

2.8 قال حدّثنا أبو خالد عبد العزيز بن معاوية بن عبد العزيز القرشى ثمّ العتّابى قال حدّثنا عبّاد بن ليث قال حدّثنى عبد المجيد أبو وهب[4] قال قال العدّاء بن خالد بن هَوْذَة أفلا أقرئك كتابا كتبه لى رسول الله عليه السلام ؟ قلت بلى فأخرج لى كتاباً فإذا فيه بسم الله الرحمن الرحيم هذا ما اشترى العدّاء بن خالد بن هَوْذَة من محمّد رسول الله اشترى عبدا أو أمة شكّ عبد
2.9 المجيد[5] بيع المسلم المسلم لا داء ولا غائلة ولا خبثة * قال حدّثنا ابن أبى عِمران قال حدّثنا إسحاق ابن أبى إسرائيل[6] وحدّثنا أبو أميّة محمّد بن إبراهيم بن مسلم قال حدّثنا إبراهيم بن محمّد بن

[1] MS المرسى
[2] MS عبد الله بن عياض
[3] MS مكاتة
[4] MS عبد الحميد أبو وهب
[5] MS شكّ عبد الحميد
[6] MS اسحاق بن اسرائيل

عَرعَرَة مثله وحدّثنا يزيد بن سنان قال حدّثنا أخى محمّد بن سنان قال حدّثنا عبّاد بن ليث ثمّ ذكروا بإسناده مثله غير أنّهم لم يقولوا ولا غائلة *

2.10 قال حدّثنا أبو عيسى موسى بن عيسى بن بشير الكوفى قال حدّثنا الحسين بن علىّ الجُعْفى عن هشام بن حسّان عن ابن سيرين عن أنس قال كان المسلمون يوصون هذا ما أوصى به فلان ابن فلان أوصى أنّه يشهد أنّه لا إله الاّ الله وحده لا شريك له وأنّ محمّداً عبده ورسوله وأنّ الساعة آتية لا ريب فيها وأنّ الله يبعث من فى القبور وأوصى من ترك بعده أن يتّقوا الله ويصلحوا ذات بينهم ويطيعوا الله ورسوله إن كانوا مؤمنين وأوصاهم بما أوصى به إبراهيم بَنيه ويعقوب
(6 b) (يا بَنِيّ إنّ اللهَ اصطَفَى // لَكمُ الدِّينَ فَلا تَموُتُنَّ إلاّ وأَنْتُم مُسلِمونَ) وأوصاهم إن حدث به حدث الموت قبل أن تغيّر وصيته هذه ومن حاجته كذا ومن حاجته كذا *

2.11 قال حدّثنا أبو جعفر محمّد بن العبّاس بن الربيع اللؤلؤىّ عن أبى يحيى زكريّاء بن مبارك الواسطى قال سمعت أبا يوسف قال حدّثنا عبيد الله بن محمّد بن عمر بن علىّ بن أبى طالب عن أبيه عن جدّه عن علىّ ابن أبى طالب أنّه كتب هذه الوصيّة هذا ما أمر به وقضى فى ماله علىّ بن أبى طالب تصدّق بِيَنْبُع ابتغاءَ بها مرضاة الله ليولجنى اللهُ بها الجنّةَ ويصرفنى عن النار ويصرف النار عنّى وهى فى سبيل الله ووجوهه تُنفَق فى كلّ نفقة من سبيل الله ووجوهه فى الحرب والسلم والجنود وذوى الرحم والقريب والغريب والبعيد لا يباع ولا يوهب ولا يورث كل مال لى بيَنْبُع ورقيقها[1] غير أنّ رَباحا وأبا نَيْزَر وجُبَيرا وان حدث[2] بى حدث فليس عليهم سبيل وهم محرّرون موال يعملون فى المال خمس حجج وفيه[3] نفقتهم ورزقهم ورزق أهاليهم فذلك الذى أقضي فيما كان لى بيَنْبُع واجبا حيّ أنا أو ميّت ومعها ما كان بِوادِى القُرَى من مال أو رقيق حيّ أنا أو ميّت ومع ذلك الأذَيْنة وأهلها حيّ أنا أو ميّت ومع ذلك بُرْقَة[4] وأهلها وأنّ رُزَيْقا له مثل ما كتبت لأبى نَيْزَر ورَباح وجُبَيْر وأنّ يَنْبُع وما لى فى وادِى القُرَى //
(7 a) والأذَيْنة وبُرْقَة[5] يُنفَق فى كلّ نفقة ابتغاء وجه الله فى سبيل الله ووجهه يوم تسودّ وجوه وتبيضّ وجوه ولا يُبعن ولا يوهبن ولا يوءدّين إلاّ الى الله هو يتقبّلهنّ وهو يرثهنّ فذلك قضيت بينى وبين الله العزيز يوم قدمت مَسْكِن حىّ أنا أو ميّت فهذا ما قضى به علىّ بن أبى طالب فى ماله واجبة بتلة يقوم على ذلك الحسن بن علىّ ما دام حيّا فإن هلك فالى حسين بن علىّ يليها ما دام حيّا فإن هلك فهى الى الأولى والأولى من ذوى السنّ والصلاح من ولدى يعدل فيها ويطعم ولدى بالمعروف غير المنكر ولا الإسراف يزرع ويغرس ويصلح كإصلاحهم أموالهم ولا تباع من أولاد نخل هذه القرى الأربع ودية حتّى تشكّل أرضها غراسا فإنّما عملتها للموءمنين

[1] MS omits ورقيقها
[2] MS ما ان حدث
[3] MS omits وفيه
[4] MS ومع ذلك رعة
[5] MS ورعة

أوّلهم وآخرهم ممّن وليها من الناس فأذكره الله إلا اجتهد نصح وحفظ أمانته ووسع هذا كتاب عليّ بن أبي طالب بيده إذ قدم مَسْكِن وقد علمتم أنّ الفقير ابن سبيل الله واجبة بتلة ومال محمّد صلّى الله عليه وسلّم يُنفَق فى كلّ نفقة فى سبيل الله ووجهه وذوى الرحم والفقراء والمساكين وابن السبيل يقوم على ذلك أكبر بنى فاطمة بالأمانة والإصلاح كإصلاحه ماله يزرع ويغرس
(7b) وينصح ويجتهد هذا ما قضى به عليّ بن أبي طالب فى هذه الأموال التى // كُتبت[1] فى هذه الصحيفة والله المستعان على كلّ حال ولا يحلّ لكلّ واحد وليها أو حكم فيها أن يعمل فيها بغير عهدى أمّا بعد فإنّ ولائدى اللاتى أتطوّف عليهنّ تسع عشرة منهنّ أمّهات أولاد أحياء معهنّ أولادهنّ ومنهنّ حبالَى ومنهنّ من لا ولد لها فقضيت إن حدث بى حدث[2] فى هذا الغزو إنّ من كان منهنّ ليس لها ولد وليس بحبلى عتيقة لوجه الله عزّ وجلّ ليس لأحد عليها سبيل ومن كان منهنّ حبلى أو لها ولد فلتمسك على ولدها وهى من حظّه فإن مات ولدها وهى حيّة فليس لأحد عليها سبيل فهذا ما قضى به فى ولائده التسع عشرة شهد على ذلك عبيد الله بن أبى رافع وهَيّاج بن أبى هَيّاج وكتب عليّ بن أبى طالب أمّ الكتاب بيده لعشر ليال خلون من جمادى الأولى من سنة تسع وثلاثين قال عبيد الله وكان بين مقتله وبين كتابه هذا أربعة أشهر وثلاث عشرة ليلة *

2.12 حدّثنا محمّد بن خزيمة قال حدّثنا أبو ربيعة قال حدّثنا أبو عوانة عن سعيد بن مسروق قال أوصى الربيع بن خُثَيم هذا ما أوصى به الربيع بن خُثَيم وهكذا كتبه رسول الله وأصحابه من بعده[3] *

2.13 (8a) وقد كتب يوسف بن خالد وهلال بن يحيى فى كتاب الإقرار والبراءات // هذا ما شهد عليه الشهود المسمّون فى هذا الكتاب ولم يكتبا هذا كتاب ما شهد عليه الشهود المسمّون فى هذا الكتاب وكان النظر على ذلك أن يكتب فى الشرى والوصايا وسائر الأشياء هذا ما اشترى وهذا ما أوصى وهذا ما اصطلح قياساً على ما أجمعوا عليه من ذلك *

2.14 قال أبو جعفر وانّما نسبنا كلّ واحد من البائع والمشترى الى أبيه والى جدّه والى قبيلته فقلنا فلان بن فلان بن فلان الفلانى ليُعرَف حضر أم غاب أم مات ولأنّ أبا حنيفة كان يقول لا يكون تعريفا الا بالنسبة الى الأب والجدّ وقال إن نُسب الى أبيه والى قبيلته ولم يُنسَب الى جدّه
2.15 لم يكن ذلك تعريفا وقال أبو يوسف هو تعريف جائز * وان نُسب الى أبيه وصناعته أو الى أبيه وتجارته فإنّ أبا حنيفة قال ليس ذلك بتعريف وقال أبو يوسف هو تعريف وقال أبو حنيفة اذا نُسب الى اسمه وصنعته فقيل فلان الخليفة أو فلان القاضى أو فلان الأمير كان تعريفا وقال
2.16 أبو يوسف مثـــل ذلك * وإن نُسب الى أبيه وكورته فإنّ أبا حنيفة كان يقول ليس ذلك

[1] MS التى كتب
[2] MS omits حدث
[3] MS بعدة

(8b) بتعريف وقال أبو يوسف هو تعريف وقال أبو حنيفة اذا نُسِب الى كلّ // ما ذكرنا إنّه تعريف وإن كان فى البلد [1] رجل آخر مثله فيما نُسِب اليه لم يكن ذلك تعريفا حتّى يوصَف بشىء آخر ليس فى صاحبه وكذلك قال أبو يوسف *

2.17 قال أبو جعفر فلمّا رأينا هذا الاختلاف نسبنا كلّ واحد من البائع والمشترى الى أبيه وجدّه وزدنا مع ذلك قبيلة إن كانت له قبيلة أو صناعة إن كانت له صناعة ليكون ذلك زيادة فى التعريف وليُبيِّن به من غيره من عسى أن يوافقه فى اسمه ونسبه *

2.18 وقد كان أبو زيد يكتب فى كتابه اشترى منه جميع الدار التي بمدينة كذا وهى فى يده وذكر أنّه إنّما فعل ذلك لأنّ بعض البصريين كان يقول اذا باع الرجل الدار أو الأرض أو ما باعه من شيء وليس فى يده لم يجز البيع وذهبوا الى أنّ ذلك بيع ما ليس عنده وانّه داخل فى نهى النبيّ عليه السلام عن بيع ما ليس عندك قال فاحتطت من قولهم وإن كان خطأ فكتبت فى كتابى ذكر اليد فى ذلك *

2.19 قال أبو جعفر ولم يكن أبو حنيفة ولا أبو يوسف ولا محمّد ولا يوسف ولا هلال يكتبون ذلك وقد ذكرنا عن رسول الله عليه السلام للعدّاء بن خالد ما قد تقدّم فى كتابنا هذا ولم يذكر فيه أنّه باعه ما باعه وهو فى يده فكان فى // ذلك حجّة قاطعة لمن ذهب الى ما كان أبو حنيفة (9a)
وأبو يوسف ومحمّد ويوسف وهلال يذهبون اليه على أبي زيد ومن ذهب مذهبه وهذا الذي ذكره أبو زيد عن بعض البصريين قد رُوى عنهم كما ذكر *

2.20 وكان أحبّ الينا ممّا ذهب اليه أبو زيد فى الاحتياط من ذلك ألاّ يذكر يد البائع على المبيع فى كتاب الشرى لأنّه لا يؤمَن أن يكون ذلك يوقع فى قلوب بعض القضاة أنّ إقرار المشترى بيد البائع على ما قد باع إقرار منه به للبائع فيكون ذلك مبطلا لوجوب الدرك له عليه فيه فى قول ابن أبي ليلى وأهل المدينة ومن قال بقولهم لأنّهم يقولون من أقرّ بشىء لرجل ثمّ ابتاعه منه ثمّ استحقّ منه مستحقّ ببيّنة شهدت له على ذلك وحكم له به القاضى إنّه لا يرجع على البائع بشىء لأنّه قد أقرّ للبائع أنّه كان مالكاً لما باعه يوم باعه فهو بإقراره ذلك عندهم مكذّب للبيّنة التى حكم بها القاضى للمدّعى *

2.21 وأمّا أبو حنيفة وأبو يوسف ومحمّد فيقولون اذا قضى القاضى بالمبيع للذى استحقّه على المبتاع بالبيّنة التى شهدت له عليه رجع المشترى على بائعه بالثمن *

3.1 قال أبو جعفر فاذا أراد رجل التوثّق من هذا القول الذى حكيناه // عمّن قاله من البصريين (9b)
كتب كتاب [2] الشرى خاليا من ذكر يد البائع على ما قد باع وأخذ شهادة الشهود على معاينة يد البائع على ما قد باع وأثبت ذلك فى كتاب غير كتاب الشرى ولا يكون للمشترى فى ذلك ذكر إقرار فإن رفع المشترى الى قاض يرى ما حكيناه من قول هؤلاء البصريين أظهر المشترى الكتاب الآخر الذى فيه شهادة الشهود على يد البائع على ما باعه يوم باعه *

[1] MS فكان فى البلد

[2] MS omits كتاب

3.0 وينبغى للمشترى إن آثر أن يفعل ذلك وإن يكتب شهادة الشهود على ما يشهد له على يـــد
البائع أن يكتب بسم الله الرحمن الرحيم هذا ما شهد عليه الشهود المسمّون فى هذا الكتاب شهدوا
جميعا أنّ جميع الدار التى بمدينة كذا فى الموضع الذى منها المعروف بكذا وهى الدار التى يحيط
بها ويجمعها ويشتمل عليها حدود أربعة أحد حدود جماعتها الحدّ الأوّل وهو كذا انتهى الى
كذا ثمّ تذكر بقيّة الحدود على ما كتبنا فى كتاب الشرى ثمّ تكتب بعقب ذلك شهد الشهود
المسمّون فى هذا الكتاب أنّ جميع الدار المحدودة فى هذا الكتاب بحدودها كلّها ثمّ تذكر الحقوق
(10 a) على مثل ما كتبنا // فى كتاب الشرى حتّى تأتى على وكلّ حقّ هو لها خارج منها فتكتب
بعقب ذلك فى يد فلان بن فلان بن فلان الفلانى يَسكنها وما شاء منها ويُسكِنها وما شاء منها
من أحبّ بأجر وغيره ويهدمها وما شاء منها ويبنى فيها ما شاء لا حائل بينه وبين ذلك يعلمونه
ولا مانع له منه يعرفونه وأنّهم قد علموا جميع ما شهدوا به على ما ذُكر من شهاداتهم فى هـــذا
الكتاب علما صحيحا وقبلوه[1] معرفة ويقينا وأنّ ذلك كان كذلك الى أن ابتاع فلان بن فلان
ابن فلان الفلانى من فلان بن فلان بن فلان الفلانى هذه الدار المحدودة فى هذا الكتاب بجميع
حدودها وحقوقها بكذا كذا دينارا مثاقيل ذهبا عينا وازنة جيادا والى أن سلّم فلان بن فلان بن
فلان الفلانى الى فلان بن فلان بن[2] فلان الفلانى جميع هذه الدار المحدودة فى هذا الكتاب بجميع
ما سُمّى لها ومنها فى هذا الكتاب والى أن قبضه منه فلان بن فلان[3] بن فلان الفلانى فصارت
فى يده وقبضه بابتياعه إيّاها منه وتسليم فلان بن فلان بن فلان الفلانى[4] إيّاها اليه وكتب فلان
ابن فلان على فلان بن فلان بذلك كتاب شرى باسمه تاريخه شهر كذا من سنة كذا ومن شهوده
(10 b) المسمّين فيه فلان بن فلان // وفلان بن فلان وفلان بن فلان وغيرهم من الشهود *

4.0 قال أبو جعفر وان شاء نسخ كتاب شرى كلّه فهو أوثق وأجود فإن آثر أن يفعل ذلك كتب
وكتب فلان بن فلان على فلان بن فلان بذلك كتاب شرى باسمه نسخته بسم الله الرّحمن الرحيم
حتّى تأتى على آخره ثمّ تكتب أسماء الشهود أو من شاء منهم على مثل مـــا ذكرنا اذا كُتب
التاريخ وأسماء بعض الشهود ولم يُنْسَخ الكتاب ثمّ تكتب على أثر ذلك شهد فلان بن فلان
وفلان بن فلان وفلان بن فلان حتّى تأتى على أسماء الشهود الذين يشهدون على يد البائع بجميع
ما ذُكر من شهاداتهم فى هذا الكتاب وأنّهم يعرفون فلان بن فلان يعنى البائع وفلان بن فلان
يعنى المشترى معرفة صحيحة بأعيانهما وأسمائهما وأنسابهما وأنّهما فلان بن فلان بن فلان الفلانى[5]
وفلان بن فلان بن فلان الفلانى المسمّيان فى الكتاب المنسوخ فى هذا الكتاب هذا إن كان نسخ
كتاب الشرى وإن كان لم ينسخه كتبت المسمّيان فى هذا الكتاب وفى الكتاب المذكور تاريخه
(11 a) وشهوده فى هذا الكتاب وأنّهم يعرفون هذا الدار المحدودة فى هذا الكتاب // ويقفون على نهاياتها

[1] MS قتلوه
[2] MS omits بن
[3] MS omits بن فلان
[4] MS omits الفلانى
[5] MS omits الفلانى

المذكورات لها فى هذا الكتاب وفى الكتاب المنسوخ فى هذا الكتاب إن كان نسخه فيه أو المذكور تاريخه وشهوده فى هذا الكتاب إن كان لم ينسخه فيه ثمّ تكتب وأشهد فلان بن فلان وفلان بن فلان حتّى تأتى على أسماء الشهود ثمّ تكتب على شهادتهم المسمّاة فى هذا الكتاب سائرَ الشهود المسمّين معهم فى هذا الكتاب أنّهم يشهدون بجميع ما ذكر من شهادتهم فى هذا الكتاب وكتبوا شهاداتهم بخطوطهم على جميع ما سُمّى ووُصف فى هذا الكتاب فى شهر كذا من سنة كذا *

4.1 قال أبو جعفر وانّما ذكرنا فى كتابنا هذا معرفة الشهود البائع والمشترى ليُعرفا باعيانهما وأسمائهما وأنسابهما وليصحّ شهادة من شهد على شهادة الشهود على ابتياع هذا وعلى بيع هذا *

4.2 وانّما ذكرنا وقوفهم على نهايات الحدود لأنّه قد يجوز أن يعرف الرجل الدار بوقوفه عليها ولا يعرف نهاياتها وكتبنا معرفة الشهود بنهايات الدار الموصوفة[1] ليتبيّن بذلك صحّة ما شهدوا عليه *

4.3 وكذلك كان أصحابنا يكتبون فى محاضرهم وسجلّاتهم التى تقع فيها الشهادة على أدر بعينها // أو (11 b) أرضين بأعيانها لا على إقرار المقرّ بها ويكتبون ذلك كذلك فى سائر العقارات التى يذكرون فيها الشهادة على معاينتها ولا يفعلون ذلك فيما تقع الشهادة فيه على الإقرار دون المعاينة *

4.4 وانّما كتبنا فى الشهادة على الشهادة ما كتبنا ولم نكتب كما يكتب بعض الناس وقالوا لهم أشهِدوا على شهاداتنا أنّا نشهد على جميع ما ذكر من شهاداتنا عليه فى هذا الكتاب لأنّ فى قولنا على إشهاد فلان بن فلان وفلان بن فلان وفلان بن فلان على شهاداتهم سائرَ الشهود المسمّين معهم فى هذا الكتاب أنّهم يشهدون على جميع ما ذكر فى شهاداتهم فى هذا الكتاب وكتاب الشهود الآخرين شهاداتهم على ذلك بخطوطهم فى آخر الكتاب وما[2] يأتى على ذلك ويغنى عنه *

4.5 وكان أبو حنيفة وأبو يوسف ومحمّد ويوسف وهلال يكتبون فى ذلك نحو ممّا كتبنا غير أنّ يوسف وهلال كانا يكتبان وعلى إشهاد فلان وفلان سائرَ الشهود المسمّين فى هذا الكتاب على شهادتهم (12 a) بجميع ما فى هذا الكتاب ولا يكتبان // أنّهم يشهدون قال أبو جعفر والذى ذهبنا اليه من هذا أجود وأصحّ فى المعنى *

2.22 قال أبو جعفر ثمّ رجعنا الى الكتاب الأوّل والى ما اختُلف فيه منه فكان أبو حنيفة يكتب فى كتابه اشترى منه الدار التى فى بنى فلان ولا يكتب التى بالكوفة وكان ذلك عنده على تلك القبيلة من ذلك المصر الذى وقع البيع فيه قال أبو جعفر سمعت أبا بكرة بكّار بن قتيبة يحكى ذلك عنه وقد حدّثنيه أيضا سليمان بن شُعَيب بن سليمان الكيسانىّ عن أبيه عن محمّد بن الحسن عن أبى حنيفة *

2.23 قال أبو جعفر وخالفه فى ذلك يوسف بن خالد وهلال وأبو زيد وسائر أصحاب الشروط وكتبوا فى ذلك نحو ممّا كتبناه فى كتابنا هذا وهذا القول أصحّ عندنا ممّا ذهب اليه أبو حنيفة لأنّه قد

[1] MS الدار الصفة

[2] MS omits وما

يجوز أن يكون ذلك على دار فى هذه القبيلة من ذلك المصر الذى تبايعا فيه أو على دار فى تلك القبيلة من مصر آخر فلمّا لم يتبيّنا مصرا بعينه كان البيع فاسدا وقد يجوز أن يقع البيع فى مصر بعينه على ما ذكرنا ثمّ يختلفان بعد فى المصر الذى وقع فيه البيع فيقول أحدهما وقع البيع بالكوفة
(12 b) على دار فى كندة وهى كندة الكوفة ويقول الآخر وقع البيع بمصرَ // على دار فى كندة وهى كندة مصرَ ولا يكون فى كتابهما معنى يدلّ على ما يقول أحدهما وقد يجوز أن تكون تلك القبيلة فى المصر الذي تبايعا فيه فى موضعَين فيقول أحدهما هذه الدار التى وقع عليها البيع[1] بمدينة كذا فى قبيلة كذا وهى القبيلة السفلى منها ويقول الآخر هذه الدار التى وقع البيع عليها بمدينة كذا فى قبيلة كذا وهي القبيلة العُليا[2] منها ولا يكون فى الكتاب الذى اكتتباه بينهما ما يدلّ على ما يقول
2.24 أحدهما فيتخالفان ويترادّان ولا يصحّ البيع ٭ قال أبو جعفر وقد اختلف الناس فما يُبْدَأ به من حدود الدار فى تحديدها وكان أبو يوسف وهلال يبتدئان بالحدّ الذى فيه باب الدار ثمّ يثنّيان بما
2.25 عن يمين الداخل منها ثمّ بما يلقى[3] وجهه ثمّ بما عن يساره ٭ وكان غيرهما[يبتدئ بالحدّ الذى عن يمين الداخل ثمّ بما يلقى][4]وجهه ثمّ بما عن يساره ثمّ بما وراء ظهره وهوالحدّ الذى فيه الباب ٭

2.26 وكل واحد من هذين المعنيين حسن جائز غير أنّه قد رُوى عن أبى حنيفة وأبى يوسف أنّهما كانا يبتدئان بحدّ القبلة[5] منها فيكتبان حدّها ممّا يلى القبلة كذا وحدّها من دبر القبلة كذا وكان هذا أحسن عندنا من القولين الأوّلين لأنّه انّما اعتبر كلّ واحد من أهل القولين الأوّلين
(13 a) باب الدار فابتدأ به بعضهم وأخّره بعضهم وقد يجوز أن يحول باب الدار // عن الموضع الذى هو فيه الى موضع آخر ومن الجانب الذى هو فيه الى جانب آخر من جوانب الدار فتذهب العلّة التى بها صار الجانب الذى كان فيه باب الدار أوّلا فى قول من جعله الأوّل وتذهب العلّة التى بها صار باب الدار آخرا فى قول من جعله الآخر وكان ما كتب أبو حنيفة وأبو يوسف ممّا لا
2.27 يحول ولا يتغيّر فكان أولى هذه الأقوال عندنا ٭ وقد كنت قبل ذلك أذهب الى ألاّ أجعل كلّ واحد من القولين الأوّلين أولى من الآخر حتّى وقعت على معنى ما ذهب اليه أبو حنيفة وأبو يوسف وكان عندى أولى من المعنيين الأوّلين وأحسن منها ٭

2.28 قال أبو جعفر وقد كان قوم يقدّمون الحدّ الشرقىّ على الغربىّ وقوم يقدّمون الغربىّ على الشرقىّ وكلّ ذلك واسع غير أنّا نبتدئ بالشرقىّ فى كتبنا على الغربىّ لأنّ القرآن قد جاء بتبدئته قال عزّ وجلّ (وللهِ المَشْرِقُ والمَغْرِبُ) وقال عزّ وجلّ (رَبُّ المَشْرِقَيْنِ والمَغْرِبَيْنِ)
2.29 وقال (فَلَا أُقْسِمُ بِرَبِّ المَشَارِقِ والمَغَارِبِ) فلهذا بدأنا بالشرقىّ قبل الغربىّ ٭ قال أبو
(13 b) جعفر وقد كان قوم يكتبون فى كتبهم حدّها الكذا دارُ فلان // وهذا عندنا فاسد لأنّه قد

[1] MS omits البيع
[2] MS القبيلة العلى
[3] MS بما تلقا
[4] يبتدئ بالحد الذى عن يمين الداخل ثم بما يلقى cut off by binder's scissors; the passage from باب الدار ثم يثنيان to الحد الذى فيه الباب was added in the margin by the copyist and is unclear.
[5] MS بحد القبلى

2.30 ابتاع الدار التى ابتاعها بحدودها لأنّ حدودها انّما هى نهاياتها * ألا ترى أنّه[1] يقول بعد هذا فى كتابه بحدودها كلّها وأرضها وبنائها فيجعله مبتاعاً لحدودها كما كان مبتاعا لبنائها فتدخل فى ذلك الدار التى جعلها حدّا لها فلا ينبغى لأحد أن يكتب هذا فى كتابه فإن جهل رجل فكتبه فإنّ أبا يوسف كان يقول لا أُبطِل به الشرى بذلك وأجعلُه على النهاية على ما تعرف العامّة *

2.31 وقال غيره من أصحابنا قد دخلت الدار التى جعلها حدّا لهذه الدار فى البيع فصار البائع بائعا لما يملك ولما لا يملك فى صفقة واحدة *

2.32 ثمّ يختلفون بعدها فى الحكم فى ذلك فكان أبو حنيفة وزُفر وأبو يوسف ومحمّد يقولون فى مثل هذا فيمن باع ما يملك وما لا يملك صفقة واحدة إنّ المشترى بالخيار إن شاء أخذ ما كان البائع يملك ممّا وقع عليه البيع بحصّته من الثمن يُقسَّم الثمنُ على قيمة هذا المملوك للبائع وعلى قيمة ما استُحِقّ على المشترى ممّا باع منه يوم وقع البيع عليهما فيكون حصّة كلّ واحد منهما من الثمن

2.33 (14 a) مقدار ما أصابه منه على هذه القسمة * وكان آخرون يقولون اذا دخل هذا // فى البيع فسد البيع لأنّه إنّما يكون ثمن ما يسلّم للمشترى من المبيع ما أصابه على هذه القسمة التى لا حقيقة معها انّما هي تحرُّز ونظر ففسد البيع من هذه الجهة فيجب الاحتراز من قولهم هذا *

2.34 قال وكان أبو يوسف ومحمّد يكتبان حدّها الكذا يلى الدار المعروفة بفلان وكان آخرون

2.35 من أصحابنا يكتبون ينتهى الى الدار المعروفة بفلان منهم يوسف وهلال وأبو زيد * وكان محمّد ابن الحسن يذهب الى أنّ يلى فى هذا أحبّ اليه من ينتهي قال لأنّه قد يقال قد انتهى فلان الى فلان وبينهما شيء ولا يقال أنّ شيئا يلى شيئا وبينهما شيء قال محمّد فلهذا اخترنـــا يلى على

2.36 ينتهى * قال أبو جعفر فلمّا اختلفوا هذا الاختلاف نظرنا فى كلام الناس الذى يتعارفونه بينهم فى هذا كيف هو فوجدناهم يقولون دار فلان تلى دار فلان وبينهما الفرجة وما أشبهها وقد قال رسول الله عليه السلام لأصحابه ليَلِينِى منكم أولو الأحـْلام والنُّهَى ولم يرد بذلك الملاصقة وقال أنس بن مالك كان رسول الله عليه السلام يحبّ أن يليه المهاجرون والأنصار ليحفظوا عنه

(14 b) فما يخاف من ينتهى شيء إلاّ خيف من يلى مثله // وكانت ينتهى أعمّ فى كلام الناس من يلى فاخترناها لذلك *

2.37 قال فإن كانت بين الدارين فرجة كتبتَ ينتهى الى الفرجة التى بينها وبين الدار المعروفة بفلان وإن شئتَ كتبتَ الى الفرجة الفاصلة التى بينها وبين الدار المعروفة بفلان وهذا أحبّ الي من الأوّل لا بـَل اذا قلنا الفرجة التي بينها وبين الدار المعروفة بفلان احتمل هذا أن يكون الفرجة من

2.38 الدارين فيكون بعضها قد دخل فى الدار المبيعة وبعضها الى الدار الأخرى[2] * قال أبو جعفر وقد كره أصحابنا أن يكتبوا فى كتبهم حدّها ينتهى الى دار فلان لأنّه لا يـُؤمن أن يبتاعها المشترى

[1] MS omits أنه ; ترى is unclear.

[2] MS وبعضها الى الفرجة

أو البائع يوما ما فيكون قد تقدّم إقراره أنّها للذى أضيفت اليه فى كتاب الشرى فلا يجب له عهدة على بائعه إيّاها فى قول ابن أبى ليلى وزفر وأهل المدينة *

2.39 قال أبو جعفر وقد كان قوم يكتبون حدّها الأوّل بأسره ينتهى الى الدار المعروفة بفلان وذهبوا الى أنّهم اذا لم يكتبوا بأسره احتمل أن يكون النهاية لبعض الحدّ ولم يكن أبو حنيفة ولا أبو يوسف
(15 a) ولا يوسف بن خالد ولا محمّد بن الحسن ولا هلال ولا أبو زيد ولا غيرهم // من أهل العلم علمناه
2.40 يكتب ذلك فى كتابه غير من أضفناه اليه وإن كنّا لم نذكره باسمه * قال أبو جعفر وقد أجمعوا أن كتبوا اشترى منه جميع الدار ولم يكتبوا بأسرها فكان ذلك عندهم على جميع الدار والحدّ فى
2.41 النظر كذلك أيضا ومحال أن يكون حدّها هو حدّ بعضها * فان قال قائل فقد ذكرتَ فى الدار ما يجمعها فقلتَ اشترى منه جميع الدار قيل له وقد كتبنا فى الحدود مثل ذلك أحد حدود جماعتها فذكرنا جماعة حدود الدار كما ذكرنا جماعة الدار فأتى ذلك على جماعة كلّ واحد منها *

2.42 قال أبو جعفر وقد اختلف الناس فيما يُكتَب بعقب البناء فكان يوسف وهلال يكتبان وبنائها سفله وعلوّه ويقولان انّما السفل والعلوّ للبناء لا لغيره من الدار وذهبا فى ذلك الى أنّهما لم يأمنا اذا قالا وسفلها وعلوّها أن يتوهّم متوهّم أنّ العلوّ هو الهواء فيكون ذلك كقوله وسمائها
2.43 وذلك يفسد البيع قالا فكتبنا سفله وعلوّه وأضفنا ذلك الى البناء لهذا المعنى * وكان أبو زيد
(15 b) وسائر أصحابنا سوى يوسف وهلال يكتبون وبنائها // وسفلها وعلوّها [بهل] و[البيع][1] على سفل الدار وعلى علوّها واحتجّ أبو زيد فى ذلك فقال اذا أضفنا السفل والعلوّ الى البناء دون الدار لم نأمن أن يتوهّم متوهّم أنّ ذلك لا ينفى أن يكون لغير البائع حقّ على هذا البناء من إحداث بناء آخر عليه *

2.44 قال فلمّا اختلفوا على ما ذكرنا ورأيناهم قد أجمعوا على أن كتبوا بعد هذا وكلّ قليل وكثير هو لها ومنها من حقوقها وكلّ حقّ هو لها داخل فيها وخارج منها فجعلوا ذلك معنى للدا ر لا للبناء ولم يكن ذلك على هواء الدار وإنّما كان على مـا كان منها ممّا يجوز اشتراطه فى البيع ووقوع البيع عليه كان كذلك وسفلها وعلوّها هما على العلوّ الذي يجوز اشتراطه فى البيع ويجوز وقوع البيع عليه وكما كان ما وصفنا مأمونا فى قوله وكلّ قليل وكثير هو لها ومنها من حقوقها كان هو كذلك فهو مأمون فى قولنا وسفلها وعلوّها وحجّة أخرى أنّا رأينا سفلها وعلوّها يشتملان على الدار كلّها من البناء والسقف وسفله وعلوّه ليسا كذلك . *

2.45 وانّما كتبنا ومسايلها فى حقوقها ومرافقها فى حقوقها وطرقها[2] التى هى لها فى حقوقها ولم نكتب
(16 a) بقولنا ومسايلها ومرافقها وطرقها حتّى قلنا فى كلّ واحد من ذلك // فى حقوقه لئلا يتوهّم متوهّم أنّ ذلك على الطرق الخارجة منها التى لا يجوز بيعها ولا اشتراطها فى البياعات أو يتوهّم فى المرافق

[1] letters obliterated in MS [2] MS ومرافقها وطرقها

أنّها الأفنية التى لا يجوز بيعها أو فى المسايل أنّها على المسايل التي يجرى فيها الماء الى الدور التى لا يجوز بيعها فاحتطنا لذلك وكتبنا فى كلّ واحد ممّا ذكرنا من حقوقها *

2.46 وقد كان يوسف وهلال وأبو زيد يكتبون فى كتبهم وكلّ حقّ هو لها داخل فيها وخارج
2.47 منها يريدون بذلك طريقا إن كان لها فى دار أخرى وما أشبه ذلك * وكان غيرهم من أصحابنا
يكتب وكلّ حقّ هو لها داخل فيها وكلّ حقّ هو لها خارج منها ويذهب فى ذلك الى أنّه اذا
قال وكلّ حقّ هو لها داخل فيها وخارج منها جعل الحقّ بكماله داخلا وجعله بكماله خارجا
قال وذلك محال لأنّه إن كان داخلا فهو غير خارج وإن كان خارجا فهو غير داخل فكتبتُ
ما كتبتُ من ذلك لهذا المعنى ليكون الداخل من تلك الحقوق غير الخارج منها ويكون الخارج
غير الداخل فيها ويدخلان جميعا فى البيع بكلام صحيح لا إحالة فيه قال أبو جعفر فكان ذلك
عندنا كلاما صحيحاً فاخترناه وكتبناه وخالفنا ما خالفه *

2.48 وكان يوسف بن خالد وهلال بن يحيى يكتبان // فى كتبهما كلّها الدار المحدودة فى هذا الكتاب (16 b)
وكان أبو حنيفة وأبو يوسف ومحمّد يكتبون الدار المحدودة [1] فى كتابنا هذا غير أنّ بشر بن الوليد
حكى عن أبى يوسف فى الإملاء أنّه كتب كتاب وقف رواه عنه الدار المحدودة فى هذا الكتاب *
2.49 وكان ما ذهب اليه أبو يوسف ومَن تابعه على ذلك أحبّ الينا لأنّا اذا قلنا فى كتابنا هذا كان
فى ذلك إضافة الكتاب الى القارئ أو الكاتب أو المشترى أو البائع *

2.50 وكان يوسف يكتب فى كتابه وكلّ قليل وكثير هو فيها ومنها وكلّ حقّ هو لها وكان أبو
2.51 زيد يكتب وكلّ قليل وكثير هو لها فيها ومنها من حقوقها * فكان ما كتب أبو زيد فى هذا
أصحّ عندنا وأحسن لأنّه قد يكون فيها ما ليس منها من سكّانها وأمتعاتهم التى لا يريدون بيعها
معها واذا قال وكلّ قليل وكثير هو لها فيها ومنها من حقوقها دخل فى ذلك كلّما كان لها من
2.52 حقّ وانتفى ما كان فيها من غير حقوقها * وقد كان أبو حنيفة يكتب وكلّ حقّ هو لها
داخل فيها أو خارج منها وكلّ قليل وكثير قال حدّثني بذلك سليمان بن شُعَيب عن أبيه عن
2.53 محمّد عن أبى يوسف عن أبى حنيفة * وكان يوسف وهلال وأبو زيد يكتبون وكلّ قليل وكثير
وكلّ حقّ هو لها داخل فيها وخارج منها فكان هذا أحبّ الينا ممّا كان أبو حنيفة يكتب فى
ذلك لأنّ « أو » فى هذا // قد يكون على أحد الأمرين * (17 a)

2.54 قال أبو جعفر وانّما كتبنا وكلّ حقّ هو لها خارج منها لأنّ أبا حنيفة كان يقول اذا وقع
البيع على دار لها ظلّة عليها وعلى دار أخرى أو لها مسيل ماء أو طريق فى دار أخرى لم يدخل
2.55 شىء من ذلك فى البيع حتّى تقول بجميع حقوقها الداخلة فيها والخارجة منها * وقال أبو يوسف
فى الطريق ومسيل الماء بقول أبى حنيفة وقال فى الظلّة بخلاف قوله فقال هى داخلة فى البيع اشترطت

[1] MS امحدودة

أو لم تشترط أو اشتُرِط للدار كلّ حقّ هو لها داخل فيها أو خارج منها أو لم يُشترط وقال أبو حنيفة وأبو يوسف ومحمّد لو لم فقل بكلّ حقّ هو لها داخل فيها أو خارج منها وقال بكلّ قليل أو كثير هو لها داخل فى ذلك الطريق والظلّة ومسيل الماء فكتبنا وكلّ حقّ هو لها خارج منها وكلّ قليل وكثير هو لها فيها ومنها من حقوقها لهذا المعنى *

2.56 وكان أبو زيد يكتب شرى صحيحا ثابتا تاما لا خيار فيه ولا شرط ولا فساد ولا عدة ولا على جهة الرهن والتلجئة ولم يكن أبو حنيفة ولا أبو يوسف ولا يوسف ولا هلال يكتبون من ذلك شيئا
2.57 ولا يصفون البيع بصحّة ولا ثبات ولا غير ذلك * فكان ترك ما كتب أبو زيد فى هذا أحوط
(17b) لأنّ فى إقرار المشترى // بصحّة البيع إقرار منه بأنّ مستحقّا إن استحقّ الدار فقد أخذها ظلما وذلك يمنعه من الرجوع على بائعه بثمن ما باعه اذا استُحقّت الدار من يده فى قول ابن أبى
2.58 ليلى وزفر وأهل المدينة * فحذفنا ذلك من كتابنا غير أنّا كتبنا شرى لا شرط فيه ولا عدة لينفى أن يدّعى واحد من المتبايعين أنّه كان فى البيع شرط *

2.59 وكتبنا ولا عدة لينفى منه العدة لأنّ الناس قد اختلفوا فى العدة فأمّا أصحابنا وأكثر أهل العلم فيقولون لا معنى لها والذي وعد بها بالخيار فى الحكم إن شاء وَفَى وإن شاء لم يَفِ وأفضل له فيما بينه وبين ربّه بأن يَفِى بها وأوجبها آخرون وجعلوا على الذى وعد بها الوفاء بها فنفيّناها
2.60 من البيع لهذا المعنى * وقد كان بعض أصحابنا يكتبون بيعاً لا خيار فيه ولا شرط ولا عدة ويحذف ما سوى ذلك ممّا كتبه أبو زيد وهذا عندنا خطأ لأنّ قوماً يقولون اذا وقع البيع فكلّ واحد من المتبايعين بالخيار على صاحبه حتّى يفارقه ببدنه ويتأوّلون ما يُروَى عن رسول الله عليه السلام من قوله البيّعان بالخيار ما لم يفترقا على ذلك فاذا نفى الخيار من البيع كان البيع فاسدا فى قول هؤلاء الذين يوجبون فيه الخيار على هذه الجهة التى وصفنا *

2.61 (18a) وكان يوسف يكتب // فبَرِئ فلان الى فلان من جميع الثمن المسمّى فى هذا الكتاب
2.62 وقبضه منه فلان بن فلان تامّا وافيا وهو كذا وكذا دينارا * وكان أبو زيد يكتب وقبض فلان ابن فلان من فلان بن فلان جميع الثمن المسمّى فى هذا الكتاب تامّا وافيا بدفع من فلان بن فلان
2.63 ذلك اليه وبرئ اليه منه فلان بن فلان وهو كذا كذا دينارا * فاجتزى يوسف بقوله فبرئ فلان الى فلان من ذكر الدفع من المشترى للثمن الى البائع ثمّ ادّعى ذكر قبض البائع للثمن وإن كان فى ذكره براءة المشترى الى البائع من الثمن ما يوجب أن يكون البائع قد قبض الثمن *

2.64 ألا ترى أصحابنا قد قالوا فى رجل قال لرجل قد بَرِئتَ اليّ ممّا لى عليك إنّه قد أقرّ له بقبض ما كان له عليه ولو قال قد أبرأتُك ممّا لى عليك إنّ ذلك ليس بإقرار منه بالقبض هكذا حدّثناه محمّد بن العبّاس بن الربيع عن علىّ بن معبد عن محمّد بن الحسن عن أبى يوسف عن أبى
2.65 حنيفة ولم يحك خلافا بينهم * وقد حدّثنا سليمان بن شعيب عن أبيه عن محمّد بن الحسن عن أبى يوسف عن أبى حنيفة بمثله أيضا غير أنّه ذكر عن أبى يوسف فى رواية محمّد هذه عنه أنّه

(18b) قال هما سواء وهما يقعان على // الإقرار بالقبض وليس هذا بالمشهور عندنا من قول أبي يوسف والمشهور عندنا هو القول الأوّل فذهب يوسف بن خالد الى أنّ قوله فبرئ فلان بن فلان من الثمن المسمّى فى هذا الكتاب بدفع المشترى وقبض البائع *

2.66 فاخترنا خلاف ما كتب يوسف وخلاف ما كتب أبو زيد ممّا هو أبين وأفهم عند العامّة فكتبنا ودفع فلان بن فلان الى فلان بن فلان جميع الثمن المسمّى فى هذا الكتاب وقبضه منه فلان ابن فلان واستوفاه منا تامّا كاملا وأبرأه من جميعه بعد قبضه ايّاه واستيفائه له وهو كذا كذا دينارا مثاقيل ذهبا عينا وازنة جيادا فجمعنا فى ذلك ذكر دفع[1] المشترى وقبض البائع وقد كان أبو يوسف يكتب فى ذلك نحو ممّا كتبنا *

2.67 وانّما احتجنا الى ذكر دفع المشترى الثمن ولم نجتز بذكر قبض البائع ايّاه لأنّ قوما يقولون لو كان لرجل على رجل مال فقبض مثله من ماله من حيث لا يعلم الذى هو عليه أنّه لا يطيب له أخذه وأصحابنا يجيزون ذلك الأخذ[2] ويحتجّون فيما يذهبون اليه من ذلك بحديث النبيّ عليه السلام لمّا سألته هند أمّ معاوية فقالت يا رسول الله إنّ أبا سفيان رجل شحيح وإنّه لا يعطيني

(19a) ما يكفيني وبنتي فهل عليَّ جناح إن آخذ من ماله سرّا // فقال رسول الله خُذي ما يكفيك

2.68 وبنتك بالمعروف * قال حدّثنا بذلك محمّد بن عمرو بن يونس السوسى قال حدّثنا أبو معاوية الضرير عن هشام بن عروة عن أبيه عن عائشة عن النبيّ عليه السلام فاخترنا دفع المشترى للثمن لهذا الاختلاف *

2.69 وكان ما كتبناه من هذا أيضا أحبّ الينا ممّا يكتبه بعض الناس وهو دفع فلان الى فلان جميع

2.70 هذه الكذا كذا الدينار فيجعل الدفع على الدنانير ولا يذكر الثمن * وكان ذكر الثمن فى هذا أحبّ الينا لأنّ تسمية الدنانير ليس فيها ذكر الوفاء بها للثمن الذى وقع بها البيع لأنّها قد يكون دنانير معيّنة من غير جنس الثمن الذى وقع به البيع واذا ذُكر الثمن كان فيه ذكر الوفاء وأغنى عن كثير من الكلام حتّى يتُوصّل به الى مثل ذلك المعنى *

2.71 ثمّ وكّدنا ذلك أيضا فكتبنا واستوفاه منه تاما كاملا ليثبت استيفاء البائع لعين الثمن ووزنه وجودته *

2.72 ثمّ وكّدنا ذلك أيضا فكتبنا وأبرأه من جميعه بعد قبضه ايّاه واستيفائه له وهو كذا كذا دينارا مثاقيل ذهبا عينا وازنة جيادا وإن زدتَ فى توكيده وأبرأه من جميعه بعد قبضه ايّاه واستيفائه له منه وهو كذا كذا دينارا كان ذلك أجود وأولى وأحوط وذلك أنّه قد يكون قبض الثمن من غيره ثمّ أبرأه منه ولا يجب له ردّه عليه إن استُحِقّت الدار من يده وانّما يجب عليه ردّه الى من كان

(19b) دفعه اليه فكان ذكر البراءة // بعد القبض والاستيفاء منه أحوط لهذا المعنى *

[1] MS omits دفع

[2] MS لاخذ

2.73 وإن لم تكتب ذلك لم يضرّ لأنّك قد كتبتَ قبل هذا ودفع فلان بن فلان الى فلان بن فلان جميع الثمن المسمّى فى هذا الكتاب وقبضه منه فلان بن فلان فكان ما ذكرتَ بعد هذا من البراءة بعد القبض والاستيفاء انّما يقع ذلك على القبض المذكور بدءًا فإن ذكرتَ هذا فى كتابك فحسن وإن اجتزأتَ بما تقدّم منك فيه ممّا قد ذكرنا فحسن *

2.74 قال أبو جعفر وانّما كتبنا فى قبض الدار وسلّم فلان بن فلان الى فلان بن فلان جميع ما وقع عليه هذا البيع المسمّى فى هذا الكتاب ولم نكتب وسلّم فلان بن فلان الى فلان بن فلان جميع هذه الدار المحدودة فى هذا الكتاب كما كان يوسف وهلال وأبو زيد يكتبون فى ذلك لأنّا اذا ذكرنا الدار احتجنا الى[1] أن نكتب ما قد ذكرناه فيما قد تقدّم من ذكر الحقوق والحدود حتّى نأتى على آخر ذلك المعنى واذا كتبنا جميع ما وقع عليه البيع أتَى ذلك على الدار على ما كان فيها وعلى ما كان منها وعلى ما سُمِّى منها ولها فيما تقدّم من الكتاب فاخترنا ذلك لأنّه أجمع وأخصر *

2.75 وانّما كتبنا وسلّم فلان بن فلان الى فلان بن فلان ولم نكتب وقبض فلان جميع ما وقع عليه هذا البيع لأنّ قوما يقولون مَن قبض ما ابتاع من يد بائعه وإن كان قد دفع ثمنه بغير تسليم //

(20 a) من بائعه ايّاه اليه فهو فى قبضه كالغاصب وعليه أن يردّه الى يد البائع حتّى يكون البائع هو الذى يخرجه من يده الى يده فاحتطنا من ذلك وإن كان خطأ لما ذكرنا *

2.76 وانّما قدّمنا ذكر قبض الثمن على ذكر قبض الدار لأنّ قوما يقولون قبض المشترى للدار بإذن البائع إقرار من البائع باستيفائه الثمن من المشترى فقدّمنا ذكر قبض البائع للثمن على ذكر قبض المشترى الدار لذلك *

2.77 قال أبو جعفر وكان يوسف يكتب وذلك بعد أن أقرّ فلان وفلان أنّهما قد رأيا جميعاً وكان أبو زيد يكتب وذلك بعد أن نظر اليه فلان يعنى المشترى وتبحّرها ورضيها ولا يكتب رؤية البائع

2.78 ولم يكن أبو حنيفة ولا أبو يوسف ولا محمّد يذكرون فى كتبهم[2] رؤية واحد المتبايعين * فكان ما كتب يوسف فى هذا أحبّ الينا لاختلاف الناس فى ذلك فكان أبو حنيفة وأبو يوسف وزفر ومحمّد يقولون للمشترى خيار الرؤية فيما اشترى ممّا لم يكن رآه قبل ذلك ولا خيار للبائع فيما باع ممّا قد كان رآه قبل ذلك وممّا لم يكن رآه *

2.79 وكان سوّار بن عبد الله العنبرى يقول لكلّ واحد من المتبايعين خيار الرؤية فيما عُقد البيع

2.80 عليه ممّا لم يكن رآه قبل ذلك * وقد رُوى عن أبى حنيفة أنّه قد كان قال هذا القول مرة //

(20 b) ثمّ رجع عنه وقد رُوى عن أصحاب رسول الله عليه السلام أنّهم كانوا قد اختلفوا فى ذلك أيضا *

2.81 قال حدّثنا بكّار بن قُتَيْبة ومحمّد بن شاذان جميعا قالا حدّثنا هلال بن يحيى بن مسلم قال حدثنا عبد الرحمن بن مهدى قال حدّثنا رَباح بن أبى معروف المكّى عن ابن أبى مُلَيكة

[1] MS omits الى

[2] MS يذكران فى كتبهما

عن عَلقَمة بن وقّاص الليثى قال اشترى طلحة بن عبيد الله من عثمان بن عفّان مالا بالكوفة
قال وهو مال آل طلحة اليوم بالكوفة فقيل لعثمان إنّك قد غُبنتَ فقال لى الخيار لأنّى بعتُ
ما لم أرَ فقال طلحة بل لى الخيار لأنّى اشتريتُ ما لم أرَ فحكّما بينهما جبير بن مطعم فقضى
أنّ الخيار لطلحة ولا خيار لعثمان *

2.82 قال أبو جعفر فكتبنا ذكر رؤية المشترى وذكر رؤية البائع احتياطاً من هذا الاختلاف *
2.83 وقد قال آخرون لا يجوز أن يتبايع رجلان شيئا غائبا عنهما فكتبنا أيضا ذكر رؤية المتبايعين لما
وقع البيع عليه ليثبت حضورهما ايّاه ولينفى غيبة كلّ واحد منهما عنه حتّى لا يفسد البيع
فى قول مَن لا يجيز بيع ما هو غائب عن المتبايعين ولا عن واحد منهما *

2.84 2.85 وكان يوسف وهلال يكتبان الرؤية التى كتبناها على إقرار المتبايعين بها * وكان أبو زيد
يكتبها على إثبات رؤية المشترى لا على إقرار منه وذهب مالك الى أنّ ما تقدّم فى كتاب الشرى
(21 a) من قبض الثمن // وقبض المبيع لم يُكتَب على الإقرار من المتبايعين به بل كُتِب على إثبات
ذلك وعلى أنّه قد كان قال فكذلك رؤية المبيع لا تُكتَب على إقرار المشترى بها [1] ولكن تُكتَب
على الإثبات وإنّها قد كانت من المشترى *

2.86 وكان من الحجّة فى ذلك ليوسف ولهلال على أبى زيد فيما ذكرناه عنه فيما احتجّ به على مَن
ذهب الى ما ذهبنا اليه أنّ قَبْض الثمن وقبض المبيع يُدْرَك ويُوقف منه على علم وعلى حقيقة
ويَعلم ذلك مَن حضره ممّن كان منه علم حقيقة كما يَعلمه الذى كان ذلك منه من نفسه فكتبتُ
2.87 ذلك على الإثبات لا على الإقرار من المتبايعين به لهذا المعنى * ورؤية الرجل للشىء ليس
ممّا يحيط بها غيرُه علما لأنّ الرجل قد يُقبِل ببصره على الشىء فيتوهّم الذى رآه أنّه قد رآه
ونظر اليه ولا يكون كذلك فى الحقيقة *

2.88 فلمّا كان ذلك كذلك كتبنا الرؤية التى وصفنا على إقرار المتبايعين بها لا على إثباتها منهما
2.89 وقد أجمعوا جميعا على مثل ذلك * ألا ترى أنّهم كتبوا فى آخر كتابهم بعد أن قُرِئ عليهما فأقرّا
أن قد فهماه ولم يكتبوا بعد أن فهماه لأنّ أحدا لا يعلم أنّ أحدا قد فهم شيئا على حقيقة كما يعلمه
الذى فهمه من نفسه فكذلك الرؤية لا تُعلَم من صاحبها عِلمَ حقيقةٍ كما يَعلمها صاحبُها //
(21 b) من نفسه فثبت بما ذكرنا أنّ كلّ شىء يُعلَم من الذى يكون منه علمَ حقيقة كما يَعلمه هو من
نفسه حتّى يكون هو وغيره ممّن حضره سواء كُتُب على الإثبات لا على الإقرار واستغنى بإثباته
من الذى كان منه عن ذكر إقراره به وكلّ ما كان لا يعلم من الذى يكون منه علم حقيقة كما يَعلَمه
هو من نفسه انّما يرجع فى علمه به الى إقراره به على نفسه والى إخباره بــه عنها كُتُب على
الإقرار منه به لا على الإثبات *

[1] MS لا تكتب اقرار المشترى بها

2.90 وكان يوسف وهلال يكتبان وذلك بعد أن أقرّ فلان بن فلان وفلان بن فلان أنّهما قد رأيا
جميعا جميع هذه الدار المحدودة فى هذا الكتاب بحدودها وجميع حقوقها وما فيها ومنها من قليل وكثير
داخل ذلك وخارجه وتبيّن لهما ذلك جميعا وعرّفاه عند عقدة هذا البيع المسمّى فى هذا الكتاب
2.91 بينهما وقبل ذلك فتبايعا على ذلك ٭ وكان أبو زيد يكتب وذلك بعد أن نظر اليها فلان بن فلان
يعنى المشترى وتبحّرها ورضيها ٭

2.92 فكان ما كتب يوسف وهلال فى هذا أحبّ وأصحّ عندنا لأنّ الناس قد اختلفوا فيما يجب
للمشترى النظر اليه فى وجوب خيار الرؤية له وفى حكم مَن باع ما لم يرَ ٭

2.93 فقال بعضهم من باع ما لم يكن معاينا له فى وقت بيعه ايّاه فبيعه باطل فكذلك من اشترى
(22 a) ما لم يكن معاينا له فى وقت شراه ايّاه // فشراه باطل فكتبنا رؤية البائع ورؤية المشترى للمبيع
2.94 فى وقت البيع لهذا المعنى ٭ وقال آخرون من اشترى ما لم يرَ فهو بالخيار اذا رآه وكانت الرؤية
التى يبطل بها الخيار عندهم فى ذلك قد اختلفوا فى كيفيّتها فكان أبو حنيفة وأبو يوسف ومحمّد
يقولون اذا نظر المشترى الى خارج الدار المبيعة فرضى ذلك منها فقد بطل بذلك خيار رؤيته ولا
2.95 يحتاج الى نظره لِما سوى ذلك منها ٭ وكان زفر بن الهذيل يقول هو على خيار رؤيته حتّى
2.96 ينظر الى ما وصفنا منها وحتّى ينظر مع ذلك الى بعض أرضها ٭ وكان الحسن بن زياد اللؤلؤىّ
يقول هو على خيار الرؤية فيها حتّى ينظر الى كلّ قليل وكثير منها والى سائر أرضها والى
سائر بنائها وغير ذلك منها ٭

2.97 فكتبنا أنّهما قد رأيا جميعا جميع هذه الدار المحدودة فى هذا الكتاب وجميع حقوقها وما فيها ومنها
من قليل وكثير وعاينا ذلك داخله وخارجه وتبيّن لهما ذلك كلّه وعرفاه عند عقدة هذا البيع المسمّى
فى هذا الكتاب بينهما وقبل ذلك فتبايعا على ذلك ليصحّ البيع فى الأقاويل التى ذكرتُ كلّها ٭

2.98 وكتبنا رؤية المتبايعين أيضا للمبيع قبل البيع ليثبت أنّ البيع // كان بينهما على ما هما معايناه
(22 b) فى وقت عقدهما البيع عليه بينهما ولمعنى غير هذا المعنى وذلك أنّ من ابتاع [شيئا][1] قد رآه قبل
البيع لم يجب له فى ذلك البيع خيار الرؤية واذا ابتاعه ولم يكن رآه قبل ذلك كان له فيه خيار
2.99 الرؤية حتّى يُحدِث المشترى فيه حدثا يقطع ذلك ٭ فكتبنا تقدّم رؤية المشترى لِما اشترى
لينفى من ذلك البيع وجوب الخيار له فى قول من يوجبه له خيار الرؤية ٭

2.100 وكان يوسف وأبو زيد يكتبان وتفرّقا جميعا بعد هذا البيع عن تراض منهما جميعا به وكان غيرهما
يكتب وتفرّقا جميعا بأبدانهما بعد هذا البيع وتصحيحه ووجوبه عن تراض منهما بجميع هذا البيع
المسمّى فى هذا الكتاب وكذلك يكتب عامّة البغداذيّين من أصحابنا ٭

[1] word obliterated

2.101 وهذا عندنا فاسد والذى كتب يوسف وأبو زيد فى ذلك أقرب الى الصواب لأنّ قوما يقولون للمتبايعين الخيار بعد البيع حتّى يتفرّقا بأبدانهما فاذا تفرّقا بأبدانهما انقطع الخيار فإذا كتب وتفرّقا جميعا بأبدانهما بعد هذا البيع وتصحيحه ووجوبه عن تراض منهما وقع ذلك على إيجاب البيع وصحّته ووجوبه

2.102 (23 a) قبل التفرّق وذلك غير جائز فى قول أهل هذا القول الذى ذكرنا * ويفسد ذلك أيضا //من جهة أخرى وذلك أنّه اذا وُصف البيع بالصحّة والجواز منعه ذلك من الرجوع بثمن ما ابتاع على بائعه اذا استُحِقّ ما باعه من يده فى قول ابن أبى[1] ليلى وأهل المدينة لأنّهم يقولون مَن أقرّ لرجل بشىء ثمّ ابتاعه منه فأقام رجل عليه بيّنة أنّه له فقضى به القاضى له ودفعه اليه لم يرجع على بائعه بشىء لأنّه أقرّ له بأنّه كان مالكا لما باعه فإنّه بذلك قد أبرأه من الرجوع عليه بشىء ومُقَرّ له أنّ القضاء الذى كان ببيّنة التى شُهدت غير جائز وقد رُوى هذا القول أيضا عن زفر *

2.103 فكتبنا وتفرّقا جميعا بأبدانهما بعد هذا البيع عن تراض منهما جميعا بجميعه وإنفاذ منهما لـــه فلم يدخل فى ذلك فساد فى قول أحد من الناس *

2.104 وكان يحيى بن أكثم يكتب فى هذا وقد رأى فلان بن فلان وفلان بن فلان جميع هذه الدار المحدودة فى هذا الكتاب وتبحّرا ذلك وأحاطا به وبجميع حقوقه ومرافقه الداخلة فيه وجميع حقوقه ومرافقه الخارجة منه معرفة وعلما ورضى ذلك كلّه فلان بن فلان وفلان بن فلان فعلى معرفتهما

(23 b) جميعا بجميع ذلك وعلمهما به فى حال تبايعهما هذه الدار تبايعاها // وتواجباها ثمّ خيّر كلّ واحد منهما صاحبه فثبت كلّ واحد منهما على إجازة هذا البيع وإمضائه ثمّ تفرّقا بعد انعقاد هذا البيع بينهما واختيار كلّ واحد منهما وإجازته للبيع المسمّى فى هذا الكتاب حتّى غاب كلّ واحد منهما

2.105 عن صاحبه عن تراض منهما بالبيع المسمّى فى هذا الكتاب * قال أبو جعفر فكان ما كتب غيره من ذكر التفرّق وحذف التخيير أحبّ الينا لأنّ التفرّق المروىّ عن رسول الله عليه السلام فى المتبايعين انّهما بالخيار حتّى تفرّقا *

2.106 قد قال الناس فيه ثلاثة أقاويل فقال قوم منهم عيسى بن أبان ذلك التفرّق هو أن كلّ واحد من المتبايعين اذا قال لصاحبه قد بِعتُك فلصاحبه قبول قوله ما لم يفارقه فاذا فارقه لم يكن له بعد

2.107 قبول ما عُقِد له على نفسه والتفرّق يبطل ذلك العقد * قال عيسى ولو لا أنّ الخبر جاء هكذا لكان للمعقود له البيعُ قبول العقد بعد سنة وأكثر من ذلك فلمّا جاء هذا الخبر على ما ذكرنا علمنا به أنّ للمعقود له البيعُ قبول ما عقد له صاحبُه ما لم يفارقه فاذا فارقه لم يكن له بعد ذلك

2.108 (24 a) قبول عقده * قال أبو جعفر // فلو وقفنا على أنّ تأويل هذا الخبر هو كما قال عيسى لما

2.109 احتجنا الى ذكر التفرّق فى كتاب الشرى * وقال قوم اذا تعاقد المتبايعان البيع فقد تفرّقا وقال آخرون اذا تعاقدا فكلّ واحد منهما بالخيار على صاحبه حتّى يتفرّقا بأبدانهما عن الموطن الذى تعاقدا فيه البيع فاذا تفرّقا عنه قبل أن يبطل البيع واحد منهما صحّ البيع بينهما *

[1] MS omits أبى

2.110 قال أبو جعفر فلمـّا كان التفرّق الذى من أجله يحتاج الى ذكر التفرّق فى كتاب الشرى
هو التفرّق الذى كان يؤوّله كلّ فريق من هذه الثلاث الفرق على ما ذكرنا كان كتابنا ايّاه
أولى من كتابنا حذف[1] التخيير الذى يقوم مقام التفرّق فى قول فرقة ولا معنى له فى قول فرقة
2.111 أخرى ✱ قال أبو جعفر ولم يكن معنى[2] لما كتبه يحيى بن أكثم من ذكر كيفيّة التفرّق وانـّه
قد غاب بعده كلّ واحد من المتبايعين عن صاحبه لأنّ إحدى الفرق اللاتى ذكرنا تجعل التفرّق
بالأقوال دون الأبدان على ما قد ذكرناه عنها ✱

2.112 وكان ما كتبناه أجمع من ذلك لأنـّا اذا ذكرنا أنـّهما تفرّقا بأبدانهما بعد البيع عن تراض منهما
(24 b) بجميعه وإنفاذ منهما له كان ما كتبنا من ذلك // إن رُفع الى من يرى البيع يتمّ بالأقوال دون
التفرّق بالأبدان جعل ما نفذ به البيع من المتبايعين هو عقدُ البائع البيعَ للمشترى وقبول المشترى
ايّاه منه وإن رُفع الى من يرى البيع لا يصحّ حتّى يتفرّقا بأبدانهما جعل ما أقرّا به من تراضيهما
ومن إنفاذهما للبيع الذى وجب بالتفرّق هو تفرّقهما بعد البيع بأبدانهما على ما يراه من غيبة كل
واحد منهما عن صاحبه وغير ذلك ✱

2.113 وكان يوسف وهلال يكتبان فما أدرك فى هذه الدار المحدودة فى هذا الكتاب وفى شىء منها
ومن حقوقها من درك من أحد من الناس كلـّهم فعلى فلان بن فلان خلاص ذلك[3] كلـّه لفلان
2.114 ابن فلان حتّى يسلـّمه له ويخلـّصه له من كلّ درك وتبعة ✱ وكان أبو زيد يكتب فما أدرك فلان
ابن فلان فى جميع ما وقع عليه البيع المذكور أو فى شىء منه ومن حقوقه من درك فعلى فلان بن
2.115 فلان تسليم ما يجب لفلان بن فلان عليه فى ذلك حتّى يسلـّم ذلك له ✱ وكان أبو حنيفة وأبو
يوسف يكتبان فما أدرك فلان بن فلان فى ذلك من درك فعلى فلان بن فلان خلاص ذلك أو ردّ
الثمن ✱

2.116 فكان ما كتب أبو حنيفة وأبو يوسف // وأبو زيد في ذلك من إضافـــة الدرك الى المشترى
(25 a) خاصّة أحبّ الينا ممـّا كتب يوسف وهلال وذلك أنّ الدرك الذى يجب على البائع بحقّ البيع
انـّما يجب للمشترى ولا يجب لغيره من وارث عنه ولا من مشترٍ منه ولا من موهب له ولا من متصدّق
عليه ولا ممن سواهم من سائر من يملكها عنه وإن كان الوارث قد يخاصم البائع فى الرجوع عليه
بحقّ ما يوجبه الاستحقاق عليه فإنـّه انـّما يخاصم فيه لوجوبه له بحقّ مورثه عن أبيه كسائر وجوب
ماله بحقّ مورثه عنه ✱

2.117 ألا ترى أنـّه لو كان على أبيه دَين كان الذى يتولّى قبض ما يجب بحقّ الدرك هو وصىّ
الميّت لا وارثه أولا ترى أنّ الوارث لو أبرأ منه البائع وعلى أبيه دَين كانت براءته ايّاه من ذلك
باطل لأنّ المال الواجب بحقّ الدرك انـّما وجب لأبيه وغرماء أبيه أحقّ بقبضه ليستوفوا دَينهم منه ✱

[1] MS omits حذف

[2] MS omits معنى

[3] MS فعلى فلان خلاص ذلك

2.118 قال أبو جعفر فاذا كتبتَ فما أدرك فى هذه الدار فقد جمعتَ فى هذا كلّ درك يدرك هؤلاء
2.119 جميعا فجعلتَه على البائع وذلك غير واجب عليه فذلك مفسد للبيع * ولكن أصحّ ذلك عندنا
(25 b) أن تكتب فما أدرك فلان بن فلان // ثمّ تنسق الذى كتبناه على ما نسقناه فى كتابنا ولا تكتب فما أدرك فلان بن فلان وكلّ واحد بسببه كما كان بعض الناس يكتبون فإنّ أسبابه هم الوارثون عنه والمتبايعون منه والمتصدّق عليهم والموهوب لهم وسائر من يملك الدار من قِبَله بتمليكه ايّاهم ايّاها والدرك ليس لهؤلاء انّما هو للمشترى خاصّة الذى وجب الثمن عليه بعقد البيع فوجبت له أسبابه وانّما يدرك الوارث فى تلك الدار ما أحدثه هو فيها بعد موت أبيه من بيعه ايّاها رجلا فيدركه فيها ما يبطل بيعه فذلك غير واجب له على البائع من أبيه ضمانه *

2.120 ولا تكتبنّ فعلى فلان ضمان ذلك كما يكتب بعض الناس فإنّ وجه ذلك على من ضمن ضمانا مستأنفا ممّا لم يكن له ضمانا قبل ذلك والدرك فى البيع ليس كذلك وهو على البائع للمشترى واجب فى عقد البيع فضمانه لذلك بعد وجوبه له عليه ليس له معنى ولكنّ وَصْف ما يوجب البيع للمشترى على البائع على ما قد وصفناه فى كتابنا أحسن *

2.121 ولا تكتب فعلى فلان عهدة ذلك كما يكتبه بعض الناس فإنّ أبا حنيفة كان يقول ضمان العهدة
(26 a) فى ذلك هو ضمان الصحيفة // قال أبو جعفر حدّثنى بذلك سليمان بن شعيب عن أبيه عن محمّد
2.122 عن أبى يوسف عن أبى حنيفة * فاذا أوجبتَ فى كتابك على البائع للمشترى ضمان صحيفة لا يوجب البيع له ضمانها عليه أفسد ذلك البيع عليه *

2.123 وانّما اخترنا ما كتبناه فى هذا الكتاب ممّا نصصناه فى التسليم على ما كان أبو حنيفة وأبو يوسف ويوسف بن خالد يكتبون فى ذلك على ما ذكرناه عنهم فى الموضوع الذى ذكرناه عنهم من هذا الكتاب لأنّ الناس يختلفون فيما يجب على البائع للمشترى اذا استُحِقّ المبيع *

2.124 فكان بعضهم يقول يجب له عليه ردّ الثمن وممّن قال ذلك أبو حنيفة وأبو يوسف وزفر ويوسف
2.125 ومحمّد بن الحسن والحسن بن زياد[1] * وكان بعضهم يقول على البائع تخليص ما باع بعَيْنه فإن لم يقدر على ذلك ضمن للمشترى دارا مثل الدار المبيعة فى موضعها فى الرِفعة والخطر وفى الذرع
2.126 والبناء كره ذلك المشترى أو طلبه وممّن قال ذلك عثمان البتّى وسوّار بن عبد الله العنبرى * وكان بعضهم يقول عليه قيمة ما باع يوم يُستحقّ إن كان ذلك أقلّ من الثمن أو أكثر *

2.127 فلمّا كان بعض الناس يرى أنّ ما يجب على البائع فى استحقاق // المبيع هو غير تخليص
(26 b) المبيع وغير ردّ ثمنه كان ما كان أبو حنيفة وأبو يوسف يكتبان من ذلك يفسد البيع فى قول من ذهب الى قول سوّار بن عبد الله وعثمان البتّى وفى قول من ذهب الى وجوب ردّ قيمة المبيع *

[1] MS ومحمد بن الحسن ومحمد والحسن بن زياد

2.128 وحجّة أخرى أنّ المستحِق اذا استحقّ الدار المبيعة من يد المشترى وقضى القاضى له بها فليس يخلو من أحد وجهين إمّا أن يجيز البيع أو لا يجيزه فإن لم يجِز البيع بطل البيع ووجب عليه ردّ الثمن فى قول أبى حنيفة وأبى يوسف ومحمّد وجميع أصحابنا فإن أجاز البيع فإنّ الناس يختلفون فى ذلك فمنهم من يقول الإجازة جائزة يصحّ بها البيع ويجب على البائع تسليم الدار الى المشترى وذلك تخليصها الذى قصد اليه أبو حنيفة وأبو يوسف فكتبا من أجله ما كتبا ممّا قد ذكرناه عنهما *

2.129 فلمّا كان فى هذا بين الناس من الاختلاف ما ذكرنا كان ذلك الشرط اذا اشتُرِط على البائع فى البيع فقد اشتُرِط عليه تخليص لا يقدر عليه أو ردّ ثمن يقدر عليه فجُعِل البائع فى ذلك مخيّرا يفعل أيّهما شاء فذلك يفسد البيع فى قول من لا يجيز البيع إلاّ بالإجازة من المستحقّ ويفسده أيضاً فى قول من يجيز البيع بالإجازة من المستحقّ لأنّ تلك الإجازة انّما كانت //

(27 a) من قِبَل المخيِّر لا من قِبَل البائع وليس فى ذلك تخليص من البائع للدار * فيكون البائع قد
2.130 برئ من تخليص الدار المبيعة ومن ردّ ثمنها ولا يؤمَن أن يتوهّم متوهّم أنّ التخليص الذى جُعِل على البائع هو ابتياع الدار وتسليمها الى المشترى بالبيع الذى عقده له على نفسه فيفسد البيع بذلك *

2.131 وقد يكون[1] أيضا أن يُستحَقّ من المبيع بعضه نصفه أو ثلثه أو جزء من أجزائه شائعا فيه
2.132 غير مقسوم منه فيكون فى ذلك بين الناس اختلاف * فمنهم من يقول المشترى بالخيار إن شاء فسخ البيع فيما بقى ورجع بالثمن على البائع وإن شاء أمسك ما بقى بحصّته من الثمن وممّن ذهب
2.133 الى هذا القول أبو حنيفة وأبو يوسف وزفر ومحمّد * ومنهم من يقول اذا استُحِقّ من المبيع شىء فسد البيع كلّه وكان على البائع ردّ جميع الثمن على المشترى *

2.134 فاذا كتبتَ ما أدرك فلان بن فلان فى هذه الدار وفى شىء منها من درك فعلى فلان بن فلان خلاص ذلك أو ردّ الثمن احتمل ذلك الثمن أن يكون هو جميع الثمن وذلك غير واجب عند أبى حنيفة وأبى يوسف ومحمّد قبل اختيار المشترى ايّاه فاذا كان ذلك شرطا واجبا فى البيع //
(27 b) كان واجبا بذلك الشرط اختاره المشترى أو لم يختره وذلك يفسد البيع *

2.135 ألا ترى أنّ رجلا لو باع رجلا دارا بألف درهم على أنّ ما استُحِقّ منها من شىء فعلى
2.136 البائع ردّ جميع ثمنها على المشترى وأخذ ما بقى منها بعد المستحقّ كان ذلك البيع فاسدا * فلمّا كان هذا الشرط يفسد البيع كان الشرط الذي يرجع اليه أيضا ويكون حكمه حكمه يفسد البيع أيضا وإن كان الثمن المشترَط ردّه هو من المستحقّ خاصّة فذلك ينفى أن يكون على البائع ردّ غيره وذلك يفسد البيع فى قول من يقول اذا استُحِقّ بعض المبيع بطل البيع فيما بقى منه ووجب ردّ ثمنه *

[1] MS omits يكون

2.137 وقد يجوز ايضا أن يُستحَقّ من الدار موضع معلوم بعينه فيكون حكمه مختلفا فيه فكان أبو حنيفة وأبو يوسف ومحمّد يقولون إن كان ذلك قبل قبض المشترى الدار المبيعة كان المشترى بالخيار إن شاء أخذ ما بقى من حصّته من الثمن وإن شاء أبطل البيع فيما بقى وأخذ جميع الثمن

2.138 وإن كان ذلك بعد القبض أخذ ما بقى بحصّته من الثمن ولا خيار له فى ذلك * وكان غيرهم

2.139 يقول يفسد البيع كلّه ويجب على البائع أن يردّ جميع الثمن على المشترى * فلمّا كان فى هذا من الاختلاف ما ذكرنا واختلف حكم استحقاق بعض المبيع عند أبى حنيفة وأبى يوسف ومحمّد

(28 a) قبل القبض وبعد القبض وكانا قد اشترطا // فيما يجب بالاستحقاق فى كتابهما شيئا واحدا لما قبل القبض ولما بعده كان ذلك مفسدا للبيع لأنّه إن كان اشترط أنّ ما يجب فى الاستحقاق قبل القبض هو ما يجب فى الاستحقاق بعد القبض أو ما يجب فى الاستحقاق بعد القبض هو ما يجب فى الاستحقاق قبل القبض كان البيع فاسدا *

2.140 قال أبو جعفر فلهذه المعانى كرهنا ما كان أبو حنيفة وأبو يوسف يكتبان ممّا قد رويناه عنهما

2.141 واخترنا ما كان أبو زيد يكتب لأنّا لا نخاف فيه شيئا من هذا * ألا ترى أنّك اذا قلتَ فعلى فلان ابن فلان تسليم ما يجب عليه فى ذلك من حقّ ويلزمه بسبب البيع المسمّى فى هذا الكتاب حتّى يسلّم ذلك الى فلان بن فلان على ما يوجبه له عليه هذا البيع المسمّى فى هذا الكتاب فاستُحِقّت الدار كلّها فرُفِع الأمر الى من يرى ردّ الثمن قضى بردّ الثمن وكان ذلك عنده هو الذى يوجبه البيع وإن رُفع الى من يرى وجها من الوجوه التى وصفنا قضى بما يرى فى ذلك وكان ما يقضى به فى ذلك هو الذى يوجبه البيع عنده وإن استُحِقّ بعض الدار شائعا فيها غير مقسوم أو استُحِقّت طائفة منها مقسومة فرُفِع ذلك الى من يرى ما ذكرناه عن أبى حنيفة وأبى يوسف وعن محمّد قضى بما ذكرناه عنهم وكان ذلك هو الذى يوجبه البيع عنده وإن رُفِع ذلك الى

(28 b) من يرى الذى يوجبه البيع // بعض ما ذكرنا فى الأقوال التى ذكرنا قضى بما يرى فى ذلك فكان ما يقضى به فى ذلك هو الذى يوجبه البيع عنده فلم نجد لفظا هو أجمع ولا أبعد ممّا يخاف منه فسخ البيع من اللفظ الذى ذكرنا وهو ما كتبناه فى هذا الموضع من كتابنا *

2.142 وقد كان أبو حنيفة وأبو يوسف يكتبان بعد فراغهما من الدرك مع قيمة ما يُحدِث فلان فى

2.143 ذلك ويحدث له بأمره من بناء وغرس وزرع * وكان غيرهما من أصحابنا يكتب مع قيمة ما يحدث فلان فيما يُستحَقّ من ذلك ويزيد فى ذلك من بناء وغرس وزرع ممّا تبلغ قيمته درهما فما فوقه الى ألف درهم وأقلّ من درهم وأكثر من ألف درهم بالغا ما بلغ بقيمة عدل يوم يُستحَقّ

2.144 ذلك وذلك البناء والغرس والزرع قائم فيما يُستحَقّ من ذلك * وكان الذى يكتب هذا ينكر على أبى حنيفة وأبى يوسف ما كانا يكتبان ممّا قد رويناه عنهما فى هذا الفصل لأنّ الاستحقاق قد يكون فى بعض الدار وقد يكون البناء والغرس والزرع فى كلّها فاذا اشترط المشترى على البائع

2.145 ضمان كلّ بنائه وكلّ غرسه وكلّ زرعه كان ذلك مفسدا للبيع * وقد كان أبو زيد خالف أبا حنيفة وأبا يوسف فى ذلك وكتب فيه مثل الذى ذكرنا عن مخالفيهما فيه *

2.146 قال أبو جعفر فكان أحبّ الأشياء إلينا فى ذلك ما كتب أبو حنيفة وأبو يوسف // وترْك
(29 a) ما كتبه مخالفها[1] ممّا قد حكيناه عنهما وعنه لأنّ الدار المبيعة اذا استُحِقّت بعد بناء المشترى
2.147 إيّاها وغرسه أو زرعه إيّاها قد اختلف الناس فى الحكم فى ذلك كيف هو * فكان بعضهم
يقول يرجع المشترى على البائع بقيمته قائما ويكون ذلك البناء والغرس والزرع قد عاد الى البائع
قائما بالقيمة التى قضى بها القاضى عليه للمشترى فيكون المستحقّ بالخيار إن شاء أخذ البائع
2.148 بقلع ذلك ورفعه عن أرضه وإن شاء احتسبه لنفسه وغرم له قيمته مقلوعا * قالوا وإن كان
البائع غائبا كان للمستحقّ أن يأخذ المشترى برفع ذلك عن أرضه وليس عليه أن ينتظر قدوم البائع
فاذا قلعه عن أرضه سلّمه المشترى الى البائع اذا قدر عليه مقلوعا وأخذ منه قيمته مقلوعا لأنّه
انّما سلّمه اليه كذلك وإن شاء المستحقّ منع المشترى قلع ذلك واحتبسه لنفسه وغرم له قيمته
مقلوعا ولم يرجع على البائع بشىء غير الثمن *

2.149 قال أبو جعفر قد رُوى هذا القول عن أصحابنا من جهة وقد رُوى عنهم خلاف هذا
حدّثنى محمّد بن العبّاس بن الربيع قال حدّثنا علىّ بن معبد عن محمّد بن الحسن أنّ المستحقّ
اذا أخذ المشترى برفع البناء عن أرضه وحكم القاضى له عليه بذلك سلّمه المشترى منقوضا الى
(29 b) البائع ورجع عليه // بقيمته قائما إن شاء وإن شاء احتبسه لنفسه منقوضا ولم يرجع على البائع
2.150 بشىء ولم يحكِ محمّد بن الحسن فى هذا خلافا بينه وبين أصحابه * فلمّا كان هذا قد يكون
على كلّ وجه من هذه الوجوه التي ذكرنا ويكون الحكم فيها مختلفا ويجب فى بعضها غير الذى
يجب فى بعض على ما قد ذكرنا من هذا الاختلاف فيها كان اشتراط المشترى على البائع فى
البيع ما يوجبه له عليه واحد من هذه الأقوال دون الذى يوجبه له عليه سواه منها يفسد البيع لأنّه
قد ألزم البائع ما قد لا يلزمه أو منع نفسه من شيء قد يجب له *

2.151 قال أبو جعفر وقد زعم أهل المدينة أنّه يقال للمستحقّ أعْطِ هذا المشترى قيمة بنائه مبنيّا
لأنّه بناه على جهالة وغرور ويكون البناء لك فإن فعلتَ ذلك وإلاّ كان دَين شريكا لك وأبرؤوا
2.152 البائع من ذلك كلّه * هذا اذا كان المشترى لا يعلم منه إقرار للبائع بملك المستحقّ ولا علمه
حتّى أحدث فى الدار ما أحدث من البناء والغرس والزرع حين أحدث ذلك فيها ولا قبل ذلك *
2.153 وإن كان المشترى بناها على علم منه أنّها لغير البائع فللمستحقّ أن يأخذ البناء من المشترى بقيمته
2.154 مقلوعا ولا شىء له على البائع * فاذا اشتُرِط على المشترى فى قولهم ما كان أبو زيد يكتبه
(30 a) ممّا قد ذكرناه // عنه من قيمة البناء والغرس أو الزرع فسد البيع على قولهم * وقد كان آخرون
2.155 يذهبون الى أنّه لا يجب على البائع للمشترى اذا استُحِقّ المبيع غير ردّ الثمن الذى قبضه منه
ولا يجب له عليه مع ذلك عندهم قيمة بناء إن كان بناه فيما استُحِقّ منه ولا قيمة غرس إن كان
غرسه ولا قيمة زرع إن كان زرعه فيه وقد رُوى هذا القول عن محمّد بن ادريس الشافعى *

[1] كتبه مخالفها words obliterated in MS

2.156 قال أبو جعفر فاذا اشتُرِط فى قول هؤلاء ما قد حكيناه عن أبى حنيفة وأبى يوسف وأبى زيد أنّهم كانوا يكتبونه فى ذلك فسد البيع فى قولهم ولكنّ أصحّ ذلك عندنا ما كتبناه فى الشرط الذى فى صدر كتابنا هذا فعلى فلان بن فلان تسليم ما يجب عليه فى ذلك ويلزمه بسبب هذا البيع المسمّى فى هذا الكتاب حتّى يسلّم ذلك الى فلان بن فلان على ما يوجبه له عليه هـذا البيع
2.157 المسمّى فى هذا الكتاب * فمتى رُفع ذلك الى من يرى مذهبا من هذه المذاهب التى ذكرنا أوجب فيه ما يذهب اليه منها ولم يكن شىء ممّا كتبناه فى كتابنا فى هذا الموضع عنده مفسدا
2.158 للبيع * قال أبو زيد وأصحّ ما يُكتَب فى هذا فعلى فلان بن فلان تسليم ما يجب عليه فى ذلك
(30 b) من حقّ ويلزمه بسبب البيع المسمّى فى هذا الكتاب حتّى يسلّم // ذلك الى فلان على ما يوجبه له عليه البيع المسمّى فى هذا الكتاب فقد رجع أبو زيد بذلك عمّا كان يكتب الى ما كتبنا *

2.159 قال أبو جعفر وقد اختلف أصحابنا فى كتاب الشهادة فى آخر كتاب الشرى فكان يوسف ابن خالد وهلال بن يحيى يكتبان شهد على فلان بن فلان وفلان بن فلان بجميع ما فى هذا الكتاب
2.160 وعلى إقرارهما ومعرفتهما بجميع ما سُمّى فيه فى صحّة منهما وجواز أمر فلان وفلان وختموا * وكان أبو زيد يكتب شهد الشهود المسمّون فى كتابنا هذا على إقرار فلان بن فلان وفلان بن فلان وفلان بن فلان بجميع ما سُمّى ووُصف فى كتابنا هذا وعلى معرفتهم جميعا بجميع ما فيه بعد أن قُرئ عليهم فأقرّوا أن قد فهموه حرفا حرفا وأشهدوهم بذلك على أنفسهم فى صحّة من عقولهم وأبدانهم وجواز من أمورهم طائعين غير مكرهين لا يولى على مثلهم فى شىء من أمورهم وهم مأمونون على أموالهم غير محجور عليهم ولا على كلّ واحد منهم فى شىء من ذلك ولا علّة بهم من مرض ولا من غيره وذلك فى شهر كذا من سنة كذا *

2.161 قال أبو جعفر فأمّا ما اختلفوا فيه من الشهادة على جميع // ما فى هذا الكتاب وعلى الإقرار
(31 a) بذلك فكتبها يوسف وهلال على جميع ما فى هذا الكتاب وكتبها أبو زيد على إقرارهما بذلك *
2.162 فانّ ما كتب أبو زيد فى ذلك أحسن لأنّ الشهادة من الشهود لا تقع على جميع ما فى هـذا الكتاب لأنّ فيه المعاينة للشىء المبيع من البائع والمشترى وذلك ممّا لا يعلم الشهود حقيقته ولا يقفون عليها وانّما يشهدون على إقرار المشترى والبائع به *

2.163 ألا ترى أنّ يوسف وهلالا قد كتبا فى كتبهما وذلك بعد أن أقرّ فلان وفلان أنّهما قد رأيا جميعا جميع هذه الدار ولم يكتبا وذلك بعد أن رأيا جميع هذه الدار لأنّ الشهود لا يتحقّقون من نظر المشترى والبائع الى الدار ما يتحقّقه كلّ واحد منهما من نظره بنفسه اليها فكتبا ذلك بالإقرار منهما بالرؤية لا على إثبات الرؤية وفى الرؤية إثبات صحّة البيع ونفى الفساد وذلك ممّا لا يعلم الشهود أنّه فى الحقيقة كذلك لأنّه قد يجوز أن يكون البائع والمشترى قد تعاقدا بينهما أنّهما يشيعان
(31 b) ببيع هذه الدار لأمر يخافانه وليس ذلك ببيع على الحقيقة وانّما هو تلجئة // ثمّ يظهران أنّهما قد تعاقدا البيع بمحضر من الشهود فيكون ظاهرا ما عقدا من البيع بينهما على الصحّة وباطنه بخلاف ذلك *

2.164 ممّا قد اختلف الناس فى الحكم فيه كيف هو فكان أبو يوسف ومحمّد يقولان يبطل البيع الذى أظهرا بالمعاقدة التى كانا تعاقداها بينهما اذا علمتَ ببيّنة قامت عليه أو بإقرار منهما بها
2.165 أو بنكول من أحدهما عن اليمين عليها بعد أن طلب صاحبه يمينه عليها * حدّثنى بذلك كلّه سليمان بن شُعَيب عن أبيه عن محمّد بن الحسن عن أبى حنيفة وأبى يوسف قال محمّد وهو قولنا وقد روى محمّد بن سماعة عن أبى يوسف عن أبى حنيفة أنّ البيع الذى تعاقدا بينهما صحيح قال ولا يكون البيع الذى أظهرا تلجئة إلاّ أن يذكرا ذلك فى عقد البيع ذكر محمّد بن سماعة هذه الرواية عن أبى يوسف عن أبى حنيفة فى نوادر محمّد بن الحسن *

2.166 قال أبو جعفر قد يجوز أيضاً أن يتعاقدا بينهما أن يظهرا البيع بثمن معلوم وهو فى الحقيقة بثمن دون ذلك الثمن فيتعاقدا البيع بمحضر من الشهود على ثمن وقد كانا تعاقدا بينهما أنّ حقيقة الثمن
2.167 (32 a) أقلّ من ذلك * فلمّا كانت // هذه الأشياء كذلك كان أولى الأشياء بنا أن يردّ الشهادة عليها الى إقرار المتبايعين بها لا الى الشهادة على حقائقها *

2.168 وأمّا ما كتب أبو زيد وعلى معرفتهما بجميع ما فيه فذلك أيضاً عندنا فاسد لأنّهما قد يقرّان أنّهما قد عرفاه ولم يعرفاه وليس يُوصَل الى حقيقة يُعرَف بها ذلك فالشهادة على الإقرار منهما به أولى *

2.169 قال أبو جعفر وأمّا ما كتب يوسف وهلال فى صحّة منهما وجواز أمر وكتب أبو زيد مكان ذلك فى صحّة من عقولهما وأبدانهما وجواز من أمورهما فانّ ما كتب أبو زيد فى هذا أقرب الى الصواب لأنّك اذا قلتَ فى صحّة منهما احتمل أن تكون تلك الصحّة وقعت على صحّة البدن أو على صحّة العقل وعليهما جميعا فتبيان ذلك وقطع الشغب فيه أحسن عندنا ممّا كتب أبو زيد فى ذلك فى قوله
2.170 فى صحّة من عقولهما وجواز من أمورهما * وقد يحتمل أيضا أن يقع ذلك على البعض لأنّ « مِن » قد تكون من الشىء على بعضه فأحسن من ذلك أن تكتب فى صحّة عقولهما وأبدانهما وجواز أمورهما *
2.171 (32 b) وقد كتب آخرون من أصحابنا فى هذا المكان[1] ما اختلف فيه يوسف وهلال وأبو زيد ممّا حكيناه // عنهم وهما صحيحا العقول والأبدان جائزا الأمور لا علّة بهما من مرض ولا غيره وزعم مَن كتب هذا « منهما » أنّه أشرح وأبين وأقرب الى فهم السامع وأقطع للشغب فكان ما كتبوا من هذا أحسن *

2.172 قال أبو جعفر ومعنى فى صحّة عقولهما وأبدانهما وجواز أمورهما هو ذلك المعنى بعينه وهو موجود فى كلام الناس يقولون « فعل فلان هذا فى مرضه » « فعل فلان هذا فى صحّته » يعنون بذلك فعله وهو مريض أو فعله وهو صحيح وقد جاء الأثر عن عمران بن حصين وعن أبى هريرة أنّ رجلا
2.173 أعتق ستة أعبد له فى مرضه يعنيان بذلك وهو مريض * فإن كتبتَ من هذا ما كتب ممّا حكيناه

[1] MS فى هذا مكان

أخيرا عمّن كتبه من أصحابنا فهو حسن وإن كتبتَ على ما كتبناه فى كتابنا الذى جعلناه صدر كتابنا هذا فهو حسن فكذلك كان عامّة أصحابنا يكتبون *

2.174 قال أبو جعفر وأمّا ما وكّد أبو زيد فى نفى الإجبار عن البائع والمشترى فكتب طائعين غير
2.175 مكرهين فذلك عندنا حسن لأنّ بيعها لو وقع على إجبار وعلى إكراه لم يجز * ألا ترى أنّ
(33 a) رجلا لو أكرهه سلطان أو غيره ممّن إكراهه كإكراه السلطان على بيع داره أو على بيع // عبده
2.176 فباع ما أكره على بيعه من ذلك إنّ بيعه غير جائز * قال أبو جعفر وذكر الطواعيّة ونفى الإكراه فى هذا أحسن كما كان ذكر الصحّة فى ذلك لينفى حكم ضدّها أحسن من ترك ذكرها *

2.177 وقد حدّثنى محمّد بن شاذان قال قلتُ لهلال بن يحيى اكتُبْ فى كتابك طائعَين غير مكرَهَين قال وما حاجتى الى ذلك قلتُ ليُعلَم أنّ البيع وقع منهما على غير إكراه قال فقد أجدهما يقولان أقررنا ونحن مكرهان غير طائعَين أنّا طائعين غير مكرهَين قال فلمّا رأيت هذا لا ينفى شيئا يوجبه السكوت رأيت أنّ السكوت عنه أحسن *

2.178 قال أبو جعفر وأمّا ما كتب أبو زيد من نفى الحجر عنهما والولاية عليهما فإنّه أغنانا عن ذلك ما كتبنا من ذكر جواز أمورهما لأنّه لا تجوز أمورهما وهما محجور عليهما ولا مولى عليهما وبعد هذا فلم ينفِ أبو زيد فى كتابه الذى وصفنا بما كتبه فيه ممّا ذكرنا عنه كلّ الأسباب التى يبطل بها البيع أو يتغيّر حكمه فيها لأنّه لم يصف المتبايعين بحريّة تنفى عنهما الرقّ ولا وصفهما ببلوغ ينفى عنهما الصغر ولا وصفهما أنّهما غير محبوسَين فى دَين يمنع ذلك الحبس بيعهما من الجواز فى
(33 b) قول من يمنعهما من البيع والإقرار // اذا كانا كذلك ولا وصفهما بأنّهما لا دَين عليهما لما يخاف عليهما من فساد إقرارهما وعليهما دَين *

2.179 الا ترى أنّ رجلا لو حُبس فى دَين عليه لرجل ثمّ باع شيئا من ماله أو أحدث فيه حدثا
2.180 من إقرار أو غيره إنّ أهل العلم قد اختلفوا فى ذلك * فأمّا أبو حنيفة وأبو يوسف فكانا يجيزان ما فُعِل من ذلك ويجعلان حكمه وهو محبوس فى ذلك الدين كحكمه قبل أن يُحبَس فيه *
2.181 وأما محمّد بن الحسن فقال ينبغى للقاضى اذا حبسه أن يُشهِد على حجره عليه وعلى منعه ايّاه من الحدث فى ماله بما يمنع غريمه من استيفاء ماله عليه إلاّ أن يبيع من ماله شيئا بثمن يكون فيه
2.182 وفاء بثمن ما يبيع من ذلك ويعاين الشهود قبضه لثمن ما باع فيجوز ما فعل من ذلك * وأمّا القاسم بن معن وشريك بن عبد الله فكانا يقولان حبس القاضي ايّاه حجر منه عليه حجر عليه بلسانه أو لم يحجر ويجعلانه بحبس القاضى ايّاه فى حكم المحجور عليه حتّى يقضى ما عليه من
2.183 دين * وأمّا أهل المدينة أو كثير منهم فكانوا يقولون اذا أدان دينا ثمّ أقرّ بعده بدين آخر أو أحدث حدثا فى ماله لم يمنع بإقراره هذا الأخير ولا يمنع غريمه[1] الأوّل من استيفاء ما كان له عليه *

[1] MS ولا يحدث غريمه

2.184 قال أبو جعفر فلمّا رأينا أبا زيد لم ينفِ // فى كتابه من ذلك شيئا عن المتبايعين واستغنى (34 a) عن نفى ذلك بوصفه المتبايعين بجواز الأمر كان النظر فى ذلك أن يكون وصفه ايّاهما بجواز الأمر يُغنيه عن ذكر نفى الحجر عليهما فى أمورهما والولاية لأنّه لمّا كان جواز الأمر ينفى الرقّ والصغر اللذين لو كانا أفسد للبيع من الحجر كان الحجر أحرى أن يستغنى بذكر جواز الأمر عن نفيه عنهما *

2.185 قال أبو جعفر ولم يكن يوسف ولا أبو زيد ولا هلال يكتبون فى كتبهم وعلى معرفتهما بأعيانهما وأسمائهما وأنسابهما وقد كتب ذلك غير واحد من أصحابنا منهم محمّد بن العبّاس وعبد الحميد ابن عبد العزيز فاخترنا ما كتبوا من ذلك ليوقف على[1] معرفة المتبايعين بأعيانهما وأسمائهما وأنسابهما ولتثبت الشهادة عليهما فى حضورهما وغيبتهما وحياتهما وموتهما وقد أجمعوا جميعا أن يكتبوا ذلك فى محاضر القضاة وسجلّاتهم والنظر على ذلك أن يُكتَب أيضا فى سائر الكتب *

2.186 فإن قال قائل إنّ ذلك لا يُكتَب فى سائر الكتب الى وقت الحاجة اليه عند شهادة الشهود به عند الحاكم فيثبت الحاكم فى شهادتهم ويشهدون به عنده من معرفة المتبايعين بأعيانهما وأسمائهما (34 b) وأنسابهما ما ينفذ ما صحّ عنده من ذلك ويقضى به // قيل له فقد كتبتَ فى كتابك فى صحّة عقولهما وأبدانهما وجواز أمورهما وفى صحّة منهما وجواز أمر ولم يؤخّر ذلك الى وقت الحاجة اليه بالشهادة عند الحاكم فيثبته الحاكم على ما يصحّ عنده ويقضى به عند ذلك فكذلك فافعَلْ فى المعرفة بالعين والاسم والنسب لأنّ ذلك ممّا يحتاج الحاكم الى الوقوف على حقيقته من الشهود كما يحتاج الى الوقوف على حقيقة صحّة عقول المتبايعين بل حاجته الى معرفة المتبايعين بأعيانهما وأسمائهما وأنسابهما أعظم من حاجته الى معرفة صحّة أبدانهما لأنّ أبدانهما قد لا تكون صحيحة ويكون لبيعهما حكم بيع المريض ويكون على الحاكم القضاء فى ذلك بما يجب عليه القضاء به فى مثله ولو جهلهما فلمّا لم يعرفهما أو لم يُعرَفا له بأعيانهما وأسمائهما وأنسابهما لم يقضِ عليهما بقليل ولا كثير *

2.187 قال أبو جعفر وهذا الذى كتبناه فى صدر كتابنا هذا واحتججنا له بما وصفناه من الاحتجاجات التى ذكرنا واخترناه من اختلاف العلماء الذى وصفنا أحوط ما قدرنا عليه لاختلاف الناس الذى
2.188 ذكرناه فى المواضع المختلف فيها * وانّما حملنا على ذلك خوف غضب مَن لا ورع له من (35 a) القضاة وتأويل مَن لا ورع له من المتفقّهة وجهل // مَن عسى أن يقع الكتاب فى يده من العامّة فيتخيّر القاضى الذى يرفع اليه الذى لا ورع له بعض هذه الأقاويل التي ذهب اليها بعض أهل العلم فيفسد بها الكتاب أو يتخيّر المتفقّه الذى يقع فى يده قولا من هذه الأقوال فيستحلّ له أمر المتبايعين أو أحدهما بتراجع فيما تبايعاه ويُفتيهما بذلك أوْ يُفتى الذى يسأله عن ذلك بهذا فيدخل ضرر ذلك على المشترى والبائع أو على أحدهما *

[1] MS ليوفق عن

2.189 ويجوز أن يكون المشترى قد بنى فيما اشترى من ذلك أو غرس أو زرع ما قد لزمه فيه أكثر
من الثمن الذى ابتاع به الدار أو الأرض أو يكون قد أحدث فيها وقفاً أو صدقة يلتمس بها وجه
الله فيُمنَع من ذلك كلّه ويبطل الكتاب [1] فالتأويل الذى خفناه من القضاة الذين وصفنا أو
2.190 من المتفقّهة الذين ذكرنا * وعسى أن يكون الموقّف لذلك قد مات فيمنع صدقته بعد موته
أن يجرى على ما قد جعل الله له أن يجريها عليه فاخترنا للناس من ذلك بما أمكنّا من الاحتياط
ممّا خفنا الله نسأله المعونة والتوفيق *

5.0 وإن كان المشترى قد أبرأ البائع من جميع عيوب الدار المبيعة كتبتَ كتاب الشرى على ما
(35 b) كتبنا غير أنّك اذا انتهيتَ // الى وتفرّقا جميعاً بأبدانهما بعد هذا البيع عن تراض منهما جميعا
بجميعه وإنفاذ منهما له كتبتَ على أثر ذلك وقد نظر فلان بن فلان يعنى المشترى الى عيوب جميع
هذه الدار المحدودة فى هذا الكتاب وعاينها وتبحـّرها عيبا عيبا وأبرأ منها فلان بن فلان يعنى البائع
بعد رؤيته لها وعلمه بها فقبـِل فلان بن فلان من فلان بن فلان جميع هذه البراءة المسمّاة فى
هذا الكتاب بمخاطبة منه ايّاه على جميع ذلك *

5.1 قال أبو جعفر هذا على نحو ما كان عليه أصحابنا البغداذيّون يكتبونه وقد كتبه غيرهم مـــن
البصريّين على خلاف هذا فكتبوا وذلك بعد أن اقرّ فلان بن فلان يعنون المشترى وفلان بن فلان
يعنون البائع أنّهما قد رأيا جميعا جميع هذه الدار المحدودة فى هذا الكتاب داخلها وخارجها وجميع
ما فيها ومنها من بناء ومنازل وقليل وكثير ووقفا على جميع عيوبها وعايناها عيبا عيبا عند عقدة هذا
البيع المسمّى فى هذا الكتاب بينهما وقبل ذلك فتبايعا على ذلك *

5.2 وقد كان هلال بن يحيى يكتب نحو من هذا وهذا أحبّ الينا من الأوّل وأوكد منه لأنّ فى
هذا رؤية المشترى للعيوب قبل البيع ووقوع البيع على علم من المشترى بها ومعرفة منه لها فذلك
يقطع أن يكون للمشترى بهذه العيوب حقّ ونقض بيع أو غيره * //

5.3 (36 a) قال أبو جعفر وانّما كتبنا الرؤية للعيوب والمعرفة بها والمعاينة لها قبل البراءة منها لاختلاف
5.4 الناس فى ذلك * فكان أبو حنيفة وزفر وأبو يوسف ومحمّد يقولون البراءة جائزة من كلّ عيب
رآه المشترى أو لم يره وقد رُوى هذا القول أيضا عن زيد بن ثابت وعن عبد الله بن عمر قال حدّثنا
يونس بن عبد الأعلى قال حدّثنا أنس بن عِياض الليثى عن يحيى بن سعيد عن سالم عن عبد الله
ابن عمر أنّه [2] باع عبدا بالبراءة من كلّ عيب فخُوصِم فيه الى عثمان بن عفّان فاستحلفه عثمان
بالله ما بعِتْهُ داء ولا علمتُه [3] ولا كتمتُه فهذا عبد الله بن عمر قد باع بالبراءة *

5.5 فدلّ ذلك أنّ مذهبه كان فى البراءة على نحو ممّا ذكرنا ممّا كان يذهب اليه أبو حنيفة ومَن
ذكرنا معه وأنّ عثمان بن عفّان رضى الله عنه أبى ذلك وخالفه فيه فلم يُجِز له البراءة ممّا علم

[1] MS omits الكتاب
[2] MS omits أنه
[3] MS ذاولا بعته

5.6 وأجازها له ممّا لم يعلم وهذا قول مالك بن أنس وعامّة أهل المدينة * وقد حدّثنا فَهْد بن سليمان قال حدّثنا محمّد بن سعيد الإصبهانى قال حدّثنا شريك بن عبد الله النخعى عن عاصم بن عبيد الله[1] عن عبد الله بن عامر بن ربيعة عن زيد بن ثابت أنّه كان يرى البراءة من كلّ

5.7 (36 b) عيب جائزة * وقال آخرون لا تجوز البراءة إلاّ بعد رؤية المشترى // العيوب ومعاينته ايّاها وهذا قول ابن أبى ليلى *

5.8 فلمّا اختلفوا فى ذلك كتبنا ما ذكرنا احتياطا من اختلافهم ووكّدنا ذلك بذكر علم المشترى ومعرفته للعيوب قبل البيع وانّما كتب مَن كتب قبول البائع البراءة من المشترى لاختلاف الناس فى عدم القبول فى ذلك *

5.9 كان أبو حنيفة يقول مَن أبرأ رجلا من حقّ له عليه من دَين أو مطالبة بعيب فى بيع أو غير ذلك فالبراءة جائزة ما لم يردّها البائع[2] وهو قول أبى يوسف ومحمّد وكان زفر يقول البراءة غير جائزة ما لم يقبلها البائع[3] فاذا قبلها جازت وكان آخرون سواهم يقولون البراءة جائزة قبلها المبرأ أو ردّها فكتبوا ما ذكروا احتياطا من ذلك *

5.10 واذا كتبتَ الرؤية والمعرفة من المشترى بالعيوب فى وقت وقوع البيع وقبل ذلك اغنى ذلك عن ذكر القبول لأنّ القبول الذى فيه الاختلاف الذى ذكرنا انّما هو القبول الذى يكون فى البراءة التى يحدثها المشترى للبائع من العيوب التى تجب له المطالبة بها بحقّ البيع لأنّه لم يكن علمها فأمّا ما كان علمه فوقع البيع على علمه به فلا نعلم فيه اختلافا أنّ البائع برئ منه *

6.0 (37 a) وإن ضمن عن البائع للمشترى ضمين جميع ما يدركه فى الدار // المبيعة من درك كتبتَ كتاب الشرى على ما كتبنا حتّى اذا انتهيتَ الى ذكر الفراغ من ذكر الدرك كتبتَ على أثر ذلك وحضر فلان بن فلان الفلانى يعنى الضمين قراءة هذا الكتاب فعرفه وأقرّ أنّ جميع ما فيه حقّ وضمن عن فلان بن فلان يعنى البائع بأمره لفلان بن فلان يعنى المشترى جميع الذى له وجميع الذى يجب له عليه من حقّ يحقّ هذا البيع المسمّى فى هذا الكتاب من تسليم ودرك وردّ ثمن وردّ قيمة بناء وقليل وكثير ممّا يجب لفلان بن فلان يعنى المشترى على فلان بن فلان يعنى البائع فى بيعه منه هذه الدار المحدودة فى هذا الكتاب على أنّ لفلان يعنى المشترى أن يأخذ بجميع الذى له وبجميع الذي يجب له من حقّ يحقّ ما ذُكر ووُصف فى هذا الكتاب فلانا يعنى البائع وفلانا يعنى الضمين وكلّ واحد منهما إن شاء أخذهما بذلك جميعا وإن شاء أخذهما شتّى كيف شاء وكلّما شاء ولا يُبرِئهما ولا واحدا منهما أخْذَه بذلك أحدهما دون صاحبه حتّى يستوفى جميع الذى له

[1] MS عاصم بن عبد الله
[2] MS ما لم يردها المسترى
[3] MS ما لم يقبلها المشترى

وجميع الذى يجب له عليهما من حقّ بحقّ البيع والضمان المسمّيَين فى هذا الكتاب وقد كفل أيضا كلّ واحد من فلان بن فلان يعنى البائع ومن فلان بن فلان يعنى الضمين بنفس صاحبه المسمّى
(37 b) معه فى هذا الكتاب بأمره لفلان بن فلان يعنى المشترى // على أنّه كلّما سلّمه اليه فهو كفيل له بنفسه كما كان قبل تسليمه إيّاه اليه ما بقى له عليه حقّ بسبب البيع والضمان المسمَّيَين فى هذا الكتاب حتّى يستوفى فلان بن فلان يعنى المشترى جميع الذى له وجميع الذى يجب له من حقّ بحقّ البيع والضمان المسمَّيَين فى هذا الكتاب وجعل أيضاً كلّ واحد من فلان بن فلان يعنى البائع ومن فلان بن فلان يعنى الضامن صاحبه المسمّى معه فى هذا الكتاب وكيله فى خصومة فلان بن فلان يعنى المشترى فيما يدّعى قِبَل صاحبه المسمّى معه فى هذا الكتاب من حقّ بسبب شىء ممّا سُمّى ووُصف فى هذا الكتاب وجعله وصيّه فى ذلك خاصّة بعد وفاته وأقامه فيما جعله اليه ممّا سُمّى ووُصف فى هذا الكتاب فى حياته وبعد وفاته مقام نفسه فى حياته على أنّ كلّ واحد منهما كلّما فسخ شيئا من هذه الوكالة ومن هذه الوصاية اللتين جعلهما الى صاحبه المسمّى معه فى هذا الكتاب فذلك الى صاحبه المسمّى معه فى هذا الكتاب وبيده عند فسخه ايّاه وبعد فسخه كما كان اليه قبل ذلك حتّى يستوفى فلان بن فلان يعنى المشترى جميع الذى له وجميع الذى يجب له من حقّ بحقّ البيع والضمان والكفالة والوكالة والوصاية المسمّى جميع
(38 a) ذلك فى هذا الكتاب فقبِل فلان بن فلان يعنى المشترى من فلان بن فلان ومن فلان // بن فلان يعنى البائع والكفيل جميع الضمان والكفالة المسمّيَين فى هذا الكتاب بمخاطبة منه ايّاهما على جميع ذلك وقبِل أيضا كلّ واحد من فلان بن فلان يعنى البائع ومن فلان بن فلان يعنى الضمين من صاحبه المسمّى معه فى هذا الكتاب جميع الوكالة والوصاية المسمّاتَين فى هذا الكتاب وتضمّن له القيام بهما بمخاطبة منه ايّاه على جميع ذلك وجميع ما فى هذا الكتاب من ضمان وكفالة ووصاية فعلى غير شرط كان بينهم فى عقدة هذا البيع المسمّى فى هذا الكتاب *

6.1 قال أبو جعفر وإنّما أفردنا ذكر ضمان الضامن من ذكر ما يجب على البائع بحقّ البيع على ما كتبنا لأنّا اذا جمعناهما جميعاً فكان ضمان الضامن قد دخل فى البيع وبه تمّ البيع *

6.2 واختلف الناس فى ذلك فقال بعضهم البيع جائز وليس هذا عندهم[1] من الشروط التى يفسد بها البيع وممّن قال ذلك أبو حنيفة وأبو يوسف ومحمّد وقال آخرون البيع فاسد بهذا الشرط وممّن
6.3 قال ذلك زفر * وأجمعوا أنّ الضمان اذا كان من الضامن للمشترى بعد تمام البيع ووجوبه وعلى غير شرط كان بينهما فى عقدته إنّه جائز لازم فكتبنا ما كتبنا لذلك *

6.4 (38 b) وإنّما كتبنا جميع الذى له وجميع الذى يجب له // على فلان بن فلان لأنّ البيع قد يوجب غرم قيمة البناء والغرس والزرع المستحدَث فيما يُستحقّ ممّا قد وقع عليه البيع فيكون ذلك ممّا يحدث وجوبه للمشترى بعد البيع على البائع بحقّ البيع المتقدّم فكتبنا ما كتبنا لذلك *

[1] MS عنده

6.5 وقد كان أبو زيد يكتب فى كتابه فى هذا الموضع من دينار وأقلّ من دينار الى كذا كذا
دينارا وأكثر من ذلك بالغا ما بلغ وكان يوسف بن خالد يكتب فى مثل هذا من دينار الى كذا
كذا دينارا ولا يكتب وأكثر من ذلك بالغا ما بلغ *

6.6 فإن اكتفيتَ بما كتبنا ممّا نسمّيه فبسبيل ذلك الاحتياط [1] وإن سمّيتَ الاختلاف فى ذلك
ممّا سَنُبَيِّنُهُ فيما بعد من كتابنا هذا فهو أجود غير أنّ ما كتب يوسف فى هذا أحبّ الينا
ممّا كتب أبو زيد لأنّا لم نأمن أن يُرفَع ذلك الى مَن لا يرى الضمان إلاّ الى مقدار من المال
معلوم فيعدّ ذلك مجهولا إذ كان ما بعد المقدار الذى سمّاه مجهولا فيجعله كذلك أيضا فيبطل
6.7 الضمان * ولكنّ أصلح ذلك عندنا أن يكون فى الدنانير فضل حتّى يغنى ذلك عن الاحتياج
الى « وأكثر من ذلك بالغا ما بلغ » وإنّما كان هذا الاحتياط عندنا بالتسمية أجود لاختلاف
الناس فى الضمان لمّا لا يُعلَم مقداره *

6.8 (39 a) فكان أبو حنيفة وأبو يوسف ومحمّد يجيزون الضمان لما يجب لفلان على فلان وإن // لم
6.9 يسمٍّ مبلغه ولم يذكر مقداره * فكان ابن أبى ليلى وسوّار بن عبد الله العنبرى لا يجيزون الضمان
فى ذلك إلاّ إن يُوقَّت للمضمون وقت معلوم أو يُذكَر له مقدار معلوم فيقال من دينار الى كذا
كذا دينارا فكتبنا ما كتبنا احتياطا من هذا الاختلاف *

6.10 قال أبو جعفر وانّما كتبنا وأقلّ من دينار لاختلاف الناس أيضا فى ذلك فكان أبو حنيفة
يقول لو أنّ رجلا قال لرجل لك علىّ من درهم الى عشرة دراهم إنّ عليه تسعة دراهم وجعل الدرهم
6.11 الآخر غاية فلم يوجبه على المُقِرّ وقال أبو يوسف ومحمّد له عليه عشرة دراهم * حدّثنا بذلك
محمّد بن العبّاس عن علىّ بن معبد عن محمّد بن الحسن عن أبى يوسف عن أبى حنيفة بما
ذكرناه عن أبى حنيفة وعن محمّد عن أبى يوسف بما ذكرناه عن أبى يوسف بموافقة محمّد له على
6.12 ذلك * وقال زفر له عليه ثمانية دراهم ما بين الدرهم الأوّل والدرهم العاشر من الدراهم فكتبنا ما
ذكرنا احتياطا من ذلك *

6.13 قال أبو جعفر وانّما كتبنا على أنّ لفلان بن فلان أن يأخذ بذلك كلّه فلانَ بن فلان وفلانَ
ابن فلان على ما كتبناه فى الموضع الذى كتبناه فيه من هذا الكتاب لأنّ الناس قد اختلفوا فى
6.14 (39 b) ذلك * فقال بعضهم اذا ضمن الرجل عن الرجل شيئا // لرجل وقبل المضمون له الضمان فللمضمون
له أن يأخذ المضمون عنه والضامن وكلّ واحد منهما وممّن قال ذلك [2] أبو حنيفة وزفر وأبو يوسف
6.15 ومحمّد * وقال بعضهم الضمان براءة للمضمون عنه وقد وجب الشىء المضمون للمضمون له على
الضامن وجعلوا ذلك كالحوالة فى قول مَن يجعل الحوالة براءة للمحيل وممّن [3] قال هذا القول الذى

[1] فبسبيل is unclear; MS omits الاحتياط

[2] وممن قال ذلك obliterated in MS

[3] وممن obliterated in MS

6.16 ذكرنا ابن ابى ليلى ومالك بن أنس * وقالوا جميعا اذا وقعت الكفالة أو الضمان على أنّ للمكفول له أو للمضمون له أن يأخذ أيّهما شاء فله أن يأخذ أيّهما شاء فكتبنا ما ذكرنا لذلك *

6.17 قال أبو جعفر وانّما كتبنا ولا يُبرِئها ولا واحدا منها أخْذه بذلك أحدهما دون صاحبه على ما كتبناه فى موضعه من هذا الكتاب لأنّ قوما كانوا يقولون اذا وقع الضمان فللمضمون له أن يأخذ به مَن شاء من الضامن أو المضمون عنه فأيّهما أخذه بذلك فقد برئ منه صاحبه فليس له مطالَبة بعد ذلك وقد ذهب الى هذا القول غير واحد من الكوفيّين فكتبنا ولا يبرئها ولا واحدا منها أخْذ فلان بن فلان بذلك وبشىء منه أحدهما دون صاحبه على ما كتبناه فى ذلك * //

6.18 (40 a) وإنّما كتبنا الكفالة بأمر المكفول عنه لمعنيَين أحدهما للكفيل ليرجع بما يلزمه فى كفالته على المكفول عنه لأنّه اذا كفل بغير أمره لم يجب له أن يرجع عليه بشىء ولا يأخذه بتخليصه ممّا كفل به عنه واذا كفل عنه بأمره وجب له أن يأخذ بتخليصه ممّا كفل به عنه ووجب له الرجوع عليه بما يؤدّيه بسبب ما كفل به عنه *

6.19 والخصلة الأخرى للمكفول له وذلك أنّ الناس قد اختلفوا فى الكفالة اذا كانت بغير أمر المكفول عنه فقال بعضهم هى جائزة ولازمة للكفيل ولا يرجع بشىء ممّا وجب عليه بسببها على المكفول عنه لأنّه لم يأمره بذلك ولم يدخله فيه وممّن قال هذا القول أبو حنيفة وزفر وأبو يوسف ومحمّد وسائر أصحابنا وعامّة أهل العلم وقال بعض الناس هو باطل وممّن قال ذلك عثمان البتّى فكتبنا ما كتبنا احتياطا من ذلك *

6.20 وانّما كتبنا قبول المضمون له للضمان لأنّ الناس يختلفون فى ذلك فكان أبو حنيفة يقول كلّ ضمان لم يكن بمخاطبة من الضامن للمضمون له وبقبول المضمون له ذلك من الضامن على
(40 b) الخطاب له منه به فهو باطل غير خوف استحسنه فى رجل حضره الموت // فقال لورثته « لفلان علىّ كذا لمال سمّاه ولفلان علىّ كذا لمال سمّاه » وضمنوا ذلك عنه بمحضره وبغيبة المضمون لهما إن
6.21 جعل الضمان جائزا لازما للورثة * وقال أبو يوسف ومحمّد الضمان فى ذلك كلّه وفيما سواه من
6.22 الضمانات جائز حضره المضمون له أو لم يحضر قَبِل أو لم يقبل * حدّثنى محمّد بن العبّاس عن علىّ بن معبد عن محمّد بن الحسن وحدّثنا سليمان بن شعيب عن أبيه عن محمّد بن الحسن بقولين جميعا غير أنّ محمّد بن العبّاس ذكر قول أبى حنيفة عن محمّد عن أبى يوسف عن أبى حنيفة فكتبنا ما كتبنا احتياطا من هذا الاختلاف *

6.23 قال أبو جعفر وانّما كتبنا كفالة كلّ واحد من البائع والضامن بنفس صاحبه للمشترى وجعلناه وكيله فيما يُدّعى قِبَله من حقّ يحقّ الكفالة والبيع لأنّ أبا حنيفة كان يقول لا يجب الدرك على الضامن حتّى يُقضَى به قبل ذلك على المضمون عنه فيكون عند ذلك للمقضى له به أن يأخذ به كلّ واحد من البائع ومن الضامن وإن شاء أخذهما به جميعا حدّثنا بذلك محمّد بن العبّاس عن علىّ بن معبد عن محمد عن أبى يوسف عن أبى حنيفة ولم يحكِ فيه خلافا *

6.24 (41 a) وقد // رُوى عن أبي يوسف فى إملائه أنّه قال الضامن خصم عن المضمون عنه ويُقضَى عليه بما يجب القضاء به على المضمون عنه لو كان حاضرا ويكون ذلك القضاء على المضمون عنه هذا كلّه إن كان الضامن بأمر المضمون عنه وإن كان الضامن بغير أمره لم يكن خصما عنه ولم يجب على الضامن شىء حتّى يجب على المضمون عنه *

6.25 فجعلنا الضامن كفيلا له ليحضره حتّى يقع القضاء عليه وجعلناه وكيلا له فى ذلك فى حياته ووصيّا له بعد وفاته ليكون خصما عنه فى حياته وبعد وفاته فيكون ما قُضِى به عليه للمشترى واجبا له على البائع وجعلنا كلّ واحد منهما كفيلا بنفس صاحبه لأنّه قد يجوز أن يكون البائع مُعدِما والكفيل مُؤسِرا فيثبت عند القاضى عدم البائع فيطلقه من السجن فجعلناه كفيلا بنفس الكفيل عنه ليحضره وليكون الحبس والمطالبة واجبين مؤسرين كانا أو معسرين غير أنّه قد رُوى عن محمّد بن الحسن فى رجل ضمن لرجل عن رجل ما وجب له على فلان أو ما ذاب له عليه أو ما قضى به له عليه بأمره أو بغير أمره ثمّ غاب فلان المضمون عنه إنّ الضامن خصم للمضمون له حتّى يثبت عليه ما وجب له على الغائب فيقضى بذلك بمحضر هذا الضامن //
(41 b) ويكون ذلك قضاء على الغائب وهذا القول فى الجامع الكبير حدّثناه محمّد بن العبّاس قال حدّثنا علىّ بن معبد عن محمّد بن الحسن *

6.26 قال أبو جعفر وانّما كتبنا على أنّ كلّ واحد منهما وكيل صاحبه فى حياته كما كان الكوفيّون والبغداذيّون من أصحابنا يكتبون فى ذلك ولم نكتب كما كان يوسف وهلال وسائر أصحابنا من البصريّين يكتبون فى ذلك وذلك أنّهم كانوا يكتبون مكان الوكيل الجرىّ ويختارون ذكر الجراية على ذكر الوكالة *
6.27 فاخترنا ما كتبنا لأنّ الوكالة أبين وأفصح فى اللغة وبها جاء القرآن وايّاها نقلت الآثار *

6.28 ألا ترى الى ما رُوى عن علىّ رحمة الله عليه قال حدّثنا سليمان بن شعيب قال حدّثنا أبى عن محمّد بن الحسن عن أبى يوسف عن محمّد بن اسحاق عن جَهْم بن أبى جَهْم عن عبد الله بن جعفر أنّ علىّ بن أبى طالب كان لا يحضر خصومته أبدا ويقول إنّ لها قُحَماً[1] وإنّ الشيطان يحضرها وكان يقول عقيل بن أبى طالب وكيلى فما قُضِىَ له فلى وما قُضى عليه فعلىَّ فلمّا
(42 a) كبر عقيل وضعف قال عبد الله بن جعفر وكيلى فما قُضى له // فلى وما قُضى عليه فعلىَّ *

6.29 وفى حديث فاطمة بنت قيس طلّقني أبو عمرو بن حفص طلاقا باتّا ثمّ خرج الى اليمن ووكّل عَيّاش بن أبى ربيعة بنفقتى فخاصمته فى ذلك الى النبىّ عليه السلام ولم تقل فجرّى عَيّاش بن أبى ربيعة وكلّ مَن فهم من الناس الجرِىّ فهم الوكيل وعلم بذكر الجرِىّ أنّه يريد به الوكيل وليس كلّ من فهم الوكيل علم أنّه الجرِىّ فأمر الوكالة أوسع وهو أقرب الى أفهام السامعين من الجراية *

[1] قحما partly obliterated

6.30 وكذلك كان أبو حنيفة وأبو يوسف ومحمّد وأبو زيد يكتبون فى ذلك غير أنّ أبا حنيفة قد رُوى عنه أنّه قال الوكيل والجرِىّ معناهما واحد فأيّهما كتبتَ فمعناه معنى صاحبه واختار فى شروطه الوكيل على الجرِىّ *

6.31 قال أبو جعفر وإنّما كتبنا فى فسخ الوكالة والوصاية ما كتبنا فى ذلك فى موضعه من هــذا الكتاب لِما نخاف على كلّ واحد من الموكّلَين من فسخ الوكالة والموصيَين من فسخ الوكالة
6.32 والوصاية * وكذلك كان اسماعيل بن حمّاد بن أبى حنيفة يكتب فى هذا غير أنّ فى ذكرنا
(42 b) وصيّة كلّ واحد منهما الى صاحبه معنى نخاف على كلّ واحد // منهما على مذهب أبى حنيفة وذلك أنّه كان يقول اذا جعل رجل رجلا وصيّا فى خاصّ من أمره بعد وفاته كان بذلك وصيّا
6.33 فى كل أموره وحلّ عنده محلّ الوصىّ المطلق الوصية * وكان أبو يوسف ومحمّد يقولان هو وصىّ فيما أوصى به اليه خاصّة غير وصىّ فيما سوى ذلك *

6.34 فينبغى لمن آثر أن يكتب شيئا من ذلك أن يوقف كلّ واحد من الضامن والمضمون عنه على ذلك لأنّه قد يجوز أن يكون صاحبه عنده غير مرضىّ لما يوجبه له بعض الناس ممّا لم يقصد به اليه فيكون ذلك براءة للكاتب من الإثم من إدخال الموصى فيما عساه لم يكن أراده وفيما لعلّه لم يعلم أحدا من العلماء قاله *

7.1 قال أبو جعفر ثمّ تكتب بعد جميع ما كتبنا ممّا احتججنا له بما وصفنا الشهادة على نحو ما ذكرناه فى الشروط المتقدّم فى كتابنا هذا غير أنّك تزيد فيها إقرار الضامن *

7.2 وقد اختلف الناس فى الموضع الذى يُوضَع فيه إقراره فقال قوم يُوضَع بعد ذكر البائع وقبل
7.3 ذكر المشترى وقد كان بعض أصحابنا يذهب الى هذا المذهب * // قال بعضهم يُوضَع بعد ذكر
(43 a) البائع والمشترى جميعا فكان هذا المذهب أصحّ المذهبين عندنا لأنّ الضمان انّما يكون بعد تمام
7.4 البيع فكذلك يكون اسم صاحبه بعد اسم مَن تولّى البيع * ألا ترى أنّهم جميعا قدّموا اسم البائع على اسم المشترى إن كان البائع هو المبتدئ بخطاب البيع والمشترى المثنّى بالقبول منه فقُدِّم
7.5 اسم البائع على اسم المشترى لذلك * فكان أيضا يجب تقديم اسم المشترى على اسم الضامن إذ كان ضمان الضامن انّما كان بعد قبول المشترى من البائع *

7.6 وقد كان يوسف بن خالد وهلال بن يحيى يكتبان وفلان كفيل على فلان وكذلك كان محمّد
7.7 ابن الحسن يكتب فيما حدّثنى سليمان بن شعيب عن أبيه * وكان أبو زيد يكتب وفلان كفيل عن فلان وكذلك مَن لقينا من أصحابنا يكتبون غير بكّار بن قُتَيبة فإنّه كان يكتب فى ذلك
7.8 مثل ما كان هلال يكتب وقد رُويت اللفظتان جميعا عن أصحابنا * وكان من حجّة يوسف فى ذلك قول الله عزّ وجلّ ﴿ وَقَدْ جَعَلْتُمُ اللهَ عَلَيكُم كَفِيلاً ﴾ وهذا الكلام الذى ذُكر كلام
(43 b) صحيح غير أنّ العامّة للمعنى الآخر أفهم منهم // لهذا المعنى فأىّ المعنيَين كتبتَ فهو حسن جائز

غير أنّ ما كان أقرب الى أفهام الناس فى كتب الشروط أولاهما عندنا لأنّه قد يقع الكتاب فى يد مَن لا فهم له باللغة من العامّة ومن غيرهم فكتبنا ما كتبنا ممّا هو أقرب الى أفهام العامّة لذلك ولأنّ الخاصّة تفهم من هذا ما تفهم العامّة والعامّة لا تفهم ما تفهم الخاصّة وبالله التوفيق *

8.0 قال أبو جعفر فإن كان للمشترى كفلاء جماعة كفلوا له عن البائع بمثل ما كفل له عنه به الكفيل الواحد ممّا ذكرنا كتبتَ وحضر فلان بن فلان وفلان بن فلان وفلان بن فلان حتّى تسمّيهم جميعا قراءة هذا الكتاب فعرفوه وأقرّوا أنّ جميع ما فيه حقّ وضمنوا عن فلان بن فلان بأمره لفلان ابن فلان جميع الذى له وجميع الذى يجب له عليه من حقّ يحقّ هذا البيع المسمّى فى هذا الكتاب من تسليم ودرك وردّ ثمن وردّ قيمة بناء[1] وما يجب له عليه ثمّ تنسق ذلك كما كتبناه فى ضمان الواحد ثمّ تكتب بعقب ذلك وكلّ واحد منهم ومن فلان بن فلان يعنى البائع كفيل بذلك عن سائر (44 a) أصحابه المسمّين معه فى هذا الكتاب بأمورهم على أنّ // لفلان بن فلان أن يأخذهم وفلان بن فلان يعنى البائع وكلّ واحد منهم بذلك كلّه وبما شاء منه إن شاء أخذهم بذلك جميعا وإن شاء أخذهم به شتّى ثمّ تنسق الكتاب فى ذلك على ما كتبناه فى ضمان الواحد غير أنّك تجعله على لفظ ضمان الجماعة *

9.1 وإن كان فى الكفلاء نساء فإنّك تنسق الكتاب على ما كتبنا غير أنّك توكّد أمور النساء بأن تكتب اذا سمّيتهنّ فى الشهادة وهنّ نسوة بالغات قد أدركن مدرك النساء وجازت أمورهنّ لهنّ وعليهنّ وكذلك كلّ موضع تقع فيه الشهادة على امرأة أو على نساء توكّده كذلك *

9.2 وكذلك كان أبو يوسف يكتب فى أمور النساء ويأمر بذلك لأنّه قد يقع فى أمورهنّ من الإشكال أكثر ممّا يقع فى أمور الرجال إلاّ أن يكون فى كتابك ما يدلّ على تاريخ ولادة[2] بعضهنّ أو على بلوغهنّ مثل أن يقول فلانة أمّ فلان بن فلان أو فلانة جدّة فلان بن فلان[3] فبضعهنّ أو بعضهنّ بمثل هذا أو يكون كتابا فيه ذكر حيض منهنّ أو من بعضهنّ أو فيه ذكر ما أتى عليهنّ من السنّ أو على بعضهنّ ممّا يدخلن به فى حكم البالغات بعد أن يكون // (44 b) متّفقا عليه لا مختلفا فيه *

9.3 فإنّ أبا حنيفة كان يقول الوقت الذى اذا بلغه الغلام ولم يكن احتلم قبله كان ببلوغه ايّاه فى حكم البالغين تسع عشرة سنة والوقت الذى اذا بلغته المرأة ولم تكن حاضت قبل ذلك ولا ولدت كانت به فى حكم البالغات فيما روى عنه أبو يوسف سبع عشرة سنة حدّثنى بذلك سليمان بن

[1] MS omits بناء

[2] MS ولاد

[3] MS جدة فلان

9.4 شعيب عن أبيه عن محمّد بن الحسن وروى الحسن بن زياد اللؤلؤى عن أبى حنيفة ثمانى عشرة
9.5 سنة فى هذا * وقال أبو يوسف من رأيه خمس عشرة سنة فى الغلام والجارية جميعا * وقال محمّد
ابن الحسن فى الغلام بقول أبى يوسف وفى الجارية بقول أبى حنيفة الذى رويناه عن سليمان
ابن شعيب فى هذا الكتاب هكذا قال فى أماليه بالرقّة وقد حدّثنا سليمان بن شعيب عن أبيه
9.6 عن محمّد فى كتاب الوكالة من الأصول أنّه وافق أبا يوسف فى قوله فى الغلام والجارية * وقد
قال قوم أيضاً الإنبات دليل على البلوغ وهذا قول قد رُوى عن جماعة من المتقدّمين *

9.7 قال أبو جعفر فإن كان فى كتابك ذكر شىء ممّا يجب به البلوغ باتّفاق أغناك ذلك عن
ذكر البلوغ وقد كان أهل العلم من أصحاب أبى حنيفة المتقدّمين يكتبون فى النساء ذكر البلوغ
9.8 إلاّ أن تكنّ قد ولدن هكذا رُوى عنهم * فكان أحبّ الأشياء الينا ذكر البلوغ // إلاّ إن (45 a)
تُذكَر الولادة لأنّه قد يجوز أن ينكرن أن قد ولدن فيحتاج فى ذلك الى تثبيت الولادة فلهذا احتجنا
الى إقرارهنّ ببلوغهنّ أو بما حكمه حكم البلوغ *

9.0 فإن كان بعض الشهود يشهد على النساء ويشهد على شهادته عليهنّ بذلك سائر الشهود معه
كتبت شهد فلان بن فلان بن فلان الفلانى ويُكْنَى أبا فلان وفلان بن فلان بن فلان الفلانى
ويُكْنَى أبا فلان حتّى تسمّى الذين يشهدون على النساء كذلك على إقرار فلانة ابنة فلان بن فلان
الفلانى حتّى تسمّى النسوة كلّهنّ كذلك ثمّ تكتب بعد أن أثبتوهنّ وعرفوهنّ معرفة صحيحة
بأعيانهنّ وأسمائهنّ وأنسابهنّ وأنّهنّ نسوة بالغات قد أدركن مدرك النساء وجازت أمورهنّ لهنّ
وعليهنّ ثمّ تنسق ذكر صحّة العقل وصحّة البدن على ما كتبنا من ذلك فى هذا الكتاب *

9.9 وقد كان بعض أصحابنا يكتب معرفة قديمة مكان معرفة صحيحة فكان ما كتبنا أحبّ الينا ممّا
9.10 كتب لأنّ المعرفة القديمة قد يختلف المقدار الذى به صارت قديمة عند أهل العلم * فكان أبو
يوسف يقول لو أنّ رجلا قال كلّ عبد لى قديم حرّ إنّه يعتق من عبيده كلّ من أتى عليه
عنده شهر وقد قال مرّة كلّ من أتى عليه ستة أشهر وأعلّ كلّ واحد من القولين فى الموضع
الذى قال بقول الله عزّ وجلّ // (وَالْقَمَرَ قَدَّرْنَاهُ مَنَازِلَ حَتَّى عَادَ كَالْعُرْجُونِ الْقَدِيمِ) * (45 b)
9.11 ولقد حدّثنى سليمان بن شعيب عن أبيه أنّه سمع محمّد بن الحسن وسأله رجل عن رجل قال كلّ
عبد لى قديم حرّ فقال له محمّد بن الحسن لا أدرى ما هذا أقديم فى[1] السنّ أو قديم فى الملك
أو قديم فى غير ذلك ولم يذكر عنه فى الجواب أكثر من هذا *

9.12 فقد أشكلتْ عليه فى ذلك الحال التى بها يكون قديما ومثل هذا يجب على العالم اجتنابه فى
كتابه لأنّه لا يأمن فى ذلك ممّن لعلّه أن يشغب فيما هو أقلّ من هذا واذا كتب معرفة صحيحة
فكلّ معنى عُرِفت المرأةُ حتّى وسِع الشاهدُ بتلك المعرفة أن يشهد على معرفتها فهى معرفة

[1] MS omits فى

صحيحة وقد يعرف الرجل الرجل أو المرأة معرفة تسعه الشهادة على المكان الذى عرفها فيه فلهذا كتبنا ما كتبنا *

9.13 وقد كان بعض أصحابنا يكتب مكان ما كتبنا من ذكر البلوغ وأقررن أنّهنّ نسوة بالغات ولا يكتب ذلك على إثبات البلوغ ثمّ يجرى كتابه على نحو ما كتبنا لأنّ البلوغ منهنّ لا يُعلَم
9.14 إلاّ بقولين وكذلك كان بعض البغداذيّين يكتب فى ذلك * وهذا عندنا فيه تقصير عمّا يجب
(46 a) لأنّ النسوة لو أقررن بالبلوغ وهنّ غير موهوم منهنّ البلوغ كان // إقرارهنّ بذلك باطلا فكان أولى الأشياء بهذا الكتاب أن يكتب وهنّ موهوم منهنّ ما أقررن به من ذلك حتى يصحّ
9.15 الإقرار * فإن كتبتَ ذلك على إثبات البلوغ فهو أجود لأنّ الرجل قد يعلم ببلوغ المرأة برؤيته ايّاها علما تسعه به الشهادة عليها أنّها بالغ وإن كتبتَ ذلك على الإقرار كتبتَ بعقبه وهنّ موهوم منهنّ ما أقررن به من ذلك *

10.0 قال أبو جعفر ثمّ تكتب بعقب ذلك ما احتججنا له بما ذكرنا وأشهد فلان بن فلان وفلان ابن فلان وفلان بن فلان يعنى الشهود الذين شهدوا على النساء على شهادتهم بذلك سائر الشهود المسمّين معهم فى هذا الكتاب أنّهم يشهدون على فلانة ابنة فلان وفلانة ابنة فلان وفلانة ابنة فلان حتّى تسمّى النسوة جميعا بجميع ما ذُكِر من شهادتهم عليهنّ فى هذا الكتاب وشهد أيضا فلان وفلان وفلان فتسمّى الشهود الذين شهدوا على النسوة خاصّة ثمّ تكتب وسائر الشهود المسمّين معهم فى هذا الكتاب على إقرار فلان بن فلان بن فلان الفلانى وفلان بن فلان بن فلان[1] الفلانى فتسمّى الباعة الرجال ثمّ تسمّى المشترين الرجال ثمّ تسمّى الضمناء الرجال بجميع
(46 b) ما سُمّى ووُصف فى هذا الكتاب // ثم تنسق الكتاب على ما ذكرنا فى الكتاب الأوّل *

10.1 وقد كان أبو يوسف يكتب وأشهدوا على شهادتهم سائر الشهود المسمّين معهم فى هذا الكتاب بجميع ما فى هذا الكتاب فكان ما كتبنا أولى عندنا من ذلك لأنّ محمّد بن الحسن قد قال فى رجل قال لرجل أشهِدْ على شهادتى لفلان بن فلان على فلان بن فلان بألف درهم له عليه إنّه لا يسعه بذلك أن يشهد على شهادته على ذلك حتّى يقول له أشهِدْ على شهادتى أنّى أشهَدُ أنّ لفلان بن فلان على فلان بن فلان ألف درهم فتسعه حينئذ الشهادة على شهادته بذلك حدّثنى بذلك محمّد بن العبّاس عن علىّ بن معبد عن محمّد بن الحسن ولم يحكِ فيه خلافا *

10.2 وكان بعض البغداذيّين من أصحابنا يكتب وأشهِدوا على شهادتهم بذلك سائر الشهود المسمّين معهم فى هذا الكتاب وقالوا لهم أشهِدوا على شهادتنا أنّا نشهَد بجميع ما فى هذا الكتاب فكان فيما كتبنا

[1] MS omits بن فلان

ما يغنينا عن هذا لأنّا كتبنا وأشهِدوا على شهادتهم على ذلك سائر الشهود المسمّين معهم فى هذا الكتاب أنّهم يشهدون على جميع ما سُمّى ووُصف فى هذا الكتاب فهذا هو الذى اذا كتبنا ما كتب البغداذيّون عاد معناه اليه ولا معنى لزيادة لفظ لا يزداد به معنى والله نسأله التوفيق *

آخر الجزء الأوّل والحمد لله على عونه وإحسانه
يتلوه فى الثانى باب بيع الجماعة من الواحد والواحد من الجماعة
وصلّى الله على سيّدنا محمّد النبىّ وآله وسلّم تسليما

الجزء الثانى من كتاب البيوع

من

الشروط الكبير

تأليف أبى جعفر أحمد بن محمد بن سلامة بن سلمة
الطحاوى الأزدى رحمه الله

بسم الله الرحمن الرحيم (48 b)

باب بيع الجماعة من الواحد والواحد من الجماعة

1.0 قال أبو جعفر واذا ابتاع رجل دارا من رجلين كتبتَ هذا ما اشترى فلان بن فلان بن فلان الفلانى من فلان بن فلان بن فلان الفلانى وفلان بن فلان بن فلان الفلانى اشترى منهما جميعا صفقة واحدة جميع الدار التى بمدينة كذا فى الموضع الكذا منها ثمّ تنسق الكتاب على نحو ما كتبنا فى شرى رجل من رجل غير أنّك تجعله على خطاب بيع الاثنين وغير أنّك اذا انتهيتَ الى وتفرّقوا جميعا بأبدانهم بعد هذا البيع المسمّى فى هذا الكتاب عن تراض منهم جميعا بجميعه وإنفاذ منهم له كتبتَ على أثر ذلك وكان بيع فلان بن فلان وفلان بن فلان جميع ما وقع عليه هذا البيع المسمّى فى هذا الكتاب من فلان بن فلان وقبضهما منه ثمنه المسمّى فى هذا الكتاب وتسليمهما اليه جميع ما وقع عليه هذا البيع المسمّى فى هذا الكتاب بإذن من كلّ واحد منهما لصاحبه المسمّى معه فى هذا الكتاب فى ذلك وأمر منه ايّاه به ثمّ تنسق الكتاب على نحو ما كتبنا فى الكتاب
(49 a) الأوّل غير أنّك تكتب فى موضع الدرك فما أدرك // فلان بن فلان فيما وقع عليه هذا البيع المسمّى فى هذا الكتاب [وفى شىء منه ومن حقوقه][1] من درك من أحد من الناس كلّهم فعلى كلّ واحد من فلان بن فلان ومن فلان بن فلان المسمّيين فى هذا الكتاب تسليم ما يجب عليه فى ذلك من حقّ ويلزمه بسبب هذا البيع المسمّى فى هذا الكتاب حتّى يسلّم ذلك الى فلان بن فلان على ما يوجبه له عليه هذا البيع المسمّى فى هذا الكتاب *

1.1 قال أبو جعفر وقد اختُلف فى كتاب الدرك فى هذا كيف يُكتَب فكان أبو بكر بن الخصّاف يكتب فيه هكذا وكان غيره من أصحابنا يكتب فعلى فلان بن فلان وفلان بن فلان تسليم ما يجب عليهما ثمّ ينسق كتابه على ذلك فكان ما كتب أبو بكر فى هذا أحبّ الينا لأنّه قد اختلف فيما وقع عليه بيع كلّ واحد من البائعين فيما وقع عليه البيع *

1.2 فقال قوم اذا كانت الدار بين البائعين نصفين فما باعه كلّ واحد منهما فهو النصف الذى له منها خاصّة وممّن قال ذلك أبو حنيفة وأبو يوسف ومحمّد بن الحسن وقال آخرون ما باعه كلّ واحد منهما فهو من النصفين جميعا وممّن قال ذلك زفر بن الهذيل *

[1] words obliterated in MS

1.3 وقد اختلف الناس مع هذا فيمن باع شيئا لغيره بأمره على من يجب عهدته وضمان الدرك فيه فقال قوم هو على البائع لم يرجع به البائع على الآمر وممّن قال ذلك أبو حنيفة وزفر وأبو يوسف ومحمّد وقال آخرون هو على المبيع له دون البائع فاذا كتبنا فعليهما تسليم ما يجب عليهما فى ذلك فقد جعلنا على كلّ واحد منهما تسليم نصف ما يجب تسليمه للمشترى على البائعين بحقّ البيع *

1.4 وقد يجوز أيضا أن يكتبوا // [لفه] [1] فيكون هذا المعنى فيه أوكد منه فى المعنى الأوّل
(49 b) [واخترنا ما كتب أبو] [1] بكر بن الخصّاف فى هذا على ما كتب غيره من العلماء [2] *

1.5 قال أبو جعفر وقد اختُلف أيضا فى الموضع الذى يُكتَب فيه ذكر إذن كلّ واحد من البائعين لصاحبه فى البيع وقبض الثمن وتسليم المبيع فكتبه غير واحد من أصحابنا فى ذلك على نحو ما كتبنا وجعلوه من كتابهم فى الموضع الذى وصفنا وقد كتبه آخرون بعد قبض المبيع وقبل ذكر الرؤية وممّن كتب ذلك يوسف بن خالد وهلال بن يحيى وكان هذا أحسن عندنا ممّا تقدّم ذكرنا له من القول الأوّل لأنه بعقب ما يحتاج الى الوكالة فيه وما بعد ذلك ممّا يُكتَب الى آخر الكتاب فليس ممّا يحتاج الى الوكالة فيه انـّما هو وصف ما كان من البائعين ومن المشترى منهما *

1.6 قال أبو جعفر ولم يكن أبو زيد يكتب فى كتابه هذا ذكر إذن كلّ واحد من البائعين لصاحبه فى البيع وكان يوسف وهلال يكتبانه على ما ذكرناه عنهما وكان ما كتبنا فى ذلك أحبّ الينـــا للاختلاف الذى ذكرناه فيما يقع عليه بيع كلّ واحد من البائعين على ما ذكرناه فى ذلك *

1.7 قال أبو جعفر ولقد حدّثنى محمّد بن شاذان قال سمعتُ هلال بن يحيى يقول كان يوسف ابن خالد يكتب فى هذا وكان بيع فلان بن فلان بن فلان وفلان بن فلان بن فلان من فلان بن
(50 a) فلان بن فلان جميع ما وقع عليه هذا البيع المسمّى فى هذا الكتاب // وقبضهما منه ثمنه المسمّى فى هذا الكتاب وتسليمهما اليه جميع ما وقع عليه هذا البيع المسمّى فى هذا الكتاب بعد إذن كلّ واحد منهما لصاحبه فى ذلك قال هلال فقلتُ له لِمَ كتبتَ هذا ؟ فقال لى للاختلاف فيما وقع عليه بيع كلّ واحد من البائعين فذكر نحو ممّا ذكرنا واحتججنا به قبل هذا قال هلال فقلتُ له فأوثق من هذا أن تكتب وكان بيع فلان بن فلان وفلان بن فلان جميع ما وقع عليه هذا البيع المسمّى فى هذا الكتاب من فلان بن فلان وقبضهما منه ثمنه المسمّى فى هذا الكتاب وتسليمهما اليه جميع ما وقع عليه هذا البيع المسمّى فى هذا الكتاب بإذن من كلّ واحد منهما لصاحبه فى ذلك فقال أبو يوسف وهل بين هذا وبين الأوّل من فروق ؟ فقلتُ له نعم أنت تقول لو قال رجل والله لا دخلتُ الدار إلاّ بعد أن يأذن لى زيد فأذن له زيد ثمّ نهاه ثمّ دخل الدار إنّه لا يحنث ولو قال والله لا دخلتُ هذه الدار إلاّ بإذن زيد فأذن له زيد ثمّ نهاه ثمّ دخل إنّه حانث فكان قوله إلاّ بعد أن يأذن لى زيد ليس فيه ثبوت الإذن حتّى يكون الدخول وقوله إلاّ بإذن زيد فيه ثبوت الإذن من زيد الى أن يكون الدخول فكذلك قوله فى هذين البائعين بعد أن أذن كلّ

[1] several words obliterated [2] العلماء unclear in MS

واحد منهما لصاحبه ليس فيه تحقيق بقاء الإذن منهما الى أن كان البيع منهما واذا قلتَ بإذن من كلّ واحد منهما لصاحبه فى ذلك كان فى ذلك تحقيق بقاء الإذن منهما الى أن كان البيع منهما

1.8 قال هلال فرجع أبو يوسف الى ذلك ٭ وهذا الذى احتجّ به هلال عندنا [من تحقيق] [1] //
(50 b) العلم والمعرفة [2] فلذلك كتبنا ما ذكرنا ٭

1.9 وكان أبو حنيفة وأبو يوسف ومحمّد يقولون اذا كانت الدار بين رجلين لأحدهما ثلثاها وللآخر ثلثها فباعاها جميعا صفقة واحدة إنّ كلّ واحد منهما بائع لنصفها فأمّا صاحب الثلثين فذلك النصف الذى باعه من نصيبه خاصّة وأمّا صاحب الثلث فذلك النصف الذى باعه هو نصيبه وهو ثلث الدار وسدسها من نصيب شريكه وجعلوا بيعه معه إذنا منه له فى البيع لما وقع عليه بيعه من نصيبه ٭

1.10 وكان الذى يخالفهم يزعم أنّ بيع كلّ واحد منهما وقع على نصف الدار فثلثا النصف الذى باعه صاحب الثلثين من نصيبه وثلثه من نصيب صاحبه وثلث النصف الذى باعه صاحب الثلث من نصيبه وثلثاه من نصيب صاحبه ولم يجعلوا بيع كلّ واحد منهما مع صاحبه إذنا منه لصاحبه فى بيع ما يقع عليه بيعه من نصيبه وهذا قول زفر فكتبتُ الإذن فى ذلك على ما كتبنا لهذا المعنى ٭

2.0 فإن أحببتَ أن تسمّى فى كتابك مقدار ما كان لكلّ واحد منهما فى الدار وما قبض من ثمنها بحقّ ما كان له فيها كتبتَ كتاب الشرى على ما كُتب حتّى اذا أتيتَ على ذكر الثمن كتبتَ على أثر ذلك على أنّ الذى باع فلان بن فلان من جميع ما وقع عليه هذا البيع المسمّى فى هذا الكتاب جميع ما ذكر فلان بن فلان أنّه جميع حقّه وحصّته وهو كذا كذا سهما من كذا كذا سهما من جميع ما وقع عليه هذا البيع المسمّى فى هذا الكتاب شائعة فيه غير مقسومة منه وعلى أنّ الذى باع فلان بن فلان من جميع ما وقع عليه هذا البيع المسمّى فى هذا الكتاب //
(51 a) جميع ما ذكر فلان بن فلان أنّه جميع حقّه وحصّته وهو كذا كذا سهما من كذا كذا سهما من جميع ما وقع عليه هذا البيع المسمّى فى هذا الكتاب شائعة فيه غير مقسومة منه فاذا أتيتَ على ذكر قبض الثمن كتبتَ من ذلك كذا كذا دينارا قبضها فلان بن فلان ثمن جميع ما ذكر فلان ابن فلان أنّه جميع حقّه وحصّته المذكور ذلك له فى هذا الكتاب وهو كذا كذا دينارا مثاقيل ذهبا عينا وازنة جيادا ومن ذلك كذا كذا دينارا قبضها فلان بن فلان ثمن جميع ما ذكر فلان بن فلان هذا أنّه جميع حقّه وحصّته المذكور ذلك له فى هذا الكتاب واذا كتبتَ هذا أغناك عن ذكر إذن كلّ من البائعين لصاحبه فى البيع وفى قبض الثمن وفى تسليم المبيع ٭

[1] words obliterated

[2] المعرفة unclear in MS

2.1 وقد اختلف الناس فى هذا وكان أبو بكر أحمد بن عمرو الخصّاف يكتب فى ذلك نحو ممّا كتبنا غير أنّه كان يكتب على أنّ الذى باع فلان بن فلان من هذه الدار المحدودة فى هــذا الكتاب كذا كذا سهما وعلى أنّ الذى باع فلان بن فلان من هذه الدار المحدودة فى هذا الكتاب

2.2 كذا كذا سهما * وكان غيره من أصحابنا لا يكتب من ذلك شيئا غير أنّه اذا أتى على قبض الثمن كتب من ذلك كذا كذا دينارا قبضها فلان بن فلان ثمن جميع ما ذكر فلان بن فلان أنّه جميع حقّه وحصّته وهو كذا كذا سهما من كذا كذا سهما من جميع ما وقع عليه هذا البيع المسمّى فى هذا الكتاب ويكتب فى الآخر مثل ذلك *

2.3 (51 b) فكان ما كتب هؤلاء // من اشتراطهم مقدار ما باع كلّ واحد من المتبايعين ممّا وقع عليه هذا البيع أحبّ الينا غير أنّه قد كان ينبغى لهم أن يجعلوا ذلك الذى باعه كلّ واحد من البائعين هو جميع ما ذكر أنّه حقّه خاصّة حتّى لا يكون شىء منه من نصيب صاحبه فى قول أحد من الناس لأنّه اذا ذكر أنّه ثلثا الدار كان فى ذلك من الاختلاف ما قد ذكرنا فى هذا الباب من وقوع بيع كلّ واحد من البائعين على مقدار نصيبه من الدار خاصّة ومن نصيبه ومن نصيب صاحبه على ما قد ذكرنا من ذلك وشرحنا وبيّنّا فيما تقدّم من هذا الباب *

3.0 واذا اشترى رجلان دارا من رجل بينهما نصفين كتبتَ هذا ما اشترى فلان بن فلان بن فلان الفلانى وفلان بن فلان بن فلان الفلانى من فلان بن فلان بن فلان[1] الفلانى اشتريا منه جميعا صفقة واحدة بينهما بالسويّة جميع الدار ثمّ تنسق الكتاب على نحو ما كتبناه *

3.1 وانّما كتبنا صفقة واحدة لاختلاف حكم الصفقة الواحدة وحكم الصفقتين فى ذلك عند بعض الناس كان أبو حنيفة يقول اذا ابتاع رجلان دارا من رجل فأصابها عيبا قبل أن يقبضاها أو بعد ما قبضاها فليس لهما أن يردّاها إلاّ جميعا وليس لأحدهما أن يردّ ما وجب له منها بالشرى دون صاحبه *

3.2 وقال أبو يوسف إن كانا لم يقبضاها فالقول فى ذلك كما قال أبو حنيفة وإن كانا قد قبضاها فلكلّ واحد منهما أن يردّ ما اشترى منها على بائعه ردّ صاحبه ما اشترى منها أو لم يردّه *

3.3 (52 a) وقال // محمّد بن الحسن لكلّ واحد منهما أن يردّ ما اشترى منها على بائعه دون صاحبه وجعل كلّ واحد منهما فى حكم من اشترى نصف الدار فى صفقة واحدة فيما يجب له من المطالبة بالعيوب وما أشبهها ولو كان البيع وقع فى الصفقتين كان لكلّ واحد منهما أن يردّ ما ابتاع منها ردّ صاحبه معه ما ابتاع منها أو لم يردّه منها *

[1] MS omits بن فلان

3.4 فكتبنا صفقة واحدة لنبيّن حكمها من حكم الصفقتين فى قول من يفرّق بين الحكمين فى ذلك ولو كتبتَ هذا فى كتب البياعات كلّها لـكان حسنا لأنّه يوكّد أنّ جميع ما وقع عليه البيع ممّا ذُكر فى كتاب العهدة المذكور ذلك فيما كان فى صفقة واحدة وأنّ حكمه فى ردّ ما يردّ منه بالعيب وما يردّ منه بخيار الرؤية حكم ما وقع البيع عليه فى صفقة واحدة لا فى صفقات مختلفات وفى ذلك أيضا ما يقطع شغب المتبايعين اذا ادّعى بعضهم أنّ البيع وقع فى صفقة واحدة أو وقع فى صفقات مختلفات *

4.0 قال أبو جعفر فإن كان البيع وقع على أنّ لأحدهما من الدار المبيعة الثلثين وللآخر الثلث ابتدأتَ الكتاب كما كتبنا حتّى اذا أتيتَ على ذكر الثمن كتبتَ على أنّ جميع ما وقع عليه هذا البيع المسمّى فى هذا الكتاب بين فلان وفلان وفلان بن فلان على ثلاثة أسهم فلفلان بن فلان سهمان منه من ثلاثة أسهم شائعان فيه غير مقسومين منه بكذا كذا دينارا مثاقيل ذهبا عينا وازنة جيادا من الثمن المسمّى فى هذا الكتاب وعلى أنّ لفلان بن فلان من جميع ما وقع عليه هذا
(52 b) البيع المسمّى // فى هذا الكتاب سهما واحدا من ثلاثة أسهم منه شائع فيه غير مقسوم منه بكذا كذا دينارا مثاقيل ذهبا عينا وازنة جيادا من الثمن المسمّى فى هذا الكتاب ودفع كلّ واحد من فلان بن فلان ومن فلان بن فلان الى فلان بن فلان جميع ثمن ما ابتاعه منه على ما سُمّى ووُصف فى هذا الكتاب وقبضه منه فلان بن فلان واستوفاه منه تامّا كاملا وأبرأه من جميعه بعد قبضه ايّاه واستيفائه له وسلّم فلان بن فلان الى فلان بن فلان وفلان بن فلان[1] جميع ما وقع عليه هـذا البيع المسمّى فى هذا الكتاب وقبضه منه فلان بن فلان وفلان بن فلان وقبض كلّ واحد منهما منه جميع ما ابتاعه منه على ما سُمّى ووُصف فى هذا الكتاب وصار فى يده وقبضه بهذا الشرى المسمّى فى هذا الكتاب ثمّ تنسق الكتاب على نحو ما كتبنا *

4.0 bis وإن شئتَ امتثلتَ فى دفع[2] الثمن ما امتثلنا فى قبض المبيع فكتبتَ ودفع فلان بن فلان وفلان ابن فلان الى فلان بن فلان جميع الثمن المسمّى فى هذا الكتاب وهو كذا كذا دينارا مثاقيل ذهبا عينا وازنة جيادا دفعها فلان بن فلان ثمن جميع ما ابتاعه من هذه الدار المحدودة فى هذا الكتاب وهو سهمان من ثلاثة أسهم منها شائعان فيها غير مقسومين منها ومن ذلك كذا كذا دينارا مثاقيل ذهبا عينا وازنة جيادا دفعها فلان بن فلان ثمن جميع ما ابتاعه من هذه الدار المحدودة فى هـذا الكتاب وهو سهم واحد من ثلاثة أسهم منها شائعا فيها غير مقسوم منها وقبض فلان بن فلان من
(53 a) فلان بن فلان وفلان بن فلان جميع الثمن المسمّى فى هذا الكتاب واستوفاه منهما[3] // فلان بن

[1] MS adds بن فلان
[2] MS omits دفع
[3] MS واستوفاه منه

فلان تامّا كاملا وأبرأهما من جميعه بعد قبضه ايّاه واستيفائه له وهو كذا كذا دينارا مثاقيل ذهبا عينا وازنة جيادا *

4.1 قال أبو جعفر وانّما كتبنا أنّ ما دفع كلّ واحد من المتبايعين من الثمن ثمن ما ابتاعه لنفسه لئلا يكون بعضه عن نفسه وبعضه عن صاحبه *

باب ضمان تسليم المبيع الى المبتاع

5.0 قال أبو جعفر واذا اشترى رجل من رجل دارًا وضمن له رجل تسليمها اليه عن البائع بأمره كتبتَ كتاب الشرى على ما كتبنا غير أنّك تمسك عن ذكر القبض للدار المبيعة فلا تذكره فاذا انتهيت الى ذكر الدار وفرغت منه كتبت بعقب ذلك وحضر فلان بن فلان الفلانى قراءة هذا الكتاب فعرفه وأقرّ أنّ جميع ما فيه حقّ وضمن عن فلان بن فلان بأمره لفلان بن فلان تسليم جميع ما وقع عليه هذا البيع المسمّى فى هذا الكتاب اليه وكفل له بنفس فلان بن فلان أيضا بأمره على أنّ فلان بن فلان يعنى الكفيل كلّما برئ الى فلان بن فلان يعنى المشترى من الكفالة بنفس فلان بن فلان يعنى البائع فهو كفيل له بنفسه حتّى يستوفى فلان بن فلان جميع ما ابتاعه ممّا سُمّى ووُصف فى هذا الكتاب ويقبضه فقبل فلان بن فلان من فلان بن فلان جميع الضمان والكفالة المسمّيين فى هذا الكتاب بمخاطَبة منه إيّاه على جميع ذلك ثمّ تكتب بعقب ذلك وجميع
(53 b) ما فى هذا الكتاب // من ضمان وكفالة فعلى غير شرط كان فى عقدة هذا البيع المسمّى فى هذا الكتاب *

5.1 وكان ابن الخصّاف يكتب فى هذا حتّى يسلّم ذلك فلان بن فلان الى فلان بن فلان ويقبّضه ايّاه أو يردّ عليه الثمن وهذا عندنا خطأ لأنّ الضامن لو جاء بالثمن فدفعه الى المشترى لـما برئ ممّا ضمن له حتّى يسلّم الدار المبيعة اليه ولو عُرفت الدار المبيعة فلم يقدر على تسليمها وذلك وجوب تسليمها عن البائع بطل البيع وانفسخ الضمان ولم يجب على الضامن ردّ الثمن *

باب ابتياع الدارين والثلاثة وأكثر من ذلك فى صفقة واحدة

6.0 قال أبو جعفر واذا اشترى رجل من رجل دورا فإن كانت مجتمعة فى مكان واحد يحيط بها ويجمعها ويشتمل عليها حدود أربعة كتبت هذا ما اشترى فلان بن فلان بن فلان الفلانى من فلان بن فلان بن فلان الفلانى اشترى منه صفقة واحدة جميع الكذا كذا الدار المتلاصقات اللاتى فى مدينة كذا فى الموضع الكذا منها ويحيط بهذه الدار الكذا كذا المسمّيات فى هذا الكتاب ويجمعها ويشتمل عليها حدود أربعة ثمّ تحدّدها ثمّ تكتب وفيه يشرع باب هذه الأدر المحدودات فى هذا الكتاب إن كانت أبوابهنّ تشرع منهنّ فى جانب واحد وإن كانت أبوابهنّ تشرع

منهنّ فى جوانب مختلفة كتبت ولهذه الكذا كذا الدار المحدودات فى هذا الكتاب كذا كذا بابا (54 a) فمنهنّ باب واحد يشرع // من هذه الأدر المحدودات فى هذا الكتاب فى حدّهنّ الكذا ومنهنّ كذا كذا بابا يشرع من هذه الأدر المحدودات فى هذا الكتاب فى حدّهنّ الكذا حتّى تأتى على الأبواب كلّها كذلك ثمّ تنسق بقيّة الكتاب على ما كتبنا *

6.1 وانّما كتبنا فى ذلك صفقة واحدة لاختلاف حكم الصفقة الواحدة وأحكام الصفقات المختلفات على ما ذكرنا من ذلك فيما تقدّم من كتابنا هذا *

6.0 bis وإن كانت الأدر فى أماكن مختلفة كتبت هذا ما اشترى فلان بن فلان الفلانى من فلان بن فلان [1] الفلانى اشترى منه صفقة واحدة جميع الكذا كذا الدار اللاتى بمدينة كذا فمنهنّ دار [2] فى الموضع الكذا ويحيط بها ويجمعها ويشتمل عليها حدود أربعة ثمّ تحدّدها وتكتب فى بقيّة الدور كذلك حتّى تأتى عليها كلّها *

6.0 ter وإن كانت منهنّ داران متلاصقتان [3] كتبت فمنهنّ داران فى موضع كذا كذا متلاصقتان يحيط بهما ويجمعهما ويشتمل عليهما حدود أربعة ثمّ تحدّها وتكتب بقيّة الدور كذلك حتّى تأتى عليها كلّها *

6.2 وقد كان بعض الناس اذا أتى على مثل هذا لم يصف الدارين أنّهما متلاصقتان ويكتب ويحيط بهاتين الدارين ويجمعهما ويشتمل عليهما حدود أربعة ويحدّهما وكان يذهب الى أنّه اذا وكّد أنّه يحيط بهما ويجمعهما ويشتمل عليهما حدود أربعة وجب بذلك أن تكونا متلاصقتين // (54 b) وهذا عندنا خطأ لأنّه قد يجوز أن تكون بينهما فرجة ليس منهما طريق [4] أو يكون جنبهما طريق وما أشبه ذلك *

باب شرى الدار إلاّ بيتا منها سفلا وعلوّا

7.0 قال أبو جعفر واذا ابتاع رجل من رجل دارا غير بيت منها كتبت هذا ما اشترى فلان بن فلان من فلان بن فلان اشترى منه جميع الدار التى بمدينة كذا فى موضع كذا ويحيط بهذه الدار ويجمعها ويشتمل عليها حدود أربعة ثمّ تحدّها ثمّ تنسق الكتاب على ما كتبنا حتّى اذا أتيتَ على وكلّ حقّ هو لها خارج منها كتبت على أثر ذلك خلا جميع البيت الذى هو من هذه الدار المحدودة فى هذا الكتاب فى الموضع الكذا منها وهو البيت الذى يحيط به ويجمعه ويشتمل عليه حدود أربعة أحد حدود جماعته ثمّ تحدّه ثمّ تكتب بحدوده كلّها وأرضه وبنائه وسفله وعلوّه

[1] MS adds بن فلان
[2] MS فنهن دارا
[3] MS داران متلاصقتين
[4] MS ليست منها طريق

ومرافقه فى حقوقه ومسايله فى حقوقه وطرقه التى هى له من حقوقه مسلّمة له فى ساحة هذه الدار التى هو منها المحدودة فى هذا الكتاب وفى دهليزها حتّى تنتهى الى الطريق الذى يشرع فيه بابها هذا إن كان بابها فى طريق وإن كان بابها فى زقاق كتبت حتّى تنتهى الى الزقاق الذى يشرع فيه بابها وكلّ قليل وكثير هو له فيه ومنه من حقوقه وكلّ حقّ هو له داخل فيه وكلّ حقّ هو له خارج منه فإنّ جميع ما وقع عليه هذا الاستثناء المسمّى فى هذا الكتاب لم يدخل ولا شىء
(55 a) منه فى هذا البيع المسمّى فى هذا الكتاب ثمّ تنسق الكتاب على نحو ما // كتبنا *

7.0 bis هذا اذا كان علوّ البيت المستثنى بَراحاً لم[1] يدخل فى البيع فإن كان علوّه بيت آخر لم يدخل فى البيع أيضا كتبت خلا البيتين اللذين أحدهما علوّ الآخر فى الجانب الكذا من هذه الدار المحدودة فى هذا الكتاب فمن هذين البيتين المستثنين فى هذا الكتاب بيت فى سفل هذه الدار المحدودة فى هذا الكتاب وهو البيت السفلىّ الذى يحيط به ويجمعه ويشتمل عليه حدود أربعة ثمّ تحدّها ومنها بيت علوّ طباق هذا البيت السفل المحدود فى هذا الكتاب ويُصعَد الى هذا البيت العلوّ الذى من هذين البيتين المستثنيين فى هذا الكتاب من الدرجة التى من هذه الدار المحدودة فى هذا الكتاب فى موضع كذا فإن ذرعتَ الدرجة وذكرت طولها وسمكها وعدد مرافقها فهو أجود وإن حدّدتَ ما هى عليه من الأرض مع ذلك فهو أوثق *

7.0 ter وإن كان البيت السفل الذى لم يدخل فى البيع قد دخل علوّه فى البيع كتبتَ الكتاب على ما كتبنا غير أنّك لا تذكر فى الاستثناء علوّ البيت المستثنى إذ كان قد دخل فى البيع ثمّ تنسق الكتاب كنحو ما ذكرنا وإن كتبتَ بعد فراغك من ذكر الاستثناء وقد دخل علوّ هذا البيت المستثنى فى هذا الكتاب فيما وقع عليه هذا البيع المسمّى فى هذا الكتاب فهو أجود *

7.0 quater وإن كان المستثنى من هذه الدار غرفة كتبت خلا الغرفة التى من هذه الدار المحدودة فى هذا
(55 b) الكتاب فى الطبقة الثانية منها // طباق المنزل السفل الذى من هذه الدار المحدودة فى هذا الكتاب فى موضع كذا وكذا وهو المنزل السفل الذى يحيط به ويجمعه ويشتمل عليه حدود أربعة ثمّ تحدّ البيت السفل الذى هذه الغرفة المستثناة طباقه ثمّ تمتثل فيما يدخل معه فى الاستثناء وفيما يخرجه من سفله ومن علوّه اللذين قد دخلا فى البيع ما كتبنا فى البيت السفلىّ المستثنى على ما كتبنا من ذلك فى هذا الكتاب ولا تحدّنّ علوّا فى شىء من كتابك ولكن صِفْه ثمّ حُدّ سفلَه وكلّما فرغتَ من ذكر شىء مستثنى فى كتاب ذكرته فيه كتبت على أثر ذلك فإنّ ذلك لم يدخل ولا شىء منه فيما وقع عليه هذا البيع المسمّى فى هذا الكتاب *

7.1 قال أبو جعفر وقد كان أبو زيد يكتب فى هذا هذا ما اشترى فلان بن فلان من فلان بن فلان اشترى منه جميع الدار التى بمدينة كذا إلاّ البيت الذى منها فى موضع كذا ثمّ يكتب الكتاب

[1] براحا لم unclear in MS

7.2 على نحو ما يكتبه فى شرى الدار الكاملة * وكان غيره من أصحابنا لا يستثنيه أوّل كتابه ثمّ يستثنيه حيث استثنيناه نحن من كتابنا *

7.3 وكان هذا أحسن عندنا ممّا كتب أبو زيد لأنّ الدار لا يُعلَم ولا يُعرَف إلاّ بحدودها فانّما يحتاج الى أن يستثنى منها ما لم يدخل فى البيع منها بعد أن يُعرَف ويُحَدّ وقد كتب أبو زيد فى بيع الخيار فأطلِقَ فى أوّل كتابه البيعَ ثمّ أشترِطُ الخيار بعد ذلك لمّا آتى على ذكر الأسباب التى وقع البيع عليها وأتبِعُ ذلك ذكر الثمن فكذلك ينبغى أن يفعل فى الاستثناء يُطلَق البيع فى أوّل الكتاب حتّى يُعلَم ويُعرَف فاذا عُلِم وعُرِف استُثنِىَ منه ما لم يدخل فيه *

(56 a) باب أشرية الدور إلاّ طريقا فيها

8.0 قال أبو جعفر واذا اشترى رجل من رجل دارا إلاّ طريقا فيها لدار أخرى كتبتَ الكتاب على ما كتبنا فاذا انتهيتَ الى وكل حقّ هو لها خارج منها كتبت على أثر ذلك خلا الطريق الذى فى هذه الدار المحدودة فى هذا الكتاب وهو الطريق الذى يتطرّق منه الى الدار التى تلاصقها من جانبها الكذا من الباب المفتوح منها اليها فى الموضع الكذا منها مسلّما ذلك فيها حتّى ينتهى الى الطريق الذى يشرع فيه بابها فإن قدرتَ على تحديد الطريق وذكر مقداره وذكر ذرعه طولا وعرضا حتّى تحصره من جميع جوانبه فقلتَ ذلك فى كتابك فهو أوثق ثمّ تكتب فإنّ ذلك من حقوق هذه الدار المحدودة فى هذا الكتاب من حقوق الدار التى تلاصقها من جانبها الكذا بالسويّة شائع بينهما غير مقسوم لم يدخل شىء من حقوق الدار الملاصقة للدار المحدودة فى هذا الكتاب فى هذا الطريق المذكور فى هذا الكتاب ولا فى شىء منه فى هذا البيع المسمّى فى هذا الكتاب *

8.1 قال أبو جعفر وقد كتب فى هذا قوم على أنّ للدار الملاصقة للدار المحدودة فى هذا الكتاب من جانبها الكذا طريقا فى ساحة هذه الدار المحدودة فى هذا الكتاب ثمّ أجرَوا الكتاب على
(56 b) نحو ما كتبنا فى ذلك فكان هذا عندى خطأ // وكان البيع عليه فاسدًا لأنّ ذلك يُخرِج من جملة الثمن يجوز ويظنّ فيبقى ما وقع عليه بعد الاستثناء مبيعاً بثمن مجهول واذا كتبتَ خلا ثمّ أتبعتَ ذلك ما لم يدخل فى البيع كان المستثنى غير داخل فى الثمن وكان الثمن بجملته ثمنا لما يبقى بعد الاستثناء *

8.2 ألا ترى أنّ رجلا لو باع دارا بألف درهم إلاّ ثلثها كان البيع واقعا على ثلثَيْها بجميع الألف ولو باعها إيّاه بألف درهم على أنّ له ثلثها كان للمشترى ثلثاها بثلثَى الثمن وكذلك كان أبو حنيفة وأبو يوسف ومحمّد وجماعة أصحابنا يقولون فى هذا فكان قوله على أنّ لى ثلثها لا يخرج ذلك الثلث من أن يكون له حصّة من الألف *

8.3 واذا قال خلا ثلثها أو إلاّ ثلثها أخرجه ذلك عن أن يكون له حصّة من الألف وكذلك قوله على أنّ لى فيها طريقا أو على أنّ للدار الملاصقة لهذه الدار المحدودة فى هذا الكتاب طريقا

فى هذه الدار المحدودة فى هذا الكتاب ثمّ وصف الطريق وسمّاه غير مخرج ذلك الطريق أن يكون له حصّة من الثمن وتلك الحصّة مجهولة وما يبقى بعدها من الثمن مجهول *

8.4 واذا قال خلا الطريق التى فيها فى موضع كذا وأخرج ذلك الاستثناء المستثنى بما وقع عليه
(57 a) البيع وصار الثمن بجملته ثمنا لما دخل فى البيع بعد المستثنى وإن شئتَ كتبتَ غير // البيت أو سوى البيت أو حاشى البيت فما كتبتَ من ذلك فهو جائز *

باب أشرية المنازل والحصص المقسومات من الدور وغيرها

9.0 قال أبو جعفر واذا اشترى رجل من رجل حجرة من دار كتبتَ هذا ما اشترى فلان بن فلان من فلان بن فلان اشترى منه جميع الحجرة التى فى الدار التى بمدينة كذا فى موضع كذا ثمّ تحدّ الدار ثمّ تكتب وهذه الحجرة التى وقع عليها هذه البيع المسمّى فى هذا الكتاب من هذه الدار المحدودة فى هذا الكتاب فى الجانب الكذا منها ثمّ تحدّد الحجرة وتذكر بابها فى أيّ حدّ هو من حدودها ثمّ تكتب بعقب ذلك اشترى فلان بن فلان من فلان بن فلان جميع هذه الحجرة المحدودة من الدار المحدودة فى هذا الكتاب وإن شئتَ كتبتَ هذه الحجرة المحدودة الموصوف جماعتها فى الدار المحدودة الموصوف جماعتها فى هذا الكتاب بحدود جميع ما وقع عليه هذا البيع المسمّى فى هـــذا الكتاب وأرضه وبنائه وسفله وعلوّه ومرافقه فى حقوقه ومسايله فى حقوقه وطرقه التى هى له من حقوقه مسلّمة له فى ساحة هذه الدار المحدودة فى هذا الكتاب وفى دهليزها حتّى تنتهى الى الطريق الذى يشرع فيه باب هذه الدار المحدودة فى هذا الكتاب هذا إن كان بابها يشرع فى طريق فإن
(57 b) كان بابها يشرع فى زقاق // كتبتَ حتّى تنتهى الى الزقاق الذى يشرع فيه بابها وكلّ قليل وكثير هو له فيه ومنه من حقوقه وكلّ حقّ هو له داخل فيه وكلّ حقّ هو له خارج منه ثمّ تنسق الكتاب على ما كتبنا *

9.0 bis وإن كان الطريق سهاما معلومة كتبتَ وطرقه التى هى له من حقوقه وهى كذا كذا سهما من كذا كذا سهما من ساحة هذه الدار المحدودة فى هذا الكتاب ومن دهليزها حتّى تنتهى الى الطريق الذى يشرع فيه بابها المذكور لها فى هذا الكتاب شائع ذلك فيما هو منه غير مقسوم منه ثمّ تحدّ الساحة والدهليز وتذكر ذرعها طولا وعرضا حتّى يوقف بذلك على نهاياتها *

9.1 وقد كان غير واحد من أصحابنا يكتبون فى هذا وطرقها التي هى له فى حقوقه مسلّمة له الى
9.2 الطريق الذى يشرع فيه باب هذه الدار المحدودة فى هذا الكتاب * وكان أبو زيد يكتب وطرقه التى هى له فى قاعة هذه الدار وفى دهليزها مسلّمة ذلك له الى الطريق الذى يشرع فيه باب
9.3 هذا الدار المحدودة فى هذا الكتاب * وكان أبو حنيفة وأبو يوسف يكتبان وطريقه فى ساحة هذه الدار الى باب هذه الدار الأعظم مسلّما داخل فى ذلك وخارج منه *

9.4 قال أبو جعفر ومعنى ما ذكرنا عن أبى حنيفة وأبى يوسف قريب من معنى ما كتبنا لأنّهما لم

(58 a) يجاوزا بما // أدخلاه فى البيع باب الدار ولا جعلا ما وراءه الى الطريق نهاية ولا غاية لما دخل فى البيع ولكنّهما جعلا باب الدار غاية وأدخلاه فى البيع *

9.5 وأمّا ما كتب الفريق الأوّل من هذه الثلاث الفرق على ما ذكرناه عنه ففاسد عندنا لأنّه يحتمل أن يكون ذلك الطريق الذى هو مسلّم له الى الطريق الذى يشرع [1] فيه باب هذه الدار الذى هو منها فى الدار الذى هو منها وقد يجوز أن يكون فى غيرها *

9.6 وأمّا أبو زيد فأثبت أنّه من الدار التى منها الحجرة التى وقع البيع عليها لأنّه كتب وطرقها فى هذه الدار المحدودة فى هذا الكتاب مسلّمة ذلك لها الى الطريق الذى يشرع فيه باب هذه الدار فكان فى هذا إثبات الطريق فى الدار المبيع منها ما وقع البيع عليه منها غير أنّه جعل ذلك مسلّما الى الطريق الذى يشرع فيه بابها فاحتمل أن يكون الطريق داخلا فى ذلك واحتمل أن يكون خارجا منه لأنّا قد رأينا الغايات قد تدخل فيما قبلها وقد تخرج ممّا قبلها قال الله عزّ وجلّ (ثُمَّ أَتِمُّوا الصِّيَامَ إِلَى اللَّيْلِ) فكان الليل غير داخل فى الصوم وقال (فَاغْسِلُوا وُجُوهَكُمْ وَأَيْدِيَكُمْ إِلَى الْمَرَافِقِ وَامْسَحُوا بِرُؤُوسِكُمْ وَأَرْجُلَكُمْ إِلَى الْكَعْبَيْنِ) فكان المرافقان والكعبان داخلين فيما قبلها *

9.7 ثمّ قد اختلف أهل العلم فى مثل هذا فى رجل قال لرجل لك علىّ من درهم الى عشرة فقال

(58 b) بعضهم عليه تسعة دراهم وممّن قال ذلك أبو حنيفة // وقال بعضهم عليه عشرة دراهم وممّن قال ذلك أبو يوسف ومحمّد بن الحسن وقال بعضهم عليه ثمانية دراهم وممّن قال ذلك زفر فكانوا مختلفين فى الغاية فى هذا فأدخلها بعضهم فيما جُعلت غاية له وأخرجها بعضهم منه *

9.8 وقال أبو حنيفة فى رجل باع عبده من رجل بألف درهم على أنّه بالخيار الى غد إنّه بالخيار الى مضىّ غد كلّه وقال أبو يوسف ومحمّد هو بالخيار الى طلوع الفجر فجعل أبو حنيفة الغاية فى هذا داخلة وجعلها أبو يوسف ومحمّد غير داخلة فلم نأمن أن يتأوّل متأوّل ذلك فى قوله مسلّما ذلك له الى الطريق الأعظم فيجعل الطريق داخلا فى البيع فيبطل البيع مع أنّ الغايات انّما اختُلف فى دخولها اذا كانت ليست بأعيان *

9.9 فأمّا اذا كانت أعيانا فهى غير داخلة عند أبى حنيفة وزفر وأبى يوسف ومحمّد لأنّهم قد أجمعوا أن رجلا لو قال لفلان من هذا الحائط الى هذا الحائط إنّه لا شىء له فى الحائطين وانّما يكون له ما بينهما فلم يجعلوا الغايات داخلة فى الأعيان كما قد جعلها بعضهم داخلة فيها اذا كانت غير أعيان ممّن قد ذكرنا ذلك عنه *

[1] MS omits الذى

9.10 فلو كتبنا كما كتب أبو زيد وكما روينا عن أبي حنيفة وأبي يوسف لكان فيه كفاية لأنّ الغاية فيه انّما هى غاية غير الأعيان[1] هى غير داخلة ولكنّا لا نأمن أن يُوقَع ذلك الكتاب الى
(59 a) من يجهل هذا // الموضوع فى الغايات فلا يفرّق بينهما فى الأعيان ولا فى غيرها *

9.11 فكتبنا مسلّما ذلك له فى ساحة هذه الدار المحدودة فى هذا الكتاب وفى دهليزها حتّى ينتهى الى الطريق الذى يشرع فيه بابها وهو نظير ما كتبوا فى الحدود يجعلوها نهاية للمبيع وجعلوا المبيع ما قبلها فكذلك الطرق تجعل نهاياتها الى الطريق الذى يشرع فيه باب هذه الدار التى هى منها فيكون منتهاها اليه ويكون البيع وقع على ما قبلها ولو وكّدتَ ذلك أيضا فكتبتَ وطرقه مسلّمة له فى ساحة هذه الدار التى هو منها المحدودة فى هذا الكتاب وفى دهليزها وفى بابها المذكور لها فى هذا الكتاب حتّى تنتهى الى الطريق الذى يشرع فيه بابها كان ذلك حسنا *

9.12 وقد كان يوسف بن خالد يكتب فى هذا وطرقها فى هذه الدار حتّى تخرج الى الطريق الذى يشرع فيه بابها وهذا أضعف من كلّ ما كُتب فى هذا المعنى ممّا قد ذكرناه فى هذا الكتاب لأنّه قد أثبت خروجه الى الطريق وقد جعله جزءا من الطريق والطريق لا يجوز بيعه ولا بيع شى منه *

9.13 قال أبو جعفر وقد كان أبو حنيفة وأبو يوسف يكتبان اشترى منه جميع الحجرة التى فى الدار وكان يوسف وأبو زيد يكتبان الحجرة التى من الدار فكان ما كتب أبو حنيفة وأبو يوسف فى
(59 b) ذلك أحبّ الينا لاجتماعهم على أن كتبوا فى الدار الكاملة اشترى منه جميع // الدار التى فى موضع كذا ولم يكتبوا الدار التى من موضع كذا *

9.14 قال أبو جعفر وإن ذرعتَ الطريق على ما كتبنا فهو أجود وإن لم يُفعَل فالبيع جائز ومقدار الطريق عند أصحابنا الى الحجرة المبيعة قدر عرض باب الدار التى هى منها مسلّما ذلك لها من باب الدار حتّى ينتهى اليها وما سوى ذلك من ساحة الدار التى منها تلك الحجرة فليس من طريق
9.15 الحجرة المبيعة * وذكر محمّد بن سماعة عن محمّد بن الحسن عن أبي يوسف قال قلتُ لأبي حنيفة كيف تكتب شرى بيت من دار فقال أكتُبُ هذا ما اشترى فلان بن فلان من فلان بن فلان[2] اشترى منه جميع البيت الذى من الدار التى بموضع كذا وحدّدها فاذا فرغتَ من حدودها كتبتَ وأحد حدود جماعة هذا البيت قال أبو يوسف فقلتُ له أولا تكتب وهذا البيت من هذه الدار فى موضع كذا كذا؟ قال لا وهذا الذى قلتَ فى الكلام حسن فاذا وقع فى الكتاب كان قبيحا *

9.16 قال أبو جعفر وقد خالف أبا حنيفة فى ذلك أبو يوسف ويوسف بن خالد وأبو زيد وجماعة أصحابنا فكتبوا فى ذلك وهذا البيت من هذه الدار المحدودة فى هذا الكتاب فى موضع كذا ثمّ

[1] MS omits الاعيان

[2] MS omits بن فلان

تحدّ حدوده وهذا أحبّ الينا لاتّفاقهم على أن يكتبوا وأحد حدود جماعة هذه الدار فلم يكن قولهم فى هذا هذه الدار قبيحا فى كتاب ولا فى لفظ فكذلك وهذا البيت من هذه الدار فى موضع كذا ليس بقبيح فى كتاب ولا فى لفظ * // وقد ذكرنا فى أمر الطريق فى الدار المبيع منها موضع (60 a) 9.17 بعينه أو حجرة بعينها كلاما فيما تقدّم من كتابنا هو أوكد ممّا كتبنا فى هذا الباب فأغنانا ذلك عن إعادته هاهنا *

باب أشرية الحصص المشاعة

10.0 قال أبو جعفر واذا اشترى رجل ثلث دار وبقيّتها للبائع كتبتَ هذا ما اشترى فلان بن فلان ابن فلان الفلانى من فلان بن فلان بن فلان[1] الفلانى اشترى منه سهما واحدا من ثلاثة أسهم من جميع الدار التى بمدينة كذا فى موضع كذا ثمّ تحدّد الدار ثمّ تكتب وهذا السهم الذى وقع عليه هذا البيع المسمّى فى هذا الكتاب شائع فى جميع هذه الدار المحدودة فى هذا الكتاب غير مقسوم منها اشترى فلان بن فلان من فلان بن فلان سهما واحدا من ثلاثة أسهم من جميع الدار المحدودة فى هذا الكتاب بحدود جميع ما وقع عليه هذا البيع المسمّى فى هذا الكتاب ثمّ تجرى الكتاب على نحو ما كتبنا فى صدر هذا الكتاب غير أنّك اذا فرغتَ من ذكر قبض المبيع كتبتَ على أثر ذلك كما يُقبَض المشاع وتكتب المعاينة والرؤية للدار كلّها على مثل ما كتبناه فى بيع الدار الكاملة لأنّ السهم المبيع لا يُعايَن *

10.1 (60 b) قال أبو جعفر وقد اختلف أصحابنا فى غير // موضع من هذا الكتاب فأمّا أبو حنيفة وأبو يوسف ومحمّد بن الحسن ويوسف بن خالد فكانوا يكتبون فى ذلك نحو ممّا كتبنا غير ما كتبنا

10.2 فى قبض المبيع كما يُقبَض المشاع فانّهم لم يكتبوا ذلك * وكان أبو زيد يكتب اشترى منه سهما واحدا من ثلاثة أسهم من جميع الدار التى بمدينة كذا مشاعا فى جميعها غير مقسوم ثمّ يحدّ

10.3 الدار بعقب ذلك * فكان ما كتب أبو حنيفة وأبو يوسف ومحمّد فى هذا أحبّ الينا لأنّهم لا يختلفون أنّ المبيع لو كان ممّا يقع عليه الحدود لقدّم تحديد الدار على تحديده ثمّ وُصف من بعد ذلك وحُدّ وكذلك اذا كان شائعا قدّم عليه تحديد الدار ثمّ وُصف من بعد ذلك *

10.4 وقد كان غيرهم من أصحابنا يقدّم تحديد الدار على ما ذكرنا عن أبى حنيفة وأبى يوسف ومحمّد ويوسف ولا يذكر السهم الذى وقع عليه البيع هاهنا كما ذكره أبو حنيفة وأبو يوسف ومحمّد ويوسف فى هذا الموضع أنّه شائع فى الدار الذى هو منها غير مقسوم ولكنّه يكتب اشترى فلان بن فلان من فلان بن فلان سهما واحدا من ثلاثة أسهم من جميع هذه الدار المحدودة فى هذا الكتاب ثمّ

[1] MS omits بن فلان

يكتب مشاعا فى جميعها غير مقسوم ثمّ يكتب فى موضع قبض المبيع كما يُقبَض المشاع على مثل ما كتبنا *

10.5 وكان يوسف يكتب اشترى فلان بن فلان من فلان بن فلان هذا السهم الذى سمّينا فى هذه
10.6 الدار المحدودة فى هذا الكتاب بحدودها كلّها ثمّ ينسق كتابه على نحو من ذلك * وكان أبو
10.7 زيد يكتب بحدود ذلك كلّه وأرضه وبنائه ثمّ ينسق كتابه على نحو من ذلك * فكان ما كتب يوسف فى هذا أقرب الى الصواب ممّا كتب أبو زيد لأنّك اذا قلتَ بحدود ذلك كلّه احتمل أن يكون ذلك قد رجع الى الدار كلّها واحتمل أن يكون قد رجع الى المبيع خاصّة دون سائر
(61 a) الدار // واذا قلتَ بحدوده كلّها كان ذلك على المبيع خاصّة دون بقيّة الدار التى هو منها *
10.8 وكان غيرهما من أصحابنا يكتب بحدود جميع ما وقع عليه هذا البيع المسمّى فى هذا الكتاب ثمّ ينسق كتابه على ذلك فكان معنى هذا قريبا من معنى ما كتب يوسف غير أنّ هذا أبين وأحوط فلذلك اخترناه على غيره *

10.9 وقد حكى يوسف أنّ أبا حنيفة كان لا يكتب فى هذا[1] بحدوده وأنّه كان يقول ليست له حدود وقال ألا ترى أنّك لم تحدّه قال وكان أبو حنيفة يكتب فى ذلك بأرضه وبنائه قال يوسف وانّما كتبتُ أنا بحدودها لأنّ الدار لمّا كان لها حدود وكان البيع قد وقع على جزء منها كان قد وقع على جزء من حدودها فذلك الجزء الذى هو المبيع من حدودها هو حدوده ألا ترى أنّك تقول بأرضه تريد بذلك بأرضه التى هى حصّته من أرض الدار التى هو منها وليست له أرض مقسومة فكذلك فقُل بحدوده يعنى حصّته من حدود الدار التى هو منها وإن لم يكن له حدود
10.10 مقسومة وهذا الذى ذهب اليه يوسف عندنا صحيح * وقد روى محمّد بن الحسن عن أبى حنيفة وعن أبى يوسف أنّهما كانا يكتبان فى ذلك كما حكينا عن أبى زيد ورُوى ذلك أيضا عن محمّد ابن الحسن أنّه كان يكتبه أيضا *

10.11 قال أبو جعفر وانّما كتبنا عند قبض المبيع كما يُقبَض المشاع لِنبيّن قبض المشترى لِما اشترى كيف هو * //

(61 b)
10.12 قال أبو زيد ولو قلتَ اشترى منه ثلث جميع الدار كان صحيحا غير أنّ ذكر السهام أحبّ الىّ لأنّ النصف وسائر الأجزاء مثل الثلث والربع وما أشبهها قد يدخل عليهم الغول والقصور[2] حتّى يعود النصف الى أقلّ من النصف وحتّى يعود الثلث الى أقلّ من الثلث وحتّى يعود الربع الى أقلّ من الربع وذلك معدوم فى السهام لأنّ السهام لا نهاية لها والنصف والثلث والربع فنهايات لا تتجاوز فكان ما ذهب اليه أبو زيد من ذلك عندنا حسن *

[1] MS لا يكتب فى هذه

[2] MS فسمصور for القصور

10.13 قال أبو جعفر وقد أنكر علينا بعض الناس قولنا كذا كذا سهما من كذا كذا سهما من جميع الدار وقد ذكر أنّ هذا لا يدلّ على أنّ هذه السهام هى جملة الدار وذكر أنّ الأحوط عنده فى ذلك أن يكتب كذا كذا سهما من كذا كذا سهما هى جميع الدار *

10.14 قال أبو جعفر وما علمتُ أحدا من أهل العلم ذهب الى ما ذهب اليه هذا المنكر علينا قد كان أبو حنيفة وأبو يوسف ومحمّد بن الحسن ويوسف بن خالد وهلال وأبو زيد وفقهاء زمننا هذا الذى جالسناهم وسائر الفقهاء الذى قرأنا كتبهم وحفظنا من أقوالهم يكتبون فى ذلك مثل ما كتبنا لا نعلم احدا من أهل العلم ولا من أهل اللغة أنكر على أحد منهم من ذلك شيئا *

10.15 ثمّ قد وجدنا ذلك موجودا فى لغة رسول الله صلّى الله عليه وسلّم حدّثنا علىّ بن معبد قال حدّثنا عبد الله بن بكر بن حبيب السهمى قال حدّثنا هشام بن حسّان وحدّثنا علىّ بن معبد
(62 a) قال حدّثنا يزيد بن هارون قال حدّثنا هشام // عن محمّد بن سيرين عن أبى هريرة قال قال رسول الله صلّى الله عليه وسلّم رؤيا المؤمن جزء من ثمانية وأربعين جزءا من النبوّة وكانت تلك الثمانية والأربعين الجزء هى جميع النبوّة ولم يقل صلّى الله عليه وسلّم من ثمانية وأربعين جزءا هى جميع النبوّة وهو صلّى الله عليه وسلّم أفصح العرب والذى أوتِى جوامعُ الكلم وخواتمه والذى لا نقص فى شىء من كلامه *

11.0 قال أبو جعفر فإن كان الذى وقع البيع عليه هو جميع حقّ البائع وحصّته كتبتَ هذا مـــا اشترى فلان بن فلان من فلان بن فلان اشترى منه جميع ما ذكر فلان بن فلان يعنى البائع أنّه جميع حقّه وحصّته وهو كذا كذا سهما من كذا كذا سهما من جميع الدار التى بمدينة كذا ثمّ تنسق الكتاب على ذلك *

11.1 وقد كان أبو زيد يكتب هكذا وكان أبو حنيفة وأبو يوسف ومحمّد بن الحسن يكتبون فى ذلك
11.2 اشترى منه جميع حقّه وحصّته وهو سهم واحد من ثلاثة أسهم * وكان يوسف وهلال وبكّار ابن قُتَيبة يكتبون فى ذلك اشترى منه سهما واحدا من ثلاثة أسهم ثمّ يجرون كتابهم على ذلك حتّى اذا انتهوا الى ذكر ما وقع عليه البيع أنّه شائع فى جميع الدار التى هو منها غير مقسوم منها كتبوا على أثر ذلك وقد دخل فيه جميع ما كان لفلان بن فلان يعنون البائع فى هذه الدار المحدودة فى هذا الكتاب من حقّ ثمّ يكتبون على أثر ذلك اشترى فلان بن فلان من فلان بن فلان ثمّ ينسقون كتابهم على ذلك *

11.3 فكان ما كتب أبو زيد فى ذلك أحسن // عندنا لأنّك اذا قلتَ وقد دخل فيه جميع ما ذُكر
(62 b) كان لفلان بن فلان فى هذه الدار المحدودة فى هذا الكتاب من حقّ احتمل أن يكون[1] الحقّ

[1] MS اشتمال ان يكون

الداخل فى المبيع هو جميع المبيع ولكنّه بعضه ففى ذلك دليل على أنّ البائع قد باع جميع ما كان له وأنّه قد باع مع ذلك ما لم يكن له *

11.4 واذا قلتَ وقد دخل فيه جميع ما كان لفلان بن فلان من حقّ ففى ذلك إقرار من المشترى أنّ البائع قد كان مالكا لذلك الداخل وفى ذلك إبطال عهدته فيه فى قول من لا يوجب عهدة المقرّ على بائع منه ما قد أقرّ أنّه له على ما قد ذكرنا من ذلك فيما تقدّم من هذا الكتاب عن ابن أبى
11.5 ليلى وأهل المدينة وزفر بن الهذيل * واذا قلتَ اشترى منه جميع ما ذكر فلان بن فلان أنّه جميع حقّه وحصّته أدخلتَ فى البيع جميع ما ذكر البائع أنّه حقّه وحصّته وأخرجتَه أن يكون له حقّ فيما بقى من الدار فذلك أجود ما كُتِب فى هذا *

11.6 وقد كتب بعض أصحابنا فى هذا اشترى منه جميع ما يُنسَب الى حقّ فلان بن فلان وهو كذا كذا سهما وليس هذا عندنا بشىء لأنّك اذا جعلتَ المبيع منسوبا الى حقّ البائع لم نأمن أن
11.7 يتوهّم متوهّم أنّ ذلك إقرار من المشترى للبائع بأنّ ذلك من حقّه فيبطل ذلك عهدته عنه * ألا ترى أنّهم قد كرهوا جميعا أن يكتبوا فى الدار الكاملة اذا تبعت المنسوبة الى حقّ فلان خوفا من هذا بعينه ولقد ذكر ابراهيم بن الجرّاح أنّ أبا يوسف نهاه عن هذا بعينه خوفا من مثل هذا فاذا
(63 a) كان هذا مكروها فى الدار الكاملة كان أيضا مكروها // فى النصف الشائع لأنّه لا يُخاف من ذلك شىء فى الدار الكاملة إلاّ خيف منه مثله فى السهام الشائعة *

11.8 قال أبو جعفر وانّما احتججنا فى هذا أن أضفنا السهام المبيعة الى ذكر البائع أنّها جميع حقّه وحصّته لما قد اختلف الناس فيه لو كتبناها سهاما مطلقة غير مضافة الى ذكر البائع أنّها جميع
11.9 حقّه وحصّته * فكان أبو حنيفة وأبو يوسف ومحمّد بن الحسن يقولون مَن باع سهما من دار
11.10 له فيها حصّة مقدارُ ذلك السهم الذى باعه منها هو الحصّة التى له فيها * وقال آخرون بل ذلك السهم شائع فى الدار كلّها فى حصّة البائع منها وفى بقيّة الدار وممّن قال بهذا منهم زفر [1] بن الهذيل فكتبنا ذلك احتياطا من هذا الاختلاف *

12.0 قال أبو جعفر فإن كان المبيع [2] بعض حقّ البائع كتبتَ اشترى منه سهما واحدا من الكذا كذا السهم التى ذكر فلان بن فلان أنّها جميع حقّه وحصّته من كذا كذا سهما من جميع الدار التى بمدينة كذا ثمّ تنسق الكتاب على ما كتبنا *

13.0 فإن كان البائع باع جميع حقّه وحصّته وهو سهم واحد من ثلاثة أسهم من جميع دار بقيّتها للمشترى كتبتَ اشترى منه جميع ما ذكر فلان بن فلان أنّه جميع حقّه وحصّته وهو سهم واحد

[1] MS وزفر

[2] MS فان كان البيع

(63 b) من ثلاثة أسهم من جميع الدار التى لفلان بن فلان يعنى المشترى منها قبل وقوع هذا // الشرى المسمّى فى هذا الكتاب بقيّتُها وهى سهمان من ثلاثة أسهم من جميعها شائعان فيها غير مقسومين منها وهى الدار التى بمدينة كذا ثمّ تنسق الكتاب على ما كتبنا *

13.1 وليس على البائع أن يقرّ للمشترى بنصيبه من هذه الدار التى ابتاع منها ما ذكرنا ابتياعه إيّاه منها لأنّه لا يُؤمَن أن يبتاع ذلك هذا البائع من المشترى بعد ذلك فيكون ما تقدّم من إقراره به له يبطل عهدته له عليه فيه فى قول ابن أبى ليلى وزفر وأهل المدينة *

13.2 وقد كان أبو حنيفة وأبو يوسف ومحمّد يكتبون فى ذلك نحو ممّا كتبنا وكان يوسف بن خالد ينسق كتابه فى ذلك على ما ذكرناه عنه على ما للبائع فيها قبل هذا الشرى فاذا فرغ من قبض المبيع كتب على أثره فقد خلُصت هذه الدار المحدودة فى هذا الكتاب بحدودها وجميع حقوقها لفلان بن فلان يعنى المشترى بما كان له فيها وبما اشترى من فلان بن فلان ممّا سُمّى ووُصف فى هذا الكتاب ثمّ يكتب بعد ذلك إقرارهما بالرؤية *

13.3 والذى كتبنا من هذا أصحّ عندنا لأنّك اذا قلتَ فقد خلُصت هذه الدار لفلان بن فلان بما كان له فيها وبما اشترى من فلان بن فلان منها حقّقتَ ملك البائع لما باعه من المشترى وذكرتَ إقرار المشترى بذلك وفى ذلك إبطال الدرك للمشترى فيما وقع عليه البيع على البائع فى قول ابن أبى ليلى وزفر وأهل المدينة وسائر من يبطل الدرك بإقرار المشترى بملك البائع لما باعه ايّاه *

13.4 وحجّة أخرى أنّ البائع قد يجوز أن يبتاع من المشترى حصّة من هذه الدار التى كانت له
(64 a) قبل ابتياع المشترى منه ما // ابتاعه منها فيكون إقرار البائع للمشترى بما أقرّ له به من ذلك ينفى وجوب الدرك له عليه فيما باعه من ذلك فى قول ابن أبى ليلى وزفر وأهل المدينة فقد ثبّتوا [1] بما ذكرنا أنّ فيما كتب يوسف ضررًا على البائع وعلى المشترى فلذلك تركناه واخترنا ما كتبناه *

14.0 قال أبو جعفر واذا ابتاع رجل من رجل جميع حقّه وحصّته بمورثه عن أبيه من دار وللبائع فى الدار حقّ سوى ذلك لم يبعه كتبتَ الكتاب على نحو ما كتبنا غير أنّك تكتب اشترى منه جميع ما ذكر فلان بن فلان أنّه جميع حقّه وحصّته بمورثه عن أبيه فلان بن فلان المتوفّى وهو كذا كذا سهما من كذا كذا سهما ثمّ تنسق الكتاب على ما كتبنا *

باب شرى المنزل والبيت وما يفترقان فيه حتّى يختلف رسمها في كتاب الشرى

15.1 قال أبو جعفر واذا اشترى رجل من رجل منزلا فوقه منزل آخر فإنّه لا يكون له منزل الأعلى مع منزل الأسفل إلاّ أن يقول أشترِى منك هذا المنزل بكلّ حقّ هو له أو يقول بمرافقه أو يقول

[1] ثبتوا obliterated in MS

بكلّ قليل وكثير هو له فيه ومنه فيكون له المنزل الأعلى مع المنزل الأسفل هكذا حدّثنا محمّد بن العبّاس عن على بن معبد عن محمّد بن الحسن عن أبى يوسف عن أبى حنيفة ولم يحكِ فيه خلافا *

15.0 (64 b) فاذا كتبتَ شرى منزل فوقه منزل قد دخل فى الشرى // كتبت اشترى منه جميع المنزل الذى من الدار التى بمدينة كذا فى الموضع الكذا منها ثمّ تحدّدها ثمّ تصف المنزل وتحدّده فاذا أتيتَ على ذلك كتبتَ بحدود جميع ما وقع عليه هذا البيع المسمّى فى هذا الكتاب وأرضه وبنائه وسفله وعلوّه وكفاك ذلك من أن تكتب اشترى منه جميع المنزلين اللذين [1] أحدهما طباق الآخر لأنّك اذا فعلتَ ذلك صار المنزلان منزلا واحدا وكذلك الحجرة والمسكن *

16.1 واذا اشترى رجل من رجل بيتا فوقه بيت فاشترى البيت الأسفل فكلّ حقّ هو له فإنّه لا يكون له البيت الأعلى هكذا حدّثنا محمّد بن العبّاس عن علىّ بن معبد عن محمّد بن الحسن عن أبى يوسف عن أبى حنيفة لم يحكِ فيه خلافا بين أحد منهم *

16.0 فاذا كتبتَ كتاب الشرى فى ذلك فاكتبْ اشترى منه جميع البيت السفل ثمّ تحدّه ثمّ تكتب بحدود جميع ما وقع عليه هذا البيع المسمّى فى هذا الكتاب ثمّ تكتب الحقوق على ما كتبنا فى ذلك فى موضعها من كتابنا هذا ثمّ تكتب خلا علوّ هذا البيت السفل الذى وقع عليه هذا البيع المذكور فى هذا الكتاب فإنّه لم يدخل ولا شىء منه فى هذا البيع المسمّى فى هذا الكتاب *

16.0 bis فإن كان البيع وقع على البيتين جميعا كتبتَ اشترى منه جميع البيتين اللذين من الدار ثمّ تحدّ الدار ثمّ تكتب وهذان البيتان اللذان وقع عليهما هذا البيع المسمّى فى هذا الكتاب من هذه الدار المحدودة فى هذا الكتاب فى الجانب الكذا منها فمنها بيت فى الطبقة السفلى من طبقاتها وهو البيت الذى يحيط به ويجمعه ويشتمل عليه حدود أربعة ثمّ تحدّده ومنها بيت من هذه الدار أيضا فى الطبقة الثانية من طبقاتها طباق البيت // السفل الذى هو منها المحدود فى هذا الكتاب ثمّ تجرى (65 a) الكتاب فى ذلك على نحو ما كتبنا *

16.2 وهذا الذى كتبنا فلا بدّ منه لأنّ الناس قد اختلفوا فى حكم البيت المبيع بحقوقه وله بيت علوّه فرُوِى فى ذلك عن أبى حنيفة وأبى يوسف ومحمّد من الجهة التي ذكرنا ما قد رويناه عنهم فى هذا الكتاب وزعم بشر بن الوليد أنّ أبا يوسف كان قد أملى عليهم هذا الباب على نحو ما ذكرنا أيضا من رواية محمّد بن الحسن وأنّه كان قد فرّق لهم بين حكم المنزل فى ذلك وبين حكم البيت قال ثمّ أملى علينا بعد ذلك هذا الباب مجمع بين حكمهما وذكر أنّ علوّ البيت يدخل فى البيع باشتراط الحقوق وباشتراط كلّ قليل وكثير لما وقع البيع عليه *

[1] MS الذان

16.3 قال فقلتُ له قد كنتَ أمليتَ علينا قبل هذا خلاف هذا القول فكأنّه حكى رجوع أبي يوسف عن ذلك الى قوله الأوّل فلمّا وقع فى هذا من الاختلاف ما ذكرنا كان أولى الأشياء بنا الاحتياط ممّا اختلفوا فيه والتمسّك بما لا يختلفون فيه وإن كان القول الصحيح عندنا فى ذلك ما قد حكيناه عن محمّد بن الحسن لأنّ المنزل قد يكون علوّا وسفلا والبيت لا يكون علوّا وسفلا انّما يكون سفلا وعلوّا *

17.0 واذا اشترى رجل من رجل بيتا من دار بطريقه فيها كتبت هذا ما اشترى فلان بن فلان من فلان بن فلان اشترى منه جميع البيت الذى من الدار التى بمدينة كذا ثمّ تحدّد الدار ثمّ تصف موضع البيت منها وتحدّده ثمّ تكتب بحدود جميع ما وقع عليه هذا البيع المسمّى فى هذا الكتاب وأرضه وبنائه ومرافقه فى حقوقه وطرقه التى هى له فى هــذه الدار التى هو منها المحدودة فى هذا
(65 b) الكتاب // مسلّمة له فيها وفى دهليزها وفى بابها الذى يشرع منها فى حــدّها الكذا حتّى تنتهى الى الطريق الذي يشرع فيه بابها هذا إن كان بابها يشرع فى طريق وإن كان يشرع فى زقاق كتبت حتّى تنتهى الى الزقاق الذى يشرع فيه بابها وكلّ قليل وكثير هو له فيه ومنه من حقوقه وكلّ حقّ هو له داخل فيه وكلّ حقّ هو له خارج منهخلا علوّ هذا البيت المحدود فى الدار المحدودة فى هذا الكتاب فإنّه لم يدخل ولا شىء منه فى هذا الشرى المسمّى فى هذا الكتاب وإن كان علوّ هذا البيت بيوتا[1] بعضها علوّ بعض كتبت خلا علوّه وخلا علوّ علوّه حتّى تأتى على ذكر الأعالى التى عليه ثمّ تكتب فإنّ جميع ما وقع عليه هذا الاستثناء المسمّى فى هذا الكتاب لم يدخل ولا شىء منه فى هذا البيع المسمّى فى هذا الكتاب ثمّ تنسق الكتاب على ما كتبنا *

17.1 قال أبو جعفر وقد كان أبو حنيفة وأبو يوسف ومحمّد يكتبون فى شرى العلوّ دون السفل بحدوده كلّها وقد خالفهم فى ذلك مخالفون فقالوا لا تكتب بحدود إلاّ لمّا هو محدود فى كتاب العهدة والعلوّ غير محدود فيها *

17.2 وكان من الحجّة عليهم فى ذلك لما كان أبو حنيفة وأبو يوسف ومحمّد يذهبون اليه فى ذلك أنّ العلوّ وإن كان غير محدود فى كتاب العهدة فليس ذلك لأنّه لا حدود له وكيف لا يكون له حدود وله نهايات والحدود انّما هى النهايات ولكنّه لا حدود له الى مواضع يقدر على التحديد اليها انّما نهاياته الى أعالى منازل أقوام والعلوّ لا يحدّ اليه وإن كانت له فى نفسه حدود فلذلك
(66 a) كتب أبو حنيفة // وأبو يوسف ومحمّد فى ذلك ما ذكرنا عنهم ولهذه العلّة التى ذكرناها لم يحدّ العلوّ ووصفناه وذكرنا سفله الذى على قرار الأرض ثمّ حدّدناه وذكرنا الطريق اليه من أيّ موضع هو وبالله التوفيق *

[1] MS بيوت

باب ابتياع البناء القائم بغير الأرض الذى هو فيها وذكر إقرار البائع أنّ أرضه فى يد المشترى دونه

18.0 قال أبو جعفر واذا اشترى الرجل من الرجل بناء دار تربتها لغير البائع كتبت هذا ما اشترى فلان بن فلان من فلان بن فلان اشترى منه[1] جميع الدار التى بمدينة كذا فى موضع كذا ثمّ تحدّد الدار ثمّ تكتب اشترى فلان بن فلان من فلان بن فلان جميع هذه الدار المحدودة فى هذا الكتاب بحدودها كلّها ثمّ تنسق الكتاب على ما كتبنا حتّى اذا انتهيت الى وكلّ حقّ هو لها خارج منها كتبت على أثر ذلك خلا أرض هذه الدار المحدودة فى هذا الكتاب فإنّها ليست لفلان بن فلان يعنى البائع ولم تدخل ولا شىء منها فى هذا الشرى المسمّى فى هذا الكتاب ثمّ تنسق الكتاب على ما كتبنا فاذا فرغتَ من ضمان الدرك كتبت على أثر ذلك وأقرّ فلان بن فلان يعنى البائع أنّه لا حقّ له فى أرض هذه الدار المحدودة فى هذا الكتاب ولا فى شىء منها ولا فى
(66 b) حقوقها ولا يد له عليها ولا على شىء منها بسبب إجارة ولا ملك ولا دعوى له فيها // ولا فى شىء منها ولا طلبة على الوجوه والأسباب كلّها وأنّها بجميع حدودها وحقوقها فى يد فلان بن فلان يعنى المشترى دونه ودون الناس كلّهم بأمر حقّ واجب لازم عرفه له ولزمه الإقرار له به وأنّ جميع ما كان فلان بن فلان يعنى البائع عقده على أرض هذه الدار المحدودة فى هذا الكتاب وعلى شىء منها وجميع ما عُقد له[2] عليها أو على شىء منها بأمره من إجارة فإنّ ذلك كلّه لفلان بن فلان يعنى المشترى بأمره إيّاه بذلك وأنّ اسم فلان بن فلان إنّما كان فى ذلك عارية منه لفلان بن فلان يعنى المشترى ومعونة فقبل فلان بن فلان من فلان بن فلان جميع ما أقرّ له به على ما سُمّى ووُصف فى هذا الكتاب بمخاطبة منه إيّاه على جميع ذلك ثمّ تكتب بعقب ذلك وجميع ما فى هذا الكتاب من إقرار فعلى غير شرط كان فى عقدة هذا البيع المسمّى فى هذا الكتاب *

19.0 وكذلك بيع بناء الحانوت الذى أرضه لغير البائع وإن شئتَ أن تكتب الكتاب فى هذا على غير ما كتبنا وهو أن تكتب هذا ما اشترى فلان بن فلان من فلان بن فلان اشترى منه جميع البناء القائم فى الدار التى بمدينة كذا فى الموضع الكذا ثمّ تحدّد الدار ثمّ تكتب اشترى فلان بن فلان من فلان بن فلان جميع البناء القائم فى هذه الدار المحدودة فى هذا الكتاب بحدوده كلّها وطرقه وخشبه وأبوابه وسقفه القائم ذلك كلّه فيه بكذا كذا دينارا مثاقيل ذهبا عينا وازنــة جيادا ثمّ تنسق الكتاب فى ذلك على نحو هذا *

19.1 وقد كان بعض الناس يكتب فى هذا اشترى منه جميع نقض // الدار ثمّ ينسق الكتاب على
(67 a)
19.2 نحو ذلك وهذا عندنا ضعيف والمعنيان الأوّلان أجود منه * وذلك أنّ محمّد بن الحسن قد

[1] MS omits منه [2] MS ما عقده له

رُوى عنه فى هذا قولان ذكرهما عنه محمّد بن سماعة فى رجل اشترى من رجل نقض دار فحكى عنه أنّه أجاز ذلك وقال هذا على أن يهدم المشترى بناء الدار فيأخذه لنفسه *

19.3 وحكى عنه قولا آخر أنّ البيع على هذا فاسد وقال قد وقع البيع ولا نقض للدار لأنّ النقض انّما يكون بعد هدم الدار فاذا وقع البيع على ما ذكرنا فقد وقع على ما لم يكن ودخل ذلك فيما نهى عنه رسول الله صلّى الله عليه وسلّم من بيع ما ليس عندك وكلّ واحد من الوجهين الآخرين صحيح المعنى فأيّهما كتبتَ فهو حسن *

20.0 قال أبو جعفر فإن كان على الحانوت الذى وقع البيع على بنائه دون أرضه علوّا لم يدخل فى البيع كتبت خلا أرض هذه الحانوت المحدود فى هذا الكتاب وخلا علوّه فإنّهما ليسا لفلان بن فلان يعنى البائع ولم يدخلا ولا شىء منهما فى البيع المسمّى فى هذا الكتاب هذا إن كان علوّه لغير البائع *

20.0 bis وإن كان علوّه للبائع كتبت خلا أرض هذا الحانوت المحدود فى هذا الكتاب فإنّها ليست لفلان بن فلان يعنى البائع ولم تدخل ولا شىء منها فى هذا البيع المسمّى فى هذا الكتاب وخلا علوّ هذا الحانوت المحدود[1] فى هذا الكتاب فإنّه لم يدخل ولا شىء منه فى هذا البيع المسمّى فى هذا الكتاب *

20.0 ter وإن كان البيع وقع على علوّ هذا الحانوت كتبتَ اشترى منه جميع الحانوت وجميع المنزل الذى علوّه
(67 b) لأنّ اسم الحانوت لا يجمع العلوّ كما يجمع اسم المنزل العلوّ // فلذلك وجب أن تكتبه فى أوّل كتابك ثمّ يوكّد ذلك بما وكّدنا به مثله ممّا تقدّم فى كتابنا *

20.1 وإنّما أخرجنا الأرض من البيع لأنّ الأرض ليست للبائع ولا ممّا وقع البيع عليه فلو لم نستثنها من البيع وأوقفنا البيع على جميع الدار لكان البيع قد وقع على ما للبائع وعلى ما ليس له ففسد ذلك البيع فى قول قوم وبطلت عن المشترى طائفة من الثمن فى قول قوم فكتبنا ما كتبنا لذلك *

20.2 وأخرجنا الأرض من يد البائع الى يد المشترى لئلا يدّعى البائع فيها حقّا بسبب ملك وإجارة
20.3 أو غيرهما * وقد حدّثنى بكّار بن قتيبة قال رأيتُ هلال بن يحيى يكتب فى شرى أرض الجرُف[2] هذا كتاب ما اشترى فلان بن فلان من فلان بن فلان اشترى منه جميع الأرض التى من أرض الجرف[2] بمكان كذا على نهر كذا وهى من أرض الجرف[2] تجرى عليها المقاسمة فى غلّاتها فيما بين أكرتها وأرباب أصلها ثمّ تحدّدها ثمّ تجرى الكتاب فى ذلك على نحو مـا تكتب فى الدور والأرضين التى ليست من الجرف[3] غير أنّه لا تُذكَر أرضها *

[1] MS المحدودة
[2] MS أرض الجون
[3] MS الجون

20.4 قال هلال وانّما جوّزتُ ذلك لأنّ للبائع فيها عمارة وغرسا وبناء وشرطا فأجعَلُ للمشترى فيها ما كان للبائع وعلى ذلك وقع البيع بينهما لأنّ اسم الجرف [1] يدلّ على ذلك قال وهذا كما قد يعارفه الناس فى بيع الدور [2] إنّ ذلك على المال الذى فيها لا على غيره وقد وقع الخطاب بينهم على الرواية *

21.0 قال أبو جعفر والاختيار عندنا فى ذلك ما كتبنا وكذلك يكتب سائر فقهاء أصحابنا من //
(68 a) البغداذيّين فإن أردتَ أن تزيد فى توكيد الكتاب أيضا بأن تذكر أنّ البائع قد جعل الى المشترى طلب ما له وطلب جميع ما يجب له بحقّ ما كان عقده أو عُقد له بأمره على هذه الأرض من إجارة ومعاملة وقليل وكثير ويجعله وكيله فى ذلك فى حياته ووصيّه فيه بعد وفاته كتبتَ الكتاب على نحو ما كتبنا ثمّ تكتب بعقب ذلك وقد جعل فلان بن فلان يعنى البائع الى فلان بن فلان يعنى المشترى جميع ما له وجميع ما يجب له ممّا عقده على أرض هذه الدار المحدودة فى هذا الكتاب وممّا كان عُقد له عليها بأمره من إجارة ومعاملة وجعله وكيله فى ذلك وفى خصومة مَن عرض له بخصومة الى القضاة والحكّام والسلطان وإثبات حجّة فيه وأخذ اليمين الذى يجب له فيه وإقامة البيّنة التى تشهد له عليه وقبض جميع ما له وجميع ما يجب له قبضه منه وجعله وصيّه فى ذلك خاصّة بعد وفاته وأقامه فيما جعله اليه من ذلك فى حياته وبعد وفاته مقام نفسه فى حياته على أنّ لفلان ابن فلان يعنى المشترى أن يتولّى ذلك بنفسه ويولّيه وما شاء منه فى حياته وبعد وفاته مَن بدا له من الوكلاء والأوصياء ويستبدل من الوكلاء والأوصياء مَن أحبّ ورأى كلّما أحبّ ورأى جائزة أمره فى ذلك فقبل فلان بن فلان من فلان بن فلان جميع الوكالة وجميع الوصاية المسمّاتين فى هذا الكتاب بمخاطبة منه إيّاه على جميع ذلك ثمّ تكتب بعقب هذا وجميع ما فى هذا الكتاب من إقرار ووكالة ووصاية فعلى غير شرط كان فى عقدة هذا البيع المسمّى فى هذا الكتاب * //

(68 b)
21.1 وهذا أحوط للمشترى غير أنّ فى بعضه حملا على البائع وذلك أنّ البائع اذا جعل المشترى وصيّه فيما جعله اليه من ذلك خيف عليه فى ذلك أن يُرفَع ذلك بعد وفاته الى مَن يرى أنّ الرجل اذا أوصى الى الرجل فى خاصّ من تركته أو فى خاصّ بما كان اليه وبيده فى حياته كان بذلك
21.2 وصيّا فى جميع تركته وفى جميع ما كان اليه وبيده فى حياته وهكذا كان أبو حنيفة يقول * وأمّا أبو يوسف ومحمّد بن الحسن فكانا يجعلانه وصيّا فيما أوصى به اليه خاصّة لا على ما سوى ذلك من أموال الموصى ولا ممّا كان اليه وبيده فى حياته *

21.3 فينبغى لمن يلِى بمثل هذا أن يعلم ما يخاف عليه ممّا ذكرنا لأنّه قد يجوز أن يكون المشترى غير موضع عنده للوصاية اليه فاذا أعلمه ذلك وما يخاف عليه فيه كان هو المختار لنفسه ما يراه لها من ذلك وكان الكاتب بريئا ممّا يخاف على مثله فى ذلك *

[1] MS الجون [2] MS الدورا

22.0 وإن أحببتَ أن تزيد فى توكيد الكتاب أيضا كتبتَ على أنّ لفلان بن فلان أن يتولّى ذلك بنفسه فى حياته ويولّيه وما شاء منه فى حياته وبعد وفاته مَن بدا له من الوكلاء والأوصياء ويستبدل من الوكلاء والأوصياء مَن أحبّ ورأى كلّما يحبّ ورأى جائزة أموره وعلى أنّ فلان بن فلان يعنى البائع كلّما فسخ شيئا من هذه الوكالة ومن هذه الوصاية المسمّاتين فى هذا الكتاب فذلك الى فلان بن فلان يعنى المشترى وبيده كما كان اليه قبل ذلك حتّى يستوفى جميع ما له وجميع ما يجب له[1] بحقّ الإقرار والوكالة والوصاية المسمّى جميع ذلك فى هذا الكتاب فإن وكّدتَ بهذا فهو حسن * //

(69 a) 22.1 قال أبو جعفر وقد اختلف الناس فى عزل البائع المشترى عن هذا بعد توكيله إيّاه به فقال قوم عزله إيّاه جائز لأنّه إنّما كان وكيلا له فيه فاذا عزله عنه كان خارجاً منه وقال آخرون لا يجب له أن يعزله عن ذلك ولا يكون المشترى خارجاً بما كان وكّله به من ذلك بعزله إيّاه عنه *

22.2 وقد رُوى هذان القولان جميعا عن محمّد بن الحسن وحكاهما عنه محمّد بن سماعة أيضا والقول الصحيح عندنا فى ذلك بطلان العزل وذلك أنّ البائع وكّل المشترى فى ذلك بما عليه أن يوكّله به وبما هو مأخوذ به شاء أو أبى فلذلك لا يجوز له أن يعزله عن ذلك وإنّما يكون له أن يعزل مَن وكّله لنفسه عمّا وكّله به لاختياره ايّاه لنفسه فأمّا مَن وكّله لغيره فليس له عزله عمّا وكّله به *

باب أشرية الدور مذارعة

23.0 قال أبو جعفر واذا اشترى رجل من رجل دارا مذارعة كتبتَ هذا ما اشترى فلان بن فلان من فلان بن فلان اشترى منه جميع الدار التى بمدينة كذا ثمّ تحدّها ثمّ تكتب اشترى فلان بن فلان من فلان بن فلان جميع هذه الدار المحدودة فى هذا الكتاب بحدودها كلّها ثمّ تنسق ذكر الحقوق وذكر جميع ما للدار على مثل ما كتبناه فى ذلك فاذا أتيت على وكلّ حقّ هو لها خارج منها كتبتَ على أثر ذلك مذارعة على أنّها كذا كذا ذِراعا مكسَّرة // بالذِراع الكذا التى (69 b) يذرع بها قسّام أهل مدينة كذا الدور والأرضين بين أهلها بكذا كذا دينارا مثاقيل ذهبا عينا وازنة جيادا فذرع هذه الدار المحدودة فى هذا الكتاب بين فلان بن فلان وفلان بن فلان بمحضرهما وإذنهما وأمرهما ذَرّاع عدول من ذَرّاع القضاة الذين يختارونهم لقسمة الدور والأرضين بين أهلها ويأمنونهم عليها فبلغ جميع ذَرعها كذا كذا ذِراعا مكسَّرة بالذراع الكذا فأقرّ فلان بن فلان وفلان بن فلان يعنى المتبايعَين أنّهما قد عرفا ذلك وقبلاه وألزماه أنفسهما ودفع فلان بن فلان الى فلان بن فلان جميع الثمن المسمّى فى هذا الكتاب ثمّ تنسق الكتاب على ما كتبنا *

[1] MS omits له

23.1 قال أبو جعفر وقد اختلف الناس فى بعض ما كتبنا وكان يوسف يكتب فى ذلك هذا كتاب ما اشترى فلان بن فلان من فلان بن فلان اشترى منه جميع الدار التى بمدينة كذا ثمّ يحدّدها

23.2 ثمّ يكتب وهى كذا كذا ذراعا مكسّرة بذراع كذا * وكان أبو زيد يكتب فى ذلك نحو ممّا كتبنا فكان ما كتب أبو زيد فى هذا أحسن عندنا ممّا كتب يوسف لأنّه اذا كتب ذلك كذلك كان الذراع مشروطا فى عقد البيع يجب على البائع أن يوفّيه المشترى كما يجب عليه أن يوفّيه سائر ما يوجبه له عليه البيع *

23.3 واذا كتبت اشترى منه جميع الدار وهى كذا كذا ذراعا فلم تجعل الذرع مشروطا فى البيع

23.4 فيجب على البائع توفية المشترى إيّاه وكتبنا ما وصفنا لذلك * وكان يوسف يكتب كذا كذا

(70 a) ذراعا مكسّرة[1] بذراع الدور بالبصرة // كان أبو زيد يكتب بالذراع الكذا الذى يذرع بها قسّام أهل مدينة كذا فكان ما[2] كتب أبو زيد من هذا أبين وأوضح فاخترناه لذلك *

23.5 وكان يوسف يكتب الذرع قبل ذكر قبض الثمن وكان أبو زيد يكتبه بعد ذكر قبض الثمن فكان ما كتب يوسف من هذا أحسن وأولى لأنّ الذرع على البائع للمشترى ولأنّ الدار المبيعة قد يكون ذرعها مثل ما شرط البائع للمشترى وقد يكون أقلّ من ذلك فإن كان أقلّ من ذلك فللمشترى فسخ البيع لنقصان الشرط ولا يلزمه الثمن فبدأنا بذرعها ليقف عليه وليُعلَم هل يجب للمشترى فسخ البيع لنقصان إن كان فى الذرع وإبطال الثمن عن نفسه أم لا ولأنّ من حجّة المشترى أن يقول للبائع اذرعْها حتّى تكون على حال اذا قبضتُها منك عليها كنتُ مستوفيا لما وجب لى عليك بحقّ البيع فبدأنا بذكر الذرع لذلك *

23.6 وكان يوسف يكتب فى كتابه فبلغ ذرع[3] هذه الدار المحدودة فى هذا الكتاب كذا كذا ذراعا مكسّرة بذراع كذا وكان أبو زيد يكتب ذلك ويكتب على أثره فأعلموا ذلك فلان بن فلان وفلان بن فلان يعنى البائع والمشترى فقبلا قولهم وصدّقاهم على ذلك بعد أن عرفاهم وتراضيا بذرعهم وألزماه أنفسهما فكان الذى أراد يوسف من هــذا تحقيق علم المشترى لذرع الدار فكتب ما ذكرنا

23.7 لذلك * وكتب أبو زيد ما ذكرناه عنه أيضا زيادة فى الشرح غير أنّه ليس فيه تحقيق ذرع

(70 b) الدار انّما فيه تصديق // البائع والمشترى للذرّاع فيما ذكروا لهما وأخبروهما به من ذرع الدار *

23.8 قال أبو جعفر فكان ما كتب يوسف فى ذلك على قلّة ألفاظه أجمع ممّا كتب أبو زيد على كثرة ألفاظه فحذونا حذو يوسف فى ذلك غير أنّا زِدنا ذلك شرحا فذكرنا أنّ الذرع كان بمحضرهما وإذنهما وأمرهما وهذا ممّا لم يكتبه يوسف ولا أبو زيد *

23.9 قال أبو جعفر وهذا عندنا ممّا لا ينبغى تركه فى مثل هذا لأنّ ذرع الدار واجب على البائع ألا ترى أنّ أجر الذرّاع إنّما يكون على البائع لا على المشترى فلمّا كان الذرع على البائع

[1] MS مسكرة

[2] MS omits ما

[3] MS فبلغ ذكر ذرع

كان الذرّاع من قبله لا من قبل المشترى فيكون ذرعهم كذرع البائع لو كان هو الذى تولّى الذرع وأخبر به المشترى فصدّقه عليه المشترى فذلك غير مبرئ له من ذرع الدار بمحضر من المشترى أو بمحضر من وكيله *

23.10 ألا ترى أنّ رجلا لو باع رجلا هذا الطعام على أنّه كذا كذا قفيزا إنّ عليه أن يوفّيه المشترى كيله ولو قال له المشترى كِلْه فكاله بغير محضر من المشترى ولا بمحضر وكيل له لم يكن ذلك كيلا يبرئه ممّا وجب عليه للمشترى من كيله له لأنّ ذلك لو كان مبرئا له من الكيل الذى وجب للمشترى عليه لكان اذا أخبر المشترى أنّ كيله كذا كذا قفيزا فصدّقه المشترى على ذلك أغناه عن كيله بعد البيع *

23.11 وليس الأمر هكذا لأنّ رسول الله صلّى الله عليه وسلّم قد قال لعثمان بن عفّان اذا اشتريتَ
(71 a) فاكْتَلْ واذا بِعتَ فكِلْ فلمّا كان // تصديق المشترى للبائع على مقدار كيل الطعام المبيع مكائلة غير مبرئ للبائع من الكيل الذى وجب عليه للمشترى بحقّ البيع ولم يجز أن يكون البائع وكيلا للمشترى فى كيله لأنّه لا يكون وكيلا فيما يبرأ به ممّا قد وجب عليه لغيره *

3.12 واحتيج الى حضور المشترى لِكيل الطعام أو الى حضور مَن يُقيمه المشترى لذلك مقام نفسه ليقرّ بذلك ويعرفه فكذلك تصديق المشترى للبائع فى ذرع الدار التى وصفنا لا يكون ذلك براءة له من وجوب ذرعها له عليه بعد ذلك ولا يجوز أن يكون البائع وكيلا للمشترى فى ذرعها *

23.13 فاحتيج الى حضور المشترى للذرع ليكون بذلك مستوفيا للذرع كما احتيج الى حضوره فى كيل الطعام الذى ذكرنا ليكون بذلك مستوفيا لِكيله ولأنّ ذرع البائع بمحضر من المشترى أو ذرع الذرّاع بأمر البائع بمحضر من المشترى ذرع للدار وذرع الذرّاع أو البائع بغير محضر من المشترى ذرع للبائع لا للمشترى فلهذا ذكرنا فى كتابنا أنّ الذرع كان بمحضر من[1] المشترى *

23.14 واحتجنا أيضا الى حضور البائع فذكرناه فى كتابنا لأنّ المشترى لا يكون وكيلا فيما يكون به مستوفيا ثمّ كتبنا بعد ذلك علمهما بمبلغ الذرع وإلزامهما ذلك أنفسهما *

24.0 قال أبو جعفر فإن كانت الدار ذُرعت وكانت أقلّ ممّا شرط البائع للمشترى كان المشترى //
(71 b) بالخيار إن شاء أخذها بجميع الثمن وإن شاء ترك فإن اختار أخْذها كتبتَ فبلغ ذرعها كذا كذا ذِراعا بذِراع كذا فأقرّ فلان بن فلان وفلان بن فلان يعنى المشترى والبائع أنّهما قد علما ذلك وعرفاه معرفة صحيحة لا ريب فيها عندهما ولا شكّ فاختار فلان بن فلان بعد ذلك يعنى المشترى أخذ هذه الدار المحدودة فى هذا الكتاب بالثمن المسمّى فى هذا الكتاب فأخذها وألزمها

[1] MS omits من

بنفسه ودفع الى فلان بن فلان جميع الثمن المسمّى فى هذا الكتاب ثمّ تنسق الكتاب على ما كتبنا *

24.1 قال أبو جعفر وانّما كتبنا علم المشترى بذرع الدار ووقوفه على ذلك ولم نختر بتصديقه الذرّاع فى الذرع للعلّة التى ذكرنا إنّ الذرّاع من قِبَل البائع ومن قِبَل أنّهم يحلّون محلّه لا محلّ المشترى ولأنّ تصديق المشترى إيّاهم فى ذلك ليس بشىء ولأنّ حضوره الذرع اذا كان به جاهلا لا معنى له وهو فى ذلك كالغائب عنه فكتبنا علمه بالذرع لنبيّن أنّ حضوره ذلك حضور قد علم به الذرع و[ناربه][1] من حكم الجاهل بالذرع *

25.0 قال أبو جعفر وإن كانت الدار لمّا ذُرعت وُجدت أكثر ممّا شرط البائع للمشترى كتبت الكتاب على ما كتبنا غير أنّك اذا انتهيتَ الى موضع الذرع كتبتَ فوُجِدت أكثر من كذا كذا ذِراعـــا يعنى المقدار الذى شرطه البائع للمشترى ولا يُحتاج أن تسمّى مقدار الزيادة لأنّه
(72 a) لا حصّة له من الثمن ولا يُحتاج أن تذكر // تسليم البائع إيّاها لأنّه لو أراد منع المشترى من الدار للزيادة التى وُجدت بها فى ذرعها على ما شرطه له فى بيعه إيّاها لم يكن ذلك له ثمّ تنسق الكتاب على ما كتبنا في هذا الكتاب وتكتب فى موضع التسليم فى جميع ما كتبنا فى هذا الباب وسلّم فلان ابن فلان الى فلان بن فلان جميع ما وقع عليه هذا البيع المسمّى فى هذا الكتاب بعد علمهما بذرع هذه الدار المحدودة فى هذا الكتاب وإن شئتَ لم تذكر ذلك فى هذا الموضع وكتبتَ فى موضع الإقرار بالرؤية وذلك بعد أن أقرّ فلان بن فلان وفلان بن فلان أنّهما قد رأيا جميعا جميع هذه الدار المحدودة فى هذا الكتاب داخلها وخارجها وجميع ما فيها ومنها من بناء ومنازل وقليل وكثير ووقفا على جميع نهاياتها المذكورات لها من جميع جوانبها المذكورة لها فى هذا الكتاب وعلى ذرع جميعها المذكور فى هذا الكتاب وقوفا صحيحا وتبيّن لهما ذلك وعرفاه جميعا *

25.1 قال أبو جعفر وانّما كتبنا هذا للخوف من شغب البائع أو المشترى ولخوف جهل مَن عسى أن يقع الكتاب فى يده فكتبنا علم البائع والمشترى لذلك ولو لم تكتبه لكان جائزا لما قد تقدّم منّا فى كتابنا ذلك ممّا يغنى عن إعادة مثله فيه * //

(72 b) [فإن كان البيع وقع على أنّ الدار ألف ذراع كلّ ذراع منهم بكذا كتبت مذارعـــة
26.0 بألف درهم على أنّها كذا كذا ذراعا ثمّ تكتب الكتاب][2] فى ذلك على ما كتبنا غير [أنّك اذا أتيتَ على ذكر جميع ما للدار من الحقوق] كتبتَ على أثر ذلك أنّ كلّ ذراع مكسّرة [بالذراع الكذا] فى هذا الكتاب شائعا فى جميعها [على أنّها ألف ذراع كلّ ذراع منهم بكذا كذا دينارا] مثاقيل ذهبا عينا وازنة جيادا وعلى [أنّ لكلّ

[1] word unclear in MS [2] obliterated in MS

ذراع منهم حصّتها] من حقوق هذا الدار الداخلة فى البيع المسمّى [فى هذا الكتاب مذارعة على ما سُمّى ووُصف] فى هذا الكتاب ثمّ تكتب فذرع هذه الدار [المحدودة فى هذا الكتاب بين فلان بن] فلان وفـلان بن فلان وبمحضرهما[1] لذلك [وإذنهما وأمرهما ذَرّاع عدول] من ذَرّاع القضاة الذين يختارونهم [لقسمة الدور والأرضين بين أهلها ويأمّنوهم] عليها وإن شئتَ كتبتَ الذين اختاروهم لقسمة الدور وائتمنوهم عليها فبلغ جميع ذرعها كذا كذا ذراعا مكسّرة بالذراع الكذا وبلغ ثمن هذه الدار المحدودة فى هذا الكتاب بحدودها كلّها وجميع حقوقها كذا كذا دينارا مثاقيل ذهبا عينا وازنة جيادا وأقرّ فلان بن فلان وفلان بن فلان أنّهما قد عرفا ذلك معرفة صحيحة وأحاطا به علما وألزماه أنفسهما وأوجبا بيع جميع هذه الدار المحدودة فى هذا الكتاب بجميع ما سُمّى لها ومنها فى هذا الكتاب على أنفسهما على ما سُمّى ووُصف فى هذا الكتاب [ثمّ تنسق بقيّة] الكتاب فى ذلك على مثل ما كتبنا ٭ //

(73 a) 26.1 قال أبو جعفر وقد اختلف أصحابنا فى بعض ما كتبنا من هذا فكان يوسف بن خالد يكتب فى ذلك من تسمية الذرع ومن تسمية ما لكلّ ذراع من الحقوق كنحو ما كتبنا ولم يكن أبو زيد يكتب من ذلك شيئا فكان ما كتب يوسف من هذا أحسن عندنا لأنّ البيع اذا وقع على هذه الدار بثمن معلوم على أنّ كلّ ذراع منها مبيعا بالثمن الذى سُمّى له ٭

26.2 ألا ترى أنّ ذرعها لو نقص من الثمن بحساب ذلك وإن زاد ذرعها على الذرع الذى اشترطه المشترى على البائع زاد الثمن بحساب ذلك فلمّا كان كلّ ذراع منها له ثمنٌ على حدة كان كلّ ذراع منها له حصّته من حقوق الدار على حدة فاخترنا ما كتب يوسف لذلك ٭

26.3 وقد كان هلال بن يحيى يكتب فى ذلك أيضا كما كان يوسف يكتب وانّما كتبنا المعرفة بينهما بإقرارهما لا بحقيقة المعرفة منهما لأنّ ذلك لا يعلمه منهما غيرهما وهذا كما قد ذكرناه فى كتابنا هذا فى رؤية المبيع ٭

26.4 وقد كان يوسف بن خالد يكتب على أنّ لفلان بن فلان يعنى المشترى مع كلّ ذراع من ذلك حصّتها ثمّ ينسق الكتاب على نحو ما ذكرنا فكرهنا ذلك وكتبنا على أنّ لكلّ ذراع ثمّ نسقنا مع ذلك ما قد ذكرنا خوفا من الإضافة الى المشترى فيكون فى ذلك إقراره بملكه ذلك من قبل البائع وفى إقراره بذلك إقراره بملك البائع لما قد باعه وفى ذلك إبطال العهدة عن البائع فى الدرك الذى يوجبه البيع عليه للمشترى لو لم يقرّ له بالمبيع فى قول قوم ٭

26.5 وانّما كتبنا على أنّها ألف ذراع كلّ ذراع منهم بكذا فسمّينا ذرع جميع الدار ولم نختر
(73 b) بأن نقول // اشترى منه جميع هذه الدار على أنّ كلّ ذراع منها بكذا لاختلاف الناس فى ذلك ٭
26.6 كان أبو حنيفة يقول اذا وقع البيع على هذه الدار كلّ ذراع منها بدرهم فانّما وقع البيع على

[1] MS ومحضرهما

ذراع واحدة غير أنّها اذا ذُرِعت فعلم المشترى ذرعها كان بالخيار إن شاء أخذها كلّ ذراع بدرهم وإن شاء ترك قال وللبائع أن يمنع المشترى منها قبل وقوفه على ذرعها واختياره لأخذها *

26.7 وأمّا أبو يوسف ومحمّد فكانا يقولان قد وجب البيع فيها للمشترى كلّ ذراع بدرهم ولا خيار له فى تركها وليس للبائع منعه منها ولا من شىء منها فكتبنا ما كتبنا لذلك *

26.8 ثمّ كتبنا من بعد ذلك تسليم البائع إيّاها الى المشترى وقبض المشترى إيّاها على ذلك وإلزامهما أنفسهما البيع فيها ليتمّ البيع فى قولهم جميعا فى جميعها *

27.0 فإن كان البيع وقع على أرض لها سَرَب كذلك كتبتَ فى كتابك على أنّ لكلّ ذراع من هذه الأذرع المسمّاة فى هذا الكتاب من هذه الأرض المحدودة فى هذا الكتاب حصّتها من حقوق هذه الأرض المحدودة فى هذا الكتاب ومن سَرَبها الخارج من حدودها الذى فى موضع كذا فإن قدرتَ على تسمية ذلك الحقّ من السَرَب فتسمّيه وهو أحوط *

28.0 قال أبو جعفر واذا كان فى هذه الأرض بقعة معلومة معروفة وقع البيع عليها بحدودها كلّها وجميع حقوقها غير مذارعة تقدّم البيع على سائر الأرض سواها كتبتَ هذا ما اشترى فلان بن فلان

(74 a) من فلان بن فلان اشترى منه جميع الأرض التى بمدينة كذا // فى موضع كذا من الأرض التى يحيط بها ويجمعها ويشتمل عليها حدود أربعة أحد حدود جماعتها ثمّ تحدّها ثمّ تكتب اشترى فلان بن فلان الفلانى من فلان بن فلان الفلانى جميع هذه الأرض المحدودة فى هذا الكتاب خلا البقعة التى منها فى موضع كذا فتحدّد البقعة ثمّ تكتب فإنّ هذه البقعة التى وقع عليها هذا الاستثناء المسمّى فى هذا الكتاب بحدودها كلّها وجميع حقوقها وطرقها فى هذه الأرض المحدودة فى هذا الكتاب مسلّمة لها فيها حتّى تنتهى الى الطريق الذى يشرع فيه بابها لم تدخل ولا شىء منها فيما وقع هذا البيع عليه من هذه الأرض المحدودة فى هذا الكتاب بحدود جميع ما وقع عليه هذا البيع المسمّى فى هذا الكتاب من هذه الأرض المحدودة فى هذا الكتاب وأرضه وبنائه وسفله وعلوّه ومرافقه فى حقوقه ومسايله فى حقوقه وطرقه التى هى له من حقوقه وكلّ قليل وكثير هو له فيه ومنه من حقوقه وكلّ حقّ هو له داخل فيه وكلّ حقّ هو له خارج منه بكذا كذا دينارا مثاقيل ذهبا عينا وازنة جيادا مذارعة على أنّ كلّ ذراع منها بكذا كذا دينارا مثاقيل ذهبا عينا وازنة جيادا وعلى أنّ لكلّ ذراع ممّا وقع عليه هذا البيع المسمّى فى هذا الكتاب مذارعة حصّتها من حقوق ما وقع عليه هذا البيع المسمّى فى هذا الكتاب مذارعة على ما سُمّى ووُصف فيه واشترى فلان بن فلان أيضا من فلان بن فلان البقعة المستثناة المحدودة من الأرض المحدودة فى هذا الكتاب بحدود جميع هذه البقعة المستثناة المحدودة فى هذا الكتاب وأرضها وبنائها

(74 b) وسفلها وعلوّها ومرافقها فى حقوقها ومسايلها // [فى حقوقها و] [1] طرقها التى هى لها من حقوقها مسلّمة لها فى ساحة الأرض التى هى منها [المحدودة] [1] فى هذا الكتاب وفى بابها الذى يشرع منها فى حدّها الكذا حتّى تنتهى الى الطريق الذى يشرع فيه بابها ثمّ تنسق الكتاب على ما كتبنا وتذكر بعقب ما كتبنا ذرع الأرض ووقوف المتبايعَين على ذلك وإقرارهما بصحّته وقبض الثمن وتفصيل ثمن الأرض دون البقعة وثمن البقعة دون بقيّة الأرض التى هى منها فتكتب فمن ذلك كذا كذا دينارا مثاقيل ذهبا عينا وازنة جيادا ثمن ما وقع عليه هذا البيع المسمّى فى هذا الكتاب مذارعة على ما سُمّى ووُصف فى هذا الكتاب ومن ذلك كذا كذا دينارا مثاقيل ذهبا عينا وازنة جيادا ثمن البقعة[2] المستثناة المحدودة من الأرض المحدودة فى هذا الكتاب ثمّ تنسق الكتاب على ما كتبنا *

28.1 وهذا إن كانت البقعة المستثناة محظرة أو كانت فى أرض بَراح غير محظرة تنتهى جانب منها أو جانبان من جوانبها الى طريق غير مملوك *

28.2 فإن كانت فى وسط الأرض المبيعة لا طريق لها إلاّ فيها والأرض المبيعة غير محظرة فلا بدّ فى هذا من أن تجعل لها طريقا معلوما [3] من موضع بعينه من الأرض التى هى منها وتسمّى مقدار الطريق وذرعها طولا وعرضا فى كتابك فإنّك إن لم تفعل ذلك كانت هذه كعرصة بِيعَت فى أرض كبيرة غير محظرة والأرض تحيط بهذه العرصة من جميع جوانبها فكان أبو يوسف يقول فى
(75 a) ذلك // البيع جائز وعلى البائع أن يجعل للمشترى طريقا فى أيّ أرضه شاء حدّثنى بذلك سليمان ابن شعيب عن أبيه عن أبى يوسف فى أماليه *

28.3 فكان محمّد بن الحسن يقول البيع فى هذا فاسد لأنّ البيع إنّما أوجب لهذه الأرض المستثناة طريقا خاصّا من موضع من هذه الأرض خاصّ بغير عينه فالبيع على ذلك فاسد وهذا أصحّ فى النظر عندنا ممّا قد حكيناه عن أبى يوسف *

28.4 قال أبو جعفر وإن كانت الأرض محظرة فالبيع جائز فى القولين جميعا وللمشترى الطريق [4] الى البقعة المستثناة من باب الأرض على مقدار الباب ما زاد الى البقعة التى ابتاعها *

29.0 واذا اشترى رجل من رجل دارا مذارعة [5] بألف درهم على أنّها ألف ذراع كلّ ذراع منها بدرهم فوقع البيع بينهما على ذلك وتقابضا أو لم تقابضا ولم يُذرَع الدار بينهما كتبتَ فى ذلك على ما كتبنا الكتاب فى ذلك *

29.0 bis وإن كانا قد [تقابضاها] [6] ذكرتَ قبض المشترى إيّاها من البائع بتسليم البائع إيّاها اليه *

[1] words obliterated in MS
[2] MS ثمن الساحة
[3] MS معلوم
[4] MS وللبائع الطريق
[5] MS دار مذارعة
[6] word obliterated in MS

29.0 ter وإن كانا لم يتقابضاها لم تذكر قبض المشترى إيّاها أو لا تذكر فى كتابك فى ذلك ذرعها لأنّهما لم يذرعاها فإن ذرعها رجال للمشترى بأمر البائع و بمحضر منه ومن المشترى فوقفوه ذرعها كتبتَ هذا ما شهد عليه الشهود المسمـّون فى هذا الكتاب شهدوا جميعا أنّ فلان بن فلان الفلا نى وفلان بن فلان
(75 b) الفلانى وقد أثبتوهما وعرفوهما معرفة صحيحة بأعيانهما وأسمائهما // [وأنسابهما وأشهداهم] [1] على أنفسهما فى صحّة عقولهما وأبدانهما وجواز أمورهما وذلك فى شهر كذا من سنة كذا أنّ فلان بن فلان الفلانى المسمّى فى هذا الكتاب كان ابتاع من فلان بن فلان الفلانى المسمّى فى هذا الكتاب جميع الدار التى بمدينة كذا فى الموضع الكذا منها وكتب عليه بابتياعه إيّاها منه كتاب شرى باسمه نسخته باسم الله الرحمن الرحيم ومن شهوده المسمّين فيه فلان بن فلان وفلان بن فلان وفلان بن فلان وغيرهم من الشهود وأنّ فلان بن فلان وفلان بن فلان المسمّيَين [2] فى هذا الكتاب يعنى المتبايعَين حضرا بعد ذلك هذه الدار المحدودة فى هذا الكتاب وأحضراها بيعهما جماعة من أهـــل المعرفة بذرع الدور من أهل الأمانة على ذلك فذرعوا بينهما هذه الدار المحدودة فى هذا الكتاب بأمرهما وإذنهما لهم فى ذلك فبلغ ذرع جميع هذه الدار المحدودة فى هذا الكتاب كذا كذا ذراعا مكسّرة بالذراع الكذا فصدّق فلان وفلان يعنى البائع والمشترى هؤلاء الذرّاع المذكورين فى هذا الكتاب على ما ذرعوا من ذلك بعد إقرارهما بالوقوف على صحّة ذلك والعلم به والمعرفة به شهد *

باب أشرية الجُدُر

30.0 قال أبو جعفر واذا اشترى رجل من رجل جدارا بأرضه كتبت هذا ما اشترى فلان بن فلان الفلانى من فلان بن فلان الفلانى اشترى منه جميع الجدار المبنىّ بالآجرّ والطين الذى من الدار التى بمدينة كذا فى موضع كذا ثم تحدّد الـــدار ثمّ تكتب وهذا الجدار الذى وقع عليه هذا البيع المسمّى فى هذا الكتاب من هذه الدار المحدودة فى هذا الكتاب فى الموضع الكذا منها ثمّ تحدّده ثمّ تكتب وطول هذا الجدار المحدود من الدار المحدودة فى هذا الكتاب كذا وكذا ذراعا بالذراع الكذا وعرضه كذا كذا ذراعا بالذراع الكذا وسمكه كذا كذا ذراعا بالذراع الكذا اشترى //
(76 a) فلان بن فلان من فلان بن فلان جميع هذا الجدار [3] المحدود من الدار التى هو منها المحدودة فى [هذا الكتاب] [4] بحدوده كلّها وأرضه وبنائه وسفله وعلوّه ومرافقه فى حقوقه وكل قليل وكثير هو له [فيه] ومنه هذا اذا كان الجدار [ملازقا لِـ] دار المشترى أو كان متّصلا بطريق للمشترى من احدى جهاته *

[1] words obliterated in MS
[2] MS المسمى
[3] MS هذه الجدار
[4] words obliterated in MS

30.1 قال أبو جعفر فإن كان الجدار [1] فى دار البائع يحيط به تربتها من جميع جوانبه لم يكن لك بدّ من أن تذكر الطريق اليه من باب دار البائع الذى هو منها لأنّه يحتاج الى أن يكون للمشترى طريق فيصل منه اليه وقد عاد ذلك الى معنى الحصص المقسومة المبيعة من الدور الكوامل التى قد تقدّم ذكرنا لها فى هذا الكتاب *

31.0 قال أبو جعفر وإن كان اشترى منه الجدار دون أرضه على أن ينقله فيذهب به كتبت اشترى منه جميع الجدار ثمّ تكتب الكتاب على ما ذكرنا غير أنّك لا تكتب بأرضه ولا بطرقه ثمّ تكتب بعقب ذلك خلا أرض هذا الجدار المحدودة فى هذا الكتاب فإنّها لم تدخل ولا شىء منها فى هذا البيع المسمّى فى هذا الكتاب *

31.1 قال أبو جعفر وقد كان بعض من كتب الشروط يكتب فى هذا اشترى منه جميع نقض الحائط ثمّ ينسق كتابه على ذلك ويقول انّما كتبت ذلك كذلك ليكون دليلا على أنّ على المشترى قلعه وهذا خطأ والبيع على ذلك فاسد عندنا لأنّه باعه نقض هذا الحائط ولا نقض له يوم وقع البيع عليه فباعه نقضا ولا نقض له ففسد البيع بذلك وكان داخلا فى نهى رسول الله صلّى الله عليه وسلّم عن بيع ما ليس عندك *

31.0 bis واذا وقع البيع على الجدار على ما ذكرنا دون أرضه فعلى المشترى أن ينقض الجدار كلّه ويحمله عن أرض البائع فإن لم تذكر ذلك فى كتابك وإن ذكرتَه أيضا فكتبتَ على أنّ على فلان بن فلان

(76 b) يعنى المشترى رفع هذا الجدار الذى وقع عليه هذا البيع المسمّى فى هذا // الكتاب عن الأرض التى هو عليها كان ذلك حسنا *

31.2 قال أبو جعفر ولم يكن أصحابنا يكتبون فى بيع الجدار ضمان الدرك فإن لم تكتب ذلك لم يضرّ وإن كتبتَه فهو أجود *

32.0 وإن كان البيع وقع على الجدار بأرضه وبنائه خلا حمولة خشبة تقوم عليه ثابتة فيه كتبت كتاب الشرى فى ذلك على ما كتبنا فى أول هذا الباب من الكتاب غير أنّك اذا أتيت على ذكر الحدود والحقوق كتبت خلا مواضع الكذا كذا الخشبة اللاتى يحملها هذا الجدار الذى وقع عليه هذا البيع المسمّى فى هذا الكتاب وهذا الجدار المحدود من هذه الدار المحدودة فى هذا الكتاب *

32.1 فإن سمّيتَ موضعها منه فحسن وإن تركتَ ذلك بعد أن تذكر وقوف البائع والمشترى على ذلك فى موضع الرؤية لم يضرّ وأحبّ الىّ أن تسمّيه وإن تسمّى موضعه من الحائط وذكر مقداره

[1] MS omits الجدار

عرضا وطولا وذرع ما فيه من الجدار فيكون ما يخرج من البيع معلوما كما كان الذى دخل فيه معلوما *

32.0 bis فإن أردتَ أن تسمّى مواضعها كتبت وهذا الخشب المستثنى مواضعه فى هذا الكتاب من هذا الجدار المحدود من الدار التى هو منها المحدودة فى هذا الكتاب على كذا وكذا ذراعا من قرار الأرض من هذا الجدار المحدود فى هذا الكتاب وهى كذا كذا خشبة أنصاف تحلّ بين كلّ خشبتَين منهم كذا كذا ذراعا بالذراع الكذا *

32.0 ter فإن كان الخشب يأخذ طرفَى الجدار قلتَ وهذا الخشب يأخذ من أوّل الجدار المحدود فى هذا الكتاب من جانبه الكذا حتّى ينتهى الى آخره من جانبه الكذا هذا على الاستواء فإن كان لا يأخذ طرفَى الجدار كتبت مواضع الخشب وسمّيتَها ووصفتَها وذكرتَ فى كتابك ما قبلها من أوّل الجدار وذرع ما بعدها منه ثمّ تكتب وهذا الخشب مسقّف بالألواح والآجرّ والجصّ والطين ويحمل أطراف هذا الخشب المذكور فى هذا الكتاب الجدار الذى وقع عليه هذا البيع المسمّى فى هذا الكتاب والجدار الذى يقابله من الدار الملاصقة له من جانبه الكذا وهى الدار التى فى السكّة المعروفة بكذا ويحيط بهذه الدار المحدودة ويجمعها ويشتمل عليها حدود أربعة أحد حدود جماعتها الحدّ الأوّل وهو كذا ينتهى الى كذا والحدّ الثانى والثالث والرابع وفيه يشرع باب هذه الدار المحدودة فى هذا الكتاب وهذا الجدار من هذه الدار المسمّى بذكرها وتحديدها

(77 a) فى هذا الكتاب // فى الموضع الكذا منها ويحيط بهذا الجدار ويجمعه ويشتمل عليه حدود أربعة أحد حدود جماعته الحدّ الأوّل وهو كذا ينتهى الى كذا والحدّ الثانى والثالث والرابع ومساحة ما بين هذين الجدارين المحدودين فى هذا الكتاب كذا كذا ذراعا بالذراع الكذا *

32.2 وإنّما كتبنا مساحة ما بينهما من الذرع احتياطا للمشترى لأنّ الجدار الذى يحمل الخشب المستثنى حمولته على جداره على ما قُدِّر من جداره كان أقلّ فى طول الخشب الذى يحمل جدارُه أطرافَها *

32.0 quater فكتبنا ذلك لذلك وإن لم تكتب هذا أو اجتزأتَ بإقرارهما برؤية ذلك والمعرفة والوقوف على نهاياته من جميع جوانبه اجزاك ثمّ تكتب فإنّ مواضع الخشب المستثنى مواضعها من الجدار المحدود من الدار[1] المبدأ بذكرها وتحديدها فى هذا الكتاب وما على هذا الخشب من حمولة فوق الجدارين اللذين يحملانها على ما سُمّى ووُصف فى هذا الكتاب لم يدخل ولا شىء منه فى هذا البيع المسمّى فى هذا الكتاب ثمّ تنسق الكتاب على ما كتبنا فى ذلك حتّى اذا انتهيتَ الى ذكر إقرار المتبايعَين برؤيتها لما وقع البيع عليه كتبت وذلك بعد أن أقرّ فلان بن فلان الفلانى وفلان بن فلان[2] الفلانى أنّهما قد رأيا جميعا جميع هذا الجدار المحدود من الدار المبدأ بذكرها فى

[1] MS الجدار المحدود الدار [2] MS adds بن فلان

هذا الكتاب وعايناه ووقفا على جميع نهاياته من جميع جوانبه وعاينا جميع مواضع الخشب المستثنى منه فى هذا الكتاب وجميع ما عليها ممّا استثنى معها من الحمولة عليه وتبيّن لهما ذلك وعرفاه جميعا عند عقدة هذا البيع المسمّى فى هذا الكتاب بينهما وقبل ذلك ثمّ تنسق الكتاب فى ذلك على مثل ما كتبنا فى أوّل هذا الباب *

32.3 وقد كان بعض الناس يكتب فى استثنائه الخشب الذى ذكرنا إلاّ حمل الكذا كذا الخشبة التى فى هذا الجدار والذى كتبنا أحسن وكذلك كان أبو زيد يكتب لأنّ صاحب الخشب

32.4 شريك فى الجدار مواضع خشبته * ألا ترى أنّ له أن يأخذ ما بيع من هذا الجدار بالسقفة فى قول من يوجب السقفة فى المقسوم والشرى فى الجدارات وما أشبهها لذلك كتبنا له حقّ فى الجدار على ما كتبناه *

تمّ الجزء الثاني من كتاب البيوع والحمد لله ربّ العالمين

يتلوه في الجزء الثالث

باب شرى القرى والأرضين الحرّة منها والخرا[جيّة][1]

[1] letters obliterated

الجزء الثالث من البيوع

من

كتاب الشروط الكبير

تأليف أبي جعفر أحمد بن محمد بن سلامة بن سلمة
الطحاوي الأزدي رحمه الله

(78 b) بسم الله الرحمن الرحيم

باب شرى القرى والأرضين الحرّة منها والخراجيّة

1.0 قال أبو جعفر واذا اشترى رجل من رجل بستانا من أرض العشر كتبت هذا ما اشترى فلان بن فلان بن فلان الفلانى من فلان بن فلان بن فلان الفلانى [1] اشترى منه جميع البستان الذى من أرض كذا من كورة كذا من قرية كذا فى الموضع الكذا من هذه القرية على أنّه حرّ عشرىّ ثمّ تنسق الكتاب فى ذلك على مثل ما كتبنا فى مثله غير أنّك اذا أتيت على وأرضه وبنائه وسفله وعلوّه كتبت على أثر ذلك ونخله وشجره وسواقيه وشربه الذى ذلك كلّه من حقوقه وطرقه التى هى له من حقوقه ومرافقه فى حقوقه وآباره فى حقوقه ومسيل مائه فى حقوقه ومغايضه فى حقوقه وعامره وغامره الداخلين فى حدوده وكلّ قليل وكثير هو له فيه ومنه من حقوقه وكلّ حقّ هو له داخل فيه وكلّ حقّ هو له خارج منه ثمّ تنسق الكتاب على مثل ما كتبنا وإن سمّيتَ هذا البستان حائطا كما يسمّيه أهل المدينة أو سمّيته جِنانا كما يسمّيه أهل مصر فذلك كلّه جائز *

1.1 (79 a) قال أبو جعفر // وقد اختلف فى بعض ما كتبنا فى كتابنا هذا فكان قوم يكتبون فيه اشترى منه جميع الجنان الحرّة العشريّة فكرهنا ذلك لأنّ فى هذا إقرارا من المشترى أنّ الجنان حرّة عشريّة كما شرط البائع وعسى أن لا يكون كذلك فيكون ما أقرّ به المشترى يبطل ما يجب له

1.2 على البائع لعدم الشرط الذى اشترطه له فيما باعه فكرهنا لك أن تكتب كما كتبوا * وكتبنا الشرط على البائع كما اشترطه عليه فى عقد البيع ليطالبه به فإن وجد المبيع كما شرط وإلاّ كان له الخيار فى ردّه وإبطال البيع فيه وفى إمساكه *

2.0 وإن كان [2] من نخل هذا البستان ثمر قائم أو فى أرضه زرع قائم لم يدخل فى البيع استثنيتَ ذلك فى كتابك فتكتب بعد وكلّ حقّ هو لها خارج منها خلا ما فى هذا البستان المحدود فى هذا الكتاب من ثمرة قائمة فى نخله القائم فيه وفى أرضه من زرع كذا كذا قائم فيها فإنّ هذه الثمرة وهذا الزرع المسمّيَين فى هذا الكتاب لم يدخلا ولا شىء منهما فى هذا البيع المسمّى فى هذا الكتاب *

2.1 قال أبو جعفر فإن قال قائل ولِمَ ذكرتَ ثمرة النخل وزرع الأرض وأخرجتها من البيع

(79 b) وهما خارجان منه غير داخلين فيه اذا لم يكن المشترى اشترطها على البائع // وقد قال رسول

[1] MS omits الفلانى

[2] MS omits كان

الله عليــه السلام مَن باع نخلا له ثمر قد أبـِّر فثمره للبائع إلاّ أن يشترط المبتاع قيل له قد رُوى ذلك عن رسول الله عليه السلام كما ذكرت واليه يذهب أصحابنا جميعاً وعامـّة أهل العلم ممّن سواهم غير أنّ ابن أبي ليلى فإنـّه قد خالفهم فى ذلك فأدخل الثمرة فى البيع اشترطه المشترى أو لم يشترطه وجعل ذلك كسعف النخل فاستثنينا ذلك فى كتابنا لهذا القول وكذلك فعلنا فى الزرع القائم فى أرض هذا البستان احتياطا من قياس قول ابن أبى[1] ليلى الذى ذكرنا فى الثمر *

2.2 واستثنينا ذلك أيضا لمعنى آخر وهو أن يُعلَم أنّ هذا الثمر وهذا الزرع قد كانا قائمين يوم وقع البيع وأنـّهما لم يدخلا فيه حذرا أن يقع بين البائع والمشترى فيهما تنازع فيدّعى البائع أنّ البيع وقع وهما قائمان على هيئتهما الآن فلم يدخلا فى البيع ويدّعى المشترى أنـّهما حدثا بعد البيع على ملكه فيكون القول فى ذلك قوله فكتبنا ما كتبنا من خروجهما من البيع وأنـّهما قد كانا يوم وقع البيع قائمين على هيئتهما الآن وأنـّهما لم يدخلا فيما وجب للمشترى بحقّ البيع *

3.0 (80 a) فإن كان المشترى قد // اشترط على البائع هذا الثمر وهذا الزرع كتبتَ الكتاب على ما ذكرنا حتـّىاذا انتهيت الى وكلّ حقّ هو له خارج منه كتبت على أثر ذلك وثمرة نخله القائمة فيه وجميع الزرع القائم فى أرض هذا البستان المحدودة فى هذا الكتاب خلا حقّ الله فى هذه الثمرة وفى هذا الزرع المذكورين فى هذا الكتاب من الصدقة وهو سهم واحد من عشرة أسهم منها هذا إن كان البستان تسقيه السماء أو كان يُسقَى فتحا *

3.0 bis وإن كان يُسقَى بغرب أو دالية كتبت خلا ما لله عزّ وجلّ فى هذه الثمرة وفى هذا الزرع المذكورين فى هذا الكتاب من الصدقة وهو سهم واحد من عشرين سهما من هذه الثمرة ومن هذا الزرع اللذين وقع هذا الاستثناء المذكور فى هذا الكتاب على ما ذكر وقوعه عليه منهما فى هذا الكتاب فإنّ جميع ما وقع عليه هذا الاستثناء المسمـّى فى هــذا الكتاب لم يدخل ولا شىء منه فى هذا البيع المسمـّى فى هذا الكتاب *

3.1 (80 b) قال أبو جعفر وقد كان أبو زيد يكتب فى ذلك وجميع مـا فيه من غلـّة قائمة والذى كتبنا أجود لأنـّك اذا قلتَ وجميع الثمرة والزرع القائمين // فيه فقد أثبتّ أنّ فى ذلك ثمرة وزرعا واذا قلتَ وجميع ما فيه من ثمرة وزرع لم يثبت هناك ثمرة ولا زرعا فيكون ذلك شرطا اشترطه المشترى على البائع فيجب على البائع أن يفى له به انـّما شرط له البائع ما فيه من ثمرة فإن كانت هناك ثمرة كانت للمشترى وإن لم يكن هناك ثمرة لم يكن البائع عارا للمشترى من شىء *

3.2 ألا ترى أنّ محمـّد بن الحسن قد قال فى رجل اشترى من رجل هذه الأرض فوجدها لا نخل فيها إنّ له أن يردّها على البائع لأنـّه لم يجد فيها النخل الذى اشترطه البائع ولو اشتراها بما يبقى

[1] MS omits أبى

من نخل أو بما فيها من النخل ثمّ أصابها فوجدها[1] لا نخل فيها إنّ البيع له لازم ولا سبيل له الى نقضه من هذه الجهة *

3.3 فكتبنا فى كتابنا الذى ذكرنا وثمرة نخله القائمة فيه وزرعه القائم فى أرضه ليدخلا فى البيع وليجب للمشترى إن لم يجدهما فى النخل والأرض كما اشترط له البائع مطالبة البائع ممّا يجب له عليه فى ذلك *

3.4 قال أبو جعفر وانّما أخرجنا حق الصدقة ممّا وقع عليه البيع لاختلاف الناس فى البيع اذا وقع
(81 a) على الثمرة // كلّها ولم يُخرَج منها حقّ الله فيها أو على الزرع كلّه ولم يُخرَج منه حقّ الله فيه فكان بعضهم يقول فى ذلك للمصدّق أن يجيز البيع فى حقّ الله منهما بحصّته من الثمن وله أن يبطل البيع فى ذلك فإن أبطل البيع بطل فى حقّ الله منهما بحصّته من الثمن وممّن ذهب الى هذا القول أبو حنيفة وأبو يوسف ومحمّد *

3.5 وكان غيرهم لا يجيز البيع فى ذلك أجازه المصدّق أو لم يجزه لأنّ عقد الشرى فإنّه بما يملك
3.6 البائع[2] وما لا يملك * ثمّ افترق الذين قالوا هذا القول فرقتين فقالت فرقة منهم لمّا بطل البيع فى هذا الجزء من الثمرة بطل فيما بقى من الثمرة وفيما ضمّته الصفقة معها وقالت فرقة منهم يجوز فيما بقى بحصّته من الثمن فلمّا اختلفوا فى ذلك هذا الاختلاف الذى ذكرناه عنهم كان الأحوط فى ذلك عندنا والله أعلم أن نخرج حقّ الله من الثمرة من البيع فنجعله غير داخل فيه *

3.7 فإن قال قائل فلِمَ لا تكتب عند اشتراط حقوق المبيع كذا كذا سهما من كذا كذا سهما من جميع الثمرة القائمة فى نخل هذا البستان المحدود فى هذا الكتاب وكذا كذا سهما من كذا كذا
(81 b) سهما // من جميع الزرع القائم فى أرض هذا البستان المحدود فى هذا الكتاب كما كان أبو زيد يكتب فى ذلك فيكون ذلك أحسن من إدخالك الثمرة كلّها والزرع كلّه فى البيع واستثنائك منهما بعضهما بعد ذلك قيل له لم نفعل فى هذا كما ذكرت لأنّا اذا جعلنا البيع واقعا على تسعة أسهم من عشرة أسهم من الثمرة ومن الزرع كما كتب أبو زيد كان حقّ الله فى الصدقة فيما وقع البيع عليه من الثمرة وفيما لم يقع البيع عليه منها وكذلك هو فى الزرع القائم فى الأرض فيدخل فيما وقع البيع عليه منهما من الاختلاف مثل الذى ذكرناه فيمَن باع نصف دار وله نصفها وقد تقدّمنا فى ذلك فى ذكر بيع الحصص المشاعة ما يغنينا عن إعادته هاهنا *

3.8 واذا ذكرنا أنّ الذى خرج من الثمرة ومن الزرع من البيع هو حقّ الله فيهما ثمّ ذكرنا مقداره كان ما وقع البيع عليه من الثمرة ومن الزرع لا صدقة فيهما فجاز البيع فيهما فلذلك أحببنا ما كتبنا على ما كان أبو زيد يكتب فى ذلك *

[1] MS omits فوجدها

[2] MS فاما يملك البائع

4.0 (82 a) قال أبو جعفر فإن أراد المشترى ابتياع الثمرة // كلّها حتّى يكون للمصدّق أن يجيز له البيع فى حقّ الله منها فى قول مَن يرى ذلك كتبتَ الكتاب على ما كتبنا وأدخلتَ الثمرة القائمة [1] فى نخل هذا الجنان أو البستان ثمّ تكتب بكذا كذا دينارا [2] مثاقيل ذهبا عينا وازنة جيادًا وعلى أنّ ثمن سائر ما وقع عليه هذا البيع المسمّى فى هذا الكتاب غير الثمن المذكور فى هذا الكتاب كذا كذا دينارا مثاقيل ذهبا عينا وازنة جيادا ثمّ تنسق الكتاب على مثل ما كتبنا وكذلك كتبتَ فى الزرع *

4.1 وانّما فصلنا ثمن الثمرة من ثمن سائر ما وقع عليه البيع عليها معها ليُعلَم بذلك أنّ حصّة الله من الثمرة من الثمن حصّة يُرجَع اليها لا يجوز ولا يظنّ غير أنّا لا نأمن أن يكون هناك من يقول اذا وقع البيع من رجل على شيئين فاستُحِق أحدهما وقد كان البيع وقع على أنّ لكلّ واحد منهما ثمنا مسمّى إنّ البيع فاسد لضمّ الصفقة ما للبائع وما ليس له *

5.0 فأحوط الأشياء فى ذلك عندنا والله أعلم أن تكتب الكتاب على ما كتبنا أوّلا من إدخال الثمرة
(82 b) كلّها فى البيع وإخراج حقّ الله منها وذكر // مقداره ثمّ تنسق الكتاب واذا أتيت على آخره قبل الشهادة كتبت حينئذ واشترى فلان بن فلان من فلان بن فلان بقيّة الثمرة المذكورة فى هذا الكتاب بعد ما وقع البيع المسمّى فى هذا الكتاب [3] عليه منها وهى سهم واحد من عشرة أسهم شائع فى هذه الثمرة غير مقسوم منها بكذا كذا دينارا مثاقيل ذهبا عينا وازنة جيادا ثمّ تنسق الشرى فى ذلك كنحو ما نسقناه [4] فيما قبله ثمّ تكتب بعقب ذلك وكان هذا البيع المثنّى بذكره فى هذا الكتاب بغير اشتراط من فلان بن فلان ومن فلان بن فلان يعنى البائع والمشترى ايّاه فى البيع المبدأ بذكره فى هذا الكتاب وكذلك تفعل فى بقيّة الزرع القائم فى الأرض المبيعة المذكورة فى هذا الكتاب حتّى لا يكون فى ذلك اختلاف بين أحد من أهل العلم ويكون المصدّق بالخيار اذا حُصد إن شاء أجاز البيع فى حقّ الله من ثمرة النخل ومن الزرع القائم فى الأرض فجاز ذلك بإجازته فى قول أبى حنيفة وأبى يوسف وزفر ومحمّد بن الحسن ولم يجز ذلك فى قول مخالفيهم * //

(83 a)
5.1 وانّما تجوز هذه الإجازة فى قول أبى حنيفة وزفر وأبى يوسف ومحمّد اذا كانت من المجيز والمبيع قائم [5] لم يُستهلَك فإن كان قد استُهلِك لم يجز بالإجازة البيع عندنا فى قول أحد ممّن سمّينا وكذلك إن مات المتبايعان أو أحدهما لم تجز الإجازة بعد موتهما ولا بعد موت مَن مات منهما فى قول مَن سمّينا وإنّما تجوز الإجازة عندهم اذا كان المتبايعان فى وقت الإجازة فى حال مَن يجوز منهما استئناف البيع والمبيع فى حال ما يجوز استئناف البيع عليه فاذا عدم معنى من هذه

[1] MS الثمرة القائم
[2] MS أو البستان كذا كذا دينارا
[3] MS المسمي فى الكتاب
[4] MS نسقنه
[5] MS والبيع قائم

المعانى فى وقت الإجازة فالإجازة باطل واذا جاز البيع بالإجازة التى ذكرنا على الشرائط التى وصفنا كان متولّى قبض ثمن ما جاز البائع بالإجازة البائعَ فى قول أبى حنيفة وزفر وأبى يوسف ومحمّد لأنّه تولّى عقد البيع ولا يستطيع المصدّق أن يتولّى قبض ثمن ذلك إلاّ بتوكيل من البائع إيّاه به *

6.0 قال أبو جعفر فإن كان فى هذا البستان ثمرة قد صُرمت من النخل وثمرة قائمة فى النخل كتبت
(83 b) عند ذكر الثمرة وجميع الثمرة القائمة فى نخل هذا // البستان المحدود فى هذا الكتاب وجميع الثمرة المصرومة من نخله المرعاة فى أرضه وكذلك إن كان الزرع الذى فيه قد حُصد بعضه كتبت وجميع الزرع القائم فى هذا البستان المحدود فى هذا الكتاب وجميع الزرع الحصيد المرعى فى أرض هذا البستان المحدود فى هذا الكتاب وان شئت كتبت فى هذا وفى الثمرة الملقاة فى أرض هذا البستان المحدود فى هذا الكتاب *

6.1 وإن جعلت للحصيد ثمنا على حدة وللثمرة المصرومة ثمنا على حدة غير ثمن ما بقى ممّا وقع البيع عليه معها كان ذلك أحوط لأنّ بعض الناس كان لا يجيز بيع السنبل الذى فيه الحنطة وليس هذا عندنا من قوله بشىء لأنّهم قد أجمعوا على جواز بيعه قبل أن يُحصَد فبيعه بعد أن يُحصَد كذلك أيضا فى النظر عندنا وقد نهى رسول الله عليه السلام عن بيع الحَبّ حتّى يشتدّ وفى ذلك دليل أنّ بيعه بعد أن يشتدّ جائز ولكن الاحتياط من أقوال الناس أحبّ الينا *

7.1 قال أبو جعفر فإن كانت أرض البستان خراجيّة فإنّ أصحّ ما كُتِب فى هذا // عندنا
(84 a) والله أعلم أن تمتثل فيه ما كتبنا فى بيع البناء القائم فى الأرض التى ليست للبائع على ما كتبنا فى ذلك فى الموضع الذى ذكرناه فيه فيما تقدّم فى كتابنا هذا *

7.2 قال أبو جعفر وقد كان أبو زيد يكتب فى بيع أرض الخراج على نحو ما يكتب فى بيع أرض العشر غير أنّه لا يصفها بخراج ولا بغيره وهذا عندنا خطأ لأنّ أهل المدينة لا يجيزون بيع أرض الخراج ولا يجعلونها مملوكة وأصحابنا يخالفونهم فى ذلك ويجعلونها مملوكة كسائر الأرضين فالأحوط عندنا لمّا وقع هذا الاختلاف أن تمتثل فيه ما كتبنا فى بيع البناء دون الأرض على ما كتبنا فى ذلك *

8.1 وإن كان فى هذه الأرض الخراجيّة ثمرة فى نخلها أو زرع فى أرضها فاشترطه المشترى معها فإنّ أبا زيد كان يكتب فى ذلك وجميع ما فى نخلها من ثمرة وجميع ما فى أرضها من زرع بكذا كذا دينارا ولا يفصله على ما ذكرناه عنه فى أرض العشر وزرعها وثمرة نخلها وزعم أنّه ذهب فى ذلك الى
(84 b) أنّ ذلك لا عشر فيه وقد أغفل فيه قول مخالفه لأنّ أهل المدينة يرون فى ذلك // العشر كما يرونه

فيه لو كان فى أرض العشر ويزعمون أنّ الخراج حقّ فى الأرض وأنّ العشر حقّ فى الزرع وفى الثمر وأنّ الخراج يُوضَع فى مواضع الخراج وأنّ العشر يُوضَع فى مواضع الصدقــات ويخالفون أبا حنيفة وأبا يوسف ومحمّدا وسائر أصحابنا لأنّ أصحابنا لا يوجبون فى ذلك عشرا ويذهبون الى أنّ العشر انّما يجب فيما لا خراج فى أرضه فأمّا ما كان فى أرضه الخراج فلا عشر فيه عندهم *

8.2 قال أبو جعفر وكان الأوثق فى ذلك عندنا والله أعلم[1] أن يُخرَج الثمرة والزرع من البيع ويُجعَل لهما ثمن على حدة فيكونان مبيعَين به فإن رُفع ذلك الى من لا يرى فى ذلك عشرا أجاز البيع فيهما وإن رُفع ذلك الى من يرى فيه عشرا امتثل فى ذلك ما يرى وكان أسهم ما قد وقع عليه سوى ذلك قد وجب وجوبا لا اختلاف بين أهل العلم فيه *

9.0 وينبغى لمن كتب هذا الكتاب أن يكتب فى آخره إقرار البائع أنّه لا حقّ لإخوانه فى أرض هذا البستان ولا فى شيء منها ولا يد له عليه بسبب إجارة ولا قبالة ولا معاملة ولا مزارعة وأنّ أرض
(85 a) هذا البستان المحدودة // فى هذا الكتاب فى يــد فلان بن فلان يعنى المشترى دونه ودون الناس كلّهم بأمر حقّ واجب لازم عرفه فلان بن فلان يعنى البائع ولزمه الإقرار به لفلان بن فلان يعنى المشترى *

8.3 فإن قال قائل قد ذكرت فيما تقدّم من هذا الفصل فى ثمرة النخل فى أرض الخراج ما يمتثل فيها اذا كانت فى أرض العشر لأنّ من الناس من يجعل فى الأرض الخراج ويجعل فى الثمرة العشر على ما ذكرته عن أهل المدينة ومن تابعهم على ذلك وقد علمتَ أنّ من الناس من لا يجعل فى هذا الثمر عشرا وهم من ذكرته من أهل الكوفة ومن تابعهم على ذلك فكان ينبغى أن لا يثبت لله حقّا تحقّ فيه الصدقة اذ كان من الناس من لا يجعل فيه حقّا قيل له إنّما أردنا بذلك أن ينفى أنّ البيع قد دخل فيه ما لا يجوز وقوع البيع عليه فى قول بعض الناس من هذين المتبايعَين فإن كتب فى ذلك خلا حقّ إن وجب لله فى ذلك بحقّ الصدقة وهو كذا كذا سهما من كذا كذا سهما من هذه الثمرة القائمة فى النخل القائم فى أرض البستان المحدود فى هذا الكتاب فإنّ
(85 b) جميع ما وقع عليه // هذا الاستثناء المسمّى فى هذا الكتاب لم يدخل ولا شيء منه فى هذا البيع المسمّى فى هذا الكتاب كان ذلك جائزا غير أنّا لا نأمن أن يتوهّم متوهّم أنّه انّما أراد به إن كان حقّا لله واجبا فلم يدخل فى البيع وإن لم يكن حقّا لله واجبا فقد وقع البيع على جميع الثمرة فيكون ذلك عنده على معنى البياعات على المخاطرة فيكون له وجه يفسد به البيع *

8.0 ولكن الأحوط فى ذلك أن تكتب خلا سهما واحدا من عشرة أسهم من جميع هذه الثمرة القائمة فى النخل القائم فى هذا البستان المحدود فى هذا الكتاب وهو السهم الذى يجب لله عزّ وجلّ بحقّ

[1] MS omits اعلم

صدقة إن وجب فى هذه الثمرة المذكورة فى هذا الكتاب فإنّ جميع ما وقع عليه هـــذا الاستثناء المسمّى فى هذا الكتاب لم يدخل ولا شىء منه فى هذا البيع المسمّى فى هذا الكتاب ثمّ تنسق الكتاب فى ذلك على ما كتبنا فى مثله ثمّ تكتب بعقب ذلك ابتاع المشترى هذا السهم من البائع بمال غير المال الأوّل على مثل ما كتبت فى أرض العشر وهذا أحوط ما قدرنا عليه فى هذا الباب وبالله التوفيق ونسأله العون * //

(86 a)

باب الشرى لمّا لا يقرّ المشترى
فى كتاب العهدة بقبضه من البائع

10.1 قال أبو جعفر واذا اشترى رجل من رجل دارا ولم يتقابضاها ولا ثمنها فأردت أن تكتب فى ذلك كتاباً تذكر فيه وجوب البيع بينهما كتبت كتاب الشرى على مثل ما كتبنا غير أنّك تحذف منه ذكر قبض الثمن وذكر قبض الدار وذكر وجوب الدرك وذلك أنّ الدرك انّما يوجب على
10.2 البائع ردّ الثمن اذا كان قد قبضه * ألا ترى أنّه لو أبرأ المشترى من الثمن وقبل المشترى منه البراءة إنّه لا يجب للمشترى على البائع ضمان الدرك فكذلك اذا لم يقبضه منه أيضا لم يجب له عليه ضمان الدرك *

11.0 قال أبو جعفر فإن أراد المشترى بعد ذلك أن يدفع الثمن الى البائع وأراد البائع أن يسلّم الدار الى المشترى ففعلا ذلك واذا [1] أرادا أن يكتبا بينهما فيه كتابا يتواصفان فيه ما كانا تعاقدا من البيع ويبرأ كلّ واحد منهما فيه الى صاحبه ممّا كان وجب له بحقّ البيع كتبت هذا ما شهد عليه الشهود المسمّون فى هذا الكتاب شهدوا جميعا أنّ فلان بن فلان بن فلان الفلانى وفلان بن فلان بن فلان
(86 b) الفلانى وقد أثبتوهما وعرفوهما معرفة صحيحة // بأعيانهما وأسمائهما وأنسابهما أقرّا عندهم وأشهداهم على أنفسهما فى صحّة عقولهما وأبدانهما وجواز أمورهما وذلك فى شهر كذا من سنة كذا أنّ فلان ابن فلان بن فلان الفلانى المسمّى فى هذا الكتاب كان ابتاع من فلان بن فلان بن فلان [2] الفلانى المسمّى فى هذا الكتاب فى شهر كذا من سنة كذا جميع الدار التى بمدينة كذا فى الموضع الكذا منها وهى الدار التى يحيط بها ويجمعها ويشتمل عليها حدود أربعة أحد حدود جماعتها الحدّ الأوّل وهو كذا ينتهى الى كذا والحدّ الثانى والثالث والرابع وفيه يشرع باب هذه الدار المحدودة فى هذا الكتاب ابتاع فلان بن فلان [3] من فلان بن فلان جميع هذه الدار المحدودة فى هذا الكتاب بحدودها

[1] MS omits اذا
[2] MS omits بن فلان
[3] MS adds بن فلان

كلّها وأرضها وبنائها وسفلها وعلوّها ومرافقها فى حقوقها ومسايلها فى حقوقها وطرقها التى هى لها من حقوقها وكلّ قليل وكثير هو لها فيها ومنها من حقوقها وكلّ حقّ هو لها داخل فيها وكلّ حقّ هو لها خارج منها بكذا كذا دينارا مثاقيل ذهبا عينا وازنة جيادا شرى لا شرط فيه ولا عدة وذلك بعد أن أقرّ فلان بن فلان وفلان بن فلان أنّهما قد رأيا جميعا جميع هذه الدار المحدودة فى هذا
(87 a) الكتاب وعايناها داخلها وخارجها وجميع // ما فيها ومنها من بناء ومنازل وقليل وكثير وتبيّن لهما ذلك وعرفاه جميعا عند عقدة هذا البيع المسمّى فى هذا الكتاب بينهما وقبل ذلك فتبايعا على ذلك وتفرّقا جميعا بأبدانهما بعد هذا البيع المسمّى فى هذا الكتاب عن تراض منهما جميعا بجميعه وإنفاذ منهما له واكتتبا بذلك كتاب شرى باسم فلان بن فلان تواصفا فيه ما كانا فعلا من ذلك تأريخه شهر كذا من سنة كذا ومن شهوده المسمّين فيه فلان بن فلان وفلان بن فلان وفلان بن فلان وغيرهم من الشهود ولم يقبض فلان بن فلان من فلان بن فلان الثمن [1] المسمّى فى هذا الكتاب وفى الكتاب المذكور تأريخه وشهوده فى هذا الكتاب ولا شيئا منه ولم يقبض فلان بن فلان من فلان ابن فلان هذه الدار المحدودة فى هذا الكتاب وفى الكتاب المذكور تأريخه وشهوده فى هذا الكتاب ولا شيئا منها وأنّ فلان بن فلان يعنى المشترى بعد ذلك دفع الى فلان بن فلان جميع الثمن المسمّى فى هذا الكتاب وفى الكتاب المذكور تأريخه وشهوده فى هذا الكتاب وقبضه منه فلان بن فلان واستوفاه تاما كاملا وأبرأه من جميعه بعد قبضه ايّاه واستيفائه له وهو كذا كذا دينارا مثاقيل ذهبا
(87 b) عينا وازنة جيادا وسلّم فلان بن فلان الى فلان بن فلان [2] جميع الدار المحدودة // فى هذا الكتاب وفى الكتاب المذكور تأريخه وشهوده فى هذا الكتاب بجميع ما سُمّى لها ومنها فى هذا الكتاب وقبضها منه فلان بن فلان وصارت فى يده وقبضه بهذا الشرى المسمّى فى هذا الكتاب وفى الكتاب المذكور تأريخه وشهوده فى هذا الكتاب فما أدرك فلان بن فلان ثمّ تنسق الدرك على مثل ما نسقناه فى موضعه فيما تقدّم من كتابنا فإذا أتيت على آخر ذلك كتبت على أثره وقد كُتب هذا الكتاب نسختين نظما واحدا ونسقا سواء لا تزيد نسخة منهما على نسخة حرفا يغيّر حكما ولا يزيل معنى فنسخة منهما فى يد فلان بن فلان ثقة له وحجّة ونسخة منهما فى يد فلان بن فلان ثقة له وحجّة ثمّ تكتب الشهادة على إقرارهما جميعا على مثل ما كتبناها فى موضعها فيما تقدّم من كتابنا هذا *

12.0 قال أبو جعفر وإن شئت كتبت الكتاب فى هذا على غير ما كتبنا وهو أن تكتب هذا ما شهد عليه الشهود المسمّون فى هذا الكتاب شهدوا جميعا أنّ فلان بن فلان بن فلان الفلانى وفلان ابن فلان بن فلان الفلانى وقد أثبتوهما وعرفوهما معرفة صحيحة بأعيانهما وأسمائهما وأنسابهما أقرّا
(88 a) عندهم وأشهداهم // على أنفسهما فى صحّة عقولهما وأبدانهما وجواز أمورهما وذلك فى شهر كذا من سنة كذا أنّهما كانا تعاقدا بينهما بيعا اكتتبا فيه على أنفسهما كتاب شرى نسخته باسم الله الرحمن

[1] MS omits الثمن

[2] MS omits بن فلان

الرحيم فتنسخ الكتاب كلّه ثمّ تكتب وأشهدا بينهما على ذلك فلان بن فلان وفلان بن فلان وفلان بن فلان وغيرهم من الشهود وكتب هؤلاء الشهود فى هذا الكتاب شهاداتهم بخطوطهم وأنّ فلان بن فلان بعد ذلك دفع الى فلان بن فلان جميع الثمن المسمّى فى هذا الكتاب ثمّ تنسق بقيّة الكتاب فى ذلك على نحو ما نسقناه فى الكتاب المنسوخ فى هذا الباب *

12.1 قال أبو جعفر وهذا أحبّ الينا من المعنى الأوّل لأنّه قد يجوز أن يدّعى أحد المتبايعين أنّ العقد الأوّل الذى كانا تعاقداه بينهما فاسد غير واجب منهما تسليم شىء الى صاحبه من مبيع ومن مبتاع به فيكون ذلك موضع شغب وكان أحوط منه نسخ الكتاب الأوّل كلّه فى هذا الكتاب ليوقف به على حقيقة ما كانا تعاقداه بينهما وهل كان جائزا أو فاسدا *

12.2 فإن قال قائل فقد سمّيت فى الكتاب الأوّل الذى لم يُنسَخ فيه الكتاب الذى فيه ذكر تعاقد
(88 b) البيع تأريخَ الكتاب الأوّل وأسماء شهوده قيل له قد يجوز أن يتّفق فى ذلك تأريخ كتابين // كانا اكتتباهما بينهما فى بيعين تعاقداهما فى ذلك فى شهر واحد وأشهدا على كلّ واحد منهما شهودا بأعيانهم فلا يكون التأريخ ولا أسماء الشهود دليلين على الكتاب الذى كان فيه ذكر البيع المؤرّخ فى هذا الكتاب إن بِيعَ من ذَيْنِكَ البَيْعَيْن المتقدِّمَيْن *

باب بيع الخيار

13.0 قال أبو جعفر واذا ابتاع الرجل من الرجل دارا على أنّ البائع فيها بالخيار ثلاثة أيّام أو على أنّ المشترى فيها بالخيار ثلاثة أيّام ولم يتقابضا الدار ولا الثمن فأرادا أن يكتبا بينهما كتابا يتواصفان ما تعاقدا بينهما من ذلك كتبت كتاب الشرى على مثل ما كتبنا فى البيع الذى لم يُقبَض غير أنّك اذا انتهيت الى ذكر الثمن الذى به وقع البيع بينهما كتبت على أثر ذلك على أنّ فلان بن فلان يعنى الذى له الخيار منهما بالخيار فى هذا البيع المسمّى فى هذا الكتاب الى انقضاء يوم كذا لكذا كذا ليلة تخلو من شهر كذا من سنة كذا وكان هذا البيع الذى تعاقداه[1] فلان بن فلان وفلان بن فلان على ما سُمّى ووُصف فى هذا الكتاب بينهما فى يوم كذا لكذا كذا ليلة خلت
(89 a) من شهر كذا من سنة كذا // ثمّ تكتب إقرارهما بالرؤية وتفرّقهما بأبدانهما بعد وقوع البيع بينهما عن تراض منهما به على مثل ما كتبنا فى ذلك فيما تقدّم من هذا الكتاب ولا تكتب فى هذا الكتاب بيعا لا شرط فيه ولا عدة لأنّ أحدهما قد اشترط فيه الخيار على صاحبه ولا تكتب فى ذلك دركا للمشترى على البائع لأنّ البيع لا يتمّ بعد *

13.1 ألا ترى أنّ المشترى إن كان هو الذى له الخيار منهما فلم يملك البائع عليه الثمن فكيف يجب له ضمان درك على البائع وانّما يوجب الدرك له ردّ الثمن أولا ترى أنّ البائع لو كان هو الذى

[1] MS عاقده

له الخيار منها إنّ المشترى لم يملك الدار بعد وإنّ الدار فى ملك البائع على حالها حتّى ينقطع خياره ويجوز بيعه فكيف يضمن له دركا فيما لم يملكه عليه *

13.0 bis قال أبو جعفر وإن شئت كتبت شرى لا شرط فيه ولا عدة غير الشرط الذى اشترطه فلان ابن فلان على فلان بن فلان فى هذا الكتاب على ما سُمّى ووُصف فيه وهذا أحبّ الينا من المعنى الأوّل لأنّه ينفى أن يكون أحد المتبايعين اشترط على صاحبه فى البيع شرطا غير ما أقرّ به له فى هذا الكتاب *

13.2 قال أبو جعفر ولم يكن أبو زيد يكتب فى كتابه ذكر اليوم الذى وقع فيه البيع بين البائع وبين المشترى // اذا كان أحدهما بالخيار على ما كتبناه نحن وهذا عندنا خطأ لأنّه اذا لم يفعل ذلك لم يدرِ متى كان البيع وقع بينهما ولا كم بين وقوع البيع بينهما وبين المدّة التى ينقطع الخيار بتقضّيها ويجب البيع به * (89 b)

13.3 وقد اختلف فى مدّة الخيار المشترطة فى البيع فقال قوم منهم أبو حنيفة وزفر إن كانت ثلاثة أيّام أو أقلّ منها فالبيع جائز وإن كانت أكثر من ثلاثة أيّام فالبيع فاسد وقال آخرون منهم أبو يوسف ومحمّد بن الحسن اذا جُعلت مدّة الخيار معلومة ثلاثة أيّام أو أقلّ من الثلاثة فالبيع فاسد واذا جُعلت ثلاثة فالبيع جائز فكتبنا ما كتبنا احتياطا من هذا الاختلاف *

13.4 وانّما كتبنا لكذا كذا ليلة خلَت من شهر كذا من سنة كذا ولم نكتب لكذا كذا ليلة بقيت من شهر كذا من سنة كذا لأنّ ما خلا من الشهر معلوم وما بقى منه مجهول لأنّه قد يكون مرّة ثلاثين ومرّة تسعة وعشرين فكتبنا ما كتبنا لذلك *

14.0 فإن أمضى صاحب الخيار البيع وأراد أن يكتب فى ذلك كتابا كتبت هذا ما شهد عليه الشهود المسمّون فى هذا الكتاب شهدوا جميعا أنّ فلان بن فلان بن فلان الفلانى وفلان بن فلان بن فلان الفلانى وقد أثبتوهما // وعرفوهما معرفة صحيحة بأعيانهما وأسمائهما وأنسابهما أقرّا عندهم وأشهداهم على أنفسهما فى صحّة عقولهما وأبدانهما وجواز أمورهما وذلك فى شهر كذا من سنة كذا أنّ فلان ابن فلان المسمّى فى هذا الكتاب كان ابتاع من فلان بن فلان المسمّى فى هذا الكتاب فى شهر كذا من سنة كذا جميع ما سُمّى ووُصف فى كتاب نسخته بسم الله الرحمن الرحيم فيُنسَخ الكتاب كلّه ومن شهوده المسمّين فيه فلان بن فلان وفلان بن فلان وفلان بن فلان وغيرهم من الشهود وأنّ فلان بن فلان بعد ذلك وقبل مضىّ مدّة الخيار التى اشترطها لنفسه فى البيع المسمّى فى هذا الكتاب وفى الكتاب المنسوخ فى هذا الكتاب أجاز هذا البيع وأمضاه وأبطل خياره فيه فصار بذلك هذا البيع المسمّى فى هذا الكتاب بيعا لا شرط فيه ولا عدة ودفع بعد ذلك فلان بن فلان يعنى المشترى الى فلان بن فلان يعنى البائع جميع الثمن المسمّى فى هذا الكتاب وقبضه منه (90 a)

فلان بن فلان واستوفاه منه تاما كاملا ثمّ تنسق الكتاب فى ذلك وفى قبض الدار المبيعة وفى
(90 b) وجوب // الدرك على مثل ما كتبنا فى ذلك فى قبض ما لم يكن ذكر قبضه فى كتاب عقد البيع *

15.0 قال أبو جعفر وان أردت أن تكتب بينهما كتاب الإجازة من غير أن تنسخ فيه كتاب المعاقدة كتبت الكتاب على ما كتبنا حتّى اذا أتيت على التأريخ الأوّل كتبت إنّ فلان بن فلان المسمّى فى هذا الكتاب يعنى المشترى كان ابتاع من فلان بن فلان المسمّى فى هذا الكتاب يعنى البائع فى يوم كذا لكذا كذا ليلة خلت من شهر كذا من سنة كذا جميع الدار التى بمدينة كذا فى الموضع الكذا منها وهى الدار التى يحيط بها ويجمعها ويشتمل عليها حدود أربعة أحد حدود جماعتها الحدّ الأوّل [1] وهو كذا انتهى الى كذا والحدّ الثانى والثالث والرابع وفيه يشرع باب هذه الدار المحدودة فى هذا الكتاب ابتاع فلان بن فلان من فلان بن فلان جميع الدار المحدودة فى هذا الكتاب بحدودها كلّها حتّى تنتهى الى وكلّ حقّ هو لها خارج منها فاذا انتهيت الى ذلك كتبت على أثره بكذا كذا دينـــارا مثاقيل ذهبا عينا وازنة جيادا شرى لا عدة فيه وعلى أنّ فلان بن فلان
(91 a) المسمّى فى هذا // الكتاب بالخيار فى هذا البيع المسمّى فى هذا الكتاب إن شاء أمضاه وإن شاء أبطله الى انقضاء كذا كذا ليلة تخلو من شهر كذا من سنة كذا وذلك بعد أن أقرّ فلان بن فلان وفلان بن فلان أنّهما قد رأيا جميعا جميع هذه الدار المحدودة فى هذا الكتاب ثمّ تنسق الكتاب فى ذلك على مثل ما كتبنا فى مثل ذلك ممّا قد تقدّم فى كتابنا هذا حتّى تأتى على عن تراض منهما جميعا بجميعه وإنفاذ منهما له فاذا أتيت على ذلك كتبت واكتتبا بينهما فى ذلك كتاب شرى باسم فلان بن فلان يعنى المشترى تواصفا فيه ما كان بينهما ممّا سُمّى ووُصف فى هذا الكتاب تأريخ ذلك الكتاب شهر كذا من سنة كذا ومن شهوده المسمّين فيه فلان بن فلان وفلان بن فلان وفلان بن فلان وغيرهم من الشهود وأحوط فى هذا أن يكون الكتاب الأوّل مؤرّخا باليوم الذى وقع فيه البيع فإن كان ذلك قد فُعل كتبت فى هذا الثانى تأريخه يوم كذا لكذا كذا ليلة خلت من شهر كذا من سنة كذا وسمّيت شهوده على مثل ما ذكرنا وتكتب بعقب ذلك ولم يقبض
(91 b) فلان بن فلان من فلان بن فلان الثمن المسمّى فى هذا الكتاب // وفى الكتاب المذكور تأريخه وشهوده فى هذا الكتاب ولم يقبض فلان بن فلان من فلان بن فلان شيئا ممّا وقع عليه هذا البيع المسمّى فى هذا الكتاب وفى الكتاب المذكور تأريخه وشهوده فى هذا الكتاب وإنّ فلان بن فلان يعنى الذى له الخيار بعد ذلك قبل انقضاء مدّة الخيار المذكورة فى هذا الكتاب وفى الكتاب المذكور تأريخه وشهوده فى هذا الكتاب أمضى هذا البيع المسمّى فى هذا الكتاب وفى الكتاب المذكور تأريخه وشهوده فى هذا الكتاب وأجازه وقطع خياره فيه ثمّ تكتب دفْع المشترى الثمن الى البائع وتسليم

[1] MS omits الحد الاول

البائع الدار الى المشترى ووجوب الدرك للمشترى على البائع على مثل ما كتبنا فى الدار التى لم يقبض عند ابتياع مبتاعها ايّاها ثمّ قُبضت من بعد ذلك على ما فى الكتاب الذى قبل هذا الكتاب *

16.0 قال أبو جعفر وإن لم يكن الذى له الخيار أجاز البيع بلسانه ولكنّ مدّة الخيار مضت فتمّ البيع بمضيّها كتبت فى الموضع الذى كتبنا فيه الإجازة ثمّ إنّ مدّة الخيار المسمّاة فى هذا
(92 a) الكتاب وفى الكتاب المذكور تأريخه وشهوده فى هذا الكتاب انقضت من قبل أن يُبطِل // فلان ابن فلان يعنى الذى له الخيار هذا البيع المسمّى فى هذا الكتاب وفى الكتاب المذكور تأريخه وشهوده فى هذا الكتاب لمضيّها فيما بين فلان بن فلان وفلان بن فلان وصار بيعا لا شرط فيه ولا عدة ثمّ تنسق الكتاب على ما كتبنا *

17.0 وإن لم يكن الذى له الخيار أجاز البيع ولكنّه أبطله فى الثلاثة الأيّام المشترطة له الخيار فيها كتبت الكتاب على ما كتبنا حتّى اذا انتهيت الى نفى قبض الدار المبيعة كتبت على أثر ذلك وإنّ فلان بن فلان يعنى صاحب الخيار بعد ذلك قبل انقضاء مدّة الخيار المذكورة فى هذا الكتاب وفى الكتاب المذكور تأريخه وشهوده فى هذا الكتاب نقض البيع المسمّى فى هذا الكتاب وفى الكتاب المذكور تأريخه وشهوده فى هذا الكتاب فيما كان هو وفلان بن فلان تعاقدا فيه البيع على ما سُمّى ووُصف فى هذا الكتاب بحقّ الخيار الذى كان له فيــه على ما سُمّى ووُصف فى هذا الكتاب وكان ذلك منه بمحضر من فلان بن فلان يعنى الذى لا خيار له من[1] المتبايعين ثمّ تكتب بعقب ذلك فلا حقّ لفلان بن فلان يعنى المشترى فى هذه
(92 b) الدار المحدودة فى هذا الكتاب ولا فى شىء منها ولا فى أرضها ولا فى بنائها // ولا دعوى له فيها ولا طلبة بسبب ملك ولا بيع ولا غيرهما على الوجوه والأسباب كلّها وكلّ دعوى يدّعيها فلان بن فلان يعنى المشترى فى هذه الدار المحدودة فى هذا الكتاب وفى الكتاب المذكور تأريخه وشهوده فى هذا الكتاب وفى شىء منها وفى أرضها وفى بنائهـــا وفيما سوى ذلك منها ويدّعى ذلك له أحد بسببه وبيّنة تُشهَد له على ذلك ووثيقة يحضرها وحجّة يحتجّ بها ويمين يدّعيها يريد استحلاف فلان بن فلان بها ومطالبة ومنازعة وعلقة وتبعة فذلك كلّه زور وباطل وإفك وظلم وفلان بن فلان من جميع ذلك كلّه برىء وفى حلّ وسعه فى الدنيا والآخرة لعلم فلان ابن فلان يعنى المشترى ولمعرفته أنّه لا يدّعى ذلك ولا شيئا منه ولا يدّعيه له أحد بسببه إلاّ تعدّيا وظلما فقبل فلان بن فلان يعنى البائع من فلان بن فلان يعنى المشترى جميع الإقرار والبراءة والتحليل

[1] MS omits من

المسمّى جميع ذلك فى هذا الكتاب بمخاطبة منه ايّاه على جميع ذلك وقد كتب هذا الكتاب نسختين نظما واحدا ونسقا سواء لا تزيد نسخة منهما على نسخة حرفا يغيّر حكما ولا يزيل معنى فنسخة منهما فى يد فلان بن فلان ثقة له // وحجّة ونسخة منهما فى يد فلان بن فلان ثقة له وحجّة * (93 a)

17.1 قال أبو جعفر وقد كان أبو حنيفة وأبو يوسف ومحمّد بن الحسن ربّما كتبوا فى مثل هذا كتابا يذكرون فيه نقض البيع الذى كان بينه وبين البائع ونحو الخيار الذى كان بينهما فيه ولا يسوقون فيه جميع الأسباب التى جرت بين البائع وبين المشترى وذهبوا فى ذلك الى أنّ الذى يحتاج اليه المشترى أن يكون فى يده حجّة له هو انتقاض البيع خاصّة حتّى لا يطالبه البائع بعد ذلك بالثمن ويدّعى عليه وجوب البيع وتمامه *

17.2 ولكنّ الأحوط فى ذلك عندنا وفى غيره ممّا يحتاج أحد المتعاقدين فيه الى حجّة تكون فى يده على صاحبه ويحتاج صاحبه أن تكون فى يده حجّة عليه أن تنسق البيع وأسبابه التى كانت بعده الى أن اكتتبا ذلك الكتاب بينهما ثمّ تجعله نسختين عند كلّ واحد منهما احداهما لما نخاف من ذلك من تغاير العقدين واختلافهما *

17.3 قال أبو جعفر وانّما ذكرنا فى كتابنا حضور الذى لا خيار له من المتبايعين نقض الذى له الخيار منهما البيع لما فى ذلك من الاختلاف كان أبو حنيفة ومحمّد بن الحسن يقولان ليس للذى له الخيار // منهما أن ينقض البيع إلاّ بمحضر من صاحبه وقد كان أبو يوسف قال بهذا القول (93 b) أيضا ثمّ رجع عنه فقال له أن ينقض الخيار حضر صاحبه أو لم يحضر *

17.4 هكذا روى محمّد بن الحسن فيما حدّثناه سليمان بن شُعَيْب عن أبيه عن محمّد بن الحسن وروى عنه بشر بن الوليد أنّه قال فى الإملاء إن كان البائع هو الذى له الخيار منهما فنقضه جائز حضر المشترى أو لم يحضر وإن كان الخيار للمشترى لم يكن له أن ينقض البيع إلاّ بمحضر من البائع وذهب فى ذلك الى أنّ الخيار اذا كان للبائع فلم يخرج المبيع من ملكه بعد البيع فله نقض البيع حضر المشترى أو لم يحضر واذا كان الخيار للمشترى فقد كان ملك المبيع على البائع بعقد البيع وهو اذا نقض البيع بحقّ خياره فيه ردّه الى ملك البائع قال فليس له ردّه الى ملك البائع إلاّ بمحضر منه *

17.5 فكان من الحجّة على هذا القول لمحمّد بن الحسن أنّ البائع اذا كان له الخيار فى المبيع فلم يملك المشترى المبيع ولكنّ البائع[1] قد يملك على المشترى الثمن اذا كان المشترى لا خيار له وإذا كان المشترى بالخيار فقد ملك على البائع المبيع ولم يملك // البائع عليه الثمن لأنّ خيار المشترى (94 a) يمنع البائع من ملك البدل عليه كما كان خيار البائع يمنع المشترى من[2] ملك المبيع عليه فلمّا

[1] MS ولكن البيع

[2] MS omits من

كان المشترى فى هذا القول ليس له نقض البيع الذى يردّ به المبيع [1] الى ملك البائع إلاّ بمحضر من البائع كان بذلك النقض الذى يردّ به البائع ملك الثمن الى المشترى اذا كان الخيار الى البائع ليس له ذلك إلاّ بمحضر من المشترى *

17.6 وحكى محمّد بن سماعة عن محمّد بن الحسن فى هذا الباب أنّ ما ذهب اليه أبو حنيفة فى ذلك أولى عنده ممّا ذهب اليه أبو يوسف لحجّة أُخرى وهى فيما ذُكر أنّه وجد الموكّل الذى يعقد الوكالة لوكيله فيما يعقدها عليه ليس له إخراج وكيله بعد منها بغير محضر من وكيله ذلك منه وكذلك وكيله بعد قبوله الوكالة منه ليس له إخراج نفسه من تلك الوكالة إلاّ بمحضر من موكّله ايّاه بها ذلك *

17.7 ألا ترى رجلا لو وكّل رجلا ببيع عبده فمضى الوكيل ببيعه ثمّ عزله الموكّل عن ذلك فباع

17.8 العبد قبل أن يعلم بقول الآمر ايّاه إنّ بيعه جائز * أولا ترى أنّ رجلا لو وكّل رجلا بابتياع

(94 b) عبد له بمال [2] معلوم من فلان بن فلان // وكالة صحيحة ثمّ ابتاع بغير ذلك المال من فلان ذلك ويرى أن يكون البيع لنفسه إنّه لا يكون له ذلك لأنّه عقد للموكّل أنّ ذلك الشرى يكون له ولا يكون له إخراج نفسه ممّا قد عقده عليها إلاّ بمحضر من عقد ذلك له عليها *

17.9 وكذلك أيضا المضارب لو أنّ رجلا دفع الى رجل ألف درهم مضاربة صحيحة على شرائط مسمّاة معلومة ثمّ أراد واحد من ربّ المال ومن المضارب إبطال العقد بغير محضر من صاحبه إنّه

17.10 لا يكون له ذلك * وكذلك الشركة لو تعاقد رجلان شركة بينهما على ما تجوز عليه الشركة ثمّ أراد أحدهما إبطال ذلك العقد بغير محضر من صاحبه إنّه لا يكون له ذلك *

17.11 فلمّا كانت هذه العقود على ما ذكرنا ليس لاحد من متعاقدَيها إخراج نفسه منها إلاّ بمحضر من صاحبه كان كذلك أيضا البيع المشترَط فيه الخيار ليس لواحد من متعاقدَيه إخراج نفسه ممّا عقده لصاحبه فيه إلاّ بمحضر من صاحبه *

17.12 وإنّما كتبنا فى نقض البيع حضور الذى لا خيار له من المتبايعَين ولم نكتب ذلك فى إجازة

(95 a) البيع لإجماعهم أنّ الإجازة من الذى له الخيار من المتبايعَين جائزة // حضر صاحبه أو لم يحضر *

18.0 فإن كان المشترى قد قبض الدار من البائع فى وقت وقوع البيع بينه وبينه ثمّ نقض الذى له الخيار منهما البيع بحقّ خياره ولم يكن البائع قبض الثمن من المشترى كتبت الكتاب فى ذلك على مثل ما كتبنا غير أنّك تذكر فيه أنّ المشترى قد كان قبض جميع ما وقع عليه البيع بتسليم من فلان بن فلان يعنى البائع ايّاه اليه وصار فى يده وقبضه ثمّ تنسق الكتاب على ما كتبنا حتّى

[1] MS يرد به البيع

[2] MS ابتاع بعبد بذلك المالى

اذا أتيت على ذكر نقض البيع كتبت على أثر ذلك وسلّم فلان بن فلان يعنى المشترى الى فلان ابن فلان يعنى البائع جميع هذه الدار المحدودة فى هذا الكتاب وفى الكتاب المذكور تأريخه وشهوده فى هذا الكتاب بجميع ما سُمّى لها ومنها فى هذا الكتاب وفى الكتاب المذكور تأريخه وشهوده فى هذا الكتاب هذا إن لم تكن نسخت الكتاب الأوّل فى هذا الكتاب وإن كتبت نسخته كتبت وفى الكتاب المنسوخ فى هذا الكتاب ثمّ تكتب وقبضها منه فلان بن فلان على هيئتها التى كان قبضها عليها منه فلان بن فلان وصارت فى يد فلان بن فلان وقبضه ثمّ تنسق الكتاب على ما
(95 b) كتبنا فى ذلك من نفى حقّ المشترى منها // من الدار على مثل ما كتبنا فى ذلك فى هذا الباب *

19.0 فان كان البائع يخاف أن يكون المشترى قد ألجأها الى غيره فأراد أن يضمنه الدرك فيها من قبله وبسببه كتبت فى آخر الكتاب قبل ذلك قبول البائع البراءة والتحليل وقد ضمن فلان بن فلان يعنى المشترى لفلان بن فلان يعنى البائع جميع الذى يدركه فى هذه الدار المحدودة فى هذا الكتاب وفى الكتاب المذكور تأريخه وشهوده فى هذا الكتاب هذا اذا لم تكن نسخت الكتاب الأوّل فى هذا الكتاب الثانى وإن كتبت نسخته كتبت وفى الكتاب المنسوخ فى هذه الكتاب من قبله وبسببه بسبب توليج وإشهاد وتمليك وإقرار وحدث إن كان فلان بن فلان أحدثه فى هذه الدار المحدودة فى هذا الكتاب وفى شىء منها أو أحدثه له محدث بأمره وحيلة إن كان احتالها فى ذلك أو احتيلت له بأمره يريد بشىء من ذلك إبطال شىء ممّا يجب عليه لفلان بن فلان يعنى البائع بحقّ البيع المذكور فى هذا الكتاب ضمانا لازما واجبا بأمر حقّ واجب لازم عرفه فلان بن فلان
(96 a) يعنى المشترى لفلان بن فلان يعنى البائع ولزمه بذلك ضمان ما ضمنه له فى هذا الكتاب // ولا براءة لفلان بن فلان إن أدرك فلانا فى ذلك درك من قبله وبسببه حتّى يخلّص من جميع الذى يدركه فى ذلك من قبله وبسببه أو يردّ عليه جميع الذى يجب له عليه ردّه ويلزمه له بحقّ الدرك والضمان المسمّيَيْن فى هذا الكتاب فقبل فلان بن فلان من فلان بن فلان جميع الإقرار والبراءة والتحليل والضمان المسمّى جميع ذلك فى هذا الكتاب بمخاطبة منه ايّاه على جميع ذلك ثمّ تكتب بعقب ذلك وقد كتب هذا الكتاب نسختين ثمّ تتبع ذلك الشهادة على مثل ما كتبنا فى مثل ذلك ممّا قد تقدّم فى هذا الباب *

20.0 فإن كان البائع قد قبض الثمن من المشترى فى وقت وقوع البيع بينهما كتبت الكتاب فى ذلك على مثل ما كتبنا وذكرت فيه أنّ البائع قد كان قبض الثمن من المشترى واستوفاه منه تامّا كاملا فإن كان الخيار للبائع [1] كتبت وأبرأه من جميعه بعد قبضه ايّاه واستيفائه له منه على مثل ما كتبنا فى مثل ذلك ممّا قد تقدّم فى هذا الكتاب *

[1] MS وان كان الخيار كان للبائع

20.1 وإن كان الخيار للمشترى لم تكتب وأبرأه من جميعه لأنّ الخيار اذا كان للبائع لم يمنعه من
(96b) ملك الثمن فقبضه ايّاه وكانت البراءة [1] للمشترى واذا كان الخيار للمشترى // لم يملك البائع المبيع [2] فقبض المشترى ايّاه منه ليس ببراءة للبائع لأنّ البراءات بالقبوض انّما تكون ممّن وجب له قبض الذى قبض قبل قبضه ايّاه *

20.2 فإن كان الخيار للبائع فنقض البيع بحقّ خياره والثمن دراهم أو دنانير أو شيء ممّا يُكال أو يُوزَن أو ممّا يُعَدّ ممّا له مثل وقد كان البيع وقع على هذا المكيل أو على هذا الموزون أو على هذا المعدود سوى الدراهم والدنانير بغير عينه ثمّ أعطاه المشترى ذلك وقبضه منه ثمّ نقض البائع البيع بحقّ خياره فيه وجب عليه أن يردّ البائع على المشترى مثل ما قبض منه وليس عليه أن يردّ عليه ما قبض منه بعينه وإن كان قائمًا فى يديه وإن كان الثمن عروضا وجب عليه أن يردّها بعينها وكذلك ينبغى أن تبيّن ذلك فى كتابك على ما ذكرنا فى كلّ صنف من هذه الأصناف *

20.3 فإن كان الخيار [3] للمشترى وجب على البائع أن يردّ عليه ما كان قبض منه عرضا أو غير عرض لأنّه لم يكن ملكه عليه وينبغى أن تبيّن ذلك فى كتابك وتكتب أنّه سلّمه الى المشترى وأنّ المشترى قبضه منه وهو على هيئته التى كان البائع قبضه منه عليها * //

(97a)

باب أشرية النخل والشجر

21.0 قال أبو جعفر واذا اشترى رجل من رجل نخلة بأرضها فأرادا أن يكتبا بينهما فى ذلك كتابا كتبت هذا ما اشترى فلان بن فلان بن فلان [4] الفلانى من فلان بن فلان بن فلان الفلانى اشترى منه جميع النخلة الكذا من البستان المحظر الذى بمدينـــة كذا فى الموضع الكذا منها ثمّ تحدّد البستان ثمّ تكتب ذكر باب البستان ليدلّ ذلك أنّه محظر ثمّ تكتب وهذه النخلة التى وقع عليها هذا البيع المسمّى فى هذا الكتاب من هذا البستان المحدود فى هذا الكتاب فى الجانب الكذا أو مستدارها كذا ويحيط بموضعها من الأرض ويجمعه ويشتمل عليه حدود أربعة ثمّ تحدّده ثمّ تنسق الكتاب فى الأرض المعروفة فإن كان هذا البستان غير محظر فقد تقدّم كلامنا فى مثل ذلك فى بيع البيت من الدار ومن الأرض المحظرة ومن الأرض غير المحظرة وبيّنّا فى ذلك ما يغنى أن يُكتَب فى هذا بفصل ذلك ووجوه الأحكام فيه ولو كان لهذه النخلة المبيعة شرب من بئر
(97b) فى هذا البستان الذى هى فيه كتبت فى موضع ذكر حقوقها وشربها الذى هو لها من البئر // من هذا البستان المحدود فى هذا الكتاب فى موضع كذا ومسيل ماء فى هذا الشرب اليها فى القناة التى

[1] MS omits وكانت البراءة
[2] MS omits المبيع
[3] MS فان الخيار
[4] MS omits بن فلان

من هذا البستان المحدود فى هذا الكتاب فى موضع كذا من أوّل هذه القناة الملاصق أوّلها لهذه البئر المحدودة فى هذا الكتاب من جانبها الكذا حتّى ينتهى ذلك الى هذه النخلة التى وقع عليها هذا البيع المسمّى فى هذا الكتاب *

22.0 وإن كان اشترى هذه النخلة على أن يقلعها بأصلها فذلك جائز فإن أرادا أن يكتبا فى ذلك كتابا كتبت هذا ما اشترى فلان بن فلان بن فلان الفلانى من فلان بن فلان بن فلان الفلانى اشترى منه جميع النخلة التى من البستان الذى بمدينة كذا فى موضع كذا ثمّ تحدّ البستان ثمّ تصف موضع النخلة وتحدّه ثمّ تكتب اشترى فلان بن فلان من فلان بن فلان جميع هذه النخلة الموصوفة المحدودة أرضها من البستان المحدود فى هذا الكتاب بأصلها وجريدها وسعفها القائمَين فيها خلا أرضها فإنّها لم تدخل ولا شىء منها فى هذا البيع المسمّى فى هذا الكتاب ثمّ تسمّى الثمن ثمّ تذكر دفع المشترى ايّاه الى البائع وقبض البائع ايّاه منه ثمّ تكتب قبض المشترى النخلة //
(98 a) من البائع بتسليم البائع ايّاها اليه وتكتب مع ذلك على أن يقلعها بأرضها ثمّ تنسق الكتاب فى ذلك على مثل ما كتبنا غير أنّك لا تحتاج فى ذلك الى ذكر ضمان الدرك *

22.1 فإن آثرت أن تكتب فى ذلك ضمان الدرك فلا تذكر لها حقوقا غير أنّ أصحابنا لا يكتبون ضمان الدرك إلاّ فى العقارات خاصّة ويجيزون فيما سواها بما توجبه الأحكام *

23.0 فإن أذن البائع للمشترى فى ترك النخلة فى أرضه عاريّة منه ايّاه ذلك كتبت على أثر ذلك التفرّق وقد أذن فلان بن فلان يعنى البائع لفلان بن فلان يعنى المشترى فى ترك هذه النخلة التى وقع عليها هذا البيع المسمّى فى هذا الكتاب فى موضعها الذى هى فيه التى من شاركها فيه فموضع هذه النخلة من البستان المحدود فى هذا الكتاب عاريّة فى يد فلان بن فلان يعنى المشترى لفلان ابن فلان يعنى البائع ويأخذه فلان بن فلان يعنى البائع برفعها عن أرضه متى شاء وعلى أنّ فلان ابن فلان يعنى المشترى لا يستحقّ بهذه العاريّة المذكورة فى هذا الكتاب من موضع هذه النخلة التى وقع عليها هذا البيع المسمّى فى هذا الكتاب من تربة هذا البستان المحدود فى هذا الكتاب //
(98 b) شيئا وجميع ما فى هذا الكتاب من إذن وعاريّة فعلى غير شرط كان فى عقدة هذا البيع المسمّى فى هذا الكتاب شهد *

باب شرى الثمرة القائمة
فى رؤوس النخل وشرى الزرع القائم فى الأرض

24.0 قال أبو جعفر واذا اشترى رجل من رجل ثمرة قائمة فى نخل كتبت هذا ما اشترى فلان بن فلان بن فلان الفلانى من فلان بن فلان بن فلان الفلانى اشترى منه جميع الثمر القائم فى النخل

الذى فى البستان الذى بمدينة كذا فى الموضع الكذا منها وهو البستان الذى يحيط به ويجمعه ويشتمل عليه حدود أربعة أحد حدود جماعته الحدّ الأوّل وهو كذا ينتهى الى كذا والحدّ الثانى والثالث والرابع وفيه يشرع باب هذا البستان المحدود فى هذا الكتاب اشترى فلان بن فلان من فلان بن فلان جميع الثمر القائم فى نخل هذا البستان المحدود فى هذا الكتاب بعد أن أزهى هذا الثمر وتناهى عظمه وحلّ بيعه خلا ما لله عزّ وجلّ فى هذا الثمر من الصدقة الواجبة وهو سهم واحد من عشرة أسهم
(99 a) من هذا الثمر المذكور فى هذا // الكتاب شائع فيه غير مقسوم منه هذا إن كانت أرضه تُسقى فتحا أو يسقيها السماء وإن كانت تُسقى بغرب أو دالية أو سانية كتبت وهو سهم واحد من عشرين سهما من هذا الثمر المذكور فى هذا الكتاب شائع فيه غير مقسوم منه فإنّ جميع ما وقع عليه هذا الاستثناء المذكور فى هذا الكتاب لم يدخل ولا شىء منه فى هذا البيع المسمّى فى هذا الكتاب ثمّ تنسق الكتاب فى ذلك على مثل ما كتبنا فى مثله ممّا قد تقدّم فى كتابنا هذا *

24.1 وقد كان أبو زيد يكتب فى هذا نحو ممّا كتبنا غير أنّه لا يذكر فى كتابه زهر الثمرة ولا تناهى عظمها ولا حلّ بيعها وذلك عندنا إغفال منه لأنّ أهل المدينة لا يجيزون بيع الثمار حتّى يزهى ويتناهى عظمها *

25.1 قال أبو جعفر فإن أراد المشترى اشتراط ترك الثمر فى رؤوس النخل الى وقت صرامه فإنّ الناس يختلفون فى ذلك فمنهم من يقول اذا وقع البيع على هذا الشرط كان البيع فاسدا وممّن ذهب الى ذلك أبو حنيفة وأبو يوسف ومنهم من يقول البيع جائز والشرط جائز لأنّ معاملات الناس على
(99 b) ذلك تجرى وممّن ذهب الى هذا القول محمّد بن الحسن // فكان أوثق الأشياء فى هذا أن يترك ذلك على العاريّة من البائع للمشترى وهو أقصى ما يقدر عليه فى هذا الباب وإن كان للبائع مع ذلك أن يأخذ المشترى برفع ذلك عن نخله متى شاء فى قول أبى حنيفة وأبى يوسف *

25.0 فإن أردت أن تبيّن ذلك فى كتابك كتبت وقد أذن فلان بن فلان يعنى البائع لفلان بن فلان يعنى المشترى فى ترك هذا الثمر الذى وقع عليه هذا البيع المسمّى فى هذا الكتاب فى رؤوس النخل الذى هو فيها الى وقت صرامه ثمّ تكتب وجميع ما فى هذا الكتاب من إذن وعاريّة[1] فعلى غير شرط كان فى عقدة هذا البيع المسمّى فى هذا الكتاب شهد *

26.1 قال أبو جعفر واذا اشترى الرجل من الرجل ثمرا فى نخل لم يتناه عظم ذلك الثمر فتركه بغير أمر من البائع حتّى تناهى فى نخله فإنّ أبا حنيفة وأبا يوسف ومحمّد بن الحسن قالوا فى ذلك الثمر كلّه للمشترى وعليه أن يتصدّق منه بما أزهى فى نخل البائع ولو اشتراه وهو بلح قد تناهى عظمه ثمّ تركه بغير إذن البائع فى النخل حتّى صار رطبا فإنّ ذلك كلّه للمشترى ولا يتصدّق منه

[1] MS omits عارية

(100 a) بشىء لأنّه هاهنا [صار] [1] شيئا انّما تغيّر فصار رطبا بعد أن كان بلحا // وكان بُسْرا ولو
26.2 تركه بإذن البائع كانت الزيادة للمشترى طيبةً فى جميع ما وصفنا * ولو استأجر رؤوس النخل من البائع شهرا معلوما بأجر معلوم أو استأجرها منه الى جذاذ الثمرة كانت الإجارة فاسدة فى الوجهين جميعا به ولم يجب للبائع على المشترى أخذ بها [2] وكانت زيادة الثمرة طيبة للمشترى لأنّ الإجارة له إن بطلت صار المشترى كأنّه ترك الثمر فى نخل البائع بإباحة [3] البائع فى ذلك له على سبيل العاريّة *

27.0 ولو أنّ رجلا اشترى من رجل زرعا قائما بغير أرض له كتبت هذا ما اشترى فلان بن فلان ابن فلان الفلانى من فلان بن فلان بن فلان الفلانى اشترى منه جميع الزرع الكذا القائم فى الأرض التى بمدينة كذا فى الموضع الكذا منها المعروف بكذا ثمّ تحدّد الأرض ثمّ تكتب اشترى فلان ابن فلان من فلان بن فلان جميع هذه الزرع الكذا القائم فى هذه الأرض المحدودة فى هذا الكتاب بعد أن تناهى عظم حبّه واشتدّ وحلّ بيعه خلا حقّ الله فى هذا الزرع المذكور فى هذا الكتاب من الصّدقة الواجبة فيه وهو كذا كذا سهما من كذا كذا سهما فإنّ جميع ما
(100 b) وقع عليه هذا الاستثناء المسمّى فى // هذا الكتاب لم يدخل ولا شىء منه فى هذا البيع المسمّى فى هذا الكتاب *

27.1 وتمثّل فى ذلك ما كتبناه فى الثمرة المبيعة فى رؤوس النخل وسواء كان هذا الزرع [4] فى أرض العشر أو فى أرض الخراج حتّى يكون الكتاب فى ذلك مجمعا على صحّته لما ذكرنا قبل هذا الباب عن أهل المدينة أنّهم يوجبون العشر فى الزرع الذى يكون فى أرض الخراج كما يوجبونه فى الزرع الذى يكون فى أرض العشر وسواء أيضا كان الزرع ممّا يكون مقداره خمسة أوسق أو أقلّ من خمسة أوسق إن أردت أن يكون كتابك مجمعا على صحته لأنّ أبا حنيفة يوجب الصدقة فى قليل ما تُخرِج الأرض وكثيره *

27.2 وقد رُوى ذلك عن ابراهيم ومجاهد وكذلك نكتب فى ثمرة النخل المبيعة فيما قلّ منها وفيما كثر على مثل ما كتبنا فيها وفى الزرع المبيع على ما ذكرنا حتّى لا يكون لاحد من أهل العلم سبيل الى نقض كتابك *

28.0 فإن أراد المشترى استئجار الأرض من البائع الى وقت معلوم كتبت الكتاب على مثل ما
(101 a) كتبنا حتّى اذا أتيت على وتفرّقا بعد هذا البيع المسمّى // فى هذا الكتاب بأبدانهما عن تراض

[1] word erased in MS
[2] MS omits بها
[3] MS باحه
[4] MS هذا كان هذا الزرع

منها جميعا بجميعه وإنفاذ منها له كتبت على أثر ذلك ثم ّ أن ّ فلان بن فلان يعنى المشترى استأجر من فلان بن فلان يعنى البائع جميع الأرض التى فيها هذا الزرع المسمّى فى هذا الكتاب وهى الأرض المحدودة فى هذا الكتاب بحدودها كلّها وجميع حقوقها كذا كذا شهرا متوالية أوّلها مستهلّ شهر كذا من سنة كذا وآخرها انقضاء شهر كذا من سنة كذا بكذا كذا دينارا مثاقيل ذهبا عينا وازنة جيادا على أن يدفع فلان بن فلان الى فلان بن فلان أجرة كلّ شهر من هذه الشهور المسمّاة فى هذا الكتاب عند انقضائه وهى كذا كذا دينارا مثاقيل ذهبا عينا وازنة جيادا وسلّم فلان بن فلان الى فلان بن فلان جميع ما وقعت عليه هذه الإجارة المسمّاة فى هذا الكتاب وقبضه منه فلان بن فلان وصار فى يده وقبضه بهذه الإجارة المسمّاة فى هذا الكتاب فى مستهلّ شهر كذا من سنة كذا بغير حائل بينه وبينه وبغير مانع له منه وذلك بعد أن أقرّ فلان بن فلان وفلان
(101 b) ابن فلان أنّهما قد رأيا جميعا جميع ما وقعت عليه هذه الإجارة // المسمّاة فى هذا الكتاب وعايناه داخله وخارجه وتبيّن لهما ذلك وعرفاه جميعا عند عقدة هذه[1] الإجارة المسمّاة فى هذا الكتاب بينهما وقبل ذلك فتعاقدا هذه الإجارة المسمّاة فى هذا الكتاب على ذلك وتفرّقا جميعا بأبدانهما بعد هذه الإجارة المسمّاة فى هذا الكتاب عن تراض منهما بها وإنفاذ منهما لها وكان استئجار فلان ابن فلان من فلان بن فلان جميع ما ذكر استئجاره ايّاه منه فى هذا الكتاب بغير شرط كان بينهما فى عقدة هذا البيع المسمّى فى هذا الكتاب وبعد أن تفرّقا بأبدانهما عن المجلس الذى تعاقدا فيه هذا البيع المسمّى فى هذا الكتاب *

28.1 وقد كان أبو زيد يكتب فى هذه الإجارة استئجار منه مواضع الزرع وهذا عندنا خطأ لأنّ ذلك على مواضع نبات الزرع دون غيره من الأرض فكان الأوثق فى ذلك عندنا والله أعلم ما كتبنا *

28.2 وكان أبو زيد يكتب أيضا فى هذه الإجارة كلّ شهر بكذا ولا يسمّى عددا لشهور وهذا عندنا خطأ لاختلاف الناس فى ذلك فكان أبو حنيفة يجعل الإجارة فى هذا على شهر واحد وكان
(102 a) أبو يوسف ومحمّد // يجعلانها إجارة جائزة كلّ شهر بما سُمّى الى أن يخرج ما وقعت اليه الإجارة من يد المستأجر فكتبنا ما كتبنا احتياطا من هذا الاختلاف *

28.3 وقد كان أبو زيد أيضا يكتب فى هذه الإجارة على أنّ لفلان بن فلان ترك هذا الزرع الذى وقع عليه هذا البيع المسمّى فى هذا الكتاب فى مواضعه الى انقضاء هذه الشهور المسمّاة فى هذا الكتاب وهذا عندنا ممّا لا يحتاج اليه لأنّ الإجارة اذا وقعت على الأرض كان للمشترى منع البائع منها ومن دخولها ولم يكن للبائع أن يأخذ المشترى برفع شىء ممّا له فيها فلا معنى لهذا الذى كتبه أبو زيد وهو أيضا عندنا على ما عقد عليه الإجارة محال لأنّه لم يعقد الإجارة على شهور معلومة فيكون لها انقضاء ينتهى اليه ويرجع اليه وانّما عقدها كلّ شهر بكذا وكذا *

[1] MS omits هذه

29.0 وإن يبرأ البائع الى المشترى من عيوب الثمرة التى باعه ايّاها فى النخل أو من عيوب الزرع القائم الذى باعه ايّاه كتبت الكتاب على ما كتبنا غير أنّك تكتب فى آخره قبل الشهادة وأقرّ
(102 b) فلان بن فلان يعنى المشترى أنّه قد نظر الى عيوب جميع ما وقع عليه هذا البيع المسمّى فى // هذا الكتاب وعرفها وعاينها عيبا عيبا وأبرأ فلان بن فلان منها يعنى البائع شهد *

باب شرى الحمّامات

30.0 قال أبو جعفر واذا اشترى رجل من رجل حمّاما بموضع زبله وموضع بئره فأراد أن يكتب فى ذلك كتابا كتبت هذا ما اشترى فلان بن فلان بن فلان الفلانى من فلان بن فلان بن فلان الفلانى اشترى منه جميع الحمّام وجميع الحجرة المعروفة بمُلقَى زبله وجميع الحجرة التى فيها بئر هذا الحمّام وساقيته وهذا الحمّام وهاتان الحجرتان بمدينة كذا فى الموضع الذى منها المعروف بكذا فإنّ ذلك يلاصق بعضه بعضا كتبت ويحيط بهذا الحمّام وبهاتين الحجرتين ويجمع ذلك ويشتمل عليه حدود أربعة وإن شئت كتبت وهذا الحمّام وهاتان الحجرتان يلاصق بعضهنّ بعضا ويحيط بهنّ ويجمعهنّ ويشتمل عليهنّ حدود أربعة *

30.1 وانّما ذكرنا ملاصقة بعضهنّ بعضا ولم نجتز بقولنا ويحيط بهنّ ويجمعهنّ ويشتمل عليهنّ حدود أربعة لأنّه قد يجوز أن تكون تلك الحدود تجمعهنّ وغيرهنّ من الطرق والدور والمنازل
(103 a) اللاتى لم يقع عليهنّ البيع فكتبنا الملاصقة لينفى ذلك // وليدلّ على أنّ ما حوَتْه الحدود قد دخل فى البيع *

30.0 bis ثمّ تكتب حدود جماعتهنّ الحدّ الأوّل وهو كذا ينتهى الى كذا والحدّ الثانى والثالث والرابع وفيه يشرع أبواب هذا الحمّام وهاتَيْن الحجرتَيْن هذا إن كانت أبوابهنّ تشرع فى حدّ واحد وإن كانت تشرع فى حدود مختلفة كتبت ولهذا الحمّام ولهاتين الحجرتين المحدودات فى هذا الكتاب ثلاثة أبواب فمنهنّ باب واحد يشرع منهنّ فى حدّهنّ الكذا ويدخل منه الى الحمّام الداخل فى الحدود المذكورة فى هذا الكتاب ومنهنّ باب واحد يشرع منهنّ فى حدّهنّ الكذا ويدخل منه الى الحجرة المعروفة بمُلقَى زبل هذا الحمّام الداخل فى الحدود المذكورة فى هذا الكتاب ومنهنّ باب واحد يشرع منهنّ فى حدّهنّ الكذا ويدخل منه الى الحجرة المعروفة ببئر هذا الحمّام[1] الداخل فى الحدود المذكورة فى هذا الكتاب وإن كانت كلّ واحدة من هاتين الحجرتين خارجة عن حدود الحمّام كتبت الكتاب على ما كتبنا حتّى اذا انتهيت الى ذكر مواضعهنّ من المدينة التى هنّ فيها كتبت على أثر ذلك ويحيط بهذا الحمّام ويجمعه ويشتمل

[1] MS omits الحمام

(103 b) عليه حدود أربعة حتّى تأتى على حدوده كلّها // ثمّ تمتثل ذلك فى كلّ حجرة من الحجرتين
اللتين دخلتا فى البيع مع الحمّام ثمّ تكتب بعقب ذلك فى هذا وفى الكتاب الأوّل اشترى فلان
ابن فلان من فلان بن فلان جميع الحمّام وجميع هاتين الحجرتين المحدود الموصوف جماعتهنّ فى
هذا الكتاب بحدودهنّ كلّها وأرضهنّ وبنائهنّ وسفلهنّ وعلوّهنّ ومرافقهنّ فى حقوقهنّ
وطرقهنّ التى هى لهنّ من حقوقهنّ ومسايلهنّ فى حقوقهنّ ومغايضهنّ فى حقوقهنّ وكلّ قليل
وكثير هو لهنّ فيهنّ ومنهنّ من حقوقهنّ وكلّ حقّ هو لهنّ داخل فيهنّ وكلّ حقّ هو
لهنّ خارج منهنّ وجميع قدور هذا الحمّام الداخل فى الحدود المذكورة فى هذا الكتاب وهو
كذا كذا قدرا فتصفهنّ وتذكر ما هنّ منه حديد أو رصاص وجميع مآزيب هذا الحمّام القائمة
فيه وجميع بئره الداخلة فى الحجرة الداخلة فى الحدود المذكورة فى هذا الكتاب وجميع الساقية القائمة
على هذه البئر[1] وجميع أداتها القائمة فيها ثمّ تنسق الكتاب فى ذلك على مثل ما كتبنا فى أشرية
الدور *

30.2 قال أبو جعفر وقد كان بعض الناس يكتب فى هذا اشترى منه جميع الحمّام ولا يذكر //
(104 a) مع ذلك حجرة البئر ولا حجرة مُلقَى الزبل ثمّ ينسق الكتاب على ذلك حتّى يصير الى ذكر
الحقوق فيكتب معها وموضع زبله وجميع الحجرة التي فيها بئر[2] الماء ثمّ يحدّ كلّ واحد منهما *

30.3 وكان أبو زيد يكتب فى ذلك مثل ما كتبنا فكان أحسن عندنا ممّا كتب الآخرون لأنّه اذا
كتب كما كتب الآخرون ما يذكر فى كتابه من الحقوق والحدود انّما يرجع على الحمّام واذا
كتب على ما كتبنا نحن وعلى ما كان أبو زيد يكتب فذكر الحمّام وذكر حجرته التى يُلقَى
فيها زبله وذكر حجرته التى فيها بئره رجع ذكر الحقوق والحدود على ذلك كلّه وقد يكون
للحجرة التى فيها البئر والحجرة التي يُلقَى فيها الزبل حقوق بائنة من حقوق الحمّام فلا تدخل
فى البيع إلاّ باشتراط المشترى ايّاها فاخترنا من هذا ما كتب أبو زيد لأنّه يأتى على ذلك كلّه
وتركنا ما كتب الآخرون لما فيه من التقصير عن ذلك *

30.4 قال أبو جعفر وقد اختلف الناس فيما يُكتَب فيما تنفرد به كلّ واحدة من هاتين الحجرتين
من الحقوق دون صاحبتها وفيما تنفرد به الحجرتان جميعا من الحقوق التى هى لهما أو فيما دون الحمّام
(104 b) وفيما ينفرد به الحمّام من الحقوق التى هى له // دون الحجرتين فكان بشر بن الوليد يجمع ذلك
كلّه فى ذكر الحقوق بكلام واحد فيكتب بحدودهنّ كلّها وأرضهنّ وبنائهنّ وقدورهنّ ومآزيبهنّ
ولا يفرد كلّ واحد من الحمّام ومن الحجرتين بما ينفرد به ممّا هو فيه وليس فى غيره ممّا وقع البيع
عليه معه وكذلك كان يكتب أيضا فى دار وحمّام بيعا جميعا صفقة واحدة فيكتب وقدورها إن
ابتدأ ذكر الحقوق والحدود بحدودها كلّها وإن ابتدأ فكتب بحدود جميع ما وقع عليه هذا البيع
كتبت وقدوره ومآزيبه ثمّ تنسق الحقوق على ذلك *

[1] MS على هذا البئر

[2] MS بئره

30.5 وكان غيره من أصحابنا يبتدئ بذكر الحقوق التى فى الدار والحمّام فيجعل ذلك نسقا واحدا حتّى ينتهى الى آخر الحقوق التى فى الجنسين جميعا ثمّ يذكر لكلّ واحد من الجنسين ما ينفرد به من الحقوق من الجنس الآخر على نحو ما كتبنا قال أبو جعفر وقد رأيت بَكّار بن قُتَيْبة يختار هذا ولا أعلمه إلاّ حكاه عن هلال بن يحيى *

باب أشرية الأرحاء

31.0 قال أبو جعفر واذا اشترى رجل من رجل بيتا فيه رحى بالرحى التى فيه وبآلتها كتبت هذا
(105 a) ما اشترى فلان بن فلان بن // فلان الفلانى من فلان بن فلان بن فلان الفلانى اشترى منه جميع البيت الذى بمدينة كذا فى الموضع الكذا منها ويحيط بهذا البيت ويجمعه ويشتمل عليه حدود أربعة فتحدّده ثمّ تكتب اشترى فلان بن فلان من فلان بن فلان جميع هذا البيت المحدود فى هذا الكتاب بحدوده كلّها وأرضه وبنائه وسفله وعلوّه ومرافقه فى حقوقه وطرقه التى هى له من حقوقه ومسايله فى حقوقه وجميع الرحى الفارسيّة القائمة فيه وجميع أحجارها وجميع خشبها وجميع أداتها وآلتها القائم ذلك كلّه فيها فإن سمّيت الأداة فحسن وإن تركت التسمية لم يضرّك ثمّ تكتب وكلّ قليل وكثير هو لهذا البيت ولهذه الرحى [1] الداخلة فى حدودها المذكورة فى هذا الكتاب من حقوقها ومن حقوق كلّ واحد منها وكلّ حقّ هو لهما وكلّ واحد منهما داخل فيهما وكلّ حقّ لهما ولكلّ واحد منهما خارج منهما ثمّ تنسق الكتاب فى ذلك على مثل ما كتبنا فى الدور والعقارات وإن شئت أيضا ابتدأت فى ذكر الحقوق فجعلت الخطاب على البيت خاصّة
(105 b) حتّى اذا انتهيت الى وكلّ حقّ هو له خارج منه كتبت على أثر ذلك // وجميع الرحى الكذا الداخلة فى حدود هذا البيت المحدود فى هذا الكتاب ببنائها وأحجارها وجميع آلتها وأداتها القائم ذلك كلّه فيها ثمّ تكتب بكذا كذا دينارا ثمّ تنسق الكتاب فى ذلك على نحو ما نسقناه فى مثله *

31.1 وقد كان أبو زيد يبدأ كتابه فى ذلك بذكر الرحى مع البيت فكتب هذا ما اشترى فلان بن فلان من فلان بن فلان اشترى منه جميع البيت الذى بمدينة كذا فى الموضع الكذا منها وجميع الرحى التى فيه بآلتها وأداتها ثمّ ينسق كتابه على ذلك *

31.2 وكان غيره من أصحابنا يكتب فى ذلك نحو ممّا كتبنا فكان من حجّة أبى زيد فيما ذهب اليه من ذلك أنّ الرحى منها ما لا يدخل فى البيع إلاّ باشتراط المشترى ايّاه قال فما لا يدخل فى البيع إلاّ باشتراط المشترى ايّاه يكون مبيعا اذا اشترطه قال فلهذا جعلت ذكر الرحى فى أوّل كتابى ثمّ ذكر البيت الذى هى فيه *

[1] MS هذا الرحى

31.3 قال أبو جعفر فيقال له قد كتبتَ في الثمرة التي لا تدخل في بيع البستان التي هي فيه لمّا اشترطها مشترى البستان فى الشرى مع ذكر حقوق البستان وأخليت أوّل كتابك من ذكرها وامتثلتَ هذا فى غير شيء من كتابك التى قدذكرنا بعضها عنك فيما قد تقدّم من كتابنا هذا فى الثمرة //
(106 a) وفى إخلاء أوّل كتابكم من ذكره ما يجب به عليكم ان تمثلوا ذلك فى بيع الرحى مع البيت التى هى فيه *

باب أشرية العيون

32.0 قال أبو جعفر واذا اشترى رجل من رجل عينا [1] فأراد أن يكتب فى ذلك كتابا كتبت هذا ما اشترى فلان بن فلان بن فلان من فلان بن فلان بن فلان اشترى منه جميع العين التى يقال لها كذا وجميع الأرض المحيطة من جميع جوانبها وهذه العين وهذه الأرض بمدينة كذا فى الموضع الكذا منها ومبتدأ هذه العين موضع كذا ومنتهاها الى موضع كذا واستدارتها كذا كذا ذراعا بذراع كذا وهى عين طاهر [2] ماؤها غير مغور ولا متغيّر وذرع هذه الأرض المحيطة بهذه العين من جميع جوانبها كذا كذا ذراعا بذراع كذا من كلّ جانب منها كذا كذا ذراعا بذارع كذا ويحيط بهذه العين وبهذه الأرض المحيطة بها من جميع جوانبها المذكورين فى هذا الكتاب ويجمعها ويشتمل عليها حدود أربعة أحد حدود جماعتها الحدّ الأوّل وهو كذا ينتهى الى كذا والحدّ الثانى والثالث والرابع ثمّ تكتب اشترى فلان بن فلان من فلان بن فلان جميع هذه العين وجميع
(106 b) هذه // الأرض المحدودة الموصوف جماعتها فى هذا الكتاب بحدودهما كلّها وأرضها فإن كان فيها بناء كتبت وبنائها سفله وعلوّه ثمّ تنسق الكتاب فى ذلك على ما كتبنا فى مثله ممّا تقدّم فى كتابنا هذا حتّى اذا أتيت على ذكر الرؤية كتبت وذلك بعد أن أقرّ فلان بن فلان وفلان ابن فلان أنّهما قد رأيا جميعا جميع هذه العين وجميع هذه الأرض المحيطة بها من جميع جوانبها المحدود ذلك فى هذا الكتاب داخلها وخارجها وجميع ما فيها ومنها من قليل وكثير ووقفا على نهايات حدودها المذكورة لها فى هذا الكتاب وعلى ما وصف به ماء هذه العين على ما سُمّى ووُصف فى هذا الكتاب وتبيّن لها ذلك وعرفاه جميعا عند عقدة هذا البيع المسمّى فى هذا الكتاب بينهما وقبل ذلك فتبايعا على ذلك وتفرّقا بأبدانهما بعد هذا البيع المسمّى فى هذا الكتاب عن تراض منهما جميعا بجميعه وإنفاذ منهما له وذرع هذه الأرض المحيطة بهذه العين المذكورة فى هذا الكتاب
(107 a) من جميع جوانبها بين فلان بن فلان وفلان بن فلان بإذنهما وأمرهما ومحضرهما ذرّاع // عدول فكان ذرعها كذا كذا ذراعا بذراع كذا على ما سُمّى ووُصف فى هذا الكتاب وكان الذى يحيط منهنّ من كلّ جانب من جوانب هذه العين ما سُمّى ووُصف فى هذا الكتاب وذكرت فيه

[1] MS عين

[2] MS ظاهر

أنّه محيط بها من كلّ جانب من جوانبها على ما سُمّى من ذلك ووُصف فى هذا الكتاب فصدّق فلان بن فلان يعنى المشترى هؤلاء الذرّاع على ذرعهم الموصوف فى هذا الكتاب بعد إحاطته به علما ووقوفه عليه وقوفا صحيحا ثمّ تكتب الدرك فى ذلك على مثل ما كتبنا فى أشرية الدور والعقارات *

32.1 قال أبو جعفر وكان أبو زيد يكتب فى هذا اشترى منه جميع العين التى يقال لها كذا وحريمها وهو مائة[1] ذراع من جميع جوانبها فكرهنا ذلك[2] وإن كان حريم العين مائة ذراع كما ذكر لأنّ ما كتبنا من ذلك أبين وأوضح وأقرب الى فهم العامّة وذلك أنّ الحريم انّما يكون للعين التى تحيا فى الأرض الميّتة وقد اختلف الناس فى إحياء الأرض الميّتة فقال بعضهم لا يكون ذلك إلاّ بأمر الإمام وبتقصير الإمام ذلك لمَن أحياه وممّن قال ذلك أبو حنيفة وقال بعضهم من أحيا أرضا ميّتة فهى له فلا يحتاج فى ذلك الى إذن الإمام ولا تقصيره ايّاه له وممّن ذهب الى ذلك أبو يوسف ومحمّد بن الحسن *

32.2 (107 b) ثمّ وصف أبو يوسف الأرض الميّتة فقال هى كلّ أرض اذا وقف رجل // على أدنى موضع منها الى أقرب الأمصار اليها فنادى بأعلى صوته لم يسمعه أقرب مَن فى المصر اليه قال فما كانت هذه صفته فهو موات مَن أحياه فهو له ومَن كان على غير ذلك فليس بموات هكذا حدّثنا سليمان بن شعيب عن أبيه عن أبى يوسف *

32.3 قال أبو جعفر فلمّا رأينا ذلك كذلك ورأينا الحريم انّما يكون فى الموات الذى وصفنا ولا يكون لغيره أخذ بها رجل فى أرضه كان أحوط الأشياء للمشترى والبائع جميعا ألا يذكرا فيما يتبايعان ما يدلّ على موات فيقع فيه من الاختلاف ما وصفنا ورأينا أن تمتثل ما يُكتَب فى الأملاك التى لا اختلاف فيها على ما كتبنا ولأنّه قد يجوز أن تكون الأرض التى فيها العين لم تكن مواتا وكانت ملكا لرجل فأحدث فيها هذه العين فلا يُستحَقّ العين بذلك حريما فيكون البائع والمشترى قد اشترطا ما لا حريم له ومثل هذا يفسد البيع *

باب شرى البئر العطن

33.0 وإذا اشترى رجل من رجل بئر عطن فأراد أن يكتب فى ذلك كتابا فإنّك تكتب هذا ما اشترى فلان بن فلان بن فلان[3] الفلانى من فلان بن فلان بن فلان الفلانى اشترى منه جميع البئر التى يقال لها كذا فى الموضع المعروف بكذا // وجميع الأرض المحيطة بها من جميع جوانبها وذرع هذه (108 a)
الأرض كذا كذا ذراعا من كلّ جانب من جوانب هذه البئر المذكورة فى هذا الكتاب وإن شئت

[1] MS وهو خمس مائة
[2] MS فكم بنا ذلك
[3] MS omits بن فلان

كتبت ذرع هذه الأرض المحيطة بهذه البئر المذكورة فى هــذا الكتاب كذا كذا ذراعا من كلّ جانب بذراع كذا من جوانب هذه البئر المذكورة فى هذا الكتاب كذا كذا ذراعا بذارع كذا وهى بئر طاهر ماؤها غير مغور ولا متغيّر ثمّ تكتب ويحيط بهذه العين وبهذه الأرض المذكورتين في هذا الكتاب ويجمعها ويشتمل عليها حدود أربعة ثمّ تحدّدهما ثمّ تنسق الكتاب على ما كتبنا فى مثل ذلك ممّا قد تقدّم فى كتابنا هذا غير أنّك تزيد فى الحقوق وعطنها فى حقوقها وحياضها التى هى لها فى حقوقها الداخلة فى حدودها المذكورة لها فى هذا الكتاب ثمّ تنسق الكتاب على مثل ما كتبنا فى ذلك فيما تقدّم فى هذا الكتاب وكذلك إن كانت البئر بئر ناضح كتبت الكتاب فى ذلك على مثل ما كتبنا فى ذلك فيما قد تقدّم فى كتابنا هذا *

33.1 قال أبو جعفر وقد كان أبو زيد يكتب فى هذا كلّه اشترى منه جميع البئر الكذا وحريمها ثمّ يكتب فى بئر العطن وهو أربعون ذراعا ويكتب فى بئر الناضح وهو ستّون ذراعا فكرهنا ذلك //
(108 b) لما قد ذكرناه فى الحريم فى الباب الذى قبل هذا الباب *

33.2 وقد قال أصحابنا فى بئر الناضح إنّ حريمها ستّون ذراعا إن كان الجبل ينتهى اليها أو ينتهى الى ما دونها ولا يبلغها وإن كان الجبل يجاوزها كان حريمها ما بلغه جبلها فقد صار الحريم على قولهم مختلفا مرّة ستّون ذراعا ومرّة أكثر من ذلك فلمّا رأينا ذلك كذلك وقد وصفنا فى الحريم ما ذكرنا رأينا أنّ الأحوط السكوت عن ذكر الحريم وإيقاع البيع على أذرع معلومة كما يمتثل فى غير الآبار على ما قد تقدّم من أمثال ذلك فى كتابنا هذا وإن أمسكت فى كتابك عن حكم العطن فلم تكتب ذكره كان أحبّ الينا *

باب أشرية الأنهار

34.0 قال أبو جعفر واذا اشترى رجل من رجل نهرا فى صحراء كتبت هذا ما اشترى فلان بن فلان ابن فلان الفلانى من فلان بن فلان بن فلان الفلانى اشترى منه جميع النهر الذى يقال له كذا فى موضع كذا وجميع الأرض التى على جانبَى هذا النهر وهو كذا كذا ذراعا فى كذا كذا ذراعا من الجانب الكذا من هذا النهر وكذا كذا ذراعا فى كذا كذا ذراعا من الجانب الكذا من هذا
(109 a) النهر[1] ومأخذه فى كذا ومصبّه فى كذا ويحيط بهذ النهر // وبهذه الأرض التى على جانبَيْه المذكورة فى هذ الكتاب ويجمعها ويشتمل عليها حدود أربعة ثمّ تنسق الكتاب فى ذلك على مثل ما كتبنا فى أشرية العقارات *

34.1 وقد كان أبو زيد يكتب فى هذا بحريمه ولا يذكر الأرض التى على جانبَى النهر وهذا عندنا خطأ لأنّ الناس قد اختلفوا فى النهر هل له حريم أم لا فكان بعضهم يقول لا حريم للنهر وانّما

[1] MS omits من الجانب الكذا من هذا النهر

الحريم للبئر العطن وبئر الناضح لحاجة العطن وحاجة الناضح الى ذلك وممّن قال هـذا القول أبو حنيفة وكان بعضهم يقول حريم النهر هو مقدار ما يحتاج اليه من جانبيْه لمُلقَى طينه وممّن قال هذا القول أبو يوسف ومحمّد بن الحسن *

34.2 فكرهنا أن نذكر فى كتابنا لهذا النهر حريما لأنّ بعض الناس يقول لا حريم له ولأنّ مَن يجعل منهم له حريما فانّما يجعله مقدار ما يُلقَى فيه الطين الخارج منه الذى لا غناء[1] بالنهر عنه فذلك مجهول غير موقوف منه على مقدار معلوم ولا حقيقة معلومة فجعلنا مكان ذلك أذرعا معروفة ليصحّ البيع فى قول الناس جميعا ولأنّا رأينا الحريم فى قول مَن جعل للنهر حريما انّما هو عنده فى أرض الموات[2] // التى يحدث فيها النهر فيجعل له من الحريم ما قد ذكرناه فى هـذا الباب * (109 b)

34.3 ولو كانت أرضا مملوكة احتفر فيها رجل نهرا لم يجعل له حريما فلمّا رأينا الأرض فى قوله قد لا يجوز أن يكون لها حريم وقد يكون لها حريم كان أولى الأشياء بنا ترك ذلك من كتابنا *

باب شرى قناة

35.0 قال أبو جعفر واذا اشترى رجل من رجل قناة فأراد أن يكتب فى ذلك كتابا كتبت هذا ما اشترى فلان بن فلان بن فلان الفلانى من فلان بن فلان بن فلان الفلانى اشترى منه جميع القناة التى بموضع كذا وهذه القناة ما بين كذا الى كذا وطولها كذا وعرضها كذا ثمّ تنسق الكتاب فى ذلك على مثل ما كتبنا فى النهر *

36.0 فإن كان على هذه القناة بيت فيه رحى تطحن بالماء كتبت هذا ما اشترى فلان بن فلان ابن فلان[3] الفلانى من فلان بن فلان بن فلان الفلانى اشترى منه جميع القناة التى من أرض كذا ما بين كذا الى كذا وجميع البيت الذى على هذه القناة ممّا يلى كذا ثمّ تكتب // ويحيط بهذه القناة وبهذا البيت ويجمعها ويشتمل عليها حدود أربعة فتحدّدهما ثمّ تنسق الكتاب فى ذلك على مثل ما كتبنا فى مثله فيما قد تقدّم فى كتابنا هذا * (110 a)

36.1 قال أبو جعفر وقد كان أبو زيد يكتب فى هذا أيضا بحريمها فكرهنا ذلك لما قـد تقدّم فى ذكر الحريم *

[1] MS التي لا غناء
[2] MS الارض الموات
[3] MS adds بن فلان

باب أشرية السفن

37.0 قال أبو جعفر واذا اشترى رجل من رجل سفينة فأراد أن يكتب فى ذلك كتابا كتبت هذا ما اشترى فلان بن فلان بن فلان الفلانى من فلان بن فلان بن فلان الفلانى اشترى منه جميع السفينة التى يقال لها كذا على أنّها من كذا وتسمّى جنس خشبها طولها كذا وعرضها كذا وعمقها كذا اشترى فلان بن فلان من فلان بن فلان جميع هذه السفينة الموصوفة فى هذا الكتاب بجميع ألواحها وعوارضها ومجاذيفها وقلوعها وبواريها وقلوسها وصواريها وجميع أداتها وآلتها الداخلة فيها والخارجة منها ممّا هو فيها وممّا هو عليها ومتّصل بها بكذا كذا دينارا ثمّ تنسق الكتاب فى
(110b) ذلك على ما كتبنا فى مثله // ممّا قد تقدّم فى كتابنا هذا *

37.1 وقد كان أبو زيد يكتب فى ذلك وهى سفينة من كذا فكرهنا نحن ذلك وكتبنا على أنّها كذا ليكون ذلك شرى ثابتا للمشترى على البائع فإن وجدها كذلك فقد استوفى شرطه وإلاّ كان له ما يجب له فى عدم الشرط *

باب شرى الرقيق والحيوان

38.0 قال أبو جعفر واذا اشترى رجل من رجل عبدا فأراد أن يكتب كتابا كتبت هذا ما اشترى فلان بن فلان بن فلان الفلانى من فلان بن فلان بن فلان الفلانى اشترى منه الغلام الذى يقال له فلان على أنّ جنسه كذا فإن وصفته فحسن وإن لم تصفه لم يضرّ ثمّ تكتب اشترى فلان ابن فلان من فلان بن فلان هذا الغلام المسمّى فى هذا الكتاب بكذا كذا دينارا مثاقيل[1] ذهبا عينا وازنة جيادا بيع المسلم المسلم لا داء ولا غائلة ولا خبثة ولا عيب ثمّ تنسق الكتاب فى ذلك على مثل ما كتبنا فيما قد تقدّم من كتابنا هذا من أشرية العقارات غير أنّك تكتب عند الرؤية //
(111a) وذلك بعـــد أن أقرّ فلان بن فلان وفلان بن فلان أنّهما قد رأيا جميعا هذا الغلام المسمّى فى هذا الكتاب وعاينا وجهه وتبيّن لهما وعرفاه عند عقدة هذا البيع المسمّى فى هذا الكتاب بينهما وقبل ذلك ثمّ تنسق الكتاب على مثل ما كتبنا فى ذلك فيما قد تقدّم من كتابنا هذا غير أنّ أصحابنا لم يكونوا يكتبون فى ذلك دركا فأن كتبتَه لم يضرّ فاذا أتيت على الشهادة على البائع وعلى المشترى كتبت على أثر ذلك وأقرّ فلان الفلانى الذى وقع عليه هذا البيع المسمّى فى هذا الكتاب أنّه كان مملوكا لفلان بن فلان يعنى البائع الى أن ملكه عليه فلان بن فلان يعنى المشترى بالبيع المسمّى فى هذا الكتاب وذلك فى شهر كذا من سنة كذا *

38.1 قال أبو جعفر وقد اختلف فى غير موضع من هذا الكتاب فكان أبو حنيفة وأبو يوسف ومحمّد ابن الحسن يكتبون فى ذلك اشترى منه المملوك الذى يُدعَى فلانا وكان يوسف بن خالد وأبو زيد

[1] MS omits مثاقيل

يكتبان اشترى منه العبد الذى يُدعَى فلانا فكان حذف ذلك كلّه عندنا أجود لما نخاف من ثبوت حرّيّة من البيع فيكون فى // إقرار المشترى أنّه مملوك وأنّه عبد ما يمنعه من وجوب الدرك (111 b) على البائع فى قول ابن أبى ليلى وأهل المدينة على ما ذكرنا عنهم فى غير هذا الموضع من هذا الكتاب *

38.2 وكان أبو حنيفة وأبو يوسف ومحمّد بن الحسن يكتبون فى ذلك لا داء ولا غائلة ولا يزيدون على ذلك شيئا وكان أبو زيد يكتب لا داء ولا غائلة ولا خبثة وكان يوسف بن خالد [1] يكتب لا داء ولا غائلة ولا خبثة ولا عيب فكان ما كتب يوسف فى هذا أجمع لأنّه قد جمع العيوب كلّها وذلك أنّ الداء انّما يقع [2] على الأمراض وتقع [3] الغائلة على السعرات وما أشبهها والخبثة تقع على رداءة الشىء [4] وقد بقيت هاهنا عيوب أبداً وليست بغائلة وليست بخبثة فمنها الأصبع الزائدة والكَي وما أشبههما ممّا لا يأتى عليه الداء ولا الغائلة ولا الخبثة والعيب يأتى على ذلك كلّه ولو ثبت لنا عن رسول الله عليه السلام حديث العداء بن خالد بن هوذة على ما قد رويناه فى صدر هذا الكتاب ممّا كتبه له رسول الله عليه السلام لا داء ولا غائلة ولا خبثة لاتّبعناه وما // جاوزناه الى (112 a) غير ذلك ولكنّه لم يثبت *

38.3 وقد كان أبو زيد يكتب الرؤية وذلك بعد أن نظر اليه فلان بن فلان ورضيه وأحبّ الينا من ذلك أن يكتب كما كتبنا إقرار البائع والمشترى بنظرهما الى وجه العبد المبيع لأنّ أبا حنيفة وأبا يوسف ومحمّد بن الحسن كانوا يقولون النظر فى الرقيق [5] الى وجوههم فى الذكور والإناث لا الى ما سوى ذلك من أبدانهم والنظر الى ما سوى بنى آدم من سائر الحيوان الى أعجازهم دون ما سوى ذلك منهم وكذلك ينبغى أن تمتثل فى كتب أشرية البهائم كلّها من الدواب وغيرها غير أنّه لا يكتب فى كتب بيع غير بنى آدم بيع المسلم المسلم لا داء ولا غائلة ولا خبثة ولا عيب *

38.4 قال أبو جعفر وإن يبرأ البائع الى المشترى من عيب ما باعه ايّاه كتبت على مثل ما كتبنا فى البراءة من العيوب فى الدور والعقارات على ما تقدّم فى كتابنا هذا *

38.5 قال أبو جعفر وقد كان أبو حنيفة لا يكتب فى شرى الرقيق فيما برئ البائع الى المشترى من عيوبه بيع المسلم المسلم لا داء ولا غائلة وانّما يكتب ذلك // فيما يكون المشترى فيه على حجّته (112 b) فى العيوب كلّها وقال أبو يوسف فقلت لأبى حنيفة لِمَ لم تكتب فى هذا بيع المسلم المسلم لا داء ولا غائلة قال لأنّى قد كتبتُ فى البراءة من كلّ داء ومن كلّ عيب فلا تحتاج فى ذلك الى أن تذكر أنّ البيع وقع بيع المسلم المسلم لا داء ولا غائلة لأنّ أحد هذين ينقض الآخر *

[1] MS omits يوسف بن خالد
[2] MS انما تقع
[3] MS omits وتقع
[4] MS رد الشيء
[5] MS النظر من الرقيق

39.0 قال أبو جعفر واذا اشترى رجل من رجل عبدا وامرأته وولده منها صفقة واحدة فأراد أن يكتب فى ذلك كتابا كتبت هذا ما اشترى فلان بن فلان بن فلان الفلانى من فلان بن فلان بن فلان الفلانى اشترى منه الغلام الذى يُدعَى فلانا على أنّ جنسه كذا والجارية التى تُدعَى فلانة على أنّ جنسها كذا زوجة هذا الغلام المسمّى فى هذا الكتاب وولدهما وهو صبىّ صغير فى حجورهما لا يعبّر عن نفسه يُدعَى فلانا صفقة واحدة بيع المسلم المسلم لا داء ولا غائلة ولا خبثة ولا عيب ثمّ تكتب الكتاب فى ذلك على مثل ما كتبنا غير أنّك تزيد فى آخره عند إقرار المبيعين
(113 a) بالرقّ للبائع إقرارهما على ولدهما بالرقّ للبائع // أيضا وتذكر مع ذلك أنّ ولدهما هذا يومئذ فى أيديهما صغير لا يعبّر عن نفسه لأنّ إقرارهما عليه بالرقّ فى هذه الحال جائز وإن كان ممّن يعبّر عن نفسه كتبت إقراره بنفسه بالرقّ بالغاً كان أو غير بالغ فإن كان بالغا لم يضرّك أن تبيّن فى كتابك ذكر بلوغه وإن كان غير بالغ كتبت وهو صغير غير بالغ لم يعبّر عن نفسه *

باب المقايضة

40.0 قال أبو جعفر واذا ابتاع رجل من رجل دارا بدار فأردت أن تكتب فى ذلك كتابا كتبت هذا ما اشترى فلان بن فلان بن فلان الفلانى من فلان بن فلان بن فلان الفلانى اشترى منه جميع الدار التى بمدينة كذا فى الموضع الكذا منها وهى الدار التى يحيط بها ويجمعها ويشتمل عليها حدود أربعة أحد حدود جماعتها الحدّ الأوّل وهو كذا ينتهى الى كذا والثانى والثالث والرابع وفيه يشرع باب هذه الدار المحدودة [1] فى هذا الكتاب اشترى فلان بن فلان من فلان بن فلان جميع هذه الدار المحدودة فى هذا الكتاب[1] بحدودها كلّها وأرضها وبنائها وسفلها وعلوّها ومرافقها فى
(113 b) حقوقها ومسايلها فى حقوقها وطرقها التى هى لها من حقوقها وكلّ قليل وكثير // هو لهـــا فيها ومنها من حقوقها وكلّ حقّ هو لها داخل فيها وكلّ حقّ [هو لها] [2] خارج منها [3] اشترى فلان ابن فلان من فلان بن فلان جميع هذه الدار [المحدودة] فى هذا الكتاب بجميع ما سُمّى لها ومنها فى هذا الكتاب بجميع الدار [التى] بمدينة كذا فى الموضع الكذا منها وهى الدار التى يحيط بها ويجمعها ويشتمل عليها حدود أربعة ثمّ تحدّدها وتذكر حقوقها وما قد دخل فى البيع منها على مثل ما كتبتَه فى الدار التى بدأتَ بذكرها وذكر حدودها وحقوقها فى كتابك هذا ثمّ تكتب بعد ذلك شرى لا شرط فيه ولا عدة وسلّم كلّ واحد من فلان بن فلان ومن فلان بن فلان الى صاحبه المسمّى معه فى هذا الكتاب جميع ما باعه ايّاه ممّا سُمّى ووُصف وحُدّ فى هذا الكتاب وقبضه منه صاحبه المسمّى معه فى هذا الكتاب وصار فى يده وقبضه بهذا الشرى المسمّى فى هذا

[1] MS omits المحدودة ... فى هذا الكتاب
[2] words obliterated in MS
[3] MS omits منها

الكتاب وذلك بعد أن أقرّ فلان بن فلان وفلان بن فلان أنّهما قد رأيا جميعا جميع هاتين الدارين المحدودتين فى هذا الكتاب داخلهما وخارجهما وجميع ما سُمّى لهما ومنهما فى هذا الكتاب من بناء
(114 a) وقليل وكثير وتبيّن لهما ذلك وعرفاه جميعا عند // عقدة هذا البيع المسمّى فى هذا الكتاب بينهما وقبل ذلك فتبايعا على ذلك وتفرّقا جميعا بأبدانهما بعد هذا البيع المسمّى فى هذا الكتاب عن تراض منهما جميعا بجميعه وإنفاذ منهما له فما أدرك كلّ واحد من فلان بن فلان ومن فلان بن فلان فيما ابتاعه من صاحبه المسمّى معه فى هذا الكتاب وفى شىء منه ومن حقوقه من درك من أحد من الناس كلّهم فعلى بائعه ايّاه المسمّى معه فى هذا الكتاب تسليم ما يجب عليه فى ذلك من حقّ ويلزمه بسبب هذا البيع المسمّى فى هذا الكتاب حتّى يسلّم ذلك الى مشتريه منه المسمّى فى هذا الكتاب على ما يوجبه له عليه هذا البيع المسمّى فى هذا الكتاب وقد كُتب هذا الكتاب نسختين نظما واحدا ونسقا سواء لا تزيد نسخة منهما على نسخة حرفا يغيّر حكما ولا يزيل معنى فنسخة منهما فى يد فلان بن فلان ثقة له وحجّة ونسخة منهما فى يد فلان بن فلان [1] ثقة له وحجّة شهد ثمّ تنسق الشهادة على مثل ما كتبنا فيما تقدّم من هذا الكتاب *

40.1 قال أبو جعفر وقد كان أبو زيد يجعل مكان الشرى فى هذا مقايضة ويجرى كتابه على ذلك والشرى الذى ذكرناه وسياقة الكتاب اليه أحبّ الينا من المقايضة وسياقة الكتاب اليها [2] لأنّه ممّا
(114 b) يفهمه // العامّة والخاصّة *

40.2 وقد كتبنا رؤية الدارين فى كتابنا هذا على ما كتبنا فإن شئت كتبتَها كذلك وإن شئت كتبت وذلك بعد أن أقرّ فلان بن فلان وفلان بن فلان أنّهما قد رأيا جميعا جميع هاتين الدارين المحدودتين فى هذا الكتاب داخلهما وخارجهما وجميع ما فى كلّ واحدة منهما ومنهما من بناء وقليل وكثير وتبيّن لهما ذلك ثمّ تنسق الكتاب على ما كتبنا *

40.3 فإن كتبت ذلك خوفا أن يتوهّم متوهّم أنّ قولك وجميع ما فيهما ومنهما من بناء وقليل وكثير انّما وقع على ما فى الدارين جميعا من الأجناس التى فيهما ومنهما جميعا وأنّ ما كان فى كلّ واحدة منهما ما ليس فى صاحبتها مثله لم يدخل فى ذلك فنسقت الكتاب فى هذا المعنى فإن احتطت من ذلك فكتبت كما كتبنا آخرا كان حسنا ظاهر المعنى وإن كتبت على ما كتبنا أوّلا كان جائزا *

40.0 bis قال أبو جعفر وإن تشاجر المتبايعان جميعا فطلب كلّ واحد منهما ألاّ يُبدأ عليه صاحبه وأن يسوى بينهما فى هذا الكتاب الذى يُكتَب بينهما فى عقدة ما لكلّ واحد منهما على صاحبه بحقّ ما ابتاع منه كتبت هذا ما شهد عليه الشهود المسمّون فى هذا الكتاب شهدوا جميعا أنّ فلان
(115 a) ابن فلان بن فلان الفلانى وفلان بن فلان بن فلان // الفلانى وقد أثبتوهما وعرفوهما معرفة صحيحة بأعيانهما وأسمائهما وأنسابهما أقرّا عندهم وأشهـداهم على أنفسهما فى صحّة عقولهما وأبدانهما وجواز

[1] MS omits بن فلان

[2] MS ساقية الكتاب عليه

أمورهما وذلك فى شهر كذا من سنة كذا أنّهما تبايعا على أن يسلّم فلان بن فلان المسمّى فى هذا الكتاب الى فلان بن فلان المسمّى فى هذا الكتاب جميع الدار التى بمدينة كذا فى الموضع الكذا منها وهى الدار التى يحيط بها ويجمعها ويشتمل عليها حدود أربعة أحد حدود جماعتها الحدّ الأوّل وهو كذا ينتهى الى كذا والحدّ الثانى والثالث والرابع وفيه يشرع باب هذه الدار المحدودة فى هذا الكتاب بحدودها كلّها وأرضها وبنائها ثمّ تنسق الكتاب فى ذلك على مثل ما كتبنا فى بيع الدار بالدراهم والدنانير حتّى اذا أتيت على وكلّ حقّ هو لها خارج منها كتبت على أثر ذلك على أن يسلّم اليه فلان بن فلان المسمّى فى هذا الكتاب جميع الدار التى بمدينة كذا فى الموضع الكذا منها وهى الدار التى يحيط بها ويجمعها ويشتمل عليها حدود أربعة ثمّ تحدّدها وتذكر حدودها وحقوقها على مثل ما ذكرتَها فى الدار التى بدأتَ بذكرها وتحديدها فى كتابك
(115 b) هذا ثمّ تكتب فقبل كلّ واحد من فلان بن فلان ومن فلان بن فلان من صاحبه // المسمّى معه فى هذا الكتاب جميع ما سلّمه اليه ووُصف فى هذا الكتاب وبذله المذكور فى هذا الكتاب وقبض كلّ واحد منهما من صاحبه المسمّى معه فى هذا الكتاب جميع ما سلّمه اليه على ما سُمّى ووُصف فى هذا الكتاب ثمّ تنسق الكتاب فى ذلك على نحو ما نسقناه فى الكتاب الذى قبل هذا *

40.4 وهكذا كان أصحابنا جميعا وسائر أصحاب الشروط يكتبون فى بيع الدارين إحداهما بالأخرى ويذكرون رؤية المتبايعين الدارين جميعا داخلها وخارجها وجميع ما فيهما ومنهما من بناء وقليل وكثير عند عقدة هذا البيع بينهما وقبل ذلك *

40.0 ter وقد يدخل فى ذلك شىء وذلك أنّ البيع قد يقع على دار بدار وكلّ واحدة من الدارين فى موضع غير الموضع الذى فيه الأخرى ولا يمكن أن يرياهما جميعا فى الوقت الذى تعاقدا فيه البيع بينهما عليه فأحوط الأشياء فى ذلك أن تكتب وذلك بعد أن أقرّ فلان بن فلان وفلان بن فلان أنّهما قد رأيا جميعا جميع هاتين الدارين المحدودتين فى هذا الكتاب داخلهما وخارجهما جميعا وجميع ما فيهما ومنهما من بناء وقليل وكثير قبل عقدة هذا البيع المسمّى فى هذا الكتاب وتبيّن لهما ذلك
(116 a) وعرفاه // جميعا حتّى لم يحقّ عليهما منه قليل ولا كثير وتعاقدا هذا البيع المسمّى فى هذا الكتاب بينهما على معرفتهما المذكورة فى هذا الكتاب ورأيا جميعا بعد ذلك هاتين الدارين المحدودتين فى هذا الكتاب وعايناهما على هيئتهما التى كانا عليها قبل هذا البيع المسمّى فى هذا الكتاب وتفرّقا جميعا بأبدانهما بعد هذا البيع المسمّى فى هذا الكتاب عن تراض منهما جميعا بجميعه وإنفاذ منهما له *

41.1 قال أبو جعفر وهذا أكثر ما قدرنا عليه فى بيع الدار بدار وكلّ واحدة منهما فى موضع سوى الموضع الذى فيه الأخرى وكذلك لو وقع البيع على أن يسلّم أحدهما الى صاحبه دارا على أن يسلّم اليه صاحبه عبدا بعينه وكرّ من حنطة بعينه وكرّ من شعير بعينه غير أنّ الأحوط فى العبد أن يمتثل فيه ما كتبناه فى شرى العبيد من حضور العبد وإقراره وتعريف المتبايعين الشهود

ايّاه بعينه وغير أنّه قد يمكن فى هذا أن يرى المتبايعان كلّ واحد من المبيعين مع رؤيته المبيع الآخر *

41.2 (116 b) فإن كان البيع وقع على كرّ من حنطة موصوف أو على كرّ من شعير موصوف كتبت الكتاب // فى ذلك على مثل ما كتبنا فى الدراهم والدنانير غير أنّك تذكر صنفه الذى هو منه وجودته إن كان جيّدا أو غير ذلك ممّا يوجب ردّه إن كان رديئا أو وسطا *

41.3 وإن كان آجلا [1] بيّنت حلول الأجل وكتبت يحلّ عليه عند انقضاء شهر كذا من سنة كذا ولا تكتب فى انسلاخ شهر كذا من سنة كذا لأنّا قد رأيناهم يقولون لآخر يوم من الشهر هو سلخ الشهر وقد يكون الشهر ثلاثين يوما ويكون تسعة وعشرين فإن كان سلخه آخر يوم منه فحلول الأجل اذا بقى من الشهر يوم أو يومان وذلك فاسد فاذا كتبت عند انقضاء شهر كذا من سنة كذا فالانقضاء لا يكون وقد بقى من الشهر المنقضى شىء فلهذا اخترنا الانقضاء على السلخ *

41.4 وقد كان بعض أصحابنا يكتب فى ذلك الى سلخ على ما ذكرنا وكان أبو زيد يكتب الى غرّة فكان ما كتبنا من ذلك أحسن عندنا والله أعلم لما ذكرنا ولأنّ الغرّة رأس الشهر فقد تكون الغرّة التى هى الغاية داخلة فى الأجل وقد تكون غير داخلة فيه *

41.5 (117 a) ألا ترى أنّ أبا حنيفة وأبا يوسف قد اختلفا فى // رجل باع عبده من رجل بألف درهم على أنّه بالخيار الى غد فقال أبو حنيفة له الخيار الى خروج غد وقال أبو يوسف له الخيار الى دخول غد وهو قول محمّد بن الحسن فلمّا اختلفوا فى الغايات على ما ذكرنا كان ما كتبنا أولى عندنا اذ لا اختلاف ولا شبهة فيه *

42.1 قال أبو جعفر واذا وقع البيع بدراهم أو دنانير أو حنطة بغير عينها أو بشعير بغير عينه فابدأْ بذكر قبض ذلك فى كتابك قبل ذكر قبض الدار المبيعة لما قد ذكرنا فى أوّل كتابنا هذا عن أهل المدينة أنّهم كانوا يقولون اذا أقرّ البائع بقبض المشترى الدار المبيعة منه بتسليمه ايّاها اليه كان فى ذلك إقرار منه بقبضه ثمنها منه قبل ذلك *

43.1 واذا وقع البيع على عرض بعرضَين فكلّ واحد من العرضين مبيع حكمه حكم صاحبه فيجب أن يكون ذكر القبض من المتبايعين معاً وإن كان أهل العلم قد اختلفوا فى العرض اذا بِيعَ بدراهم أو بدنانير أو بحنطة موصوفة بغير عينها أو بشعير موصوف بغير عينه [2] متى يجب لكلّ واحد من المتبايعين قبض ما ابتاع من صاحبه والله نسأله التوفيق والعون برحمته * //

[1] MS وان كان اجل

[2] MS omits عينه

(117b) 43.2 فكان أبو حنيفة وأبو يوسف ومحمّد بن الحسن يقولون على المشترى أن يدفع الثمن أوّلا فاذا قبضه منه البائع دفع اليه العرض المبيع قالوا ولا يجب على المشترى دفع الثمن وحده وكان سفيان الثورى يقول يجب على البائع تسليم العرض المبيع الى المشترى فاذا سلّمه اليه وجب على المشترى دفع الثمن اليه وكان أهل المدينة يقولون يتقابضان معاً لا يتقدّم أحدهما فى القبض صاحبه وجعلوا ذلك فى حكم العرضين أحدهما بصاحبه *

44.1 قال أبو جعفر واذا ابتاع رجل من رجل دارا بثياب سُمّى طولها وعرضها ورفعتها وحلول أجلها فإنّ أبا حنيفة وأبا يوسف ومحمّد بن الحسن كانوا يجيزون ذلك وإن لم يسمّ لها أجلا لم يجز ذلك البيع عندهم وقد خالفهم فى ذلك مخالف فقال لا يجوز البيع على ما ليس بعينه إلاّ أن يكون ممّا لم يحصره مكيال أو ميزان فيعرف بذلك مقدار كيله ومقدار وزنه فما كان ليس كذلك فلا يجوز البيع به ولا يتهيّأ فى هذا الكتاب اذ كان فيه من الاختلاف ممّا قد ذكرنا وانّما تُكتَب الكتب
(118a) احتياطا من الاختلاف فاذا لم // يقدر على ذلك فلا معنى لاكتتابها والله نسأله التوفيق *

44.2 قال أبو جعفر وقد كان أصحابنا يسمّون بيع الدار بالدار والعبد بالعبد والعرضين سوى ذلك كلّ واحد منهما بصاحبه مقايضة ويكتبون العهدة فى ذلك على ذكر المقايضة لا على ذكر البيع وقد أنكر ذلك عليهم منكر ودفع المقايضة أن يكون لها معنى فكان من حجّتنا لهم عليه فى ذلك أنّا قد وجدنا من كلام رسول الله عليه السلام فى العرض بالعرض المقايضة [1] وهو أنّ علي بن عبد الرحمن بن محمّد بن المغيرة قال حدّثنا عبد الله بن يوسف قال حدّثنا عيسى بن يونس ابن أبي اسحاق السبُيَعى قال حدّثنى أبى عن أبيه عن ذى الجَوْشَن الضبابى قال أتيت النبيّ عليه السلام بعد أن فرغ من أهل بدر بابن فرسى يقال لها القرحاء فقلتُ يا محمّد إنّى قد جئتك بابن القرحاء لتتّخذه قال لا حاجة لى فيه وإن أردت أن أقضيك منه المختارة من دروع بدر فقلتُ ما كنت أقضيه بغيره قال لا حاجة لى فيه فبهذا [2] رسول الله عليه السلام قد ذكر المقايضة وسمّى بيع الفرس بالدرع مقايضة * //

(118b) 44.3 فثبت بذلك استقامة ما ذهب اليه أصحابنا فى ذلك وصحّته وانتفاء الآجال غير أنّا كتبنا ما كتبنا فى هذا الباب من ذكر ما جرى فى ذلك على سبيل الشائع اذ كان من شَأْننا فى الشروط أن نقطع الاختلاف عنها ما قدرنا على ذلك وأن نمتثل فيها ما لا اختلاف فيه فكتبنا فى هذا مـــا كتبنا لإجماعهم عليه وتركنا ما سواه فيه وإن كان جائزا صحيحا مستقيما والله نسأله التوفيق والعون على ذلك برحمته [3] *

من كتاب الشروط والحمد لله على عونه وتوفيقه
وصلواته على سيدنا محمد النبي وآله وتسليمه
يتلوه فى الرابع باب الرجل يشترى الشىء لغيره

[1] MS بالمقايضة
[2] MS فهذا
[3] MS adds آخر الجزء الثالث من البيوع

باب الرجل يشترى الشيء لغيره

45.0 قال أبو جعفر واذا ابتاع رجل دارا لرجل بأمره فأراد أن يكتب فى ذلك كتابا كتبت هذا ما اشترى فلان بن فلان بن فلان الفلانى لفلان بن فلان بن فلان الفلانى بأمره من فلان بن فلان
(119 a) ابن فلان الفلانى اشترى له منه جميع الدار التى بمدينة كذا فى الموضع الكذا وهى الدار // التى يحيط بها ويجمعها ويشتمل عليها حدود أربعة أحد حدود جماعتها الحدّ الأوّل وهو كذا ينتهى الى كذا والثانى والثالث والرابع وفيه يشرع باب هذه الدار المحدودة فى هذا الكتاب اشترى فلان ابن فلان[1] الفلانى لفلان بن فلان الفلانى بأمره من فلان بن فلان الفلانى جميع هذه الدار المحدودة فى هذا الكتاب بحدودها كلّها وأرضها وبنائها ثمّ تنسق الكتاب على مثل ما كتبنا فى مثل ذلك على ما تقدّم فى كتابنا حتّى اذا أتيت على وكلّ حقّ هو لها خارج منها كتبت على أثر ذلك بكذا كذا دينارا مثاقيل ذهبا عينا وازنة جيادا شرى لا شرط فيه ولا عدة ودفع فلان بن فلان يعنى المشترى من مال فلان بن فلان يعنى الآمر الى فلان بن فلان جميع الثمن المسمّى فى هذا الكتاب وقبضه منه فلان بن فلان واستوفاه منه تامّا كاملا وأبرأه وأبرأ فلان بن فلان يعنى الآمر من جميعه بعد قبضه ايّاه واستيفائه له وهو كذا كذا دينارا مثاقيل ذهبا عينا وازنة جيادا وسلّم فلان بن فلان الى فلان بن فلان جميع ما وقع عليه هذا البيع المسمّى فى هذا الكتاب وقبضه منه
(119 b) فلان بن فلان وصار // فى يده[2] وقبضه بهذا الشرى المسمّى فى هذا الكتاب وبأمر فلان يعنى الآمر ايّاه بذلك واذنه له فيه وذلك بعد أن أقرّ فلان بن فلان وفلان بن فلان يعنى المتبايعين أنّهما قد رأيا جميعا جميع هذه الدار المحدودة فى هذا الكتاب فتذكر رؤيتهما لها مثل ما كتبنا فى ذلك ممّا قد تقدّم فى كتابنا هذا وتذكر مع ذلك تفرّقهما جميعا بأبدانهما بعد البيع عن تراض منهما به وإنفاذ منهما له ثمّ تكتب على أثر ذلك فما أدرك فـــلان بن فلان[3] فيما وقع عليه هذا البيع المسمّى فى هذا الكتاب وفى شيء منه من حقوقه من درك من أحد من الناس كلّهم فعلى فلان ابن فلان يعنى البائع تسليم ما يجب عليه فى ذلك من حقّ ويلزمه من سبب هذا البيع المسمّى فى هذا الكتاب حتّى يسلّم ذلك الى الذى يجب له قبضه منه بحقّ هذا البيع المسمّى فى هذا الكتاب من فلان بن فلان يعنى المشترى ومن فلان بن فلان يعنى الآمر بحقّ هذا البيع المسمّى فى هذا الكتاب على ما يوجبه له عليه هذا البيع المسمّى فى هذا الكتاب شهد على إقرار فلان بن فلان الفلانى يعنى البائع وفلان بن فلان الفلانى[4] يعنى المشترى بجميع ما سُمّى ووُصف فى هذا
(120 a) الكتاب ثمّ تنسق الشهادة // على مثل ما كتبناه فيها فيما قد تقدّم من كتابنا هذا *

45.0 bis قال أبو جعفر وإن أراد المشترى تقديم اسم الآمر فى كتاب الشرى قبل اسمه كتبتَ هذا ما

[1] MS adds بن فلان
[2] MS omits فى يده
[3] MS omits فلان بن فلان
[4] MS omits الفلانى

اشترى لفلان بن فلان الفلانى [1] بأمره فلان بن فلان الفلانى من فلان بن فلان الفلانى ثمّ تنسق الكتاب فى ذلك على مثل ما كتبناه *

45.1 قال أبو جعفر وقد اختُلف فى غير موضع من هذا الكتاب فكان أبو حنيفة وأبو يوسف ومحمّد ابن الحسن يكتبون فيه هذا ما اشترى فلان بن فلان لفلان بن فلان بأمره من فلان بن فلان ولا يذكرون المال وكان أبو زيد يكتب هذا ما اشترى فلان بن فلان لفلان بن فلان بماله وأمره فيزيد ذكر المال ويقدّمه على ذكر الأمر وكان غيرهم من أصحابنا يكتبون بأمره وماله فيقدّمون ذكر الأمر على ذكر المال *

45.2 فكان ما كتب أبو حنيفة وأبو يوسف ومحمّد بن الحسن فى ذلك أحبّ الينا ممّا كتب الآخرون لأنّ الشرى اذا وقع فانـّما يجب ثمنه للبائع على الوكيل لأنـّه هو الذى تولـّى الشرى منه فهو من مال الوكيل ويجب للوكيل مثله على الآمر هذا قول أبى حنيفة وزفر وأبى يوسف ومحمّد بن الحسن

(120 b) وأكثر أهل العلم فإذا كتبت أنّ الذى وقع به الشرى ووجب // للبائع على المبتاع هو من مال الآمر كان الشرى فى قول أبى حنيفة وزفر وأبى يوسف ومحمّد بن الحسن فاسدا *

45.3 وكان مخالفهم يقول الثمن واجب للبائع على المبتاع له فلم يضرّ الشرى فى قوله سكوتنا عن ذكر الثمن أنـّه من مال المشترى أو من مال المشترى له بل السكوت عن ذلك أولى حتّى إن رُفـع الكتاب [2] الى مَن يرى أنّ الثمن وجب على المبتاع له بحقّ البيع جعله على المبتاع له وإن رُفع الى مَن يرى أنّ الثمن كان وجب على المبتاع بحقّ ما تولّى من عقد البيع جعل الثمن عليه *

45.4 قال أبو جعفر وقد كان بعض أصحابنا يكتب ودفع فلان بن فلان يعنى الوكيل جميع الثمن المسمـّى فى هذا الكتاب من مال فلان بن فلان يعنى الآمر الى فلان بن فلان يعنى البائع وقبضه منه فلان بن فلان واستوفاه منه تامـّا كاملا وأبرأه من جميعه بعد قبضه ايـّاه واستيفائه له وهو كذا كذا دينارا مثاقيل ذهبا عينا وازنة جيادا *

45.5 وكذلك كان أبو زيد يكتب فى ذلك المال من الآمر [3] فى دفع الثمن على ما كتبنا وهو أحبّ الينا لما قد ذكرناه فى أوّل كتابنا هذا عن بعض الناس من أهل العلم أنـّهم كانوا يقولون إنّ مَن

(121 a) قبض مالا من مال رجل له عليه مثله دين بغير أمره // لم يملكه بذلك القبض ولم يبرأ الذى عليه الدين من الدين الذى عليه بذلك القبض حتّى يكون الذى عليه الدين هو الذى يتولّى دفعه الى الذى هو له عليه أو يأمره بقبضه من ماله *

45.6 ويتأوّلون فى ذلك ما قد رُوى عن رسول الله عليه السلام أنـّه قال أدِّ الى مَن ائتمنك ولا تَخُن مَن خانك فلذلك ذكرنا فى كتابنا هذا أنّ دفع المشترى الثمن الى البائع من مال الآمر كان بأمر

[1] MS omits الفلانى

[2] MS ان وقع الكتاب

[3] MS ذلك الأمر من الآمر

الآمر حذرا من هذا القول وإن كان عندنا ليس بشىء لأنّ معنى قول رسول الله عليه السلام أدِّ الى مَن ائتمنك ولا تَخُن مَن خانك انّا وجهه عندنا على أن يكون عشرة دراهم على رجل فقبض مكانها عن ماله أكثر منها فإذا فعل ذلك فقد خانه بتزيّده على ما له عليه فإذا قبض مقدار ما له عليه لم يخنه *

45.7 وقد رُوى عن رسول الله إباحة مثل هذا قالت عائشة رضى الله عنها جاءت أمّ معاوية الى رسول الله فقالت يا رسول الله إنّ أبا سفيان رجل شحيح وإنّه لا يعطينى ما يكفينى وبنتى فهل علىّ جناح إن آخذ من ماله وهو لا يعلم فقال رسول الله خُذِى ما يكفيك وبنتك بالمعروف *

45.8 وقال الشَعْبى عن المِقدام أبى كريمة الشامى قال قال رسول الله عليه السلام ليلة للضيف حقّ على كلّ مسلم أصبح بفنائه // دين له عليه صحّ إن شاء اقتضاه وإن شاء تركه * (121 b)

45.9 وقال يزيد عن أبى الخير عن عقبة بن عامر الجهنى قال قلنا يا رسول الله إنّك تبعثنا فننزل بقوم فلا يأمرون لنا بحقّ الضيف فقال رسول الله عليه السلام خذوا من أموالهم ففى هذه الآثار التى ذكرنا إباحة مَن له دين على رجل أن يأخذ من ماله مثله أباحه ذلك الذى له عليه الدين أو لم يبحه *

45.10 ألا ترى أنّ رسول الله عليه السلام قال لهند خُذِى ما يكفيك وبنتك بالمعروف إذ كان ذلك واجبا لها ولهم فى مال أبى سفيان ولم يأمرها بالوقوف عن ذلك الى دفع أبى سفيان ايّاه اليها وجعل ليلة الضيف فى حديث المِقدام دينا للضيف فى مال من أصبح بفنائه ثمّ جعل له فى حديث عقبة أخذه وإن كان الدين ذلك عليه أباحه أو لم يبحه ذلك من ماله وهذه آثار صحاح ثابت مجيئها فهى أولى من الخبر الأوّل ولا يثبت أهل العلم بالإسناد إسناده ولأنّه لو ثبت إسناده لم يخرج معناه عن معنى غيره ممّا قد رويناه فى هذا الباب *

45.11 ولكن التحرّز من أقوال العلماء فى الشروط أولى الأشياء بنا فلذلك كتبنا فى ذلك ما كتبنا وجعلنا للمأمور وللآمر من الثمن جميعا لأنّ قوما من العلماء يجعلون الثمن // للبائع على المشترى (122 a)
وإن كان المشترى اشترى لغيره منهم أبو حنيفة وزفر وأبو يوسف ومحمّد بن الحسن وقوم يجعلونه على المشترى له فوفّينا كلّ واحد من المشترى ومن المشترى له ما يجب له من البراءة بدفع الثمن فى قول جميع العلماء ولم ننتقص واحدا منهما براءة تجب له فى قول أحد من الفقهاء *

45.12 قال أبو جعفر وكان أبو زيد وغيره من أصحابنا لا يذكرون فى قبض المشترى الدار المبيعة من البائع أمر الآمر ايّاه بذلك وكان هذا عندنا خطأ لأنّ قوما يجعلون قبض الدار المبيعة فى هذا للآمر دون المأمور وقوم يجعلونه للمأمور دون الآمر منهم أبو حنيفة وزفر وأبو يوسف ومحمّد وكان المأمور إذا قبض الدار فى قول مَن يجعل قبضها للآمر بغير أمر الآمر متعدّيا ويوجبون عليه ردّها الى مَن يجب عليه ردّها اليه من البائع أو الآمر فكتبنا أمر الآمر المأمور بقبضها احتياطا للمأمور لا يلحقه تعدٍّ فى قبضها واحتياطا للبائع ليبرأ بتسليمها الى المأمور *

45.13 قال أبو جعفر وكان أبو زيد يكتب فى موضع الدرك من هذا الكتاب فما أدرك فلان بن فلان
(122b) يعنى الآمر من درك فيما ابتاع له فلان بن فلان ممّا سُمّى ووُصف فى // هذا الكتاب فعلى فلان بن فلان يعنى البائع تسليم ما يجب لكلّ واحد من فلان بن فلان يعنى الآمر ومن فلان بن فلان يعنى المأمور عليه فى ذلك من حقّ حتّى يسلّم ذلك له *

45.14 وكان غيره من أصحابنا يكتب فى ذلك فما أدرك فيما وقع عليه هذا البيع المسمّى فى هذا الكتاب وفى شىء منه ومن حقوقه من درك من أحد من الناس كلّهم فعلى فلان بن فلان يعنى البائع تسليم ما يجب عليه فى ذلك من حقّ ويلزمه بسبب هذا البيع المسمّى فى هذا الكتاب حتّى يسلّم ذلك الى الذى يجب له قبضه منه بحقّ هذا البيع المسمّى فى هذا الكتاب من فلان بن فلان يعنى المشترى ومن فلان بن فلان يعنى المشترى له على ما يوجبه له عليه هذا البيع المسمّى فى هذا الكتاب *

45.15 وكان أبو حنيفة وأبو يوسف يكتبان الدرك فى ذلك للمشترى دون المشترى له وكان محمّد ابن الحسن يكتب الدرك فى ذلك لهما جميعا فلمّا اختلفوا فى ذلك أردنا أن ننظر الى وجوب الدرك فى الحكم فى هذا البيع لمن هو فوجدنا أبا حنيفة وأبا يوسف وزفر ومحمّدا يقولون هو للمشترى دون
(123a) المشترى له ووجدنا آخرين من أهل العلم يقولون هو للمشترى له // دون المشترى فكُنّا إن جعلنا الدرك لواحد من المشترى أو من المشترى له بطل بذلك البيع فى قول من يجعل الدرك للآخر منهما وإن جعلنا الدرك لهما جميعا بطل البيع فى القولين جميعا لأنّه انّما يجب الدرك بكفالة المشترى دون المشترى له أو يجب بكفالة المشترى له دون المشترى فإذا كتبتَه لهما جميعا فقد جُعل بعضه لمن لا يجب له وصار ذلك شرطا فى البيع فأبطل البيع فى قول من يبطل البيع بالشروط التى ليست منه إذا اشتُرِط فيه فكان أصحّ ما كُتب فى هذا عندنا ما اخترناه ممّا قد كتبه المقدّمون قبلنا ممّا قد ذكرناه عنهم فى هذا الكتاب لأنّه متى رُفع هذا الكتاب الى من يجعل الدرك بحقّ ذلك البيع للمشترى جعل الذى يجب له الدرك المذكور فى ذلك الكتاب هو المشترى ومتى رُفع ذلك الى من يجعله للمشترى له جعل الذى يجب له هو المشترى له وزدنا فى شرى ذلك فكتبنا فى كتابنا فيه فجُعل لفلان[1] بن فلان تسليم ما يجب عليه فى ذلك من حقّ ويلزمه بسبب هذا البيع المسمّى
(123b) فى هذا الكتاب // حتّى يسلّم ذلك الى الذى يجب له قبضه منه من فلان بن فلان يعنى المشترى ومن فلان بن فلان يعنى المشترى له على ما يوجبه له عليه هذا البيع المسمّى فى هذا الكتاب *

46.0 قال أبو جعفر وإن أحببت أن تزيد فى كتابك هـذا وكالة المشترى للآمر المشترى له فى المطالبة بحقوق البيع ليجب للمشترى له المطالبة بذلك فى حياة الموكّل وبعد وفاته[2] وفى غيبته فى قول من يجعل حقوق البيع للمشترى على البائع دون المشترى له كتبت الكتاب على ما كتبنا حتّى اذا انتهيت الى آخر الدرك كتبت بعقب ذلك قبل الشهادة وقد جعل فلان بن فلان يعنى

[1] MS فجعل فلان

[2] MS فى حياة الوكيل بعد وفاته

المشترى الى فلان بن فلان يعنى المشترى له جميع ما اليه وجميع ما يجب له بحقّ هذا البيع المسمّى
فى هذا الكتاب والخصومة والمنازعة الى القضاة والحكّام والسلطان وإثبات حججه فى ذلك وأخذ
اليمين التى تجب له فيه وإقامة البيّنة التى تُشهَد له عليه وحبس مَن يجب له حبسه بحقّ هذا
البيع المسمّى فى هذا الكتاب كلّما رأى وإطلاقه من بعد حبسه كلّما رأى وقبض جميع ما اليه
وجميع ما يجب له قبضه بحقّ هذا البيع المسمّى فى هذا الكتاب وجعله وكيله فى جميع ما جعله
(124 a) اليه // وممّا سُمّى ووُصف فى هذا الكتاب فى حياته ووصيّه فى ذلك خاصّة بعد وفاته وأقامه
فى جميع ما جعله اليه ممّا سُمّى ووُصف فى هذا الكتاب فى حياته وبعد وفاته مقامَ نفسه فى حياته
على أنّ لفلان بن فلان يعنى المشترى له أن يتولّى ذلك بنفسه فى حياته ويولّيه وما شاء منه فى
حياته وبعد وفاته مَن بدا له من الوكلاء والأوصياء ويستبدل من الوكلاء والأوصياء ما أحبّ ورأى
كلّما أحبّ ورأى جائز أمره فى ذلك وعلى أنّ فلان بن فلان يعنى المشترى كلّما فسخ شيئا
من هذه الوكالة ومن هذه الوصاية المسمّاتين فى هذا الكتاب فذلك الى فلان بن فلان يعنى المشترى
له وبيده عند فسخ فلان بن فلان يعنى المشترى ذلك وبعد فسخه كما كان اليه قبل ذلك حتّى يستوفى
فلان بن فلان يعنى المشترى له جميع ما له وجميع ما يجب له من حقّ بحقّ البيع والإقرار والوكالة
والوصاية المسمّى جميع ذلك فى هذا الكتاب فقبل فلان بن فلان يعنى الآمر من فلان بن فلان
يعنى المشترى جميع الإقرار والوكالة والوصاية المسمّى جميع ذلك فى هذا الكتاب بمخاطبة منه
(124 b) ايّاه على جميع ذلك وجميع ما فى هذا // الكتاب من وكالة ووصاية فعلى غير شرط كان فى
عقدة هذا البيع المسمّى فى هذا الكتاب شهد على إقرار فلان بن فلان[1] يعنى البائع وفلان بن فلان
يعنى المشترى بجميع ما سُمّى ووُصف فى هذا الكتاب ثمّ تنسق الشهادة فى ذلك على مثل ما
كتبناها فى مثله ممّا قد تقدّم فى كتابنا هذا حتّى اذا أتيت على ذكر معرفة البائع والمشترى كتبت
بعقب ذلك وعلى معرفتهم فلان بن فلان بن فلان الفلانى المسمّى فى هذا الكتاب يعنى الآمر
المشترى له بعينه واسمه ونسبه وذلك فى شهر كذا من سنة كذا *

46.1 قال أبو جعفر وقد كان اسمعيل بن حمّاد بن أبى حنيفة يكتب فى ذلك نحو ممّا كتبنا بألفاظ
أقلّ من هذه الألفاظ وكان أبو زيد يكتب شيئا من ذلك يوكّده هذا التوكيد غير أنّهما جميعا
لم يكونا يكتبان ذكر معرفة المشترى له بعينه واسمه ونسبه فكتبنا ما كتبنا على ما وصفنا احتياطا
من اختلاف أهل العلم وكتبنا معرفة الشهود بالآمر المشترى له بعينه واسمه ونسبه ليكون ذلك حجّة
على المشترى إن حجره يوما وليكون ذلك حجّة له فى تثبيت وكالة المشترى ايّاه بما وكّله به وفى
تثبيت وصايته بما أوصى به اليه *

46.2 وقد كان بعض أصحابنا يمتثل فى ذلك // نحو ممّا كتبنا غير أنّه لا يكتب وكلّما فسخ فلان
(125 a) ابن فلان شيئا من هذه الوكالة ومن هذه الوصاية على ما كتبنا فى ذلك فكان ما كتبنا فى ذلك

[1] MS adds بن فلان

أحبّ الينا لأنّ أصحابنا قد اختلفوا فى فسخ المأمور هذه الوكالة وفى إخراج الأمر عنها بعد عقده ايّاها على نفسه للآمر فذكر محمّد بن سماعة عن محمّد بن الحسن أنّه قال فى ذلك هى كسائر الوكالات وللمأمور أن يعزل الأمر عنها متى أحبّ قال وكذلك الوصاية فى ذلك من المأمور الى الآمر فللمأمور أن يخرج الأمر عنها متى أحبّ *

46.3 قال أبو جعفر وقال محمّد بن الحسن مرة أخرى ليس للمأمور أن يعزل الأمر عنها جميعا لأنّه وكّله بما وجب عليه توكيله به وبما لو أبى المأمور أن يفعله أخذ بأن يفعله وأخبر على ذلك فى الوكالة والوصاية قال وانّما يكون للموكّل عزل ما وكّله فيما وكّله به بنفسه ويكون للموصى عزل الوصىّ عمّا أوصى به اليه فيما أوصى به اليه لنفسه وفيما على نفسه من وكالة ووصاية هو مأخوذ بها فليس له أن يعزله عنها *

46.4 وهذا هو أصحّ القولين عندنا وأولاهما بمذهب محمّد بن الحسن ولكنّا كتبنا فى الوكالة وفى
(125 b) الوصاية ما كتبنا // احتياطا من الاختلاف الذى ذكرناه فى ذلك وانّما ذكرنا أنّ للآمر أن يتولّى ذلك بنفسه وأن يولّيه فى حياته وبعد وفاته منَ بدا له الوكلاء والأوصياء ليتّسع له ما جعل اليه من ذلك ولأنّ مَن جعله فى ذلك كالوكيل للمأمور لم يكن له فى قوله أن يتعدّى ما جعله اليه المأمور من ذلك ولا يفوّضه الى غيره وينبغى لمن كتب هذا الكتاب أن يبيّن للمأمور ما يلزمه فى توصيته الأمر بذلك وما بين الناس فيه من الاختلاف إن آثر أن يفعل ذلك فإنّ أبا حنيفة كان يقول مَن أوصى لرجل بشىء خاصّ بعد وفاته كان وصيّا فى سائر أموره فى ماله وفى حقّ ما كان يتولّاه لغيره بسبب وصاية كانت منه اليه اذا كان قد توفّى قبله وخالفه فى ذلك أبو يوسف ومحمّد فقالا هو وصىّ فيما أوصى اليه به خاصّة دون ما سواه *

46.5 قال أبو جعفر والصحيح عندنا من القولين فى هذا هو قول أبى يوسف ومحمّد غير أنّا لا نأمن أن يختار غيرنا ما ذهب اليه أبو حنيفة فيدخل المأمور بوصيّته الى الأمر بما أوصى اليه به فيما لا
(126 a) يجب ويجعله وصيّا فى مال المأمور // ولعلّه لا يكون لذلك عنده موضع فأحوط الأشياء أن يبيّن الكاتب للمأمور عند سؤاله ايّاه اكتتاب الوصيّة للآمر ما يخاف عليه فى ذلك ممّا قد رويناه عن أبى حنيفة *

46.6 قال أبو جعفر وقد كان يوسف بن خالد لا يذكر الوكالة فى كتابه هذا ويجعل مكانها جراية ويختار هذا اللفظ على الوكالة وكان أبو حنيفة وأبو يوسف ومحمّد وأبو زيد يختارون فى كتبهم الوكالة على الجراية وهذا المذهب أحبّ الينا وايّاه نختار لأنّ القرآن قد جاء به قال الله عزّ وجلّ (وَتَوَكَّلْ عَلَى الحَيِّ الذى لا يَمُوتُ) و (قَالُوا حَسْبُنَا اللهُ وَنِعْمَ الوَكِيلُ) وجرت بذلك ألفاظ رسول الله عليه السلام عند سؤال عُكاشة بن مِحْصَن[1] ايّاه عن قوم وصفهم وذكر دخولهم الجنّة فقال مَن هم يا رسول الله قال له رسول الله هم الذين لا يَكْتَوون[2] ولا يسترقون ولا يتطيّرون وعلى ربّهم يتوكّلون وجرت به ألفاظ أصحاب رسول الله قال عبد الله بن

[1] MS عكاشة بن حصن

[2] MS الذى لا يكتبون

جعفر كان عليّ بن أبي طالب لا يحضر خصومة أبدا ويقول أنّ لها قُحَم وأنّ الشيطان يحضرها
(126b) وكان يقول عقيل // ابن أبي طالب وكيلي فما قُضي له من شيء فلي فما قُضي عليه فعليّ فلمّا كبر عقيل قال عبد الله بن جعفر وكيلي فما قُضي له من شيء فلي وما قُضي عليه فعليّ وقالت فاطمة ابنة قيس طلقني زوجي طلاقا باتّا ثمّ خرج نحو اليمن ووكّل عياش بن أبي ربيعة بنفقتي ثمّ ذكرت الحديث *

46.7 وهؤلاء هم الفصحاء الذين تُؤخَذ عنهم اللغة ويُرجَع فيها اليهم والوكالة أعمّ وأشهر وأظهر معنى من الجراية وكلّ مَن فهم معنى الجراية فهم معنى الوكالة وليس كلّ مَن فهم معنى الوكالة فهم معنى الجراية فما قرب من أفهام الناس أولى أن يُستعمَل فى الكتب ممّا بعد وكان أبو حنيفة وأبو يوسف ومحمّد فيما حدّثني سليمان بن شعيب عن أبيه يقولون فيمن قال فلان جريّي إنّ معنى ذلك معنى وكيلي ويختارون فى كتبهم مثل الذى اخترناه *

46.8 قال أبو جعفر وينبغي أن تكتب الشهادة فى آخر هذا الكتاب على إقرار البائع والمشترى والمشترى له إن كان المشترى له حاضرا لأنّ البائع قد أقرّ بقبض الثمن من مال الآمر وأقرّ المشترى
(127a) بدفعه ايّاه اليه من مال الآمر أيضا فإن // لم يقرّ الآمر بوجوب ذلك له كان له أن يأخذ كلّ واحد من البائع ومن المشترى بردّ الثمن عليه إذ كان يقول أنّه قبضه بغير أمره فيعظم بينهما فى ذلك ويطول أمرهما ويأثم تارك الاحتياط لهما فيما كان صار اليه من أمرهما *

47.0 فإن كان المشترى له غائبا كان الأحوط فى ذلك أن تكتب هذا ما اشترى فلان بن فلان لفلان بن فلان بأمره ثمّ تنسق الكتاب على مثل ما كتبنا غير أنّك تكتب [1] أنّ الثمن الذى قبضه البائع من مال الآمر ولكنّك تكتبه على مثل ما تكتبه فى الشرى لو كان المشترى اشترى المبيع لنفسه ثمّ تنسق بقيّة الكتاب على ما كتبنا والشهادة فى آخره على ما وصفنا حتّى اذا أتيت على التاريخ كتبت وأشهد فلان بن فلان المسمّى فى هذا الكتاب يعنى المشترى خاصّة سائر الشهود المسمّين فى هذا الكتاب بعد أن غاب فلان بن فلان يعنى البائع عن المجلس الذى أقرّ فيه بما شهد به عليه الشهود المسمّون فى هذا الكتاب أنّ جميع الثمن الذى دفعه الى فلان بن فلان
(127b) المسمّى فى هذا الكتاب وهو كذا كذا دينارا // مثاقيل ذهبا عينا وازنة جيادا من مال فلان بن فلان يعنى الآمر وأنّه لا حقّ له قِبل فلان بن فلان يعنى الآمر فى ثمن هذه الدار التى ابتاعها له المحدودة فى هذا الكتاب ولا فى شيء من هذه الدار المحدودة فى هذا الكتاب ولا فى أرضها ولا فى بنائها ولا فيما سوى ذلك منها ولا دعوى له فيها ولا طلبة قليل ولا كثير قديم ولا حديث على الوجوه والأسباب كلّها وذلك بأمر حقّ واجب لازم عرفه فلان بن فلان يعنى المشترى لفلان ابن فلان يعنى الآمر ولزمه الإقرار له به شهد على إقرار فلان بن فلان يعنى المأمور بهذا الإقرار المذكور فى هذا الكتاب بعد الشرى المسمّى فى هذا الكتاب بعد أن قُرئ عليه ثمّ تنسق الشهادة

[1] MS omits تكتب

فى ذلك على ما كتبنا فيكتب الشهود شهاداتهم على إقرار كل واحد من فلان بن فلان يعنون
البائع ومن فلان بن فلان يعنون الوكيل بما ذُكر من إقرار كلّ واحد منهما على ما أقرّ به فى هذا
الكتاب وإن شئتَ أجريتَ الكتاب فى ذلك على نحو ما كتبنا أوّلا وذكرت فيه أنّ الثمن الذى
(128 a) دفعه المشترى الى البائع من // مال الآمر فأذا أتيت على موضع الشهادة نسقتها على ما كتبنا
حتّى اذا فرغت منها كتبت قبل التاريخ غير ما فى هذا الكتاب ممّا ذُكر فيه من دفع فلان
ابن فلان يعنى المشترى الى فلان بن فلان يعنى البائع من مال فلان بن فلان يعنى الآمر جميع
الثمن المسمّى فى هذا الكتاب فإنّ فلان بن فلان يعنى البائع لم يقرّ أنّ ذلك الثمن الذى قبضه
من مال فلان بن فلان يعنى الآمر ثم تكتب وكتب الشهود المسمّون فى هذا الكتاب شهاداتهم
بخطوطهم على جميع ما سُمّى ووُصف فى هذا الكتاب فى شهر كذا من سنة كذا *

47.1 قال أبو جعفر وينبغى أيضا أن يعلم الوكيل أنّه غير مأمون عليه إنكار الآمر أن يكون أمره
بالشرى وأنّه يجب له عند ذلك أن يضمّنه ما أقرّ أنّه دفعه من ماله ويسلّم الدار اليه ولا يؤمَن
عليه أيضا من قِبله ما هو أغلظ من هذا وهو أن يقول أمّا الدار فلى ليس بابتياعك ايّاها بأمرى
ولكن بملكى لها قبل ذلك فلا يكون للمشترى أخذ الدار منه ويكون للمشترى له أخذ الثمن من
(128 b) المشترى وتضمينه ايّاه فينبغى أن يُنبَّه على هذا الموضوع // ليحتاط لنفسه بما يؤمنه العاقبة فى ذلك *

47.2 قال وكان بعض أصحابنا يكتب فى هذا الكتاب ولا دعوى له فيها ولا طلبة على كلّ وجه
وسبب وكان أبو زيد يكتب على وجه من الوجوه ولا سبب من الأسباب وكان يوسف بن خالد
يكتب على الوجوه والأسباب كلّها فهذا عندنا أحسن وأجمع وايّاه اخترنا فى كتبنا كلّها التى
ذكرناه فيها وذلك أنّه اذا كتبت على كلّ وجه وسبب احتمل أن يكون كلّ لم تقع على كلّ
الوجوه ولا على كلّ الأسباب وانّما وقعت على سبب واحد وعلى وجه واحد كما قد كان أبو
حنيفة يقول فى مثل هذا فى رجل ابتاع من رجل كلّ قفيز من هذا الطعام بدرهم إنّ ذلك البيع
انّما وقع على قفيز واحد واذا كتبنا على ما كتب الآخرون ممّا ذكرناه عنهم وهو على كلّ وجه من
الوجوه وسبب من الأسباب كان ذلك أقرب الى أن يكون على وجه واحد وعلى سبب واحد من
قولنا على كلّ وجه وسبب فكرهنا هذين المعنيين للنقص الذى فى أحدهما ولاحتمال الآخر أن
(129 a) يكون ذلك النقص فيــه أيضا // واخترنا ما هو أجمع منهما وهو ما كتبنا على الوجوه والأسباب
كلّها وكذلك كان هلال بن يحيى يكتب فإن كرهت ذلك خوفا أن يتأوّل متأوّل قولك على
الوجوه والأسباب كلّها على ما جمع الوجوه والأسباب كلّها لا على ما يفرد ببعضها دون بعض
وإن كان هذا فى اللغة بعيدا وفى الأوهام معه وما كتب على وجه من الوجوه وعلى سبب من الأسباب
وعلى الوجوه والأسباب كلّها فيكون ذلك نفيا لما خفته من ذلك والله نسأله التوفيق *

آخر الجزء الثالث والحمد لله على نصره وإحسانه
يتلوه فى الرابع باب الرجل يشترى الدار باسمه
ثمّ يقرّ بعد ذلك أنّه اشتراها لغيره بأمره *

الجزءُ الرّابع مِن كتاب البُيوع

مِن

الشّروط الكبير

تأليف أبي جعفر أحمد بن محمد بن سلامة الأزدى الطحاوى

ومعه كتاب الشفع والإجارات

(130b) بسم الله الرحمن الرحيم

باب الرجل يشترى الدار باسمه ثمّ يقرّ بعد ذلك أنّه اشتراها لغيره بأمره

1.0 قال أبو جعفر واذا اشترى رجل من رجل دارا وقبضها ودفع ثمنها ثمّ أقرّ بعد ذلك أنّه ابتاعها لغيره بأمره فأراد أن يقرّ له بذلك فى ظهر كتاب العهدة الذى كان اكتتبها باسمه على البائع ويقرّ فيما يكتب من ذلك أنّه ابتاعها لهذا المقرّ له بأمره كتبت هذا ما شهد عليه الشهود المسمّون فى هذا الكتاب شهدوا جميعا أنّ فلان بن فلان الفلانى المسمّى فى بطن هذا الكتاب وقد أثبتوه وعرفوه معرفة صحيحة بعينه واسمه ونسبه أقرّ عندهم وأشهدهم على نفسه فى صحّة عقله وبدنه وجواز أمره وذلك فى شهر كذا من سنة كذا أنّه ابتاع لفلان بن فلان بن فلان الفلانى بأمره جميع ما وقع عليه هذا البيع المسمّى فى هذا الكتاب وأنّه دفع جميع الثمن المذكور فى بطن هذا الكتاب الى بائعه المسمّى فى بطن هذا الكتاب من مال فلان بن فلان بأمره وأنّه قبض جميع ما وقع عليه هذا البيع المسمّى فى هذا الكتاب من بائعه المسمّى فى بطن هذا الكتاب لفلان بن فلان بأمره وأنّ اسمه كان فيما تولّى من ذلك لفلان بن فلان الفلانى عاريّة منه له ومعونة وأنّه لا حقّ له فيما وقع
(131 a) عليه هذا // البيع المسمّى فى بطن هذا الكتاب ولا دعوى له فيه ولا طلبة على الوجوه والأسباب كلّها وأنّه لا حقّ له قِبل فلان بن فلان يعنى الآمر فى شىء من الثمن المسمّى فى بطن هذا الكتاب ولا عليه ولا عنده ولا بيده على الوجوه والأسباب كلّها وأنّ جميع ما أقرّ به لفلان بن فلان ممّا سُمّى ووُصف فى ظهر هذا الكتاب بأمر حقّ واجب لازم عرفه لفلان بن فلان ولزمه الإقرار له به وأنّه قد سلّم الى فلان بن فلان يعنى المقرّ له جميع ما ابتاعه له ممّا سُمّى ووُصف وحُدّ فى بطن هذا الكتاب وقبضه منه فلان بن فلان وصار فى يده وقبضه على هيئته التى كان قبضه له عليها فلان بن فلان من بائعه المسمّى فى بطن هذا الكتاب وأنّه قد ضمن لفلان بن فلان يعنى المقرّ له جميع الذى يدركه فيما ابتاعه له ممّا سُمّى ووُصف فى بطن هذا الكتاب من قبله وبسببه بسبب إقرار وإشهاد وتلجئة وتمليك وحدث وحيلة إن كان احتالها فى ذلك أو احتيلت له بأمره يريد بذلك إبطال شىء ممّا أقرّ به لفلان بن فلان المسمّى [1] فى ظهر هذا الكتاب ولا براءة له إن أدرك فلان بن فلان فى ذلك درك من قبله وبسببه حتّى يخلّصه وجميع الذى يدركه فى ذلك من قبله وبسببه أو يردّ عليه جميع الذى يجب له عليه ردّه ويلزمه له بحقّ الدرك والضمان

1 MS omits المسمى

المسمّيين فى هذا الكتاب وأنّه قد جعل الى فلان بن فلان يعنى الآمر جميع الذى اليه وجميع الذى
(131 b) يجب له من حقّ بسبب البيع المسمّى فى هذا الكتاب // والخصومة والمنازعة فى ذلك الى القضاة والحكّام والسلطان وإثبات حججه فى ذلك وإقامة البيّنة التى تُشهَد له على ذلك وحبس كلّ من وجب حبسه بسبب شىء من ذلك كلّما رأى وإطلاقه من بعد حبسه ايّاه كلّما رأى وقبض جميع الذى اليه وجميع الذى يجب له قبضه بحقّ البيع المسمّى فى بطن هذا الكتاب وجعله وصيّه فى ذلك خاصّة بعد وفاته وأقامه فى جميع ما جعله اليه ممّا سُمّى ووُصف فى ظهر هذا الكتاب فى حياته وبعد وفاته مقـــام نفسه فى حياته على أنّ لفلان بن فلان يعنى المقرّ له أن يتولّى ذلك بنفسه فى حياته ويولّيه فى حياته وبعد وفاته مَن بدا له من الوكلاء والأوصياء ويستبدل من الوكلاء والأوصياء مَن أحبّ ورأى كلّما أحبّ ورأى جائزة أموره فى ذلك وعلى أنّ فلان بن فلان يعنى المقرّ كلّما فسخ شيئا من هذه الوكالة ومن هذه الوصاية المسمّاتين فى هذا الكتاب فذلك الى فلان بن فلان يعنى المقرّ له وبيده عند فسخ فلان بن فلان يعنى المقرّ ذلك وبعد فسخه كما كان اليه قبل ذلك حتّى يستوفى فلان بن فلان يعنى الآمر جميع الذى له وجميع الذى يجب له من حقّ بحقّ البيع والإقرار والضمان والوكالة والوصاية المسمّى جميع ذلك فى هذا الكتاب وحضر فلان بن فلان يعنى المقرّ له قراءة هذا الكتاب فعرفه وأقرّ أنّ جميع ما فيه حقّ على ما سُمّى
(132 a) ووُصف // وقبل من فلان بن فلان يعنى المقرّ جميع الإقرار والضمان والوكالة والوصاية المسمّى جميع ذلك فى ظهر هذا الكتاب بمخاطبة منه ايّاه على جميع ذلك وأقرّ فلان بن فلان أيضا يعنى المقرّ له أنّه قد قبض من فلان بن فلان يعنى المقرّ جميع ما ابتاعه له ممّا سُمّى ووُصف وحُدّ فى بطن هذا الكتاب هيئته التى كان فلان بن فلان يعنى المقرّ قبضه له عليها من بائعه المسمّى فى هذا الكتاب شهد على إقرار فلان بن فلان الفلانى[1] يعنى المقرّ وفلان بن فلان الفلانى يعنى المقرّ له بجميع ما سُمّى ووُصف فى ظهر هـــذا الكتاب وبجميع ما سُمّى ووُصف فى بطنه بعد أن قُرئ عليهما جميعا جميع ما فيهما فأقرّا أن قد فهماهما وعرفا جميع ما فيهما حرفا حرفا فى صحّة عقولهما وأبدانهما وجواز أمورهما طائعين غير مكرهين وعلى معرفتهما بأعيانهما وأسمائهما وأنسابهما وذلك فى شهر كذا من سنة كذا *

2.0 قال أبو جعفر وإن لم يرد المقرّ أن يكتب الإقرار فى ظهر العهدة التى كان اكتتبها على البائع باسمه ولكنّه أراد أن يكتب كتابا بدفعه الى المقرّ له يكون ثقة فى يده ويحتبس الكتاب عنده إذ كانت الصحيفة له كتبت هذا مـــا شهد عليه الشهود المسمّون فى هذا الكتاب شهدوا جميعا
(132 b) أنّ فلان بن فلان بن فلان الفلانى // وقد أثبتوه وعرفوه معرفة صحيحة بعينه واسمه ونسبه أقرّ عندهم وأشهدهم على نفسه فى صحّة عقله وبدنه وجواز أمره وذلك فى شهر كذا من سنة كذا أنّه كان

[1] MS omits الفلانى

ابتاع من فلان بن فلان الفلانى فى شهر كذا من سنة كذا جميع الدار التى بمدينة كذا فى الموضع الكذا منها واكتتب عليه بابتياعه ايّاها منه كتاب شرى نسخته بسم الله الرحمن الرحيم فتنسخ الكتاب كلّه ثمّ تكتب ومن شهوده المسمّين فيه فلان بن فلان وفلان بن فلان وفلان بن فلان حتّى تسمّى الشهود كلّهم أو مَن شئتَ منهم ثمّ تكتب على أثر ذلك أقرّ فلان بن فلان يعنى المقرّ أنّه ابتاع جميع هذه الدار المحدودة فى هذا الكتاب وفى الكتاب المنسوخ فى هذا الكتاب بحدودها كلّها وبجميع حقوقها المسمّى جميع ذلك لها فى هذا الكتاب المنسوخ فى هذا الكتاب لفلان ابن فلان بن فلان الفلانى يعنى المقرّ له وأنّه قد دفع جميع ثمنها المسمّى فى هذا الكتاب وفى الكتاب المنسوخ فى هذا الكتاب الى بائعه المسمّى فى هذا الكتاب وفى الكتاب المنسوخ فى هذا الكتاب من مال فلان بن فلان يعنى المقرّ له بأمره وأنّه قد قبض جميع ما وقع عليه هذا البيع المسمّى فى هذا الكتاب وفى الكتاب المنسوخ فى هذا الكتاب لفلان بن فلان يعنى المقرّ له بأمره وأنّ اسمه كان
(133 a) فيما تولّى من ذلك لفلان بن فلان عاريّة منه له // ومعونة ثمّ تنسق بعقب ذلك جميع ما كتبناه فى الكتاب الأوّل الذى ذكرناه فى هذا الباب حتّى إذا أتيت على آخر الدرك كتبت على أثر ذلك وشهد فلان بن فلان بن فلان الفلانى ويكنى أبا فلان وفلان بن فلان بن فلان الفلانى ويكنى أبا فلان حتّى تسمّى الشهود الذين كانوا شهدوا على البائع بإقراره بالبيـــع المذكور[1] فى العهدة المنسوخة فى هذا الكتاب أنّهم يعرفون فلان بن فلان بن فلان الفلانى الرجل المسمّى فى هذا الكتاب وفى الكتاب المنسوخ فى هذا الكتاب يعنى البائع بعينه واسمه ونسبه معرفة صحيحة وأنّه أقرّ عندهم وأشهدهم على نفسه فى صحّة عقله وبدنه وجواز أمره فى شهر كذا من سنة كذا لفلان ابن فلان بن فلان الفلانى الرجل المسمّى فى هذا الكتاب وفى الكتاب المنسوخ فى هذا الكتاب يعنى المشترى بجميع ما فى الكتاب المنسوخ فى هذا الكتاب بعد أن قُرِئَ عليه بمحضرهم فأقرّ لهم أنّه قد فهمه وعرف جميع ما فيه حرفا حرفا وهو يوم أقرّ بذلك عندهم صحيح العقل والبدن جائز الأمر وأشهدوا على شهاداتهم على جميع ذلك الشهود المسمّين معهم فى هذا الكتاب أنّهم يشهدون على إقرار فلان بن فلان بن فلان الفلانى يعنى البائع بجميع ما ذُكر من شهادتهم به على إقراره فى هذا الكتاب وشهدوا هم وسائر الشهود المسمّين معهم فى هذا الكتاب على إقرار فلان بن فلان الفلانى يعنى المقرّ له بجميع ما سُمّى ووُصف فى هذا الكتاب ثمّ تنسق بقيّة الكتاب على ما كتبنا فى مثله ممّا قد تقدّم فى كتابنا هذا *

1.1 (133 b) قال أبو جعفر // وقد كان بعض أصحابنا يكتب فى الكتاب المنسوخ فى ظهر كتاب العهدة الذى بدأنا بذكره فى هذا الباب أنّ جميع الدار المحدودة فى بطن هذا الكتاب لفلان بن فلان يعنى المقرّ له ففى يده وملكه ملكا صحيحا وحقّا واجبا وأنّه كان ابتاعها له بأمره وماله من فلان بن فلان

[1] MS المذكورة

يعنى البائع فكرهنا نحن ذلك ورأينا أنّ تركه أصلح لأنّ المقرّ إذا زعم أنّ المقرّ له قد ملك الدار المبيعة بحقّ ابتياعه ايّاها له ممّن باعه ايّاها كان فى ذلك ما يوجب جواز بيع البائع بإقراره وفى ذلك ما يمنعه من الرجوع بالثمن عليه إن استُحِقّت الدار فى يده فى قول ابن أبى ليلى وزفر وأهل المدينة على ما قد ذكرناه عنهم فيما تقدّم من كتابنا هذا *

1.2 وقد كان بعض أصحابنا يكتب فى ذلك مكان معرفة صحيحة معرفة قديمة فكرهنا ذلك للاختلاف فى مقدار القدم ألا ترى أنّ رجلا لو قال كلّ عبد لى قديم فهو حرّ إنّ الناس قد اختلفوا فى ذلك فكان بعضهم يقول كلّ عبد له قد أتى عليه فى ملكه شهر فهو قديم وكلّ عبد له لم يأت عليه فى ملكه شهر فليس بقديم وقد رُوى هذا القول عن أبى يوسف وقال بعضهم كلّ عبد له فى ملكه ستة أشهر أو أكثر من ذلك فهو قديم وكلّ عبد له فى ملكه أقلّ من ستة أشهر فليس بقديم وقد رُوى هذا القول أيضا عن أبى يوسف ورُوى عنه أنّه احتجّ فى ذلك بقول الله جلّ وعزّ (وَالقَمَرَ قَدَّرْنَاهُ مَنَازِلَ حَتَّى عَادَ كَالعُرْجُونِ القَدِيمِ) فرُوى عنه أنّه قال القدم //

(134 a) فى هذا أيضا وقع على العرجون وهو ما أتى عليه ستة أشهر ولقد حدّثنا سليمان بن شعيب عن أبيه قال سمعتُ محمّد بن الحسن وسأله رجل قال كلّ عبد لى قديم فهو حرّ فقال محمّد بن الحسن ما أدرى ما هذا أقديم فى الملك أو قديم فى السنّ أو قديم فى كذا وأشكل ذلك عليه حتّى لم يقطع فيه بمعنى *

1.3 فإذا كان ما ذكرنا كذلك لم ينبغِ أن يكلّف الشاهد أن يشهد أنّه يعرف فلان بن فلان معرفة قديمة لأنّه قد يجوز أن يعرفه منذ مدّة قد يقع عليها اسم القدم وقد يجوز أن يعرفه منذ مدّة لا يقع عليها اسم القدم فيكون قد كلّف ما لا يجب عليه أو ما عسى أن يكون اذا شهد به شهد على ما لا علم له به أو على ما هو فى الحقيقة على خلاف ذلك وقد دفع الله عزّ وجلّ ذلك عنه وأباح له الشهادة بغيره ووافقه المسلمون على ذلك وأجمعوا له عليه *

1.4 ألا ترى أنّ رجلا لو حضر رجلا لم يره قطّ ولم يعرف له اسما ولا نسبا وحضر معه جماعة يعرفهم ويرجع الى قبول قولهم فعرّفوه هذا الرجل الذى حضر بعينه واسمه ونسبه ووقع فى قلبه تصديقهم ولم يتّهم شيئا ممّا كان منهم انّه واسع له أن يشهد على معرفة الرجل الذى عرّفوه ايّاه بعينه واسمه ونسبه حضر أو غاب أو مات أولا ترى أنّه إن لم يعرّفه ايّاه قوم بأعيانهم ولكن جاءت الأخبار متواترة أنّ هذا فلان بن فلان ولم يره قبل ذلك إنّه يسعه أن يشهد على أنّه فلان بن فلان لأنّه قد علم ذلك // وقد قال الله عزّ وجلّ (إِلاَّ مَنْ شَهِدَ بِالحَقِّ وَهُمْ يَعْلَمُونَ) فهذا (134 b)

ممّن قد علم ما قد وقف عليه ممّا ذكرناه وحان له أن يشهد به ولا اختلاف علمنا بين أهل العلم فى ذلك ولا قدم معه فى المعرفة فما حاجتنا أن نكتب ما يحمل فيه الشاهد على ما لا يسعه *

باب الرجل يشترى لابنه الصغير دارا أو غيرها

3.0 قال أبو جعفر واذا اشترى الرجل دارا لابنه وهو صغير فى حجره ودفع ثمنها من مال كان لابنه فى يده فأراد أن يكتب بذلك كتاباً كتبت هذا ما اشترى فلان بن فلان الفلانى لابنه فلان بن فلان الفلانى بحقّ ولايته عليه لأنّه طفل صغير فى حجره ولمّا رأى له فيما ابتاعه له من ذلك من حسن النظر والحياطة له فيه والتوفير عليه من فلان بن فلان بن فلان الفلانى اشترى له منه جميع الدار ثمّ تنسق الكتاب فى ذلك على مثل ما كتبناه فيما تقدّم من كتابنا هذا حتّى اذا أتيت على ذكر باب الدار المبيعة كتبت اشترى فلان بن فلان لابنه فلان بن فلان بحقّ ولايته عليه لأنّه طفل صغير فى حجره ولما رأى له فيما ابتاعه له ممّا سُمّى ووُصف وحُدّ فى هذا الكتاب من حسن النظر والحياطة له والتوفير عليه من فلان بن فلان جميع هذه الدار المحدودة فى هذا الكتاب بحدودها كلّها ثمّ تنسق ذكر الحقوق التى لها على مثل ما نسقناه فى مثل ذلك حتّى اذا أتيت على وكلّ حقّ هو لها خارج منها كتبت على أثر ذلك بكذا كذا دينارا مثاقيل ذهبا عينا وازنة جيادا شرى لا شرط فيه ولا عدة ودفع فلان بن فلان من مال ابنه فلان بن فلان بحقّ ولايته عليه //

(135 a) الى فلان بن فلان جميع الثمن المذكور فى هذا الكتاب وقبضه منه فلان بن فلان واستوفاه منه تامّا كاملا وأبرأه وأبرأ ابنه فلان بن فلان من جميعه بعد قبضه ايّاه واستيفائه له وهو كذا كذا دينارا مثاقيل ذهبا عينا وازنة جيادا وسلّم فلان بن فلان الى فلان بن فلان جميع ما وقع عليه هذا البيع المسمّى فى هذا الكتاب وقبضه منه فلان بن فلان [1] وصار فى يده وقبضه بهذا الشرى المسمّى فى هذا الكتاب بحقّ ولايته على ابنه فلان بن فلان وذلك بعد أن أقرّ فلان بن فلان يعنى المشترى وفلان بن فلان يعنى البائع فتذكر إقرارهما برؤيتهما الدار المبيعة وتنسق الكتاب على مثل ما كتبناه فى مثل ذلك حتّي تأتى على ذكر التفرّق ثمّ تكتب بعقب ذلك فما أدرك فيما وقع عليه هذا البيع المسمّى فى هذا الكتاب وفى شىء منه ومن حقوقه من درك من أحد من الناس كلّهم فعلى فلان ابن فلان يعنى البائع تسليم ما يجب عليه فى ذلك من حقّ ويلزمه هذا البيع المسمّى فى هذا الكتاب حتّى يسلّم ذلك الى الذى يجب له قبضه منه بحقّ هذا البيع المسمّى فى هذا الكتاب من فلان ابن فلان يعنى المشترى ومن فلان بن فلان يعنى الابن المشترَى له بعد بلوغه وأنس رشده

(135 b) واستحقاقه قبض ماله على ما يوجبه له عليه هذا البيع المسمّى فى هذا الكتاب // وقد جعل فلان ابن فلان ابنه فلان بن فلان بعد بلوغه وأنس رشده واستحقاقه قبض ماله وكيله بجميع ما اليه وبجميع ما يجب له من حقّ بحقّ البيع المسمّى فى هذا الكتاب والخصومة والمنازعة فى ذلك الى القضاة والحكّام والسلطان ثمّ تنسق بقيّة الكتاب فى ذلك على مثل ما كتبنا فى شرى الوكيل

[1] MS adds, after فلان بن فلان واستوفاه منه تاما كاملا وأبرأه وأبرأ ابنه فلان بن فلان من جميعه بعد قبضه اياه واستيفائه له وهو كذا كذا دينارا مثاقيل ذهبا عينا وازنة جيادا وسلم فلان بن فلان الى فلان بن فلان جميع ما وقع عليه هذا البيع المسمى فى هذا الكتاب وقبضه منه فلان بن فلان

غير أنّك لا تذكر للصبيّ فى ذلك قبولا لأنّه صغير لا قبول له *

4.0 فإن خاف الأب أن يكبر الصبيّ فيدّعى أنّ الشرى لم يكن من أبيه له فى صغره وإنّه كان بعد بلوغه وخروجه من ولايته أو يدّعى أنّه كان فى صغره وأنّه لم يكن فيما ابتاعه له وَفَى بما ابتاعه له به أو خاف البائع ذلك فإنّك تكتب الكتاب على مثل ما كتبنا حتّى اذا أتيت على الدرك كتبت على أثره شهد فلان بن فلان بن فلان الفلانى ويكنى أبا فلان وفلان بن فلان بن فلان الفلانى ويكنى أبا فلان وفلان بن فلان بن فلان الفلانى ويكنى أبا فلان حتّى تسمّى من الشهود كذلك من أردت شهاداته على ذلك ثمّ تكتب على معرفة فلان بن فلان بن فلان الفلانى الصبىّ المسمّى فى هذا الكتاب بعينه واسمه ونسبه معرفة صحيحة وأنّ أباه فلان بن فلان بن فلان الفلانى الرجل المسمّى فى هذا الكتاب ابتاع له جميع ما وقع عليه هذا البيع المسمّى فى هذا الكتاب بالثمن المسمّى فى هذا الكتاب ودفع الثمن المسمّى فى هذا الكتاب الى بائعه المسمّى فى هذا الكتاب وأنّ [1] فلان بن فلان بن فلان الفلانى يعنى المشترَى له يُقصَد طفل صغير فى حجر أبيه فلان ابن فلان ويتولّى عليه القيام لصغره عن القيام بنفسه وأنّ فيما وقع عليه هذا البيع المسمّى فى هذا الكتاب وَفَى بالثمن المسمّى // فى هذا الكتاب وأنّ فى ابتياع ذلك لفلان بن فلان يعنى الصبىّ (136 a) صلاحا ونظرا له وحياطة وتوفيرا عليه وأشهد فلان بن فلان وفلان بن فلان وفلان بن فلان على شهاداتهم على ذلك سائر الشهود المسمّين معهم فى هذا الكتاب أنّهم يشهدون على جميع ما سُمّى ووُصف من شهاداتهم عليه فى هذا الكتاب وشهدوا هم وسائر الشهود المسمّين معهم فى هذا الكتاب على إقرار فلان بن فلان يعنى البائع وفلان بن فلان يعنى المشترى بجميع ما سُمّى ووُصف فى هذا الكتاب ثمّ تنسق بقيّة الشهادة على مثل ما كتبنا فى مثل ذلك فيما قد تقدّم فى كتابنا هذا *

3.1 قال أبو جعفر وكان أبو حنيفة وأبو يوسف ومحمّد يبتدئون هذا الكتاب هذا ما اشترى فلان ابن فلان لابنه فلان بن فلان بماله وهذا عندنا غير صحيح على مذاهبهم لما قد ذكرناه عنهم ممّا كانوا يبتدئون به كتاب شرى رجل لرجل بأمره وتركهم ذكر ماله وذكرنا مالهم فى ذلك من الحجّة على من كتب بأمره وماله فأغنانا ما ذكرناه من ذلك فيما هناك عن إعادته هاهنا *

5.0 قال أبو جعفر فإن كان الأب انّما ابتاع الدار لابنه من نفسه كتبت هذا ما اشترى فلان ابن فلان بن فلان الفلانى[2] لابنه فلان بن فلان بن فلان الفلانى وهو طفل صغير فى حجره يتولّى عليه القيام لصغره عن القيام بنفسه ولما رأى له // فيما ابتاعه له من ذلك من حسن النظر والحياطة (136 b) له والتوفير عليه اشترى له من نفسه جميع الدار التى بمدينة كذا ثمّ تنسق الكتاب فى ذلك على

[1] MS omits أن

[2] MS omits بن فلان الفلانى

مثل ما كتبنا حتّى اذا انتهيت الى قبض الثمن كتبت وقبض فلان بن فلان من مال ابنه فلان ابن فلان جميع الثمن المسمّى فى هذا الكتاب واستوفاه منه[1] تامّا كاملا وأبرأ منه ابنه فلان بن فلان بعد قبضه ايّاه واستيفائه له وهو كذا كذا دينارا مثاقيل ذهبا عينا وازنة جيادا وقبض فلان بن فلان لابنه فلان بن فلان من نفسه جميع ما وقع عليه هذا البيع المسمّى فى هذا الكتاب فصار ذلك فى يده وقبضه بهذا الشرى المسمّى فى هذا الكتاب وبحقّ ولايته على ابنه فلان بن فلان ثمّ تكتب ذكر الدرك بعقب ذلك ولا تكتب للفرقة ذكرا لأنّ البائع انّما باع من نفسه فلا يجوز أن يكون مفارقا لها وتوكّد الدرك فتكتب فما أدرك فيما وقع عليه هذا البيع المسمّى فى هذا الكتاب وفى شىء منه ومن حقوقه من درك من أحد من الناس كلّهم فعلى فلان بن فلان يعنى الأب البائع تسليم ما يجب عليه فى ذلك من حقّ ويلزمه بسبب هذا البيع المسمّى فى هذا الكتاب حتّى يسلّم ذلك الى من يجب له قبضه منه بحقّ هذا البيع المسمّى فى هذا الكتاب على ما يوجبه له عليه البيع المسمّى فى هذا الكتاب شهد *

5.1 (137 a) قال أبو جعفر وانّما كتبنا فى الدرك // ما كتبنا وجعلنا قبض المبيع من الأب[2] البائع الى الذى يجب له قبضه منه ولم نصمد فى ذلك الى الابن بعينه فنجعل اليه قبض ذلك بعد بلوغه وأنس رشده واستحقاقه قبض ماله على مثل ما كتبناه فيما ابتاعه الأب لابنه الصغير من غيره لأنّ ذلك ممّا الى الأب قبضه قبل بلوغ ابنه إمّا بحقّ ما يوجبه له البيع وإمّا بحقّ ولايته على ابنه على ما فى ذلك من الاختلاف بين العلماء على ما قد ذكرناه عنهم فى ذلك فيما قد تقدّم من كتابنا هذا *

5.2 واذا كان الأب هو البائع من نفسه لابنه وابنه صغير فقد يجوز أن تُستحَقّ الدار قبل بلوغ الابن ويُبطَل البيع فيها فيجب على الأب ردّ الثمن فلا يمكنه قبضه من نفسه ولا يستطيع أن يبرأ ممّا وجب عليه لابنه إلاّ بأن يقى له القاضى أمينا من أمنائه يتولّى قبض ما وجب عليه لابنه فيبرأ الأب بقبض ذلك الأمين منه ما يقبضه للابن وقد يجوز أن تُستحَقّ الدار بعد بلوغ الابن فيكون ما يجب بالدرك الى الابن فى قول بعض العلماء وفى قول آخرين يجب على الأب تفويض ذلك الى الابن *

5.3 فلمّا كان ذلك كذلك لم نجعل قبض ما يجب بالدرك الى الابن وجعلناه الى الذى يجب له بحقّ البيع فمتى رُفع ذلك الى مَن يرى فى ذلك شيئا جعل الذى يجب له القبض هو الذى يرى وجوب القبض له بحقّ البيع فى مذهبه مع أنّ شرى الأب // لابنه من نفسه بين أهل العلم فيه (137 b) تنازع *

5.4 فكان أبو حنيفة وأبو يوسف ومحمّد بن الحسن يجيزون ذلك كما يجيزون ابتياعه له من الغريب وكذلك يجيزون بيعه ما لابنه من نفسه كما يجيزون بيعه ايّاه من الغريب وكان زفر بن الهذيل

[1] MS omits منه

[2] MS وجعلنا قبضه من الأب

وجماعة من أهل العلم لا يجيزون من ذلك شيئا ويقولون لا يكون الأب بائعا من نفسه ولا مبتاعا منه على حال *

5.5 وانّما كتبنا هذا الكتاب الذى ذكرنا هذا الكلام على أثره على نحو ما كتبه أصحابنا على مذهبهم خاصّة [ ] [1] ولا نكتب مثله إذ كان فيه من الاختلاف ما ذكرنا وأحبّ الينا ممّا كتبوا إذا آثر الأب أن يبيع داره من ابنه أن يبيعها من رجل بالغ صحيح العقل والبدن جائز الأمر ويسلّمها اليه ويقبضها منه الغريب فإذا فعل ذلك ابتاعها منه حينئذ لابنه وكتب عليه فى ذلك كما يكتب فيما ابتاعه من الغريب لابنه فلا نعلم فيما يفعل من ذلك بين أهل العلم اختلافا *

باب شرى المضارب

6.0 قال أبو جعفر واذا دفع الرجل الى الرجل ألف درهم مضاربة صحيحة بالنصف فابتاع المضارب // (138 a) بالمال دارا للمضاربة وقبضها فأراد أن يكتب فى ذلك كتابا كتبت كتاب الشرى على مثل ما كتبنا فيمن ابتاع دارا لنفسه فاذا فرغت من الدرك كتبت الشهادة أيضا على البائع والمشترى على نحو ما كتبنا فاذا أتيت على التاريخ كتبت على أثر ذلك وأقرّ فلان بن فلان يعنى المشترى أنّ فلان بن فلان بن فلان الفلانى يعنى ربّ المال [2] كان دفع اليه ألف درهم فضّة صحاحا وزن سبعة مضاربة صحيحة على أنّ ما أطعم الله فيها من شىء كان بينهما نصفين وأنّه قبضها منه على ذلك فلم تزل فى يده الى أن ابتاع جميع ما وقع عليه هذا البيع المسمّى فى هذا الكتاب والى أن دفعها الى فلان بن فلان يعنى البائع قَبضًا مِن الثمن المسمّى فى هذا الكتاب فإنّ هذه المضاربة المذكورة فى هذا الكتاب لم تنفسخ مذ يوم تعاقدها فلان بن فلان يعنى المشترى وفلان بن فلان يعنى ربّ المال فى المال المذكور فى هذا الكتاب الى أن أقرّ فلان بن فلان بالإقرار المذكور فى هذا الكتاب بأنّه ابتاع[3] جميع هذه الدار المحدودة فى هذا الكتاب بجميع ما سُمّى لها فى هذا الكتاب للمضاربة المذكورة فى هذا الكتاب وأنّ الثمن الذى دفعه الى فلان بن فلان المسمّى فى هذا الكتاب // يعنى البائع هو الألف الدرهم المضاربة المذكورة فى هذا الكتاب وأنّه لا حقّ (138 b) له فى هذه الدار المحدودة فى هذا الكتاب ولا فى أرضها ولا فيما سوى ذلك منها ولا دعوى له فيها ولا طلبة على الوجوه والأسباب كلّها خلا ما له وخلا ما يجب له بحقّ المضاربة المذكورة فى هذا الكتاب شهد ثمّ تمتثل الشهادة فى ذلك على مثل ما كتبناها فيمن اشترى دارا باسمه ثمّ أقرّ فى آخر كتابه أنّه ابتاعها لغيره بأمره على مثل ما كتبنا فى ذلك فيما قد تقدّم فى كتابنا هذا غير

[1] words illegible in MS (لأنا نراه ؟)
[2] MS رب المال المضاربة
[3] MS وانه ابتاع

أنّك لا تحتاج فى هذا الى أن تكتب ذكر وكالة من المضارب لربّ المال فى المطالبة بأسباب البيع لأنّ الذى يجب له ذلك بحقّ البيع هو المضارب دون ربّ المال لا اختلاف بين العلماء فى ذلك *

6.1 وكذلك لو اشتراها المضارب باسمه ثمّ قبضها ثمّ أراد بعد ذلك أن يقرّ بأنّه ابتاعها للمضاربة وأنّ الثمن الذى كان دفعه الى بائعها ايّاه هو المال المضاربة وقد كان قبل ذلك اكتتب على بائعها ايّاه كتاب شرى باسمه ووقعت الشهادة بينهما على جميع ما فيه امتثلت فى ذلك ما كتبنا
(139 a) فى مثله ممّا قد تقدّم فى كتابنا هذا فيمن اشترى دارا واكتتب على بائعها كتابا باسمه // ثمّ أراد أن يقرّ أنّه ابتاعها لغيره بأمره غير أنّك لا تحتاج فى ذلك الى وكالة ولا الى وصاية لأنّ ذلك انّما توجبه المضاربة للمضارب لا لربّ المال *

باب الإقالة

7.0 قال أبو جعفر واذا اشترى رجل من رجل دارا وقبضها وقبض بائعها منه ثمنها ثمّ تقايلا فيها بعد ذلك فأرادا أن يكتبا بينهما فيها كتاب إقالة كتبت هذا كتاب لفلان بن فلان بن فلان الفلانى كتبه له فلان بن فلان بن فلان الفلانى وأقرّ له بجميع ما فيه وأشهد له على ذلك كلّه شهودا سُمّوا فى هذا الكتاب فى صحّة عقله وبدنه وجواز أمره وذلك فى شهر كذا من سنة كذا أنّى كنت ابتعت منك فى شهر كذا من سنة كذا جميع الدار بمدينة كذا فى الموضع الكذا منها ثمّ تحدّدها ثمّ تكتب بعقب ذلك كنت ابتعت منك جميع هذه الدار المحدودة فى هذا الكتاب بحدودها كلّها وأرضها وبنائها ثمّ تنسق ذلك على مثل ما نسقناه فى كتب أشرية العقارات على مثل ما تقدّم فى كتابنا هذا حتّى اذا أتيت على وكلّ حقّ هو لها خارج منها كتبت على أثر ذلك بكذا كذا دينارا مثاقيل ذهبا عينا وازنة جيادا شرى لا شرط فيه ولا عدة ودفعت اليك جميع الثمن
(139 b) المسمّى فى هذا الكتاب وقبضتَه // منّى واستوفيتَه تامّا كاملا وأبرأتنى من جميعه بعد قبضك ايّاه واستيفائك له وهو كذا كذا دينارا مثاقيل ذهبا عينا وازنة جيادا وسلّمت الىّ جميع ما ابتعته منك ممّا سُمّى ووُصف فى هذا الكتاب وقبضته منك وصار فى يدى وقبضى بابتياعى ايّاه منك من ذلك بعد أن أقررت أنا وأنت أنّا قد رأينا جميعا جميع هذه الدار المحدودة فى هذا الكتاب داخلها وخارجها وجميع ما فيها ومنها من بناء ومنازل وقليل وكثير وتبيّن لنا ذلك وعرفناه جميعا عند عقدة هذا البيع المسمّى فى هذا الكتاب بيننا وقبل ذلك فتبايعنا على ذلك وتفرّقنا جميعا بأبداننا بعد هذا البيع المسمّى فى هذا الكتاب عن تراض منّا بجميعه وإنفاذ منا له وكتبتُ عليك بذلك كتاب شرى باسمى تاريخه شهر كذا من سنة كذا ومن شهوده المسمّين فيه فلان بن فلان وفلان بن فلان وفلان بن فلان وغيرهم من الشهود ثمّ إنّك يا فلان بن فلان بعد ذلك سألتنى أن أقيلك ببيعك ايّاى هذه الدار المحدودة فى هذا الكتاب بجميع حدودها وحقوقها المسمّى جميع

ذلك لها فى هذا الكتاب على أن تردّ علىّ جميع ثمنها الذى كنتَ قبضته منّى بحقّ بيعك ايّاها
(140 a) منّى المذكور فى هذا الكتاب وفى الكتاب // المذكور تاريخه وشهوده فى هذا الكتاب وهو كذا
كذا دينارا مثاقيل ذهبا عينا وازنة جيادا فأجبتك الى ما سألتنى من ذلك وأقلتك جميع البيع المسمّى
فى هذا الكتاب وفى الكتاب المذكور تاريخه وشهوده فى هذا الكتاب على أن تردّ علىّ جميع الثمن
المسمّى فى هذا الكتاب وفى الكتاب المذكور تاريخه وشهوده فى هذا الكتاب وعلى أن أردّ عليك
جميع ما كنت ابتعته منك على ما سُمّى ووُصف فى هذا الكتاب فقبلتَ منّى جميع هذه
الإقالة المذكورة فى هذا الكتاب بمخاطَبة منك ايّاى على جميعها ودفعتَ الىّ جميع الثمن المسمّى
فى هذا الكتاب وقبضته منك واستوفيته تامّا كاملا وأبرأتك من جميعه بعد قبضى ايّاه واستيفائى
له وهو كذا كذا دينارا مثاقيل ذهبا عينا وازنة جيادا وسلّمت اليك جميع هذه الدار المحدودة فى
هذا الكتاب وفى الكتاب المذكور تاريخه وشهوده فى هذا الكتاب بجميع ما سُمّى لها ومنها فى
هذا الكتاب وفى الكتاب المذكور تاريخه وشهوده فى هذا الكتاب وقبضتها منّى على هيئتها التى
كانت عليها يوم قبضتها منك بحقّ ابتياعى ايّاها منك المذكور[1] فى هذا الكتاب لم يتغيّر
(140 b) عنها بعيب ولا غيره // وذلك بعد أن أقررت أنا وأنت جميعا أنّا قد رأينا جميعا جميع هذه الدار
المحدودة فى هذا الكتاب داخلها وخارجها وجميع ما فيها ومنها من بناء ومنازل وقليل وكثير وتبيّن
لنا ذلك وعرفناه جميعا عند عقدة هذه الإقالة المسمّاة فى هذا الكتاب بيننا وقبل ذلك فتقايلنا
على ذلك وتفرّقنا جميعا بأبداننا بعد هذه الإقالة المسمّاة فى هذا الكتاب عن تراض منّا بها وإنفاذ
منّا لها فلا حقّ لى فى هذه الدار المحدودة فى هذا الكتاب وفى الكتاب المذكور تاريخه وشهوده
فى هذا الكتاب ولا فى شىء منها ولا فى حقوقها وفى قبلك من ثمنها المسمّى فى هذا الكتاب على
الوجوه والأسباب كلّها فما أدركك فيما وقعت عليه هذه الإقالة المسمّاة فى هذا الكتاب وفى شىء
منه ومن حقوقه من درك من قبلى وبسببى بسبب إقرار وإشهاد وتلجئة وتمليك وحدث وحيلة إن
كنت احتلتها فى ذلك أو احتيِلت لى بأمرى تبطل بذلك هذه الإقالة المسمّاة فى هذا الكتاب
أو شيئا منها أى ذلك كان فعلىّ لك تسليم ما يجب لك علىّ فى ذلك من حقّ ويلزمنى لك بحقّ
هذه الإقالة المسمّاة فى هذا الكتاب حتّى أسلّم ذلك لك على ما يوجبه لك علىّ[2] الإقالة المسمّاة
فى هذا الكتاب شهد على إقرار فلان بن فلان الفلانى يعنى المشترى المقيل وفلان بن فلان الفلانى //
(141 a) بجميع ما سُمّى ووُصف فى هذا الكتاب ثمّ تنسق الشهادة عليها على مثل ما كتبناها على
المتبايعين على ما تقدّم فى كتابنا هذا *

7.1 قال أبو جعفر فإن كان البائع لم يكن قبض الثمن حتّى تقايلا كتبت الكتاب على ما كتبنا
وذكرت فيه أنّ البائع لم يكن قبض الثمن المسمّى فى هذا الكتاب وفي الكتاب المذكور تاريخه
وشهوده فى هذا الكتاب ولا شيئا منه وكذلك إن كان المشترى لم يكن قبض الدار كتبت ذلك فى

[1] MS البيع المذكور [2] MS omits على

كتابك أيضا غير أنّ الناس قد اختلفوا فى الإقالة فى الدار المبيعة قبل قبض مبتاعها ايّاها فأجاز بعضهم الإقالة فيها وجعلوها فسخ بيع وممّن ذهب الى ذلك أبو حنيفة وأبو يوسف ومحمّد بن الحسن وأبطل بعضهم الإقالة فيها وجعلوها كالبيع المستأنف من المشترى الذى لم يقبضها فاعرفْ هذا الموضع فإنّه لا [ ] [1] الكتاب معهم على ما اختـُلِف فيه[2] *

7.2 قال أبو جعفر وقد اختـُلِف فى غير موضع من هذا الكتاب فكان يوسف بن خالد يبتدئ به هذا كتاب لفلان بن فلان يعنى البائع المستقيل كتبه له فلان بن فلان // يعنى المشترى المقيل (141 b) إنّى كنت اشتريت منك جميع الدار ثمّ يجرى كتابه على ذلك وكان أبو زيد يبتدئ به هذا ما شهد عليه الشهود المسمّون فى هذا الكتاب شهدوا جميعـــا انّ فلان بن فلان بن فلان الفلانى وفلان بن فلان بن فلان الفلانى وقد أثبتوهما وعرفوهما معرفة صحيحة بأعيانهما وأسمائهما وأنسابهما أقرّا عندهم وأشهداهم على أنفسهما فى صحّة عقولهما وأبدانهما وجواز أمورهما وذلك فى شهر كذا من سنة كذا أنّ فلان بن فلان الفلانى الرجل المسمّى فى هذا الكتاب كان ابتاع من فلان بن فلان ابن فلان الفلانى الرجل المسمّى فى هذا الكتاب فى شهر كذا من سنة كذا جميع الدار التى بمدينة كذا فى الموضع الكذا منها ثمّ ينسق كتابه على ذلك *

7.3 قال أبو جعفر هذا معناه وإن لم تكن هذه ألفاظه ولكنّها ألفاظ غيره من فقهاء أصحابنـــا البغداذيّين فكان من الحجّة لأبى زيد فيما كتب من ذلك أنّا قد رأيناهم جميعا ابتدؤوا كتاب الشرى بهذا ما اشترى فلان بن فلان بن فلان ثمّ تنسقوا الكتاب على ذلك ولم ينسقوه على إقرار أحد المتبايعين للآخر فيكتبون هذا كتاب لفلان بن فلان كتبه له فلان بن فلان // إنّك سألتنى (142 a) أن أبيعك الدار فلمّا كتبوا الشرى منسوقا على الإخبار عن البائع كيف كان لا على الإقرار من أحد المتبايعين بذلك للآخر فكتاب الإقالة فى النظر كذلك أيضا *

7.4 وكان من الحجّة ليوسف بن خالد على أهل هذا القول أنّا رأينا كتاب الشرى هذا ما اشترى فلان بن فلان كما ذكر هذا المحتجّ وقد رأينا كتاب الإقالة ثمّ يمتثل فيه هذا المعنى فيكتب فيه هذا ما استقال فلان بن فلان كما كتب الشرى هذا ما اشترى فلان بن فلان وابتدائى بخلاف ذلك فابتدأه بعضهم بمثل ما ابتدأه به يوسف وابتدأه بعضهم بمثل ما ابتدأه به أبو زيد وردّوا ذلك جميعا الى الإقرار الذى كتبه أبو زيد فيه إقرار المتبايعين جميعا والذى كتبه يوسف فيه إقرار المقيل *

7.5 فأردنا أن ننظر فى المعانى التى تبتدئ بها الكتب كيف هى فنستخرج منها بهذا الموضع الذى اختلفوا فيه معنى صحيحا فنظرنا فى ذلك فوجدنا الشرى قد كتبوا فيه جميعا هذا ما اشترى فلان ابن فلان وهو // أمر قد تعاقده المتبايعان فيما بينهما ابتداء إنّه إيجاب حقّ لكلّ واحد منهما على (142b)

[1] words illegible in MS

[2] MS ما اختلاف فيه

صاحبه ولم يخبرا فيه عن سبب متقدّم لمّا تعاقدا بينهما من البائع وكذلك امتثل فى نظير ذلك فكتب هذا ما أصدق فلان بن فلان على هذا المعنى بعينه وهذا ما أوصى به فلان بن فلان على هذا المعنى بعينه ورأينا كتبا أخرى [1] تخبر فيها عن أسباب متقدّمة منها الخلع يخبر فيه عن نكاح متقدّم لا يصحّ إلاّ به ومنها العتاق يخبر فيه عن ملك المعتِق للعبد المعتَق ولولا ذلك الملك لم يقع العتاق وفى أشباهه لذلك يطول الكتاب بذكرها فكتبوا جميعا ومنهم يوسف وأبو زيد هذا كتاب لفلان ابن فلان كتبته له فلانة ابنة فلان ثمّ أجروا كتاب الخلع على ذلك وهذا كتاب لفلان بن فلان كتبه له مولاه فلان بن فلان ثمّ أجروا كتاب العتاق على ذلك وكتاب الإقالة يخبر فيها عن سبب متقدّم وهو البيع ولولا ذلك البيع لم يكن إقالة للنظر على ذلك أن يردّ ما اختلفوا فيه منه الى ما أجمعوا عليه من كتب الخلع وكتب العتاقات وأشباهها فتكتب ذلك على إقرار المقيل لا
(143 a) على إقرار المتقايلين فتكتب بما ذكرنا على ما كتب يوسف // وكذلك ينبغى لك أن تمتثل فى كتبك كلّها فما كان منها ليس فيه إخبار عن سبب متقدّم ابتدأتَه كنحو ما يُبتدأ الخلع والعتاق اللذين ذكرنا *

7.6 قال أبو جعفر هذا هو القياس على ما أجمعوا عليه فما كان من كتابنا هذا قد حملناه على هذا المعنى فقد حملناه على ما يوجبه القياس وما كان منه قد حملناه على غير ذلك فإنّ القياس فيه ما ذكرنا هاهنا والله الموفّق *

7.7 وكان يوسف يكتب فى كتابه فى الإقالة التى ذكرنا بحدودها وجميع حقوقها وما فيها ومنها من بناء وقليل وكثير وكان أبو زيد يكتب بحدودها كلّها وأرضها ثمّ ينسق بقيّة ذكر حقوقها على ما ينسق ذلك فى كتاب الشرى حتّى يأتى على وكلّ حقّ هو لها داخل فيها وكلّ حقّ هو لها خارج منها فكان ما كتب أبو زيد فى هذا أجود عندنا ممّا كتب يوسف لأنّهم قد أجمعوا جميعا على أن كتبوا فى الشرى بحدودها كلّها وأرضها وبنائها حتّى أتوا على حقوقها كلّها على
(143 b) ما كتبوا فى كتاب الشرى ولم يكتبوا وما كان فيها من بناء // وقليل وكثير فكان ما اختلفوا فيه هاهنا فى كتاب الإقالة معطوفا على ما أجمعوا عليه هناك فى كتاب الشرى وقد ذكرنا فيما قد تقدّم فى كتابنا هذا على أبى زيد نحو ممّا كتب يوسف هاهنا فى باب بيع الثمار وكتب وما فى ذلك من ثمرة قائمة وقد كتبنا نحن هناك فساد هذا الكلام والحجّة عليه فأغنانا ذلك عن إعادته هاهنا *

7.8 وكان يوسف يكتب فكتبت عليك كتاب عهدة شرائها باسمى ولم يكن أبو زيد يكتب فى كتابه من ذلك شيئا فكان ما كتب يوسف فى ذلك أحبّ الينا وأحسن عندنا ليُعلَم متى كان هذا البيع الذى كانت هذه الإقالة منه غير أنّى أكره أن يكتب فى ذلك وكتبت عليك كتاب عهدة شرائها باسمى كما كتب يوسف لأنّ أبا حنيفة كان يقول عهدة الشرى هى الصحيفة المكتوب

[1] MS كتبا اخر

فيها الشرى وكتاب عهدة الشرى فى ذلك فى قوله غير كتاب الشرى وثمّ تكتب [1] فى ذلك وكتبت عليك بذلك كتاب شرى باسمى ثمّ تذكر تاريخه وشهوده على ما كتبنا لينتفى ما فيه من التنازع والاختلاف *

7.9 وكان يوسف يكتب وإنّك سألتنى أن أقيلك بيعك منّى هذه الدار وأردّها عليك وكان
(144 a) أبو زيد يكتب ثمّ إنّ فلان بن فلان سأل // فلان بن فلان أن يفاسخه البيع فى القبض فقال بعضهم هى فسخ بيع وليست ببيع مستقبل وممّن قال ذلك أبو حنيفة وقال آخرون هى بيع مستقبل وممّن قال ذلك أبو يوسف ومحمّد بن الحسن *

7.10 فلمّا اختلفوا فى الإقالة كما ذكرنا لم يجز لنا أن نسمّيها فسخا لأنّ بعضهم يأبى ذلك ولم نسمّها بيعا لأنّ بعضهم لا يقول ذلك وسمّيناها إقالة وذكرناها باسمها الذى لا يختلفون فيه أنّه اسمها وإن كانوا يختلفون فى حكم المعنى الواجب به على ما ذكرناه عنهم فمتى رُفع ذلك الى من يرى الإقالة بيعا جعلها بيعا وأجرى فيها حكم البيع ومتى رُفع الى من يرى الإقالة فسخا جعلها فسخا وأجرى فيها حكم الفسخ *

7.11 وكان يوسف يكتب فى كتابه وإنّك سألتنى بعد ذلك أن أقيلك بيعك منّى هذه الدار وأردّها عليك وانّى أطلبتُك ذلك وأقيلك بيعك منّى هذه الدار المحدودة فى هذا الكتاب ورددتها عليك بالثمن الذى كنت بعتنيها به فقبلت منّى إقالتى ايّاك هذه الدار وردّى ايّاها عليك *

7.12 وكان أبو زيد يكتب فى كتابه ثمّ إنّ فلان بن فلان سأل فلان بن فلان أن يفاسخه البيع //
(144 b) فى هذه الدار المحدودة فى هذا الكتاب فأجابه فلان بن فلان والذى كتب يوسف فى هذا أحسن عندنا ممّا كتب أبو زيد لأنّ الناس قد اختلفوا فى الإقالة بعد القبض على ما ذكرنا فجعلها قوم بيعا وجعلها قوم فسخا وكان مَن يجعلها بيعا منهم أبو يوسف ومحمّد يقولون اذا عُقدت بدون الثمن الذى كان البيع عُقد به أو بأكثر منه جارت على ما عُقدت عليه من ذلك قلّ أو كثر وكان مَن يجعلها فسخا وهو أبو حنيفة ومَن ذهب مذهبه فى ذلك يردّها الى الثمن الذى وقع به البيع *

7.13 حدّثنا سليمان بن شعيب عن أبيه عن محمّد بن الحسن بما ذكرناه عن أبى حنيفة وعن أبى يوسف وعن محمّد فى الإقالة وفى الزيادة على ثمن المبيع المتقدّم لها وفى التقضية منه *

7.14 فلمّا كان ذلك كذلك كان أولى الأسباب بنا أن نجعل سؤال البائع المشترىَ الإقالةَ كسؤال المساوم بالعرض ربَّ العرض البيعَ وكما كان ذلك لا يكون إلاّ بثمن معلوم وكذلك هو فى الإقالة لا يكون الاّ بثمن معلوم غير أنّ يوسف قد كان ينبغى له أن يتبيّن الثمن فى موضع السؤال

[1] MS ولم تكتب

(145 a) من المستقيل قبل // الإجابة من المقيل ايّاه الى ذلك فتكتب ذلك على مثل ما كتبنا ثمّ تتبعه فأجابه فلان بن فلان الى ذلك *

7.15 قال أبو جعفر ولم يكن يوسف ولا أبو زيد يكتبان فى كتابهما فى الإقالة الرؤية للدار من المقيل والمستقيل فى وقت وقوع الإقالة بينهما فى ذلك ولا التفرّق بعدها وذلك عندنا إغفال منهما لما قد ذكرناه فى الإقالة أنّها عند بعض الناس بيع المستقبل فمَن جعلها كذلك فلم يكمل فيها أسباب البيع التى يجوز البيع كمالها بطلت فى قوله وكان أولى الأشياء بهما الاحتراز من ذلك بأن يذكر الرؤية والتفرّق فى ذلك كما يذكر أنّها فى البيع على نحو ما كتبنا فتصحّ عند مَن يراها بيعا ولا يضرّها ذلك عند مَن يراها فسخا *

7.16 وكان يوسف يكتب فى كتابه فما أدركك فى هذه الدار المحدودة فى هذا الكتاب وفى شىء منها ومن حقوقها من درك من أحد من الناس كلّهم من قبلى وبسببى من قبل شىء كنت أحدثته أو أحدثه لى محدث بأمرى وبسببى بوجه من الوجوه يدركك من قبله فى ذلك درك *

7.17 وكان أبو زيد يكتب فى ذلك فما أدرك فلان بن فلان فى ذلك من درك من قبل إقرار وتلجئة وهبة وبيع وحدث كان من فلان بن فلان يعنى المشترى فى ذلك قبل كتابنا هذا استُحِقّ به
(145 b) ذلك // أو شيئا منه فعلى فلان بن فلان فكان ما كتب يوسف فى ذلك أجمع ممّا كتب أبو زيد وكان ما كتبنا نحن فى ذلك فى كتابنا أحسن ممّا كتبا وأجمع وأشرح لأنّك اذا كتبت من قبل إقرار وتلجئة وهبة وبيع وحدث فقد يجوز أن يكون الدرك من قبل صدقة كانت من المقيل أو من قبل تزويج على الدار أو من قبل ما سوى ذلك ممّا تُستحَقّ به الأشياء وتُملَّك على مالكَيْها *

7.18 فكان أولى الأشياء فى ذلك وأحوطها أن تكتب من قبل إقرار وتلجئة وتمليك وحدث فيكون ذلك قد أتى على الهبات والصدقات وعلى جميع الأشياء التى تُملَّك بها العقارات على مالكَيها فلا نقض فى ذلك غير أنّا نكره فى ذلك أن تكتب كما كتب يوسف فى كتابه من درك من أحد من الناس كلّهم من قبلى وبسببى لأنّ الدرك لا يجب على المقيل من قبل الناس كلّهم لأنّه انّما ملك العوض الذى أقال فيه من قبل المستقيل لا من قبل غيره وانّما يجب عليه ضمان الدرك فيما كان منه وبسببه لا ممّا سوى ذلك *

7.19 فإن قال قائل فقد أعقب ذلك يوسف وكتب فيه من قبلى وبسببى قيل له فما كانت حاجته أن يقول من أحد من الناس كلّهم ثمّ يرفع ذلك عن كلّ الناس غير نفسه والدرك فانّما يجب عليه من قبل نفسه لا من قبل غيره فإن قال فإنّه وإن كان انّما يجب عليه من قبل نفسه فانّما
(146 a) ذلك فيما يعقده لغيره من سائر // الناس فيكون الدرك من قبل المعقود له قيل هذا وهذا أيضا فغير جائز لأنّ الدرك انّما يدرك المستقيل من قبل عقد المقيل لغيره من قبل إقالته ايّاه وقد يجوز أيضا أن يكون الدرك من قبل وقف كان أحدثه فى الدار التى أقال فيها فلا يكون ذلك دركك من قبل

أحد من الناس غير المقيل فيكون قوله من أحد من الناس كلّهم ناقضا عن هـــذا المعنى لأنّ الوقف انـما يجب لله عزّ وجلّ ويتصرّف غلاّته ومنافعه فى الوجوه التى سبّلها الموقف فاذا كتبت فما أدرك فى ذلك من درك من قبلى وبسببى على ما كتبنا أتيت على هذه المعانى كلّها بألفاظ أخصر ممّا كتب يوسف وأجمع للمعانى التى ذكرنا فيها *

7.20 قال أبو جعفر فإن كانا تقايلا قبل قبض المشترى الدار المبيعة فإنّ يوسف وأبا زيد كانـــا يكتبان فى ذلك على مثل ما كانا يكتبان فى الإقالة اذا تقدّمها قبض المشترى الدار المبيعة غير أنّهما كانا يكتبان بعد الفراغ من ذكر البيع من غير أن يكونا تقابضا وزاد يوسف على أبى زيد فى ذلك فكتب فإنّك سألتنى أن أقيلك بيعك منّى هذه الدار من غير أن أكون نقدتك شيئا من ثمنها ولا قبضت منك شيئا منها ولا كتبت عليك لها عهدة * //

7.21 (146 b) فكان ما كتب يوسف فى هذا أحسن عندنا ممّا كتب أبو زيد غير أنّ بعض أهل العلم قد حكينا عنه فيما قد تقدّم من هذا الباب أنّ الإقالة فيما لم يُقبَض باطل وجعل ذلك في حكم بيع ما لم يُقبَض فلمّا كان بيع ما لم يُقبَض لا يصحّ فكذلك الإقالة فيما لم يُقبَض لا يصحّ عنده أيضا وكان أحوط الأشياء عندنا فى ذلك أن يسلّم البائع الدار الى المشترى ويقبضها منه المشترى ثمّ يتقايلان فيها بعد ذلك ويكتبان الكتاب على ما كتبنا فى الدار المبيعة اذا تقايل متبايعاها فيها بعد أن تقابضاها على ما كتبنا فى أوّل هذا الباب وليس على المشترى فى قبضه ايّاها ضرر فيبيع من أجل ذلك مَن قبضها لأنّه وإن كان فى الإقالة بعد القبض كالبائع فى قول من يجعلها بيعا فإنّه انّما باعها ممّن كان ابتاعها منه ولا يجب له عليه فى ذلك ضمان درك إلاّ من قبله وبسببه خاصّة *

7.22 قال أبو جعفر وقد ذكرنا فى غير هذا الباب ممّا قد تقدّم من هذا الكتاب أنّ أحوط الأشياء فى الكتاب الذى قد تقدّم ذكره ووقعت الشهادة فيه اذا احتيج الى ذكره فى كتاب كتب بعده أن تنسخ كلّه فيه ليوقف بذلك على فساد إن كان فيه فأغنانا ذلك عن إعادته فى هذا الباب غير أنّا نستحبّ أيضا فى كتاب الإقالة الذى كتبنا فى أوّل هذا الباب أن تنسخ الكتاب //

(147 a) الأوّل فى هذا الكتاب الأخير ليوقف بذلك على حقيقة ما كان فيه ولئلا يدّعى واحد من المتقايلين أنّه كان فى الكتاب الأوّل ما يمنع من الإقالة والله نسأله التوفيق *

باب الشركة فى البيع

8.0 قال أبو جعفر واذا اشترى رجل من رجلا دارا وقبضها ودفع ثمنها واكتتب على بائعها كتاب شرى باسمه ثمّ أشرك فيها رجل بالنصف فأرادا أن يكتبا بينهما فى ذلك كتابا فإنّك تكتب هذا كتاب لفلان بن فلان بن فلان [1] الفلانى كتبه له فلان بن فلان بن فلان الفلانى وأقرّ له بجميع

[1] MS omits بن فلان

ما فيه وأشهد له على ذلك كلّه شهودا سمّوا فى هذا الكتاب فى صحّة عقله وبدنه وجواز أمره وذلك
فى شهر كذا من سنة كذا أنّى ذكرتُ لك أنّى ابتعتُ من فلان بن فلان جميع الدار التى بمدينة
كذا فى الموضع الكذا منها وهى الدار التى يحيط بها ويجمعها ويشتمل عليها حدود أربعة ثمّ
تحدّدها ثمّ تكتب ذكرت لك[1] أنّى ابتعت من فلان بن فلان الفلانى جميع هذه الدار المحدودة فى
هذا الكتاب بحدودها كلّها ثمّ تذكر حقوقها على مثل ما كتبناها فيما تقدّم من كتابنا هذا حتّى
(147 b) تأتى على وكلّ حقّ هو لها خارج منها فاذا أتيت على ذلك كتبت على أثره // بكذا كذا دينارا
مثاقيل ذهبا عينا وازنة جيادا ودفعت جميع ثمنها المسمّى فى هذا الكتاب الى بائعها منّى المسمّى
فى هذا الكتاب وقبضه منّى واستوفاه منّى تامّا كاملا وأبرأنى من جميعه بعد قبضه ايّاه واستيفائه
له وهو كذا كذا دينارا مثاقيل ذهبا عينا وازنة جيادا وقبضت جميع ما وقع عليه هذا البيع المسمّى
فى هذا الكتاب بتسليم من بائعى المسمّى معى فى هذا الكتاب ذلك الىّ وذلك بعد أن أقررتُ أنا
وبائعى المسمّى معى فى هذا الكتاب أنّا قد رأينا جميعا جميع هذه الدار المحدودة فى هذا الكتاب
داخلها وخارجها وجميع ما فيها ومنها من بناء ومنازل وقليل وكثير وتبيّن لنا ذلك وعرفناه جميعا
عند عقدة هذا البيع المسمّى فى هذا الكتاب بيننا وقبل ذلك وتفرّقنا جميعا بأبداننا بعد هذا البيع
المسمّى فى هذا الكتاب عن تراض منّا جميعا بجميعه وإنفاذ منّا له وكتبت على بائعى المسمّى
فى هذا الكتاب بابتياعى منه هذه الدار المحدودة فى هذا الكتاب كتاب شرى باسمى تاريخه كذا
ومن شهوده المسمّين فيه فلان بن فلان وفلان بن فلان وفلان بن فلان وغيرهم من الشهود وإنّك
يا فلان بن فلان بعد ذلك سألتَنى أن أشركك فى جميع هذه الدار المحدودة فى هذا الكتاب النصف
(148 a) من جميعها شائع فيها // غير مقسوم منها بحدود هذا النصف الذى سألتَنى أن أشركك به وأرضه
وبنائه وسفله وعلوّه ومرافقه فى حقوقه ومسايله فى حقوقه وطرقه التى هى له من حقوقه وكلّ قليل
وكثير هو له فيه ومنه من حقوقه وكلّ حقّ هو له داخل فيه وكلّ حقّ هو له خارج منه بحصّة
هذا النصف المسمّى فى هذا الكتاب من الثمن المسمّى فى هذا الكتاب وفى الكتاب المذكور
تاريخه وشهوده فى هذا الكتاب وهى كذا كذا دينارا مثاقيل ذهبا عينا وازنة جيادا فأجبتُك الى
ما سألتَنى من ذلك وأشركتُك فى جميع ما وقع عليه هذا البيع المسمّى فى هذا الكتاب وفى الكتاب
المذكور تاريخه وشهوده فى هذا الكتاب بينى وبين بائعى المسمّى فيها بالنصف شائع فيما هو منه
غير مقسوم منه بحدود هذا النصف الذى أشركتك فيه على ما سُمّى ووُصف فى هذا الكتاب
وجميع حقوقه بحصّته من الثمن المسمّى فى هذا الكتاب وفى الكتاب المذكور تأريخه وشهوده فى
هذا الكتاب وهى كذا كذا دينارا مثاقيل ذهبا عينا وازنة جيادا فقبلت منّى هذه الشركة الموصوفة
فى هذا الكتاب بمخاطبة منك ايّاىَ على [جميع ذلك][2] ودفعتَ الىّ جميع الثمن الذى تعاقدنا
(148 b) به هذه الشركة // المسمّاة فى هذا الكتاب بيننا وقبضته منك واستوفيته منك تامّا كاملا وأبرأتك
من جميعه بعد قبضى ايّاه واستيفائى له وهو كذا كذا دينارا مثاقيل ذهبا عينا وازنة جيادا وسلّمت

[1] MS ذكر لك

[2] words illegible in MS

اليك جميع هذا النصف الذى أشركتك به المسمّى فى هذا الكتاب وقبضته منّى فصار فى يدك وقبضك بهذه الشركة المسمّاة فى هذا الكتاب كما يُقبَض المشاع وذلك بعد أن أقررت أنا وأنت أنّا قد رأينا جميعا جميع هذه الدار المحدودة فى هذا الكتاب وفى الكتاب المذكور تأريخه وشهوده فى هذا الكتاب داخلها وخارجها وجميع ما فيها ومنها من بناء ومنازل وقليل وكثير وتبيّن لنا ذلك وعرفناه جميعا عند عقدة هذه الشركة المسمّاة فى هذا الكتاب بيننا وقبل ذلك فتعاقدنا هذه الشركة المسمّاة فى هذا الكتاب فى هذه الدار المحدودة فى هذا الكتاب بيننا على ذلك وتفرّقنا جميعا بأبداننا بعدها عن تراض منّا بها وإنفاذ منّا لها فما أدركك يا فلان بن فلان فى هذا النصف الذى أشركتك به فى هذه الدار المحدودة فى هذا الكتاب وفى شىء منه ومن حقوقه من درك من أحد من الناس كلّهم فعلىّ تسليم ما يجب لك علىّ فى ذلك من حقّ ويلزمنى لك بحقّ هذه الشركة المسمّاة فى
(149 a) هذا الكتاب // حتّى أسلّم ذلك اليك على ما توجبه لك علىّ هذه الشركة المسمّاة فى هذا الكتاب شهد فلان بن فلان[1] الفلانى ويكنى أبا فلان وفلان بن فلان الفلانى ويكنى أبا فلان وفلان بن فلان الفلانى ويكنى أبا فلان أنّهم يعرفون فلان بن فلان الفلانى يعنى البائع الرجل المسمّى فى هذا الكتاب وفى الكتاب المذكور تأريخه وشهوده فى هذا الكتاب معرفة صحيحة بعينه واسمه ونسبه وأنّه أقرّ عندهم وأشهدهم على نفسه فى صحّة عقله وبدنه وجواز أمره فى شهر كذا من سنة كذا ببيعه من فلان بن فلان الفلانى[2] المسمّى فى هذا الكتاب يعنى المشترى جميع هذه الدار المحدودة فى هذا الكتاب بجميع ما سُمّى لها ومنها فى هذا الكتاب بالثمن المسمّى فى هذا الكتاب وهو كذا كذا دينارا مثاقيل ذهبا عينا وازنة جيادا وأنّه قد قبض من فلان بن فلان يعنى المشترى جميع الثمن المسمّى فى هذا الكتاب واستوفاه منه تامّا كاملا وأبرأه من جميعه بعد قبضه ايّاه واستيفائه له منه وهو كذا كذا دينارا مثاقيل ذهبا عينا وازنة جيادا وأنّه قد سلّم الى فلان بن فلان جميع
(149 b) ما وقع عليه هذا البيع المسمّى فى هذا الكتاب // وفى الكتاب المذكور تأريخه وشهوده فى هذا الكتاب وقبضه منه فلان بن فلان وأشهدوا على شهاداتهم سائر الشهود المسمّين معهم فى هذا الكتاب أنّهم يشهدون على فلان بن فلان يعنى البائع بجميع ما ذُكر من شهادتهم عليه فى هذا الكتاب وشهدوا هم وسائر الشهود المسمّين معهم فى هذا الكتاب على إقرار فلان بن فلان وفلان ابن فلان يعنى اللذين تعاقدا الشركة المسمّاة فى هذا الكتاب بجميع ما سُمّى ووُصف فى هذا الكتاب ثمّ تنسق الشهادة على ما كتبنا فى مثل ذلك ممّا تقدّم فى هذا الكتاب *

8.1 قال أبو جعفر وانّما كتبنا أنّ الشركة كانت بالنصف ولم نكتب أنّها كانت فى النصف لأنّها اذا وقعت فى النصف فانّما تقع على الربع واذا وقعت بالنصف وقعت على النصف بكماله فلذلك كتبنا بالنصف ولم نكتب فى النصف *

[1] MS adds بن فلان

[2] MS omits الفلانى

8.2 وانّما كتبنا ذلك على جهة الشركة ولم نكتب على جهة البيع لأنّ الشركة اذا وقعت فانّما
(150 a) تقع بنصف // الثمن فهى ضرب من التولية فإن وقعت ذلك فى خيانة فزيد على هذا الدخيل فى الثمن فإنّ أبا حنيفة وابن أبى ليلى وأبا يوسف قالوا يحطّ عن الدخيل الخيانة *

8.3 وقال زفر بن الهذيل ومحمّد بن الحسن لا ينحطّ عنه منها شىء ولكنّه يكون له الخيار فيما ملّكه إن شاء احتبسه بالثمن الذى سمّاه له الذى ملّكه ايّاه وإن شاء ردّ التمليك فيه وأبطله فبيّنّا فى كتابنا أنّ ذلك كان شركة لاختلاف حكم الشركة والبيع المستقبل فى قول أبى حنيفة وابن أبى ليلى وأبى يوسف وليجب للدخيل حكم الشركة فى الأقوال كلّها وانّما سمّينا البائع فى هذا الكتاب وذكرنا وقوع الشهادة عليه ببيعه والشهادة على من شهد عليه بذلك احتياطا ليُعلَم أنّ هذا البيع الذى وجبت فيه[1] هذه الشركة هو البيع الذى كان بين البائع الأوّل وبين المبتاع منه ليجب لهذا الدخيل حكم الشركة فى بيع معلوم ولتجب له حطيطة إن كانت من البائع الأوّل عن الذى أشرك هذا الدخيل فى قول من يوجب الحطيطة فى ذلك عن[2] هذا الدخيل *

8.4 ألا ترى أنّ رجلا لو اشترى من رجل دارا بألف درهم وقبض الدار ثمّ أشرك فيها ثمّ حطّ البائع عن المشترى طائفة من الثمن إنّ على المشترى أن يحطّ الذى أشركه بحصّته منها فى قول أبى حنيفة وأبى يوسف ومحمّد بن الحسن ويجعلون ذلك كالتولية فى نصف الدار وقد خولفوا فى ذلك
(150 b) فكان زفر بن الهذيل وغيره من أهل العلم يقولون هذه الحطيطة // هى عن المحطوط عنه خاصّة ولا يجب عليه أن يحطّ شيئا منها عن الذى أشركه *

8.5 فلمّا اختلفوا فى ذلك على ما ذكرنا سمّينا البائع وذكرنا وقت بيعه ليُعلَم أىّ بيع هو وأشهدنا على شهادة من شهد عليه بالبيع لئلا يحضر فيقول قد أقرّ لى الذى كانت الدار فى يده وأشرك فيها فإنّها كانت فى يدى وادّعى علىّ بيعا لم يكن منّى فكتبنا الشهادة على إقراره بالبيع وأشهدنا على شهادة الشهود عليه بذلك لهذا المعنى *

8.6 وكذلك قبضه الثمن ذكرناه فى كتابنا لئلا يحضر فيقول قد بعت الدار ولم أقبض ثمنها فارْدُدْها الى يدى حتّى استوفى ثمنها *

8.7 وكذلك تسليمه الدار الذى ذكرناه فى كتابنا حذرا أن يقول قبض المشترى الدار بغير تسليم ايّاها اليه وقد ذكرنا فى صدر كتابنا هذا عن بعض الناس أنّه كان يقول ليس لرجل أن يقبض دارا قد ابتاعها بغير أمر بائعها وإن كان قد دفع ثمنها حتّى يكون البائع هو الذى سلّمها اليه وإن كان هذا القول خطأ فإنّ الاحتياط منه أصلح *

8.8 وحجّة أخرى لاختيارنا ذكر الشركة فى هذا الكتاب على ذكر البيع وهى أنّ رجلا لو أشرك رجلا
(151 a) فى دار قد ابتاعها ودفع ثمنها // وقبضها وسلّم الى الدخيل معه ما أشركه بـه فيها ثمّ أصاب

[1] MS الذى وجب فيه

[2] MS omits عن

الدخيل بما أشركه به عيبا لم يكن علمه ولا برئ اليه البائع منه إنّ له ردّ الشركة والرجوع على الذى أشركه بالثمن الذى قبضه منه وتسليم ما أشركه به اليه ولو كان بعد أن قبض ما وجب له بحقّ الشركة وصار فى يده حدث به عيب ثمّ أصاب به عيبا كان به قبل الشركة لم يبرأ اليه الذى أشركه منه لم يكن له أن يرجع على هذا الذى أشركه بشىء إلاّ ان يشاء الذى أشركه أن يقبض منه الذى أشركه به معيب العيبين جميعا ويردّ عليه ثمنه وذلك كالتولية *

8.9 ألا ترى رجلا لو اشترى من رجل دارا بألف درهم وقبضها ثمّ ولاّها رجلا بثمنها الذى ابتاعها به ثمّ أصاب بها هذا المولى عيبا كان في يد الذي ولاّها وقد حدث بها عيب فى يده إنّ الذى ولاّها بالخيار إن شاء قبلها منه معيبة العيبين جميعا وردّ عليه ثمنها الذى قبضه منه وإن شاء أبى قبولها ولا حقّ عليه للمولى لأنّ من حجّته أن يقول انـّما دفعت اليك هذه الدار تولية ليكون لى عليك من الثمن مثل ما كان للبائع علىّ فاذا طلبتنى بنقصان عيب فقد طلبت
(151 b) منّى إخراج ما كان بيننا من التولية وردّه الى غير التولية وليس كذلك // عقدت لك على نفسى والبيع ليس كذلك لأنّ رجلا لو ابتاع من رجل دارا وقبضها فحدث بها عيب فى يده من السماء ثمّ أصاب بها عيبا كان فى يد البائع فأبى البائع قبولها منه بهذا العيب الحادث بعد بيعه ايـّاها كان عليه ردّ حصّته من الثمن على المشترى *

8.10 فلمـّا رأينا أحكام الشركة قد تخالف أحكام البيع فيما ذكرنا فى قول أبى حنيفة وأبى يوسف ومحمـّد بن الحسن وتخالفه أيضا فى قول أهل المدينة لأنـّهم يجيزونها قبل قبض المبتاع ولو كان طعاما لا يحلّ بيعه قبل قبضه فكتبنا ما جرى بين هذين المتعاقدين على ما سمّيناه فيما عقده كلّ واحد منهما لصاحبه بما سمّيناه ليكون كلّ واحد من هؤلاء المختلفين متى رُفع اليه هذا الكتاب يمضى فيه ما يرى *

8.11 قال أبو جعفر ولو نسخت الكتاب الذى كان اكتتبه المشترى على بائعه فى كتاب الشركة لأغناك عن كثير ممـّا قد كتبنا فى كتابنا الذى نسخناه فى هذا الباب لأنّ ذلك الكتاب فيه ذكر البائع وذكر البيع وقبض الثمن وتصحيح الأسباب التى بها يتمّ البيع *

8.12 ولم يكن أبو حنيفة // ولا أبو يوسف ولا محمـّد بن الحسن ولا يوسف بن خالد ولا هلال ولا
(152 a) أبو زيد يؤكـّدون هذا التوكيد فى هذا الكتاب ولكنـّا ذكرناه وأكـّدناه نحن ليوفـّى فى الدخيل ما توجبه له الشركة من الوجوه التى ذكرنا والله نسأله التوفيق *

باب التولية

9.0 قال أبو جعفر واذا اشترى رجل من رجل دارا وقبضها ودفع ثمنها ثمّ ولاّها رجلا فأرادا أن يكتبا بينهما فى ذلك كتابا كتبت على مثل ما كتبنا فى كتاب الشركة حتّى اذا أتيت على تأريخ الكتاب الأوّل وعلى ذكر شهوده كتبت على أثر ذلك وانـّك يا فلان بن فلان سألتنى أن أولـّيك

هذه الدار المحدودة فى هذا الكتاب بجميع ما سُمّى لها ومنها فى هذا الكتاب بالثمن الذى ذكرت لك أنّى ابتعتها به من بائعى المسمّى فى هذا الكتاب ثمّ تنسق الكتاب على ذلك على لفظ
9.1 التولية كنحو ما نسقناه على لفظ الشركة * وقد اختلف الناس فى التولية فى البيع الذى لم يُقبَض فقال بعضهم لا يجوز ذلك وجعلوه كالبيع المستقبل وممّن قال ذلك أبو حنيفة وأبو يوسف وزفر
(152 b) ومحمّد بن الحسن ومحمّد بن ادريس الشافعى // وكان بعضهم يجيز التولية فيما قُبِض وفيما لم يُقبَض فى سائر البياعات *

10.0 قال أبو جعفر فإن كان المشترى قد بنى فى هذه الدار بناء قبل أن يولّيها هذا الرجل ثمّ ولّاها ايّاه بثمنها الذى كان ابتاعها به وبقيمة بنائها[1] الذى كان أحدثه فيها فإنّ يوسف بن خالد قد كان يكتب فى ذلك الكتاب بينهما على هذا المعنى وهذا المعنى عندنا فاسد لأنّ البناء يكون مبيعا بهذه التولية ولا يجوز بيع شىء بقيمة ولكنّ الأوثق عندنا فى ذلك أن تكتب إنّى ذكرتُ لك أنّى ابتعت من فلان بن فلان جميع الدار التى بمدينة كذا ثمّ تنسق الكتاب على ما ذكرنا انّه يُكتَب فى التولية فإذا أتيت على وكلّ حقّ هو لها خارج منها كتبت على أثر ذلك خلا البناء القائم فيها فى الموضع الكذا منها وهو الموضع الذى يحيط به ويجمعه ويشتمل عليه حدود أربعة ثمّ تحدّده ثمّ تكتب فإنّ هذا البناء خاصّة دون أرضه المحدودة فى هذا الكتاب لم يدخل ولا شىء منه[2] فيما ذكرت لك أنّى كنت ابتعته من فلان بن فلان المسمّى فى هذا الكتاب //
(153 a) وذكرت لك أنّى أحدثته لنفسى بعد ابتياعى هذه الدار المحدودة فى هذا الكتاب من فلان بن فلان وأنّك يا فلان بن فلان سألتنى أن أولّيك جميع ما ذكرت لك أنّى كنت ابتعته من فلان ابن فلان فيما سُمّى ووُصف وحُدّ فى هذا الكتاب بالثمن الذى ذكرت لك أنّى ابتعته به وهو كذا كذا دينارا مثاقيل ذهبا عينا وازنة جيادا فأجبتك الى ذلك ثمّ تنسق الكتاب على ما كتبنا حتّى اذا فرغت من ذكر الثمن كتبت على أثر ذلك وابتعت منّى يا فلان بن فلان جميع هذا البناء القائم الذى ذكرت لك أنّى أحدثته أنا فى هذه الدار المحدودة فى هذا الكتاب وهو البناء المستثنى المحدودة أرضه فى هذا الكتاب بجميع الأبواب والخشب والسقف والأجرّ والطين القائم ذلك كلّه فيه بكذا كذا دينارا مثاقيل ذهبا عينا وازنة جيادا ثمّ تنسق الكتاب على ذلك ثمّ تكتب ودفعت الىّ يا فلان بن فلان جميع الثمن المسمّى فى هذا الكتاب وقبضته منك واستوفيته تامّا كاملا وأبرأتك من جميعه بعد قبضى ايّاه واستيفائى له وهو كذا كذا دينارا مثاقيل ذهبا عينا وازنة جيادا[3] من ذلك كذا كذا دينارا ثمن ما وقعت عليه هذه التولية المسمّاة فى هذا الكتاب ومن ذلك كذا كذا دينارا ثمن البناء الذى وقع عليه هذا البيع المسمّى فى هذا الكتاب ثمّ تذكر

[1] MS بقيمه بنائه
[2] MS منها
[3] MS جياد

(153 b) قبض المشترى على نحو ما كتبنا فى كتاب الشركة // وتنسق الكتاب على ذلك حتّى اذا انتهيت الى ذكر الإقرار بالرؤية كتبت وذلك بعد أن أقررنا جميعا أنّا قد رأينا جميع ما وقعت عليه هذه التولية المسمّاة فى هذا الكتاب وجميع ما وقع عليه هذا البيع المسمّى فى هذا الكتاب داخلها وخارجها وجميع ما فيها ومنها من بناء ومنازل وقليل وكثير وتبيّن لنا ذلك ووقفنا على نهاية كلّ صنف ممّا يقع عليه هذا البيع وهذه التولية المسمّيان فى هذا الكتاب من جميع جوانبه وقوفا صحيحا وتبيّن لنا ذلك وعرفناه جميعا عند عقدة هذه التولية وعند عقدة هذا البيع المسمّيين فى هذا الكتاب بيننا وقبل ذلك فتعاقدناهما بيننا على ذلك وتفرّقنا جميعا بأبداننا عن تراض منّا بجميعهما وإنفاذ منّا لهما فما أدركك يا فلان بن فلان فيما وقعت عليه هذه التولية وفيما وقع عليه هذا البيع المسمّيان فى هذا الكتاب وفى شىء منها وفى شىء من كلّ واحد منهما من درك من أحد من الناس كلّهم فعلىّ لك تسليم ما يجب لك علىّ فى ذلك من حقّ ويلزمنى بسبب التولية وبسبب البيع
(154 a) المسمّيين فى هذا الكتاب حتّى أسلّم ذلك اليك على ما توجبه لك علىّ هذه التولية // وعلى ما يوجبه لك علىّ هذا البيع المسمّيان فى هذا الكتاب ثمّ تنسق الكتاب على نحو ما كتبنا فى الشركة *

10.1 قال أبو حنيفة وأبو يوسف ومحمّد لو أنّ رجلا اشترى من رجل دارا بثمن مسمّى وقبضها ثمّ ولّاها رجلا ولم يسمّ له ثمنها ثمّ علم المولى بعد ذلك بثمنها كان بالخيار إن شاء أخذها وإن شاء ترك *

10.2 وقال آخرون لا يجوز التولية حتّى يُسمَّى الثمن فى عقدها كما يُسمَّى فى سائر البياعات فلمّا اختلفوا فى ذلك كتبنا فى كتابنا التولية ذكر الثمن الذى كان البيع وقع به بين المتبايعين من أجل هذا الاختلاف *

باب المرابحة والمواضعة

11.0 قال أبو جعفر واذا اشترى رجل من رجل دارا بمائة دينار وقبضها ثمّ باعها من رجل مرابحة بربح عشرة دنانير فأرادا أن يكتبا بينهما فى ذلك كتابا كتبت هذا كتاب لفلان بن فلان كتبه له فلان بن فلان ثمّ تنسق الكتاب فى ذلك على مثل ما كتبنا فى الشركة وفى التولية حتّى اذا فرغت من ذكر تأريخ الكتاب الأوّل وذكر شهوده كتبت على أثر ذلك وانّك سألتنى يا فلان ابن فلان أن أبيعك جميع الدار المحدودة فى هذا الكتاب بجميع ما سُمّى لها ومنها فى هذا الكتاب
(154 b) مرابحة بثمنها المسمّى فى هذا الكتاب وهو كذا كذا دينارا مثاقيل ذهبا عينا وازنة // جيادا وبكذا كذا دينارا مثاقيل ذهبا عينا وازنة جيادا ربحا لى فأجبتك الى ما سألتنى من ذلك ثمّ تنسق الكتاب على ذكر المرابحة على نحو ما كتبنا فى الشركة وفى التولية *

11.1 قال أبو جعفر وانّما كتبنا بثمنها المسمّى فى هذا الكتاب وهو كذا كذا دينارا مثاقيل ذهبا عينا وازنة جيادا وبكذا كذا دينارا مثاقيل ذهبا عينا وازنة جيادا ربحا لى فوصفنا الربح ولم نجتزِ[1] بوصف الثمن الأوّل لأنّ أبا حنيفة ومحمّدا وأبا يوسف كانوا يقولون فى رجل باع من رجل دارا بألف درهم وضح ثمّ باعها المشترى من رجل بربح عشرة دراهم إنّ على المشترى ألفا وضحا مثل الثمن الأوّل وعليه عشرة دراهم نقد البلد الذى تبايعا فيه[2] ولم يجعلوا الربح من جنس الثمن فكتبنا ما كتبنا من ذلك احتياطا من قولهم *

11.2 وإن كان البيع وقع فى المسألة الأولى بمائة دينار وبربح العشرة أحد عشر كتبت ذلك فى كتابك وذكرت جنس الثمن وأمّا الربح فى هذا فإنّ أبا حنيفة وأبا يوسف ومحمّدا كانوا يقولون هو من جنس الثمن الأوّل وإن أمسكت عن وصف الربح فى كتابك بما وصفت به الثمن الأوّل من أجل هذا القول فذلك جائز وإن وصفته بما وصفت به الثمن الأوّل على جهة التوكيد فهو حسن [ثمّ تكتب بعقب][3] ذلك فبلغ ثمن هذه الدار المحدودة فى هذا الكتاب كذا كذا
(155 a) دينارا مثاقيل ذهبا عينا وازنة جيادا // ثمّ تنسق الكتاب على نحو ذلك *

11.3 وانّما كتبنا فى هذا وفى التولية وفى الشركة قبول السائل من المسؤول ما كان سأله ايّاه منهنّ لأنّ أبا حنيفة وأبا يوسف ومحمّدا كانوا يقولون لو أنّ رجلا قال لرجل بِعنى عبدك هذا بألف درهم فقال قد فعلت لم يجب البيع بذلك حتّى يقبل السائل فذكرنا فى كتابنا القبول فى الموضع الذى ذكرناه فيه لهذا المعنى *

11.4 وأحبّ الينا من وقوع البيع بربح العشرة أحد عشر أن يقع بربح العشرة دراهم درهم وتكتب الكتاب على ذلك وتذكر فيه نوع الدراهم ثمّ تنسق الكتاب على ذلك فإنّ أبا حنيفة وأبا يوسف ومحمّدا قالوا اذا وقع البيع بربح العشرة أحد عشر وإنّ القياس فى ذلك أن يكون الربح لكلّ عشرة دراهم من الثمن أحد عشر درهما قالوا ولكنّا نستحسن فنجعله درهما واحدا لكلّ عشرة دراهم فلمّا اختلف استحسانهم فى هذا وما يوجبه القياس عندهم لم نأمن أن يذهب ذاهب فى ذلك الى القياس فيوجب على المشترى أكثر ممّا يرى أنّه يجب عليه فكان أحوط الأشياء فى ذلك أن تكتب الكتاب على ما ذكرنا ليأمن المشترى فى ذلك من اختلاف أهل العلم ومن قول من يذهب منهم الى القياس الذى ذكرنا *

12.0 قال أبو جعفر ولو لم يقع البيع مرابحة ولكنّه وقع مواضعة كتبت الكتاب على ما كتبنا
(155 b) حتّى اذا انتهيت الى ذكر تأريخ الكتاب // الأوّل وأسماء شهوده كتبت على أثر ذلك فسألتنى ان أبيعك هذه الدار المحدودة فى هذا الكتاب بجميع ما سُمّى لها ومنها فى هذا الكتاب مواضعة

[1] MS ولم نجتزى
[2] MS التى تبايعا فيه
[3] words illegible in MS

بوضيعة كذا كذا دينارا من ثمنها المسمّى فى هذا الكتاب وهو كذا كذا دينارا مثاقيل ذهبا عينا وازنة جيادا فأجبتك الى ما سألتنى من ذلك ثمّ تنسق الكتاب على ما كتبنا وتكتب فيه فكان الذى صار اليه ثمن هذه الدار المحدودة فى هذا الكتاب بهذه المواضعة المذكورة فى هذا الكتاب كذا كذا دينارا مثاقيل ذهبا عينا وازنة جيادا ثمّ تنسق الكتاب على ما كتبنا *

12.1 وإن كان البيع وقع فى ذلك بوضيعة العشرة أحد عشر فإنّ أبا حنيفة وأبا يوسف ومحمّدا قالوا فى ذلك كان القياس أن يكون الثمن عشرة أجزاء من أحد وعشرين جزءًا من الثمن الذى كان البيع الأوّل وقع به قالوا ولكنّا نستحسن فنجعله عشرة أجزاء من أحد عشر جزءًا من الثمن الأوّل فأحوط الأشياء عندنا فى هذا اذا وقع البيع على ذلك أن تنظر الى مقدار الوضيعة التى تجب فى هذا البيع فتجعل البيع واقعا بينهما مواضعة بوضيعـــة كذا كذا دينارا من الثمن الأوّل فأحوط لما نخاف فى ذلك من الاختلاف حكم الاستحسان وحكم القياس *

12.2 وانّما كتبنا كتُبُنا هذه على ذكر المرابحة وعلى ذكر المواضعة ولم نجعلها على بيوع مستأنفة وأثمان مستأنفة لأنّا لا نأمن أن يكون البائع قد زاد على المشترى فى الثمن فإنّه إن كان فعل ذلك فإنّ أبا حنيفة وزفر ومحمّدا كانوا يقولون المشترى بالخيار إن شاء أخذ المبيع بثمنه الذى سمّياه[1]

12.3 (156 a) بينهما فى عقد البيع وإن شاء ترك * وكان // ابن أبى ليلى وأبو يوسف يقولان يحطّ عنه الخيانة وحصّتها من الربح إن كان البيع وقع مرابحة *

12.4 ولما نخاف أيضا أن يحدث فى يد المشترى فى هذا المبيع عيب ثمّ يحدث به عيبا كان فى يد بائعه ايّاه لم يبرأ اليه منه ولم يعلم به المشترى فيختلف حكم ذلك وحكم البيع لأنّه فى المرابحة انّما يكون للبائع الخيار إن شاء قبض المبيع وردّ جميع الثمن على المشترى وإن شاء أبى ذلك ولا شىء عليه لأنّ من حجتّه على المشترى منه أن يقول له انّما بعتك بيعا مرابحة فإن جُعل لك علىّ الرجوع ببعض الثمن خرج البيع الذى كان بيننا من حكم المرابحة وصار الى حكم بيع المساومة ولم أبعك كذلك ولست بقادر أن تردّ المبيع على حال ما قبضته منّى لأنّه قد حدث به عيب فى يدك لم يكن فى يدىّ والبيع ليس كذلك البائع بالخيار إن شاء قبل من المشترى المبيع على حال ما هو عليه وردّ عليه الثمن الذى قبضه منه وإن شاء أبى ذلك وردّ على المشترى نقصان العيب الذى كان بالمبيع يوم قبضه منه من الثمن الذى كانا تبايعا به فلذلك كتبنا بينهما ما تعاقدا على مثل ما تعاقدا بينهما من مرابحة ومواضعة وبيّنّا ذلك فى كتابنا ليجب لكلّ واحد منهما عند كلّ فريقة هؤلاء المختلفين ما يجب له فى قوله من الوجوه التى ذكرنا فى هذا الباب *

[1] MS ثمنه التى سمياه

باب الرجل يشترى دارا من رجل ثمّ يهب له ثمنها قبل أن يقبضه منه

13.0 (156 b) قال أبو جعفر واذا اشترى الرجل من أبيه[1] دارا فوهب له أبوه // ثمنها فأراد أن يكتب عليه بذلك كتابا كتبت هذا ما اشترى فلان بن فلان بن فلان الفلانى من أبيه فلان بن فلان بن فلان الفلانى اشترى منه جميع الدار التى بمدينة كذا ثمّ تنسق الكتاب فى ذلك على ما كتبنا فى مثله ممّا قد تقدّم فى كتابنا هذا حتّى اذا أتيت على ذكر الثمن كتبت بعقب ذلك وأبرأ فلان بن فلان ابنه فلان بن فلان من جميع الثمن المسمّى فى هذا الكتاب وهو كذا كذا دينارا مثاقيل ذهبا عينا وازنة جيادا وقبل فلان بن فلان من أبيه فلان بن فلان هذه البراءة المسمّاة فى هذا الكتاب بمخاطبة منه ايّاه على جميع ذلك وسلّم فلان بن فلان الى ابنه فلان بن فلان جميع ما وقع عليه هذا البيع المسمّى فى هذا الكتاب ثمّ تنسق الكتاب فى ذلك على مثل ما كتبنا فى البيع الذى لا براءة فيه من الثمن فيما تقدّم من كتابنا هذا غير أنّك لا تكتب فى ذلك دركا لأنّ البائع لم يقبض من المشترى ثمنا والدرك انّما يوجب ردّ الثمن *

13.1 قال أبو جعفر وقد كان يوسف يكتب فى هذا مثل ما كتبنا غير أنّه كان يكتب فوهب فلان بن فلان لابنه فلان بن فلان جميع الثمن المسمّى فى هذا الكتاب ويختار ذلك على البراءة فكان ذكر البراءة هاهنا أحبّ الينا من ذكر الهبة لأنّ قوما يقولون هبة الدين باطل ويذهبون فى ذلك الى أنّ الهبة لا تجوز إلاّ مقبوضة وليس الدين بقائم بعينه فيكون مقبوضا وكانت البراءة من الدين جائزة فى قولهم جميعا فلذلك اخترنا البراءة على الهبة فى هذا *

13.2 (157 a) قال وكان يوسف يقدّم ذكر قبض الدار فى هذا على ذكر هبة الثمن فى الكتاب // الذى كان يكتبه فى ذلك وكان تقديم البراءة من الثمن على قبض الدار المبيعة فى هذا أحبّ الينا لأنّ قوما يقولون قبض المشترى الدار من البائع بإذن البائع إقرار من البائع بقبض ثمنها من المشترى ولهذا المعنى قدّم ذكر قبض البائع الثمن فى كتاب الشرى على ذكر قبض الدار المشتراة ففى قول هؤلاء اذا كُتب الكتاب على ما ذهب اليه يوسف انّما كان البائع واهبا للثمن بعد أن صار فى حكم القابض له فهبته ايّاه للمشترى لا ينفى عنه ضمان الدرك للمشترى فيما باعه ايّاه اذ كان قد أقرّ له بما يكون به فى حكم المقرّ بقبض ثمن ما باعه فلهذا المعنى اخترنا فى كتابنا هذا تقديم البراءة من الثمن على قبض المشترى[2] للدار المبيعة *

13.3 ولم يكن يوسف يكتب فى كتابه هذا ذكر الرؤية للدار من المتبايعين ولا من واحد منهما ولا تفرّقهما بعد تبايعهما ايّاها وكان ذكر ذلك كلّه عندنا أحسن بل هو ممّا لا بدّ من ذكره لأنّ البائع انّما ملّك المشترى الدار المبيعة بالبيع الذى باعه ايّاها فإن صحّت أسباب ذلك البيع صحّ ذلك التمليك وإن بطلت أسباب ذلك البيع بطل ذلك التمليك والبيع لا يصحّ فى قول بعض

[1] MS من ابنه

[2] MS على قبض البائع

الناس إلاّ برؤية البائع والمشترى لما وقع عليه البيع عند وقوع البيع بينهما وتفرّقهما بأبدانهما من بعد البيع وقد ذكرنا ذلك وما يليه فيما تقدّم من كتابنا هذا فلهذا المعنى احتجحنا[1] أن يُكتَب ذلك فى كتابنا هذا *

13.4 (157b) وحجّة أخرى وهى أنّ سوّار بن عبد الله[2] // قد كان يقول للبائع خيار الرؤية فيما باعه اذا لم يكن رآه قبل بيعه ايّاه وقد كان أبو حنيفة مرّة قال هذا القول وقد احتجّ به عثمان بن عفّان على طلحة بن عبيد الله فى حديث علقمة بن وقاص اذ قال لطلحة بن عبيد الله لى الخيار لأنّى بعت ما لم أرَ وقد ذكرنا ذلك بإسناده فى بدء كتابنا هذا فإذا لم تكتب فى هذا إقرار البائع برؤية الدار التى باعها كان له فى هذا القول أن يقول انّما وقع بيعى على ما لم أرَ فيكون القول قوله فى ذلك ويكون له إبطال البيع وارتجاع الدار بخيار الرؤية فى قول هؤلاء القائلين *

13.5 قال أبو جعفر وقد اختلف الناس فى إبراء البائع المشترى من الثمن قبل أن يقبضه منه وكان أبو حنيفة وأبو يوسف ومحمّد بن الحسن يقولون البراءة جائزة ولا يكون البائع بها فى معنى قابض الثمن فإن استحِقّ المبيع من يد المشترى لم يرجع على البائع بشىء فى قولهم وكذلك لو أصاب المشترى بها عيبا لم يكن له على البائع سبيل إلاّ أن يشاء المشترى أن يردّها على البائع ولا يأخذ منه شيئا *

13.6 وكان آخرون يقولون فى ذلك إبراء البائع المشترى من الثمن يقوم مقام قبضه ايّاه منه لأنّه هو الذى أبطله عن المشترى بإبرائه ايّاه منه وقد روى عيسى بن أبان عن محمّد بن الحسن أنّه قال هذا القول قال ولكنّا استحسنّا القول الأوّل فإن استحِقّ المبيع فى قول هؤلاء الذين جعلوا البراءة قبضا لم يجب // للمشترى فى قولهم على البائع شىء لأنّ المبيع لمّا استحِقّ عُلِم أنّ (158a)
البيع لم يجب به للبائع على المشترى ثمن لأنّه باعه ما لا يملك وانّما أبرأه ممّا يجب له عليه وإن أصاب المشترى بالمبيع عيبا ردّه فى قولهم على البائع وأخذ الثمن ولم يكن للمشترى على البائع إن استحِقّ المبيع من يده شىء فى قول أبى حنيفة وأبى يوسف ومحمّد ولا فى قول هؤلاء الآخرين مطالبة من الثمن للمعنيَيْن اللذين ذكرناهما فلهذا المعنى لم نكتب فى كتابنا فى هذا دركا للمشترى على البائع *

14.1 فإن كان البائع قبض الثمن من المشترى[3] وهو دراهم أو دنانير أو حنطة لم يقع البيع عليها بعينها أو شعير لم يقع البيع عليه بعينه أو ما أشبه ذلك من الأشياء المكيلات والموزونات لم يقع البيع عليها بعينها ثمّ وهبه البائع للمشترى وسلّمه اليه وقبضه منه المشترى ثمّ حضرا ليكتبا بينهما

[1] MS اجتجنا
[2] MS عبد اله
[3] MS فان كان المشترى قبض الثمن من البائع

كتابا يصفان فيه البيع والهبة كتبت الكتاب بينهما فى ذلك مثل ما تكتبه فى البيع الذى لم يهب البائع ثمنه للمشترى فإن ذكرت الهبة فيه فحسن وإن لم تذكرها فحسن غير أنّك اذا ذكرتها وجب لها حكم الهبة ووجب لواهبها أن يرجع فيها على ما يرجع فى الهبة فى قول مَن يجعل ذلك له وعلى ما سنُبَيِّنُهُ فى باب الهبة ان شاء الله *

14.2 فإن كان الثمن عرضا من العروض قبضه البائع من المشترى ثمّ وهبه له وسلّمه اليه وقبضه
(158 b) منه // المشترى كتبت فى كتابك ذلك كلّه ولم تكتب فيه دركا لأنّ هبة البائع للمشترى الثمن العرض بعد قبضه ايّاه منه وقبل قبضه ايّاه منه سوى فى قول أبى حنيفة وأبى يوسف ومحمّد وهو مثل الدراهم والدنانير والثمن الذى ليس بعرض الذى وهبه البائع للمشترى قبل قبضه ايّاه منه فى جميع ما وُصف *

14.3 وإن كانا تعاقدا البيع بينهما على دراهم بعينها أو دنانير بعينها ثمّ وهبها البائع للمشترى بعد أن قبضها منه وقبل ذلك منه المشترى وقبض منه الدراهم أو الدنانير بتسليمه ايّاها اليه فإنّ أبا حنيفة وأبا يوسف ومحمّدا كانوا يقولون فى ذلك إنّ البيع لم يقع على أعيان الدراهم ولا على أعيان الدنانير وإن كان المتبايعان قد أضافا البيع اليها وانّما وقع البيع على مثلها فى ذمّة المشترى للبائع فهبة البائع الدراهم أو الدنانير التى قبضها من المشترى للمشترى ليست بمنزلة ثمن البائع فيما وجب عليه[1] للمشترى من ردّه الثمن عليه إن استحِقّ المبيع من يده أو من ردّ الثمن عليه إن أصاب بالمبيع عيبا كان به قبل البيع فردّه على البائع *

14.4 وكان زفر بن الهذيل ومالك بن أنس ومحمّد بن ادريس الشافعى وعامّة أهل المدينة يذهبون الى أنّ البيع الذى أضيف الى دراهم بأعيانها أو الى دنانير بأعيانها فقد وقع البيع عليها بأعيانها ويجعلونها كالعروض *

14.5 والأحوط فى هذا الكتاب اذا وهب البائع للمشترى الثمن بعد أن قبضه منه[2] // أن يكون ذلك
(159 a) كلّه مذكورا فى كتاب العهدة وإن تذكر فيها أنّ البيع قد أضافه المتبايعان الى الدراهم بأعيانها أو الى الدنانير بأعيانها وأنّ هبة البائع ايّاها للمشترى كان بعد قبضه ايّاها منه فمتى رُفع الكتاب الى مَن يذهب الى مذهب من هذين المذهبين اللذين ذكرنا جعل البائع[3] والمشترى على ما يذهب اليه فى ذلك ولم يكن فى الكتاب عنده نقيصة عن المعانى التى يحتاج اليها فيه *

[1] MS ليست بمنزلة عن البائع ما وجب عليه
[2] MS ان قبض منه
[3] MS حمل البائع

باب شرى الأعمى وبيعه

15.1 قال أبو جعفر ولو أنّ رجلا أعمى اشترى دارا من رجل غير أعمى فأراد أن يكتب عليه بذلك كتابا فإنّ يوسف بن خالد كان يكتب كتاب الشرى فى ذلك على مثل ما كان يكتبه فى شرى البصير غير أنّه اذا انتهى الى موضع الرؤية كتب وذلك بعد أن أقرّ فلان بن فلان وفلان بن فلان يعنى المتبايعين أنّه قد رأى مع فلان بن فلان يعنى البائع لفلان بن فلان يعنى المشترى وكيلٌ لفلان بن فلان يعنى المشترى الأعمى[1] هذه الدار المحدودة فى هذا الكتاب ثمّ ينسق الكتاب على مثل ما كان ينسقه فى شرى البصير فاذا انتهى الى قوله عند عقدة هذا البيع المسمّى فى هذا الكتاب بينهما وقبل ذلك كتب على أثر ذلك فأعلمَ الوكيل[2] فلانُ بن فلان فلانَ بن فلان يعنى المشترى جميع ما رأى من ذلك كلّه ووصفه له فقبل فلان بن فلان يعنى المشترى ذلك ورضى به فتبايع فلان بن فلان // وفلان بن فلان يعنى المتبايعين بعد ذلك كلّه من الرؤية الموصوفة فى (159 b) هذا الكتاب ومن علم فلان بن فلان يعنى المشترى بها وتفرّقا بعد البيع عن تراض منهما جميعا به وهكذا كان يوسف يكتب فى هذا الكتاب ولم نرَ أبا زيد ذكر فى كتابه من ذلك شيئا *

15.2 وكان هذا الذى كتب يوسف من ذلك عندى ضعيفا لمعنيَيَيْن أمّا أحدهما فإنّ الناس قد اختلفوا فى شرى الأعمى فأجازه بعضهم وممّن أجازه منهم أبو حنيفة وأبو يوسف ومحمّد بن الحسن ثمّ اختلفوا فيما يقوم لها الضرير مقام النظر من الصحيح فقال محمّد بن الحسن فيما حكاه عنه محمّد بن سماعة اذا وقف الأعمى من الدار المبيعة حيث لو كان بصيرا رآها فذلك رؤية له وقال غيره منهم اذا وُصفت له فكانت كما وُصفت له فذلك كرؤيته لها لو كان بصيرا فالذى كتب يوسف ليس على محلّ الرؤية من البصير فى قول محمّد بن الحسن *

15.3 قال أبو جعفر وفى ذلك معنى آخر وهو أنّ أبا يوسف ومحمّد بن الحسن قد قالا فى الرجل البصير اذا اشترى دارا من رجل بصير فوكّلا رجلا بصيرا بقبضها والنظر اليها ففعل ذلك إنّ نظر هذا الوكيل ليس كنظر هذا المشترى وإنّ الوكالة فى ذلك غير جائزة حدّثنا بذلك محمّد ابن العبّاس بن الربيع عن علىّ بن معبد عن محمّد بن الحسن عن أبى يوسف *

15.4 قال أبو جعفر فالنظر على ذلك أن يكون الأعمى كذلك فى قول أبى يوسف ومحمّد بن الحسن ولا يكون وكيله فى ذلك يقوم مقامه لو كان بصيرا ثمّ رجعنا الى تمام ذكر اختلاف الناس فى شرى // الأعمى فحدّثنا ابراهيم بن أبى داود قال حدّثنا عبد الحميد بن صلح قال حدّثنا على (160 a) ابن مسهر قال سألت أبا حنيفة عن شرى الأعمى فأجازه وسألت سفيان الثورى عنه فأبطله قال علىّ وقول سفيان فى هذا أحبّ الىّ *

[1] MS يعنى المشترى بصير

[2] MS فاعلم وكيل

15.5 قال أبو جعفر وقد وافق سفيان على ما قال من ذلك مالك بن أنس ومحمّد بن ادريس الشافعى وكان أوثق الأشياء عندنا فى هذا أن يوكّل الأعمى وكيلا بصيرا يشترى له هذه الدار ثمّ يكتب الوكيل الكتاب فى ذلك على مثل ما يكتب فى شرى الرجل للرجل على مثل ما كتبنا فى ذلك فيما تقدّم فى كتابنا هذا حتّى لا يكون بين أهل العلم فى ذلك اختلاف وكذلك اذا أراد أن يبيع دارا وكّل غيره من البصراء يبيعها لما نخاف فى ذلك من الاختلاف الذى ذكرنا *

باب شرى الأخرس وبيعه

16.0 قال أبو جعفر واذا اشترى رجل غير أخرس من رجل أخرس دارا فأراد أن يكتب عليه بذلك كتاب شرى فإنّه يكتب هذا ما شهد عليه الشهود المسمّون فى هذا الكتاب شهدوا جميعا أنّ فلان بن فلان بن فلان الفلانى وقد أثبتوه وعرفوه معرفة صحيحة بعينه واسمه ونسبه أخرس لا يتكلّم أصمّ لا يسمع بصير عاقل يعرف بتدبير نفسه [المضرّة] [1] والمنفعة والأخذ والإعطاء والبيع والشرى
(160b) وما له فيه الحظّ والتوفير وما عليه فيه الغبن والوكس وأنّه يخالط الناس // فيفاوضهم الأمور ويعرف الناس بأعيانهم وكناهم وأنسابهم وعشائرهم من القبائل وأوطانهم من البلدان كلّ ذلك بإشارة منه فيومئ بإشارته بذلك الى مَن حضر بما حضره منها ويعرف بإشارته ما غاب عنه منها وأنّ ذلك من إشارته قائم فيه دائم منه لا يختلف حتّى صار ذلك عندهم بما قد تلوا منه وخبروا كاللغة التى لا يجهل سامعها ما أراد به قائلها وأنّه يبايع الناس بتلك الإشارة فيبيع ويشترى ويأخذ ويعطى وإن نقص فى كيل أو وزن أو عدد عرف ذلك وأشار به الى مَن حضره حتّى يعرف ذلك منه وما نقم على مَن فعل ذلك به من انتقاصه ايّاه وإن زيد على ماله فى ذلك زيادة عرفها وأشار بوصف ما زيد منها وأنّ ذلك منه عامّ فى معرفة الأمور حتّى يشير فى صفة ذى العيب بعيبه وصفة ما لا عيب فيه [2] بصفته وكلّ ذلك من أمره معروف أنّه أقرّ عندهم وأشهدهم على نفسه بالإشارة الموصوفة فى هذا الكتاب بعد الذى عرفوه به ممّا سُمّى ووُصف فى هذا الكتاب أنّه باع من فلان بن فلان بن فلان الفلانى بمحضر من فلان بن فلان هذا وإشارة منه اليه جميع الدار التى بمدينة كذا فى الموضع الكذا منها فتصفها وتحدّدها بمحضر منه ايّاها وإشارة منه اليها ووقوف
(161a) منه على جميع // جوانبها ونهاياتها كلّها بحدودها وأرضها وبنائها ثمّ تنسق الكتاب فى ذلك على مثل ما كتبنا فى الشرى من غير الأخرس فيما تقدّم من كتابنا هذا حتّى تأتى على وكلّ حقّ هو لها خارج منها فتكتب على أثر ذلك بكذا كذا دينارا مثاقيل ذهبا عينا وازنة جيادا فقبل منه فلان بن فلان يعنى المشترى ما باعه ايّاه من ذلك بمخاطبة منه ايّاه على ذلك ودفع فلان بن فلان الى فلان بن فلان جميع الثمن المسمّى فى هذا الكتاب وقبضه منه فلان بن فلان وصار فى يده

[1] word illegible in MS

[2] MS وصفة لا عيب فيه

وقبضه بمحضر من الشهود المسمّين فى هذا الكتاب ذلك ورؤية أعينهم ايّاه وأبرأه[1] فلان بن فلان من جميعه بالإشارة الموصوفة فى هذا الكتاب بعد قبضه ايّاه واستيفائه له منه بمحضرهم ورؤية أعينهم وهو كذا كذا دينارا مثاقيل ذهبا عينا وازنة جيادا وسلّم فلان بن فلان يعنى الأخرس الى فلان بن فلان بمحضر من الشهود المسمّين فى هذا الكتاب ورؤية أعينهم جميع ما وقع عليه هذا البيع المسمّى فى هذا الكتاب وقبضه منه فلان بن فلان وصار فى يده وقبضه بهذا الشرى المسمّى فى هذا الكتاب ثمّ تنسق الكتاب فى ذلك على مثل ما كتبنا فى بيع غير الأخرس فيما تقدّم من كتابنا هذا غير أنّك كلّما ذكرت فيه إقرار الأخرس كتبت بعقب ذلك بالإشارة الموصوفة فى هذا الكتاب وتكتب فى آخر الكتاب بعد أن أشير الى فلان بن فلان يعنى الأخرس بجميع ما
(161 b) فيه فأقرّ بالإشارة الموصوفة // فى هذا الكتاب أنّه قد فهمه وعرف جميع ما فيه بعد أن قُرئ على فلان بن فلان يعنى المشترى فأقرّ أن قد فهمه وعرف جميع ما فيه حرفا حرفا وفلان بن فلان يعنى الأخرس وفلان بن فلان يعنى المشترى صحيحا العقول والأبدان جائزا الأمور طائعان غير مكرهين وقد عرفها الشهود المسمّون فى هذا الكتاب وأثبتوهما معرفة صحيحة بأعيانهما وأسمائهما وأنسابهما وكتبوا شهاداتهم بخطوطهم فى شهر كذا من سنة كذا *

16.1 قال أبو جعفر وإن شئت كتبت وكتبت شهاداتهم على جميع ما سُمّى ووُصف فى هذا الكتاب فى شهر كذا من سنة كذا وهكذا كان محمّد بن الحسن يختار فى مثل هذا وقال من الشهود مَن عسى ألاّ يكتب بخطّه ويكتب له غيره حدّثنا بذلك سليمان بن شعيب عن أبيه عن محمّد بن الحسن *

16.2 وقد كان يوسف بن خالد وهلال بن يحيى يكتبان العهدة على الأخرس على مثل ما كتبنا وما علمنا أحدا من أهل العلم يقدمهما فى ذلك غير أنّهما لم يكونا يكتبان فى بدء كتابهما وقد عرفوه وأثبتوه معرفة صحيحة بعينه واسمه ونسبه فكتبنا نحو ذلك لأنّ بنا من الحاجة الى معرفته بعينه واسمه ونسبه أكثر ما بنا من الحاجة الى معرفة ما وصفنا من أحواله فيما ذكرناه عنهما فى كتاب العهدة الذى كتبناه عليه وغير أنّهما كانا يكتبان وما له فيه الحظّ وعليه فيه الغبن فكرهنا نحن ذلك لئلا
(162 a) يحمل على // النقصان ويتوهّم متوهّم أنّه أُريد بذلك شىء واحد له فيه الحظّ وعليه فيه الغبن وهذا محال فكتبنا ما له فيه الحظّ وما عليه فيه الغبن لنبيّن أنّ ما له فيه الحظّ غير ما عليه فيه الغبن وغير أنّهما لم يكونا يكتبان فى ذكر الدار المبيعة إشارة البائع اليها فكتبنا نحن ذلك لأنّه انّما يعرف قصده الى الدار بإشارته اليها كما يعرف قصده الى البائع منه والى المشترى منه بإشارته اليه *

16.3 وكما كانت إشارته الى بائعه والى المبتاع منه ممّا لا بدّ من ذكرها فى كتاب الشرى عندهما وكذلك إشارته الى الدار المبيعة وكذلك تُكتَب فى جميع ما يعامل به الأخرس وفيما يجب له وفيما

[1] MS وأبرأ

يجب عليه من الديون والشفع والإجارات وفيما يعقده على نفسه من رهن وغيره وفيما يعقد له من ذلك على نحو ما كتبنا *

باب البيع اذا وقع على أنّ المشترى إن لم ينقد للبائع الثمن الى كذا وكذا يوما فلا بيع بينهما أو وقع على أنّ البائع إن ردّ الثمن على المشترى الى كذا كذا يوما فلا بيع بينهما

17.1 قال أبو جعفر واذا اشترى الرجل من الرجل دارا بألف درهم على أنّ المشترى إن لم ينقد للبائع
(162 b) الثمن الى ثلاثة أيّام فلا بيع بينهما // فإنّ أبا حنيفة وأبا يوسف ومحمّد بن الحسن كانوا يجيزون ذلك ويجعلونه فى حكم البيع اذا وقع على أنّ المشترى بالخيار ثلاثة أيّام قالوا لأنّ المشترى إن شاء نقد الثمن فى الثلاثة الأيّام فتمّ البيع وإن شاء منع ذلك فبطل البيع فجعلوا ذلك البيع كالبيع اذا وقع على أنّ المشترى بالخيار ثلاثة أيّام حدّثنا سليمان بن شعيب عن أبيه عن محمّد بن الحسن عن أبى حنيفة وعن أبى يوسف بما ذكرناه عنهما وعن محمّد من رأيه بما ذكرناه عنه *

17.2 وحدّثنا محمّد بن العبّاس قال حدّثنا علىّ بن معبد قال أخبرنا محمّد بن الحسن قال أخبرنا يعقوب بن ابراهيم عن أبى حنيفة بما ذكرناه عنه وعن أبى يوسف وعن محمّد بما ذكرناه عنهما وكان زفر بن الهذيل لا يجيز هذا البيع ويجعله فاسدا فاعرِفْ هذا فأنّه قد اختلِف فيه *

17.3 وقال أهل العلم فيه ما قد رويناه عمّن ذكرناه منهم وافترقوا فيه فرقتَيْن فقالت كلّ فرقة منهم واحدا من هذين القولين ولا يخرج فى ذلك كتاب متّفق عليه *

17.4 فإن أحبّ هذان المتبايعان اذ قد وقع فى بيعهما هذا الاختلاف أن يتناقضاه ويعقدا بينهما بيعا بألف درهم وانّما أخذا من الأثمان الجائزة على أنّ المشترى بالخيار ثلاثة أيّام كان ذلك أصلح وأحوط وكان بيعهما على الخيار ثلاثة أيّام بيعا صحيحا غير مختلف فيه والمشترى يصل بذلك البيع
(163 a) الجائز الذى لا اختلاف فيه الى مثل ما يصل اليه بالبيع الأوّل الذى ذكرناه // المختلف فيه فى
17.5 قول مَن يجيز له * قال فإن كان البيع وقع بينهما على أنّ المشترى إن لم ينقد البائع الثمن فيما بينه وبين أربعة أيّام فلا بيع بينهما فإنّ أبا حنيفة قال هذا البيع فاسد ولا يجوز البيع فى هذا اذا اشترط فيه مدّة أكثر من ثلاثة أيّام على مثل ما كان يقول فى الخيار وأمّا محمّد بن الحسن فأجاز الشرط فى ذلك اذا كان الى وقت معلوم ثلاثة أيّام أو أقلّ منها أو أكثر منها كنحو ما كان يقول فى الخيار وأمّا أبو يوسف فلم يجز الشرط فى هذا أكثر من ثلاثة أيّام ووافق أبا حنيفة فى ذلك وخالفه فى الخيار حدّثنا سليمان بن شعيب عن أبيه عن محمّد بن الحسن عن أبى حنيفة وعن أبى يوسف بما ذكرناه عنهما وحدّثنا محمّد بن العبّاس عن علىّ بن معبد عن محمّد بن الحسن عن أبى يوسف عن أبى حنيفة بما رويناه عنه *

17.6 واذا اشترى الرجل من الرجل دارا بألف درهم ودفع المشترى الى البائع الثمن واشترطا فى عقد البيع بينهما أنّ البائع إن ردّ على المشترى الثمن فيما بينه وبين ثلاثة أيّام فلا بيع بينهما فإنّ أبا حنيفة وأبا يوسف ومحمّد بن الحسن كانوا يجيزون ذلك أيضا ويجعلون هذا الشرط كالشرط الذى يشترطه البائع لنفسه فى عقد البيع أنّه بالخيار // ثلاثة أيّام حدّثنا بذلك محمّد بن العبّاس (163 b)
عن علىّ بن معبد عن محمّد عن أبى يوسف ممّا قد رويناه عنه *

17.7 حدّثنا سليمان بن شعيب عن أبيه عن محمّد عن أبى حنيفة عن أبى يوسف بذلك على مثل ما ذكرناه فى الاشتراط للمشترى فى الفصل الذى قبل هذا من هذا الباب وفى حكم الاشتراط اذا كان أربعة أيّام أو أكثر من ذلك على مثل ما ذكرناه فى ذلك فى الفصل الذى قبل هذا *

17.8 وأمّا زفر بن الهذيل فكان لا يجيز هذا الشرط ويفسد به البيع فاعرفْ ذلك فإنّه لا يتهيّأ فى ذلك كتاب متّفق عليه ولكن الأحوط فى ذلك أن يتناقض المتبايعين ما كانا يعاقدا بينهما من ذلك ويستأنفان بيعا بثمن معلوم على أنّ البائع بالخيار فيما باع ثلاثة أيّام على مثل ما كتبنا فى ذلك فى باب بيع الخيار الذى قد مضى فيما تقدّم من هذا الكتاب *

باب كتاب العهدة يضيع من المشترى فسأل البائع أن يجدّد له فى ذلك كتابا آخر

18.0 قال أبو جعفر واذا اشترى الرجل من الرجل دارا بمائة دينار وتقابضا جميعا واكتتب المشترى على البائع بذلك كتابا وأشهد له على نفسه بذلك شهودا وذكر المشترى للبائع أنّ الكتاب قد ضاع منه وسأله أن يجدّد له فى ذلك كتابا فإنّ هذا لا يجب على البائع فإن أجاب البائع المشترى الى ذلك وأراد أن يكتب له به على نفسه // كتابا يصف فيه ما كان عقد له على نفسه من بيع (164 a)
هذه الدار ومن قبضه منه ثمنها ومن تسليمه ايّاها اليه وممّا كان اكتتبه له على نفسه فى ذلك فى الكتاب الأوّل كتبت هذا كتاب لفلان بن فلان بن فلان الفلانى يعنى المشترى كتبه له فلان ابن فلان بن فلان الفلانى وأقرّ له بجميع ما فيه وأشهد له على ذلك كلّه شهودا سمّوا فى هذا الكتاب فى صحّة عقله وبدنه وجواز أمره وذلك فى شهر كذا من سنة كذا إنّك كنتَ ابتعتَ منّى جميع الدار التى بمدينة كذا فى الموضع الكذا منها وهى الدار التى يحيط بها ويجمعها ويشتمل عليها حدود أربعة أحد حدود جماعتها الحدّ الأوّل وهو كذا ينتهى الى كذا والحدّ الثانى والثالث والرابع ثمّ تذكر باب الدار فى أىّ حدّ هو من حدودها ثمّ تكتب كنت ابتعت منّى جميع هذه الدار المحدودة فى هذا الكتاب بحدودها كلّها ثمّ تنسق ذكر الحقوق التى هى لها على مثل ما نسقناه فى مثل ذلك ممّا قد تقدّم من كتابنا هذا حتّى اذا أتيت على وكلّ حقّ هو لها خارج منها كتبت بعقب ذلك بكذا كذا دينارا مثاقيل ذهبا عينا وازنة جيادا شرى لا شرط فيـه ولا عدة

ودفعت الىّ جميع الثمن المسمّى فى هذا الكتاب وقبضته منك واستوفيته تامّا كاملا وأبرأتك من
(164 b) جميعه بعد قبضى ايّاه واستيفائى له وهو كذا كذا دينارا مثاقيل // ذهبا عينا وازنة جيادا وسلّمت
اليك جميع ما وقع عليه البيع المسمّى فى هذا الكتاب بينى وبينك وقبضته منّى وصار فى يدك
وقبضك بالشرى المسمّى فى هذا الكتاب وذلك بعد أن أقررت أنا وأنت أنّا قد رأينا جميعا جميع
هذه الدار المحدودة فى هذا الكتاب داخلها وخارجها وجميع ما فيها ومنها من بناء ومنازل وقليل
وكثير وتبيّن لنا ذلك وعرفناه جميعا عند عقدة هذا البيع المسمّى فى هذا الكتاب بيننا وقبل ذلك
فتعاقدنا هذا البيع المسمّى فى هذا الكتاب بيننا على ذلك فتفرّقنا جميعا بأبداننا بعد أن تعاقدناه
بيننا عن تراض منّا جميعا بجميعه وإنفاذ منّا له وضمنت لك جميع ما يدركك فيما وقع عليه البيع
المسمّى فى هذا الكتاب بينى وبينك وفى شىء منه ومن حقوقه من درك من أحد من الناس كلّهم
حتّى أسلّم ذلك اليك على ما يوجبه لك علىّ هذا البيع المسمّى فى هذا الكتاب وكتبت لك على
نفسى بابتياعك منّى جميع ما وقع عليه البيع المسمّى فى هذا الكتاب كتاب شرى باسمك تأريخه
شهر كذا من سنة كذا ومن شهوده المسمّين فيه فلان بن فلان وفلان بن فلان وفلان بن فلان
وغيرهم من الشهود وإنّك يا فلان بن فلان ذكرت لى أنّ ذلك الكتاب الذى كنت اكتتبته لك
على نفسى المذكور تأريخه وشهوده فى هذا الكتاب ضاع منك وسألتنى أن أكتب لك على نفسى
كتابا أقرّ لك بشراك منّى جميع هذه الدار المحدودة فى هذا الكتاب بجميع ما سُمّى لها ومنها فى
(165 a) هذا الكتاب وبقبضى منك ثمنها المسمّى فى هذا الكتاب وبتسليمى ايّاها اليك // ليكون ثقة
لك وحجّة فى يدك فأجبتك الى ما سألتنى من ذلك وكتبت لك على نفسى هذا الكتاب فلا حقّ
لى فى هذه الدار المحدودة فى هذا الكتاب ولا فى شىء منها ولا فى أرضها ولا فى بنائها ولا فى حقوقها
ولا قبلك فى شىء من ثمنها ولا عليك ولا عندك ولا بيدك على الوجوه والأسباب كلّها فما أدركك
يا فلان بن فلان فيما ذُكر ابتياعك ايّاه منّى ممّا سُمّى ووُصف فى هذا الكتاب من أحد من
الناس كلّهم فعلىّ لك تسليم ما يجب علىّ فى ذلك من حقّ ويلزمنى لك حتّى أسلّم اليك جميع
الذى يجب لك علىّ فى ذلك على ما يوجبه لك علىّ هذا البيع المسمّى فى هذا الكتاب وفى الكتاب
المذكور تأريخه وشهوده فى هذا الكتاب فقبل فلان بن فلان من فلان بن فلان جميع الإقرار المسمّى
فى هذا الكتاب وصدّقه على ذلك كلّه بمخاطبة منه ايّاه على جميع ذلك *

باب الرجل يبتاع لأبيه دارا بأمره ويكتب على بائعه ايّاها كتاب عهدة باسمه ثمّ يوصى أبوه بثلثها لرجل ثمّ يموت بعد ذلك ويترك ابنه المشترى وابنا آخر معه لا وارث له غيرهمـا

19.0 قال أبو جعفر واذا اشترى الرجل دارا لأبيه بأمره وكتب عهدتها باسمه ثمّ مات أبوه وقد كان
أوصى بثلثها لرجل وترك ما بقى منها ميراثا بين ابنيَه أحدهما المشترى ولم يترك وارثا غيرهما فأراد

(165 b) المشترى أن يكتب فى ذلك كتابا // تنسق فيه ذلك كلّه وتجعله نسختين ليكون [1] إحداهما فى يد أخيه بحقّ ما وجب له بمورثه عن أبيه والأخرى فى يد الموصى له بحقّ ما وجب له بوصيّة الموصى فإنّك تكتب هذا كتاب لفلان [2] بن فلان الفلانى يعنى الموصى له ولفلان بن فلان الفلانى يعنى ابن الميّت الذى لم يتولّ الشرى كتبه لهما فلان بن فلان بن فلان الفلانى وهو أخو فلان بن فلان المسمّى فى هذا الكتاب لأبيه وأقرّ لهما بجميع ما فيه وأشهد لهما على ذلك كلّه شهودا سمّوا فى هذا الكتاب فى صحّة عقله وبدنه وجواز أمره وذلك فى شهر كذا من سنة كذا أنّى كنت ابتعت من فلان بن فلان بن فلان الفلانى فى شهر كذا من سنة كذا جميع الدار التى بمدينة كذا فى الموضع الكذا منها ثمّ تحدّدها ثمّ تكتب كنت ابتعت من فلان بن فلان جميع هذه الدار المحدودة فى هذا الكتاب بحدودها كلّها ثمّ تنسق ذكر حقوقها على مثل ما نسقناها فيما تقدّم من كتابنا هذا حتّى اذا أتيت على وكلّ حقّ هو لها خارج منها كتبت على أثر ذلك بكذا كذا دينارا مثاقيل ذهبا عينا وازنة جيادا ودفعت جميع ثمنها المسمّى فى هذا الكتاب الى بائعها منّى المسمّى فى هذا الكتاب وقبضه منّى واستوفاه منّى تامّا كاملا وأبرأنى من جميعه بعد قبضه ايّاه واستيفائه له وهو كذا كذا دينارا مثاقيل ذهبا عينا وازنة جيادا وسلّم الىّ بائعى المسمّى فى هذا الكتاب جميع هذه الدار المحدودة فى هذا الكتاب وجميع ما سُمّى لها ومنها فى هذا الكتاب وقبضتُ ذلك منه وصار فى يدى وقبضى بابتياعى ايّاه منه وأقررت أنا وهو أنّا قد رأينا جميعا جميع هذه الدار المحدودة فى هذا الكتاب داخلها وخارجها

(166 a) وجميع ما فيها ومنها من بناء ومنازل وقليل وكثير // وتبيّن لنا ذلك وعرفناه جميعا عند عقدة هذا البيع المسمّى فى هذا الكتاب بيننا وقبل ذلك وتفرّقنا جميعا بأبداننا بعد هذا البيع المسمّى فى هذا الكتاب عن تراض منّا جميعا بجميعه وإنفاذ منّا له وضمن لى بائعى المسمّى فى هذا الكتاب جميع الذى يدركنى فيما ابتعته منه ممّا سُمّى ووُصف فى هذا الكتاب من درك من أحد من الناس كلّهم حتّى يسلّم ذلك الىّ على ما يوجبه لى عليه البيع المسمّى فى هذا الكتاب واكتتب على نفسه بذلك [3] كلّه كتاب شرى باسمه تأريخه شهر كذا من سنة كذا ومن شهوده المسمّين فيه فلان بن فلان وفلان بن فلان بن فلان وغيرهم من الشهود وانّما كان ابتياعى جميع ما ذُكر ابتياعى ايّاه فى هذا الكتاب لأبى فلان بن فلان بأمره ايّاى بذلك وإذنه لى فيه ودفعت جميع الثمن المسمّى فى هذا الكتاب فى حياة أبى فلان بن فلان من مال أبى فلان بن فلان بأمره وقبضت جميع ما وقع عليه هذا البيع المسمّى فى هذا الكتاب فى حياة أبى فلان بن فلان لأبى فلان بن فلان بأمره وانّما كان اسمى فيما تولّيت من ذلك عاريّة منّى لأبى فلان بن فلان ومعونة وإنّه لا حقّ لى قبل أبى فلان بن فلان فى الثمن الذى ابتعت له به هذه الدار المحدودة فى هذا الكتاب وإنّ أبى فلان بن فلان بعد ذلك تُوُفّى وقد كان أوصى قبل وفاته فى صحّة عقله وبدنه [4] وجواز

[1] MS يكون

[2] MS هذا كتاب فلان

[3] MS واكتتب عليه بذلك

[4] MS عقله وبد

أمره هذا إن كان أوصى فى صحّة عقله وبدنه وإن كان انـّما أوصى فى مرضه الذى [1] تـُوُفـِّى فيه
كتبت فى صحّة عقله وجواز أمره فى مرضه الذى تـُوُفـِّى فيه بعد ابتياعى له جميع ما ذُكر ابتياعى
ايـّاه له فى هذا الكتاب لفلان بن فلان المسمـّى فى هذا الكتاب يعنى الموصى له بثلثها شائع فيها
(166 b) غير مقسوم منها // بحدود هذا البيت الذى أوصى له به وأرضه وبنائه وتذكر حقوقه على مثل ما
تذكرها فى كتاب الشرى حتـّى اذا أتيت على وكلّ حقّ هو له خارج منه كتبت على أثر ذلك
ثمّ تـُوُفـِّى أبى فلان بن فلان ولم يرجع عن شىء من ذلك ولم يغيـّره ولم يبدله ولم يخرج هذه الدار
المحدودة فى هذا الكتاب وفى الكتاب المذكور تأريخه وشهوده فى هذا الكتاب ولا شىء منها من
ملكه الى أن تـُوُفـِّى وقد كان قبل وفاته بعد وصيـّته هذه المذكورة فى هذا الكتاب رجع عن كلّ
وصيـّة كان أوصى بها فى هذه الدار المحدودة فى هذا الكتاب وأبطلها وفسخها وأخرج مـَن كان
أوصى بها اليه عمـّا كان أوصى به اليه منها غير ما كان أوصى به منها لفلان بن فلان المسمـّى
فى هذا الكتاب [2] ممـّا سـُمـّى ووُصف فى هذا الكتاب فإنـّه لم يرجع عن ذلك ولا عن شىء منه
الى أن تـُوُفـِّى وإن شئت كتبت ولم يكن أبى فلان بن فلان أوصى بهذه الدار المحدودة فى هذا
الكتاب ولا بشىء منها لأحد من الناس الى أن تـُوُفـِّى غير ما أوصى به منها لفلان بن فلان المسمـّى
فى هذا الكتاب على ما سـُمـّى ووُصف فى هذا الكتاب فقبل فلان بن فلان من أبى فلان بن
فلان جميع ما أوصى به له من ذلك فوجب ثلث هذه الدار المحدودة فى هذا الكتاب الذى كان
أبى فلان بن فلان أوصى به على ما سـُمـّى ووُصف فى هذا الكتاب لفلان بن فلان بحقّ وصيـّة
أبى فلان بن فلان له به بعد أن كان جميع ما أوصى به أبى فلان بن فلان لفلان بن فلان ممـّا سـُمـّى
(167 a) ووُصف فى هذا الكتاب ومن سائر ما أوصى به أبى فلان بن فلان ممـّا سوى ذلك فيه // خارجا
من ثلث ماله وبعد أن قبضت أنا وأخى فلان بن فلان من مال أبينا فلان بن فلان بحقّ مورثنا عنه
اذ لا وارث له غيرنا أكثر من مثلـَىْ وصاياه وصار ما بقى من هذه الدار المحدودة فى هذا الكتاب
بعد ما وجب منها لفلان بن فلان المسمـّى فى هذا الكتاب بحقّ وصيـّة أبى فلان بن فلان المسمـّاة
فى هذا الكتاب بينى وبين أخى فلان بن فلان المسمـّى فى هذا الكتاب فسلـّمت الى فلان بن
فلان يعنى الموصى له جميع ما وجب له من هذه الدار المحدودة فى هذا الكتاب بجميع حدوده
وحقوقه بحقّ وصيـّة أبى فلان بن فلان له به وهو سهم واحد من ثلاثة أسهم شائع فى هذه الدار
المحدودة فى هذا الكتاب غير مقسوم منها وقبضه منـّى فلان بن فلان وصار فى يده وقبضه كما
يـُقبـَض المشاع وأبرأنى وأخى فلان بن فلان من جميعه بعد قبضه ايـّاه وسلـّمت الى أخى فلان
ابن فلان جميع ما وجب له من هذه الدار المحدودة فى هذا الكتاب بحقّ مورثه عن أبيه فلان بن
فلان الفلانى وقبضه منـّى وصار فى يده وقبضه وهو كذا كذا سهما من كذا كذا سهما من جميع
هذه الدار المحدودة فى هذا الكتاب شائعة فيها غير مقسومة منها فلا حقّ لى فى شىء ممـّا سلـّمته

[1] MS فى مرضه التى

[2] MS فى الكتاب

الى فلان بن فلان يعنى الموصى له ممّا وجب له من هذه الدار المحدودة فى هذا الكتاب بحقّ وصيّة أبى فلان بن فلان المتوفّى له به ولا فى شىء ممّا سلّمته الى أخى فلان بن فلان ممّا وجب له بحقّ مورثه عن أبيه فلان بن فلان من هذه الدار المحدودة فى هذا الكتاب وهو كذا كذا سهما من
(167 b) كذا كذا سهما // من جميعها شائعة فيها غير مقسومة منها وقد جعلتُ أخى فلان بن فلان المسمّى فى هذا الكتاب وكيلى فى جميع ما الىّ وفى جميع ما يجب لى ممّا سلّمته اليه من هذه الدار المحدودة فى هذا الكتاب بحقّ ابتياعى ذلك لأبى فلان بن فلان على ما سُمّى ووُصف فى هذا الكتاب ثمّ تنسق الوكالة بذلك والوصاية به على مثل ما كتبناهما فيمن اشترى لرجل دارا وكتب عهدتها باسمه ثمّ أقرّ بها له وإنّه كان ابتاعها له بأمره ثمّ تكتب بعقب ذلك وحضر فلان بن فلان وفلان بن فلان المسمّيان فى هذا الكتاب يعنى ابن الميّت والموصى له قراءة هذا الكتاب فعرفاه وأقرّا أنّ جميع ما فيه حقّ وصدّقا فلان بن فلان على جميع ما أقرّ به فى هذا الكتاب على ما سُمّى ووُصف فى هذا الكتاب وأقرّا أنّهما قد قبضا من فلان بن فلان يعنى المقرّ جميع ما ذُكر قبضهما اياه منه فى هذا الكتاب وصار فى أيديهما وقبضهما وأبرآه منه بعد قبضهما ايّاه وأنّه لم يبق لهما قبل فلان بن فلان ولا عليه ولا عنده ولا بيده فى هذه الدار المحدودة فى هذا الكتاب ولا فى شىء منها حقّ ليست وصيّة ولا مورث ولا قليل ولا كثير على الوجوه والأسباب كلّها فقبل فلان بن فلان من فلان بن فلان ومن فلان بن فلان جميع الإقرار والبراءة المسمّيَين فى هذا الكتاب بمخاطبة منه ايّاهما على جميع ذلك وقبل أيضا فلان بن فلان من فلان بن فلان جميع ما جعل اليه من الوكالة والوصاية المسمّاتَين فى هذا الكتاب بمخاطبة منه ايّاه على جميع ذلك وقد كتب هذا الكتاب ثلاثة نسخ نظما واحدا ونسقا سواء لا تزيد نسخة منهنّ على نسخة //
(168 a) حرفا يغيّر حكما ولا يزيل معنى فنسخة منهنّ فى يد فلان بن فلان يعنى المقرّ ثقة له وحجّة ونسخة منهنّ فى يد فلان بن فلان يعنى الموصى له ثقة له وحجة ونسخة منهنّ في يد فلان بن فلان يعنى الابن المقرّ له ثقة له وحجّة شهد على[1] إقرار فلان بن فلان يعنى الابن المقرّ وفلان ابن فلان يعنى الموصى له وفلان بن فلان يعنى المقرّ له بجميع ما سُمّى ووُصف فى هذا الكتاب ثمّ تنسق الشهادة على مثل ما كتبنا فى مثل ذلك ممّا قد تقدّم فى كتابنا هذا *

19.1 وهكذا كان يكتب يوسف بن خالد غير أنّه لم يكن يوكّد هذا التوكيد الذى ذكرناه نحن وإنّ أحبّ الأشياء الينا فى هذا الكتاب أن يحذف منه الأشياء التى توجب ملك الميّت لهذه الدار فلا تكتب فيه ولم تخرج هذه الدار المحدودة فى هذا الكتاب ولا شىء منها من ملكه الى أن تُوفّى وإلاّ تكتب فوجب ثلث هذه الدار الذى كان أبى أوصى به لفلان بن فلان لأنّ الميّت انّما ملك الدار بإقرار الابن أنّه كان ابتاعها له بأمره وفى تثبيت كلّ واحد من الابنين بملك أبيهما[2] الدار تثبيت ملك البائع ايّاها وإزالة وجوب الدرك فى قول ابن أبى ليلى وأهل المدينة وزفر وانّما

[1] MS omits على   [2] MS من ملك ابيهما

كتبنا هذا الكتاب على مثل ما كتبناه عليه وإن كان أحبّ الأشياء فى بعضه ما قد ذكرناه بعده لأنّ أصحابنا كانوا يكتبونه على نحو ما كتبناه فكتبناه على نحو ما كانوا يكتبون ثمّ بيّنّا من بعده كيف الاختيار فيه *

19.2 وانّما كتبنا وبعد أن قبضت أنا وأخى فلان بن فلان من مال أبى فلان بن فلان بحقّ مورثنا
(168 b) عنه // أكثر من مثلَى وصاياه ولم نجتز بإقرارهما بقبضهما ثلثَى الدار اللذين هما مثلا ما قبضه الموصى له منها لأنّا قلنا فى كتابنا وكان جميع ما أوصى به أبى فلان بن فلان من ذلك وسائر وصاياه خارجا من ثلث ماله فأثبتنا وصايا غير هذه الوصيّة واحتجنا من أجل ذلك الى أن يقبض الورثة لأنفسهم مثلَيْها *

19.0 bis فإن لم يكن للميّت وصيّة سوى ذلك لم تكتب فى كتابك من هذا شيئا وكتبت مكانه وذلك بعد أن كان أبى فلان بن فلان تُوُفِّى ولا وصيّة له غير ما أوصى به لفلان بن فلان على ما سُمّى ووُصف فى هذا الكتاب *

20.0 وإن شئت أجريت الكتاب فى ذلك على غير ما وصفنا وهو أن تكتب هذا ما شهد عليه الشهود المسمّون فى هذا الكتاب شهدوا جميعا أنّ فلانا وفلانا ابنَى فلان بن فلان بن فلان الفلانى وفلان بن فلان بن فلان الفلانى وقد أثبتوهم وعرفوهم معرفة صحيحة بأعيانهم وأسمائهم وأنسابهم أقرّوا عندهم وأشهدوهم على أنفسهم فى صحّة عقولهم وأبدانهم وجواز أمورهم وذلك فى شهر كذا من سنة كذا أنّ فلان بن فلان بن فلان الفلانى الرجل المسمّى فى هذا الكتاب قد كان فى صحّة عقله وبدنه وجواز أمره فى شهر كذا من سنة كذا ابتاع من فلان بن فلان بن فلان[1] الفلانى جميع الدار التى بمدينة كذا فى الموضع الكذا منها وهى الدار التى يحيط بها ويجمعها ويشتمل عليها حدود أربعة فحدّدها وتذكر بابها فى أىّ حدّ هو من حدودها على مثل ما كتبنا فى مثل ذلك ثمّ تكتب بعقب ذلك كان فلان بن فلان المسمّى فى هذا الكتاب ابتاع من فلان بن فلان جميع هذه الدار المحدودة فى هذا الكتاب بحدودها كلّها ثمّ تنسق ذكر حقوقها وذكر ثمنها على مثل ما نسقناهما
(169 a) فيما تقدّم // قبل ذلك فى كتابنا هذا ثم تكتب ودفع فلان بن فلان جميع الثمن المسمّى فى هذا الكتاب الى فلان بن فلان وقبضه منه فلان بن فلان واستوفاه منه تامّا كاملا وأبرأه من جميعه بعد قبضه ايّاه واستيفائه له وهو كذا كذا دينارا مثاقيل ذهبا عينا وازنة جيادا وسلّم فلان بن فلان الى فلان بن فلان جميع هذه الدار المحدودة فى هذا الكتاب بجميع ما سُمّى لها ومنها فى هذا الكتاب وقبضها منه فلان بن فلان وصار فى يده وقبضه بابتياعه ايّاها منه وذلك بعد أن أقرّ فلان ابن فلان وفلان بن فلان أنّهما قد رأيا جميعا جميع هذه الدار المحدودة فى هذا الكتاب داخلها وخارجها وجميع ما فيها ومنها من بناء ومنازل وقليل وكثير وتبيّن لهما ذلك وعرفاه جميعا عند عقدة البيع الذى

[1] MS omits بن فلان

كانا تعاقداه بينهما المسمّى فى هذا الكتاب وقبل ذلك وتفرّقا جميعا بأبدانهما بعد هذا البيع الذى كانا تعاقداه بينهما عن تراض منهما جميعا بجميعه وإنفاذ منهما له وضمن فلان بن فلان يعنى البائع لفلان بن فلان يعنى المشترى جميع الذى له وجميع الذى يجب له عليه من حقّ بحقّ ابتياعه منه جميع ما ذكر ابتياعه ايّاه منه فى هذا الكتاب حتّى يسلّم ذلك اليه على ما يوجبه له عليه هذا البيع المسمّى فى هذا الكتاب واكتتب فلان بن فلان على بائعه المسمّى فى هذا الكتاب كتاب شرى باسمه تأريخه شهر كذا من سنة كذا ومن شهوده المسمّين فيه فلان وفلان وغيرهم من الشهود وانّما كان فلان بن فلان ابتاع جميع ما ذكر ابتياعه ايّاه فى هذا الكتاب لأبيه فلان ابن فلان بأمره ايّاه بذلك وهو صحيح العقل والبدن وجائز الأمر وبإذنه له فيه ودفع جميع ثمنه المسمّى فى هذا الكتاب الى بائعه المسمّى فى هذا الكتاب من مال أبيه فلان بن فلان بأمره وقبض جميع
(169b) ما وقع عليه البيع // المسمّى فى هذا الكتاب من بائعه المسمّى فى هذا الكتاب لأبيه فلان بن فلان بأمره وكان اسمه فيما تولّى من ذلك عاريّة منه لأبيه فلان بن فلان ومعونة له وانّ أباه فلان ابن فلان بعد ذلك أوصى وهو صحيح العقل والبدن وجائز الأمر لفلان بن فلان المسمّى فى هذا الكتاب بسهم واحد من ثلاثة أسهم من جميع هذه الدار المحدودة فى هذا الكتاب ثمّ تُوُفّىَ فلان ابن فلان ولا وصيّة له فى هذا الدار المحدودة فى هذا الكتاب غير ما أوصى به منها لفلان بن فلان المسمّى [1] فى هذا الكتاب على ما سُمّىَ ووُصف فى هذا الكتاب فقبل فلان بن فلان من فلان ابن فلان جميع ما أوصى به له ممّا سُمّىَ ووُصف فى هذا الكتاب فقبض جميع ما أوصى به له فلان بن فلان ممّا سُمّىَ ووُصف فى هذا الكتاب وصار فى يده وقبضه بتسليم من فلان بن فلان المسمّى فى هذا الكتاب ذلك وهو سهم واحد من ثلاثة أسهم من جميع هذه الدار المحدودة فى هذا الكتاب شائع فيها غير مقسوم منها ولم يكن فلان بن فلان أبو فلان وفلان ابنى فلان المسمَّيَيْن فى هذا الكتاب ترك وارثا يوم تُوُفّىَ غير ابنيَه فلان وفلان المسمّين فى هذا الكتاب وقبض فلان بن فلان لنفسه كذا كذا سهما من كذا كذا سهما من جميع هذه الدار المحدودة فى هذا الكتاب وصارت فى يده وقبضه كما يُقبَض المشاع بحقّ ما أقرّ به له أخوه فلان بن فلان المسمّى فى هذا الكتاب وبتسليم أخيه فلان بن فلان المسمّى فى هذا الكتاب اليه وذلك بعد أن أقرّ فلان
(170a) وفلان ابنا فلان بن فلان المسمّيان فى هذا الكتاب // أنّ جميع ما أوصى به أبوهما فلان بن فلان لفلان بن فلان خارج من ثلث ماله وجعل فلان بن فلان الى أخيه فلان بن فلان جميع ما اليه وجميع ما يجب له فى شىء إن وجب لفلان بن فلان يعنى المقرّ له فى هذه الدار المحدودة فى هذا الكتاب بحقّ مورثه عن أبيه فلان بن فلان على ما أقرّ به له أخوه فلان بن فلان المسمّى فى هذا الكتاب والخصومة والمنازعة فى ذلك الى القضاة والحكّام والسلطان ثمّ تنسق بقيّة الكتاب فى ذلك على مثل ما كتبناه فيما تقدّم من كتابنا هذا فى رجل اشترى دارا باسمه ثمّ أقرّ بعد ذلك أنّه كان ابتاعها لغيره بأمره *

[1] MS omits المسمى

باب الرجل يبتاع دارا من رجل ثمّ يموت المشترى قبل أن يدفع ثمنها وقبل أن يقبضها

21.0 قال أبو جعفر ولو أنّ رجلا ابتاع دارا من رجل ثمّ مات المشترى قبل أن يدفع الثمن الى البائع وقبل أن يقبض منه الدار وقبل أن يكتب عليه فيها عهدة فأراد ابن المشترى وهو وارثه لا وارث له غيره أن يدفع الثمن الى البائع وأن يقبض منه الدار وأن يكتب عليه بها عهدة فإنّك تكتب هذا كتاب لفلان بن فلان بن فلان الفلانى يعنى المشترى كتبه له فلان بن فلان بن فلان الفلانى يعنى البائع وأقرّ له بجميع ما فيه وأشهد له على ذلك كلّه شهودا سمّوا فى هذا الكتاب فى صحّة
(170b) عقله وبدنه وجواز أمره وذلك فى شهر كذا من سنة كذا أنّ أباك فلان بن فلان // قد كان فى صحّة عقله وجواز أمره فى شهر كذا من سنة كذا فى مرضه الذى تُوُفّى فيه ابتاع منّى جميع الدار التى بمدينة كذا فى الموضع الكذا منها ثمّ تحدّدها ثمّ تكتب على أثر ذلك ابتاع أبوك فلان ابن فلان منّى جميع هذه الدار المحدودة فى هذا الكتاب بحدودها كلّها ثمّ تنسق الكتاب على مثل ما كتبنا فى كتاب الشرى حتّى تأتى على شرى لا شرط فيه ولا عدة فتكتب على أثر ذلك وذلك بعد أن أقررت أنا وأبوك فلان بن فلان أنّا قد رأينا جميعا جميع هذه الدار المحدودة فى هذا الكتاب داخلها وخارجها وجميع ما فيها ومنها من بناء ومنازل وقليل وكثير وتبيّن لنا ذلك وعرفناه جميعا عند عقدة هذا البيع المسمّى فى هذا الكتاب بيننا وقبل ذلك فتبايعنا على ذلك وتفرّقنا جميعا بأبداننا بعد هذا البيع المسمّى فى هذا الكتاب عن تراض منّا جميعا بجميعه وإنفاذ منّا له ثمّ تُوُفّى أبوك فلان بن فلان بعد ذلك فى شهر كذا من سنة كذا ولم يدفع الىّ شيئا من الثمن المسمّى فى هذا الكتاب ولم يقبض منّى شيئا ممّا وقع عليه هذا البيع المسمّى فى هذا الكتاب بينى وبينه ولم يكتب علىّ فى ذلك كتاب شرى باسمه ولا كتبه له غيره علىّ بأمره باسمه ولم يترك وارثا يوم تُوُفّى غيرك وإنّك يا فلان بن فلان بعد وفاة أبيك فلان بن فلان دفعت الىّ جميع الثمن المسمّى فى هذا الكتاب من مال أبيك فلان بن فلان وقبضته منك واستوفيته منك تامّا كاملا وأبرأتك وأباك فلان بن فلان من جميعه بعد قبضى ايّاه واستيفائى له وهو كذا كذا دينارا
(171a) مثاقيل // ذهبا عينا وازنة جيادا وسلّمت اليك جميع هذه الدار المحدودة فى هذا الكتاب بجميع ما سُمّى لها ومنها فى هذا الكتاب وقبضت ذلك منّى وصارت فى يدك وقبضك بابتياع أبيك فلان بن فلان ايّاه منّى وبحقّ وراثتك ايّاه على ما سُمّى ووُصف فى هذا الكتاب فما أدركك وأباك[1] فلان بن فلان فيما وقع عليه هذا البيع المسمّى فى هذا الكتاب وفى شىء منه ومن حقوقه من درك من أحد من الناس كلّهم فعلىّ تسليم ما يجب علىّ فى ذلك من حقّ ويلزمنى بسبب البيع المسمّى فى هذا الكتاب حتّى أسلّم ذلك الى من يجب له قبضه منّى على ما يوجبه علىّ البيع المسمّى فى هذا الكتاب فقبلت منّي يا فلان بن فلان لنفسك ولأبيك فلان بن فلان المتوفّى جميع الإقرار والبراءة المسمّيين فى هذا الكتاب بمخاطبة منك ايّاى على جميع ذلك شهد *

[1] MS فما أدركك أباك

21.0 bis قال أبو جعفر وهذا اذا كان البيع فى صحّة المشترى فإن كان البيع فى مرضه الذى تُوُفّىِّ فيه كتبت الكتاب على نحو ما كتبنا غير أنّك تزيد فيه اذا أتيت على قولك وقبضت منّى جميع ما وقع عليه هذا البيع المسمّى فى هذا الكتاب وصار فى يدك وقبضك بابتياع أبيك فلان بن فلان ايّاه منّى وذلك بعد أن كان فى قيمة جميع ما وقع عليه البيع المسمّى فى هذا الكتاب وَفَى بثمنه المسمّى فى هذا الكتاب *

21.1 وانّما كتبنا دفع الثمن من مال الميّت احتياطا للبائع وللمشترى جميعا فأمّا ما حطْنا به المشترى //
(171 b) فإنّ الدين انّما كان للبائع على الميّت لأنّه هو المشترى منه لا على ابنه الذى ورثه فإن أقرّ البائع أنّه قبض الثمن من مال الابن لا من مال الميّت فإنّ أبا حنيفة وأبا يوسف ومحمّدا كانوا يجعلون هذا الثمن دينا للابن على أبيه ولا يجعلون الابن متبرّعا بذلك الأداء عن أبيه فاذا جعلوه دينا للابن على الأب احتيج الى قائم يقوم بمال الميّت ليقضى منه الابن ماله على أبيه من الدين وذلك لا يكون إلاّ من قِبل وصىّ ثابت الوصيّة أو من قبل مَن يقيمه القاضى فى ذلك مقام الأمين أو مقام الوصىّ فيكون البائع فى هذا القول قد دفع الدار الى الابن وليس الى الابن قبضها منه فلا يبرأ إلاّ بدفعها اليه *

21.2 فحطنا البائع فى هذا القول فجعلناه قابضا للثمن من مال الميّت ليكون الميّت بريئا ممّا كان له عليه من الثمن الذى وجب البيع به بينهما ولم يجب للابن على أبيه دينا *

21.3 وقال قوم اذا دفع الابن الثمن من ماله كان متبرّعا به عن أبيه وكان فى دفعه ايّاه عن أبيه كغريب لو تبرّع به فقضاه عن الميّت هذا اذا دفع الابن الثمن من ماله فاذا جعل الابن متبرّعا بدفع الثمن من ماله وحكم له فيه كحكم الغريب[1] لو أدّاه من ماله عن الميّت *

21.4 وقد رأينا رجلا لو ابتاع عبدا من رجل بألف درهم فجاء رجل فتبرّع بالمال ودفعه عن المشترى من ماله بغير أمر المشترى فبرئ المشترى من الثمن ثمّ أصاب المشترى بالعبد عيبا فردّه على البائع
(172 a) فقضى قاض أنّه لا سبيل له على البائع // فى الثمن الذى قبضه البائع من المشترى لأنّه لم يكن قبضه منه ولا من ماله انّما كان قبضه من غيره واذا ردّه عليه بغير قضاء قاض كان ذلك الردّ يقوم مقام الإقالة والإقالة تقوم مقام البيع المستقبل فله أن يرجع عليه بثمن ما باعه ايّاه بتلك الإقالة فيأخذه منه من ماله فكذلك الابن الذى وصفنا لو جعلنا ما قبض البائع منه فى المسألة التى ذكرنا من مال الابن ثمّ أصاب الابن بالعبد عيبا يطالب البائع بردّه كان انّما يطالبه بردّه لأبيه والبائع فلم يقبض شيئا من مال أبيه وللبائع أن يقول لا خصومة بينى وبينك لأنّك انّما تطالبنى لأبيك ولم أقبض من أبيك بدلا من البيع الذى بعته فى حياته ولا قبضته من ماله بعد وفاته فيكون فى بيعه مَن دفع خصومته عن نفسه فجعلنا مال الأب احتياطا من هذا القول[2] فجعلنا

[1] MS بحكم الغريب

[2] MS فحملنا الابن من هذا القول

ما قبض البائع من الثمن من مال الميّت ليكون اذا أصاب بالمبيع عيبا ردّه عليه الميّت وارتجع منه ثمنه فردّه الى ما للميّت *

22.0 وإن شئت كتبت الكتاب فى ذلك على غير هذا المعنى وهو أن تكتب هذا ما شهد عليه الشهود المسمّون فى هذا الكتاب شهدوا جميعا أنّ فلان بن فلان بن فلان الفلانى يعنى البائع وفلان ابن فلان بن فلان الفلانى يعنى ابن المشترى المتوفّى وقد أثبتوهما وعرفوهما معرفة صحيحة بأعيانهما وأسمائهما
(172 b) وأنسابهما أقرّا عندهم وأشهداهم على أنفسهما فى صحّة // عقولهما وأبدانهما وجواز أمورهما وذلك فى شهر كذا من سنة كذا أنّ فلان بن فلان بن فلان الفلانى أبا فلان بن فلان المسمّى فى هذا الكتاب قد كان فى صحّة عقله وبدنه وجواز أمره فى شهر كذا من سنة كذا ابتاع من فلان بن فلان المسمّى فى هذا الكتاب جميع الدار التى بمدينة كذا فى الموضع الكذا منها وهى الدار التى يحيط بها ويجمعها ويشتمل عليها حدود أربعة ثمّ تحدّدها ثمّ تكتب بعقب ذلك ابتاع فلان ابن فلان أبو فلان بن فلان المسمّى فى هذا الكتاب من فلان بن فلان المسمّى فى هذا الكتاب جميع هذه الدار المحدودة فى هذا الكتاب بحدودها كلّها ثمّ تنسق بقيّة الكتاب على ما كتبناه فى مثل ذلك ممّا قد تقدّم فى كتابنا هذا حتّى تأتى على وكلّ حقّ هو لها خارج منها فاذا أتيت على ذلك كتبت على أثره بكذا كذا دينارا مثاقيل ذهبا عينا وازنة جيادا شرى لا شرط فيه ولا عدة وذلك بعد أن أقرّ فلان بن فلان أبو فلان بن فلان المسمّى فى هذا الكتاب وفلان بن فلان يعنى البائع المسمّى فى هذا الكتاب أنّهما قد رأيا جميعا جميع هذه الدار المحدودة فى هذا الكتاب داخلها وخارجها وجميع ما فيها ومنها من بناء ومنازل وقليل وكثير وتبيّن لهما ذلك وعرفاه جميعا عند عقدة هذا البيع المسمّى فى هذا الكتاب بينهما وقبل ذلك فتبايعا على ذلك وتفرّقا جميعا بأبدانهما بعد هذا البيع المسمّى فى هذا الكتاب عن تراض منهما جميعا بجميعه وإنفاذ منهما له ثمّ تُوُفِّى فلان بن فلان بعد ذلك فى شهر كذا من سنة كذا ولم يدفع الى فلان بن فلان من الثمن المسمّى فى هذا
(173 a) الكتاب شيئا ولا برئ منه ولا من شىء منه ولم يقبض شيئا ممّا وقع عليه هذا // البيع المسمّى فى هذا الكتاب ولم يكتتب به ولا اكتتب له بأمره على فلان بن فلان فى ذلك كتاب شرى ولم يترك وارثا يوم تُوُفِّى غير ابنه فلان بن فلان المسمّى فى هذا الكتاب وإنّ فلان بن فلان يعنى البائع بعد ذلك قبض من تركة فلان بن فلان المتوفّى جميع الثمن المسمّى فى هذا الكتاب واستوفاه تامّا كاملا بدفع من فلان بن فلان يعنى الابن ذلك اليه وأبرأ فلان بن فلان يعنى المشترى وابنه فلان ابن فلان المسمّى فى هذا الكتاب من جميعه بعد قبضه ايّاه واستيفائه له وهو كذا كذا دينارا مثاقيل ذهبا عينا وازنة جيادا وقبض فلان بن فلان يعنى الابن المسمّى فى هذا الكتاب جميع ما وقع عليه هذا البيع المسمّى فى هذا الكتاب وصار فى يده وقبضه بتسليم من فلان بن فلان يعنى البائع ذلك اليه فما أدرك فلان بن فلان يعنى المشترى الابن [1] فيما وقع عليه هذا البيع المسمّى فى

[1] MS omits الابن

هذا الكتاب وفى شىء منه ومن حقوقه من درك من أحد من الناس كلّهم فعلى فلان بن فلان يعنى البائع تسليم ما يجب عليه فى ذلك من حقّ ويلزمه بسبب هذا البيع المسمّى فى هذا الكتاب حتّي يسلّم ذلك الى مَن يجب له قبضه منه بحقّ هذا البيع المسمّى فى هذا الكتاب على ما يوجبه له عليه هذا البيع المسمّى فى هذا الكتاب شهد *

22.1 قال أبو جعفر وإن كان البيع كان فى مرض المشترى كتبت ذلك فى كتابك وذكرت فيه (173 b) أنّ فى قيمة ما وقع عليه // هذا البيع المسمّى فى هذا الكتاب وَفَى بجميع الثمن المسمّى فى هذا الكتاب *

22.2 وانّما كتبنا ذلك الوفاء من الابن إن يرجع على البائع فيقول انّما كان أبى ابتاع منك هذه الدار فى مرضه الذى تُوُفِّىَ فيه فحاباك فيما كان ابتاعه منك به والثمن غير خارج من ثلث ماله ولا مال له غيره فيلحقه فى ذلك كما يلحق المحاباة فى المرض من وارث المريض المحابى ولا يكون إقرار الابن بجميع ما فى الكتاب إقرارا بأنّ فى قيمة المبيع وَفَى بثمنه الذى ابتيع به *

باب الرجل يبتاع دارا من رجل ثمّ يموت البائع قبل أن يقبض ثمنها وقبل أن يسلّمها الى المشترى

23.0 قال أبو جعفر واذا ابتاع الرجل من الرجل دارا بمال معلوم فلم يتقابضا حتّى تُوُفِّىَ البائع وترك ابنا وهو وارثه لا وارث له غيره فأراد المشترى أن يدفع الثمن الى ابن البائع وأن يقبض منه الدار وأن يكتب عليه فى ذلك كتابا يتواصفان فيه ما كان بين المشترى والبائع وما أحدث المشترى وابن البائع بعد موت البائع من التقابض كتبت هذا ما شهد عليه الشهود المسمّون فى هذا الكتاب شهدوا جميعا // أنّ فلان بن فلان[1] بن فلان الفلانى يعنى المشترى وفلان بن فلان بن فلان الفلانى يعنى البائع وقد أثبتوهما وعرفوهما معرفة صحيحـــة بأعيانهما وأسمائهما وأنسابهما أقرّا عندهم وأشهداهم على أنفسهما فى صحّة عقولهما وأبدانهما وجواز أمورهما وذلك فى شهر كذا من سنة كذا أنّ فلان بن فلان الفلانى المسمّى فى هذا الكتاب قد كان فى صحّة عقله وبدنه وجواز أمره فى شهر كذا من سنة كذا ابتاع من فلان بن فلان الفلانى أبى فلان بن فلان المسمّى فى هذا الكتاب جميع الدار التى بمدينة كذا فى الموضع الكذا منها ثمّ تنسق الكتاب على مثل ما كتبنا فى الباب الذى قبل هذا الباب حتّي تأتى[2] على شرى لا شرط فيه ولا عدة فاذا أتيت على ذلك كتبت على أثره ولم يقبض كلّ واحد من فلان بن فلان يعنى المشترى ومن فلان بن فلان يعنى البائع المسمّى فى هذا الكتاب شيئا ممّا وقع عليه هذا البيع المسمّى فى هذا الكتاب ولا من الثمن المسمّى فى هذا الكتاب الى أن تُوُفِّىَ فلان بن فلان المسمّى فى هذا الكتاب ولم يترك وارثا يوم تُوُفِّىَ (174 a)

[1] MS omits أن and بن فلان

[2] MS على تاتى

غير ابنه فلان بن فلان الفلانى المسمّى فى هذا الكتاب وقد كان فلان بن فلان وفلان بن فلان يعنى المشترى والبائع بعد أن تبايعا جميع ما ذكر تبايعهما ايّاه فى هذا الكتاب أقرّا جميعا فى صحّة عقولهما وأبدانهما وجواز أمورهما أنّهما قد رأيا جميعا جميع هذه الدار المحدودة فى هذا الكتاب داخلها وخارجها وجميع ما فيها ومنها من بناء ومنازل وقليل وكثير[1] وتبيّن لهما ذلك وعرفاه عند عقدة //
(174 b) هذا البيع المسمّى فى هذا الكتاب بينهما وقبل ذلك فتبايعا على ذلك وتفرّقا جميعا بأبدانهما بعد هذا البيع المسمّى فى هذا الكتاب عن تراض منهما جميعا بجميعه وإنفاذ منهما له ثمّ إنّ فلان بن فلان يعنى المشترى دفع الى فلان بن فلان يعنى ابن البائع بعد وفاة أبيه فلان بن فلان جميع الثمن المسمّى فى هذا الكتاب وقبضه منه فلان بن فلان واستوفاه منه تامّا كاملا وأبرأه من جميعه بعد قبضه ايّاه واستيفائه له وهو كذا كذا دينارا مثاقيل ذهبا عينا وازنة جيادا وسلّم فلان بن فلان بعد ذلك الى فلان بن فلان جميع ما وقع عليه البيع المسمّى فى هذا الكتاب وقبضه منه فلان بن فلان وصار فى يده وقبضه بهذا الشرى المسمّى فى هذا الكتاب فما أدرك فلان بن فلان فيما وقع عليه المسمّى فى هذا الكتاب وفى شىء منه ومن حقوقه من درك من أحد من الناس كلّهم فعلى فلان بن فلان يعنى البائع الميّت تسليم ما يجب له[2] عليه فى ذلك من حقّ ويلزمه بسبب هذا البيع المسمّى فى هذا الكتاب حتّى يقبض ذلك فلان بن فلان يعنى المشترى لمَن يجب له قبض ذلك منه بعد موت فلان بن فلان بحقّ البيع الذى كان من فلان بن فلان فى حياته على ما سُمّى ووُصف فى هذا الكتاب شهد *

23.1 قال أبو جعفر وانّما منعنا أن يضيف الواجب للمشترى بحقّ الدرك الى تركة الميّت كما نضيف اليها دينا لو كان عليه الى أن تُوُفّى لأنّ الدين معلوم ما هو فهو دين فى التركة فيجب
(175 a) ان يضاف اليها والواجب بالدرك غير معلوم ولا متّفق عليه بل هو مختلف فيه // وبيّنّا ذلك وما قد قيل فيه فى أوّل كتابنا هذا بيانا يغنينا عن إعادته فى هذا الموضع فلمّا كان الواجب عند بعضهم ردّ ثمن يكون دينا فى مال الميّت والواجب عند آخرين منهم تخليص دار ليس من مال الميّت لم يجز أن يضيف الواجب الى تركة الميّت اذ كان قد جعله بعضهم فى غيرها وجعلناه منهما غير مضاف الى شىء فإن رُفع الى مَن يرى الواجب للمشترى ردّ الثمن جعله دينا فى التركة وإن رُفع الى مَن يرى غير ذلك جعله حيث يراه *

23.2 فإن كان البيع لم يقع فى صحّة البائع ولكنّه وقع فى مرض موته كتبت الكتاب على ما كتبنا وذكرت فيه وقوع البيع فى المرض وأنّ فى الثمن الذى وقع به البيع وفاء بقيمة جميع ما وقع عليه البيع المسمّى فى هذا الكتاب *

آخر الجزء الرابع والحمد لله ربّ العالمين
يتلوه فى الخامس باب الرجل يبتاع دارا
ثمّ يبيعها من بائعها قبل قبضه منه ثمنها *

[1] MS omits وقليل وكثير

[2] MS omits له

الجزء الخامس من البيوع

من

كتاب الشروط الكبير

(المفقود)

تأليف أبي جعفر أحمد بن محمد بن سلامة بن سلمة
الطحاوي الأزدي رحمه الله

(176b) بسم الله الرحمن الرحيم

باب الرجل يبتاع دارا ثمّ يبيعها من بائعها قبل قبضه ثمنها

1.1 قال أبو جعفر واذا اشترى الرجل من الرجل دارا فقبضها ولم يدفع ثمنها ثمّ باعها من بائعها ايّاه بثمن مسمّى من جنس الثمن الأوّل فإنّ أبا حنيفة وزفر ومحمّدا قالوا فى ذلك إن باعها بمثل ثمنها الذى ابتاعها به منه أو أكثر منه فالبيع جائز وإن باعها منه بمثل ثمنها الأوّل أو بأقلّ منه أو بأكثر منه فالبيع جائز لأنّ هذا بيع مستأنف غير البيع الأوّل فإن باعها منه بدنانير وقد كان ابتاعها منه بالدراهم والدنانير التى باعها منه قيمتها بأقلّ من قيمة الدراهم فإنّ أبا حنيفة وأبا يوسف ومحمّدا قالوا فى ذلك البيع فى هذا فاسد فجعلوا الدنانير والدراهم فى ذلك جنسا واحدا استحسانا وقال زفر البيع فى هذا جائز *

1.2 وإن لم يبعها المشترى من بائعها ايّاه حتّى حدث بها عيب فى يده ينقص من قيمتها[1] التى كانت عليها يوم قبضها منه بحقّ ابتياعه ايّاها منه شيئا قليلا كان ذلك النقصان أو أكثر منه ثمّ باعها من بائعها[2] منه بأقلّ من الثمن الذى كان ابتاعها به منه فالبيع جائز فى قولهم جميعا *

1.0 (177a) واذا اشترى الرجل من الرجل دارا بمائة دينار وقبض المشترى // الدار ولم يقبض البائع الثمن فباعها المشترى من بائعها منه بمائة دينار وخمسين دينارا فأرادا أن يكتبا بينهما فى ذلك كتابا تكتب هذا ما اشترى فلان بن فلان الفلانى من فلان بن فلان الفلانى[3] اشترى منه جميع الدار التى كان فلان بن فلان المسمّى فى هذا الكتاب ابتاعها من فلان بن فلان المسمّى فى هذا الكتاب بمائة دينار واحدة مثاقيل ذهبا عينا وازنة جيادا وسلّمها اليه فلان بن فلان وقبضها منه وصارت فى يده بحقّ ابتياعه ايّاها منه من غير أن يكون فلان بن فلان قبض من فلان بن فلان الثمن المسمّى فى هذا الكتاب ولا شيئا منه وهى الدار التى بمدينة كذا ثمّ تنسق الكتاب على مثل ما كتبناه فى مثل ذلك ممّا قد تقدّم فى كتابنا هذا حتّى اذا أتيت على ذكر التفرّق وفرغت منه كتبت على أثره فما أدرك فلان بن فلان يعنى المشترى فيما وقع عليه هذا البيع المسمّى فى هذا الكتاب وفى شىء منه ومن حقوقه من درك من قبل فلان بن فلان يعنى البائع وبسببه فعلى فلان بن فلان يعنى البائع تسليم ما يجب عليه فى ذلك من حقّ ويلزمه بسبب هذا البيع المسمّى فى هذا الكتاب

[1] MS يقبضها من قيمتها
[2] MS اسم بائعها من بائعها
[3] MS omits الفلانى

(177b) حتّى يسلّم ذلك الى فلان بن فلان يعنى المشترى على ما يوجبه // له عليه هذا البيع المسمّى فى هذا الكتاب شهد *

1.3 قال أبو جعفر وانّما ضمنّنا البائع الدرك من قبله وبسببه خاصّة لأنّه انّما ملك الدار من قِبل هذا الذى ابتاعها منه فانّما يجب له عليه ضمان الدرك من قبله خاصّة وكذلك لو كان هذا المشترى اشتراها من مشتريها منه بمثل الثمن الذى كان اشتراها به منه كتبت الكتاب على نحو ما كتبنا وبيّنت الثمن وسمّيت مقداره *

1.0 bis ولا يصلح أن تكتب فى ذلك كتابا اذا ابتاعها بأقلّ ممّا كان باعها به منه للاختلاف الذى قد ذكرنا بين أهل العلم فى ذلك فى أوّل هذا الكتاب إلاّ أن يكون الدار قد نقصت فى يد مبتاعه عمّا كانت عليه فى الوقت الذى كان قبضها منه من بائعها فإن كان ذلك كذلك كتبت الكتاب على ما كتبنا حتّى اذا أتيت على ذكر الثمن كتبت على أثر ذلك وكان بيع فلان بن فلان هذه الدار المحدودة فى هذا الكتاب بجميع ما سُمّى لها ومنها فى هذا الكتاب من فلان بن فلان بعد أن حدث بها فى يد فلان بن فلان بعد ابتياعه ايّاها من فلان بن فلان البيع المذكور فى صدر هذا الكتاب
(178a) عيب نقصها وغيّرها عن حالها الذى كانت عليه فى وقت قبضه // ايّاها من فلان بن فلان بحقّ ابتياعه ايّاها منه البيع الأوّل المذكور فى هذا الكتاب ثمّ تكتب بقيّة الكتاب على مثل ما كتبنا فى هذا الكتاب *

1.0 ter وإن كان باعها منه بدنانير وانّما كان ابتاعها منه بدراهم كتبت الكتاب على مثل ما كتبنا حتّى اذا أتيت على ذكر الثمن كتبت على أثر ذلك وذلك بعد أن كانت هذه الكذا كذا الدينار المسمّاة فى هذا الكتاب فى قيمتها من الورق أكثر من الكذا كذا الدرهم التى كان فلان ابن فلان ابتاع بها من فلان بن فلان هذه الدار المحدودة فى هذا الكتاب البيع المذكور فى صدر هذا الكتاب وإن كان المشترى قد برئ الى البائع من الثمن الذى كان ابتاع منه الدار به وقبضه منه البائع والمسألة على حالها كتبت الكتاب فى ذلك على مثل ما كتبنا غير أنّك تكتب فى أوّله الدار التى كان ابتاعها فلان بن فلان من فلان بن فلان بكذا كذا دينارا مثاقيل ذهبا عينا وازنة جيادا ودفع فلان بن فلان الى فلان بن فلان ثمنها المسمّى فى هذا الكتاب وقبض فلان بن فلان من فلان بن فلان جميع الدار المذكورة فى هذا الكتاب بتسليم من فلان بن فلان ايّاها اليه واكتتب فلان بن فلان ممّا كان ابتاعه منه من ذلك كتاب شرى باسمه تأريخه شهر كذا من سنة كذا ومن
(178b) شهوده المسمّين فيه فلان بن فلان وفلان // بن فلان وفلان بن فلان[1] وغيرهم من الشهود وهى الدار التى بمدينة كذا ثمّ تنسق الكتاب على نحو ما كتبنا فى رجل اشترى دارا من رجل وتقابضا قيمتها ولم يكن ابتاعها منه قبل ذلك غير أنّك تكتب فى الدرك فى ذلك على نحو ما كتبناه فى

[1] MS omits وفلان بن فلان

هذا الباب وتجعله للمشترى على البائع فيما كان من البائع وبسببه لا فيما كان من قبل غيره من سائر الناس *

2.0 وإن كان البائع ابتاعها من المشترى هى ودارا أخرى[1] لم يكن البائع باعها من المشترى ولم يكن المشترى قبض من البائع ثمن الدار التى كان باعها ايّاه والثمن الذى تعاقدا عليه هذا البيع الثانى من جنس الثمن الذى تعاقدا عليه البيع الأوّل كتبت هذا ما اشترى فلان بن فلان من فلان بن فلان صفقة واحدة اشترى منه جميع الدارين اللتين بمدينة كذا فمن هاتين الدارين الدار التى فى موضع كذا وهى الدار التى كان فلان بن فلان ابتاعها من فلان بن فلان بكذا كذا دينارا مثاقيل ذهبا عينا وازنة جيادا وقبضها وصارت فى يده بتسليم فلان بن فلان ايّاها اليه من غير أن يكون فلان بن فلان قبض منه ثمنها المسمّى فى هذا الكتاب ولا شيئا منه فإن كان كتب
(179 a) عليه بها كتاب شرى // كتبت وكتب عليه بابتياعه ايّاها منه كتاب شرى تأريخه شهر كذا من سنة كذا ومن شهوده المسمّين فيه فلان بن فلان وفلان بن فلان وفلان بن فلان وغيرهم من الشهود ويحيط بهذه الدار ويجمعها ويشتمل عليها حدود أربعة ثمّ تحدّدها ثمّ تكتب بعقب ذلك ومنها الدار التى فى موضع كذا ثمّ تحدّدها ثمّ تنسق الكتاب على مثل ما كتبنا فى مثل ذلك فى ابتياع الدارين صفقة واحدة من رجل حتّى اذا أتيت على ذكر الثمن كتبت على أثر ذلك على[2] أنّ ثمن جميع الدار المُبدأ بذكرها وتحديدها فى هذا الكتاب من الثمن المسمّى فى هذا الكتاب كذا كذا دينارا مثاقيل ذهبا عينا وازنة جيادا فتسمّى ثمنها الأوّل أو أكثر منه على ما تعاقدا بينهما فى ذلك وعلى أنّ ثمن الدار المثنى بذكرها وتحديدها فى هذا الكتاب من الثمن المسمّى فى هذا الكتاب كذا كذا دينارا مثاقيل ذهبا عينا وازنة جيادا ثمّ تنسق الكتاب فى ذلك على مثل ما كتبناه فى الكتاب الذى قبل هذا الكتاب حتّي اذا أتيت على وتفرّقا جميعا بأبدانهما
(179 b) بعد هذا البيع المسمّى فى هذا الكتاب عن تراض منهما جميعا بجميعه وإنفاذ // منهما له كتبت على أثر ذلك فما أدرك فلان بن فلان فى هذا الدار المُبدأ بذكرها وتحديدها فى هذا الكتاب من قبل فلان بن فلان وبسببه ثمّ تنسق فى ذلك ما كتبنا فى ذلك فى تضمين الدرك من قبله وبسببه خاصّة فاذا فرغت من ذلك كتبت وما أدرك فلان بن فلان فى هذه الدار المثنى بذكرها وتحديدها فى هذا الكتاب وفى شىء منها ومن حقوقها من درك من أحد من الناس كلّهم ثمّ تنسق بقيّة الكتاب فى ذلك على ما كتبنا فيمن باع دارا من رجل لم يكن ابتاعها منه *

2.1 وانّما فصلنا ثمن الدارين جميعا فجعلنا ثمن كلّ واحدة منها غير ثمن الأخرى لأنّ أبا حنيفة وأبا يوسف ومحمّدا كانوا يقولون فى هذا لا يجوز البيع حتّى يكون الذى بيعت به الدار التى كان هذا المشترى ابتاعها من هذا المبتاع منه الثمن الأوّل أو أكثر من ذلك فقسمنا الثمن لهذا المعنى

[1] MS هى دار اخرى

[2] MS omits على

لأنّه [ ][1] القسم على القيمة التى لا تُعرَف ولا يجوز ويظنّ وإن شئت كتبت الكتاب فى ذلك على خطاب المشترى الأوّل على مثل ما كتبنا فى بيع المرابحة والتولية والله نسأله التوفيق *

باب الشرى بالدين

(180 a) 3.0 قال أبو جعفر واذا كان لرجل على رجل دنانير دين فابتاع منه بها دارا فأراد أن يكتب عليه كتاب شرى فإنّك تكتب هذا ما اشترى فلان بن فلان بن فلان الفلانى من فلان بن فلان بن فلان الفلانى ثمّ تنسق الكتاب على مثل ما كتبنا فى الشرى بغير الدين فيما تقدّم من كتابنا هذا حتّى اذا أتيت على كلّ حقّ هو لها خارجا منهــا كتبت على أثر ذلك بالكذا كذا الدينار المثاقيل الجياد التى لفلان بن فلان على فلان بن فلان دينا ثابتا لازما بصكّ تأريخه شهر كذا من سنة كذا ومن شهوده المسمّين فيــه فلان بن فلان وفلان بن فلان وفلان بن فلان وغيرهم من الشهود فبرئ فلان بن فلان يعنى البائع من هذه الدنانير المسمّاة فى هذا الكتاب وفى الكتاب المذكور تأريخه وشهوده فى هذا الكتاب وسلّم فلان بن فلان يعنى البائع الى فلان بن فلان جميع ما وقع عليه هذا البيع المسمّى فى هذا الكتاب ثمّ تنسق الكتاب على مثل ما كتبنا فى الشرى بغير الدين فيما تقدّم من كتابنا هذا *

3.0 bis (180 b) قال أبو جعفر فأن كان الشرى وقع بهذه الدنانير وبدنانير سواها كتبت الكتاب // على مثل ذلك حتّى اذا انتهيت الى وكلّ حقّ هو لها خارج منها كتبت على أثر ذلك بالكذا كذا الدينار التى لفلان بن فلان على فلان بن فلان بصكّ تأريخه شهر كذا من سنة كذا ومن شهوده المسمّين فيه فلان بن فلان وفلان بن فلان وفلان بن فلان وغيرهم من الشهود وبكذا كذا دينارا مثاقيل ذهبا عينا وازنة جيادا سوى هذه الكذا كذا الدينار المذكورة فى هذا الكتاب وفى الكتاب المذكور تأريخه وشهوده فى هذا الكتاب فبرئ فلان بن فلان يعنى البائــع من هذه الكذا كذا الدينار المسمّاة فى هذا الكتاب وفى الكتاب المذكور تأريخه وشهوده فى هذا الكتاب ودفع فلان ابن فلان الى فلان بن فلان بقيّة الثمن المسمّى فى هذا الكتاب وقبضها منه فلان بن فلان واستوفاها منه تامّة كاملة وأبرأه من جميعها بعد قبضه ايّاها واستيفائه لها وهى كذا كذا دينارا مثاقيل ذهبا عينا وازنة جيادا ثمّ تنسق الكتاب على مثل ما كتبنا فى الشرى بما ليس بدين على ما تقدّم من كتابنا هذا *

4.0 قال أبو جعفر وإن كان البيع كان من غير الذى عليه الدين بالدين على أن يبرأ الذى هو
(181 a) عليه منه كتبت هذا كتاب لفلان بن فلان الفلانى // يعنى البائع كتبه له فلان بن فلان يعنى الذى له

[1] word illegible in MS

الدين وأقرّ له بجميع ما فيه وأشهد له على ذلك كلّه شهودا سمّوا فى هذا الكتاب فى صحّة عقله وبدنه وجواز أمره وذلك فى شهر كذا من سنة كذا أنّه كان لى على فلان بن فلان الفلانى كذا كذا دينارا مثاقيل ذهبا عينا وازنة جيادا دينا ثابتا لازما حالا بصكّ تأريخه شهر كذا من سنة كذا ومن شهوده المسمّين فيه فلان بن فلان وفلان بن فلان وفلان بن فلان وغيرهم من الشهود وأنّك بعتنى جميع الدار التى بمدينة كذا فى الموضع الكذا منها ثمّ تحدّدها ثمّ تكتب بعتنى جميع هذه الدار المحدودة فى هذا الكتاب بحدودها كلّها ثمّ تنسق الكتاب فى ذلك على مثل ما كتبنا فى مثله ممّا تقدّم فى كتابنا هذا حتّى اذا اتيت على وكلّ حقّ هو لها خارج منها كتبت على أثر ذلك بهذه الكذا كذا الدينار التى لى على فلان بن فلان المسمّى فى هذا الكتاب وهى الكذا كذا الدينار المسمّاة فى هذا الكتاب وفى الكتاب المذكور تأريخه وشهوده فى هذا الكتاب على أن يبرأ منها فلان بن فلان فلا يكون عليه منها قليل ولا كثير فقبلتُ منك ما بعتَنى من ذلك بمخاطبة منّى

(181 b) ايّاك على جميعه وبرئ فلان بن فلان يعنى الذى كان // عليه الدين من هذه الكذا كذا الدينار التى كانت لى عليه[1] ببيعك منّى البيع المسمّى فى هذا الكتاب وقبضته منك وصار فى يدى وقبضى وذلك بعد أن أقررت أنا وأنت أنّا قد رأينا جميعا جميع ما وقع عليه هذا البيع المسمّى فى هذا الكتاب داخله وخارجه وجميع ما فيه ومنه من بناء وقليل وكثير وتبيّن لنا ذلك وعرفناه جميعا عند عقدة هذا البيع المسمّى فى هذا الكتاب بيننا وقبل ذلك فتبايعنا على ذلك وتفرّقنا جميعا بأبداننا بعد هذا البيع المسمّى فى هذا الكتاب عن تراض منّا جميعا بجميعه وإنفاذ منّا له فلم يبق لى على فلان بن فلان من هذه الكذا كذا الدينار التى كانت لى عليه المسمّاة فى هذا الكتاب وفى الكتاب المذكور تأريخه وشهوده فى هذا الكتاب ولا من شىء منها ولا دعوى لى فى ذلك ولا طلبة إلاّ وقد برئ منه فلان بن فلان بما بعتنى ممّا سُمّى ووُصف فى هذا الكتاب فما أدركنى فيما وقع عليه هذا البيع المسمّى فى هذا الكتاب وفى شىء منه ومن حقوقه من درك من أحد من الناس كلّهم فلى ما يوجبه لى هذا البيع المسمّى فى هذا الكتاب على كلّ واحد منك يا فلان بن فلان ومن فلان بن فلان يعنى الذى كان عليه الدين على ما يوجبه لى البيع المسمّى فى هذا الكتاب

(182 a) شهد على إقرار فلان بن فلان يعنى البائع وفلان بن // فلان يعنى المبتاع بجميع ما سُمّى ووُصف فى هذا الكتاب بعد أن قُرئ عليهما جميعا جميع ما فيه من أوّله الى آخره فأقرّا أن قد فهماه وعرفا جميع ما فيه حرفا حرفا فى صحّة عقولهما وأبدانهما وجواز أمورهما طائعين غير مكرهين وعلى معرفتهما ومعرفة[2] فلان بن فلان يعنى الذى كان عليه الدين بأعيانهم وأسمائهم وأنسابهم وذلك فى شهر كذا من سنة كذا *

4.1 قال أبو جعفر وانّما كتبنا الدرك فى هذا على ما كتبنا لأنّ قوما يقولون فى هذا لو استُحِقّت الدار المبيعة رجع المشترى على مطالبه بدينه كما كان[3] قبل الشرى فيكون ذلك الرجوع على الذى

[1] MS التى كانت لى عليك

[2] MS omits معرفة

[3] MS كما قال

كان عليه الدين لا على البائع وممّن قال هذا القول أبو حنيفة وزفر وأبو يوسف ومحمّد بن الحسن وقال آخرون يرجع المشترى على البائع بقيمة الدار المبيعة أو بدار مثلها على مثل ما ذكرناه عنهم فى ذلك من الاختلاف فى صدر هذا الكتاب *

4.2 فلمّا كان الرجوع فى الاستحقاق فى قول قوم على الذى كان عليه الدين وفى قول قوم آخرين على البائع كتبنا الدرك فى ذلك على ما كتبنا حتّى إن رُفع ذلك الى واحد من الفريقين قضى فيه بما يرى *

5.0 وإن شئت ابتدأت الكتاب فى ذلك فكتبت هذا ما اشترى فلان بن فلان من فلان بن فلان
(182 b) اشترى منه // جميع الدار التى بمدينة كذا ثمّ تنسق الكتاب على مثل ما كتبنا فى الشرى بغير الدين على ما تقدّم فى كتابنا هذا حتّى اذا أتيت على وكلّ حقّ هو لها خارج منها كتبت على أثر ذلك بالكذا كذا الدينار التى لفلان بن فلان المسمّى فى هذا الكتاب على فلان بن فلان بصكّ تأريخه شهر كذا من سنة كذا ومن شهوده المسمّين فيه فلان بن فلان وفلان بن فلان وفلان بن فلان وغيرهم من الشهود وعلى أن يبرأ فلان بن فلان من هذه الكذا كذا الدينار المسمّاة فى هذا الكتاب وفى الكتاب المذكور تأريخه وشهوده فى هذا الكتاب ولا يكون عليه منها قليل ولا كثير ثمّ تكتب بعقب ذلك وسلّم فلان بن فلان الى فلان بن فلان جميع ما وقع عليه هذا البيع المسمّى فى هذا الكتاب ثمّ تنسق الكتاب فى ذلك على مثل ما نسقناه فى الشرى بالمال العين فيما تقدّم من كتابنا هذا غير أنّك تكتب فيه الدرك على مثل ما كتبنا فى هذا الباب فى الشروط التى قبل هذا الشرط ثمّ تنسق الشهادة على مثل ما كتبناها فى الشرط الذى قبل هذا الشرط *

5.1 قال أبو جعفر وهذا القول عندنا أحسن من الكتاب الأوّل وأحوط لكلّ واحد من المتبايعين فيه وذلك أنّك اذا ذكرت فى كتابك أنّ المطلوب قد برئ من الدين بالبيع الذى تعاقده هذان
(183 a) المتبايعان // بينهما كان فى ذلك إقرار من المبتاع أنّ الدار المبيعة للبائع لأنّ الذى عليه الدين لا يبرأ من الدين إلّا[1] وهذا البيع الأوّل بيع صحيح وفى إقرار المبتاع بصحّة البيع نفى وجوب الدرك على البائع إن استُحِقّت الدار المبيعة فى قول ابن أبى ليلى وأهل المدينة فكرهنا ذلك واكتفينا باشتراط البراءة لأنّ البيع اذا صحّ وجبت واذا بطل انتفت *

5.2 وانّما بدأنا بالكتاب الأوّل فذكرناه فى هذا الباب فإنّ أصحابنا كذلك كانوا يكتبونه وفيه حمل على المبتاع فخالفنا ذلك الى هذا الكتاب الآخر ليأمن المبتاع من اختلاف الناس فى ذلك *

[1] MS omits الا

باب بيع المريض واشترائه

6.0 قال أبو جعفر واذا ابتاع رجل مريض من رجل صحيح دارا فأراد أن يكتب فى ذلك كتاب شرى فإنّك تكتب كتاب الشرى على مثل ما كتبنا فى بيع الصحيحَين أحدهما من صاحبه فاذا انتهيت الى آخر كتابك كتبت شهد على إقرار فلان بن فلان وفلان بن فلان يعنى المتبايعين بجميع ما سُمّى ووُصف فى هذا الكتاب بعد أن قُرئ عليهما جميعا جميع ما فيه فأقرّا أن قد فهماه وعرفا جميع ما فيه حرفا حرفا طائعين غير مكرهين وعلى معرفتهما بأعيانهما وأسمائهما وأنسابهما وفلان ابن فلان يعنى المشترى[1] صحيح العقل جائز الأمر وذلك فى شهر كذا من سنة كذا * //

(183 b) 6.1 قال أبو جعفر وقد كان بعض أصحابنا يكتب فى مثل هذا وفلان بن فلان يعنى المريض مريض صحيح العقل جائز البيع ولا يكتب جائز الأمر وكذلك كان يكتب فى وصيّة المريض فى صحّة عقله وجواز وصيّته وكان عيسى بن أبان وغيره من أصحابنا يكتبون فى ذلك وجواز أمره على مثل ما كتبنا *

6.2 قال أبو جعفر فإن قال قائل انّما كتبتُ وجواز بيعه فى البيع وجواز وصيّته فى الوصيّة لأنّى اذا كتبت وجواز أمره جمعت أموره كلّها وليست أمور المريض كلّها بجائزة كما تجوز أمور الصحيح قيل له وليس كلّ وصايا المريض جائزة ولا كلّ بياعاته جائزة فاذا كان قولك وجواز وصيّته انّما يريد الوصيّة التى تجوز له أن يوصى بها وكذلك قولك وجواز بيعه انّما هو على البيع الذى يجوز أن يبيعه فما أنكرتَ على مخالفك أن كتب وجواز أمره وأراد بذلك أمره الذى يجوز منه فى مرضه وعلى هذا أريد فيما يُكتَب للصحيح وجواز أمره انّما أراد والأمر الذى يجوز من الصحيح ولم يريدوا كلّ أموره لأنّه قد يعقد البيع الجائز وقد يعقد البيع الفاسد وكذلك سائر عقوده من غير البياعات قد يعقدها على الفاسد وقد يعقدها على الجواز فيكون ما يعقدها على الجواز جائزا وما يعقدها على الفساد[2] فاسدا ولا يجب بقولنا وجواز أموره جواز // كلّ أموره لأنّه انّما يقع ذلك على ما يجوزه له الحكم فكذلك اذا كتب على مريض فإنّما يقع على أموره التى يجوزها له الحاكم * (184 a)

6.3 قال أبو جعفر واذا صحّ هذا المريض من مرضه بعد ذلك قام فيما ابتاعه فى مرضه مقام الصحيح وسواء كانت فيه محاباة أو لم يكن فيه محاباة *

7.0 فإن كانت فيه محاباة فكانت الدار المبيعة تساوى مائة دينار فابتاعها المريض بمائتَى دينار ثمّ صحّ من ذلك المريض فأراد البائع أن يكون فى يده حجّة لتصحّ له المحاباة فانّك تكتب هذا

[1] MS بمعنى البائع

[2] MS وما عقدها على الفساد

ما شهد عليه الشهود المسمّون فى هذا الكتاب شهدوا جميعا أنّ فلان بن فلان يعنى المشترى وهم يعرفونه بعينه واسمه ونسبه معرفة صحيحة وأنّه ابتاع بمحضرهم من فلان بن فلان بن فلان الفلانى وهم يعرفونه أيضا بعينه واسمه ونسبه معرفة صحيحة جميع الدار التى بمدينة كذا فى الموضع الكذا منها ثمّ تحدّدها ثمّ تكتب بعقب ذلك ابتاع فلان بن فلان من فلان بن فلان بمحضرهم جميع هذه الدار المحدودة فى هذا الكتاب ثمّ تحدّدها كلّها ثمّ تنسق ذكر حقوقها على مثل ما نسقناه فى مثل ذلك ممّا قد تقدّم فى كتابنا هذا حتّى تأتى على وكلّ حقّ هو لها خارج منها فتكتب
بعقب ذلك بكذا كذا دينارا مثاقيل ذهبا // عينا وازنة جيادا ودفع فلان بن فلان الى فلان بن (184 b)
فلان جميع الثمن المسمّى فى هذا الكتاب وقبضه منه فلان بن فلان بمحضرهم ورؤية أعينهم واستوفاه منه تامّا كاملا وأبرأه من جميعه بعد قبضه ايّاه واستيفائه له وهو كذا كذا دينارا مثاقيل ذهبا عينا وازنة[1] جيادا وسلّم فلان بن فلان الى فلان بن فلان جميع ما وقع عليه هذا البيع المسمّى فى هذا الكتاب وقبضه منه فلان بن فلان بمحضرهم ورؤية أعينهم وصار فى يده وقبضه بهذا الشرى المسمّى فى هذا الكتاب وأقرّ عندهم[2] فلان بن فلان وفلان بن فلان أنّهما قد رأيا جميعا جميع هذه الدار المحدودة فى هذا الكتاب داخلها وخارجها وجميع ما فيها ومنها من بناء ومنازل وقليل وكثير وتبيّن لهما ذلك وعرفاه جميعا عند عقدة هذا البيع المسمّى فى هذا الكتاب بينهما وقبل ذلك وتفرّقا جميعا بأبدانهما بمحضرهم ورؤية أعينهم بعد هذا البيع المسمّى فى هذا الكتاب عن تراض منهما جميعا بجميعه وإنفاذ منهما له واكتتب فلان بن فلان على فلان بن فلان بذلك كتاب شرى باسمه تأريخه شهر كذا من سنة كذا ومن شهوده المسمّين فيه فلان وفلان وغيرهم من الشهود
وأنّ فلان بن فلان المسمّى فى هذا الكتاب يعنى المشترى كان يوم وقع // هذا البيع المسمّى (185 a)
فى هذا الكتاب مريضا صحيح العقل جائز الأمر وأنّه بعد ذلك برئ من مرضه المذكور فى هذا الكتاب وخرج منه فصار صحيح البدن لا علّة به من مرض ولا غيره وكتبوا شهاداتهم على ذلك بخطوطهم فى شهر كذا من سنة كذا [وأشهدهم فلان بن فلان يعنى المشترى أنّه قد جعل فلان ابن فلان وصيّه فى ذلك بعد وفاته وأقامه فيما جعله اليه][3] من ذلك فى حياته وبعد وفاته مقام نفسه فى حياته[4] وأنّه قد رجع عن كلّ وصيّة كان أوصى بها قبل ذلك وأبطلها وفسخها وأخرج مَن كان أوصى بها اليه عمّا كان أوصى به اليه منه[5] وأنّه تُوُفّى[6] بعد ذلك ولا يعلمونه رجع عن شىء من ذلك ولا أبطله ولا غيّره وأنّه قد ترك عليه ديونا لفلان بن فلان ولفلان بن فلان وهى كذا كذا دينارا لكلّ واحد منهما منها ما ذُكر له منها فى هذا الكتاب وأنّ لفلان بن فلان يعنى الميّت

[1] MS ذهبا عينا معربه
[2] MS واقر لهم
[3] After وسنة كذا a white space of half a line was left in the MS by the copyist, and بانى اشهدت على شهادات الشهود was inserted by another hand. The rest of the insertion is illegible. The phrases between brackets are based on the sense of the clauses that follow.
[4] MS omits فى حياته و
[5] MS omits عما كان أوصى به اليه منه
[6] MS فيها وانه توفى

هذه الدار[1] المحدودة فى هذا الكتاب وفى ملكه وأنّه ترك من الورثة يوم تُوُفِّى بَنيه وهم فلان ابن فلان وفلان بن فلان وفلان بن فلان لا يعلمون له وارثا غيرهم وأنّهم من أهل العلم بجميع ما شهدوا[2] به من ذلك والخبرة به وأنّ فلانا وفلانا ابنَى فلان بن فلان صبيّان صغيران لم يدركا ولا واحد منهما وأنّهما فى ولاية وصيّهما فلان بن فلان المسمّى فى هذا الكتاب بحقّ توصية أبيهما
(185 b) فلان بن فلان // المتوفّى ايّاه عليهما وأنّ فلان بن فلان بالغ صحيح العقل جائز الأمر وأنّ فلان ابن فلان يعنى الوصىّ مأمون على هؤلاء لفلان بن فلان وعلى ما ولى لابنَيه فلان وفلان ابنَى فلان بن فلان يعنى الصغيرين وعلى جميع ما أسند اليه فلان بن فلان من وصيّته اليه جائز أمره وبيعه فيما وقع عليه بيعه المسمّى فى هذا الكتاب وأنّ فلان بن فلان يعنى الوصىّ قد كان قبل من فلان بن فلان جميع ما أوصى به اليه ممّا سُمّى ووُصف فى هذا الكتاب وأنّ فى هذا الثمن المسمّى فى هذا الكتاب وَفَى بجميع ما وقع عليه هذا البيع المسمّى فى هذا الكتاب لا وكس فيه ولا شطط وأنّ بيع فلان بن فلان يعنى الوصىّ من فلان بن فلان يعنى المشترى جميع ما وقع عليه هذا البيع المسمّى فى هذا الكتاب وقبضه منه جميع الثمن المسمّى فى هذا الكتاب وتسليمه اليه جميع ما وقع عليه هذا البيع المسمّى فى هذا الكتاب كان بسؤال فلان وفلان وفلان يعنى الغرماء ايّاه ذلك ليقتضوا ديونهم المسمّاة لهم فى هذا الكتاب من الثمن المسمّى فى هذا الكتاب وبإذن فلان بن فلان يعنى الابن البالغ[3] لفلان بن فلان يعنى الوصىّ له[4] فى ذلك وأمر منه ايّاه فما أدرك //
(186 a) فلان بن فلان يعنى المشترى فيما وقع عليه هذا البيع المسمّى فى هذا الكتاب وفى شىء منه ومن حقوقه من درك من أحد من الناس كلّهم فلفلان بن فلان يعنى المشترى تسليم[5] ما يجب له فى ذلك من حقّ ويلزمه على مَن يجب ذلك له عليه بحقّ هذا البيع المسمّى فى هذا الكتاب حتّى يسلّم ذلك الى فلان بن فلان يعنى المشترى على ما يوجبه له عليه هـــذا البيع المسمّى فى هذا الكتاب وقد كتب هذا الكتاب نسختين متّفقتَيْن نظما واحدا ونسقا سوى لا تزيد نسخة منهما على نسخة حرفا يغيّر حكما ولا يزيل معنى فنسخة منهما فى يد فلان بن فلان يعنى البائع ثقة له وحجّة ونسخة منهما فى يد فلان بن فلان يعنى المشترى ثقة له وحجّة شهد فلان بن فلان الفلانى ويكنى أبا فلان وفلان بن فلان الفلانى ويكنى أبـــا فلان حتّى تسمّى الشهود الذين ذُكرت شهاداتهم فى صدر هذا الكتاب بجميع ما ذُكر من شهاداتهم فى هذا الكتاب على فلان بن فلان المتوفّى وبجميع ما شهدوا فى هذا الكتاب من وفاة فلان بن فلان ومن عدد ورثته ومن صغر مَن ذُكر صغره منهم فى هذا الكتاب ومن بلوغ مَن ذُكر بلوغه منهم فى هذا الكتاب وبجميع
(186 b) ما ذُكر من شهادتهم عليه ممّا سوى ذلك فى هذا الكتاب وأشهدوا على شهاداتهم بذلك // سائر الشهود المسمّين معهم فى هذا الكتاب أنّهم يشهدون على جميع ما ذكر من شهاداتهم عليه

[1] MS وان فلان بن فلان يعنى الميت وهذه الدار
[2] MS بجمع ما شهدوا
[3] MS الابن البائع
[4] يعنى الوصية
[5] MS omits تسليم

فى هذا الكتاب وشهدوا هم وسائر الشهود المسمّون[1] معهم فى هذا الكتاب على إقرار فلان بن فلان يعنى البائع وفلان بن فلان يعنى المشترى وفلان وفلان حتّى تسمّى الغرماء وفلان بن فلان يعنى الابن البالغ بجميع ما سُمّى ووُصف فى هذا الكتاب ثمّ تنسق الشهادة على مثل ما كتبنا فى ذلك فيما قد تقدّم من كتابنا هذا حتّى اذا أتيت على وأنسابهم كتبت على أثر ذلك غير ما فى هذا الكتاب ممّا ذكره فلان بن فلان يعنى الوصىّ من ملك فلان بن فلان يعنى الميّت لهذه الدار المحدودة فى هذا الكتاب ومن وصيّته اليه بجميع ما ذُكر من وصيّته به اليه فى هذا الكتاب فإنّ فلان بن فلان يعنى المشترى لم يقرّ بذلك ولا شىء منه وكتب الشهود المسمّون فى هذا الكتاب شهاداتهم بخطوطهم على جميع ما سُمّى ووُصف فى هذا الكتاب فى شهر كذا من سنة كذا *

7.1 قال أبو جعفر وقد اختُلف فى غير موضع من هذا الكتاب فكان يوسف بن خالد يكتب فى ذلك هذا كتاب ما اشترى فلان بن فلان من فلان بن فلان اشترى منه بعد وفاة فلان بن فلان جميع الدار التى بمدينة كذا ثمّ ينسق كتابه على ذلك ولا يذكر إقرار البائع أنّ الدار للميّت

(187 a) فكان أحبّ الينا من ذلك // أن تذكر أنّ هذه الدار التى باعها فلان بن فلان يعنى[2] الوصىّ ذُكر أنّها لفلان بن فلان الى أن تُوُفّى وتنسق مع ذلك ما قد نسقناه معه فى كتابنا لأمرين *

7.2 أمّا أحدهما فإنّ أهل المدينة كانوا يقولون اذا باع الوصىّ شيئا من تركة الميّت على أنّه وصىّ لم يجب عليه فى ذلك ضمان درك وإن لم يبيّن أنّه وصىّ وجب عليه فيه ضمان الدرك وإن كان فى الحقيقة وصيّا وكتبنا ذكر هذا الوصىّ أنّه وصىّ للميّت ليكون بيعه قد وقع على ذلك فيجب له أن يثبت أنّه وصىّ ما يجب للأوصياء فى [ ][3] من سقوط ضمان الدرك عنهم فى قول أهل المدينة *

7.3 والأمر الآخر أنّا ذكرنا أنّه باعها فى قضاء دين فلان بن فلان فقد يجوز أن يبيع دارا هى له فى قضاء دين على الميّت ويجب له الرجوع بذلك فى مال الميّت فى قول مَن يرى ذلك فكتبنا ما كتبنا احتياطا من ذلك فإن قال قائل فإنّ يوسف قد كتب فى آخر كتابه حيث ذكر شهادة الشهود أنّ الميّت قد ترك هذه الدار ميراثا وكذلك كان يكتب قيل له ذكر هذا فى أوّل الكتاب أصلح فإن أشهدت على شهادات الشهود على ذلك كان أوثق *

8.1 قال أبو جعفر وإن لم يكن المشترى مريضا ولكنّ البائع هو المريض والمسألة على حالها //

(187 b) كُتب كتاب الشرى على نحو ما كتبنا وذكرتَ فيه مرض البائع وصحّة المشترى وإن برئ البائع

[1] MS omits المسمون

[2] MS omits يعنى

[3] word illegible in MS

من مرضه فأراد المشترى أن يكتب كتابا يذكر ذلك فيه أو كان فى البيع محاباة كان البائع حابى بها المشترى كتب له كتابا فى ذلك على نحو ما كتب للبائع فى المسألة الاولى *

8.2 وقال أبو حنيفة وأبو يوسف ومحمّد فيمن يبيع دارا أو عبدا من رجل غريب صحيح ثمّ يقرّ فى مرضه أنّه قد استوفى منه الثمن ولم يعاين الشهود ذلك منه ثمّ يموت من مرضه ذلك إنّ القول قوله والمشترى برئ من الثمن وسواء كان على البائع دين أو لم يكن عليه دين ولو لم يكن البيع فى المرض ولكنّه كان فى الصحّة ثمّ أقرّ البائع فى مرضه الذى تُوُفِّى فيه أنّه قد استوفى الثمن كلّه من المشترى فإنّ ذلك منه يقوم مقام البراءة بغير قبض فإن كان عليه دين كان أصحاب ذلك الدين أولى بما على هذا الغريم وإن لم يكن عليه دين كان ذلك كالوصيّة منه للذى أقرّ له بقبض الدين منه *

8.3 هذا روى عنهم محمّد بن الحسن وروى الحسن بن زياد اللؤلؤىّ عن أبى يوسف أنّه قال لا أجعل إقراره بقبض الدين فى مرضه يقوم مقام البراءة بغير قبض ولكن أجعله قابضا لذلك المال من المشترى ثمّ أجعله قضاء ما كان له عليه فإن كان عليه دين فى الصحّة لقوم // [آخرين (188 a) يبيّنه][1] جعلت دين الصحّة أوّلا فإن فضل من ماله شىء أنفذت لهذا فيه *

8.4 قال أبو جعفر وهذا القول أصحّ على هذا فيهم من القول الأوّل وقد كان جماعة من أهل العلم منهم محمّد بن ادريس الشافعى يقولون إقرار المريض بالدين فى مرضه كإقراره فى صحّته ويحاصّ المقرّ له بما أقرّ به له أصحاب دين الصحّة *

8.5 قال أبو جعفر فكان الأوثق عندنا فيما وجب للمريض من ثمن عرض باعه وفيما وجب له من ثمن عرض ابتاعه أن يُكتَب فيه عليه وله كتاب يُذكَر فيه معاينة الشهود قبضه ما وجب له قبضه حتّى لا يكون له فى ذلك تنازع بين أهل العلم *

9.1 قال أبو جعفر ولو أنّ رجلا ابتاع دارا من أبيه فى مرضه بثمن فيه وفاء بقيمة الدار فأراد أن يكتب عليه بذلك عليه كتاب شرى كتبت على نحو ما كتبنا من كتاب شرى الغريب الصحيح من المريض فإن برئ الأب من مرضه ذلك وأراد أن يكتب بذلك كتابا ليكون ثقة له وليصحّ له بيعه ويجوز لابنه المحاباة إن كانت فى الدار كتبت له فى ذلك كنحو ما كتبنا للغريب بعد برء بائعه من مرضه *

9.2 وإن مات الأب من مرضه ذلك فإنّ أبا حنيفة كان يقول إن كان له ورثة سوى هذا الابن المبتاع فلم يجيزوا للابن ذلك البيع فالبيع مردود وسواء كان فى ثمن الدار نقص // عن قيمة الدار أو (188 b) كان وفاء بقيمة الدار *

[1] words obscured in MS

9.3 قال أبو يوسف فإن كان الثمن وفاء بقيمة الدار فقد جاز البيع للابن[1] وإن كان فى الثمن نقص عن قيمة الدار فلم يجز ذلك بقيّة الورثة للابن فالابن إن شاء ردّ تمام قيمة الدار من ماله إلاّ ما يجب له منه بحقّ الميراث الى بقيّة الورثة معه وإن شاء أبطل البيع *

9.0 فإن أجاز الورثة للابن البيع الذى باعه ايّاه أبوه فأراد أن يكتب عليهم بذلك كتابا كتبت هذا كتاب لفلان بن فلان يعنى المشترى كتبه له أخواه فلان وفلان ابنا فلان بن فلان الفلانى وأقرّا له بجميع ما فيه وأشهدا له على ذلك شهودا سمّوا فى هذا الكتاب فى صحّة عقولهما وأبدانهما وجواز أمورهما وذلك فى شهر كذا من سنة كذا أنّك كنتَ ابتعتَ من أبينا وهو أبوك فلان بن فلان فى صحّة عقله وجواز أمره فى شهر كذا من سنة كذا فى مرضه الذى تُوُفِّى فيه جميع الدار التى بمدينة كذا فى الموضع الكذا منها وكتبتَ[2] عليه بذلك كتاب شرى باسمك نسخته باسم الله الرحمن الرحيم ثمّ تنسخ الكتاب كلّه ثمّ تكتب ومن شهوده المسمّين فيه فلان وفلان وفلان وغيرهم من الشهود وأنّ أبانا فلان بن فلان تُوُفِّى بعد ذلك وبعد قبضه منك جميع الثمن المسمّى فى هذا الكتاب وفى الكتاب المنسوخ فى هذا الكتاب وهو كذا كذا دينارا مثاقيل ذهبا عينا وازنة
(189 a) جيادا وبعد قبضك // منه جميع ما وقع عليه هذا البيع المسمّى فى هذا الكتاب وفى الكتاب المنسوخ فى هذا الكتاب ولم يترك وارثا يوم تُوُفِّى غيرنا وغيرك وأنّا أجزنا لك بعد وفاته بيعه منك المسمّى فى هذا الكتاب وفى الكتاب المنسوخ فى هذا الكتاب وكتبنا ذلك فلا حقّ لنا فى هذه الدار المحدودة فى هذا الكتاب وفى الكتاب المنسوخ فى هذا الكتاب ولا فى شىء منها ولا فى أرضها ولا فى بنائها ولا فيما سوى ذلك منها ولا قبلك من ثمنها المسمّى فى هذا الكتاب وفى الكتاب المنسوخ فى هذا الكتاب على الوجوه والأسباب كلّها فقبل فلان بن فلان من أخويه فلان وفلان ابنَى فلان بن فلان جميع الإقرار والبراءة المسمّيين فى هذا الكتاب بمخاطبة منه ايّاهما على جميع ذلك شهد ثمّ تكتب الشهادة فى ذلك على مثل ما كتبنا فى مثله ممّا قد تقدّم من كتابنا هذا *

9.4 قال أبو جعفر وانّما ذكرنا الإجازة أنّها كانت من هذين المجيزين بعد موت أبيهما لاختلاف الناس فى إجازتهما لذلك قبل موت أبيهما فكان أبو حنيفة وزفر وأبو يوسف ومحمّد يقولون فى ذلك الإجازة باطلة لانّهما أجازا قبل أن يجب لهما شىء فيما وقع البيع عليه *

9.5 وكان أهل المدينة يقولون فى ذلك // الإجازة جائزة وليس لهما أن يرجعا بعد وفاة أبيهما فيما كانا
(189 b) أجازاه فى حياته لأخيهما وكذلك كان الفريقان جميعا يقولون فى سائر الوصايا المجاوز لها الثلث اذا أجازها الورثة فى حياة الموصى ثمّ مات الموصى بعد ذلك على ما ذكرنا عن كلّ فريق منهم فكتبنا الإجازة على ما وصفنا من هذا الاختلاف *

[1] MS فقد كان البيع للابن [2] MS واكتبت

9.6 قال أبو جعفر وانّما كتبنا بإجازة هذين الابنين لأخيهما ما كان لأبيهما ولم نكتب قبول أخيهما الإجازة [1] لأنّ هذا لا يحتاج فيه الى قبوله لذلك منهما لأنّه لا يملك بإجازتهما ذلك شيئا من قِبلهما وانّما يملك من قِبل أبيه *

9.7 ألا ترى أنّ مريضا لو أعتق فى مرضه عبدا ثمّ مات من مرضه ذلك والعبد لا يخرج من بيته فأجاز الورثة ذلك إنّ العبد حرّ وأنّ ولائه للميّت دون ورثته إذ كان هو المعتق دونهم ولم يجعلوا فيما أجازوا مقام النفس شيئا [2] من العبد يجب لهم به ولاؤه *

9.8 وكذلك ما ذكرنا من إجازة الوارثين اللذين ذكرنا لأخيهما ما كان ابتاعه من أبيهما فى مرض وفاته لم يملك الابن شيئا من قِبل أخويه فلا يحتاج [3] الى قبوله ذلك منهما وانّما ملكه من قِبل أبيه بعقد قد قبله منه وكان لأخويه ألا يجيزا فيكون لهما ما يجب لهما بتركهما الإجازة فلمّا أجازا بطل ما كان //
(190 a) لهما جاز العقد من الميّت الذى قد قبله الابن فى حياته من أبيه *

10.0 ولو أنّ رجلا صحيحا ابتاع من رجل مريض دارا بدين عليه يبيّنه فأراد أن يكتب عليه بذلك كتابا فإنّك تكتب فى ذلك كما كتبنا فى بيع المريض الصحيح حتّى اذا أتيت على وكلّ حقّ هو لها خارج منها كتبت على أثر ذلك بالكذا كذا الدينار التى لفلان بن فلان على فلان بن فلان بصكّ باسم فلان تأريخه شهر كذا من سنة كذا ومن شهوده المسمّين فيه فلان وفلان وغيرهم من الشهود وسلّم فلان بن فلان الى فلان بن فلان جميع ما وقع عليه هذا البيع المسمّى فى هذا الكتاب ثمّ تنسق بقيّة كتاب الشرى على مثل ما كتبنا فى ذلك فاذا فرغت من الكتاب كتبت وشهد فلان بن فلان الفلانى ويكنى أبا فلان وفلان بن فلان الفلانى ويكنى أبا فلان [4] يعنى شهود الصكّ أنّ فلان بن فلان الفلانى يعنى البائع قد كان فى صحّة عقله وبدنه وجواز أمره فى شهر كذا من سنة كذا أقرّ عندهم وأشهدهم على نفسه لفلان بن فلان الفلانى يعنى المشترى بجميع ما فى هذا الكتاب المذكور تأريخه وشهوده فى هذا الكتاب وأنّ هذه الكذا كذا الدينار المسمّاة فيه دين عليه لفلان بن فلان وأنّهم لا يعلمون فلان بن فلان منذ أشهدهم على ذلك برىء من هذه
(190 b) الدنانير // المسمّاة فى هذا الكتاب وفى الكتاب المذكور تأريخه وشهوده فى هذا الكتاب ولا من شىء منها الى وقوع هذا البيع المسمّى فى هذا الكتاب وأنّهم يعرفون فلان بن فلان وفلان بن فلان يعنى المشترى والبائع ويثبتونهما معرفة صحيحة بأعيانهما وأسمائهما وأنسابهما قبل إقرارهما عندهم بجميع ما فى هذا الكتاب المذكور تأريخه وشهوده فى هذا الكتاب وبعد ذلك الى أن شهدوا بهذه الشهادة المذكورة فى هذا الكتاب وأشهدوا على شهاداتهم بذلك سائر الشهود المسمّين معهم فى هذا الكتاب أنّهم يشهدون على فلان بن فلان لفلان بن فلان بما ذُكر من شهاداتهم له عليه

[1] MS omits الاجازة
[2] MS شىء
[3] MS فيحتاج
[4] MS omits وفلان بن فلان ويكنى أبا فلان

فى هذا الكتاب فى صحّة عقله وبدنه وجواز أمره فى شهر كذا من سنة كذا قبل مرضه المذكور فى هذا الكتاب وكتبوا شهاداتهم بخطوطهم على جميع ما سُمّى ووُصف فى هذا الكتاب فى شهر كذا من سنة كذا *

10.1 قال أبو جعفر وانّما كتبنا الشهادة على الدين لأنّ البائع مريض فإن لم يكن الدين الذى باع الدار به بيّنة فى الصحّة وإلاّ كان غرماؤه الذى له عليهم الدين الذى على أصله بيّنة أو على
(191 a) إقراره به لهم فى الصحّة بيّنة أولى بثمن // هذه الدار المبيعة ممّن باعها منه يعنى الذى أقرّ له به فى مرضه [1] *

10.2 ألا ترى أنّ أبا حنيفة وأبا يوسف ومحمّدا كانوا يقولون فى رجل أقرّ لرجل وهو مريض مرض يموّته بدين ثمّ مات وعليه دين قد كان أقرّ به فى الصحّة أو علم وجوبه عليه فى الصحّة بغصب غصبه أو وديعة استهلكها إنّ غرماء الصحّة أولى ممّن أقرّ له فى مرضه *

10.3 وكانوا يقولون أيضا لو وجب عليه دين فى المرض وعلم وجوبه عليه بمال استهلكه أو بغصب غصبه كان أصحاب دين الصحّة يتحاصّون جميعا فى مال الميّت وقال غيرهم غرماء الصحّة وغرماء المرض سواء فكتبنا ما ذكرنا احتياطا ممّا وصفنا *

10.4 قال أبو جعفر ولم نكتب فبرئ فلان بن فلان من هذه الكذا كذا الدينار لأنّ فى ذلك إقرارا بصحّة البيع لأنّ المشترى بالدين لا يبرأ من الدين اشترى به عرضا إلاّ أن يكون شراه ايّاه شرى صحيحا فى إقراره ببراءته من الدين بذلك إقرار منه بصحّة البيع[2] وفى إقراره بصحّة البيع إبطال العهدة فيه على البيع فى قول ابن أبى ليلى وأهل المدينة *

10.5 قال أبو جعفر وقد كنّا ذكرنا فى بعض ما تقدّم من كتابنا هذا البراءة من الدين المبتاع به
(191 b) وهذا الذى كتبنا هاهنا // واخترناه أصحّ من ذلك وأوثق عندنا والله نسأله التوفيق *

باب بيع الأوصياء

11.0 قال أبو جعفر ولو أنّ رجلا مات وعليه دين وترك دارا وأولادا صغارا وكبارا وأوصى الى رجل فباع الوصىّ الدار من رجل ولم يكن الحاكم أنفذ له الوصيّة وقد كان البيع بسؤال الغرماء ايّاه ذلك وإذن البالغين من الورثة له فيه فأراد المشترى والوصىّ أن يكتبا فى ذلك كتابا يكون نسختين إحداهما فى يد المشترى والأخرى فى يد الوصىّ فإنّك تكتب هذا ما اشترى فلان بن فلان بن فلان الفلانى من فلان بن فلان بن فلان الفلانى اشترى منه بعد وفاة فلان بن فلان الفلانى جميع الدار التى ذكر فلان بن فلان يعنى الوصىّ أنّ فلان بن فلان تُوُفّى وهو يملكها وأنّ فلان بن فلان

[1] MS ممن باعها منه ىرى اقر به عليه فى مرضه   [2] MS بذلك البيع اقرار منه

هذا قد كان فى صحّة عقله وجواز أمره فى شهر كذا من سنة كذا فى مرضه الذى تُوُفِّى فيه إن
كان أوصى اليه وهو مريض وإن كان أوصى اليه وهو صحيح كتبت فى صحّة عقله وبدنه وجواز
أمره فى شهر كذا من سنة كذا جعله وصيّه فى جميع تركته وفى اقتضاء ما له من دين وفى قضاء
(192 a) ما عليه من دين وجعله // وصيّا على أصغار ولده وأقامه فى جميع ما أوصى به اليه من ذلك بعد
وفاته مقام نفسه فى حياته ورجع عن كلّ وصيّة كان أوصى بها قبل ذلك وأبطلها وفسخها وأخرج
مَن كان أوصى بها اليه عمّا كان أوصى به اليه من ذلك وكتب فلان بن فلان يعنى الميّت لفلان
ابن فلان يعنى الوصىّ بجميع ما أوصى به اليه ممّا سُمّى ووُصف فى هذا الكتاب كتاب وصيّة
تأريخه شهر كذا من سنة كذا ومن شهوده المسمّين فيه فلان وفلان وفلان وغيرهم من الشهود
وأنّ فلان بن فلان يعنى الوصىّ قد كان فى صحّة عقله وبدنه وجواز أمره قبل من فلان بن فلان
جميع ما أوصى اليه من ذلك وتضمّن له القيام به بعد وفاته بمخاطبة منه ايّاه على جميعه ثمّ تُوُفِّى
فلان بن فلان بعد ذلك ولم يرجع عن شىء ممّا سُمّى ووُصف فى هذا الكتاب ولم يغيّره ولم
يبدله ولم يخرج فلان بن فلان ممّا كان أوصى به اليه من ذلك ولم يخرج فلان بن فلان نفسه ممّا
كان أوصى به اليه فلان بن فلان من ذلك وهى الدار التى بمدينة كذا فى الموضع الكذا منها
ويحيط بهذه الدار ويجمعها و يشتمل عليها حدود أربعة ثمّ تحدّدها وتذكر حقوقها حتّى تأتى
على وكلّ حقّ هو لها خارج منها فتكتب بعقب ذلك بكذا كذا دينارا مثاقيل ذهبا عينا وازنة
جيادا ثمّ تنسق قبض الثمن وقبض المبيع على مثل ما كتبناه فيمن باع دارا لنفسه فيما تقدّم //
(192 b) من هذا الكتاب ثمّ تكتب بعقب ذلك الرؤية والتفرّق على مثل ما كتبنا فيما تقدّم من كتابنا
هذا ثم تكتب بعقب ذلك وذلك [1] بعد أن ذكر فلان بن فلان وفلان بن فلان وفلان بن فلان
يعنى غرماء الميّت أنّ فلان بن فلان الفلانى تُوُفِّى ولهم عليه كذا كذا دينارا مثاقيل ذهبا عينا وازنة
جيادا دينا ثابتا لازما من ذلك لفلان بن فلان بصكّ كان اكتتبه باسمه على فلان بن فلان فى
حياته وفلان بن فلان يومئذ صحيح العقل جائز الأمر بكذا كذا دينارا تأريخ ذلك الصكّ شهر
كذا من سنة كذا ومن شهوده المسمّين فيه فلان وفلان وفلان وغيرهم من الشهود ومن ذلك لفلان
ابن فلان كذا كذا دينارا حتّى تسمّى ما لكلّ واحد من الغرماء كما كتبت ما للأوّل منهم وبعد
أن حضر فلان بن فلان وفلان بن فلان وفلان بن فلان فشهدوا جميعا أنّ فلان بن فلان الفلانى
يعنى الميّت تُوُفِّى وهم يعرفونه بعينه واسمه ونسبه معرفة صحيحة وأنّه كان قبل ذلك فى صحّة عقله
وبدنه وجواز أمره هذا إن ذكروا أنّه كان أشهدهم وهو صحيح وإن ذكروا أنّه كان أشهدهم
وهو مريض كتبت فى صحّة عقله وجواز أمره فى مرضه الذى تُوُفِّى فيه وتبيّن تأريخ الوصيّة فى
الوجهين جميعا إنّه جعل فلان بن فلان المسمّى فى هذا الكتاب يعنى البائع بمحضر من فلان
(193 a) ابن فلان هذا // إن شهدوا أنّه كان حاضرا يوم وقعت الوصيّة وإن لم يشهدوا على ذلك كتبت

[1] MS omits وذلك

وهم يعرفونه بعينه واسمه ونسبه معرفة صحيحة بعد وفاته فى جميع تركته وفى اقتضاء ما له من دين وفى قضاء ما عليه من دين وعلى أصاغر ولده وأنّه أقامه فى جميع ما جعله اليه [1] *

11.1 ألا ترى أنّ رجلا لو باع دارا لغيره بأمره وذكر فى أوّل كتابه ذلك فقيل الدار التى ذكر فلان بن فلان أنّها لفلان بن فلان وأنّ فلان بن فلان هذا قد وكّله ببيعها فإن آثر بعد ذلك أن يذكر شهادة الشهود فى آخر كتابه على الوكالة ذكرها *

11.2 أولا ترى أنّ رجلا لو اشترى لرجل دارا بأمره كتب فى أوّل كتابه هذا ما اشترى فلان بن فلان لفلان بن فلان بأمره فلمّا كان [2] الأمر فى هذا مقدّما فى أوّل هذين الكتابين كان ذلك كذلك ذكر وصيّة الميّت وذكر ملكه للدار المبيعة مقدّما فى أوّل الكتاب *

11.3 قال أبو جعفر ولم يكن يوسف يكتب فى شهادة الشهود فى كتابه هذا رجوع الميّت عن كلّ
وصيّة كان أوصى بها قبل وصيّته الى هذا الوصىّ البائع وكان أحبّ الأشياء الينا فى ذلك أن تكتب
11.4 ذلك على ما كتبناه لاختلاف الناس فى ذلك * فكان أبو حنيفة وأبو يوسف ومحمّد بن الحسن
يقولون اذا أوصى رجل الى رجل وقد كان قبل ذلك أوصى الى رجل آخر أنّهما وصيّان جميعا //
(193 b) حتّى يرجع عن وصيّته الأولى وكان أهل المدينة يقولون وصيّته الى هذا الثانى رجوع منه عن
وصيّته الأولى فكتبنا ما كتبنا فى ذلك احتياطا من هذا الاختلاف وكان يوسف يكتب فى
الشهادة على عدد الورثة وأنّه لم يدّعِ وارثا غير ولده *

11.5 قال أبو جعفر وهذا عندنا خطأ لأنّ الشهود فى مثل هذا انّما عليهم أن يشهدوا على أنّهم لا يعلمون لفلان المتوفّى وارثا يوم تُوُفِّى غير ولده ثمّ يسمّونهم وقد يَعلم غيرهم غير ذلك فيكونون هم لا يعلمون ما قد علم وقد كره أصحابنا أن يكتبوا أنّ لا وارث له غيرهم لأنّ ذلك ظنّ والشهادة على عيب *

11.6 قال أبو يوسف ولو شهدوا بذلك عند القاضى فإنّ الناس فى ذلك لا يجـيزون شهادتهم لأنّهم
يشهدوا بما لا يعلمون قال ولكن أستحسن [فأجيزُها وأرى معناهم فى معنى الشهادة] [3] على
العلم فاذا كتب وأنّه لم يدّعِ وارثا يُعلَم غير ولده كان قد أدخل الشهود فى الشهادة [4] على ما لا
يعلمون لأنّهم قد يُعلَم من ولده مَن لا يعلمون ولأنّه لا يؤمن أن يُرفَع ذلك الكتاب الى القاضى
11.7 فيرى القياس فى ذلك على ما كتبناه * قال أبو جعفر وقد كان عيسى بن أبان [5] يكتب فى
11.8 (194 a) مثل هذا ولم يترك يوم تُوُفِّى يعلمونه غير ولده ثمّ يسمّيهم * قال أبو جعفر // فهذا أحسن
ممّا كتبه يوسف والذى كتبناه نحن أحسن عندنا من هذا الذى [6] كان عيسى بن أبان يختاره *

[1] Marginal correction or addition illegible at end of paragraph.
[2] MS فلما ان كان
[3] words obscure in MS
[4] MS فى الشهود
[5] MS omits عيسى بن ابان
[6] MS عندنا وهذا الذى

11.9 قال أبو جعفر وقد قال أصحابنا فى رجل قال والله ما ضربت أحدا غير زيد ولم يكن ضرب زيدا ولا غيره إنّه لا يحنث وكذلك لو قال والله ما أملك من الدراهم غير خمسين درهما فلم يكن يملك خمسين ولا غيرها لم يحنث فكانت يمينه فى ذلك انّما تقع على أنّه لا يملك سوى الخمسين وعلى أنّه لم يضرب غير زيد وليس فى ذلك تحقيق ملكه للخمسين ولا إثبات ضربه لزيد فكان النظر على هذا أن يكون كذلك أيضا شهادة الشهود انّما الشهادة [1] على أنّ فلان بن فلان لم يترك وارثا يوم تُوُفّى يعلمونه غير زيد ولا يريد [2] أن يكونوا يعلمونه وارثا للميّت وليس فيها تحقيق أمر زيد أنّه وارث للميّت *

11.10 وقال ولم يكن يوسف بن خالد يكتب وهم من أهل العلم والخبرة بذلك وكان بكّار بن قتيبة يكتبه ويوقف الشهود [3] عليه فى شهاداتهم فكان ما كتب بكّار بن قتيبة فى ذلك أحبّ الينا لما فيه من التأكيد والدلالة على أنّ الشهود يبطنون أمر الميّت وأمر مَن ورثه ولم يكن يوسف يكتب فى كتابه هذا ضمان الدرك أصلا *

11.11 (194 b) قال أبو جعفر وذِكره على ما كتبنا أحسن عندنا // لأنّا رأينا كتب بياعات العقارات لا تَخلَى من ذكر ضمانات الدرك إمّا على مَن تولّى البيع وإمّا على مَن تُولّى له فى قول من يكتب فى ذلك كذلك وإمّا إن يُقصَد بها الى من تجب عليه بحقّ البيع وإمّا إن يُقصَد بها الى من اشترى ذلك لنفسه واشتُرِى له بأمره أو يُقصَد به الى الواجب له ذلك منها وإن يسمّى بعينه *

11.12 قال أبو جعفر وكتبنا الدرك فى كتابنا هذا على ما كتبنا قياسا على ذلك ولم نجعل ضمان الدرك فى مال الميّت ولا على وصيّه لاختلاف الناس فى ذلك فكان أبو حنيفة وأبو يوسف ومحمّد يقولون فى هذا ضمان الدرك على الوصىّ ثمّ يرجع الوصىّ على الغرماء إن كانوا أمروه بالبيع ولم يكن فى الثمن الذى يباع به فضل عن ديونهم الذى يضمن على الميّت *

11.13 وقال آخرون ضمان ذلك فى مال الميّت لا على وصيّه وقال آخرون ضمان ذلك على الوصىّ ولا يرجع به فى مال الميّت ولا على غرمائه ولا على أحد ممّن ورثه لأنّه أدخل نفسه فى ذلك ولم يجعل الميّت اليه أن يبيع شيئا لغيره *

11.14 قال أبو جعفر فكتبنا ما كتبنا احتياطا من هذا الاختلاف فمتى رُفع ذلك الى مَن يرى ضمان الدرك فى مال الميّت جعل الذى وجب ذلك الدرك عليه المقصود به اليه فى كتاب العهدة الميّت وإن رُفع ذلك الى غيره ممّن يرى واحدا من القولين الآخرين جعل الذى وجب عليه ضمان الدرك هو الذى يرى واجبا عليه *

11.15 (195 a) قال أبو جعفر // وقد قال أبو حنيفة وأبو يوسف ومحمّد إنّ هذه الدار المبيعة إن كان فى ثمنها الذى بيعت به فضل عن الدين الذى على الميّت وقد باع الوصىّ الدار بأمر البالغين من

[1] MS omits انما الشهادة

[2] ولا يريد unclear

[3] MS ويوقف الشهادة

الورثة رجع الوصىّ بما لحقه من ضمان الدرك فيها بمقدار ما صار من الغرماء من ثمنها على الغرماء ورجع على البالغين من الورثة بمقدار ما أخذوا من ثمنها بحقّ مورثهم عن الميّت وذلك أنـّها ضامن الدرك مَن هو فى كتابنا *

11.16 قال أبو جعفر ولم يكن يوسف يكتب فى كتابه أسماء الغرماء ولا مقدار ديونهم وهذا عندى ممّا لا بدّ من تسميته لأنـّه انـّما احتيج الى شهادتهم على الدين ليجوز أخذ [1] الغرماء للعرض فى البيع فمتى لم يسمّ الدين وأهله لم تثبت الشهادة ولم يقبلها القاضى *

11.17 وإن كان البيع وقع بغير أمر البالغ من الورثة فأثبِتْ فى كتابك فى موضع الذكر بما شهد عليه الشهود وبعد إن كان ما على فلان بن فلان من الدين المسمّى فى هذا الكتاب أكثر من قيمة هذه الدار المحدودة فى هذا الكتاب وأكثر من ثمنها الذى بيعت به هذا إن [ ] [2] من ذكر الثمن فحسن وإن لم تفعـــل لم يضرّ لأنـّك قد ذكرت فى كتابك مقدار ثمن الدار ومقدار ما على الميّت من الدين *

11.18 قال أبو جعفر وانـّما ذكرنا قيمة الدار ولا بدّ منه لأنـّه إن كان الدين يفى بالقيمة لم يحتج الى إذن الورثة ولا الى إقرارهم لأنّ على الميّت من الدين ما لا ميراث لهم معه ولا يُعلَم ذلك ولا يُوقَف عليه إلاّ بذكر قيمة الدار *

11.19 (195 b) وأمّا اذا كان الدين على الميّت دون قيمة الدار // فلا بدّ فى هذا من ذكر إذن البالغين من الورثة لاختلاف الناس فى البيع إن وقع بغير أمرهم كان أبو حنيفة يقول للوصىّ أن يبيع جميع عقارات الميّت اذا كان على الميّت دين قليلا كان ذلك الدين أو كثيرا صغارا كان الورثة أو

11.20 كبارا * وكان أبو يوسف ومحمّد يقولان ليس له أن يبيع من عقار الميّت إلاّ مقدار ما على الميّت من الدين وإلاّ بإذن أيضا من الورثة [3] فكتبنا إذن البالغين من الورثة للوصىّ فى البيع احتياطا من هذا الاختلاف *

11.0 bis قال أبو جعفر فإن كان الورثة جميعا صغارا فباع الوصىّ الدار كلـّها والذى على الميّت من الدين أقلّ من مقدار قيمتها الذى باعها به كتبت وذلك بعد أن رأى فلان بن فلان يعنى الوصىّ لفلان وفلان وفلان بنى فلان بن فلان اذ كان وليـّا عليهم بحقّ وصاية أبيهم فلان بن فلان المتوفّى اليه اذ كانوا صغارا لم يبلغوا ولاواحد منهم الحظّ والتوفير لهم من هذه الدار المحدودة فى هذا الكتاب ممّا كان وجب لهم منها بحقّ مورثهم عن أبيهم فلان بن فلان المتوفّى *

11.21 قال أبو جعفر ولم يكن يوسف يستثنى فى الإقرار الذى كان يكتبه فى الشهادة فى آخر الكتاب شيئا من الإقرار فلا يدخله فى إقرار المشترى كما استثنيناه نحن فى كتابنا وكان استثناؤنا ذلك وإخراجه

[1] اخذ illegible in MS
[2] word illegible
[3] MS والا مقدار أيضا فى الورثة

ممّا كان أقرّ به المشترى أحوط للمشترى وأثبت لضمان الدرك له على مَن يجب له ضمان الدرك
(196 a) عليه // بحقّ البيع على ما وصفنا *

12.0 وإذا كان الميّت أوصى بوصايا مسمّاة فباع الوصىّ هذه الدار ليصرف ثلث ثمنها فى الوصايا ويحتبس ما بقى من ثمنها فى يده بعد ذلك للورثة وهم جميعا صغار كتبت هذا ما اشترى فلان ابن فلان من فلان بن فلان ثمّ تنسق الكتاب فى ذلك على ما كتبنا فى الكتاب الذى قبل هذا حتّى اذا أتيت على وكتب له بذلك كتاب وصيّة كتبت على أثر ذلك نسخته بسم الله الرحمن الرحيم فتنسخ كتاب الوصيّة كلّه ثمّ تكتب على أثره ومن شهوده المسمّين فيه فلان وفلان وفلان وغيرهم من الشهود ثمّ تنسق الكتاب فى ذلك حتّى اذا أتيت على ذكر التفرّق كتبت بعقب ذلك وذلك بعد أن شهد فلان بن فلان ويكنى أبا فلان وفلان بن فلان ويكنى أبا فلان وفلان بن فلان ويكنى أبا فلان أنّهم يعرفون فلان بن فلان المسمّى فى هذا الكتاب يعنى الميّت معرفة صحيحة بعينه واسمه ونسبه وأنّه أقرّ عندهم وأشهدهم على نفسه فى صحّة عقله وبدنه وجواز أمره فى شهر كذا من سنة كذا هذا إن كان أشهدهم وهو صحيح البدن وإن كان أشهدهم وهو مريض كتبت فى صحّة عقله وجواز أمره فى شهر كذا من سنة كذا فى مرضه الذى تُوُفّىَ فيه بجميع ما
(196 b) فى هذا الكتاب المنسوخ فى هذا الكتاب // بعد أن قُرئ عليه بمحضرهم فأقرّ لهم أنّه قد فهمه وعرف جميع ما فيه حرفا حرفا وأنّهم يعرفون أيضا فلان بن فلان الرجل المسمّى فى هذا الكتاب يعنى الوصىّ [1] ثمّ تنسق الكتاب على ما كتبنا فى الكتاب الذى قبل هذا وتحذو [2] فيما تريده فى هذا الكتاب نحو ما كتبناه فى الكتاب الذى قبل هذا *

11.22 قال أبو جعفر ولا بدّ فى هذا من ذكر أمر الورثة وإذنهم فى البيع وفى قبض الثمن وفى تسليم المبيع الى مبتاعه لأنّ أبا يوسف ومحمّدا كانا لا يجيزان بيع الوصىّ جميع الدار فى مثل هذا وانّما
11.23 يجيزان له بيع مقدار ثلثها الذى يجب ثمنها لأهل الوصايا * وكان أبو حنيفة يجيز له بيعها كلّها فذكرنا إذن الورثة للوصىّ فى ذلك وأمرهم ايّاه به وإقرارهم بجميع ما كان منهم فى ذلك احتياطا من هذا الاختلاف *

11.24 وكان أصحابنا يكتبون فى الدين ويذكرونه على المتوفّى فى كتبهم دينا ثابتا لازما ولا يكتبون حالا قالوا وذلك أنّه لو كان الى أجل فمات الذى هو عليه حلّ الدين بموته فلا معنى لذكر أجل
11.25 فيما لا يكون له أجل * قال أبو جعفر وأحبّ الأشياء فى هذا الينا أن تذكر الدين حالا لاختلاف الناس فى ذلك اذا كان له أجل وما عليه قبل حلول أجله فكان أكثرهم يقول قد حلّ بموته وبطل
(197 a) أجله وقد قال آخرون بل هو فى أجله قد رُوى ذلك // عن محمّد بن سيرين وعن سعيد بن ابراهيم وعن غيرهما فأولى الأشياء بنا أن نحتاط من اختلاف العلماء *

[1] MS omits يعنى الوصى

[2] MS وتحدوا

باب شرى الأوصياء

13.0 قال أبو جعفر واذا أوصى رجل الى رجل بشرى نسمة وعتقها عنه بعد وفاته فابتاعها الوصىّ بعد موت الموصى وأعتقها عنه فأراد أن يكتب لها بذلك كتابا يُذكَر فيه شراوءه ايّاها وعتقه لها وإقرار بائعها بذلك ويجعله نسختين نسخة فى يده ونسخة فى يد النسمة فإنّك تكتب هذا ما اشترى فلان بن فلان الذى ذكر أنّه وصىّ فلان بن فلان المتوفّى فى جميع تركته بعد وفاته وفى إنفاذ وصاياه[1] ذكر أنّه قد كان أوصى بها اليه فى حياته منها شرى نسمة من ثلث تركته بكذا كذا دينارا مثاقيل ذهبا عينا وازنة جيادا وعتقها عنه من فلان بن فلان[2] الفلانى اشترى منه الغلام الذى يُدعَى فلانا وهو الغلام الذى صفته كذا ثمّ تنسق الكتاب فى ذلك على مثل ما كتبنا فى اشتراء الرقيق فيما تقدّم من كتابنا هذا غير أنّك تكتب الدرك فى ذلك على مثل ما كتبنا فيمن اشترى شيئا لغيره بأمره على ما قد تقدّم فى كتابنا هذا فاذا أتيت على آخر الكتاب كتبت على أثر ذلك

(197 b) وأقرّ فلان بن فلان يعنى الوصىّ أنّ جميع الثمن الذى نقده فلان بن فلان // على ما سُمّى ووُصف فى هذا الكتاب كان من ثلث تركة فلان بن فلان المتوفّى وأنّ ذلك وجميع ما أوصى به المتوفّى خارج من ثلث مال فلان بن فلان وأنّ ورثة فلان بن فلان[3] الفلانى المتوفّى قد قبضوا من تركة فلان بن فلان الفلانى المتوفّى بحقّ موروثهم عنه أكثر من مثل وصاياه هذا إن كان الورثة بالغين فقبضوا لأنفسهم وإن كانوا صغارا فى حجر هذا الوصىّ كتب بعد أن كان ذلك وجميع ما أوصى به فلان بن فلان خارجا من ثلث تركة فلان بن فلان وبعد أن صار فى يد فلان بن فلان يعنى الوصىّ لورثة فلان بن فلان بحقّ ولايته عليهم لصغرهم عن القيام بأنفسهم من تركة فلان بن فلان بحقّ موروثهم عن فلان بن فلان أكثر من مثل وصاياه وهذا اذا كانت الوصايا دون الثلث فإن كانت تفِى بالثلث كتبت مثل وصاياه ثمّ تكتب بعقب ذلك وشهد هوءلاء الشهود المسمّون فى هذا الكتاب أيضا أنّ فلان بن فلان يعنى الوصىّ أقرّ عندهم وأشهدهم على نفسه أنّه أعتق هذا الغلام المسمّى فى هذا الكتاب عن فلان بن فلان المتوفّى بحقّ ما ذكر من وصايته اليه على ما سُمّى ووُصف فى هذا الكتاب وأنّه لا سبيل له ولا لأحد من الناس عليه بسبب رقّ

(198 a) ولا خدمة ولا سعاية // ولا قليل ولا كثير إلاّ سبيل الولاء فإنّ ولائه لفلان بن فلان المتوفّى ولم يقرّ فلان بن فلان يعنى البائع بشىء ممّا أقرّ به فلان بن فلان من ذلك وأقرّ فلان الفلانى يعنى الغلام أنّه كان مملوكا الى أن عتق بالعتاق المسمّى فى هذا الكتاب وقد كُتب هذا الكتاب كذا كذا نسخة فتذكر عدد النسخ وفى أيدى مَن تكون *

13.1 قال أبو جعفر وكان أحبّ أن يُجمع[4] العتاق والشرى فى مثل هذا فى كتاب واحد تكون نسخته فى يد البائع لأنّه قد يكون فيه إقرار المشترى أنّ العبد المشترَى كان شراه ايّاه ملكا للميّت وأنّه

[1] MS وانفاذ وصايا
[2] MS omits بن فلان
[3] MS adds بن فلان
[4] MS وكاحب ان يجمع

صار حرّا بعتاقه ايّاه عنه وفى ذلك وجوب ملك البائع وفى وجوب ملكه انتفاء لضمان الدرك عنه فى قول قوم ولكنّ الأحوط فى هذا أن تكتب الشرى ثمّ تكتب بعقبه إقرار المشترى أنّه اشتراه بحقّ وصيّة الميّت اليه من ثلث مال الميّت ولا تزيد على ذلك شيئا *

14.0 وإن آثرت أن تجمع ذلك فى كتاب واحد ممّا لا يكون فيه خوف من إبطال ضمان الدرك كتبت هذا ما اشترى فلان بن فلان من فلان بن فلان اشترى منه الغلام الفلانى الكذا الذى يُدعَى فلانا بيع
(198 b) المسلم المسلم لا داء ولا غائلة ولا خبثة ولا عيب بكذا كذا دينارا // مثاقيل ذهبا عينا وازنة جيادا شرى لا شرط فيه ولا عدة ودفع فلان بن فلان الى فلان بن فلان جميع الثمن المسمّى فى هذا الكتاب وقبضه منه فلان بن فلان واستوفاه منه تامّا كاملا وأبرأه من جميعه بعد قبضه ايّاه واستيفائه له وهو كذا كذا دينارا مثاقيل ذهبا عينا وازنة جيادا وسلّم فلان بن فلان الى فلان بن فلان هذا الغلام المسمّى فى هذا الكتاب وقبضه منه فلان بن فلان وصار فى يده وقبضه بهذا الشرى المسمّى فى هذا الكتاب وذلك بعد أن أقرّ فلان بن فلان وفلان بن فلان يعنى المتبايعين أنّهما قد رأيا جميعا هذا الغلام المسمّى فى هذا الكتاب وعايناه ونظرا الى وجهه عند وقوع هذا البيع المسمّى فى هذا الكتاب بينهما وقبل ذلك فتبايعا على ذلك وتفرّقا جميعا بأبدانهما بعد هذا البيع المسمّى فى هذا الكتاب عن تراض منهما جميعا بجميعه وإنفاذ منهما له فما أدرك فلان بن فلان فى هذا الغلام المسمّى فى هذا الكتاب من درك من أحد من الناس كلّهم فعلى فلان بن فلان تسليم ما يجب عليه فى ذلك من حقّ ويلزمه بسبب هذا البيع المسمّى فى هذا الكتاب حتّى يسلّم ذلك الى فلان بن
(199 a) فلان على ما يوجبه له عليه هذا البيع المسمّى فى // هذا الكتاب ثمّ إنّ فلان بن فلان يعنى المشترى بعد ابتياعه الغلام المسمّى فى هذا الكتاب من فلان بن فلان وبعد دفعه الثمن اليه منه المسمّى فى هذا الكتاب أقرّ وهو صحيح العقل والبدن جائز الأمر أنّ فلان بن فلان الفلانى المتوفّى قد كان فى صحّة عقله وبدنه وجواز أمره أوصى اليه بجميع تركته وإنفاذ وصاياه ثمّ تُوُفِّى ولم يرجع عن شىء ممّا أوصى به اليه ولم يبطله ولم يغيّره وتُوُفِّى يوم تُوُفِّى ولا وصىّ له غيره ولا وصيّة له غير وصيّته اليه وأنّ فيما كان أوصى به اليه من ذلك أن يبتاع ممّا يصير فى يده بعد وفاته من تركته نسمة بكذا كذا دينارا مثاقيل ذهبا عينا وازنة جيادا فيعتقها عنه وأنّه ابتاع النسمة المذكورة فى هذا الكتاب فى البيع المذكور [1] فى هذا الكتاب لفلان بن فلان المتوفّى بحقّ ما كان أوصى به اليه ممّا سُمّى ووُصف فى هذا الكتاب وأنّه دفع ثمنها المسمّى فى هذا الكتاب من مال فلان ابن فلان المتوفّى بعد أن كان جميع الثمن المسمّى فى هذا الكتاب وسائر وصايا فلان بن فلان المتوفّى خارجة من ثلث تركته وبعد أن صار فى يد فلان بن فلان الفلانى بحقّ وصاية فلان
(199 b) ابن فلان الفلانى اليه من تركة فلان بن فلان أكثر من مثل وصاياه // وأنّه بعد ذلك أعتق هذا

[1] MS فى هذا الكتاب بيع المذكور

الغلام المسمّى فى هذا الكتاب عن فلان بن فلان المتوفّى بحقّ وصايته اليه على ما سُمّى ووُصف فى هذا الكتاب ولا يردّ على ذلك شيئا ثمّ تكتب الشهادة على إقرار البائع والمشترى بجميع ما فى هذا الكتاب حتّى اذا أتيت على آخر الشهادة كتبت على أثر ذلك غير ما فى هذا الكتاب ممّا ادّعاه فلان بن فلان يعنى الوصىّ من وصاية فلان بن فلان المتوفّى اليه ومن ابتياعه هذا الغلام المسمّى فى هذا الكتاب لفلان بن فلان بحقّ وصايته اليه ومن دفعه الثمن المسمّى من مال فلان ابن فلان المتوفّى فإنّ فلان بن فلان يعنى البائع لم يقرّ بشىء من ذلك *

14.1 قال أبو جعفر وهذا أحسن من الأوّل وانّما منعنا أن تذكر فى هذا الكتاب ولاء النسمة المعتقة للميّت لأنّ فى ذلك تصحيح البيع الذى كان بين المتبايعين وإقرار المبتاع منها أنّ النسمة كانت للبائع وفى ذلك إبطال ضمان الدرك له عليه فى قول قوم فتركنا ذلك وذكرنا العتاق ولم نذكر وجوب الولاء لأحد فإن استُحقّت النسمة كان للمشترى أن يرجع بثمنها على البائع فى قول أهل العلم جميعا وإن لم تُستحَقّ فهى عتيقة بحقّ عتاق المشترى ايّاها وفى ذلك وفيما أقرّ به المشترى ممّا ذكرنا من وصاية الميّت اليه // بالابتياع والعتاق اللذين ذكرنا ما يجب به الولاء للميّت * (200 a)

باب بيع الوكلاء

15.0 قال أبو جعفر ولو أنّ رجلا وكّل رجلا ببيع دار له وأشهد له على ذلك شهودا فباعها هذا الوكيل فإن أراد أن يُكتَب له فى ذلك كتاب يذكر له فيه الوكالة فإنّك تكتب هذا ما اشترى فلان بن فلان من فلان بن فلان اشترى منه جميع الدار التى ذكر فلان بن فلان يعنى البائع أنّ فلان بن فلان الفلانى وكّله ببيعها ممّن رأى بكذا كذا دينارا مثاقيل ذهبا عينا وازنة جيادا وبقبض ثمنها من مبتاعها منه وبتسليمها الى مبتاعها منه وأنّه أشهد له على ذلك شهودا منهم فلان بن فلان وفلان بن فلان وفلان بن فلان وغيرهم من الشهود وهى الدار التى بمدينة كذا فى الموضع الكذا منها ويحيط بهذه الدار ويجمعها ويشتمل عليها حدود أربعة ثمّ تحدّدها ثمّ تكتب بعقب ذلك اشترى فلان بن فلان من فلان بن فلان جميع هذه الدار المحدودة فى هذا الكتاب بحدودها كلّها ثمّ تنسق الكتاب على مثل ما كتبنا فيمن باع دار نفسه فيما تقدّم من كتابنا هذا حتّى اذا أتيت على ذكر التفرّق كتبت بعقب ذلك بعد أن شهد فلان وفلان وفلان يعنى الشهود // الذين سمّيتهم فى صدر كتابك أنّ فلان بن فلان يعنى الموكّل[1] وقد أثبتوه وعرفوه معرفة صحيحة بعينه واسمه ونسبه أقرّ عندهم وأشهدهم على نفسه فى صحّة عقله وبدنه وجواز أمره فى شهر كذا من سنة كذا أنّه جعل الى فلان بن فلان يعنى البائع بيع هذه الدار المحدودة فى هذا الكتاب بحدودها كلّها وجميع حقوقها ممّن رأى بكذا كذا دينارا مثاقيل ذهبا عينا وازنة جيادا وقبض ثمنها ممّن يبتاعها (200 b)

[1] MS يعنى الوكيل

منه وتسليمها الى مبتاعها منه وأنّ فلان بن فلان يعنى البائع قبل من فلان بن فلان جميع ما جعل اليه من ذلك بمخاطبة منه ايّاه على جميعه ثمّ تكتب بعقب ذلك فما أدرك فلان بن فلان يعنى المشترى فيما وقع عليه هذا البيع المسمّى فى هذا الكتاب وفى شىء منه ومن حقوقه من درك من أحد من الناس كلّهم فعلى الذى يجب ذلك عليه من فلان بن فلان يعنى البائع ومن فلان بن فلان يعنى الآمر بحقّ هذا البيع المسمّى فى هذا الكتاب تسليم ما يجب عليه فى ذلك من حقّ ويلزمه بسبب هذا البيع المسمّى [1] فى هذا الكتاب حتّى يسلّم ذلك الى فلان بن فلان على ما يوجبه له عليه هذا البيع المسمّى فى هذا الكتاب شهد فلان وفلان وفلان يعنى الشهود الذين ذكرت

(201 a) شهادتهم فى هذا الكتاب أنّهم يشهدون على فلان بن فلان يعنى الآمر // بجميع ما ذكر من شهادتهم عليه فى هذا الكتاب وأشهدوا على شهادتهم بذلك سائر الشهود المسمّين معهم فى هذا الكتاب أنّهم يشهدون على فلان بن فلان يعنى الآمر بجميع ما ذكر من شهادتهم عليه فى هذا الكتاب وشهدوا هم وسائر الشهود المسمّين معهم فى هذا الكتاب على إقرار فلان بن فلان وفلان ابن فلان يعنى المتبايعين بجميع ما سُمّى ووُصف فى هذا الكتاب بعد أن قُرئ عليهما جميعا جميع ما فيه من أوّله الى آخره فأقرّا أن قد فهماه وعرفا جميع ما فيه حرفا حرفا ثمّ تنسق الكتاب فى ذلك على مثل ما كتبنا فى مثله ممّا قد تقدّم فى كتابنا هذا *

15.1 قال أبو جعفر وإن زِدت فى كتابك هذا معرفة الشهود الذين شهدوا على وكالة الدار بعينها والوقوف على نهايات حدودها من جميع جوانبها والشهادة على شهادتهم بذلك كان أحوط *

15.2 قال أبو جعفر وإنّا كتبنا الدرك فى ذلك على ما ذكرنا لاختلاف الناس فيه فكان بعضهم يقول يجب على الموكّل لأنّ البيع انّما كان بأمره وقال بعضهم يجب على الوكيل ثمّ يرجع به الوكيل على

(201 b) الموكّل فكتبناه على ما كتبنا // احتياطا من هذا الاختلاف *

15.0 bis فإن كان الموكّل لم يسمّ للوكيل شيئا ولكنّه أطلق له بيع الدار كتبت الكتاب على مثل ما كتبنا غير أنّك تحذف من الوكالة ذكر مقدار ثمن الدار وغير أنّك تكتب فى آخر كتابك وشهد فلان وفلان وفلان حتّى تسمّى شهود الوكالة أنّهم يعرفون هذه الدار المحدودة فى هذا الكتاب ويقفون على نهاياتها المذكورات لها فى هذا الكتاب وقوفا صحيحا وأنّ فى الثمن الذى باعها به فلان بن فلان من فلان بن فلان وفاء بقيمتها لا وكس فيه ولا شطط *

15.3 قال أبو جعفر وانّما كتبنا أنّ فى الثمن الذى بيعت به الدار وفاء بثمنها لاختلاف الناس فى الثمن لو كان لا وفاء فيه بثمنها فكان أبو حنيفة يقول البيع جائز وجعل بيع الوكيل ايّاها كبيع

15.4 مالكها ايّاها وأجاز بيعه ايّاها فيما باعها [2] به من قليل الثمن ومن كثيره * وكان أبو يوسف ومحمّد بن الحسن يقولان لا يجوز بيع الوكيل ايّاها إلّا بدراهم أو بدنانير يكون فيها وفاء بثمنها أو تقصير عن ذلك بمقدار ما يتغابن الناس فيه فكتبنا ما كتبنا من ذلك احتياطا من هذا الاختلاف *

[1] MS omits المسمى

[2] MS فما باعها

15.5 قال أبو جعفر وإنّى أحبّ [1] أن يوكّد أيضا فى كتاب شرى الوكيل مثل ذلك بل هو فى //
(202 a) الشرى أولى منه فى البيع لأنّ الناس قد اختلفوا فى البيع بالثمن الذى لا يتغابن الناس فيه من الوكلاء على ما وصفنا ولم يختلفوا في الشرى اذا وقع من الوكلاء بما لا يتغابن الناس فيه إنّه[2] لا يلزم الوكيل شيء *

باب شرى العبد على أنّه يصنع صنعة من الصناعات

16.0 قال أبو جعفر واذا اشترى الرجل من الرجل عبدا على أنّه خبّاز أو على أنّه خيّاط أو ما أشبه ذلك فأراد أن يكتب فى ذلك كتابا فإنّك تكتب هذا ما اشترى فلان بن فلان بن فلان الفلانى من فلان بن فلان بن فلان الفلانى اشترى منه الغلام الفلانى الذى يُدعَى فلانا على أنّه خبّاز بيع المسلم المسلم لا داء ولا غائلة ولا خبثة ولا عيب بكذا كذا دينارا مثاقيل ذهبا عينا وازنة جيادا ثمّ تنسق الكتاب فى ذلك على مثل ما كتبنا فيه فى باب شرى الرقيق فإن أراد البائع أن يُوفِي المشترى الشرط الذى شرطه له فى هذا الغلام الذى باعه ايّاه كتبت الكتاب على مثل ما كتبنا حتّى اذا أتيت على ذكر الثمن كتبت فخبز هذا الغلام المسمّى فى هذا الكتاب بمحضر من فلان ومن فلان يعنى المتبايعين خبزا يقع عليه به اسم خبّاز [3] هذا إن كان البيع وقع على أنّه
(202 b) خبّاز وإن كان // البيع وقع على أنّه خيّاط كتبت فخاط هذا الغلام المسمّى فى هذا الكتاب بمحضر من فلان ومن فلان خياطة يقع عليه بها اسم خيّاط ثم تكتب ودفع فلان بن فلان الى فلان بن فلان جميع الثمن المسمّى فى هذا الكتاب ثمّ تنسق الكتاب على مثل ما كتبنا حتّى اذا أتيت على ذكر إقرار البائع والمشترى برؤية العبد كتبت على أثر ذلك وبعد أن أقرّ فلان ابن فلان يعنى المشترى باستيفائه من فلان بن فلان يعنى البائع جميع ما يجب له عليه بحقّ ما اشترطه من الصناعة المسمّاة فى هذا الكتاب فى الغلام المسمّى ثمّ تنسق الكتاب على مثل ما كتبنا وكذلك تكتب فى سائر الصناعات من البناء والقصارة [ ] [4] وغير ذلك لأنّ على البائع أن يُوفِي المشترى ما اشترطه له من صناعة الغلام الذى قد باعه ايّاه وشرطها له فيه فلذلك كتبنا استيفاء المشترى لذلك وبراءة البائع اليه منه *

[1] MS وانى لاحنه
[2] MS omits انه
[3] MS يقع عليه عبره اباه اسم خباز
[4] word illegible in MS

باب الرجل يبتاع الدار من رجل ويقبضها منه ويقبض بائعها منه ثمنها ثمّ يقرّان أنّ ذلك البيع كان تلجئة

17.0 (203 a) قال أبو جعفر واذا اشترى الرجل من الرجل دارا وقبضها // وقبض بائعها منه ثمنها ثمّ أقرّا بعد ذلك أنّ البيع الذى كان أظهراه فيها لم يكن بيعا وإنّه كان تلجئة لأمر كان البائع خافه فأرادا أن يكتبا فى ذلك كتابا كتبت هذا ما شهد عليه الشهود المسمّون فى هذا الكتاب شهدوا جميعا أنّ فلان بن فلان الفلانى وفلان بن فلان الفلانى وقد أثبتوهما وعرفوهما معرفة صحيحة بأعيانهما وأسمائهما وأنسابهما أقرّا عندهم وأشهداهم على أنفسهما فى صحّة عقولهما وأبدانهما وجواز أمورهما وذلك فى شهر كذا من سنة كذا أنّهما كانا أظهرا أنّ فلان بن فلان المسمّى فى هذا الكتاب ابتاع من فلان بن فلان الفلانى جميع الدار التى بمدينة كذا فى الموضع الكذا منها وهى الدار التى يحيط بها ويجمعها ويشتمل عليها حدود أربعة ثمّ تحدّدها ثمّ تكتب أظهرا أنّ فلان بن فلان المسمّى فى هذا الكتاب اشترى من فلان بن فلان [1] جميع هذه الدار المحدودة فى هذا الكتاب بكذا كذا دينارا مثاقيل ذهبا عينا وازنة جيادا بيعا لا شرط فيه ولا عدة وأنّ فلان بن فلان المسمّى فى هذا الكتاب دفع الى فلان بن فلان المسمّى فى هذا الكتاب جميع الثمن المسمّى فى هذا الكتاب وأنّ فلان بن فلان يعنى البائع قبضه من فلان بن فلان واستوفاه منه تامّا كاملا وأبرأه من جميعه بعد
(203 b) قبضه ايّاه واستيفائه له وهو كذا كذا دينارا مثاقيل ذهبا عينا وازنة جيادا // وأنّ فلان بن فلان قبض من فلان بن فلان جميع هذه الدار المحدودة فى هذا الكتاب وقبضه بتسليم من فلان بن فلان ايّاها اليه وكُتب بينهما فى ذلك كتاب شرى نسخته بسم الله الرحمن الرحيم فينسخه كلّه ومن شهوده المسمّين فيه فلان بن فلان وفلان بن فلان وفلان بن فلان وغيرهم من الشهود وأنّهما لم يكونا تعاقدا بينهما بيعا صحيحا وانّما كان ذلك تلجئة منهما لأمر كانا خافاه وأنّ ملك فلان بن فلان لم يزل عن هذه الدار المحدودة فى هذا الكتاب وفى الكتاب المنسوخ فى هذا الكتاب بشىء ممّا سُمّى ووُصف فى هذا الكتاب لأنّ ذلك لم يكن بيعا صحيحا وأنّ فلان بن فلان لم يكن قبض من فلان بن فلان شيئا من الثمن الذى كان أقرّ له بقبضه ايّاه منه فى هذا الكتاب وفى الكتاب المنسوخ فى هذا الكتاب وأنّ فلان بن فلان يعنى الذى أقرّ بالشرى قد ردّ على فلان بن فلان يعنى الذى أقرّ بالبيع جميع هذه الدار المحدودة فى هذا الكتاب وقبضها منه فلان بن فلان على هيئتها التى كانت عليها يوم قبضها فلان بن فلان من فلان بن فلان على ما سُمّى ووُصف فى هذا الكتاب وفى الكتاب المنسوخ فى هذا الكتاب وأنّ فلان .ن فلان يعنى الذى كان أقرّ
(204 a) بالشرى ضمن لفلان بن فلان يعنى الذى كان أقرّ بالبيع // جميع الذى يدركه فى هذه الدار المحدودة فى هذا الكتاب وفى شىء منها ومن حقوقها من درك من قبله وبسببه بسبب إقرار وتلجئة وإشهاد وتمليك وحدث وحيلة إن كان احتالها فيما أقرّ به لفلان بن فلان ممّا سُمّى ووُصف فى

[1] MS omits اشترى من فلان بن فلان

هذا الكتاب أو احتيلت له بأمره يريد بشىء من ذلك إبطال شىء مماّ أقرّ به لفلان بن فلان فى هذا الكتاب ضمانا واجبا لازما بأمر حقّ واجب لازم عرّفه له ولزمه به ضمان ما ضمنه له فى هذا الكتاب ولا براءة لفلان بن فلان إن أدرك فلان بن فلان فى ذلك درك من قِبله وبسببه حتّى يخلّصه من جميع الذى يدركه فى ذلك من قِبله وبسببه أو يردّ عليه جميع الدرك الذى يجب له عليه ردّه ويلزمه له بحقّ الدرك والضمان المسمّيَين فى هذا الكتاب وكلّ دعوى يدّعيها كلّ واحد من فلان بن فلان ومن فلان بن فلان قبل صاحبه المسمّى معه فى هذا الكتاب وعليه وعنده وبيده يريد بشىء من ذلك إبطال شىء مماّ أقرّ له به فى هذا الكتاب ويدّعى ذلك له أحد بسببه وبيّنة تُشهَد له على ذلك ووثيقة يحضرها وحجّة يحتجّ بها ويمين يدّعيها يريد استحلافه بها ومطالبة ومنازعة وعلقة وتبعة فذلك كلّه كذب وزور وباطل وإفك وظلم والمدّعى عليه منها من جميع
(204 b) ذلك كلّه // برىء وفى حلّ وسعه فى الدنيا والآخرة لعلم كلّ واحد منهما ولمعرفته أنّه لا يدّعى ذلك ولا شيئا منه ولا يدّعيه له أحد بسببه إلاّ تعدّيا وظلما فقبل كلّ واحد من فلان ومن فلان من صاحبه المسمّى معه فى هذا الكتاب جميع الإقرار والضمان والبراءة والتحليل المسمّى جميع ذلك فى هذا الكتاب بمخاطبة منه ايّاه على جميع ذلك وقد كُتِب هذا الكتاب نسختين نظما واحدا ونسقا سواء ولا تزيد نسخة منهما على نسخة حرفا يغيّر حكما ولا يزيل معنى فنسخة منهما فى يد فلان ثقة له وحجّة ونسخة منهما فى يد فلان ثقة له وحجّة شهد *

18.0 قال أبو جعفر وإن شئتَ أن تكتب الكتاب فى ذلك فتنسقه على إقرار المقرّ له بالشرى كتبت هذا كتاب لفلان بن فلان كتبه له فلان بن فلان وأقرّ له بجميع ما فيه وأشهد له على ذلك شهودا سمّوا فى هذا الكتاب فى صحّة عقله وبدنه وجواز أمره وذلك فى شهر كذا من سنة كذا أنّك ألجأتَ الىّ جميع دارك التى بمدينة كذا فى الموضع الكذا منها وتحدّدها ألجأتَ الىّ جميع دارك المحدودة فى هذا الكتاب بحدودها كلّها ثمّ تنسق ما لها ومنها على ما نسقناه فى كتاب الشرى فيما تقدّم
(205 a) من كتابنا هذا حتّى اذا // أتيت على وكلّ حقّ هو لها خارج منها كتبتَ على أثر ذلك وكتبتَ لى بذلك على نفسك كتاب شرى باسمى تأريخه شهر كذا من سنة كذا ومن شهوده المسمّين فيه فلان وفلان وغيرهم من الشهود وأقررتَ لى فيه أنّك قبضتَ جميع الثمن المسمّى فيه وهو كذا كذا دينارا مثاقيل ذهبا عينا وازنة جيادا وأنّك قد سلّمتَ جميع ما ذُكر أنّه وقع عليه هذا البيع المسمّى فى هذا الكتاب بينى وبينك وأنّى قبضته منك وصار فى يدى وقبضى ولم يكن ذلك شرى صحيحا ولا أمرا واجبا ولا خرجت هذه الدار المحدودة فى هذا الكتاب وفى الكتاب المذكور تأريخه وشهوده فى هذا الكتاب ولا شىء منها من ملكك بما أقررتَ لى به من ذلك وانّما كان ذلك الإقرار منك تلجئة منك الىّ ولم تكن قبضتَ منّى من الدنانير المسمّاة فى هذا الكتاب وفى الكتاب المذكور تأريخه وشهوده فى هذا الكتاب شيئا قليل ولا كثير وانّما كان ما أقررنا به من ذلك تلجئة لأمر خفناه فهذه الدار المحدودة فى هذا الكتاب وفى الكتاب المذكور

(205 b) تأريخه وشهوده فى هذا الكتاب لك وفى يدك وملكك ملكا صحيحا وحقّا واجبا دونى // ودون الناس كلّهم بأمر حقّ واجب لازم [عرّفتهُ لك بإقرار منّى لك] [1] به وإنّى بعد ذلك سلّمتُ اليك جميع هذه الدار المحدودة فى هذا الكتاب[2] وفى الكتاب المذكور تأريخه وشهوده فى هذا الكتاب بجميع حقوقها وحدودها وقبضتَها منّى وصارت فى يدك وقبضك على هيئتها التى كنتُ قبضتُها منك على ما سُمّى ووُصف فى هذا الكتاب وفى الكتاب المذكور تأريخه وشهوده فى هذا الكتاب وضمنتُ لك جميع الذى يدركك فى هذه الدار المحدودة فى هذا الكتاب وفى شىء منها ومن حقوقها من درك من قِبلى وبسببى ثمّ تنسق ذلك على مثل ما قد كتبناه فى مثله ممّا قد تقدّم فى كتابنا هذا ثمّ تكتب بعقب ذلك وكلّ دعوى أدّعيها عليك بعد هذا الكتاب وقبلك وعندك وفى يدك فى هذه الدار المحدودة فى هذا الكتاب وفى شىء منها ويدّعى ذلك أحد بسببى ثمّ تنسق الكتاب على ذلك على خطاب الواحد فى نفى الدعوى والبيّنة واليمين على ما تقدّم فى مثل ذلك من كتابنا هذا والله نسأله التوفيق *

باب السلم

19.0 قال أبو جعفر واذا أسلم رجل الى رجل دنانير مسمّاة فى أرادب من قمح معلومة فأراد أن يكتب

(206 a) فى ذلك كتابا // كتبت هذا كتاب لفلان بن فلان الفلانى يعنى المسلِم كتبه له فلان بن فلان يعنى المسلَّم اليه وأقرّ له بجميع ما فيه وأشهد له على ذلك كلّه شهودا سمّوا فى هذا الكتاب فى صحّة عقله وبدنه وجواز أمره وذلك فى شهر كذا من سنة كذا إنّك كنتَ أحضرتَنى كذا كذا دينارا مثاقيل ذهبا عينا وازنة جيادا فأسلمتَها الىّ فى كذا كذا إردبّا قمح نقِىّ جيّد أسمر مدوَّر يابس من قمح مدينة كذا سلما صحيحا جائزا واجبا على أن أفِيك ذلك عند انقضاء شهر كذا من سنة كذا فى الموضع الكذا الذى بمدينة كذا المعروف هذا الموضع بكذا فقبلتُ منك ما أسلمتَ الىّ من ذلك بمخاطبة منّى ايّاك على جميعه ودفعتَ الىّ هذه الكذا كذا الدينار التى أحضرتَنيها المسمّاة فى هذا الكتاب وقبضتُها منك فى المجلس الذى تعاقدنا فيه هذا السلم فى هذا الكتاب بيننا قبل افتراقنا بأبداننا ثمّ افترقنا بعد ذلك منه بأبداننا وهذه الدنانير المسمّاة فى هذا الكتاب قائمة بعينها فى يدى لم استهلكها ولا شيئا منها عن تراض منّا جميعا بجميع ما فى هذا الكتاب وإنفاذ منّا له فقد وجب لك علىّ جميع هذا القمح المسمّى فى هذا الكتاب على ما سُمّى ووُصف فى

(206 b) هذا الكتاب من جودته وصفة عينه ومقدار كيله وحلول أجله وموضع قبضه // فلا براءة لى من ذلك ولا مخرج ولا مدفع إلاّ بالخروج اليك منه على ما يوجبه لك علىّ هـذا السلم المسمّى فى هذا الكتاب فقبل فلان بن فلان من فلان بن فلان جميع ما أقرّ له به فى هذا الكتاب وصدّقه

[1] partly erased in MS [2] MS omits فى هذا الكتاب

على الأجل المسمّى فيه بمخاطبة منه ايّاه على جميع ذلك شهد على إقرار فلان بن فلان الفلانى يعنى المسلِّم وفلان بن فلان الفلانى يعنى المسلَّم اليه بجميع ما سُمّى ووُصف فى هذا الكتاب ثمّ تنسق الشهادة فى ذلك على مثل ما كتبناها فى سائر ما تقدّم من كتبنا التى ذكرناها فى هذا الكتاب *

19.1 وانّما كتبنا أنّك أحضرتَنى كذا كذا دينارا فأسلمتَها الىّ بالإردبّ المعروف بكذا أو بالوَيبة المعروفة بكذا وأسلمتَها الى كذا وإن كان أصحابنا لا يكتبون ذلك كذلك لاختلاف الناس فيه لو لم يحضر المسلِّمُ المسلَّمَ اليه الدنانير التى أسلمها اليه فى وقت السلم *

19.2 فكان بعضهم يقول اذا أسلم رجل الى رجل دنانير فى كَيل مسمّى أو فيما سوى ذلك ممّا يجوز فيه السلم ولم يسمّ دنانير بعينها ولا يقصد به [1] اليها وكانت عنده دنانير أو لم يكن عنده دنانير فاستقرضها فدفعها الى المسلَّم اليه فقبضها المسلَّم اليه فى المجلس الذى يعاقدا فيه السلم قبل أن يتفرّقا منه فالسلم جائز * //

(207 a)
19.3 قالوا وانّما يكون الدنانير دينا لو تفرّقا عن موطن السلم قبل قبض المسلَّم اليه ايّاها فتكون دينا ويدخل ذلك فى نهى رسول الله عليه السلام عن بيع الكالِى بالكالِى وهو بيع الدين بالدين وممّن ذهب الى هذا القول أبو حنيفة وأبو يوسف ومحمّد بن الحسن فقالوا لو قصد بالسلم الى دنانير بعينها لم يقع السلم عليها بعينها ووقع على مثلها فى ذمّة المسلَّم اليه وقبضها المسلَّم اليه [2] فى موطن السلم قبل أن يتفرّقا منه بأبدانهما جاز السلم وإن تفرّقا منه قبل ذلك بأبدانهما بطل السلم *

19.4 وخالفهم زفر فى حرف من هذا فقال اذا تعاقدا السلم على دنانير بعينها صمدا بالعقد اليها فقد وقع السلم عليها بعينها وليس للمسلِّم أن يمنع المسلَّم اليه منها وإن لا يعطيه غيرها وليس للمسلَّم اليه أن يأخذ المسلِّم بغيرها وجعلها فى معنى القرض اذا تعاقدا السلم عليه بعينه *

19.5 فقال وإن ضاعت فى يد المسلِّم قبل قبض المسلَّم اليه ايّاها منه بطل السلم ووافق أبا حنيفة
19.6 وأبا يوسف ومحمّدا فى سائر ما حكيناه عنهم فى هذا الفصل * وقال آخرون لا يجوز السلم فى هذا إلاّ إن يُعقَد على دنانير بعينها أو على دراهم بعينها يُقصَد به اليها فيكون السلم واقعا على
(207 b) عينها وإن ضاعت // فى يد المسلِّم قبل أن يقبضا منه المسلَّم اليه بطل السلم فى قولهم وهى عندهم [3]
19.7 فى حكم العروض * قالوا وإن عُقد السلم على دنانير موصوفة وعلى دراهم موصوفة ولم يصمد به الى دنانير بعينها ولا الى دراهم بعينها فالسلم فاسد وكان ذلك عندهم فى معنى بيع الدين بالدين الذى نهى عنه رسول الله عليه السلام *

19.8 فلمّا اختلفوا فى هذا على ما وصفنا فقال كلّ فريق منهم ما ذكرناه عنه كتبنا إنّك أحضرتَنى كذا كذا دينارا فأسلمتَها الىّ فى كذا كذا إردبّا [4] فإن رُفع ذلك الى من يرى السلم وجب بغير

[1] MS omits يقصد به
[2] MS omits وقبضها المسلم اليه
[3] MS وهم عندهم
[4] MS omits اردبا

الدنانير المقصود بالسلم اليها جعل قبض المسلَّم اليه ايّاها من المسلِّم اقتضاء ممّا وجب له عليه من رأس مال السلم الذى تعاقدا وصحّ السلم ولم يضرّه عنده قصد المسلِّم والمسلَّم اليه بالسلم الى دنانير بعينها وذكرها عقد السلم عليها وإن رُفع الى من يرى السلم وقع على الدنانير [1] المقصود بالسلم اليها جعل السلم واقعا عليها بعينها وصحّ السلم وجعلها الذى وجب اليه على المسلِّم بحقّ السلم الذى تعاقداه *

19.9 (208 a) وكان أبو زيد يكتب فى ذلك إنّك // أسلمتَ الىّ كذا كذا دينارا فى كذا كذا ولا يذكر
19.10 فى كتابه صمدا بالسلم الى دنانير بأعيانها * قال أبو جعفر وهذا عندنا إغفال منه لما قد ذكرناه من اختلاف أهل العلم فى السلم اذا لم يقصد به الى دنانير بأعيانها ولا الى دراهم بأعيانها *

19.11 وانّما كتبنا بقاء الدنانير وسلامتها فى يد المسلَّم اليه القابض لها حتّى يتفرّق هو والمسلِّم عن موطن السلم وإن لم يكن أصحابنا كتبوا ذلك فى كتبهم [2] لأنّ قوما يقولون اذا استهلك المسلَّم اليه الدراهم بعد ما قبضها من المسلِّم قبل أن يفترقا ثمّ افترقا وهى مستهلكة فبافتراقهما يتمّ السلم بينهما لو كانت عينا فأمّا اذا كانت دينا فقد صار السلم فى قمح دين بدنانير دين فذلك يفسد السلم فى قولهم ويدخله فى نهى النبىّ عليه السلام عن الكالىِ بالكالىِ *

19.12 قال أبو جعفر وانّما كتبنا فى ذكر القمح نقىٍ جيّد ولم نكتب نقىٍ من المدر والغلث والقصل كما كان أصحابنـــا يكتبون لأنّا اذا كتبنا نقىّ من القصل والمدر والغلث لم يوجب بذلك أن يكون نقيّا من غير ذلك واذا كتبنا نقيّا جيّدا أغنانا ذلك عن النقاء من المدر والغلث والقصل والطين
(208 b) ومن كلّ شىء سوى القمح ثمّ وصفنا القمح بالسمرة // لأنّ فى القمح الأسمر وغير الأسمر فوصفناه بالسمرة ليتبيّن بذلك من سائر أنواع غير هذا النوع وكذلك إن كان القمح الذى وقع عليه السلم أبيض بيّنت ذلك فى كتابك *

19.13 قال أبو جعفر ثمّ وكّدنا ذلك فقلنا يابس لتُنفى عنه الرطوبة ثمّ كتبنا مدوّر ليُعلَم أنّه غير يوسفىّ فإن كان القمح الذى وقع عليه هذا السلم غير مدوّر بيّنتَ ذلك فى كتابك أيضا *

19.14 ثمّ كتبنا من قمح مدينة كذا لتفاضل قمح المدن بعضه على بعض وليُعلَم أنّ السلم قد وقع على قمح يُعرَف ويُبيَّن من سائر أنواع القمح سوى النوع الذى هو منه حتّى يصحّ السلم ويجوز هذا إن كانت تلك المدينة مدينة توءمّن على قمحها أن لا يفقد ولا ينقطع من أيدى الناس ولا يقدر عليه وإن كان قمحا ممّا يجوز أن يفقد وينقطع من أيدى الناس حتّى لا يُوجَد منه مـــا وقع عليه السلم فالسلم فاسد *

19.15 ثمّ ذكرنا حلول السلم الى أجل لأنّ السلم لا يجوز بغير أجل فى قول أكثر أهل العلم ومقدار ذلك الأجل الذى لا بدّ منه فى السلم ثلاثة أيّام فصاعدا فإن كان أجل السلم ما بين مقداره //

[1] MS وقع على غير الدنانير

[2] MS وان يكن اصحابنا كتبوا فى كتبهم

(209 a) مثل أن يكون وقع فى شهر وحلوله بعد الشهر [1] اكتفيت بذلك عن ذكر اليوم الذى تعاقدا فيه السلم وإن كان عقد السلم فى شهر وحلوله فى ذلك الشهر ذكرتَ [2] الوقت الذى تعاقدا فيه السلم وامتثلت فى ذلك ما كتبناه فى بيع الخيار الى أجل معلوم فيما قد تقدّم من كتابنا هذا *

19.16 وكذلك إن كان السلم فى شهر وحلوله فى شهر آخر عند مستهلّه بيّنتَ فى كتابك اليوم الذى وقع فيه السلم أىّ يوم هو غير أنّك إن كنتَ ذكرتَ تأريخ كتابك هذا أنّه مستهلّ شهر كذا من سنة كذا ثمّ ذكرت حلول السلم فى الشهر الذى بعده دلّ ذلك أيضا على مدّة أجل السلم وعلى أنّها مدّة يجوز بها السلم فى قول مَن قدّر المدّة التى يجوز بها السلم كما ذكرنا *

19.17 قال أبو جعفر ولم نجد عن أصحابنا فى مدّة أجل السلم التى لا بدّ منها وقتا وانّما ذُكر ذلك عن قوم فأجزنا من قولهم ما كتبنا *

19.18 ثمّ ذكرنا الموضع الذى يوفيه فيه لاختلاف الناس فى ذلك لو لم يسمّ الموضع فكان بعضهم يقول السلم فاسد قلّ مقداره أو كثر كان لحمله مؤنة أم لم تكن وقد كان أبو حنيفة قال بهذا القول ثمّ رجع عنه فقال إن كان لحمل السلم مؤنة فالسلم فاسد // وإن كان لا مؤنة لحمله (209 b) فالسلم جائز ويوفيه ايّاه فى الموضع الذى وقع فيه السلم هذا إن كان وقع السلم فى مدينة أو قرية وقد جعل بعضهم السلم جائزا فى ذلك كلّه ويوفيه ايّاه حيث وقع السلم اذا كانا تعاقداه فى مدينة أو فى قرية وممّن قال بهذا القول مالك بن أنس وأبو يوسف ومحمّد بن الحسن *

19.19 وإن كان السلم وقع بينهما فى غير مصر ولا مدينة ولا قرية فيما لا مؤنة لحمله فى قول أبى حنيفة الأخير وفيما لحمله مؤنة أو لا مؤنة لحمله فى قول أبى يوسف ومحمّد فإنّهم يختلفون فى ذلك ويُروى عنهم فيه قولان أمّا أحدهما فيوفيه حيثما لقيه وأمّا الآخر فيوفيه فى أقرب الأمصار والقرى من ذلك الموضع الذى تعاقدا فيه السلم فكتبنا ذكر الموضع الذى يوفى المسلَّم اليه المسلِّم فيه ما وجب له عليه بحقّ السلم ليصلح السلم فى هذه الأقوال كلّها *

19.20 ثمّ ذكرنا دفع المسلِّم رأس مال السلم الى المسلَّم اليه فى المجلس الذى تعاقدا فيه السلم وقبض المسلَّم اليه ذلك منه قبل أن يتفرّقا بأبدانهما لأنّ أبا حنيفة وأبا يوسف ومحمّد بن الحسن وأكثر أهل العلم قالوا إن تفرّقا من مجلس السلم قبل أن يتقابضا // رأس المال بطل السلم وقد كان (210 a) أهل المدينة لا يفسدون السلم بهذا التفرّق اذا تقابضا رأس المال بعد ذلك قبل أن يتطاول الأمر فكتبنا قبض المسلَّم اليه رأس مال السلم بدفع من المسلِّم ايّاه اليه قبل أن يتفرّقا عن موطن السلم لذلك *

19.21 قال أبو جعفر وقد كتب قوم فى ابتداء هذا الكتاب فى كذا كذا إردبّ قمح نقىّ جيّد
19.22 اسمر حديث لينفوا بذلك أن يكون عتيقا وقد كتب بعضهم حديث عام كذا * قال أبو جعفر وهذا على معنى قول الشافعى وأمّا أصحابنا فما علمتُ أحدا منهم كتب ذلك فى كتبه فى السلم

[1] MS بعد اشهر [2] MS omits ذكرت

وانّما منعنا من اكتتاب ذلك واخترنا [1] الاحتراز فيه من هذا الاختلاف الذى ذكرناه لأنّا لم نقدر على ذلك وكنّا إن كتبناه احتياطا ممّا ذهب اليه الشافعى أفسدنا به السلم فى قول أبى حنيفة وأبى يوسف ومحمّد لأنّهم كانوا يقولون لا يجوز عقد السلم إلاّ على ما يكون موجودا فى وقت عقد السلم وفى وقت حلول السلم وفيما بينهما فإن كان معدوما فى شىء من ذلك فالسلم عندهم فاسد
(210 b) قالوا لأنّه قد يجوز أن يموت المسلَّم اليه قبل حلول الأجل والمسلَّم فيه غير موجود // فيبطل السلم ويعود الى معنى بعده مَن أسلم فيه *

19.23 قال أبو جعفر وقد خولفوا فى هذا فقيل اذا كان حلول السلم فى وقت يكون المسلَّم فيه موجودا فالسلم جائز وإن كان المسلَّم فيه معدوما فى وقت وقوع السلم واعتلّ مخالفهم فى ذلك بحديث أبى منهال عن ابن عبّاس أنّ رسول الله عليه السلام قدم المدينة والناس يُسلمون فى الثمار السنة والسنتين فقال صلّى الله عليه وسلّم أسلِموا فى كَيل معلوم ووزن معلوم الى أجل معلوم قالوا فلم يقل لهم رسول الله صلّى الله عليه وسلّم أسلِموا فيما يكون موجودا فى وقت ما أسلمتم وغير معدوم الى وقت حلوله لكم فقد دلّ ذلك على جواز السلم فيما يكون موجودا فى وقت عقد السلم وفيما يكون غير موجود حين حلّ حلول السلم [2] لأنّ الحديث الذى ذكرنا لم يذكر ذلك *

19.24 قيل لهم هذا الحديث كما ذكرتم ولم يأتِ على جميع أسباب السلم التى لا يجوز السلم إلاّ بها ألا ترون أنّكم تقولون لا يجوز السلم حتّى يُسمَّى موضع قبض السلم وليس هذا فى الحديث
(211 a) ولم تجعلوا الحديث مانعا من // هذا القول إذ كان النبىّ عليه السلام لم يذكره فيه *

19.25 أولا ترون أيضا أنّكم تقولون لا بدّ من قبض رأس المال فى موطن السلم قبل أن يتفرّق منه المسلِّم والمسلَّم اليه ولم يمنع النبىّ عليه السلام من ذلك فى غير هذا الحديث أولا ترون أيضا أنّه لا يجوز السلم إلاّ بما كان عينا ولم يمنع النبىّ عليه السلام من ذلك فى غير هذا الحديث *

19.26 فإن قلتم إنّه وإن لم يمنع ذلك فى هذا الحديث فقد منع منه فى غيره فى نهيه عن بيع الكالِى بالكالِى قيل لكم فقد دلّ هذا الحديث على أنّ حديث أبى المنهال لم يستوعب الأسباب التى لا يجوز السلم إلاّ بها وإنّه قد بقيت من الأسباب التى لا يجوز السلم إلاّ بها أسباب تؤخذ من غير هذا الحديث *

19.27 فقد حدّثنا محمّد بن خُزيمة قال حدّثنا عبد الله بن رجاء الغدانىّ قال أخبرنا شعبة عن عمرو ابن مرّة قال سمعت أبا البخترىّ الطائىّ قال سألت ابن عبّاس عن السلم فقلت إنّا ندع أشياء لا نجد لها فى كتاب الله تحريما فقال إنّا نفعل ذلك نهى رسول الله عليه السلام عن بيع النخل حتّى يؤكل منه *

19.28 فكان سؤال أبى البخترىّ ابنَ عبّاس عن السلم فأجابه ابن عبّاس // بأن قال نهى رسول
(211 b) الله عليه السلام عن بيع النخل حتّى يُؤكَل منه فأخبر أنّ نهى رسول الله عن بيع النخل حتّى

[1] MS omits اخترنا

[2] MS omits حل حلول السلم

يـُؤكـَل منه قد دخل فيه السلم[1] وأنّ السلم لا يجوز أن يُعقـَد على تمر نخل إلاّ فى حال ما يكون الثمن مقدورا عليه وفى ذلك وجوب ما ذهب اليه أبو حنيفة وأبو يوسف ومحمّد بن الحسن ووجوب استعمال هذه الزيادة التى فى حديث أبى البخترىّ على ما فى حديث أبى المنهال مع ما فى حديث

19.29 أبى المنهال ولا يـُترَك لأنّ الزائد أولى من الناقص * ولابن عبّاس الذى رجع اليه فى حديث أبى المنهال هو الذى أجاب أبا البخترىّ بهذا الجواب فوجب بذلك استعمال ما رُوى عنه فى حديث أبى البخترى وفى حديث أبى المنهال جميعا ولا يـُترَك شىء من ذلك *

19.30 وقد رُوى عن عمر مثل ذلك أيضا حدّثنا ابراهيم بن مرزوق قال حدّثنا وهب بن جرير قال حدّثنا شعبة عن عمرو بن مرّة عن أبى البخترىّ قال سألت ابن عمر عن السلف فى التمر

19.31 فقال نهى عمر عن بيع التمر حتّى يصلح * وقد رُوى عن جابر بن عبد الله وعن رجل من الأنصار من أصحاب رسول الله عليه السلام مثل ذلك أيضا *

19.32 (212 a) حدّثنا روح بن الفرج قال حدّثنا يحيى بن عبد الله بن بكير // قال أخبرنا المفضّل بن فضالة عن خالد أنّه سمع عطاء بن أبى رباح يسأل عن الرجل يبيع ثمرة أرض رطبا كان أو عنبا يسلف فيها قبل أن تطيب فقال لا يصلح إنّ ابن الزبير باع ثمرة أرض له ثلاث سنين فسمع بذلك جابر بن عبد الله الأنصارىّ فخرج الى المسجد فقال فى أناس منعنا رسول الله أن نبيع الثمرة حتّى تطيب *

19.33 قال أبو جعفر قوله ذلك إنّ نهى رسول الله عليه السلام عن بيع الثمار قبل أن تطيب قد دخل فيه بيع الثمار المضمونة وإنّه لا يجوز البيع المضمون فيها إلاّ وهى موجودة وإن كانت[2] تحلّ فى وقت آخر قد تكون فيه موجودة اتباعا لهذه الآثار وتمسّكنا[3] بها فلمّا كان السلم لا يجوز فيما قد جاء عن رسول الله وعن أصحابه الذين ذكرنا إلاّ والمسلَّم فيه موجود كتبنا فى كتابنا حديث عام كذا العام لم يُجِز فسد السلم فى ذلك بهذه الآثار ولكنّا لم نكتب ذلك وتمسّكنا بهذه الآثار وتركنا ما خالفها ولو قدرنا على الاحتراز منه كان أحبّ الينا ولكنّا[4] لم نقدر على ذلك *

20.0 (212 b) قال أبو جعفر ولو أنّ رجلا أسلم الى رجل دنانير فى قمح وشعير فأرادا أن يكتبا فى ذلك كتابا فإنّك تكتب هذا كتاب لفلان // بن فلان الفلانى[5] كتبه له فلان بن فلان الفلانى ثمّ تنسق الكتاب على ما كتبنا فى الشرائط التى فى أوّل هذا الباب حتّى اذا أتيت على التأريخ الأوّل كتبت إنّك أحضرتَنِى كذا كذا دينارا مثاقيل ذهبا عينا وازنة جيادا فأسلمتَ الىّ منها كذا كذا دينارا بعينها فى كذا كذا إردبّا قمح فتصفه على مثل مـــا وصفناه فى الكتاب الأوّل ثمّ

[1] MS قد دخل فيه السلام
[2] MS هى موجودة ان كانت
[3] MS تمسكا
[4] MS omits ولكنا
[5] MS omits الفلانى

تكتب [1] وأسلمت الىّ منها كذا كذا دينارا بعينها فى كذا كذا إردبّا شعير فتصفه بما يوصف به الشعير على أن أوفيك هذا القمح وهذا الشعير الموصوفين فى هذا الكتاب عند انقضاء شهر كذا من سنة كذا فى الموضع المعروف بكذا ثمّ تنسق الكتاب على مثل ما كتبنا فى الشرط الأوّل فى هذا الباب *

20.1 قال أبو جعفر وانّما فصلنا رأس مال كلّ واحد من القمح والشعير من رأس مال الآخر منهما لاختلاف الناس فى ذلك لو جمعا فى مال واحد غير مفصول رأس مال كلّ واحد منهما منه من رأس مال الآخر فكان بعضهم يقول اذا وقع السلم كذلك فهو فاسد وممّن قال ذلك أبو حنيفة وسفيان بن سعيد وكان بعضهم يقول السلم جائز ورأس مال كلّ واحد منهما ما يصيبه من رأس //
(213 a) المال اذا قُسم رأس المال على قيمته وعلى قيمة النوع الآخر المضمون معه فى السلم ويجعلون ذلك كعرضين بيعا معا صفقة واحدة بمال واحد وممّن قال ذلك أبو يوسف ومحمّد فذكرنا لكلّ واحد من الحنطة ومن الشعير رأس مال معلوم لهذا المعنى *

20.2 وانّما جعلنا رأس مال كلّ واحد منهما بعينه ولم نجعل الدنانير بكلّيّتها رأس مال لهما لأنّ قوما يقولون لا يجوز السلم وإن كان رأس المال فيه دراهم مسمّاة حتّى تكون دراهم مفردة ودنانير مفردة مصمودا بالسلم اليها فكتبنا ما كتبنا لذلك *

21.0 قال أبو جعفر واذا أسلم رجل الى رجل دنانير فى رطب موصوف الى أجل موصوف فأرادا أن يكتبا فى ذلك كتابا كتبت على مثل ما كتبناه فى الشرط الأوّل من هذا الباب حتّى اذا انتهيت الى التأريخ الأوّل كتبت إنّك أحضرتَنِي كذا كذا دينارا مثاقيل ذهبا عينا وازنة جيادا فأسلمتَها الىّ فى كذا كذا قفيز رطب برنىّ جيّد غير محشف ولا معيب على أن أوفيك ذلك عند انقضاء شهر كذا من سنة كذا فى الموضع الكذا من مدينة كذا المعروف هذا الموضع بكذا وذلك بعد
(213 b) أن صار الرطب موجودا فى أيدى الناس // قبل وقوع هذا السلم المسمّى فى هذا الكتاب بيننا وفى وقت وقوع هذا السلم المسمّى فى هذا الكتاب بيننا وغير معدوم من أيديهم الى بعد حلول هذا الأجل المسمّى فى هذا الكتاب فقبلت منك ما أسلمت الىّ من ذلك ثمّ تنسق الكتاب على مثل ما كتبنا فى الشرط الأوّل من هذا الباب وإن كان الرطب البرنىّ مختلفا فى البلدان أضفته الى المدينة التى هو منها وإن كان غير مختلف فى البلدان أهملت ذلك فلا [2] تضيفه الى مدينة *

21.1 قال أبو جعفر وانّما كتبنا أنّ السلم وقع بعد وجوب الرطب فى أيدى الناس وأنّه غير معدوم من أيديهم الى بعد حلول أجل السلم لما قد ذكرناه عن أبى حنيفة وأبى يوسف وعن محمّد بن الحسن أنّ السلم لا يجوز إلاّ فى موجود فى وقت عقد السلم وفى وقت حلول السلم وفيما بين ذلك فكتبنا ما وصفنا احتياطا من قولهم هذا *

[1] MS omits ثمّ تكتب [2] MS فلو

19.34 واعلم أنّ الأحوط فى المسلِّم أن يكون المبدأ فى الإقرار المكتوب فى آخر الشهادة ثمّ يُثنى بالمسلَّم اليه لأنّا لو بدأنا بالمسلَّم اليه ثمّ أقرّ [1] لم نأمن أن يقول المسلِّم أنّ السلم حال فيكون القول قوله فى قول أبى حنيفة وأبى يوسف ومحمّد ويفسد السلم على قولهم ولكن يُبدَأ فى ذلك بالمسلِّم ثمّ يُثنّى // بالمسلَّم اليه ليكون المسلِّم قد أقرّ بالأجل الذى عليه فيما وجب له بحقّ السلم قبل إقرار المسلَّم اليه له بالسلم ❊ (214 a)

19.35 وكذلك رجل لو أقرّ لرجل بمال على نفسه الى أجل وكتب به على نفسه كتابا ذكر الأجل فإنّه يُبدَأ فيه بإقرار المقرّ له ليثبت الأجل ❊ وكذلك بيع باعه رجل بمال الى أجل فكتب فى ذلك كتابا فالأحوط فيه أن يُبدَأ بإقرار مَن عليه الأجل قبل إقرار مَن له الأجل ❊
19.36

19.37 فإن قال قائل فإنّ أبا حنيفة وأبا يوسف ومحمّدا قد خولفوا فى ذلك فقال مخالفهم وهو ابن أبى ليلى وأهل المدينة والشافعىّ فقالوا القول لقول المقرّ أنّ المال الى الأجل الذى وصله بالإقرار بالمال لقول المقرّ له قيل له قد علمنا أنّ ذلك كذلك وأنّ أهل العلم قد اختلفوا فيه كما ذكرت ولكنّا لو كتبناه على أن بدأنا بإقرار الذى عليه الشىء أمن عليه فى قول أهل المدينة وابن أبى ليلى والشافعىّ ولم يؤمَن عليه فى قول الآخرين وإن بدأنا بالمقرّ له أمن عليه فى قول جميع الناس وكان أولى الأشياء بنا ما كان فيه الاحتياط من أقوال جميع الناس والتمسّك به ❊

19.38 قال أبو جعفر وكذلك امرأة طلّقها زوجها على مال أو عبد أعتقه مولاه // على مال فكتب فى ذلك كتابا فإنّه يبتدئ فيه عند الشهادة بالعبد والمرأة لأنّهما لو أنكرا فقالا انّما كان الطلاق والعتاق بغير مال كان القول قولهما فى ذلك مع إيمانهما فى قول أبى حنيفة وأبى يوسف ومحمّد فيبتدئ بهما ليكون المال قد تقدّم إقرارهما به على أنفسهما ثمّ يسأل بعد ذلك الذى له المال وهو الزوج والمولى فإن أقرّا بما قالا وجب لهما المال وإن أنكرا لم يجب لهما شىء ولم يضرّ المقرّين قبلهما ما أقرّا به على أنفسهما من وجوب المال عليهما بالطلاق والعتاق الذى ذكرنا وأمّا سائر الكتب فانّما نبتدئ فيها بإقرار البائع وبإقرار مَن حكمه حكم البائع فيها ثمّ ثنّينا بعد ذلك بالمشترى أو بمَن حكمه [2] حكم المشترى فيها والله نسأله التوفيق ❊ (214 b)

آخر البيوع من كتاب الشروط الكبير والحمد لله
على عونه وإحسانه وتوفيقه وصلّى الله على
سيّدنا محمّد النبىّ وآلـه وسلّم تسليما ❊

[1] MS لو بدأنا بالمسلم ثم اقر

[2] MS او لمن حكمه

CONTENTS OF THE "KITĀB AL-BUYŪ'"